Riffs & Choruses

A New Jazz Anthology

Edited by Andrew Clark

CONTINUUM
London and New York

Continuum
The Tower Building, 11 York Road, London SE1 7NX
370 Lexington Avenue, New York, NY 10017–6503

This selection and introductory material © 2001 Andrew Clark
First published 2001 by arrangement with Bayou Press Ltd

British Library Cataloguing-in-Publication Data
A catalogue record for this book is available from the British Library.

ISBN 0-8264-4755-4 (hardback)
       0-8264-4756-2 (paperback)

Library of Congress Cataloging-in-Publication Data
Riffs & choruses: a new jazz anthology/edited by Andrew Clark.
     p. cm.
   Includes bibliographical references (p.) and index.
   ISBN 0-8264-4755-4—ISBN 0-8264-4756-2 (pbk.)
     1. Jazz–History and criticism. I. Title: Riffs and choruses. II. Clark, Andrew, 1938–

ML3507.R54 2000
781.65–dc21

                                                                                    00-043025

Typeset by BookEns Ltd, Royston, Herts.
Printed and bound in Great Britain by Cromwell Press, Trowbridge

CONTENTS

Acknowledgements   xiii

Heads   1
Introduction   3

Riff 1   11
Chorus I The Delirium Tremens of Syncopation:
Jazz and definition (origin, terms, early reception)   13

  1 Compendium: Jazz – formal definitions (1913–99)   18
  2 Avril Dankworth: 'Introductory: Jazz' (1968)   22
  3 Robert Hendrickson: 'Come on, Jazz!' (1987)   23
  4 Eileen Southern: 'The Jazz Age' (1983)   24
  5 James Reese Europe: 'A negro explains "Jazz"' (1919)   25
  6 Alan P. Merriam and Fradley H. Garner: 'Jazz – the word' (1968)   26
  7 Ferdinand 'Jelly Roll' Morton: 'I created jazz in 1902' (1938)   27
  8 Gunther Schuller: "The origins" and "The beginnings" (1968)   30
  9 Anonymous: 'The appeal of the primitive jazz' (1917)   32
 10 Anonymous: 'Delving into the genealogy of jazz' (1919)   35
 11 Henry O. Osgood: 'These cacophonic combinations' (1926)   37
 12 Anne Shaw Faulkner: 'Does jazz put the sin in syncopation?'
     (1921)   38
 13 Clive Bell: 'Plus de jazz' (1921)   40
 14 Ernst-Alexandre Ansermet: 'Bechet and jazz visit Europe, 1919'
     (1919)   42
 15 Olin Downes: 'A concert of jazz' (1924)   44
 16 Roger Pryor Dodge: 'Negro jazz' (1929)   46
 17 Svend Gade: 'Baptized by jazz' (1927)   50
 18 Jean-Paul Sartre: 'I discovered jazz in America' (1947)   51
 19 Sybil Kein: 'Jazz' (1984)   53

Riff 2   55
Chorus II Nothin' Over There But Critics: Jazz and history
(criticism, canon, historiography)   57

 20 David Meltzer: 'Jazz history-making' (1993)   61
 21 John Gennari: 'Jazz criticism: Its development and ideologies' (1991) 62
 22 Martin Williams: 'Introduction: A matter of fundamentals' (1970)   68

23 Winthrop Sargeant: "Hot jazz" vs. "Fine art" (1946)   71
24 André Hodeir: 'The essence' (1956)   75
25 Scott DeVeaux: 'Constructing the jazz tradition: Jazz historiography'
    (1991)   79
26 Krin Gabbard: 'Writing the other history' (1995)   85
27 Gary Tomlinson: 'The jazz canon as monological canon' (1991)   87
28 Amiri Baraka [LeRoi Jones]: 'Jazz and the white critic' (1963)   91
29 Linda Dahl: 'Preface, *Stormy Weather*' (1984)   96
30 Nat Shapiro and Nat Hentoff: 'Introduction, *Hear Me Talkin' to Ya*'
    (1955)   99
31 Charles Mingus: 'I don't see nothin' over there but critics' (1971)   101

Riff 3   103
Chorus III 'The Sound of Surprise': Jazz and style (convention,
repertoire, improvisation)   105

32 Joachim Berendt: 'The styles of jazz' (1959)   109
33 Geoff Dyer: 'Tradition, influence and innovation' (1991)   110
34 Bruce Lippincott: 'Aspects of the jam session' (1958)   116
35 Ingrid Monson: 'The ensemble and the soloist' (1996)   120
36 Hayden Carruth: 'Three paragraphs' (1978)   124
37 Ross Russell: 'Seein' Red' (1961)   126
38 Mary Lou Williams: 'The battle of the tenor kings' (1954)   128
39 Art Pepper and Laurie Pepper: 'That's what it's all about' (1979)   129
40 J.C. Thomas: 'John Coltrane is practicing' (1975)   130
41 Nathan W. Pearson: 'Kansas City jazz style' (1988)   133
42 Barry Ulanov: 'Moldy figs vs. moderns!' (1947)   137
43 Martin Gardner: 'The fall of Flatbush Smith' (1947)   139
44 Gary Giddins: 'Jazz turns neoclassical' (1985)   141
45 Martin Williams: 'How long has this been going on?' (1989)   144

Riff 4   147
Chorus IV A People's Music: Jazz and culture (context, audience,
social practice)   149

46 Charles Nanry: 'Jazz as social history' (1979)   153
47 Harold Horowitz: 'The American jazz audience' (1986)   154
48 David W. Stowe: 'Understanding swing' (1994)   158
49 Kathy J. Ogren: 'The significance of the jazz controversy for
    twenties America' (1989)   164
50 Neil Leonard: 'Acceptance of jazz in the twenties' (1962)   170
51 Morroe Berger: 'Jazz: Resistance to the diffusion of a culture-
    pattern' (1947)   177
52 Alan P. Merriam and Raymond W. Mack: 'The jazz community'
    (1960)   178
53 Amiri Baraka: 'Where's the music going and why?' (1987)   180
54 Lawrence W. Levine: 'Jazz and American culture' (1989)   183
55 Burton W. Peretti: 'Epilogue: Jazz as American history' (1997)   185

Riff 5   191
Chorus V So Black and Blue: Jazz and race (colour, identity, otherness)   193

56   Sascha Feinstein: 'Miss Brown to you (1915–1959)' (2000)   197
57   Charley Gerard: 'Battling the black music ideology' (1998)   198
58   Amiri Baraka: 'Masters in collaboration' (1987)   203
59   James Lincoln Collier: 'Black, white, and blue' (1993)   208
60   Gene Lees: 'Jazz black and white' (1994)   212
61   Leonard Feather: 'The jazzman as critic: the blindfold test ("Riddle of the races")' (1960)   215
62   Nat Hentoff: 'Archie Shepp: The way ahead' (1968)   216
63   Arthur Taylor: Interviews with Charles Tolliver, Freddie Hubbard, Hazel Scott and Betty Carter (1970–2)   220
64   Langston Hughes: 'Bop' (1961)   223
65   Billie Holiday: 'Travelin' light' (1956)   225
66   Mezz Mezzrow: 'Out of the gallion' (1946)   227
67   Michael Harper: 'Here where Coltrane is' (1977)   230
68   Albert Murray: 'Epilogue, *Stomping the Blues*' (1976)   231
69   Charles Mingus: 'The final set for this afternoon' (1971)   232
70   Ross Russell: 'Minstrelsy' (1961)   234

Riff 6   235
Chorus VI Young Man with a Horn': Jazz and myth (narrative, romance, fabulation)   237

71   Robert Sargent: 'Touching the past' (1987)   241
72   Frederick Ramsey, Jr. and Charles Edward Smith: 'New Orleans: Callin' our chillun home' (1939)   242
73   William Matthews: 'The Buddy Bolden cylinder' (1991)   244
74   Dana Gioia: 'Bix Beiderbecke (1903–1931)' (1986)   245
75   Otis Ferguson: 'Young man with a horn' (1936)   245
76   Dorothy Baker: 'from *Young Man With a Horn*' (1938)   248
77   Al Young: 'Lester leaps in' (1982)   250
78   François Postif: 'Lester Paris 59' (1959)   251
79   Frank Büchmann-Møller: 'He wanted to look down on Broadway' (1990)   254
80   Geoff Dyer: 'Dying in a hotel room' (1991)   256
81   William Matthews: 'Listening to Lester Young' (1978)   259
82   Ross Russell: 'At Billy Berg's' (1973)   260
83   Amiri Baraka: 'A tribute to Bird' (1987)   263
84   Michael Harper: ' "Bird Lives": Charles Parker' (1977)   264
85   Baroness Pannonica de Koenigswarter: 'The death of Bird' (1962)   266
86   Tony Scott: 'Destination K.C.' (1960)   268
87   John Clellon Holmes: 'The horn still blows' (1958)   270

Riff 7   273
**Chorus VII Hear Me Talkin' to Ya: Jazz and the jazz
life (orality, autobiography, mediation)**   275

88   Christopher Harlos: 'Jazz autobiography: Theory, practice,
     politics' (1995)   279
89   Whitey Mitchell: 'Getting there is half the fun' (1963)   284
90   Dicky Wells: 'The hazardous road' (1971)   286
91   Mary Lou Williams: 'Music everywhere' (1954)   289
92   Mike Zwerin: 'Claude Thornhill: The square on the lawn' (1983)   292
93   Eddie Condon: 'The poorest 7-piece orchestra on Earth' (1947)   299
94   Mezz Mezzrow: 'Them first kicks are a killer' (1946)   302
95   Ferdinand 'Jelly Roll' Morton: 'Street parades' (1950)   304
96   Hampton Hawes: 'Watts burning' (1974)   305
97   Dizzy Gillespie: 'Beboppers ... the cult' (1979)   307
98   Art Pepper and Laurie Pepper: 'Heroin' (1979)   310
99   Louis Armstrong: 'Storyville' (1955)   313

Riff 8   315
**Chorus VIII Reetie Vouties with a Little Hot Sauce: Jazz
and language (vernacular, argot, hipness)**   317

100   Robert S. Gold: 'Introduction, *Jazz Talk*' (1975)   321
101   Neil Leonard: 'The jazzman's verbal usage' (1986)   324
102   Anatole Broyard: 'A portrait of the hipster' (1948)   332
103   Robert G. Reisner: 'Cool' (1959)   335
104   Amiri Baraka [LeRoi Jones]: 'Be cool' (1963)   336
105   Jack Kerouac: 'Just one big orooni' (1957)   337
106   Anonymous: 'Vipers, tea, and jazz' (1946)   338
107   Zora Neale Hurston: 'Story in Harlem slang' (1942)   339
108   Steve Allen: 'Crazy Red Riding Hood' (1954)   347
109   Mary Lou Williams and Milton Orent: 'In the Land of
      Oo-Bla-Dee' (1949)   349
110   Lawrence Ferlinghetti: 'Sometime during eternity' (1958)   350
111   Cab Calloway: '*The New Cab Calloway's Hepster's Dictionary:
      Language of Jive*' (1944)   351
112   Dan Burley: 'Advanced reading in jive – Sam D. Home's
      soliloquy' (1944)   356
113   King Pleasure [Clarence Beeks]: 'Parker's mood' (1953)   358
114   Angela Jackson: 'Make/n my music' (1973)   359

Riff 9   361
**Chorus IX Spontaneous Bop Prosody: Jazz and literature
(word, text, performance)**   363

115   Leland H. Chambers: 'Improvising and mythmaking in
      Eudora Welty's "Powerhouse"' (1995)   368
116   Ann Petry: 'Solo on the drums' (1947)   372

117 Frank London Brown: 'McDougal' (1961)   376
118 Al Young: 'Chicken Hawk's dream' (1966)   378
119 Donald Barthelme: 'The king of jazz' (1977)   380
120 Whitney Balliett: 'Imagining music' (1990)   383
121 Jack Baird: 'A jazzman's heaven' (1956)   387
122 'Jean-Louis' [Jack Kerouac]: 'Jazz of the Beat Generation' (1955)   390
123 Kenneth Rexroth: 'Married blues' (1966)   392
124 Kenneth Patchen: 'Lonesome boy blues' (1957)   392
125 Kenneth Patchen: 'Opening the window' (1957)   393
126 Lawrence Ferlinghetti: from 'Autobiography' (1958)   394
127 Etheridge Knight: 'For Eric Dolphy' (1980)   397
128 Sascha Feinstein: 'Blues villanelle for Sonny Criss' (2000)   398
129 Michael Harper: 'Brother John' (1970)   399
130 Harryette Mullen: 'Playing the invisible saxophone *en el
     Combo de las Estrellas*' (1981)   400
131 Larry Neal: 'Don't say goodbye to the porkpie hat' (1969)   401

Riff 10   405
**Chorus X All the Usual Pitfalls: Jazz and film (cliché, stereotype,
ambience)**   407

132 Kenneth C. Spence: 'Jazz digest' (1988)   411
133 Krin Gabbard: 'Questions of influence in the white jazz biopic'
     (1996)   416
134 Donald Bogle: 'Louis Armstrong: The films' (1994)   421
135 Jean-Pierre Coursodon: '*Round Midnight*: An interview with
     Bertrand Tavernier' (1986)   425
136 Francis Davis: 'At the movies: Everycat' (1986)   431
137 Gary Giddins: 'Birdman of Hollywood' (1988)   433
138 Francis Davis: 'Birdland, Mon Amor' (1988)   437
139 James Agee: 'Films' (1944)   441
140 Charles Emge: 'On the beat in Hollywood' (1944)   442
141 Jackie Lopez: 'Is Hollywood yielding?' (1945)   443
142 Whitney Balliett: '*The Sound of Jazz*' (1983)   444
143 Hal Hinson: '*Let's Get Lost*: Baker as icon' (1989)   446
144 James Berardinelli: '*A Great Day in Harlem*' (1995)   448

Out-Chorus   451
Suggested Reading   453
Bibliography   463
Index of Names   475
Index of Jazz (and Jazz-related) Names   486

Acknowledgements

Every effort has been made to trace or contact the copyright holders of original material contained in this volume. Grateful acknowledgement is made to the following for permission to reprint copyrighted material.

Anonymous: 'Vipers, Tea, and Jazz', From *Newsweek*, 28 October 1946 © 1946 Newsweek, Inc. All rights reserved, reprinted by permission.

Ernst-Alexandre Ansermet: Ernst-Alexandre Ansermet: 'Bechet and Jazz Visit Europe, 1919.' © 1962 by Frederic Ungar, reprinted by permission of the Continuum International Publishing Group Ltd.

Whitney Balliett: 'Imagining Music.' Reprinted by permission of Harold Ober Associates Incorporated. First published in *The New Yorker*, © 1990 by Whitney Balliett. *The Sound of Jazz*, St Martin's Press and Harold Ober Associates Incorporated, first published in *The New Yorker*. © 1983 by Whitney Balliett. © 2000 by Whitney Balliett. From *Collected Works: A Journal of Jazz, 1954–2000*, by Whitney Balliett, reprinted by permission of St Martin's Press, LLC.

Amiri Baraka: All excerpts reprinted by permission of Sterling Lord Literistic, Inc. Copyright by Amiri Baraka.

Donald Barthelme: 'The King of Jazz.' © 1981 by Donald Barthelme. Reprinted by permission of the Wylie Agency.

James Berardinelli: *A Great Day in Harlem.* © 1995, used by permission of author.

Joachim Berendt: Excerpt from *The New Jazz Book: A History and Guide* by Joachim Berendt, © 1962 Peter Owen Ltd., London.

Morroe Berger: 'Jazz: Resistance to the Diffusion of a Culture-Pattern.' Reprinted by permission of *Journal of Negro History*.

Donald Bogle: 'Louis Armstrong: The Films.' From Marc H. Miller, *Louis Armstrong: A Cultural Legacy*, University of Washington Press, © 1994, reprinted by permission of the University of Washington Press.

Anatole Broyard: 'A Portrait of the Hipster' by Anatole Broyard first appeared in *Partisan Review*, vol. XV, no. 6, 1948.

Frank Büchmann-Møller: *You Just Fight for Your Life: The Story of Lester Young.* Frank Büchmann-Møller. © 1990 by Frank Büchmann-Møller, reproduced with permission of Greenwood Publishing Group, Inc., Westport, CT.

Hayden Carruth: 'Three Paragraphs.' Reprinted from *Sitting In: Selected Writings on Jazz, Blues, and Related Topics*, by Hayden Carruth, by

Gary Giddins: From *Rhythm-a-ning,* © 1985 by Gary Giddins. Reprinted by permission of Georges Borchardt, Inc. All rights reserved. From *Faces in the Crowd,* © 1992 by Gary Giddins. Reprinted by permission of Georges Borchardt, Inc. All rights reserved. From *Faces in the Crowd: Players and Writers* by Gary Giddins. © 1992 by Gary Giddins. Used by permission of Oxford University Press, Inc.

Dizzy Gillespie and Al Fraser: From *To Be or Not to Bop* by Dizzy Gillespie. © by John Birks Gillespie and Wilmot Alfred Fraser, used by permission of Doubleday, a division of Random House, Inc.

Dana Gioia: 'Bix Beiderbecke (1903–1931)' © 1986 by Dana Gioia. Reprinted from *Daily Horoscope* with the permission of Graywolf Press, Saint Paul, Minnesota.

Christopher Harlos: Excerpt from 'Jazz Autobiography: Theory, Practice, Politics,' in Krin Gabbard (ed.), *Representing Jazz.* © 1995, Duke University Press. All rights reserved, reprinted with permission.

Michael Harper: 'Here Where Coltrane Is,' '"Bird Lives": Charles Parker,' 'Brother John.' From *Images of Kin: New and Selected Poems.* © 1977 by Michael S. Harper, used with permission of the Poet and the University of Illinois Press.

Robert Hendrickson: Entry from *The Encyclopedia of Word and Phrase Origins,* by Robert Hendrickson, Macmillan, 1987, reprinted by permission of Macmillan Publishers Ltd.

Hal Hinson: '*Let's Get Lost*: Baker as Icon.' © 1989, *The Washington Post,* reprinted with permission.

André Hodeir: 'The Essence.' From André Hodeir, *Jazz: Its Evolution and Essence.* © 1956 by Grove Press, used by permission of Grove/Atlantic, Inc.

Billie Holiday: Excerpt from *Lady Sings the Blues* by Billie Holiday and William F. Dufty. © 1956 by Eleanora Fagan and William F. Dufty. Used by permission of Doubleday, a division of Random House, Inc.

John Clellon Holmes: Excerpt from *The Horn.* Reprinted by permission of Sterling Lord Literistic, Inc., © 1958 by Estate of John Clellon Holmes.

Harold Horowitz: 'The American Jazz Audience.' From *New Perspectives on Jazz,* edited by David N. Baker, published by the Smithsonian Institution Press, Washington, DC, © 1991, used by permission of the publisher.

Langston Hughes: 'Bop' from *The Best of Simple* by Langston Hughes. Farrar, Straus and Harold Ober Associates Incorporated. © 1961 by Langston Hughes. Copyright renewed 1989 by George Houston Bass. Reprinted by permission of Hill and Wang, a division of Farrar, Straus and Giroux, LLC.

Zora Neale Hurston: 'Story in Harlem Slang' as taken from *The Complete Stories* by Zora Neale Hurston. Introduction © by Henry Louis Gates, Jr. and Sieglinde Lemke. Compilation © 1995 by Vivian Bowden, Lois J. Hurston Gaston, Clifford Hurston, Lucy Ann Hurston, Winfred Hurston Clark, Zora Mack Goins, Edgar Hurston, Sr., and Barbara Hurston Lewis. Afterword and Bibliography © 1995 by Henry Louis Gates. Reprinted by permission of HarperCollins Publishers, Inc. 'Story in Harlem Slang' was originally published in *The American Mercury,* July 1942.

Albert Murray: Excerpt from *Stomping the Blues.* © 1971 by Albert Murray, reprinted with permission. No changes shall be made to the text of the above work without the express consent of The Wylie Agency, Inc.

Charles Nanry: Excerpt from *The Jazz Text,* 1979. Reprinted by permission of Charles Nanry.

Larry Neal: 'Don't Say Goodbye to the Porkpie Hat.' From the book *Visions of a Liberated Future* by Larry Neal. © 1989, appears by permission of the publisher, Thunder's Mouth Press.

Kathy J. Ogren: Excerpt from *The Jazz Revolution: Twenties America and the Meaning of Jazz* by Kathy J. Ogren. © 1992 by Kathy J. Ogren, used by permission of Oxford University Press, Inc.

Henry O. Osgood: Excerpt from *So This is Jazz* by Henry Osgood. © 1926 by Henry O. Osgood, by permission of Little, Brown and Company (Inc).

Kenneth Patchen: 'Lonesome Boy Blues,' and 'Opening the Window,' by Kenneth Patchen, from *Selected Poems by Kenneth Patchen.* © 1954, 1957 by New Directions Publishing Corp. Reprinted by permission of New Directions Publishing Corp.

Art Pepper and Laurie Pepper: Excerpts from *Straight Life* reprinted by permission of Arthur Pepper Music Corp. and Laurie Pepper.

Burton W. Peretti: Excerpt from *Jazz in American Culture,* © 1997 by Burton W. Peretti, by permission of Ivan R. Dee, Publisher.

Ann Petry: 'Solo on the Drums.' Reprinted by the permission of Russell & Volkening as agents for the author. © 1947 by Ann Petry, renewed 1975 by Ann Petry. Originally appeared in *The Magazine of the Year,* 1947.

King Pleasure [Clarence Beeks]: 'Parker's Mood'. Words by Clarence Beeks, music by Charlie Parker. © 1976 Screen Gems-EMI Music Inc., U.S.A. Screen Gems-EMI Music Ltd, London WC2H 0EA. Reproduced by permission of International Music Publications Ltd.

Frederic J. Ramsey Jr. and Charles Edward Smith: Excerpt from *Jazzmen* by Frederic J. Ramsey Jr. and Charles Edward Smith, © 1939, by Harcourt, Inc. and renewed 1967 by Frederic J. Ramsey Jr., reprinted by permission of the publisher.

Robert G. Reisner: Excerpt from *The Jazz Titans,* by Robert George Reisner. © 1960 Doubleday, a division of Random House. Reprinted by permission.

Kenneth Rexroth: 'Married Blues,' by Kenneth Rexroth, from *The Collected Shorter Poems.* © 1963 by Kenneth Rexroth, reprinted by permission of New Directions Publishing Corp.

Ross Russell: Excerpts from *The Sound,* 1962, reprinted by permission of Cassell & Co.

Winthrop Sargeant: Excerpt from *Jazz: Hot and Hybrid.* Originally published in *The New Yorker.* Reprinted by permission of Jane Sargeant.

Robert Sargent: 'Touching the Past,' from his collection *Aspects of a Southern Story.* Reprinted by permission of Robert Sargent and The Word Works, Inc.

Jean-Paul Sartre: 'I Discovered Jazz in America.' From Ralph de Toledano (ed.), *Frontiers of Jazz,* Frederick Ungar, 1962. Reprinted by permission of The Continuum International Publishing Group Ltd.

To my family

Heads[1]

We'd have a jam session, this guy sets a riff[2] over here and this one sets a riff over here and another one sets a riff, and the guys just go on swinging. Each chorus[3] they'd build it up. (Jazz guitarist Gene Ramey, on 'Riffs,' in Nathan W. Pearson, *Goin' to Kansas City*, 1988)

Jazz is a very big word. (Leonard Feather, 'The World of Jazz,' CBS telecast, 1955)

All the complex forces of American life which ... focus in jazz. (Ralph Ellison, 'The Golden Age, Time Past,' *Esquire*, 1959)

Jazz is the symbol of the triumph of the human spirit, not of its degradation. It is a lily in spite of the swamp. (Archie Shepp, in Valerie Wilmer, *Jazz People*, 1970)

There are probably more anthologies devoted to jazz than to any other twentieth-century musical genre. (Robert Walser (ed.), *Keeping Time: Readings in Jazz History*, 1999)

Everyone has his or her vision of jazz, and this is mine. (Gary Giddins, *Visions of Jazz: The First Century*, 1998)

---

1 Basic arrangements (sometimes themes or melodies) worked out and memorized by band or group, without being written down – hence, 'in the head.'
2 Brief melodic phrase (or simple theme), repeated rhythmically and used as background for soloist – hence, 'setting up a riff.'
3 Musical form outlining chord structure or progression which forms basis for improvised solo – hence, 'taking, building or blowing a chorus.'

Introduction

> ... just a whole lotta fun
> You could take any old riff
> And make a real long run

Head arrangements: *Riffs & Choruses*

Jazz singer Eddie Jefferson's 'vocalized' bebop lines provide an analogy to the impetus and methodology of *Riffs & Choruses*. The book's content takes off, jazz-like, from a number of 'riff' starting-points – 'head' themes like jazz history, style, culture, language, myth, life and race; it constructs a number of extended, exploratory 'choruses' from the accumulated material written *on* and *to* jazz. What is offered here are interpretative variations – improvisations – on topics central to jazz's musical and cultural repertoire and its defining practice. This book reflects Jefferson's celebration of the large possibilities of jazz, its creative and critical opportunities in 'long' texts.

The ten content sections, or 'Choruses,' of the anthology encompass a number of approaches to jazz study, and provide a comprehensive overview of jazz writing. Assembled here for examination are varied and representative texts: e.g. jazz history, musicological analysis, cultural study, sociology and sociolinguistics, essay, journalism, interview, review, (auto)biography, fiction, poetry and film. The organization of material by topic and genre, rather than chronology, is central to the book's strategy. Chronology offers but one kind of methodology – and a limiting one, at that; *Riffs & Choruses* is more interested in inter-relationship, simultaneity and the kind of synergism that manifests itself in the variety and inventiveness of jazz. The rationale for selection also involves theoretical and ideological concerns. These lead to a wider demonstration of how jazz is approached and understood, and, as activity and process, pervades a variety of forms and discourses. Ultimately, *Riffs & Choruses* encompasses the nature and dimension of the 'world' of jazz, both as music and in its relation to American culture and society. As Ralph Ellison has remarked, much of that life and culture is 'jazz-shaped.'[1]

Constructing Choruses: jazz histories (Choruses I–III)

The issues of who 'owns' jazz history and the authority of its construction are crucial to versions of the 'story' or narrative of jazz and are embedded in *Riffs & Choruses*. Attempts at definition, claims for origin, accounts of evolution, descriptions of stylistic phases, provisions of context, interpretations of meaning – all subject the music to particular readings and agendas. In turn, jazz has become a ground of debate about its cultural significance, not least as an artefact of a modernizing world and emblem of that modernity; the competing discourses on the nature and early reception of jazz, for example, are testimony to such controversy and profound difference (see **Chorus I**).

The history of jazz is partly one of definition and analysis of style. Jazz can be more rather than less adequately defined. Certainly, there is a measure of agreement on its recognizable characteristics – views of jazz have got rather beyond the pejorative 'syncopated riot' or 'nigger music' of early responders.[2] Yet noise, apparent shapelessness and absence of 'tune' are still a problem with reception by the listening public. *Ah, but where's the melody?* Part of this book's intention is to define jazz and establish its features and essential properties; in doing so, it presents the dynamics of playing conventions and procedures – the jazz process. Some earlier selections here, concerning jazz appreciation (**Chorus I**) and musicians' improvisation, their playing styles and repertoire (**Chorus III**), suggest that a language of convention, form and spirited narrative telling – an alternative 'story,' no less – is present in most jazz performance and style. Indeed, *one* version of jazz history rests most securely in jazz recordings and their musical analysis – rather than oral recounting, reports of 'the jazz life,' or extramusical myths and biographies. A history of the music has been constructed from an argument about the origin, evolution and development of jazz style (**Chorus III**).

This argument, in turn, has produced a vigorous polemic as to what constitutes definable and valued style in jazz. The purist 'style war' of the 1940s, a clash of classic New Orleans jazz with the progressive innovations of bebop, has been one such focal point. Another, in more recent decades, and still in progress, is the eclecticism of modern and avant-garde jazz. Post-modernist assaults on the jazz tradition have included the stylistic syntheses of fusion, 'world music,' rock, funk and rap – with commodities like 'acid jazz' and 'smooth jazz' compounding style mix and confusion. The struggle to win the argument between forward innovation (synthesis) and a return to jazz tradition (consolidation) continues.[3] And with it, perhaps, the likely future of the music.

In theoretical and interpretative terms, jazz is often understood as a *performance* music, an artefact based on the aesthetic, dynamic and spontaneity of improvisation, and treated as autonomous art object. This formal, stylistic analysis, which employs an essentially *internalist* aesthetic, is traceable to jazz critics like André Hodeir, in *Jazz: Its Evolution and Essence* (1956), and has continued, principally, in the work of Gunther Schuller (*The History of Jazz*, 2 vols, 1968, 1989) and Martin Williams (*The Jazz Tradition*, 1970/1993; *The Smithsonian Collection of Classic Jazz*, 1973/1987). Such a musicological approach to the 'jazz tradition' and its canon (**Chorus II**) has a distinguished and durable history; it is what comes most readily to hand in analysing and teaching jazz *as music*. But jazz is also understood as the product of particular cultural and socio-economic factors, contexts, and environments; it has affinity with its practitioners, public and larger society. An *externalist* approach, or contextualized aesthetic for jazz, has received considerable impetus of late, especially from the sociological and cultural analysis of historians and musicologists like Scott DeVeaux, Gary Tomlinson, and Krin

Gabbard, whose essay collections *Jazz Among the Discourses* and *Representing Jazz* (both 1995) have opened up new dimensions for jazz as discipline and study. Surveying jazz criticism, John Gennari persuasively argues that jazz recordings need to be 'understood as documents created in specific socio-historical contexts,' rather than autonomous works of art.[4] While *Riffs & Choruses* features and compares material from both these approaches (**Chorus II**), its methodology and content favour the more culturally based model of jazz history and historiography. Moreover, it sees jazz as a musical and cultural phenomenon particularly reflecting (or 'signifying') the dominant African-American contribution to the music: in terms of racial difference, aesthetics, agency and what might be called coping strategy. One argument – early advanced by writers like Amiri Baraka (LeRoi Jones) – has been for the inseparability of jazz from the conditions of black culture which long preceded its emergence.[5] To suggest jazz displays an omnipresent relation to the culture of race and racism is to repeat a truism. This book repeats it.

Variant jazz histories are also constructed through generic typologies, such as autobiography and the strong tradition in jazz narrative of oral history, involving the increasing provision/use made of archival resources. Ever since the ground-breaking compilation *Hear Me Talkin' to Ya* (1955) – itself billed as a 'story' from the 'makers' – writers on the jazz life and scene have sought the oral testimony of the musicians themselves. 'Jazz talk' and 'talking jazz' have become histories in the vernacular, with all the authority – if partiality – of first-hand experience. Versions of jazz history, too, are clearly determined by factors like sociology, race and gender. For example, several more recent histories, including those of Linda Dahl (1984) and Leslie Gourse (1995), focus on women's roles in and contributions to jazz, a timely feminizing of the jazz life and experience in contexts which, historically, have been resolutely masculine. If jazz, and jazz history, is to be institutionalized and made more professionally responsive to a nascent *discipline* of jazz studies, then these and other discourses are likely to have increasing sway, and the parameters of understanding jazz duly extended. *Riffs & Choruses* contributes to this process.

Playing changes: jazz cultures (Choruses IV–VII)

Essentially, the argument for a contextual approach to jazz can be made through a study of its pervasiveness in American history and culture. Here, *Riffs & Choruses* assembles a variety of material on jazz's relationship with the overlapping areas of culture, race, myth, and the jazz life. Analogies between the changing phases and styles of jazz music and socio-political and cultural change in America itself (**Chorus IV**) are broadly suggested by full-length studies like Burton Peretti's *Jazz in American Culture* (1997) – and in articles on the reception and politics of the music, by writers like Lawrence Levine (1989), Bernard Gendron (1994) and Eric Lott (1995).[6] In James Collier's words, jazz has been a 'theme song' for the American century.[7] Other cultural historians, too, have followed the example set by Neil Leonard's *Jazz and the White Americans* (1962), and interpreted specific periods of jazz in terms of socio-cultural history and change, through factors like performance contexts, production and audience reception. So, for David Stowe (1994), 1930s and 1940s American culture is 'swing-shaped;' and, in the researches of Kathy Ogren (1989), Scott Fitzgerald's 'jazz age' takes on more precise meaning. Others, like Irving Horowitz, Alan Merriam and Charles Nanry, have also brought a sociological perspective to jazz. Studies of deviant and outsider behavioural patterns in jazz musicians, and case histories of professional activity, have helped analyse what it means to talk of a jazz profession and community.

At the centre of much of the cultural manifestation of jazz lies the issue of race, and a continuing debate on how to evaluate the contributions and achievements of black jazz musicians in a predominantly white culture. (**Chorus V**). Racial 'otherness' and issues of identity, creativity and representation underlie this debate, as does black musicians' concern with the ownership of jazz in an exploitative power structure. Arthur Taylor's earlier interviews with black jazz musicians, and more recent studies from Burton Peretti (1992), Gene Lees (1994), Jon Panish (1997) and Charley Gerard's aptly-titled *Jazz in Black and White* (1998), all centre on race and American culture. To such ideological struggles may be added the musical and linguistic dimension of 'signifying.' African-American literature and music improvises with emotional force and creative expressiveness on its own experience. For black writers and musicians like Amiri Baraka, Henry Louis Gates, Charles Mingus and Albert Murray, jazz is an inter-textual vernacular of extraordinary inventive power, an index of racial ethos and temper.

Alternative jazz histories situated in socio-cultural contexts have also produced aficionado accounts and hagiographies of jazz musicians (**Chorus VI**). These take shape as personal stories and (auto)biographies which share the elevating tendencies of myth; they convert jazz lives into narratives of romance (success) and tragedy (failure) – and often heroism. The fascination of myths and their fabulation is turned into a mystique in the cases of certain jazz musicians' careers and lives. This process is illustrated here in case 'stories' centred on Bix Beiderbecke, Lester Young and Charlie Parker – with the emanation of the 'jazz myth' in legendary Buddy Bolden and his New Orleans 'chillun.'

The culture of the jazz life in the contexts of musical profession and experience has found inscription and mediation in some distinctive autobiographies (**Chorus VII**). Jazz writing from musicians themselves involves issues like authorship and authenticity in translating orality into written texts, frequently with the collaboration of others – a kind of double mediation. Christopher Harlos' article on the theory, practice and politics of jazz autobiography (Gabbard 1995b) is a major contribution here. If many autobiographies enlarge the cultural dimensions of jazz, they also provide an invaluable supplement – even alternative – to formal histories. Live testimony of jazz musicians, like Hampton Hawes, Mezz Mezzrow, Art Pepper and Mike Zwerin, give authentic, personal voice to versions of the jazz experience and the demanding business of 'payin' dues.' Such authenticity, with its first-hand recounting, and the vitality and persistence of an oral tradition, are essential to a fuller picture of the music. The culture of jazz is rendered more vibrantly human and accessible in this way.

Improvising lines: jazz extensions (Choruses VIII–X)

A recent multi-disciplinary anthology by Robert O'Meally, *The Jazz Cadence of American Culture* (1998), presages what will, hopefully, be an increasing interest in examining other cultural practices and arts which draw on jazz music and 'the jazz factor,' e.g. history, painting, photography, dance, poetry, fiction and film.[8] This suggests that a 'jazz-shaped' culture reflects distinctive features of the music – democratic and co-operative participation, protean change, improvisation, flexibility, rhythmic vitality, emotional intensity, directness – and embodies or correlates them in other forms. Here, *Riffs & Choruses* explores permeations of the spirit and properties of jazz in three overlapping areas: language, literature and film. It views them as valuable and significant extensions of the 'world' of jazz.

Together with the technical terms employed by jazz as music, it has developed a language specific to its sociological and cultural contexts, which serves as a kind of insider vernacular and code (**Chorus VIII**). As Robert Gold's *Jazz Talk* (1975) demonstrates, jazz parlance and lingo, prolific and inventive, mostly derive from black idiom and the argot of crime and urbanism. Its specialized jargon sets it apart from the mainstream and majority, though it has made permanent contributions here. Anthology selections focus on the 1940s–1950s, a period of especial fecundity. They illustrate jazz language's propensity for signalling semantic and often cultural–racial difference, as well as subverting conventional linguistic and literary practice. This is found in samples of vernacular autobiography, parodies of fairy tale and popular song, and Beat poetry. 'Hip' terms and 'jive' talk are also presented in lexicon and 'translation,' and as part of vocal strategy in scat, vocalese and jazz-related poetry.

Literary analogues of jazz, or 'literary jazz,' employing the synergy of a jazz aesthetic, can be most nearly found in the forms of fiction and poetry, which is where selections here concentrate (**Chorus IX**). Much of this literary writing describes jazz in momentary performance, simulating its effects in an attempt to imitate or reproduce in linguistic terms the sounds and spirit of the music; other fiction more effectively interprets jazz through the displacement of metaphor, rather than direct description. A degree of success attends the better short stories and novellas (Eudora Welty's 'Powerhouse' and Julio Cortázar's 'The Pursuer' are widely admired), though literary texture can only imperfectly approximate to music – as Jack Kerouac's 'spontaneously' composed prose and prosody demonstrate. The closer synthesis of jazz form with poetry, which emphasizes voice, orality and performance, is exhibited through selections from the 'jazz-and-poetry' movement of the 1950s. A variety of other, later poems also demonstrate the influence of jazz, in subject and/or technique; they appropriate or replicate the aura and ambience of the music.

The confluence of jazz with film has not always been a fortunate one, despite the potential for fruitful encounter (**Chorus X**). The contexts of canon, art and ideology colour the filmic representation of jazz, and determine much of the racial stereotyping of black characters who perform jazz in white environments. Here, Krin Gabbard's study of jazz in American cinema (1996) is a seminal contribution. Jazz has been particularly used – as well as abused – in white biopics dealing with both white and black subjects, where it has been too readily equated with sordidness and sleaze and larded with the clichés of myth-making. The problems which beset jazz feature film – as well as some of its relative successes – are illustrated in the critical reception given *Round Midnight* (1986) and *Bird* (1988). Numerous jazz documentary and performance vehicles have arguably fared better in privileging jazz and its musicians, and representative choices from these genres complete *Riffs & Choruses'* consideration of cultural practices with affinity to jazz.

'A real long run': using this book

Riffs & Choruses is a reader anthology and resource tool. The book meets the interests of a broad readership, but it is also intended to be used in classrooms involving a variety of courses in jazz music, jazz history, and writing on the cultural dimensions of – and approaches to – jazz. The primary sources assembled here complement and expand on historically-orientated jazz texts – and especially on the accompanying volume to this book: Alyn Shipton's *A New History of Jazz* (2001). The anthology also complements those texts which emphasize jazz appreciation and the perspectives of jazz style. *Riffs & Choruses*, too, provides supplementary readings for popular music, African-American, American and Cultural Studies, history and sociology courses.

The book organizes its selections on a topic and genre basis, and by analytical-descriptive category. The threefold division of content suggested above (*Jazz Histories, Jazz Contexts, Jazz Extensions*) identifies potential groupings of Choruses in the anthology; the latter run as a continuum, 1 to 10. Each Chorus is prefaced by Riffs of appropriate 'head' quotation; they are followed by an edited, critical overview, which offers contextualized, linked commentary on the significance of each of the subsequent items of content, and identifies certain issues for discussion. These overviews provide *essential* prefatory matter for a reading of the anthology's content and are a guide to the order and grouping of the 144 items. Individual content items and their authors are identified in bold type (e.g. **Morton (7)**); cross-references to other Choruses employ roman numerals, which may be followed by an item number (e.g. **IX/ 125**). All content items are sourced in footnotes and give, where known, dates of first publication; where items have been excerpted, exact page numbers are provided. Textual referencing follows standard procedure – e.g. (Ulanov 1952: 5) – with identification of author, publication date, and page or chapter number; full details are given in the Bibliography. The anthology's content is followed by a comprehensive Suggested Reading overview. This tracks the sequence of anthology Choruses, making recommendations which are tied in with issues, themes and subject areas of the main text. The Select Bibliography provides details of all suggested reading (excluding title-lists of fiction, poetry and film); it also records all other works quoted or referred to, as well as a number of other titles useful for a study of jazz. Editorial matter largely dispenses with foot- and endnotes – except when retained, sometimes edited, from an original source item – and relies on the comprehensive Bibliography to provide readers with *all* relevant information. A Name Index concludes the anthology.

Coda: acknowledgements

The first – and last – acknowledgement is to myself: *Riffs & Choruses* has been thirty years in my head and five years in the making. It has been a long birthtime. I first taught jazz and literature courses at Clark University, Massachussets, in the late 1960s; in 1978 I was appointed by the Polytechnic of Wales to teach American Literature/Studies, which later, as the University of Glamorgan, supported me in offering new Jazz Studies modules; colleague-historian Neil Wynn encouraged me in teaching American Studies in ways interdisciplinary across many years of shared practice; the British Association for American Studies favoured me with delivery of synchronic papers on jazz culture and literature; more recently, research labours have been supported with the University of Glamorgan's excellent inter-library loan service, namely through staff Lynda Edwards, Ceri Ham and Rachael Morgan. In the preparation of such a large anthology, the following authors and individuals have given their generous help and support: Richard Albert, Whitney Balliett, Linda Dahl, Scott DeVeaux, Geoff Dyer, Sascha Feinstein, Krin Gabbard, John Gennari, Gary Giddins, Toby Gleason, Michael Harper, Gene Lees, Neil Leonard, Sue Mingus, Ingrid Monson, Dan Morgenstern, Harryette Mullen, Charles Nanry, Laurie Pepper, Lewis Porter, Ken Spence, Al Young and Mike Zwerin. With numerous copyright permissions, the following were especially considerate in negotiating fees: Kay Robin Alexander (Duke University Press), Perry Cartwright (Chicago University Press), Carole Christiansen (Doubleday), Sara Crowe (Wylie Agency), Sari Globerman (Russell & Volkening), Donald Graham (*Washington Post*), DeAnna Heindel (Georges Borchardt), Norma Johnson (Greenwood Pub. Group), Mary Beth Keane (Sterling Lord Literistic), Yvonne Knight (University of Illinois Press), Eve Lazovitz (St. Martin's Press), Richard Nash (Oxford University Press), Dennis Palmore (New Directions), Mimi Ross (Henry Holt) and Craig Tenney (Harold Ober). Finally, this project has only seen day through the belief and enthusiasm of editorial director Janet Joyce at Continuum, and jazz writer, editor, broadcaster and publisher Alyn Shipton, at Bayou Press. The rest, as they say, has been and is very much my own. Copyright permissions excepted, *a whole lotta fun* in making *a real long run*.

Notes

1 Ralph Ellison: 'What America would be like without blacks,' *Time*, 95 (6 April, 1970): 33.
2 The first phrase was Damon Runyon's, in 1917 (see Tirro: *Jazz: A History* [1993]: 88); the second was commonplace.
3 For an anthology of the controversies and critical issues involving understanding and reception of jazz, see Robert Walser's *Keeping Time: Readings in Jazz History* (1999).
4 John Gennari, 'Jazz criticism: its development and ideologies,' *Black American Literature Forum*, 25, 3 (Fall, 1991): 459.
5 See Krin Gabbard, 'Introduction: the jazz canon and its consequences,' *Jazz Among the Discourses* (1995a): 25, n. 27.

6 For details, see entries in Bibliography.
7 James Lincoln Collier, *Jazz: The American Theme Song* (1993).
8 Distinctions in racial uses of jazz and their representation in postwar American culture are welcomingly examined in Jon Panish's *The Color of Jazz* (1997). See also *Seeing Jazz: Artists and Writers on Jazz*, compiled Marquette Folley-Cooper *et al.* (1997).

Riff 1

I have an ear for music,
Almost everybody has;
But what is there that's Beautiful,
In a howling band of jazz?
(Teddy Morse, *New York Clipper*, 1917)

A number of niggers surrounded by noise. (*The Etymological Dictionary of Modern English*, quoted Charles S. Johnson, 'Jazz,' *Opportunity*, 1925)

The genesis myth of jazz as word, practice, symbol, and history. (David Meltzer (ed.), *Reading Jazz*, 1993)

Jazz is primarily a performance art that takes place in an ensemble context of collective improvisation. (Stanley Crouch, 'Jazz criticism and its effect on the art form,' in *New Perspectives on Jazz*, ed. D.N. Baker, 1990)

The First Sensational Amusement Novelty of 1917
'THE JASZ BAND'
Direct from its amazing success in Chicago,
where it has given modern dancing new life and a new thrill.
The Jasz Band is the latest craze that is sweep-
ing the nation like a musical thunderstorm ...
You've Just Got to Dance When You Hear It.
(Quoted H.O. Brunn,
The Story of the Original Dixieland Jazz Band, 1960)

Come on, boys! Give it a lick! What do you think you are – a symphony orchestra or something? (Henry Osgood, 'The anatomy of jazz,' 1926)

Chorus I

The Delirium Tremens of Syncopation: Jazz and definition

(origin, terms, early reception)

Neil Powell introduces his dictionary, *The Language of Jazz* (1997: 1), by observing that jazz has 'the distinction of being an art-form almost exactly of the twentieth century: born into the modern world, defined by and defining its epoch, subject to irrevocable and quite possibly terminal change as the millennium closes.' In the end lies always a beginning, and the birth beginnings of jazz – in origin and definition – have received considerable attention and debate. **Chorus I** introduces formal and working definitions of jazz; musicological conventions; etymology and musical origins; and the discourses and ideologies of early reception.

Jazz may be easy to recognize – uncharitably, an early critic called it 'ordered and calculated noise' (see **10**) – but it is 'treacherously difficult to analyse: it both invites and repels exegesis' (Powell 1997: 2*). The New Grove Dictionary of Jazz* confidently defines it (in part) as 'a music created mainly by black Americans in the early 20th century through an amalgamation of elements drawn from European-American and tribal African musics' (Kernfeld 1994: 580). This is James Collier speaking, a white jazz historian. Most jazz musicians would not disagree with this provenance, but many have resisted definitions, or ignored them. For Max Roach, for example, 'jazz' is synonymous with 'shit' (as in 'don't give me all that …'), and redolent of bawdy houses and an unsavoury past. Hampton Hawes and Charles Tolliver, among other black musicians, have equated naming with control by white business – nomenclature as possession (Taylor 1993: 109–10, 76, 185). Duke Ellington consistently disclaimed playing or writing 'jazz,' in favour of a broader 'music' and 'folk music' (e.g. Tucker 1993: 44–5, 218, 249). Many musicians simply proclaim their lack of interest in or inherent difficulty with definition. Famously, Louis Armstrong is reputed to have advised one lady enquirer against 'messing' with it (Horowitz 1973: 58), while others take refuge in vernacular or metaphor. 'It's like lovin' a girl, and havin' a fight, and then seein' her again,' proffered bandleader Chick Webb (Ulanov 1952: 5). He was, after all, a drummer.

The reluctance of musicians themselves has not deterred others from attempting definition of jazz and analyses of its nature and process. Behind definition, too, lie particular ideologies, especially of cultural and racial politics. Sociologists Horowitz and Nanry (1975: 24) observe that under the rhetoric about the etymology of the word are disputations on the nature of jazz, and the contribution made by black Americans to the idiom. In this sense, meanings have been constructed for, and imposed on the music. They are 'readings' which create their own discourse and reflect a vigorous debate over jazz and its reception by early modern America.

The historicity of jazz may suggest it is a collective activity, where 'its meaning is defined by its social context' (Horowitz and Nanry 1975: 25). It is worth emphasizing this claim when considering definitions, since to date there have been many more *musicological* definitions than sociological ones. It is hardly surprising jazz has been primarily defined as *music*, according to formal elements and characteristic features, with styles and performances related to an established canon (**II**). This is where the burden of definition falls, utilizing what Horowitz and Nanry call 'the boundary maintenance approach' (ibid.: 26) of inclusion/exclusion, or the 'recognition-model', which Francis Newton (1975: 15–21) offers as a check-list of defining characteristics.

The initial compendium of **jazz definitions** (**1**) ranges across a broad period (1913–99), with representation of varied commentators, white and black, American and European, musician and non-musician. From a musicological viewpoint, there is considerable agreement on the *features* and *elements* of jazz. The working context of jazz activity is an informal, performance one, with ritual inter-action between musicians and audience; it is primarily improvised, a music of spontaneous, sometimes collective creativity; its 'swing' and rhythmic emphases – syncopation – are a marked feature of its momentum; it has distinct timbral qualities in instrumentation, voice and style; and it is a complex blending of European, African and African-American musical traditions – in (respectively?) harmony, rhythm and melodic form.

If the musicology and formal aesthetic of jazz are to have application, this must lie in the technical basis of appreciation, an awareness for listeners of *how* jazz works, and *what* it is doing. (See also **III**.) In an introduction to jazz, Avril **Dankworth** (**2**) economically outlines the 'musical basis' of the jazz process, identifying the techniques of form, improvisation and rhythm. Additionally, Martin Williams, in *Where's the Melody?* (1966: 6–15),* has provided a lay 'listener's introduction' to the essentials of jazz rhythm and improvisation. While jazz rhythm (or 'swing') is largely a recognizable quality, improvisation is not. What Williams explains is that jazz musicians, in improvising, offer *new melodies*, made up on the spot; these may involve embellishment of a written melody (or theme) or invention of new melodies, patterned on the chord structure, or harmonic base, of the original. Essential to the whole practice is the notion of *variation*, both rhythmical and melodic. The final answer to Williams' initial question is: 'the melody is the one the player is *making*' (my italics). Jazz melody is inherently in jazz improvisation itself. This is an essential point to grasp in any understanding of the jazz process and it combats the often-heard accusation from listeners that jazz is tuneless or lacks melodic content.

Clearly, definition here is confined to jazz's technical properties, resulting in the particular 'feel' or 'spirit' in which it is conceived and played. However,

---

* Copyright charges prevent reprinting.

certain musicologists and cultural historians, like Krin Gabbard – editor of several essay collections on jazz – have expressed conviction that any attempt to arrive at definition 'must be based on a sociocultural analysis of jazz rather than on its internal aesthetics' (Gabbard 1995a: 22, n.1). Horowitz's sociological 'paradigm' for jazz (1973: 58) similarly suggests a number of 'vectors,' some extra-musical; these again argue for a plural and multi-dimensional context, and one which deserves growing recognition (**II**).

'Whence comes jass?' (Kingsley 1917) Etymologically, derivation of the word 'jass' or 'jazz' has invited much fruitless conjecture (**3–6**). However, apparently conflicting etymologies may be mutually reinforcing ones: e.g. *jaser*, as in chat or gossip; corruptions and variations of musicians named as Jasper, Jazzbo, Razz, Charles and Chas; black slang for sexual intercourse; onomatopoeically, energy and excitement (see Powell 1997: entry, 67–8). Robert **Hendrickson**'s encyclopaedic entry (**3**) provides a useful summary of the word; it is expanded by Eileen **Southern** (**4**) to suggest 'jazz' entered print/printable meaning by at least *c.* 1915–16, with references to band music, vaudeville, song publication and early recording; and it receives specific focus in James **Europe**'s explanatory, 1919 account of Razz's New Orleans band and 'jazzing [up]' the new music (**5**). Semantic and linguistic derivation of 'jazz' has been exhaustively researched by ethnomusicologists Alan **Merriam** and Fradley **Garner**, who examine suggested sources (1917–58). Their conclusion, reproduced here (**6**), decides there is no compelling evidence for the claims of one over another.

Historical uncertainty over the origins of 'jazz' is compounded by Ferdinand 'Jelly Roll' **Morton**'s audacious claim as creator of the music in 1902 (**7**). This was made in a riposte in *Down Beat* magazine in 1938, when Morton took vehement issue with a radio broadcast, which had attributed composer W.C. Handy with jazz's origin. Other than providing an amusing portrait of *braggadocio* Morton, the letter testifies to the sheer earliness of developed 'jazz' music activity in America – dates, locations, personnel, titles, styles. No wonder that Morton could claim 'Originator of Jazz & Stomps' and 'World's Greatest Hot Tune Writer' on his business cards. His was a large, important influence, not least in virtuosic piano improvisation, early jazz composition and small group orchestration, and the dating of some of Morton's work may lend part-credence to his bold claim (Tirro 1993: 155–8).

That jazz originated from a complex fusion of cultural influences and musical styles is not in question, and a number of jazz-like musics had surely evolved in many American locales before application of the word 'jazz' in the 1910s. Musicologist Gunther **Schuller**'s huge study, *Early Jazz* (1968), is centred on 'roots and musical development,' and is one of the most influential works to emphasize the value of detailed musical analysis over sociological and historical investigation (**8**). Schuller's starting point is the relatively primitive and lowly nature of early jazz (its 'nadir'), following as he does an evolutionary model of development for its growth into 'a world music.' This agenda privileges a formalist and aesthetic view of jazz, its conventions, repertoire and – above all – recordings. From such a standpoint, unfortunately, other historical and certainly contextual considerations are largely excluded.

'Jazz is upon us, everywhere' (Engel 1922: 182). The **early reception of jazz** (**9–17**) ranges from ecstatic approval and proselytizing zeal to outright hostility and moral condemnation. It illustrates – as both Leonard (1962) and Ogren (1989) have shown – the controversy surrounding jazz in the context of early twentieth-century culture, of which it was a central, modernizing part (**IV**). Here, responses to the new music provide a vehicle for various agendas and ideologies. Jazz can appeal in its folkloric, primitive vitality and beneficent noise – force and emblem of the modern (**9–10**), where it becomes 'a sign and symbol of the American pace, of its moving spirit,' 'the natural expression of the times' (Porter 1997: 123, 124). As one writer notes (**10**), the music's joyous, virile energy constitutes 'a large part of its compelling force and appeal.' Conversely, jazz is seen as tainted and immoral deviance: its raw, syncopating rhythms are seductively lustful and decadent, 'jungle' music that 'makes savages of us all' (Anon: 1918).

'So this is jazz ... that peculiar word!' Although a subsequent convert, Henry **Osgood**'s first introduction to the new music (**11**) recollects 'a nerve-harrowing, soul-wrenching noise.' The Ted Lewis orchestra – leader in 'mildewed evening clothes' and playing a 'pitiless' clarinet – is memorably 'cacophonic.' Anne **Faulkner** (1922) rubbishes jazz as destructive dissonance, asking if the music 'put the sin in syncopation' (**12**); she quotes with approval the opinion of a Dr Henry van Dyke, who viewed it as 'an unmitigated cacophony,' 'a species of music invented by demons for the torture of imbeciles' (Porter 1997: 122). If Faulkner appealed to the General Federation of Women's Clubs to popularize 'Good Music,' John McMahon's articles on 'the dangers of jazz' in *The Ladies' Home Journal* enlisted the aid of national Dancing Masters, urging them to reform steps and positions in 'the case of the Commonwealth of Decency versus the Jazz' – before the latter put music on the 'path of degradation' (McMahon 1921, 1922). For outraged European classicists and aesthetes like Clive **Bell** (**13**), jazz is arrogantly dismissed as music of coarse impudence, essentially irreverent and philistine. 'Jazz rags everything ... *plus de Jazz*,' insists his onslaught of 1921. 'Toujours Jazz,' was another critic's combative response (Seldes 1924).

Yet if jazz was welcomed and vilified with equal vigour, there were also the encomiums and appreciations. These sought to legitimize jazz's status and give it recognition as a new and timely American art form; they also reveal some prescience of the nature of the genre. Swiss conductor Ernst-Alexandre **Ansermet**'s eulogistic praise of 'extraordinary clarinet virtuoso' Sidney Bechet is well known, but he also provides an informed account of the art of ragtime, as epitomized by the Southern Syncopated Orchestra, touring Europe in 1919 (**14**). Part of the intention to make jazz respectable involved assimilation into the mainstream culture of the 1920s. This is the motive behind the 'sweet' orchestral music of white bandleader Paul Whiteman. Ostensibly the 'King of Jazz,' Whiteman's activist role promoted a coalescence of various musical styles, across a broad spectrum of popular taste. Olin **Downes** reviews Whiteman's 'symphonic' style in a famous (and grandiose) 1924 concert given by Whiteman's Palais Royal Orchestra in Aeolian Hall, New York (**15**). The 'educational' intention, announced Whiteman's press release, was to illustrate the strides made in popular music from 'the discordant jazz' to 'the really melodious music of to-day, which – for no good reason – is still called jazz' (Osgood 1926: 144–5). From Palais to Concert Hall, from discord to melody, from jazz to music ...

Some of the genuine distinctions between jazz and popular music and 'the true nature of the embryonic form now developing amongst us' are investigated by discerning critic Roger Pryor **Dodge**, in 'Negro Jazz' (1929) (**16**). Dodge offers a riposte to the 'pseudo-jazz' of Whiteman's symphonic performances, in that he re-establishes – indeed, re-creates – the rhythmic and structural essentials of 'Negro' music, which carry melody through to conclusion with a fundamental, natural force. Under attack are the bogus or diluted imitations of jazz – Dodge instances Whiteman and popular composers Gershwin and Berlin – which 'bring about its fusion or confusion with the windbag symphony or trick programme closing rhapsody.' A veritable roll-call of 'true' jazz pioneers – disseminated through recordings – is ranged against 'the bastard children of the polite orchestras.' Dodge rests his case on the innate *negritude* of jazz, which resists dilution and assimilation.

Three views of the essential American-ness of jazz—its energy and movement—conclude the Chorus. Svend **Gade**'s (**17**) Doctor Hausmann, a German composer, comes to America (1927) with his new symphony – only to find the 'characteristic voice' of America is *jazz*. Another European visitor, Jean-Paul **Sartre** (**18**), discovers jazz at Nick's Bar, in New York of 1947. Jazz is a consuming force: hellish, nervous and frenzied is how it leaves its listeners. There is nothing else like it – and it is America's 'national pastime.' Sybil **Kein**, in a poem translated from French (**19**), lays down in 'sassy syncopation' the melting-pot origins, forms and influences that make up 'Jazz.' It is surely worth 'One Mo' Time!'

1 Compendium: Jazz – Formal definitions (1913–99)*

1.1 Ernest J. Hopkins: 'In praise of "Jazz," a futurist word which has just joined the language' (1913)

'Jazz' ... can be defined, but it cannot be synonymized. If there were another word that exactly expressed the meaning of 'jaz,' 'jazz' would never have been born. A new word, like a new muscle, only comes into being when it has been long needed. This remarkable and satisfactory-sounding word, however, means something like life, vigor, energy, effervescence of spirit, joy, pep, magnetism, verve, virility, ebulliency, courage, happiness – oh, what's the use? – JAZZ.

1.2 Henry O. Osgood: *So This is Jazz* (1926)

Jazz: (*orig.* Africa) *v.* to enliven; *pop.* to pep up; *adj.* jazzy, applied to manners, morals, and especially music; *n.* jazz, pepped-up music – or pepped-up most anything else.

1.3 Wilder Hobson: *American Jazz Music* (1939)

The natural language, what may be called genuine jazz, is often an intricate, innovating, spirited music. It would be convenient to give a succinct definition of its form, but attempts to do so have led only to such statements as 'a band swings when its collective improvisation is rhythmically integrated.' The reason why jazz cannot be defined is the fact that it *is* a language. It is not a collection of rhythmic tricks or tonal gags, but a distinctive rhythmic-melodic-tonal idiom – as is, say, Japanese *gaga-ku* or Balinese gong music. And a language of course cannot be defined. A rude sense of it may be had by hearing it. Beyond that, what it communicates will be involved with what the hearer knows of its form.

Jazz springs out of folk music and it still has many folk-musical qualities. It is relatively brief, spontaneous, full of improvisation and the frequent lyric subtlety of men speaking a loved language with enthusiasm. In its lyricism are suggestions of the intense Negro folk spirituals, of revival hymn shouting, blues, folk ballads, popular songs old and new (which it sometimes uses as themes), marches, West Indian strains, and hard music beaten out for hard dancing. And this music moves in unprecedented, extremely varied, and persuasive rhythms.

1.4 Hugues Panassié: *The Real Jazz* (1942)

It will be useful once for all to understand what we mean by the word 'jazz' ... Above all it must not be forgotten, as it too often has been, that jazz was created by the Negro people – more precisely by the Negroes of the United States ... We

---

* *Sources*: See author/date entries in Bibliography.

have here the reason for the extraordinary lack of comprehension authentic forms of jazz have had to battle against, on the rare occasions when jazz has succeeded in reaching the public at all: it is the music of another race, and when confronted with this music, the white race has found itself completely bewildered. This does not mean that white people are unable to understand jazz. We know that there are good jazz musicians belonging to the white race. But in general the Negroes prove more gifted, and while the Negro masses among themselves have an instinctive feeling for this music, white people approach it with resistance and assimilate it slowly.

1.5   Marshall Stearns: *The Story of Jazz* (1956)

We may define jazz tentatively as a semi-improvisational American music distinguished by an immediacy of communication, an expressiveness characteristic of the free use of the human voice, and a complex flowing rhythm; it is the result of a three-hundred-years' blending in the United States of the European and West African musical traditions; and its predominant components are European harmony, Euro-African melody, and African rhythm.

1.6   Joachim Berendt: *The New Jazz Book* (1959)

Jazz is a form of art music which originated in the United States through the confrontation of the Negro with European music. The instrumentation, melody, and harmony of jazz are in the main derived from western musical tradition. Rhythm, phrasing and production of sound, and certain elements of blues harmony are derived from African music and from the musical conception of the American Negro. Jazz differs from European music in three basic elements:

1   A special relationship to time, defined as 'swing.'
2   A spontaneity and vitality of musical production in which improvisation plays a role.
3   A sonority and manner of phrasing which mirror the individuality of the performing jazz musician.

1.7   Francis Newton [E.J. Hobsbawm]: *The Jazz Scene* (1975 [1959])

There can be no firm or adequate definition of jazz ... Nevertheless, as a rough guide, it may be said that jazz ... is music which contains the following five characteristics ... 1. Jazz has certain musical peculiarities [e.g. 'blue' and common major scales] ... 2. Jazz leans heavily, and probably fundamentally, on another African element, rhythm [e.g. 'beat' and syncopation] ... essential to jazz [and] ... the organizing element in the music ... 3. Jazz employs peculiar instrumental and vocal colours [or 'tone' and 'voices'] ... 4. Jazz has developed certain specific musical forms and a specific repertoire [e.g. blues and ballad] ... 5. Jazz is a player's music [e.g. individual and collective improvisation].

1.8   Leroy Ostransky: *Understanding Jazz* (1977)

Jazz is the comprehensive name for a variety of specific musical styles generally characterized by attempts at creative improvisation on a given theme (melodic or harmonic), over a foundation of complex, steadily flowing rhythm (melodic or percussive) and European harmonies; although the various styles of jazz may on occasion overlap, a style is distinguished from other styles by a preponderance of those specific qualities peculiar to each style.

1.9 Max Roach: in Taylor, *Notes and Tones* (1993 [1977])

What do you think about the word jazz?

Jazz is a word that came from New Orleans. It came from the French. It was spelled *j-a-s-s*. A jass house was a house of ill repute. In those days they also called them bawdy houses ... Our music was first known as the music that came from these bawdy houses ... Therefore, when it moved up the Mississippi to Chicago, they made it into jazz. Louis Armstrong always referred to his music as New Orleans style. When someone decided to capitalize on it, they would call it Dixieland, presumably to take the taint of jazz off. There is a lot of truth in the saying that when you name something, you claim it ... It was named jazz, which is why today when you hear people in a film or a television show saying: 'Don't give me all that jazz,' it's synonymous with saying: 'Don't give me all that shit.' Some of us accept this title, though there are many who don't. Personally I resent the word unequivocally because of our spirituals and our heritage; the work and sweat that went into our music is above shit. I don't know whether anybody else realizes what this means, but I really do, and I am vehement about it. The proper name for it, if you want to speak about it historically, is music that has been created and developed by musicians of African descent who are in America ... So for a title I would call it African-American music.

1.10 Jerry Coker: *How to Listen to Jazz* (1978)

Jazz. A musical style that evolved in the United States around 1900, chiefly played by Afro-Americans, though the music has since been produced and consumed interracially and internationally. Jazz was, in the earliest stages, a brewing of many stylistic influences – African rhythms and 'blue tones,' European instruments and harmonies, marches, dance music, church music, and ragtime – all played with an exaggerated, emotional pulse (or beat). The twelve-bar blues form originated in jazz and has always been prevalent in jazz performance. The most important characteristic of jazz, however, is improvisation. Virtually every jazz selection will focus on improvisation, even when many other characteristics remain optional. Jazz continues to develop, absorb new styles and techniques, and change with great rapidity, but improvisation, the blues, and the vigorous pulse remain reasonably constant throughout its history of development from folk music to art music.

1.11 Frank Tirro: *Jazz: A History* (1993 [1977])

As a working definition, we will consider jazz to be the music that came into being through the African-American experience in the southern part of the

United States during the late nineteenth century and first blossomed in the vicinity of New Orleans at the turn of the twentieth century. This music, which has undergone many stylistic changes, may be considered to include ragtime, blues, classic jazz, Chicago-style jazz, swing, boogie-woogie, Kansas City-style jazz, bebop, progressive jazz, free jazz, and fusion-jazz, as well as others. Certain musical elements are common to all, and the musical sound produced in combination is usually recognizable as jazz even by the untrained listener. These elements may be present in varying proportions, depending upon the style, the performers, and sometimes accidental circumstances, but the common features usually are:

1 improvisation, both group and solo;
2 rhythm sections in ensembles (usually drums, bass, and chordal instrument such as piano, banjo, or guitar);
3 metronomical underlying pulse to which syncopated melodies and rhythmic figures are added (in this regard, additive rhythm is frequently employed);
4 reliance on popular song form and blues form in most performances;
5 tonal harmonic organization with frequent use of the blues scale for melodic material;
6 timbral features, both vocal and instrumental, and other performance-practice techniques that are characteristic of particular jazz substyles, such as vibratos, glissandi, articulations, etc.; and
7 performer or performer-composer aesthetic rather than a composer-centered orientation.

1.12 Krin Gabbard: *Jazz Among the Discourses* (1995)

I would define jazz as a music that is rooted primarily in the confrontation between African American traditions and European music, involving some improvisation and syncopation, and performed more often in nightclubs and dance halls than in concert halls. The music has changed too quickly throughout its history to accommodate a more precise definition. I am convinced that any attempt to arrive at such a definition must be based on a sociocultural analysis of jazz rather than on its internal aesthetics.

1.13 Mark Gridley: *Jazz Styles* (1999 [1978])

Defining Jazz: Four Views

1 For many people, music need only *be associated with the jazz tradition* to be called jazz. Defining jazz in this way is circular. According to this approach, jazz can be anything that anyone ever called 'jazz.' In other words, the meaning of the term resides in the use to which the term has been put. In the view of these people, to know what jazz is, we merely go by how the word is used. Many individuals say that jazz cannot be defined. They just use the term, and then whatever they used it for becomes its meaning. So if someone calls a particular kind of music jazz, that particular kind of music really *is* jazz. In fact, some people apply the term to almost

any music that displays characteristics that have ever been associated with anything ever called jazz. For example, music might be called jazz just because it has a bluesy flavor, or just because it uses instruments that have been associated with jazz, such as saxophones and drums, or just because it has 'jazzy rhythms,' or just because it displays manipulations of pitch and tone quality associated with jazz ... This means that a given performance might fall into the jazz category even though it uses no improvisation and conveys no swing feeling. When people use the term that loosely, they rarely distinguish between jazz and other kinds of music to which we might best apply the term 'jazz-like.'

2   For many other people, a performance need only *convey jazz swing feeling* in order to be called jazz. These people tend to say, 'Jazz is a feeling more than anything else,' or 'Jazz is not *what* you play but *how* you play it.'

3   For some people, a performance need only *be improvised* in order to qualify as jazz. Note, however, that if we define jazz this way, we overlook characteristics that can distinguish jazz from other kinds of music that also employ improvisation, such as rock, and the music of India and Africa.

4   The most common definition for jazz requires that a performance *contain improvisation* and *convey jazz swing feeling*.

2 **Avril Dankworth** Introductory: Jazz (1968)

Source: Avril Dankworth, 'Introductory,' in *Jazz: An Introduction to Its Musical Basis* (London: Oxford University Press, 1968: 1–2). (Editor's title)

Most jazz is in the form of melodic and rhythmic variations upon a theme. The theme is usually a twelve-bar blues melody, the chorus of a popular dance-tune, or a specially composed theme. The basic form is usually simple, with square-cut four- or eight-bar phrases.

There is often a short introduction; then the theme is played by the entire group – combo or band ('combo' is the term for a small combination of players) – followed by a series of variations known as 'choruses'. The first chorus is often pretty close to the theme, only slightly decorated; but with each successive chorus comes further embellishment of melody and rhythm, according to the inspiration, desire, and skill of the player. The more the embellishment, the less obvious is the relationship of the variation to the first statement of the theme: the later choruses often break away from it entirely and become new melodies over the existing harmonies. The final variation, as in 'classical' music, either recaptures the clear-cut spirit of the opening as a final reminder of the original, or works up to an exciting coda or summing-up of all that has gone before.

The improvisation may be solo or collective. When a soloist improvises, he is free to do as he pleases, while the other players combine to accompany him in a harmonic-rhythmic background. But in many performances there are times when everyone improvises simultaneously; this is called collective or group improvisation ('jam sessions'), and here, obviously, each player carries the responsibility of disciplining himself to become part of the whole, and not playing in a way that is conspicuous. The result is a kind of polyphony: only the rhythm section maintains the steady harmonic-rhythmic beat, while the melodic instruments improvise in counterpoint above it. Since they all work on the same harmonic progressions everything fits – or should fit! – together.

A 'break' is a small cadenza which occurs at the end of a phrase with a long note or rest, at which point the soloist is left high and dry without the support of the other instruments. A 'riff' is a short phrase – usually of two or four bars – many times repeated over the changing harmonies of the theme. Greatly favoured as a device for accompaniment, especially during the Swing era, it may also be used by an instrumentalist in the course of his solo.

On the whole, traditional (New Orleans) jazz favours collective improvisation, but in music of the Swing era and since, solo variations have held prime place. Further, traditional jazz is entirely spontaneous, each musician working without music –'ad-libbing' in musicians' language. But since the late twenties, much of the collective work and accompaniment of swing, bop, and modern jazz have been 'arranged' – that is, written down in improvisatory style. In this case, the soloist has a prepared background over which he works. 'Composition' – except for some modern works – usually implies the 'theme' upon which the variations are built. The musician who writes down variations upon this theme is known as the 'arranger'.

3 **Robert Hendrickson** Come on, Jazz! (1987)

Source: Robert Hendrickson, entry 'Jazz' in *The Encyclopedia of Word and Phrase Origins* (London: Macmillan, 1987: 286). (Editor's title)

Enough men to form a good *jazz* group are credited with lending their names to the word. One popular choice is a dancing slave on a plantation near New Orleans, in about 1825 – *Jasper* reputedly was often stirred into a fast step by cries of 'Come on, Jazz!' Another is Mr. *Razz*, a band conductor in New Orleans in 1904. Charles, or *Chaz*, Washington, 'an eminent ragtime drummer of Vicksburg, Mississippi circa 1895,' is a third candidate. A variation on the first and last choices seems to be Charles Alexander, who, according to an early source, 'down in Vicksburg around 1910, became world famous through the song asking everyone to "come on and hear Alexander's Ragtime Band." Alexander's first name was Charles, always abbreviated Chas. and pronounced Chazz; at the hot moments they called, "Come on, Jazz!", whence the *jazz* music.' Few scholars accept any of these etymologies, but no better theory has been offered. Attempts to trace the word *jazz* to an African word meaning hurry have failed, and it is doubtful that it derives from either the *chasse* dance step; the Arab *Jazib*, 'one who allures'; the African *jaiza*, 'the sound of distant drums'; or the Hindu *jazba*, 'ardent desire.' To complicate matters further, *jazz* was first a verb for sexual intercourse, as it still is today in slang.

4 **Eileen Southern** The Jazz Age (1983)

Source: Eileen Southern, 'The Jazz Age,' in *The Music of Black Americans: A History* (New York: Norton, 1983 [1971]: 361–2) (excerpt).

There are numerous theories about the origin of the word *jazz*. One to which several authorities subscribe is that the word is somehow related to an intinerant black musician named Jazbo Brown, who was well known in the Mississippi River Valley country. It was said that when Brown played in the honky-tonk cafés, the patrons would shout, 'More, Jazbo! More, Jaz, more!' Another theory is that the word can be traced to a sign painter in Chicago who, in about 1910, produced a sign for the black musician Boisey James stating that 'Music will be furnished by Jas.' Band.' James, a purveyor of hot music and particularly of the blues, became known as 'Old Jas,' and the music he played, 'Jas's music.' Eventually the music was simply called jazz.

Many varied theories have been advanced over the years. James Europe denied, for example, having given an explanation that was attributed to him in the press – that the word *jazz* represented a corruption of 'razz,' the name of a Negro band active in New Orleans about 1905. It is noteworthy, however, that all of the theories suggest that the word is to be associated in one way or another with the folk mores of black men, either in the United States or in Africa.

Ironically, the first groups to formally introduce jazz to the public were white dance orchestras from New Orleans. In 1915 the Lamb's Club of Chicago hired a white band, under the direction of Tom Brown, that was billed as 'Brown's Dixieland Jass Band, Direct from New Orleans, Best Dance Music in Chicago.' Two years later an orchestra led by Nick LaRocca, the 'Original Dixieland Jazz Band,' opened at the Reisenweber Café in New York and made musical history, for during the same year LaRocca's band made the first recordings of jazz music. According to legend, the Victor Recording Company offered a contract to Freddie Keppard and his Original Creole Band, but Keppard refused it for fear that other trumpet players might steal his musical ideas. But Victor did make a test recording of a black band, the Creole Jass Band playing *Tack 'em Down*, on December 2, 1918 ...

In the black tenderloin districts of villages and large cities throughout the nation, black ensembles (or 'combos') continued to play the kind of music they had been playing for many years, a blues-rag kind of music, most frequently performed by a pianist, drummer, and banjoist or harmonica player or by a lone pianist. Few of the players were aware that their kind of music was invading the dance spots of white America, and there is no evidence that they consistently used the word 'jazz' in reference to their music before the 1920s. The leaders of large black dance orchestras in such places as New York, Chicago, Denver, Memphis, St. Louis, and Kansas City must have known that the term *jazz* was being applied to dance orchestras, but they did not make immediate changes in the names of their groups. They were doing quite well, after all, as 'syncopated orchestras.'

There were, however, a few exceptions; as early as 1916 pianist-songwriter W. Benton Overstreet used the term *jass* in reference to support groups he directed for the vaudeville acts of Estelle Harris at the Grand Theatre in Chicago. And the songs that Harris featured in her act included two with the word *jazz* in their titles – *Jazz Dance* (copyrighted 1917, 1918) and *That Alabama Jazbo Band*. According to the black press, *Jazz Dance* was used by more black vaudeville acts than any other song ever published. In September 1917 W.C. Handy recorded a song titled *The Jazz Dance*, which may have been the Overstreet song; and in March 1919 James Reese Europe recorded the song with his Hell-Fighter's Band.

By 1918, of course, the term *jazz* had moved into common usage. Black regimental bands fighting overseas in World War I were identified as jazz bands, and both black and white newspapers published articles about the new music. In April 1918 W.C. Handy staged a 'jass and blues concert' at the Selwyn Theatre in New York, assisted by Fred Bryan, 'the Jazz Sousa.' And the Smart Set toured with a musical comedy, *Bamboula*, that was described as a jazzonian opera.

5 James Reese Europe A negro explains 'Jazz' (1919)

Source: James Reese Europe, 'A Negro Explains "Jazz",' *Literary Digest*, 26 April (1919: 28–9).

I believe that the term 'jazz' originated with a band of four pieces which was found about fifteen years ago in New Orleans, and which was known as 'Razz's Band.' This band was of truly extraordinary composition. It consisted of a barytone horn, a trombone, a cornet, and an instrument made out of the chinaberry-tree. This instrument is something like a clarinet, and is made by the Southern negroes themselves. Strange to say, it can be used only while the sap is in the wood, and after a few weeks' use has to be thrown away. It produces a beautiful sound and is worthy of inclusion in any band or orchestra. I myself intend to employ it soon in my band. The four musicians of Razz's Band had no idea at all of what they were playing; they improvised as they went along, but such was their innate sense of rhythm that they produced something which was very taking. From the small cafés of New Orleans they graduated to the St. Charles Hotel, and after a time to the Winter Garden, in New York, where they appeared, however, only a few days, the individual musicians being grabbed up by various orchestras in the city. Somehow in the passage of time Razz's Band got changed into 'Jazz's Band,' and from this corruption arose the term 'jazz.'

The negro loves anything that is peculiar in music, and this 'jazzing' appeals to him strongly. It is accomplished in several ways. With the brass instruments we put in mutes and make a whirling motion with the tongue, at the same time blowing full pressure. With wind instruments we pinch the mouthpiece and blow hard. This produces the peculiar sound which you all know. To us it is not discordant, as we play the music as it is written, only that we accent strongly in this manner the notes which originally would be without accent. It is natural for us to do this; it is, indeed, a racial musical characteristic. I have to call a daily rehearsal of my band to prevent the musicians from adding to their music more than I wish them to. Whenever possible they all embroider their parts in order to produce new, peculiar sounds. Some of these effects are excellent and some are not, and I have to be continually on the lookout to cut out the results of my musicians' originality.

6 Alan P. Merriam and Fradley H. Garner
Jazz – the word (1968)

Source: Alan P. Merriam and Fradley H. Garner, 'Jazz – the word,' *Enthnomusicology*, 68, V, 12 (1968): 373, 392–3 (excerpts).

The history of the word *jazz* is indeed a fascinating one. Variously derived from Africa, Arabia, the Creole, French, Old English, Spanish, the Indians, the names of mythical musicians, old vaudeville practices, associations with sex and vulgarity, onomatopoeia, and other sources, its real origin has been, and may well remain, a mystery. Yet a study of the problems that have been associated with it, and a tracing of the suggestions and viewpoints that have been advanced in the literature from 1917 through 1958, provide a real journey into the background not only of the word, but of jazz itself.

A number of summary articles concerning the word have appeared in the past, but for the most part these have added nothing new to the controversy which surrounds the word. Of more importance are the original suggestions which provided the material for such summaries; thus an article by Walter Kingsley in the New York *Sun* (1917) laid down some of the basic ideas concerning African and minstrel origins of the word which have been copied, either with or without acknowledgment of the source, time and time again. A series of articles in the *Etude* in August and September, 1924, while rehashing some previous suggestions, led to one of the most extended discussions of the problem which raged through several allied journals. A third set of articles, again stressing the African origin, was set off by an anonymous piece in the New York *Times* (1934) which led to numerous rejoinders and further suggestions. We have come to a point in the study of the word where it seems wise to review the past theories although even now it is probably impossible to decide surely which will ultimately prove to be correct ...

We have reviewed ... the various suggested sources for the word jazz revealed in the literature of the past forty-one years, and it is clear that the evidence for one is for the most part no better than for another. It seems to the present authors that the stories of variously named musicians probably have little basis in fact, while the original use of the word as a minstrel or vaudeville term leaves us only a little closer to the original source. The African and Arabic theories remain a possibility and deserve further research, while the English, Indian, and Spanish origins are fairly clearly unbased. The relationship to the French *jaser* remains a distinct possibility, given the French influence in the Southern United States and in New Orleans in particular, as does the early idea that jazz as a minstrel term involved notions somewhat similar to the French translation of that word. The reference to the French, *chasse beaux*, is indeed an intriguing one which should be vigorously pursued. The onomatopoetic and spontaneous origins are highly speculative at very best, but the association of the word jazz in its vulgar sense remains a distinct possibility.

The earliest associations of the word with music so far as locale is concerned refer, surprisingly, to San Francisco, a possibility which remains but which does not seem logical in view of our knowledge of the beginnings of jazz as a musical form. In any event it is reasonably clear that the term came into wide usage in a relatively restricted period between 1913 and 1915. Most early spellings seem to be a figment of the imaginations of the authors who devised them, and suggestions for new words have been spectacularly unsuccessful.

We suggest the need for linguistic and philological research although we are not at all sure that the origin of jazz, the word, can ever be found.

7 Ferdinand 'Jelly Roll' Morton
I created jazz in 1902 (1938)

Source: Ferdinand 'Jelly Roll' Morton, 'I created jazz in 1902, not W.C. Handy,' *Down Beat*, August, 1938: 3, 31; September, 1938: 4 (excerpts). (Reprinted in Ralph de Toledano, *Frontiers of Jazz* [1962]: 104–8.)

It is evidently known, beyond contradiction, that New Orleans is the cradle of *jazz*, and I, myself, happened to be the creator in the year 1902, many years before the Dixieland Band organized. *Jazz* music is a style, not compositions, any kind of music may be played in *jazz*, if one has the knowledge. The first stomp was written in 1906, namely *King Porter Stomp. Georgia Swing* was the first to be named *swing*, in 1907. You may be informed by leading recording companies. *New Orleans Blues* was written in 1905, the same year *Jelly Roll Blues* was mapped out, but not published at that time. New Orleans was the headquarters for the greatest Ragtime musicians on earth. There was more work than musicians, everyone had their individual style. My style seemed to be the attraction. I decided to travel, and tried Mississippi, Alabama, Florida, Tennessee, Kentucky, Illinois and many other states during 1903–04, and was accepted as sensational ...

In 1912 I happened to be in Texas, and one of my fellow musicians brought me a number to play – *Memphis Blues*. The minute I started playing it, I recognized it. I said to James Milles, the one who presented it to me (trombonist, still in Houston, playing with me at that time), 'The first strain is a Black Butts strain all dressed up.' Butts was strictly *blues* (or what they call a Boogie Woogie player), with no knowledge of music. I said the second strain was mine. I practically assembled the tune. The last strain was Tony Jackson's strain, *Whoa B-Whoa*. At that time no one knew the meaning of the word *jazz* or *stomps* but me. This also added a new word to the dictionary, which they gave the wrong definition. The word *blues* was known to everyone. For instance, when I was eight or nine years of age, I heard blues tunes entitled *Alice Fields, Isn't It Hard to Love, Make Me A Palate on the Floor* – the latter which I played myself on my guitar ...

I still claim that *jazz* hasn't gotten to its peak as yet. I may be the only perfect specimen today in *jazz* that's living. It may be because of my contributions, that gives me authority to know what is correct or incorrect. I guess I am 100 years ahead of my time ... *Jazz* may be transformed to any type of tune, if the transformer has doubt, measure arms with any of my dispensers, on any instrument (of course I'll take the piano). If a contest is necessary, I am ready.

The whole world was ignorant of the fact that *blues* could be played with an orchestra (with the exception of New Orleans). One of my protégés, Freddie Keppard, the Trumpet King of all times, came to Memphis on an excursion from New Orleans. I had him and his band play the *New Orleans Blues*, one of my numbers. *That* was the first time Memphis heard *blues* played by an orchestra ...

Happy Galloways played blues when I was a child. Peyton with his accordion orch, Tick Chambers orch, Bob Frank and his piccolo orch. Their main tunes were different pairs of blues. Later Buddy Bolden came along, the first great powerful cornetist. On still or quiet nights while playing Lincoln Park, he could be heard on the outskirts of the City, Carrolton Ave. Section, from 12 to 14 miles away. When he decided to fill the park, that's when he would exert his powerful ability. This man also wrote a *blues* that lived a very long time (thought I heard Buddy Bolden say, '—, —, take it away.') This tune was copyrighted by someone else under the name of *St. Louis Tickler*, and published about 1898. Buddy was older than I. I wrote a *blues* in 1907 entitled *Alabama Bound*. Someone heard the number and had it published in New Orleans ...

Paul Whiteman claimed to be the 'King of Jazz' for years, with no actual knowledge of it. Duke Ellington claimed the title of 'Jungle Music,' which is no more than a flutter tongue on a trumpet or trombone, to any denomination of chord, which was done by Keppard, King Oliver, Buddy Petit and many more, including myself when I played trombone, no doubt before he knew what music was ... For many years I was Number One man with the Victor Recording Company. *Tiger Rag* was transformed into *jazz* by me, from an old French Quadrille, that was played in many tempos. I also transformed many light operas such as *Sextet, Melody in F, Humoresque*, etc., and *After the Ball, Back Home in Indiana*, etc., and all standards that I saw fit, more than 35 years ago ...

In New Orleans we used a regular combo of violin, guitar, bass violin, clarinet, cornet, trombone and drums. Freddie Keppard and his band were employed at a dance hall by the name of the Tuxedo. This went badly and he had to cut two men off. Keppard let out violin, guitar and bass and hired Buddy Christian on piano. That was the first formation of the so-called Dixieland combo. Wm. Johnson, Morton's brother-in-law, wanted to come to California with a band. Morton's wife immediately financed the trip. On arriving in Los Angeles, they were hired by Pantages for his circuit, on circuit tour. They came east the latter part of 1914 or early 1915 and invaded New York City. Played at the Palace Theatre for two weeks, breaking all box office records. They were booked by Harry Weber. The personnel of this orchestra was: Wm. Johnson, bass; Eddie Vincent, trombone; Freddie Keppard, cornet; George Bakay, clarinet; Gee Gee Williams, guitar; Jimmy Palao, violin; Morgan Prince, comedian. This was the first all-New Orleans orch to invade New York. They later joined the show (Town Topics) as just another act, and positively stole the show. This was the greatest organization in history until they disbanded ...

When I first started going to school, at different times I would visit some of my relatives per permission, in the Garden district. I used to hear a few of the following blues players, who could play nothing else – Buddy Canter, Josky Adams, Game Kid, Frank Richards, Sam Henry and many more too numerous to mention – what we call 'ragmen' in New Orleans. They can take a 10c Xmas horn, take the wooden mouthpiece off, having only the metal for mouthpiece, and play more *blues* with that instrument than any trumpeter I had ever met through the country imitating the New Orleans trumpeters ...

Speaking of jazz music, anytime it is mentioned musicians usually hate to give credit but they will say, 'I heard Jelly Roll play it first.' I also refer you to Clarence Jones, in the early days around Chicago and musicians (pianists) like Tony Jackson, Albert Cahill, 'Slap Rags' White, Santoy, Blue, George Hall, Chas. Hill, Black Paderewski, etc. I am sure he remembers when different musicians would say 'there's something peculiar,' referring to my playing and arranging, but all who heard me play would immediately become copy-cats, irregardless of what instrument they played. My figurations – well – I guess, were impossible at that time, and arguments would arise, stating that no one could put this idea on a sheet. It really proved to be the fact for years. Even Will Rossiter's crack arranger, Henri Klickman, was baffled, but I myself figured out the peculiar form of mathematics and harmonics that was strange to all the world but me ...

My contributions were many: First clown director, with witty sayings and flashily dressed, now called master of ceremonies; first glee club in orchestra; the first washboard was recorded by me; bass fiddle, drums – which was supposed to be impossible to record. I produced the fly swatter (they now call them brushes). Of course many imitators arose after my being fired or quitting. I do not hold you responsible for this. I only give you facts that you may use for ammunition to force your pal to his rightful position in fair life. Lord protect us from more Hitlers and Mussolinis. Very truly yours, (signed) JELLY ROLL MORTON, *Originator of Jazz and Stomps, Victor Artist, World's Greatest Hot Tune Writer.*

8 **Gunther Schuller** 'The origins' and 'The beginnings' (1968)

Source: Gunther Schuller, 'The Origins,' and 'The Beginnings,' in *Early Jazz: Its Roots and Musical Development* (New York: Oxford University Press, 1968: 3–4, 63–4) (excerpts).

'The origins'

During the second decade of our century, while the world was engaged in its first 'global' war, and European music was being thoroughly revitalized by the innovations of Arnold Schoenberg and Igor Stravinsky and the radical experiments of the musical 'futurists' and 'dadaists,' America was quietly, almost surreptitiously, developing a distinctly separate musical language it had just christened with a decidedly unmusical name: jazz. The developments in Europe, following a centuries-old pattern in 'art music,' were generated by the visions of single individuals – what the romantic century liked to call the inspirations of 'creative genius.' Jazz, on the other hand, was at this point not the product of a handful of stylistic innovators, but a relatively unsophisticated quasi-folk music – more sociological manifestation than music – which had just recently coalesced from half a dozen tributary sources into a still largely anonymous, but nevertheless distinct, idiom.

This new music developed from a multi-colored variety of musical traditions brought to the new world in part from Africa, in part from Europe. It seems in retrospect almost inevitable that America, the great ethnic melting pot, would procreate a music compounded of African rhythmic, formal, sonoric, and expressive elements and European rhythmic and harmonic practices. Up to the present time these jazz antecedents have been discussed and documented (in so far as documentation has been possible) only in sociological and historical terms. The main events, leading from the importation of Negro slaves into the United States through the rituals of the Place Congo in New Orleans to the spread of 'jazz' as a new American music, have been well substantiated, but the details of this historical development must await much more research and documentation. Our knowledge of the links between certain important events – such as the dances at the Place Congo in the mid-nineteenth century and the emergence of the generation of jazz musicians after Buddy Bolden following the turn of the century – is largely dependent upon educated guessing rather than the sifting of factual data.

While further historical information may or may not be forthcoming, we can now define quite accurately the relationship of jazz to its antecedents on the basis of *musical analysis*. Through such studies it is possible to establish the musical links between earliest jazz and the various tributary African and European musical sources.

It is tempting to categorize this or that aspect of jazz as deriving exclusively from either the African or the European tradition, and many a jazz historian has found such temptation irresistible. Jazz writing abounds with such over-simplifications as that jazz rhythm came by way of Africa, while jazz harmonies are exclusively based on European practices; and each new book perpetuates the old myths and inaccuracies. From writing based on well-meant enthusiasm and amateur research, as much jazz criticism has been, more accurate analysis cannot be expected. But it now is possible to look at the music seriously and to put jazz's antecedents into much sharper focus. In the process the African and European lineages will become somewhat entangled, as is inevitable in the study of a hybrid that evolved through many stages of cross-fertilization over a period of more than a century.

'The beginnings'

It is impossible to establish the exact beginnings of jazz as a distinct, self-contained music. Some historians use the year 1895 as a working date; others prefer 1917, the year that the word *jazz* seems to have become current and the year that the Original Dixieland Jazz Band made what are generally considered the first jazz recordings; still others prefer dates in between. But whatever date is picked, it is safe to say that in purely musical terms the earliest jazz represents a primitive reduction of the complexity, richness, and perfection of its African and, for that matter, European antecedents. Once we get past the fascinating stories and legends of early jazz, once we penetrate beyond jazz as a reflection of certain crucial changes in the social evolution of the American Negro, we are left with a music which in most instances can hold the musician's attention only as a museum relic. The purely musical qualities, heard without regard to their historical and social trappings, have lost their particular, almost topical meaning for us; and as musical structures, in performance and conception, much of the earliest jazz sounds naïve or crude or dated.

This is not to say that we cannot or should not listen to early jazz in the context and aura of its historical past. Indeed, if we as individuals can be conscious of the historic interest, we surely can enjoy early jazz more than its purely musical qualities warrant. Objective discussion of early jazz is made more difficult because no large body of recordings exists. The problem of assessing the quality of early jazz is compounded further by the fact that the pre-1923 recordings that do exist (or even those that are presumed to exist) cannot all be considered jazz in the strictest sense. Most of these recordings were made by society orchestras, novelty bands, or jazz groups who were forced by the companies recording them to play novelty or polite dance music.

The beginnings of film coincide roughly with those of jazz. Yet by 1915 the cinema had already produced its first great artist, D. W. Griffith. In jazz – as far as recorded proof goes – we have to await the recordings of King Oliver and Louis Armstrong for comparable achievement. We may assume, of course, that King Oliver was playing nearly as well in 1916 as in 1923, and that players such as Jelly Roll Morton, Freddie Keppard, Bunk Johnson, and Buddy Petit were producing above-average jazz in the decade before jazz recording began in earnest. But we lack proof. The unfortunate circumstances that placed a social barrier between a colored performer and the white recording companies have robbed us of the evidence forever.

But even if we could find isolated examples of great enduring jazz in this formative period, we would still have to admit that early jazz represents, speaking strictly musically, a relatively low point in the Negro's musical history. Indeed, how could it have been otherwise? Circumstances such as segregation and extreme race prejudice forced the music to be what it was. That it was as much as it was, and that it had enough strength to survive and eventually grow into a world music, is abundant proof of its potential strength and beauty.

From this nadir, jazz gradually developed not only in quality but also in basic conception and intent. The musicians who produced it were undergoing some very profound social changes, and their music obviously had to reflect this. Many jazz followers accept the necessity of these social changes but are unwilling to accept the corollary changes in the music itself. Such a contradiction in position, is, needless to say, untenable.

9 **Anonymous** The appeal of the primitive jazz (1917)

Source: Anonymous, 'The appeal of the primitive jazz,' *Literary Digest*, 55, 25 August (1917: 28–9).

A strange word has gained wide-spread use in the ranks of our producers of popular music. It is 'jazz,' used mainly as an adjective descriptive of a band. The group that play for dancing, when colored, seem infected with the virus that they try to instil as a stimulus in others. They shake and jump and writhe in ways to suggest a return of the medieval jumping mania. The word, according to Walter Kingsley, famous in the ranks of vaudeville, is variously spelled jas, jass, jaz, jazz, jasz, and jascz; and is African in origin. Lafcadio Hearn, we are told, found the word in the creole patois and idiom of New Orleans and reported that it meant 'speeding up things.' The creoles had taken it from the blacks, and 'applied it to music of a rudimentary syncopated type.' In the New York *Sun* [1917], Mr. Kingsley rehearses many of the curious facts and customs associated with the word:

'In the old plantation days, when the slaves were having one of their rare holidays and the fun languished, some West-Coast African would cry out, "Jaz her up," and this would be the cue for fast and furious fun. No doubt the witch-doctors and medicine-men on the Kongo used the same term at those jungle "parties" when the tomtoms throbbed and the sturdy warriors gave their pep an added kick with rich brews of Yohimbin bark – that precious product of the Kameruns. Curiously enough the phrase "Jaz her up" is a common one to-day in vaudeville and on the circus lot. When a vaudeville act needs ginger the cry from the advisers in the wings is "put in jaz," meaning add low comedy, go to high speed and accelerate the comedy spark. "Jasbo" is a form of the word common in the varieties, meaning the same as "hokum," or low comedy verging on vulgarity.

'Jazz music is the delirium tremens of syncopation. It is strict rhythm without melody. To-day the jazz bands take popular tunes and rag them to death to make jazz. Beats are added as often as the delicacy of the player's ear will permit. In one-two time a third beat is interpolated. There are many half notes or less and many long-drawn, wavering tones. It is an attempt to reproduce the marvelous syncopation of the African jungle.'

Contribution is drawn from Prof. Wm. Morrison Patterson's 'pioneering experimental investigation of the individual difference in the sense of rhythm.' Thus: 'The music of contemporary savages taunts us with a lost art of rhythm. Modern sophistication has inhibited many native instincts, and the mere fact that our conventional dignity usually forbids us to sway our bodies or to tap our feet when we hear effective music has deprived us of unsuspected pleasures.' Professor Patterson goes on to say that the ear, keenly sensible of these wild rhythms, has 'rhythmic aggressiveness.' Therefore of all moderns the jazz musicians and their auditors have the most rhythmic aggressiveness, for jazz is based on the savage musician's wonderful gift for progressive retarding and acceleration guided by his sense of 'swing.' He finds syncopation easy and pleasant. He plays to an inner series of time-beats joyfully 'elastic' because not necessarily grouped in succession of twos and threes. The highly gifted jazz artist can get away with five beats where there were but two before. Of course, besides the thirty-seconds scored for the tympani in some of the modern Russian music, this doesn't seem so intricate, but just try to beat in between beats on your kettle-drum and make rhythm and you will think better of it. To be highbrow and quote Professor Patterson once more:

'With these elastic unitary pulses any haphazard series by means of syncopation can be readily, because instinctively, coordinated. The result is that a rhythmic tune compounded of time and stress and pitch relations is created, the chief characteristic of which is likely to be complicated syncopation. An arabesque of accentual differences, group-forming in their nature, is superimposed upon the fundamental time divisions.'

There is jazz precisely defined as a result of months of laboratory experiment in drum-beating and syncopation. The laws that govern jazz rule in the rhythms of great original prose, verse that sings itself, and opera of ultra modernity. 'Imagine Walter Pater, Swinburne, and Borodin swaying to the same pulses that rule the moonlit music on the banks of African rivers.'

For years, we are told, jazz has ruled in the underworld resorts of New Orleans. It has emancipated itself in part from its original surroundings: 'There in those wonderful refuges of basic folk-lore and primeval passion wild men and wild women have danced to jazz for gladsome generations. Ragtime and the new dances came from there, and long after jazz crept slowly up the Mississippi from resort to resort until it landed in South Chicago at Freiburg's, whither it had been preceded by the various stanzas of "Must I Hesitate?" "The Blues," "Frankie and Johnny," and other classics of the levee underworld that stir the savage in us with a pleasant tickle. Freiburg's is an institution in Chicago. If you "go South" you must visit that resort.

'Now let me tell you when jazz music was first heard on the Great Wine Way. I forgot to tell you that it has flourished for hundreds of years in Cuba and Haiti, and, of course, New Orleans derived it from there. Now when the Dollys danced their way across Cuba some years ago they now and again struck a band which played a teasing, *forte* strain that spurred their lithe young limbs into an ecstasy of action and stimulated the paprika strain in their blood until they danced like mænads of the decadence. They returned to New York, and a long time later they were booked on the New Amsterdam roof for the "Midnight Frolic," and Flo said:

' "Haven't you something new? My kingdom for a novelty." And Rosie and Jenny piped up and said that in Cuba there was a funny music that they weren't musicians enough to describe for orchestration, but that it put little dancing devils in their legs, made their bodies swing and sway, set their lips to humming and their fingers to snapping. Composers were called in; not one knew what the girls were talking about; some laughed at this "daffy-dinge music." Flo Ziegfeld, being a man of resource and direct action, sent to Cuba, had one of the bands rounded up, got the Victor people to make records for him, and the "Frolic" opened with the Dollys dancing to a phonograph record. Do you remember? Of course you do. That was canned jazz, but you didn't know it then. First time on Broadway, my dear. My own personal idea of jazz and its origin is told in this stanza by Vachel Lindsay:

> Fat black bucks in a wine-barrel room,
> Barrel house kings with feet unstable,
> Sagged and reeled and pounded on the table,
> Pounded on the table;
> Beat an empty barrel with the handle of a broom,
> Hard as they were able,
> Boom, boom, BOOM,
> With a silk umbrella and the handle of a broom,
> Boomlay, boomlay, boomlay, BOOM.

'Lindsay is then transported to the Kongo and its feats and revels and he hears, as I have actually heard, a "thigh-bone beating on a tin-pan gong."

'Mumbo Jumbo is the god of jazz; be careful how you write of jazz, else he will hoodoo you.

'I add to this the opinion of a highbrow composer on jazz. He is a great technical master of music and does not want his name used. He hates jazz.

"Jazz differs from other music, as it wants to appeal to the eye as much as to the ear.

"The dancing is done simultaneously with performing music. Either the violinist, trombone- or saxophone-player will dance (contortional) while playing.

"Acrobatics are performed with the instruments themselves, as, for example, the violinist throwing the bow and catching it to the tune or rhythm of the music." '

10 **Anonymous** Delving into the genealogy of jazz (1919)

Source: Anonymous, 'Delving into the genealogy of jazz,' *Current Opinion*, 67 (August, 1919: 97) (excerpt).

Good or bad, fad or institution, Jazz was born in Chicago, developed in New Orleans, exploited in New York and glorified in Paris. So writes one of the many authorities who have recently delved into this latest manifestation of American music that has conquered a place in the western world. Howard Brockway, the American composer, attempts to explain, in the N. Y. *Review*, the characteristics and origin of Jazz, but its origin still remains obscure. Chicago claims it, and, according to E. M. King, Chicago still holds the strongest title. But Jazz, claims Mr. Brockway, though it is new to us in the United States and through us to both England and France, is not absolutely new to the world. He attempts an analysis of this newest musical phenomenon:

'Just what is Jazz? In striving to answer this query, I can not hope to imitate the admirable brevity of the word. Jazz is ordered and calculated noise. It is a compound of qualities, both rhythmic and melodic. It seeks, and with absolute success be it said, to sweep from our minds all simultaneous consideration of other things, and to focus our attention upon its own mad, whirling, involved self. Herein lies a large part of its compelling force and appeal. It may well be that General Gouraud could find the hideous load of responsibility lightened, perhaps even put aside for the moment, as he listened to Europe's jazzing, and that he felt his pulse responding to the virile rhythm, and his emotions joining in the rush of the humorous care-free mood. Certain it is that our dough-boys, fresh from the trenches, with days and weeks of grim endeavor and physical strain behind them, turned to the Jazz furnished by their bands and found in it relaxation and solace and cheer which enabled them to forget what was past and to abandon themselves wholeheartedly to the joyous hilarity of the present moment.

'There is not the slightest doubt in this maelstrom of rhythm there abides a powerful tonic effect. Through the medium of the physical, it reaches and influences the psychological attitude. I have been convinced of the truth of this fact by personal experience, undergone not once but many times.'

Jazz is composed of rhythm, melody and a certain modicum of contrapuntal inner voices, continues Mr. Brockway. But the greatest of these is rhythm. The Jazz band starts out to 'get you' and leaves nothing to chance. 'It is fairly well established that only an oyster can resist the appeal of syncopated rhythm when it is performed with masterful abandon which absolutely controls dynamic gradations and vital accents.' Here is the real secret of Jazz:

'The howitzers of the Jazz band's artillery are stationed in the "traps." Under this heading we find all the instruments of percussion, such as the big drum, the snare drum, cymbals, triangle, wooden blocks played upon with drumsticks, xylophone, cowbells, rattles, whistles for the production of various weird noises, and a host of other implements, often the personal conceptions of individual players of the traps. The trombones may represent field guns, while the clarinets, oboes, saxophones, alto horns and cornets furnish the rapid-fire batteries. The range being point-blank, it is easy to see why the effect of the "drum-fire" is complete!

'The melody will always be borne by sufficient instruments to ensure its "getting over." Then, in the inner voices of the band, will take place a combination of effects which adds enormously to the total drive of the number. Here are certain of the contrapuntal features which are mentioned above. They consist of a variety of hilarious effects, produced by trombones or saxophones, attained by a curious sliding from note to note. This creates an extremely comical result. This characteristic and droll portamento has become so well known and so popular that it has achieved a specific name – "blues," a humorously apt designation. A striking contrast is made by the mournful soughing of the trombones in the midst of the joyous riot of the rest of the band. Sharp rhythmic ejaculations arise from out the welter of sound, and over the whole tumult the traps-player spreads his array of dazzling accents, brought forth with absolute virtuosity from his motley army of noise producers. It almost seems, at times, like a case of "each for himself and the devil take the hindmost." But it is not so, and there is definite purpose and ordered means in it all.'

11 **Henry O. Osgood** These cacophonic combinations (1926)

Source: Henry O. Osgood, 'Preambular,' in *So This Is Jazz* (Boston: Little, Brown, 1926: 3–6) (excerpt). (Editor's title)

'*Do* come,' said my friend. 'You'll enjoy it. Ted Lewis and his orchestra are going to play.' And, to add to the lure of the invitation, he produced a Ted Lewis record and played it on the machine in his office.

I went – nevertheless. After food and speeches were over, came Ted Lewis and his orchestra, four men besides himself and his clarinet – a piano player, a cornetist, a trombonist and the drums and traps man, who had less drums than his brother of to-day, but more traps, such as frying pans, rattles, tin cans, cow bells and whistles, plain and fancy, including a siren. It was no worse than the record, except that it was louder. It was, to be candid, very loud indeed.

The cornetist was the most reasonable member of the aggregation. Less often mute and less often muted than to-day, he contented himself as a rule with playing the tune, indulging only occasionally in disturbing extravaganza.

The pianist was diligent. An adapt at syncopation, he supplied the groundwork, occasionally playing the melody *solo*, when the cornetist so far forgot himself as to be imaginative or stopped for breath; occasionally doubling it when circumstances seemed to demand that.

The trombonist was a merry wight and strictly impartial. Wherever he could find a little niche or cranny in the piece that seemed to need filling up, he filled it, and didn't seem to care much what he filled it with. He blew loud, he blew soft, he glissandoed, he counterpointed. He pointed the bell of his machine in the air, he slanted it at the ground, he waved it about indiscriminately. It sounded equally bad in every position.

His activity, however, was nothing to that of the drummer. When it came to the final repeat of a chorus, *fortissimo,* this individual became the embodiment of an insane Alexander, sighing – no, not sighing – clamoring for more instruments to conquer. For the final dash under the wire he would hastily stick a whistle between his teeth, then, devoting his left hand to its legitimate business of playing the snare drum and pounding out the rhythm on bass drum and cymbal with his right foot, he would, like a spiritualistic medium at a séance, free his right hand for illegitimate purposes, beating or shaking the cow bells, pummeling the wood block or the tin cans, assaulting the suspended cymbal or winding the rattle with a zeal, persistency and determination worthy of a better cause.

Aiding and abetting all this disturbance, himself the most strident note in it, Ted Lewis, in mildewed evening clothes, stood front center against the background of his fellow bandits, a battered top hat cocked on one side of his head, in his hands and on his lips that instrument which, in the hands of an unscrupulous performer, is the most ruthless of all – a clarinet. And Lewis was not only unscrupulous and ruthless, he was absolutely pitiless. The remarks of

the traditional pig under the gate are as the whispers of a soloist in the Celestial
Choir compared to the anguished, agonizing sounds he forced from that
tortured instrument. It is a wonder the S.P.C.A. never interfered. The part he
chose for himself in the ensemble was to supply an impromptu, irresponsible,
unrelated *obligato* to what went on about him, always in the shrieking,
squawking upper register of the instrument and always at its full power.

Improvisation and irresponsibility were the keynotes of jazz as performed in
those days. In a combination like Lewis' band no one except the pianist really
needed to *know* whatever piece was being subjected to performance. The
cornetist, with the pianist's assistance, easily scraped acquaintance with the
melody. The other three had no interest in it. While the drummer performed his
simple duties – and, though occasionally multifarious, they are simple – the
trombone below and the clarinet above wove about the tune improvised
arabesques that were sometimes ingenious, sometimes utterly inappropriate,
never subdued, all the players jolting up and down and writhing about in
simulated ecstasy, in the manner of Negroes at a Southern camp-meeting
afflicted with religious frenzy.

The net result was, to sensitive ears, the most nerve-harrowing, soul-
wrenching noise ever produced in the name of music. The old forty horse-
power, all-brass circus and minstrel bands were as nothing compared to it. The
perambulating steam calliope of old circus days seemed in contrast
Shakespeare's 'concord of sweet sounds' itself.

Not that all the blame lay upon Ted Lewis. There were hundreds and
hundreds of these cacophonic combinations all over the country. Lewis is
selected as the particular example of the development of this school of jazz to
the *n*th power – and also because he was my first introduction to it. If, as it
seems likely, he was the original offender from whom all others derived, the
load of responsibility on his shoulders is a mighty one.

12 **Anne Shaw Faulkner** Does jazz put the sin in syncopation? (1921)

Source: Anne Shaw Faulkner, 'Does jazz put the sin in syncopation?'
Ladies' Home Journal, 38, 8 (August 1921: 16, 34) (excerpts).

We have all been taught to believe that 'music soothes the savage breast,' but
we have never stopped to consider that an entirely different type of music
might invoke savage instincts ...

America is facing a most serious situation regarding its popular music ...
Never in the history of our land have there been such immoral conditions
among our young people, and in the surveys made ... the blame is laid on jazz
music and its evil influence on the young people of to-day. Never before have

such outrageous dances been permitted in private as well as public ballrooms, and never has there been ... such a strange combination of tone and rhythm as that produced by the dance orchestras of to-day.

Certainly, if this music is in any way responsible for the condition and for the immoral acts which can be traced to the influence of these dances, then it is high time that the question should be raised: 'Can music ever be an influence for evil?' ...

To-day ... the first great rebellion against jazz music and such dances as the 'toddle' and the 'shimmy' comes from the dancing masters themselves ... The National Dancing Masters' Association, at their last session, adopted this rule: 'Don't permit vulgar cheap jazz music to be played. Such music almost forces dancers to use jerky half-steps, and invites immoral variations. It is useless to expect to find refined dancing when the music lacks all refinement, for, after all, what is dancing but an interpretation of music?' ...

Many people classify under the title of 'jazz' all music in syncopated rhythm, whether it be the ragtime of the American Negro or the csardas of the Slavic people. Yet there is a vast difference between syncopation and jazz. To understand the seriousness of the jazz craze, which, emanating from America, has swept over the world, it is time that the American public should realize what the terms ragtime and jazz mean ...

The Encyclopedia Britannica sums up syncopation as 'the rhythmic method of tying two beats of the same note into one tone in such a way as to displace the accent' ... This curious rhythmic accent on the short beat is found in its most highly developed ... intense forms among the folk of ... Slavic countries ... It was [also] the natural expression of the American Negroes, used by them as the accompaniment for their bizarre dances and cakewalks. Negro ragtime, it must be frankly acknowledged, is one of the most important and distinctively characteristic American expressions to be found in our native music ... Many of the greatest compositions by ... American composers have been influenced by ragtime. Like all other phases of syncopation, ragtime quickens the pulse, it excites, it stimulates; but it does not destroy ...

What of jazz? It is hard to define jazz, because it is neither a definite form nor a type of rhythm; it is rather a method employed by the interpreter in playing the dance or song. Familiar hymn tunes can be jazzed until their original melodies are hardly recognizable. Jazz does for harmony what the accented syncopation of ragtime does for rhythm. In ragtime the rhythm is thrown out of joint, as it were, thus distorting the melody; in jazz exactly the same thing is done to the harmony. The melodic line is disjointed and disconnected by the accenting of the partial instead of the simple tone, and the same effect is produced on the melody and harmony which is noticed in syncopated rhythm. The combination of syncopation and the use of these inharmonic partial tones produces a strange, weird effect, which has been designated 'jazz.'

The jazz orchestra uses only those instruments which can produce partial, inharmonic tones more readily than simple tones – such as the saxophone, the clarinet and the trombone, which share honors with the percussion instruments that accent syncopated rhythm. The combination of the syncopated rhythm, accentuated by the constant use of the partial tones sounding off-pitch, has put syncopation too off-key. Thus the three simple elements of music – rhythm, melody and harmony – have been put out of tune with each other.

Jazz originally was the accompaniment of the voodoo dancer, stimulating the half-crazed barbarian to the vilest deeds. The weird chant, accompanied by the syncopated rhythm of the voodoo invokers, has also been employed by other barbaric people to stimulate brutality and sensuality. That it has a demoralizing effect upon the human brain has been demonstrated by many scientists.

There is always a revolutionary period of the breaking down of old conventions and customs which follows after every great war; and this rebellion against existing conditions is to be noticed in all life to-day. Unrest, the desire to break the shackles of old ideas and forms are abroad. So it is no wonder that young people should have become so imbued with this spirit that they should express it in every phase of their daily lives. The question is whether this tendency should be demonstrated in jazz – that expression of protest against law and order, that bolshevik element of license striving for expression in music.

The human organism responds to musical vibrations ... What instincts then are aroused by jazz? Certainly not deeds of valor or martial courage ... Jazz disorganizes all regular laws and order; it stimulates to extreme deeds, to a breaking away from all rules and conventions; it is harmful and dangerous, and its influence is wholly bad ...

In a recent letter to the author, Dr. Henry van Dyke says of jazz: 'As I understand it, it is not music at all. It is merely an irritation of the nerves of hearing, a sensual teasing of the strings of physical passion. Its fault lies not in syncopation, for that is a legitimate device when sparingly used. But "jazz" is an unmitigated cacophony, a combination of disagreeable sounds in complicated discords, a willful ugliness and a deliberate vulgarity.'

Never in the history of America have we more needed the help and inspiration which good music can and does give ... The General Federation of Women's Clubs has taken for its motto: 'To Make Good Music Popular, and Popular Music Good.' Let us carry out this motto in every home in America firmly, steadfastly, determinedly, until all the music in our land becomes an influence for good.

13 **Clive Bell** Plus de jazz (1921)

Source: Clive Bell, 'Plus de jazz,' *New Republic*, 28 (21 September 1921: 92–3, 94, 95, 96) (excerpts).

On the first night of the Russian ballet in Paris, somewhere about the middle of May, perhaps the best painter in France, one of the best musicians, and an obscure journalist were sitting in a small bistrot on the Boulevard St. Germain.

They should all have been at the spectacle; all had promised to go; and yet they sat on over their alcools and bocks and instead of going to the ballet, began to abuse it. And from the ballet they passed to modern music in general, and from music to literature: till, gradually, into the conversation came, above the familiar note of easy denigration, a note of energy, of conviction, of aspiration, which so greatly astonished one at least of the three that, just before two o'clock – the hour at which the patron puts even his most faithful clients out of doors – he exclaimed with an emphasis in him uncommon 'Plus de Jazz!'

It was the least important of the three who said it, and, had it been the most, I am not suggesting that, like the walls of Jericho, a movement would have tottered at an ejaculation. Jazz will not die because a few clever people have discovered that they are getting sick of it; Jazz is dying, and the conversation to which I have referred is of importance only as an early recognition of the fact. For the rest, it was unjust, as such conversations will be; the Jazz movement, short and slightly irritating though it was, having served its turn and added its quota to the tradition. But Jazz is dead, or dying at any rate, and the moment has come for someone who likes to fancy himself wider awake than his fellows to write its obituary notice. In doing so he may, adventitiously, throw light on something more interesting than the past; for, since always movements are conditioned to some extent by their predecessors, against which, in some sort, they must ever be reactions, he may adumbrate the outline of that which is to come.

The Jazz movement is a ripple on a wave; the wave – the large movement which began at the end of the nineteenth century in a reaction against realism and scientific paganism – still goes forward. This wave is essentially the movement which one tends to associate, not very accurately perhaps, with the name of Cézanne: it has nothing to do with Jazz: its most characteristic manifestation is modern painting which, be it noted, Jazz has left almost untouched. The great modern painters – Derain, Matisse, Picasso, Bonnard, Friesz, Braque, etc. – were firmly settled on their own lines of development before ever Jazz was heard of. Only the riff-raff has been affected. Italian futurism is the nearest approach to a pictorial expression of the Jazz spirit.

The movement bounced into the world somewhere about the year 1911. It was headed by a band and troupe of niggers, dancing. Appropriately it took its name from music – the art that is always behind the times ... Impudence is its essence – impudence in quite natural and legitimate revolt against Nobility and Beauty: impudence which finds its technical equivalent in syncopation: impudence which rags ... After impudence comes the determination to surprise: you shall not be gradually moved to the depths, you shall be given such a start as makes you jigger all over ... Its fears and dislikes – for instance its horror of the Noble and the Beautiful – are childish; and so is its way of expressing them. Not by irony and sarcasm, but by jeers and grimaces does Jazz mark its antipathies. Irony and wit are for the grown-ups. Jazz dislikes them as much as it dislikes Nobility and Beauty. They are products of the cultivated intellect, and Jazz cannot away with intellect or culture. Niggers can be admired artists without any gift more singular than high spirits: so why drag in the intellect? Besides, to bring intellect into art is to invite home a guest who is apt to be inquisitive and even impartial. Intellect in Jazz circles is treated rather as money was once in polite society – it is taken for granted. Nobility, Beauty and intellectual subtlety are alike ruled out: the two first are held up to ridicule, the last is simply abused. What Jazz wants are romps and fun and to make fun; that is why, as I have said, its original name Rag-time was the better. At its best, Jazz rags everything ...

And of course it was delightful for those who sat drinking their cocktails and listening to nigger-bands to be told that, besides being the jolliest people on earth, they were the most sensitive and critically gifted. They, along with the children and savages whom in so many ways they resembled, were the possessors of natural, uncorrupted taste. They first had appreciated rag-time and surrendered themselves to the compelling qualities of jazz. Their instinct might be trusted: so, no more classical concerts and music lessons ...

What, I believe, has turned so many intelligent and sensitive people against Jazz is the encouragement it has given to thousands of the stupid and vulgar to fancy that they can understand art and to hundreds of the conceited to imagine that they can create it ...

Even to understand art a man must make a great intellectual effort. One thing is not as good as another; so artists and amateurs must learn to choose. No easy matter that: discrimination of this sort being somewhat altogether different from telling a Manhattan from a Martini. To select as an artist or discriminate as a critic are needed feeling and intellect and – most distressing of all – study. However, unless I mistake, the effort will be made. The age of easy acceptance of the first thing that comes is closing. Thought rather than spirits is required, quality rather than color, knowledge rather than irreticence, intellect rather than singularity, wit rather than romps, precision rather than surprise, dignity rather than impudence, and lucidity above all things: *plus de Jazz*.

14 **Ernst–Alexandre Ansermet** Bechet and jazz visit Europe, 1919 (1919)

Source: Ernst-Alexandre Ansermet, 'Bechet and jazz visit Europe, 1919' (1919), in Ralph de Toledano (ed.), *Frontiers of Jazz* (New York: Frederick Ungar, 1962 [1947]: 115–16, 116–17, 119–20, 121–2) (excerpts).

This is not about African Negroes but about those of the Southern states of the U.S.A., who have created the musical style commonly known as the rag. Rag music is founded essentially on rhythm and in particular on the qualities of syncopation in rhythm. Rag music first came to Europe in the form of the cake-walk, as I recall, and then with the one-step, two-step, fox-trot, and all the American dances and songs to which the subtitle of rag-time is applied.

America is full of small instrumental ensembles devoted to rag-time, and if the national music of a people is none other than its popular music, one can say that rag-time has become the true national popular music of America ...

The first thing that strikes one about the Southern Syncopated Orchestra is the astonishing perfection, the superb taste, and the fervor of its playing. I couldn't say if these artists make it a duty to be sincere, if they are penetrated by the idea that they have a 'mission' to fulfill, if they are convinced of the 'nobility' of their task, if they have that holy 'audacity' and that sacred 'valor' which our code of musical morals requires of our European musicians, nor indeed if they are animated by any 'idea' whatsoever. But I can see they have a very keen sense of the music they love, and a pleasure in making it which they communicate to the hearer with irresistible force – a pleasure which pushes them to outdo themselves all the time, to constantly enrich and refine their medium. They play generally without notes, and even when they have some, it only serves to indicate the general line, for there are very few numbers I have heard them execute twice with exactly the same effects. I imagine that, knowing the voice attributed to them in the harmonic ensemble, and conscious of the role their instrument is to play, they can let themselves go, in a certain direction and within certain limits, as their heart desires. They are so entirely possessed by the music they play, that they can't stop themselves from dancing inwardly to it in such a way that their playing is a real show, and when they indulge in one of their favorite effects which is to take up the refrain of a dance in a tempo suddenly twice as slow and with redoubled intensity and figuration, a truly gripping thing takes place, it seems as if a great wind is passing over a forest or as if a door is suddenly opened on a wild orgy ...

The desire to give certain syllables a particular emphasis or a prolonged resonance, that is to say preoccupations of an expressive order, seem to have determined in Negro singing, their anticipation or delay of a fraction of rhythmic unity. This is the birth of syncopation. All the traditional Negro songs are strewn with syncopes which issue from the voice while the movement of the body marks the regular rhythm. Then, when the Anglo-Saxon ballad or the banal dance forms reach the Dixieland land of the plantations, the Negroes appropriate them in the same fashion, and the rag is born. But it is not enough to say that Negro music consists in the habit of syncopating any musical material whatsoever. We have shown that syncopation itself is but the effect of an expressive need, the manifestation in the field of rhythm of a particular taste, in a word, the genius of the race. This genius demonstrates itself in all the musical elements, it transfigures everything in the music it appropriates. The Negro takes a trombone, and he has a knack of vibrating each note by a continual quivering of the slide, and a sense of glissando, and a taste for muted notes which make it a new instrument; he takes a clarinet or saxophone and he has a way of hitting the notes with a slight *inferior appoggiatura,* he discovers a whole series of effects produced by the lips alone, which make it a new instrument. There is a Negro way of playing the violin, a Negro way of singing. As for our orchestra tympani, needless to say with what alacrity the Negro runs out to greet them, he grasps all the paraphernalia instantaneously including the most excessive refinements, to set up an inexhaustible jugglery.

The banjo itself (string instrument strummed with a pick) is perhaps not the invention of the Negro, but the modification for his use of a type of instrument represented elsewhere by the mandolin.

By the grouping of these chosen instruments, following the most diversified combinations, a more or less definite type of Negro orchestra constituted itself, of which the Southern Syncopated Orchestra is as the first milestone – an attempt at a synthesis of great style. Composed of two violins, a cello, a saxophone, two basses, two clarinets, a horn, three trumpets, three trombones, drums, two pianos, and a banjo section, it achieves by the manner in which the instruments are played, a strangely fused total sonority, distinctly its own, in which the neutral timbres like that of the piano disappear completely, and which the banjos surround with a halo of perpetual vibration. Now the fusion is such (all brasses muted) that it is difficult to recognize the individual timbres, now a very high clarinet emerges like a bird in flight, or a trombone bursts out brusquely like a foreign body appearing. And the ensemble displays a terrific dynamic range, going from a subtle sonority reminiscent of Ravel's orchestra to a terrifying tumult in which shouts and hand-clapping is mixed ...

There is in the Southern Syncopated Orchestra an extraordinary clarinet virtuoso who is, so it seems, the first of his race to have composed perfectly formed blues on the clarinet. I've heard two of them which he had elaborated at great length, then played to his companions so that they are equally admirable for their richness of invention, force of accent, and daring in novelty and the unexpected. Already, they gave the idea of a style, and their form was gripping, abrupt, harsh, with a brusque and pitiless ending like that of Bach's second *Brandenburg Concerto*. I wish to set down the name of this artist of genius; as for myself, I shall never forget it – it is Sidney Bechet. When one has tried so often to rediscover in the past one of those figures to whom we owe the advent of our art – those men of the 17th and 18th centuries, for example, who made expressive works of dance airs, clearing the way for Haydn and Mozart who mark, not the starting point, but the first milestone – what a moving thing it is to meet this very black, fat boy with white teeth and that narrow forehead, who is very glad one likes what he does, but who can say nothing of his art, save that he follows his 'own way,' and when one thinks that his 'own way' is perhaps the highway the whole world will swing along tomorrow.

15 **Olin Downes** A concert of jazz (1924)

Source: Olin Downes, 'A concert of jazz,' *New York Times*, 13 February 1924: 16 (excerpt).

A concert of popular American music was given yesterday afternoon in Aeolian Hall by Paul Whiteman and his orchestra of the Palais Royal. The stage setting was unconventional as the program. Pianos in various stages of déshabillé stood about, amid a litter of every imaginable contraption of wind and percussion instruments. Two Chinese mandarins, surmounting pillars, looked down upon a scene that would have curdled the blood of a Stokwoski or a Mengelberg. The golden sheen of brass instruments of lesser and greater dimensions was caught up by a gleaming gong and carried out by bright patches of an Oriental back-drop. There were also lying or hanging about frying pans, large tin utensils and a speaking trumpet, later stuck into the end of a trombone – and what a silky, silkly tone came from that accommodating instrument! This singular assemblage of things was more than once, in some strange way, to combine to evoke uncommon and fascinating sonorities.

There were verbal as well as programmatic explanations. The concert was referred to as 'educational,' to show the development of this type of music. Thus the 'Livery Stable Blues' was introduced apologetically as an example of the depraved past from which modern jazz has risen. The apology is herewith indignantly rejected, for this is a gorgeous piece of impudence, much better in its unbuttoned jocosity and Rabelasian laughter than other and more polite compositions that came later.

The pianist gathered about him some five fellow-performers. The man with the clarinet wore a battered top hat that had ostensibly seen better days. Sometimes he wore it, and sometimes played into it. The man with the trombone played it as is, but also, on occasion, picked up a bath tub or something of the kind from the floor and blew into that. The instruments made odd, unseemly, bushman sounds. The instrumentalists rocked about. Jests permissible in musical terms but otherwise not printable were passed between these friends of music. The laughter of the music and its interpreters was tornadic. It was – should we blush to say it? – a phase of America. It reminded the writer of some one's remark that an Englishman entered a place as if he were its master, whereas an American entered as if he didn't care who in blazes the master might be. Something like that was in this music.

There were later remarkably beautiful examples of scoring for a few instruments; scoring of singular economy, balance, color and effectiveness; music at times vulgar, cheap, in poor taste, elsewhere of irresistible swing and insouciance and recklessness and life; music played as only such players as these may play it. They have a technic of their own. They play with an abandon equalled only by that race of born musicians – the American negro, who has surely contributed fundamentally to this art which can neither be frowned nor sneered away. They did not play like an army going through ordered manoeuvres, but like the melomaniacs they are, bitten by rhythms that would have twiddled the toes of St. Anthony. They beat time with their feet – lèse majesté in a symphony orchestra. They fidgeted uncomfortably when for a moment they had to stop playing. And there were the incredible gyrations of that virtuoso and imp of the perverse, Ross Gorman. And then there was Mr. Whiteman. He does not conduct. He trembles, wabbles, quivers – a piece of jazz jelly, conducting the orchestra with the back of the trouser of the right leg, and the face of a mandarin the while.

16 **Roger Pryor Dodge** Negro jazz (1929)

Source: Roger Pryor Dodge, 'Negro jazz,' *The Dancing Times,* 229 (1929: 32–5).

Ernest Newman, the eminent musical critic of the *London Times,* some short time since allowed his keen judgment to be overthrown in the violence of a controversy for and against jazz. A reading of the remarks of Mr. Newman and the answers of his opponents convinces me that jazz needs protection not so much against its enemies as against its friends.

The word 'jazz' is being used too loosely and too indiscriminately by persons who have little perception of the true nature of the embryonic form now developing amongst us. It is no wonder that critics are unable to agree when no two of them are discussing the same thing. The word 'jazz' as it is currently used seems to cover both true jazz and popular music in general. It covers Paul Whiteman, George Gershwin and Irving Berlin, none of whom I consider as belonging to the ranks of jazz at all. But if these men are not exponents of jazz, who are? And what is jazz?

It has been said that there is no such thing as jazz music and that what is commonly called jazz is only a manner of playing music. This is partly true. Any composition can be transformed into a sort of imitation jazz, either by an instrumental technique that applies to the melody, stunts that cannot be notated, or by subjecting it to a jazz-like rhythmical treatment that is susceptible of notation. Critics lay stress on the appearance in jazz of instrumental stunts that cannot be notated as evidence of its ephemeral nature; but this, it seems to me, is a perfectly natural condition. Because these effects cannot be notated now is no proof that they will always be incapable of notation. Those that prove to have value will so develop that in time they will come to be written down, either within our own notation or by creating one of their own. In fact, it seems almost inevitable that a type of music arising from the folk and not from the academies should give vent to sounds that have not yet been foreseen by our present system of notation.

There are two styles of jazz as we have it now which combine to form the most perfect type of jazz – the rhythmic treatment which can give a jazz flavour to any composition and the 'blues.' It is this rhythmic treatment which is generally referred to as jazz, and it is a technique which, once acquired, can be applied to any type of music. The most familiar variety is that which adds the thinnest possible veneer of jazz to the original composition, which, as a rule, is a popular song or a mediocre classic. The melody of the selected composition either undergoes a slight rhythmical distortion to obtain the jazz effect, or is provided with a background of jazz accompaniment; but in both cases enough, unfortunately, of the original is left so that the result of this treatment, as applied to the lesser classics, is the loss of whatever small value the original possessed.

The blues have developed from the spirituals, which had their genesis in the simple but powerful four-part harmonies of our hymns. They are the result of straining a formal and highly-cultivated music through the barbaric and musical mind of the negro. The spirituals are the negros' digestion of our hymn tunes. The blues, in turn, are another step in the development, as Handy's book does not neglect to explain, and it is this material that constitutes the basis of true jazz. Into the negros' singing or playing of the spirituals crept the savage rhythms that had shaped or been shaped by the ancestral dances of the tribe and these formed in time a definite playing style; and in recognising this style we recognise jazz.

As I have implied above, the point at which pseudo-jazz stops and jazz begins is largely a matter of degree only. The negro bands often take music foreign to their own culture and base their jazz on the very popular songs or classics which form the foundation of certain of the Whiteman performances. The result is most interesting. But it is very different from the civilised and elegant versions of the symphonic jazz band. For the negro has taken the least possible contribution from the notes of the melody. He distorts it beyond recognition, makes of it an entirely new synthesis and his product is a composition – whereas that of the symphonic band is no more than a clever arrangement. This is indeed interesting, but vastly more so are the two forms entirely negroid, entirely born of the jazz impulse, the blues themselves and that faster form, the stomp.

A common criticism of jazz is that it is nothing but rhythm; that if the drums were removed there would be nothing left. This is an argument that will hardly hold water. The rhythmical peculiarity of jazz is not superimposed upon it by the drums; instead the whole orchestra is engaged in creating the rhythm; and though this rhythm may have been introduced at first by the drums, it is not their sole property. Take away the tom-toms and the steady tom-tom beat can still be heard in the rhythmical pulsations of accompaniment and melody. The development from the hymn and spiritual to the blues and stomp is paralleled in the history of classical music by the development of the fundamental chant as influenced by the rhythms of the dance tunes; a movement which culminated in the rhythmic, but certainly not drum-like, works of Bach.

Up to the time of Bach, music was an art of the people which found expression through individual geniuses, of whom Bach was one and the last. Jazz is certainly, as was the contrapuntal music, a music of the people. And like the music of the contrapuntal period, it is distinguished by the same bare melodies, stripped to fundamentals, driving with a continuous flow of musical thought to a natural and inevitable conclusion. There is no pause, no turning to one side, no attempt to lift the music to uncertain heights, as in romantic music of the pre-decadent period. Jazz melodies, like contrapuntal melodies, inspire both melodic and contrapuntal development and do not depend on full-throated orchestration to cover a lack of fundamental virility. Just as a fugue carries in its melody the rhythmic beat that never ceases to pulsate until the end of the composition is reached, so a jazz melody contains a rhythm that carries it through to its conclusion without pausing for false emotional effects.

This old contrapuntal music is marked by a steady pulsating rhythm that holds it to its purpose of musical development. The compositions are masterpieces of structural beauty; they have an inevitability about them the

Romantic school has never attained, due to its constant vacillation in both tempo and content – its melodies that refuse to stand alone without the aid of expressive 'interpretation.' Since the time of Bach, music has ceased to be a high development of folk art, and become merely a vehicle for self-expression. It is a decadent art and as is the general rule in arts that are in a decadent state it has created for itself forms that are at once the result and the proof of its decadence.

Let us take the old chant as a beginning, and carry the academic line to Bach, its highest contrapuntal development. Down from this strong and vital line fell constant little lines to the people. It is these adulterated offshoots which the people seized upon, revitalized and finally sent back to the academy. Thus the new school was slowly seeded, rising contemporaneously with the old school which was nearing its highest point of development. This impregnation of the people by the contrapuntal school resulted in the birth of the Romantic school; the second beginning. It was around these folk tunes Haydn built his little variations – these tunes which have a long musical line, and are not to be confused or associated with the primitive chants. From Haydn through Strauss the Romantic school has thrived upon and now practically exhausted, occidental folk tunes. From Haydn through Strauss men have been expressing themselves by means of variations on a folk tune, be they impromptu or symphonic – variations never intrinsically musical, depending as they do on expressive 'interpretation.' This school has tapered out to its logical and decadent conclusion. It was ripe under Beethoven. It is now and has been for a long time rotten. Consequently jazz which was born out of the first beginning and has been kept by the negro in the same stern school, is of an altogether different calibre than the themes that are treated by the Romantic school. To subject jazz to Romantic treatment is an outrage comparable only to romantising the pre-Bach music.

Now what have our jazz reformers done? The writers in America have not tried to develop jazz, but have applied it to other ends than its own. Gershwin selected that stalest of decadent forms, the rhapsody; an episodic form that allows the furthest possible departure from the logical carrying to completion of a single musical idea, and hence, probably the form more remote from the genuine jazz ideal than any other. He produced an episodic and disjointed composition of which the separate parts resembled jazz, but which had not, as a whole, the continuity and directness of true jazz music. It was no more than we should have expected, however, from a composer who is not, whatever his publishers may think, a jazz writer, but simply a first-rate popular song writer. The jazz contribution of Whiteman's famous orchestra consists in the application of little jazz rhythms or syncopation to popular songs and popular classics. This method is in direct contradiction to that of a certain composer who used two blues as themes for a symphonic work. Both took a part of jazz to use for other ends; but neither of them wrote jazz. Some moderns who have been influenced by jazz, as almost all of them have been, have shown better taste in avoiding classical forms when they approached jazz. Stravinsky, it is true, wrote a concerto very much in the medium of jazz, but as a rule he makes no attempt, when he composes a jazz piece, to drape it on the structural form of a symphony or an opera.

Between those who seize upon such superficialities as syncopation to mean jazz to them, and those who give the word a broader definition we discern a decided difference in viewpoint. We may suspect that the term 'lively art' as applied to jazz, means for the first, 'frivolous art,' and for the second, 'vital art.' Whiteman, Gershwin, Berlin, and others are exponents of frivolous art; if there is anything bogus about jazz it is certain to be found in their type of jazz. Taking popular songs that are hand-me-downs from the romantic classics and 'heart songs,' Whiteman's orchestra paints them with a jazz rhythm, and is forthwith acclaimed a pioneer of jazz. To these jazz artists who confine themselves to syncopating the classics, I have only to say that their conduct is a mild outrage. I do not care for the jazz players who do it, but it is difficult to get excited if the 'Anvil Chorus' from *Il Travatore*, the 'March' from *Aida*, or even the 'Moonlight Sonata' are jazzed. Those classics which would be in any sense desecrated by being jazzed have never been touched.

It is this syncopation of jazz which has led so many of its imitators astray. There is a great deal of syncopation in jazz, but it is all subordinate to the more important steady two-four or four-four beat. Composers imitating jazz – Stravinsky is again an example – produce syncopation a great deal more intricate and less dependent on the main beat than that found in true jazz. The treatment is the result of the natural impression of the novice in a new type of music, who has seized upon one of its features and exaggerated it. As we become better acquainted with jazz rhythms, our new jazz compositions will undoubtedly incorporate a more natural type of syncopation and abandon tricks of rhythm that may be momentarily amusing but are without permanence. It seems that the development of jazz lies not so much along the lines of further syncopation as it does in the possibility of harmonic and contrapuntal advance – counterpoint, a device which is already used abundantly in jazz. Much as jazz is supposed to dominate our modern music, it is really rare in its pure state. Since its appeal is still to the few, except in adulterated form, the big cities in America are not rich in fine jazz orchestras. Instead, the chief jazz orchestras are scattered all over the country and the only feasible way to hear good jazz in quantity is through phonograph records.

What, then, is the condition and status of jazz? To my mind the creative playing found in *low-down* jazz is establishing a stronger form than any that has arisen for centuries. It is a musical form produced by the primitive innate musical instinct of the negro and of those lower members of the white race who have not yet lost their feeling for the primitive. It is appreciated not only by these primitives but by those who can participate in the enjoyment of a stern school and can appreciate its vitality while it is still in the process of development. It is disliked by those who know it only in its diluted form and who, often under the impression that they are defending it, desire to bring about its fusion or confusion with the windbag symphony or the trick programme closing rhapsody. There is no important similarity between the orchestras of Paul Whiteman, Jack Hylton, etc., and such organisations as *Ted Lewis and his Band, Fletcher Henderson, and his Orchestra, Mound City Blue Blowers, King Oliver's Jazz Band, Thomas Morris and his Seven Hot Babies, Red Nichols and his Five Pennies, Duke Ellington and his Orchestra, Louis*

Armstrong and his Hot Five, and *Jimmy O'Bryant's Famous Original Washboard Band.*

Also, among the many soloists who have contributed to the development of virile non-emasculated jazz may be mentioned the singers, *Bessie* and *Clara Smith*; the pianists, *Seger Ellis* and *Jimmy Johnson*; the clarinetists, *Boyd Senter* and *Wilton Crawley*; the cornetists, *Miley, Swasey, Johnny Dunn,* and *Louis Armstrong*; the trombonist, *Joe Williams*; the guitarist, *Ed Lang* and the team *Bobby Leecan* and *Robert Cooksey* playing the harmonica and guitar. These are a few of the pioneers, scattered far and wide over the country, only to be brought together through the medium of the phonograph. But their music will grow; the confusion between true jazz and its bastard children of the polite orchestras will become less; musical publications will begin to recognise the existence of the true jazz; and it will no longer be necessary to defend jazz from its defenders. Not that it really requires defence; for it will exist so long as the negro lives *in* our civilisation but not *of* it.

17 **Svend Gade** Baptized by jazz (1927)

Source: Svend Gade, 'Baptized by jazz' in *Jazz Mad* (New York: Jacobsen-Hodgkinson Corp., 1927: 13–22) (abridged excerpts). (Reprinted from Lewis Porter, *Jazz: A Century of Change* [1997]: 149–50.)

A jerk. A jerk. A jerkee rhythm. A moan. A wail. A jerkee rhythm. A bing! A clash! A wail! A mo-o-oan. A jerk. A whine. A jerk. A jerkee rhythm. Pounding, pounding. Beating. Groaning. Music for the feet. A feverish pulsation. A savage undulation. Music for the feet. Nothing for the heart. Nothing for the head. A jerk. A jerk –

And its name was jazz ...

[I]t was this weird yet characteristic voice of America that the Hausmanns first heard ...

And everywhere around them whanged, and moaned and blared, the jazz of nervous America. Jazz on the records in the boarding house parlor. Jazz over the radio in the boarding house dining room. Jazz breathed by the little colored boy on the street through his harmonica as the other little colored boy charlestoned to it. Jazz winked the signs on Broadway, proclaiming stage bands. Jazz stared [from] the painted signs, announcing delirious dancing with dinner.

But this was no concern of the Hausmanns, no, not any more say, than the gumchewing in which so many people seemed interested.

So, lightheartedly and confident of his reception Doctor Hausmann set out to bestow his great symphony on this captivating America ...

But day followed day, all pretty much like the first.

'Is it jazz?' someone would ask with a sudden flash of interest, when the name of the symphony was mentioned. But the interest winked right out when a negative answer was made. And came the stereotyped reception: 'Suppose you write us a letter about it.' Or, 'Well, you might leave it here and we'll look over it.' Or, 'No, we don't examine the works of unknown composers.' Or, in the vast majority of organizations devoted to music less austere than the few symphony orchestras, 'We haven't any use for that kind of stuff. Why don't you write jazz, man? Jazz is the music to-day. Wouldn't give you a nickel for anything else.' Hausmann wrote letters. They were never answered ...

Hausmann hunted for work as a leader – theatre orchestra, band, anything. But always they demanded jazz, jazz, jazz. With his genius for transcribing into sound all the emotion of which a man is capable, he could not truckle to the cheap desire for mere motion.

Jazz, which he had thought was no concern of theirs, became the bitter topic of their meal-time conversations. It haunted his dreams at night. 'This fine country is jazz-mad!' he exclaimed in despair.

18 **Jean–Paul Sartre** I discovered jazz in America (1947)

Source: Jean-Paul Sartre, 'I discovered jazz in America,' in Ralph de Toledano (ed.), *Frontiers of Jazz* (New York: Frederick Ungar, 1962 [1947]: 66–8). (Originally published in *Saturday Review of Literature*, XXX [29 November 1947]: 48–9, with above title.) (Translated by Ralph de Toledano.)

Jazz is like bananas – it must be consumed on the spot. God knows there are recordings in France, and some sad imitators. But all they do is give us an excuse to shed a few tears in pleasant company. Like everyone else, I really discovered jazz in America. Some countries have a national pastime and some do not. It's a national pastime when the audience insists on complete silence during the first half of the performance and then shouts and stamps during the second half. If you accept this definition, France has no national pastime, unless it is auction sales. Nor has Italy, except stealing. There is watchful silence while the thief works (first half) and when he flees there is stamping and shouts of: 'Stop, thief' (second half). Belgium has its cockfights, Germany vampirism, and Spain its *corridas*.

I learned in New York that jazz is a national pastime. In Paris, it is a vehicle for dancing, but this is a mistake: Americans don't dance to jazz; instead they have a special music, heard also at marriages and First Communions, called: Music by Muzak. In apartments there is a faucet. It is turned on and Muzak musics: flirtation, tears, dancing. The faucet is turned off, and Muzak musics no more: the lovers and communicants are put to bed.

At Nick's bar, in New York, the national pastime is presented. Which means that one sits in a smoke-filled room among sailors, Orientals, chippies, society women. Tables, booths. No one speaks. The sailors come in fours. With justified hatred, they watch the smoothies who sit in booths with their girls. The sailors would like to have the girls, but they don't. They drink; they are tough; the girls are also tough; they drink, they say nothing. No one speaks, no one moves, the jazz holds forth. From ten o'clock to three in the morning the jazz holds forth. In France, jazzmen are beautiful but stupid, in flowing shirts and silk ties. If you are too bored to listen, you can always watch them and learn about elegance.

At Nick's bar, it is advisable not to look at them; they are as ugly as the musicians in a symphony orchestra. Bony faces, mustaches, business suits, starched collars (at least in the early part of the evening), no velvety looks, muscles bunching up under their sleeves.

They play. You listen. No one dreams. Chopin makes you dream, but not the jazz at Nick's. It fascinates, you can't get your mind off it. No consolation whatsoever. If you are a cuckold, you depart a cuckold, with no tenderness. No way to take the hand of the girl beside you, to make her understand, with a wink, that the music reflects what is in your heart. It is dry, violent, pitiless. Not gay, not sad, inhuman. The cruel screech of a bird of prey. The musicians start to give out, one after the other. First the trumpet player, then the pianist, then the trombonist. The bass player grinds it out. It does not speak of love, it does not comfort. It is hurried. Like the people who take the subway or eat at the Automat.

It is not the century-old chant of Negro slaves. Nor the sad little dream of Yankees crushed by the machine. Nothing of the sort: there is a fat man who blows his lungs out to the weaving motion of his trombone, there is a merciless pianist, a bass player who tortures the strings without listening to the others. They are speaking to the best part of you, the toughest, the freest, to the part which wants neither melody nor refrain, but the deafening climax of the moment. They take hold of you, they do not lull you. Connecting rod, shaft, spinning top. They beat you, they turn, they crash, the rhythm grips you and shakes you. You bounce in your seat, faster and faster, and your girl with you, in a hellish round.

The trombone sweats, you sweat, the trumpet sweats, you sweat some more, and then you feel that something has happened on the bandstand; the musicians don't look the same: they speed ahead, they infect each other with this haste, they look mad, taut, as if they were searching for something. Something like sexual pleasure. And you too begin to look for something. You begin to shout; you have to shout; the band has become an immense spinning top: if you stop, the top stops and falls over. You shout, they shriek, they whistle, they are possessed, you are possessed, you scream like a woman in childbirth. The trumpet player touches the pianist and transmits his hypnotic obsession. You go on shouting. The whole crowd shouts in time, you can't even hear the jazz, you watch some men on a bandstand sweating in time, you'd like to spin around, to howl at death, to slap the face of the girl next to you.

And then, suddenly, the jazz stops, the bull has received the sword thrust, the oldest of the fighting cocks is dead. It's all over. But you have drunk your whiskey, while shouting, without even knowing it. An impassive waiter has brought you another. For a moment, you are in a stupor, you shake yourself, you say to your girl: Not bad. She doesn't answer, and it begins all over again. You will not make love tonight, you will not be sorry for yourself, you will not even be surfeited, you won't get real drunk, you won't even shed blood, and you'll have undergone a fit of sterile frenzy. You will leave a little worn out, a little drunk, but with a kind of dejected calm, the aftermath of nervous exhaustion.

Jazz is the national pastime of the United States.

19 Sybil Kein Jazz (1984)

Source: Sybil Kein, 'Jazz,' in *Delta Dancer* (Detroit: Lotus Press, 1984: 63).

(For Vernel Bagneris)

From Storyville, vaudeville, cabarets
and tonks, we played blues, marches, spirituals
and rags. We laid down that burden
of massa, slave, and bastard. We laid it down
in sassy syncopation.
Old New Orleans danced with
quadrilles, rhumbas, shimmies, and grinds.
We laid that burden down.
Jassbo and Jassebelle,
congo drums and Creole songs,
we laid that burden down.
No need to study war no more. When those saints go
marching, we will be in that
number: Satchmo and Jelly Roll,
Salty Dog and Sale Dame
Playing sweet sweet harmony,

'One Mo Time!'

Riff 2

The truth is that there is not a single satisfactory history of jazz – anywhere. (James Collier, *Jazz: The American Theme Song*, 1993)

Art does not reflect society and environment and consciousness so much as it tells us what environment and society and consciousness do not know. (Martin Williams, 'The meaning of a music,' *The Jazz Tradition*, 1970)

It is curious how the concept of the jazz tradition tends to leach the social significance out of the music, leaving the impression that the history of jazz can be described satisfactorily only in aesthetic terms. (Scott DeVeaux, 'Constructing the jazz tradition: jazz historiography,' *Black American Literature Forum*, 1991)

In effect, the official history of jazz is that which appears in print, taking the form of a coherent story of progress, of 'continuity and change,' certified by its canonical hierarchy of 'major figures' who are compelled to recite a tale of evolutionary destiny. (Jed Rasula, 'The media of memory: the seductive menace of records in jazz history,' in Krin Gabbard [ed.], *Jazz Among the Discourses*, 1995)

Melting Down the Iron Suits of History. (Stanley Crouch, *The All-American Skin Game, or, The Decoy of Race*, 1995)

There are no critics except musicians. (Charles Tolliver, in Arthur Taylor, *Notes and Tones*, 1977)

CHORUS II
Nothin' Over There but Critics: Jazz and history
(criticism, canon, historiography)

Who owns and makes jazz history? David Meltzer's anthology, *Reading Jazz* (1993), argues for a white 'invention' of jazz and the struggle to 'own' the music across a 'contested turf' of competing histories (21–2). White American culture has constructed histories or narratives which legitimize and commodify – even demonize – jazz and claim ownership to its development. Meltzer rightly argues that jazz history narratives reflect opposing or contesting ideologies ('racisms') and these are a formulating principle in writing about jazz. **Chorus II** assembles examples of such 'historical' writing and the various critical discourses used to construct narratives – and canons – for jazz.

Meltzer's view of the jazz canon as a 'partial' and 'malleable' art form (**20**) reflects the challenge to the culture of recorded jazz as official history and institutional power. What is under question is the dominant influence of an internalist musicology, represented by historians like Martin Williams and Gunther Schuller. Their established canon of major figures and master works, and the autonomous methodologies that support it, have been duly institutionalized in Williams' own compilation, *The Smithsonian Collection of Classic Jazz* (1973/1987). This is widely used by jazz historians as the standard discography and is the canonical bible for jazz educators – though a revision or alternative is greatly overdue. The Smithsonian 'classics' are a major source of privileged texts and effectively constitute 'the jazz tradition': Williams' Introduction (1987: 6) claims they underwrite jazz's 'aesthetic durability' and 'honorable' history. Musicological analysis of selected jazz recordings is also demonstrated, at exhaustive length, by Gunther Schuller's history, whose analysis of jazz as 'musical language' (1968: viii) and 'ongoing process' (1989: xi) has been as influential as Williams in establishing the canon.

This formalist approach and narrative of a tradition have exerted continued influence on many standard jazz histories. Historians like Stearns (1956/1970), Tirro (1977/1993), Collier (1978), Gridley (1978), Megill and Demory (1984), Sales (1984), Porter, Ullman and Hazell (1993) and Gioia (1997) have largely replicated the seamlessly linear New Orleans-to-Fusion, Armstrong-to-Marsalis account of jazz period, style and soloist. Regrettably, most of these works omit any ideological or sociological basis for jazz history – larger, extra-musical contexts and issues – or subordinate them to considerations of musical style.

This internalist approach, too, insists on the simplifications of a coherent, univocal narrative. A history of jazz becomes the 'story' of the music's growth

(Stearns), pulling into a 'comprehensible form the vast body of information on jazz and its players' (Collier 1978: ix), and insisting on 'a logical developmental scheme ... that unfolds in a rather orderly fashion' (Tirro 1993: xix). Even Gioia's 'updated' *History of Jazz* (1997) 'tells the story of this music,' rehearses the conventional stylistic frame ('Prehistory' to 'Freedom and Beyond') and offers what its jacket calls 'the giants of jazz and the great moments of jazz history.' What the 'jazz tradition' and its privileged versions of narrative offer is a perpetual re-telling: one history's content, and its methodology, soon comes to read like another's. A strong smell of mutual derivation hovers over these works, prompting the question: 'Ah yes, but *whose* history is this?'

One response may lie in John **Gennari**'s excellent comprehensive survey of jazz criticism, published in *Black American Literature Forum* (1991). Gennari ultimately develops a model placing less emphasis on close readings of recordings as 'autonomous aesthetic works' (ibid.: 459) and more on the view that situates the music in a black ethos and context. In one section (III) (**21**), he examines the institutional criticism of André Hodeir and Williams, emphasizing their affinities with literary New Criticism's practice of close scrutiny of texts and formal concern with art's autonomy and transcendence. While Gennari readily acknowledges the efforts of these key critics in the acceptance of jazz as legitimate art, he argues the social significance of the music deserved/s more timely attention.

The role of **Williams** as jazz canon-keeper is demonstrated in *The Jazz Tradition* (1970/1993), a collection of essays on individual jazz artists. In the opening essay (**22**), Williams introduces the 'fundamental' ideas that support his investigation of the nature and history of jazz. These are (a) the related contributions made by major figures (e.g. Morton, Armstrong, Ellington) to an evolving tradition; and (b) the stylistic developments resulting from rhythmic innovation. Williams admits imposing a pattern of evolutionary development on jazz, in discerning an alternating process of innovation and consolidation. As an argument for the evolution of style, the essays are persuasive and important; they may well offer 'a more comprehensive and perhaps more *musical* view' of jazz development than previously available (ibid.: 5; my italics). Yet jazz here is rendered almost wholly aesthetic and abstract; Williams' opening recognition of jazz as an African-American idiom (ibid.: 3) is rarely translated into a concern with the cultural and social experience of black musicians themselves.

Earlier attempts at jazz criticism and the construction of historical narrative had largely anticipated Williams' perfection of the evolutionary model. Yet some argued that in jazz's departure from its primal sources lay the seeds of eventual decadence. Critics of the 1930s and 1940s – some of them white Europeans – engaged in a transatlantic debate on the authentic primitivism of jazz and purity of its alleged African and folkloric origins. Competing agendas emerged between those who argued for jazz's growing maturation and legitimation as potentially serious art music (e.g. Hodeir) and others who argued the spontaneous 'hotness' of jazz was its essential identity and sought to distinguish between 'true and false' versions of the music (e.g. Panassié, *Le Jazz Hot* [1934], *The Real Jazz* [1942]). This debate was but a forerunner of the acrimonious 'style wars' between traditionalists and modernists, set off by 1940s bebop and New Orleans revivalism (**III**).

Musicologist Schuller's *Early Jazz* (1968: viii) gave an approving nod to the analytical skills of one such contributor to the debate, Winthrop **Sargeant**. His *Jazz: Hot and Hybrid* (1946), after a detailed explication of technical features, reinforces its premise that jazz is essentially folk music, not to be confused (or competing) with 'classical' or 'highbrow' art music. Sargeant's 'Conclusions' (**23**), while they identify jazz's uniqueness, also propound an anti-developmental, anti-modernist view in arguing for the unchanging 'essence' of jazz and its radical differences from 'concert' music (see DeVeaux 1991: 534–6).

Such anachronistic views were surely challenged by French critic André **Hodeir**. In seeking the 'essence' of jazz (**24**), he applies the emerging standards of formal criticism to what he calls 'esthetic evolution' and the 'criterion of taste' (1956: Preface). Essentialism, for purist Hodeir, resides in 'only those characteristics that are at once specific and constant' (ibid.: 234). This is a rigorous, if self-conscious, analytic method and Hodeir's concluding emphasis – on jazz's mix of relaxation (swing) and tension (hot playing) – makes a discerning contribution to the nature of jazz style. Hodeir's influence was large: he was the first to periodize jazz history, propose a performance canon, and devise a technical vocabulary for discussion of the music (Gennari 1991: 482).

The opening section of Scott **DeVeaux**'s admirable essay on jazz historiography (1991) (**25**) demonstrates the conventional narrative of jazz history is an accepted and enduring one, and not lightly deconstructed – especially in view of its recentness and evident utility. DeVeaux suggests the construction of a unitary narrative of continuous evolution has persisted because it confers respectability and validation on a music that would otherwise be marginalized. In the pervasive issues of race, ethnicity and economics, jazz is an 'oppositional discourse' (ibid.: 530). The jazz tradition rescues and reifies the music, giving it a simplified universality and autonomy.

If this provides the *raison d'être* for the essentialist notion of jazz history, DeVeaux demonstrates (in the essay's remainder) how that framework has proved inadequate and outmoded for current explanation of the music. If the struggle is over possession of jazz history – and within this, definition – what is crucially at issue are the *boundaries* within which jazz is situated. DeVeaux concludes it is timely for 'an approach that is less invested in the ideology of jazz as aesthetic object and more responsive to issues of historical particularity' (ibid.: 553). New narratives are needed to reconstitute the jazz tradition.

This is the ground emphatically occupied by recent developments in jazz studies, particularly the interpretative work done by cultural historians and others engaged in cross-disciplinary approaches. Krin **Gabbard**, editor of two ground-breaking anthologies (1995a, 1995b), applies critical theory to the discourses and representation of jazz, with particular concentration on its cultural and mythical contexts. Noting that his contributors have placed jazz 'much more securely within specific cultural moments' (**26**), Gabbard lays claim to a furthering of Meltzer's agenda – the 'colonization and permissible racism' of jazz. This in turn opens up jazz study to a variety of contexts and through related disciplines: it challenges the history model of the music and the stability of the canon.

The application of theory and use made of cross-disciplinary contexts have had important outcomes for the identification of the history of jazz with African-American culture. DeVeaux observes ethnicity provides a core, 'a center of gravity' for the narrative of jazz, and that race is a crucial social factor in any formulation of jazz's evolution (1991: 529, 545). The application of an African-American aesthetic to jazz has been advanced by the use made of black literary theory, which has challenged the dominant white canon in creating a distinctly vernacular approach to black experience. Henry Louis Gates, in using 'the signifying monkey' (1988) of African-American folklore, explains signifyin(g) as a rhetorical or linguistic strategy, employing particular oral devices, and used extensively in black American discourse. To 'signify' is to be 'double-voiced' or engage in double play, involving repetition and revision, in the creative 'space' between the two linguistic areas of white and black culture. It is, again, the 'two-ness' of being African-*and*-American. Gary **Tomlinson** suggests extra-canonical uses for this analytic criticism, especially in the propensity for jazz playing and writing to engage in 'signification.' In 'Cultural Dialogics and Jazz' (**27**), Tomlinson, a self-described 'white historian', argues for the fluid cross-referencing and vernacular 'repetition-with-difference' of black discourse in jazz itself. The article overall identifies the *dialogical* aspect of signifying – that is, of dialogue or 'mediation between or among texts or languages' (1991: 231). Such 'doubleness' – flexible, playful, indirect, informal and improvisatory – also belongs naturally to *jazz* playing. It is not available in *monological* versions of the canon, where the jazz tradition is white, imitatively Eurocentric and hierarchical; and where the formalist aesthetic controls possibilities of meaning and value. For Tomlinson, the restrictive positions adopted by the 'monological canon' are well illustrated in the hostile critical reception to Miles Davis' 'dialogic' rock-jazz fusion of the late 1960s and early 1970s – which he examines in the last part of the article. (See also **III/45**.)

Amiri **Baraka**'s (LeRoi Jones) warnings of the institutionalizing of jazz, through 'white middle-brow' criticism, serve as a preface to the extract from Tomlinson's essay. Their source is Baraka's collection, *Black Music* (1967), an early attempt by a black writer to insist on an African-American vernacular aesthetic for an understanding of jazz. In 'Jazz and the White Critic' (1963) (**28**), Baraka pursues the notion that jazz's meaning lies not in the music as such (appreciation), but in the music's essential expression of 'an attitude, or a collection of attitudes, about the world.' Though Baraka does not allude to the 'signifying' practice of black culture, he clearly has such a negotiating strategy in mind when he refers to 'the validity of redefined emotional statements' which reflect 'the changing psyche' of the black American. Like Meltzer, Baraka poses the question of who is authorized to define jazz; he ends with the hope that only those who know and understand indigenous black philosophy and culture will attempt the task.

Historical accounts of jazz, then, may be formal, aesthetic, contextual and racial. They can also be supplemented with two further narratives, one constructed from a gender perspective, the other drawing on the oral testimony of musicians themselves. Linda **Dahl**, in *Stormy Weather* (1984), records 'the music and lives' of 'jazzwomen' and their contribution to the community of jazz: as bandleaders, arrangers, managers, instrumentalists and vocalists. Dahl's 'Preface' (**29**) lists the factors that have largely excluded women from the mostly masculine, often sexist world of jazz and pays tribute to jazzwomen's struggle, determination and success in playing the music, as well as identifying the major practitioners. As if to confirm Dahl's exclusionist claims, Nat **Shapiro** and Nat **Hentoff**'s celebrated *Hear Me Talkin' to Ya* (1955) assembles the 'story' of jazz, 'as told by the *men* who made it' (my italics) (**30**). This compendium draws on 'first-person accounts' by musicians – as opposed to 'academic histories' – and offers a strain of informal interview and personal reminiscence. Shapiro and Hentoff still intend to 'indicate the perspective of jazz evolution', even if this is 'seen by the musicians themselves.' This essentially human face of jazz history is closely linked to the personalized, self-inscribed narrative found in jazz autobiography (**VII**). It illustrates, too, how constructions of jazz history turn readily enough into myth and romance, once they focus on the lives of individual musicians (**VI**).

Orrin Keepnews once said, 'jazz criticism is a bad idea, poorly executed' (1987: 219). In his autobiography, *Beneath the Underdog* (1971), Charles **Mingus** lampoons a clique of jazz critics through a New York jam session, where they become the performers – with Martin Williams playing everything (**31**). Their 'schitt,' however, is replaced by the real thing: 'God' Tatum, 'Bird' Parker and Mingus play 'Lover.' 'Dig the critics over there still talking to each other. Don't hear a thing.'

20 **David Meltzer** Jazz history-making (1993)

Source: David Meltzer (ed.), *Reading Jazz* (San Francisco: Mercury House, 1993: 14). (Editor's title)

The history of jazz, its canon, is as partial and malleable as that of any other art form.

A history buried beneath the weight of its mythology: there's a consumer-simple über-myth cutting time into movements like Classic Jazz, Swing, Bebop, Free Jazz; each of these invented eras has a cast of significant and defining Heroes and Martyrs. It's a history reiterated by the recording industry with a subdivision allotted for the reinvention and/or resurrection of rediscovered (or re-foregrounded) players Francis Davis calls 'outcats,' those who fell beneath the first-wave steamroller of mythopoesis. There's an axial history and culture of recorded jazz that presents regional artists and groups, the so-called 'territory bands,' whose impact was localized, and whose rediscovery opens up a 'thicker' history of jazz and the possibility that many players, arrangers, vocalists, bands might have been (or were) of equal originality and brilliance as those icons of the pantheon.

21 **John Gennari** Jazz criticism: Its development and ideologies (1991)

Source: John Gennari: 'Jazz criticism: its development and ideologies,' *Black American Literature Forum*, 25, 3 (Fall, 1991: 476–7, 477–8, 480–5) (excerpts).

In 1958 Martin Williams, soon to join Nat Hentoff in launching the excellent *Jazz Review,* wrote an article for *Down Beat* entitled 'Criticism: The Path of the Jazz Critic' in which he lamented the mediocre state of jazz criticism and suggested how jazz critics might improve their craft. Too much jazz criticism, Williams complained, was public relations pablum or amateur journalism being palmed off as informed opinion, and this was incongruent with the high quality of the music: 'We assure ourselves that jazz is an "art," and often proceed to talk about it as if it were a sporting event.' Arguing that critical tools must be 'trained, explored, disciplined and tested like any other talent,' Williams urged a stronger analytical approach to the music and more of an emphasis on content and meaning. The jazz critic should have a strong background in the liberal arts, a firm grasp of Plato and Aristotle as well as Eliot and Jung, and familiarity with the best criticism in all fields. With this learning and awareness, the critic could then analyze jazz works using the same questions that Matthew Arnold argued should be applied in literary criticism: What is the work trying to do? Does it succeed? How and why? Is it worth doing? How does it compare with the best works in the field? Following such a method, Williams hoped, would help jazz criticism achieve at least some of the distinction of the top-level literary criticism that was being produced in the United States ...

Whether Williams aspired to this level of high seriousness is doubtful, but he did want jazz criticism to raise its intellectual standards and procedures. In jazz circles, though a consensus might have developed around the idea that Armstrong's Hot Fives were better than his Hot Sevens, the only tangible evidence of this consensus might have been a file of scattered *Down Beat* clippings and Columbia liner notes. The limited development of the jazz critical infrastructure at this time was such that the single most penetrating analysis ever produced of a particular artist or record could conceivably have perished, before seeing the light of publication, in the very moment of its expression in some New York or Chicago tavern. The virtual nonexistence of 'jazz studies,' not only as an educational curriculum but as a *concept,* made it next to impossible to discern intellectual authority in the expression of jazz opinion. To be sure, some opinions carried more weight than others, but the basis of such critical weight had as much to do with force of personality as with force of reason. Jazz critics knew who they liked, and perhaps why, but they did not spell out the specific criteria to be used in evaluating and interpreting the music.

The 1950s was a crucial decade for jazz, and not only because the music itself was in the process of assimilating and transforming the momentous aesthetic advances of bebop; not only because the cool, Third Stream, and free experiments were taking jazz to places it had never been before. Increased visibility and status of a certain kind were represented by expanded and more diverse audiences, the advent of the Newport Jazz Festival, college concert bookings, and exemplary recording and packaging of the music by labels such as Blue Note, Riverside, and Prestige ...

Between 1955 and 1963 the jazz bibliography expanded to include *Hear Me Talkin' to Ya: The Story of Jazz as Told by the Men Who Made It* (1955), a compilation by Nat Shapiro and Nat Hentoff of richly evocative remembrances culled from the jazz press; Marshall Stearns's *The Story of Jazz* (1956), a witty, smooth-reading account, drawing on the research of ethnomusicologists, as well as ample personal familiarity with the New York scene, of jazz's evolution from West African, Caribbean, European, and native sources into the cosmopolitan complexities of bebop; André Hodeir's *Jazz: Its Evolution and Essence* (1956), the first serious formalist study of jazz ... Francis Newton's *The Jazz Scene* (1959), an astute analysis of the social underpinnings of jazz which, in arguing that 'no bar of coloured jazz has ever made sense to those who do not understand the Negro's reaction to oppression,' foreshadowed the arguments ... of Amiri Baraka's highly influential 1963 book *Blues People*; Nat Hentoff's *The Jazz Life* (1961), a collection of Hentoff's essays from *Harper's*, *Esquire*, *Dissent*, and *Down Beat*, whose higher-journalism sensibility and enlightened perspective on social and cultural matters raised the quality of the jazz discourse several notches; Whitney Balliett's *The Sound of Surprise* (1959), the first collection of his beautifully written *New Yorker* pieces; Martin Williams's *Jazz Panorama* (1962), which includes Gunther Schuller's famous piece on Sonny Rollins's *Blue Seven* and a Nat Hentoff interview with Miles Davis that is one of the most incisive statements ever made about jazz; and Williams's *King Oliver* (1960), *Jelly Roll Morton* (1962), and the essays from the *Evergreen Review*, *Saturday Review*, and *Down Beat* – later collected in *The Jazz Tradition* (1970) – in which Williams explored key artists' complete oeuvres and the entire jazz tradition for ideas about how jazz has evolved as an individual and collective endeavor.

Clearly jazz writing had taken a giant step beyond the 'hot, gassy prose, provincialism, inaccuracy, and condescension' Whitney Balliett described as constituting jazz's unimpressive critical tradition to that time (*Sound* 14). The music was beginning to achieve the kind of serious critical recognition that it had long suffered for, and the criticism began better serving readers who were looking for intelligent musicological analysis as well as insight into jazz's connection with broader intellectual and political currents. This flowering of serious thought and commentary on jazz was a stanching of the wounds that had been inflicted on jazz in its long history of degradation and margin-alization, and it came at a time when American society, in the intersecting trajectories of the Cold War and the Civil Rights movement, had much to gain from increasing the status of its most important native art form. In this climate, it became possible and necessary for jazz criticism to scrutinize itself more seriously than it had in the past. Should it follow literary New Criticism in the privileging of texts – in this case, recordings – as the primary focal point of analysis? Should it consider racial identity and the historical experience of blacks as issues central to the development of jazz aesthetics, or as separate issues altogether? Most importantly, who was it that qualified for the position of jazz critic? What kind of experience and education did it take to qualify someone as an authoritative critical voice? Whose interpretations of jazz were the most valuable?

Hodeir's *Jazz: Its Evolution and Essence*, as a pioneer effort in scholarly, formalist jazz criticism, begins with an effort to underline its author's authority and justify his method. Hodeir, in a piece of neo-primitivist logic that recalls the earlier French engagement with jazz, argues that only artists can judge other artists, but since jazz musicians demonstrate no capacity for the kind of thought process that goes into criticism, he is stepping in to do it for them:

> Who has spoken of Schoenberg with more warmth and competence than Alban Berg? Who has given us a more clear-sighted analysis of *Le Sacre du Printemps* than Pierre Boulez? However, it is characteristic of the European composer to meditate. It is not rare to see him become truly aware of a problem at the very moment when he is in the act of creation. The jazz musician does not meditate. If he happens to listen attentively to the work of another musician, he grasps what it has to offer through intuitive assimilation rather than by reflection. (*Jazz* 18)

But Hodeir's perspective on jazz easily escapes the pitfalls of Panassié's primitivism. A serious effort to elucidate the technical features of jazz musicianship is evident on every page of the book; there is no room in Hodeir's resolute search for the truth of Armstrong's aesthetic for flighty speculation on subconscious urges or powers of self-hypnosis. Hodeir does, however, share with Panassié an ideological framework that posits a distinction between 'primitive' and 'civilized' (or what Hodeir refers to as 'modern') modes of cultural expression. Whereas Panassié considered jazz itself a primitive art form, Hodeir sees jazz as rooted in primitive art but ever straining to transcend it and achieve more and more of the systematic intellectual coherence of civilized art.

Hodeir makes much in this book of how much jazz musicians have taken from the European musical tradition: fixed time meters and tonal scales, the architecture of song form, a certain kind of syncopation. Essentially correct in his assertion that jazz has profited mightily from its assimilation of European musical principles, Hodeir also is well-qualified to define these principles. Like all true artists, like the European modernist composers who were borrowing heavily from jazz, jazz musicians have used as many of the cultural resources at their disposal as possible, and the European musical tradition has been one of them. But what Hodeir does not contemplate – and in this his neo-primitivism is most marked – is the possibility that jazz musicians have taken from African music something more than an intuitive, natural approach to their art, such as important technical principles and distinct concepts of musicianship.

Hodeir's book was the first to propose under one cover a periodization of jazz history, a canon of jazz performances, a technical vocabulary for discussing the music, and a theory of the music's aesthetic essences. The book's form *itself* is an impressive and illuminating act of criticism: an introductory suggestion of jazz's place in contemporary culture; an outline of the evolution of jazz, highlighting key individual achievements (Armstrong's Hot Five recordings, Ellington's *Concerto for Cootie*, Charlie Parker's bop, and Miles Davis's cool recordings) and the search for a common musical language; and a discussion of the essential characteristics of jazz. Some American jazz writers and musicians found the book rarified and laborious – Balliett called it a 'dry and difficult semi-musicological study' and objected to the 'hyper-intensity that leads Mr. Hodeir into the hushed zones of French theoretical criticism' *(Sound* 19) – and a few suggested that Hodeir's remoteness from the American jazz scene and his experience as a composer in the European tradition led him to misunderstand the music's fundamental properties. These critics – notably Balliett and pianist Billy Taylor – took particular issue with Hodeir's argument that improvisation and the blues are not essential to jazz.

Martin Williams was more receptive to Hodeir, in part perhaps because the French composer and critic represented for him the kind of highbrow sensibility that he thought jazz criticism could use, but equally because he found Hodeir's systematic approach to jazz history and his effort to define the aesthetic essences of jazz excellent models for emulation. He was also won over by Hodeir's perception that Charlie Parker had deeply enriched and replenished jazz by burrowing deep into the organic roots of the music, particularly in regard to rhythm, at the same time as he was crafting innovations out of the harmonic and melodic languages of European music (Panassié, the former high priest of French jazz criticism, had, by contrast, regarded Parker as 'an extremely gifted musician' who 'gradually gave up jazz in favor of bop' [18]).

Williams went on to shape Hodeir's ideas into a framework for thinking about the entire jazz tradition, arguing that all of the key stylistic innovations have resulted from changes in rhythmic conception, and showing how the jazz tradition broke down into alternating periods of innovation and consolidation. In the late '50s, when Ornette Coleman took the advances of Charlie Parker a step further – subverting conventional chord structures, bar lines, and ways of fingering and blowing a saxophone, but keeping his experiments firmly embedded in the blues – Williams wrote exceptionally fine, even prescient, criticism which argued that Coleman, more than any other of his contemporaries (including the more celebrated John Coltrane), was developing the implicit resources of jazz and pointing to a fruitful path for jazz's future. Since assuming a curatorial position at the Smithsonian in the early 1970s, Williams had been keeper of the jazz canon for the United States' (and the world's) heritage. In *The Smithsonian Collection of Classic Jazz*, first released in 1973 and still undergoing revision and extension, jazz has its answer to the *Norton Anthology of Literature* and Morton Adler's Great Books series.

Williams's *The Jazz Tradition* is the best representation of his view of jazz history. In this collection of essays, Williams offers portraits of the jazz masters and, by tracing the thread of influence that has connected them, gives credence to his notion of an evolving tradition. Williams shows that he not only listens closely to the music, but thinks hard about the creative processes by which major artists find where their specialness lies … His writing is clean and unadorned, and he shifts easily (sometimes too easily) from one recording to the next, one idea to the next. The essays fall somewhere between the levity of record reviews and the gravity of scholarly analyses. Here are a couple of representative passages:

> Miles Davis's earliest records were sometimes able and occasionally faltering, but they showed a very personal approach to the modern jazz idiom. From time to time he did espouse the virtuoso manner of Gillespie, and on occasion he showed a perceptive ability almost to abstract Gillespie's style, as on *A Night in Tunisia* with Charlie Parker. But more often he was involved in a simple, introspective but sophisticated lyricism which seemed to refute the ideas that many people had about modern jazz as a virtuoso music whose simple passages had to alternate with a sustained barrage of sixteenth-notes. And he was sometimes so good a lyricist as to be able to follow, for example, Charlie Parker's superb solo on *Embraceable You* without sounding a hopeless anti-climax. (*Jazz Tradition*: 203)

> [Charlie Parker's] *Koko* may seem only a fast-tempo showpiece at first, but it is not. It is a precise linear improvisation of exceptional melodic content. It is also an almost perfect example of virtuosity *and* economy. Following a pause, notes fall all over and between this beat and that beat: breaking them asunder, robbing them of any vestige of monotony; rests fall where heavy beats once came, now 'heavy' beats come between beats and on weak beats. *Koko* has been a source book of ideas and no wonder; now that its basic innovations are familiar, it seems even more a great performance in itself. (*Jazz Tradition*: 149–50)

Whether sketching a musician's career or focusing on a single solo, there is a seamless quality to this writing that is at once seductive and frustrating: seductive in its gliding readability, frustrating in its lack of sustained argument. It is not easy to disprove Williams, but that may mean that he hasn't offered enough substance for an argument. Though not given to the densely analytical style of literary New Criticism, Williams shares the New Critics' belief that art transcends its surroundings and exists for its own sake. The jazz world delineated in these essays seems to have no tensions other than creative ones, no aspirations other than aesthetic ones, no purpose other than the evolution of style.

Perceiving the need to reflect more deeply on the meaning of the jazz experience, Williams appended an essay to *The Jazz Tradition* entitled 'The Meaning of a Music: An Art for the Century' which offers the clearest exposition of his philosophy of jazz. Williams assails Marxist interpretations of the music for turning art 'into a reductive "nothing but" proposition, robbed of its complexities and its humanity … Art does not reflect society and environment and consciousness,' Williams writes, 'so much as it tells us what environment and society and consciousness do not know' (251). And what jazz has told us – what makes jazz *the* quintessential twentieth-century art – is that we must continually remake, reinvent ourselves through action. His argument, reminiscent of both Dewey and existentialism, is that jazz has uniquely fused thought and feeling, reflection and emotion, into the act of doing. With their emphasis on performance and improvisation, on individual creativity in a group context, on constantly changing approaches to their material, jazz musicians, in Williams's view, have fashioned the best aesthetic response to the twentieth century's assault on humanistic values.

There is no gainsaying the formidable efforts of the key jazz critics of the 1950s in pushing for the acceptance of jazz as a legitimate art, and in initiating the process of forging the tools for its serious discussion. If jazz enjoyed the position in American culture it deserves, Martin Williams might now enjoy a reputation similar to those of the Abstract Expressionist critics Clement Greenberg and Harold Rosenberg, who are praised widely for their insight into modern painting's illumination of the twentieth-century human condition. But the problem with Williams's philosophical claims for jazz – and with Rosenberg's and Greenberg's claims for abstract painting – is that they tell us much more about the critic's consciousness than about the artist's. How does Williams know that the modern jazz musician shares Williams's philosophical concerns? To be sure, many jazz musicians have expressed a fundamental faith in the virtues of doing, in the value of improvisation as a way to reinvent oneself through direct action. But the meaning of this experience might be very different for the jazz artist who is undergoing it than it is for the critic who is interpreting it. In Williams's essays there is not enough evidence of the jazz musicians' own voices, not enough of their personal testimony, to substantiate the meaning that Williams imposes on their art.

Williams is far from ignorant of the social implications of jazz – 'Jazz,' he has written, 'is the music of a people who have been told by their circumstances that they are unworthy. And in jazz, these people discover their own worthiness' (*Jazz Tradition*: 256) – and as a critic sincerely committed to the idea that African-American musical culture deserves far more cultural and intellectual prestige than it has hitherto received, he has played no small role in the struggle for black equality. But at a moment in American history when black people were engaging in a heroic effort to free themselves from the constraints of segregation, it was inevitable that, for many blacks, the discovery of 'their own worthiness' in jazz was a process that demanded far more attention to the social significance of the music.

Works cited

Balliett, Whitney. *The Sound of Surprise: 46 Pieces on Jazz*. New York: Dutton, 1959.
Hodeir, André. *Jazz: Its Evolution and Essence*. New York: Grove, 1956.
Panassié, Hugues. *Guide to Jazz*. New York: Houghton, 1956.
Williams, Martin. *The Jazz Tradition*. New York: Oxford UP, [1970] 1983.

22 **Martin Williams** Introduction: A matter of fundamentals (1970)

Source: Martin Williams, 'Introduction: a matter of fundamentals,' in *The Jazz Tradition* (New York: Oxford University Press, 1993 [1970]: 3–8).

One observer has suggested that jazz music – or all jazz music but the most recent – represents a kind of cultural lag in which the devices of nineteenth-century European music have been domesticated and popularized in the United States, adding that at the same time these devices were inevitably influenced by an African-derived rhythmic idiom.

I am sure that proposition is untrue. It assumes that European ideas of harmony and melody are fundamental to jazz and used in jazz in the same way that they were in Europe, whereas the truth may be that in jazz, rhythm is fundamental.

Jazz did not exist until the twentieth century. It has elements which were not present either in Europe or in Africa before this century. And at any of its stages it represents, unarguably it seems to me, a relationship among rhythm, harmony, and melody that did not exist before. Whatever did not exist before the twentieth century is unlikely to express that century.

If we undertake a definition of jazz, we would begin with the fact that it is an Afro-American musical idiom, and we would already be in trouble, for almost all our music is in an Afro-American or Afro-influenced idiom.

And so, to digress for a moment, is much of our culture Afro-influenced? Most of our slang comes from the gallion (as the black ghetto was once called), although numbers of our population continue to believe it is the invention of the teenagers in the corridors of our largely white high schools. So does most of our dancing. And how many Americans realize the origins of the strutting and baton twirling of our drum majorettes – and how would they react if they did know? More than one foreigner has observed that Americans do not walk like their European and Asian relatives, and one observer has gone far enough to declare that they walk more like Africans. Modes of comedy in America have been deeply influenced by our minstrelsy, which, however much it was distorted by white blackface, was still black in origin and, more important, in device, in attitude, and in outlook.

To return to our music, it might surprise the patrons at the Nashville Grand Old Opry to learn how deeply their so-called 'Country and Western' idiom has been influenced by an Afro-American one, but their reaction would not change the facts. And it should be widely acknowledged that no one in any musical idiom any longer writes for (let us say) the trumpet as he once did because of what jazzmen have shown that instrument can do. Most of our musicians also know that American symphonic brassmen generally have an unorthodox vibrato because of the pervasiveness of the jazzman's vibrato.

It should be acknowledged that today jazz is not *the* popular idiom of

American black men. And jazz shares such contributions as its 'blues scale' and its unique musical form, the twelve-bar blues, with other popular idioms. But jazz is the most respected Afro-American idiom, the most highly developed one, and the idiom to which improvisation is crucially important.

I hope that from the chapters that follow two ideas will emerge of how jazz has evolved. One has to do with the position of certain major figures and what they have contributed to jazz. The other has to do with rhythm.

I should say at this point that I did not begin with these ideas as preassumptions. They emerged in my own mind and related themselves to the theories of other commentators only as I undertook to write the chapters themselves. They offer, I hope, a more comprehensive and perhaps more musical view of the way jazz has developed than has previously been available.

If we take the most generally agreed-upon aesthetic judgments about jazz music, the first would undoubtedly be the dominant position and influence of Louis Armstrong – and that influence is not only agreed upon, it is easily demonstrable from recordings.

If we take a second generally agreed-upon opinion, it would concern the importance of Duke Ellington, and most particularly Ellington in the maturity of 1939–42.

And a third opinion? Surely the importance of the arrival of Charlie Parker. And after Parker, what made jazz history was the rediscovery of Thelonious Monk. And after that, the emergence of Ornette Coleman – or so it would be if one were looking for evidence of originality after Parker and Monk.

The pattern that emerges from those judgments would be a kind of Hegelian pendulum swing from the contributions of an innovative, intuitive improviser (Armstrong, Parker), who reassessed the music's past, gave it a new vocabulary, or at least repronounced its old one, and of an opposite swing to the contributions of a composer (Ellington, Monk), who gave the music a synthesis and larger form – larger, but not longer.

And before Armstrong? As I hope my essay demonstrates, Jelly Roll Morton's music represented a synthesis and summary of what jazz, and Afro-American music in general, had accomplished up to the moment of his arrival.

There remain the matter of the direct influence of the great figures on some of their immediate followers, and the matter of the few players whom one might call dissenters.

Following Armstrong I have written of Bix Beiderbecke, whose ends were comparable with Armstrong's but whose means and origins were somewhat different. I have spoken of the direct but very different effect of Armstrong on Coleman Hawkins and on Billie Holiday, and of the somewhat less direct effect of his work on the Count Basie orchestra. Similarly, I have tried to discuss Charlie Parker's effect on Miles Davis and on Horace Silver, and to discuss their own contributions. I have endeavored to point out the things that Monk, John Lewis, and Sonny Rollins have in common, along with the things they do not.

The question of where a study like this stops becomes fairly arbitrary at some point. One's final word on where it stops must be that it had to stop somewhere, and it stopped where I stopped it. I have here added chapters on King Oliver, Sidney Bechet, Art Tatum, Charlie Mingus, and Sarah Vaughan.

Were I to continue, my next choices might include Earl Hines, Fletcher Henderson, Roy Eldridge ... But, as I say, my book stops where it stops.

If we examine the innovations of Armstrong and Parker, I think we see that each of them sprang from a rhythmic impetus. Similarly, if we look at pre-New Orleans – cakewalk tunes, then ragtime – we can again identify a definite and almost logical rhythmic change. Similarly, looking beyond Parker to more recent developments we see important changes in rhythm.

Dizzy Gillespie has said that when he is improvising he thinks of a rhythmic figure or pattern and then of the notes to go with it, and I am sure that any important jazz musician from any style or period would give us a similar statement. Indeed, the musicians and fans give us the key to the changes in the music in the style-names themselves: cakewalk, ragtime, jazz, swing, bebop. Casual as they are, regrettable as they sometimes may seem, these words do not indicate melodies or harmonies. They indicate rhythms.

In all the stylistic developments of jazz a capacity for rhythmic growth has been fundamental. And in saying that, I believe we are saying more than we may seem to be saying. There is nothing in the outer environment of the music, nor in the 'cultural influences' upon its players, to guarantee such growth. Quite the contrary. One might say that during the past hundred years of jazz and the African-American music that preceded it, American black men have relearned a rhythmic complexity (in different form) which was commonplace to their African ancestors.

And here we find ourselves up against the 'liberal' bugaboo of 'natural rhythm' and whether Negroes have it or not – up against the position which holds that Negroes do not and could not have something called 'natural rhythm,' and that it is insulting and even racist to say that they do.

Negroes certainly could not have *un*natural rhythm. The music ultimately comes from people, not alone from their environment or their cultural influences. Certainly blacks must have a rhythm natural to their own music and their own dances (which does not of course mean that 'all' Negroes have such a thing, nor that others may not acquire it). Nor is the rhythm simply personal to certain musicians, otherwise there would not be such a wide response to it on the part of others – other musicians, dancers, listeners.

My sense of human justice is not, I hope, dependent on the assumption that black men *could* not have a natural rhythm. Differences among peoples do not make for moral inequality or unworthiness, and a particular sense of rhythm may be as natural as a particular color of skin and texture of hair. No, it does no damage to my sense of good will toward men or my belief in the equality of men, I trust, to conclude that Negroes as a race have a rhythmic genius that is not like that of other races, and to concede that this genius has found a unique expression in the United States.

It is worth pointing out that the rhythmic capacities of a jazz musician are not directly dependent on other aspects of technique in the traditional sense. Players either *think* rhythmically in a particular style, or they do not. Oscar Peterson had prodigious facility as a pianist but rhythmically he does not think in the manner of 'modern' jazz, and when he undertakes a Parker-esque run we may hear an incongruous fumbling in the fingers. Similarly, Buddy Rich, an astonishingly accomplished drummer technically, still plays swing era drums rhythmically.

I think that a rhythmic view of jazz history provides the most valuable insight into its evolution. But I do not mean to set up absolute standards in pointing it out, and there are contradictions when one comes down to individual players, particularly white players. Thus, such harmonic and linear modernists as Stan Getz, Gerry Mulligan, and even Art Pepper think in an older rhythmic idiom of alternate strong and weak accents or heavy and light beats, within a 4/4 time context. Still, pianist Al Haig, for example, who is white, grasped quite early the rhythmic idiom of Gillespie and Parker. Coleman Hawkins, on the other hand, once he had absorbed early Armstrong and begun to develop his own style, became almost European in his emphasis of the 'weak' and 'strong' beats. (I expect, by the way, that this is because Hawkins is not a blues man.)

Any theory of how an art has evolved holds its dangers. The life of an art, like the life of an individual, resists schematic interpretations, and the interpreter who proposes one risks distorting his subject to suit his theories. It should go without saying that I hope that my view of jazz history does not involve distortions. But it is my further hope that, the theoretical aspects aside, the individual essays herein may stand on their own as tributes to their subjects.

23 **Winthrop Sargeant** 'Hot jazz' vs. 'fine art' (1946)

Source: Winthrop Sargeant, 'Conclusions,' in *Jazz: Hot and Hybrid* (New York: Da Capo, 1975 [1946]: 268–75) (excerpt). (Editor's title)

A great deal of recent writing about jazz has assumed for it the status of a fine art. The eloquent defenders of '*le jazz hot*' have held jazz concerts in the most impressively conservative American concert halls, and have discussed these concerts in lofty critical language. They have written books and published magazines dealing solemnly with the aesthetics of jazz and the artistry of the popular virtuosos who play it. They have even argued that the great musical issue of the day is that of jazzism vs. 'classicism,' that jazz is in some way the American successor to the venerable art of concert music, its tunesmiths and improvising virtuosos the latter-day equivalents of so many Beethovens and Wagners. Bach, after all, used to improvise too.

The enormous popularity of jazz, coupled with the prevailing decadence of concert and operatic music, has given this view a superficial appearance of weight. Considered merely as a social phenomenon jazz leaves its unfriendly critics in the position of King Canute. You can't ignore an art that makes up seventy per cent of the musical diet of a whole nation, even if its primitive thumps and wails fail to fit the aesthetic categories of refined music criticism.

Jazz has often been innocently described as a 'folk music.' And, considered purely as music, it is one. But its powers over the common man's psyche are not even vaguely suggested by that term. No other folk music in the world's history has ever induced among normal people such curious psychopathic aberrations as the desire to wear a zoot suit, smoke hashish or jabber cryptic phrases of 'jive' language. None, probably, has ever produced waves of mass hysteria among adolescents like those recently associated with the swing craze. Nor has any folk music ever before constituted the mainstay of half a dozen nation-wide publishing, recording, broadcasting and distributing industries.

Yet when you try to approach jazz from a critical point of view, you are immediately struck by a curious split which divides almost every aspect of jazz from any real correspondence with so-called 'classical' music. For all the attempts of Paul Whiteman, Benny Goodman and others to bridge the gap, it still remains generally true that jazz players can't play 'classical,' and that 'classical' players can't play jazz. Not one jazz *aficionado* in a thousand has any interest in 'classical' music, and very few serious concertgoers feel anything more cordial than mild irritation when they listen to jazz. Attempted mixtures of the two idioms invariably act like oil and water. Jazzed classics and symphonies with jazz themes have a tendency to ruffle tempers in both camps. Even the impartial critic is at a loss for any similar scale of standards in the two arts. Though many a jazz aesthete has tried to, you can't compare a Louis Armstrong solo to a Josef Szigeti sonata performance, or a Bessie Smith blues to an aria from *Rigoletto*. There isn't any common ground.

The disregard of this distinction among jazz critics has led to some curious concert ventures and to a vast amount of amazing aesthetic double-talk. Jazz concerts in Carnegie Hall and the Metropolitan Opera House have been hailed as cultural milestones when, in fact, they only proved that jazz can be played in uncongenial surroundings especially designed for the wholly different requirements of *Traviata* or the New York Philharmonic – if that needed proving. Ever since the pundit Hugues Panassié discovered *le jazz hot* in a French chateau full of phonograph records, the world of intellectual jazz addicts has been calling a spade a *cuiller à caviar*. The ebullient, hit-or-miss ensemble of a New Orleans stomp is reverently described as 'counterpoint'; the jazz trumpeter's exuberant and raucous lapses from true pitch are mysteriously referred to as 'quarter tones' or 'atonality.' Jazz, as an art with a capital A, has become something to be listened to with a rapt air that would shame the audiences of the Budapest Quartet. To dance to it (which is just what its primitive Negro originators would do) becomes a profanation.

Highbrow composers have also tried bridging the gap. The idea that an amalgamation of jazz with such traditional forms as the sonata or the symphony might result in an American style of concert music is too attractive to be ignored. American composers have repeatedly written jazz symphonies, jazz concertos and jazz fugues. But they usually discard the idea after a few experiments, and they never succeed in using jazz as anything but a superficial ornamental embellishment, as they might, say, use a Balinese or Algerian tune for local color. Their so-called jazz composition is not jazz at all – as any jitterbug can tell from the first note. Its rigid highbrow musical structure prohibits the very type of improvisation that makes jazz fun to listen to. It remains a 'classical' composition with jazz-style trimmings, something about as American and about as homogeneous as a Greek temple with a shingle roof. The outstanding exception to this rule is probably Gershwin's mildly jazzy opera *Porgy and Bess,* which came close to artistic success. But Gershwin's opera is saved, as far as the appropriateness of its music is concerned, mainly because it is a folk opera with a Negro setting. It is, in other words, a highly specialized type of opera, if, indeed, it can properly be considered an opera at all. The use of the same idiom in connection with the generality of operatic drama would be unthinkable.

Why does this peculiar split exist? The answer, I think, will be found by clearing away the pseudo-classical verbiage of the jazz critic and looking at the aesthetic nature of jazz itself. Jazz, for all the enthusiasms of its intellectual *aficionados,* is not music in the sense that an opera or a symphony is music. It is a variety of folk music. And the distinction between folk music and art music is profound and nearly absolute. The former grows like a weed or a wildflower, exhibits no intellectual complexities, makes a simple, direct emotional appeal that may be felt by people who are not even remotely interested in music as an art. It is often beautiful to listen to, whether it is jazz, or Irish or Welsh ballad singing, or Spanish *flamenco* guitar playing, or New England sea chanties, or Venetian gondolier songs. But it is not subject to intellectual criticism, for it lacks the main element toward which such criticism would be directed: the creative ingenuity and technique of an unusual, trained musical mind.

Art music, on the other hand, is an art as complicated as architecture. It begins where folk music leaves off, in the conscious creation of musical edifices that bear the stamp, in style and technique, of an individual artist. Its traditions – the rules of its game – are complicated and ingenious. They are the result of centuries of civilized musical thinking by highly trained musicians for audiences that are capable of judging the finer points of such thought. Art music is no field of wildflowers. It is a hothouse of carefully bred and cultivated masterpieces, each one the fruit of unusual talent and great technical resourcefulness. You may prefer the open fields of folk music to the classical hothouse. That is your privilege. But if so, you are simply not interested in music as a fine art. And it is no use getting snobbish about your preference and pretending that your favorite musical wildflower is a masterpiece of gardening skill. It isn't.

Thus, the remarks 'I prefer early Chicago-style jive to *Tristan and Isolde,*' or 'I prefer Kirsten Flagstad to Ethel Waters' are not really critical or evaluative statements. They are like saying 'I prefer percherons to race horses' – an understandable preference, but one that would be meaningless to a racing enthusiast. 'But after all, hasn't jazz got melody, rhythm and harmony, and aren't these attributes of concert music?' Of course. But the uses to which these materials are put differ greatly in the two arts. Jazz harmony ... is restricted to four or five monotonous patterns which support the florid improvisations of the soloist like a standardized scaffolding. These patterns never differ, never make any demands on creative ingenuity. Virtually every blues, and every piece of boogie woogie pianism, uses precisely the same harmony as every other blues or boogie woogie piece. Rhythmically, jazz is somewhat more ingenious, but not much more varied. It is limited to four-four or two-four time, and its most interesting effects are the result of blind instinct rather than thought.

Melodically, jazz is often strikingly beautiful and original. But jazz melody, like all folk melody, is of the amoebic rather than the highly organized type. Jazz melody, unlike most highbrow melody, consist of tunes rather than themes. These tunes are as simple and self-contained as one-cell animals. They can be repeated, sometimes with embellishments and variations, but they are incapable of being formed into higher musical organisms. Cell for cell, or melody for melody, they often compare favorably with the themes of highbrow music. The melody of Bessie Smith's *Cold in Hand Blues,* for example, is a much more beautiful tune than the 'V for Victory' theme of Beethoven's *Fifth Symphony.* But when you have played it, that is all there is – a beautiful, self-sufficient amoeba. Beethoven's crusty little motif is a cell of a different sort, almost without significance by itself, but capable of being reproduced into a vast symphonic organism with dramatic climaxes and long range emotional tensions.

The jazz artist, like all folk musicians, creates his one-cell melodies by instinct and repeats them over and over again, perhaps with simple variations. The composer of art music, on the other hand, is interested in one-cell melodies only as raw material. His creative mind begins where the instinct of the folk musician leaves off, in building such material into highly organized forms like symphonies and fugues. It is the technique and ingenuity with which he accomplishes this job that is the main subject of music criticism, as it applies to composition. And this is why music criticism is apt to sound pompous and miss its mark when it is applied to the creative side of a folk art like jazz. There is, to be sure, a large amount of concert music and of opera that is related to folk-music sources, and that sometimes scarcely rises above the folk-music level. Chopin waltzes, Brahms Hungarian dances, Tchaikovsky ballet tunes, Grieg songs, old-fashioned Italian operatic arias, and so on, sometimes fall under this heading. But the sophisticated music world has long thought of these items as belonging to a special, 'semi-popular' category. They are not the backbone of symphonic or operatic art. And they are seldom the subject of serious music criticism.

One of the most striking features of jazz as compared with art music is its lack of evolutionary development. Aside from a few minor changes of fashion, its history shows no technical evolution whatever. The formulas of the jazz musical language ... were nearly all used in the earliest of jazz and still constitute, with minor modifications, the basis of jazz technique. Occasionally, as in the piano rag, these formulas have taken on a special character due to the popularity of certain instruments or combinations of instruments. But the formulas themselves have remained constant. Jazz today remains essentially the same kind of music it was in 1900. Its simple forms – the blues, the eight-bar barbershop phrases – have been characteristic of it from the very beginning. This lack of evolution, which is an attribute of all folk music, is another of the main differences between jazz and concert music. The history of the latter shows a continuous development of structural methods. Few important highbrow composers have left the technique of music where they found it.

24 **André Hodeir** The essence (1956)

Source: André Hodeir, 'The Essence,' in *Jazz: Its Evolution and Essence* (New York: Grove, 1956: 234–41).

1   What is not essential

We have looked over the conceptions of rhythm and the handling of sound as they apply to the jazz musician. Our search for what is essential to this music now obliges us to ask a series of questions concerning other factors that appear to be equally important. What we have to do is distinguish between the vital center of jazz and the part that is just connected with it. African holdovers, the spirit and form of the blues, the repertory, improvisation, arrangements, melody, harmony – are these simply elements of jazz? Do they constitute its essence? The importance of these questions is obvious. We shall regard as essential only those characteristics that are at once specific and constant. For instance, the growl is part of the language of jazz. It arose from a need to express certain sensations that do not exist outside this music. However, the growl is not essential, since innumerable works that are undeniably jazz make no use whatsoever of this effect. With a few exceptions, jazz uses only a two- and four-beat meter. But this meter is not specific; it existed long before the first Negro slaves set foot in America. Nevertheless, both the growl and the 2/2 or 4/4 bar are part of larger conceptions (sound and rhythm) that we may be obliged to regard as essential.

Melodic holdovers from Africa are not essential to jazz. There is, for example, no trace of them in Coleman Hawkins' *Body and Soul*. This same piece authorizes us to disqualify, as essential characteristics, the language and spirit of the blues, which played a great role in the gestation of jazz but do not seem to be constant and necessary elements. The form of the blues is even less important than the style. The principle of the four-bar unit of construction, which was introduced into Negro-American folklore at an undetermined epoch and subsequently adopted by jazzmen as an unchangeable rule, is called into question in certain modern works. This observation brings us to a considera- tion of the twofold problem of repertory and form. The pieces that are referred to, in a regrettable misuse of the term, as 'jazz classics' are not at all an essential part of this music. André Kostelanetz has produced a version of *Tiger Rag* that is completely outside the realm of jazz. On the other hand, any piece that lends itself to the conditions of infrastructure that jazz requires can be assimilated. Jazzmen have borrowed innumerable themes from different repertories and have treated them with great liberty without thereby altering the essence of their art ... The example of *Concerto for Cootie* shows that jazz can very well get away from the theme-and-variations form that almost all its works follow. Improvisation, whether individual or collective, is not essential either. We have seen that jazz can be expressed by means of arrangements. And arrangements themselves are merely a device the jazz musician uses as the need arises. Counterpoint is a form of thought and of expression that is found in a small number of works, especially if the word is taken in a strict sense. The same thing is not true, of course, in the case of harmony and melody, which figure in virtually all recorded works. It might be claimed that both disappear in certain drum solos, but such solos are only an episodical part of jazz. Melody and harmony would therefore be essential if they didn't have, in jazz, a non-specific character that is not completely offset by the phrase-chorus idea and the blues mode, which are ... the only real contributions of the Negro-American genius in this domain. In both cases, borrowings are more numerous if not more evident than innovations.

Our study of rhythm and sound brought out the existence of two phenomena, swing and the hot manner of playing. Are these two elements constant and specific enough to satisfy the criteria for what is essential? As to whether they are sufficiently specific, there can be no doubt about the answer. Sometimes one of the two elements is enough by itself to place a musical fragment in the world of jazz. [Don] Byas' initial inflection in *Laura* identifies the performance as being jazz even before rhythmic values and the infrastructure produce the sensation of swing. Inversely, a slow piano solo by John Lewis or Erroll Garner may be made up of sounds that could figure in a European composition, but its pulsation will show that it is jazz. But doesn't this twofold example suggest that a careful examination of how constant these swing and hot phenomena are might lead to unexpected conclusions?

2   Historic persistence of the swing and hot phenomena

It seems certain that the solution to the problem we are considering – what constitutes the essence of jazz – lies in the tension-relaxation duality. What remains to be seen is whether these two elements have always existed side by side in equal proportions or whether one has been more important than the other at different times.

Reconstitutions of primitive jazz seem to show clearly not only that the Louisiana pioneers had very little swing but also that their rhythmic conceptions made it impossible for swing to appear in more than an embryonic stage. The jazzmen who did honor to the New Orleans style between 1920 and 1928 represented a definite advance over their predecessors ... but frequent slips in performance and certain backward rhythmic conceptions prevented most of them from matching the fullness of swing achieved by Armstrong and his disciples. The element of relaxation is accordingly much weaker in the primitive and oldtime styles than the element of tension, which reaches a level of paroxysm. At least during the primitive period, hot language may be said to outweigh swing in a proportion of nine to one. But as time went on, this proportion continued to change in favor of swing. An equilibrium was established between 1935 and 1940, at the beginning of the classical period. Jazz lost some of its early savageness; it became organized and polished, its violence was put under control. At the same time, conceptions and means of execution were modified, and both the soloist and the accompanist were able to express a more intense swing. That was when thousands of young pianists, white and colored, took Teddy Wilson as an example. People began to be less interested in playing hot than in swinging. However, two opposing trends were in the process of being born. The first was a reaction and included a whole series of screaming tenor saxophonists like Illinois Jacquet. These musicians re-emphasized the elements of tension, but without sacrificing the quality of swing that the preceding generation had acquired. Still, their dynamism was more often than not expressed at the expense of the strictly musical quality of their solos. At the other extreme, Lester Young took over the element of relaxation at the high degree of perfection to which Armstrong and Hodges had brought it and carried it even further by developing muscular relaxation and suitable rhythmic conceptions. This step forward may, however, have been accompanied by a certain weakening of vital drive. The type of swing created by Young is what cool musicians identify themselves with. But the price paid by the followers of this movement for their adherence to these conceptions and their legitimate desire to go beyond them has been an almost total abandonment – a necessary abandonment, freely consented to and even solicited – of the element of tension. The same elements are to be found in ultramodern as in primitive jazz, but the proportions are reversed. The element of relaxation is now very much in evidence, whereas the element of tension is considerably subdued.

3 Must jazz be divided into compartments?

Is it reasonable to give the name of jazz to successive musical conceptions in which the proportions of the two elements we have regarded as essential are so variable? Wouldn't it be better to dissociate them? If 1952 jazz had almost nothing in common with 1917 jazz, the reason may be that there had been a change of essence between those two dates. If we consider only the hot manner of playing as essential, certain solos of Lester Young lose almost all title to being called jazz; but the same thing is true of the greater part of New Orleans jazz if we consider swing as the essential element. Certain theoreticians have crossed this Rubicon. They affirm that New Orleans music (which they call 'jazz') is essentially different from classical jazz (which they call 'swing'), just as the latter is absolutely different from modern jazz (which they refer to as 'bebop'). According to their way of seeing things, Ella Fitzgerald is not a jazz singer, she is a 'swingwoman'; Charlie Parker and Miles Davis are no more related than she is to such 'real jazzmen' as King Oliver and Johnny Dodds. The weakness of this theory is immediately apparent in the superpositions it involves. Where does Louis Armstrong come? Is he a jazzman or a swingman? Thanks to him, doesn't the phenomenon of swing, which the pioneers felt only vaguely, appear at the height of the New Orleans period? In our introduction, we wondered whether it was legitimate to divide the history of jazz into several distinct periods. A procedure that may be acceptable in the interest of clarifying an explanation ceases to be valid when used as the starting point for what is supposed to be a demonstration of historical truth. Under such circumstances, the arbitrariness of making radical separations between styles that obviously intermingle becomes evident.

4   Toward a change of essence?

We have observed that the elements of relaxation and tension, which we consider conjointly essential, exist permanently side by side, but that the element of tension has grown smaller as the other element increased. In works belonging to the cool movement, tension is very weak. There is reason, then, to consider the possibility that one of the two poles between which the electricity of jazz is concentrated may disappear. The public, as we have seen, is more sensitive to tension than to relaxation, and its current attitude might incline us to pessimistic considerations. But quite apart from those, it behooves us to wonder whether such a total effacement of one of its major components would not entail the effacement of all jazz. In other words, can it be that we are witnessing a change of essence? Probably so. If the curve of its two elements were to continue bending in the same direction, the evolution of jazz would find a logical conclusion in its own disappearance. Bernard Heuvelmans would be closer to the truth than Boris Vian. Jazz would seem to have been just a lucky accident. But doesn't European musical thought itself, considered at a distance, have the appearance of an accident without parallel in history? The important thing would be for jazz to have a successor in some kind of Negro-American music that would offer as much as jazz without actually being the same thing. Some people believe that this has happened, and that what we call cool jazz is nothing other than the new art that has come to take the place of the old form, which is about to disappear. Considering all the great jazzmen who are still alive – some of them hardly over thirty – talk of this imminent demise strikes me as premature.

By our definition, jazz consists essentially of *an inseparable but extremely variable mixture of relaxation and tension* (that is, of swing and the hot manner of playing). Defined in this way, jazz has an incredibly rich past, considering the briefness of its history. It has involved the most varied forms of expression – vocal and instrumental, monodic and polyphonic, individual and collective, improvised and worked out. After remaining a music of the common people for a long time, some of Ellington's works put it in the ranks of highbrow music; Armstrong gave it mystical overtones, and Miles Davis added to it a chamber music character that it had lacked before. It has something to offer to every mood and can be sometimes light, sometimes serious. There is nothing like it for dancing, but it is also at home in the concert hall. Although it is the music of the American Negro, its universality has long since been established. Its disappearance would be deplorable unless a worthy successor arose to take its place. For it is doubtful that recordings made in our time will be enough to give men in later centuries an adequate idea of its beauty. Of course, richer and nobler art forms have died out over the centuries, leaving only meager hints of their greatness. It is only natural to hope that a more favorable destiny awaits one of the most vital musical manifestations of our time. Or could it be that this enormous vitality is precisely what makes it so hard to imagine its ever being dead? In any case, the only answer to this question, as to any other question about the future, is a large interrogation point. Tomorrow's music will be whatever tomorrow's men are.

25 **Scott DeVeaux** Constructing the jazz tradition: Jazz historiography (1991)

Source: Scott DeVeaux, 'Constructing the jazz tradition: jazz historiography,' *Black American Literature Forum*, 25, 3 (Fall, 1991: 525–31) (excerpt).

I don't know where jazz is going. Maybe it's going to hell. You can't make anything go anywhere. It just happens. (Thelonious Monk)

To judge from textbooks aimed at the college market, something like an official history of jazz has taken hold in recent years. On these pages, for all its chaotic diversity of style and expression and for all the complexity of its social origins, jazz is presented as a coherent whole, and its history as a skillfully contrived and easily comprehended narrative. After an obligatory nod to African origins and rag-time antecedents, the music is shown to move through a succession of styles or periods, each with a conveniently distinctive label and time period: New Orleans jazz up through the 1920s, swing in the 1930s, bebop in the 1940s, cool jazz and hard bop in the 1950s, free jazz and fusion in the 1960s. Details of emphasis vary. But from textbook to textbook, there is substantive agreement on the defining features of each style, the pantheon of great innovators, and the canon of recorded masterpieces.

This official version of jazz history continues to gain ground through the burgeoning of jazz appreciation classes at universities and colleges. It is both symptom and cause of the gradual acceptance of jazz, within the academy and in the society at large as an art music – 'America's classical music,' in a frequently invoked phrase.[1] Such acceptance, most advocates of jazz agree, is long overdue. If at one time jazz could be supported by the marketplace, or attributed to a nebulous (and idealized) vision of folk creativity, that time has long passed. Only by acquiring the prestige, the 'cultural capital' (in Pierre Bourdieu's phrase) of an artistic tradition can the music hope to be heard, and its practitioners receive the support commensurate with their training and accomplishments. The accepted historical narrative for jazz serves this purpose. It is a pedigree, showing contemporary jazz to be not a fad or a mere popular music, subject to the whims of fashion, but an autonomous art of some substance, the culmination of a long process of maturation that has in its own way recapitulated the evolutionary progress of Western art.

The added twist is that this new American classical music openly acknowledges its debt not to Europe, but to Africa. There is a sense of triumphant reversal as the music of a formerly enslaved people is designated a 'rare and valuable national American treasure' by the Congress, and beamed overseas as a weapon of the Cold War.[2] The story of jazz, therefore, has an important political dimension, one that unfolds naturally in its telling. Louis Armstrong, Duke Ellington, and John Coltrane provide powerful examples of black achievement and genius. Their exacting discipline cannot be easily marginalized, *pace* Adorno, as 'mere' popular entertainment, or as the shadowy replication of European forms. The depth of tradition, reaching back in an unbroken continuum to the beginning of the century, belies attempts to portray African Americans as people without a past – hence the appeal of an unambiguous and convincing historical narrative: If the achievements that jazz represents are to be impressed on present and future generations, the story must be told, and told well.

For all its pedagogical utility, though, the conventional narrative of jazz history is a simplification that begs as many questions as it answers. For one thing, the story that moves so confidently at the outset from style to style falters as it approaches the present. From the origins of jazz to bebop there is a straight line; but after bebop, the evolutionary lineage begins to dissolve into the inconclusive coexistence of many different, and in some cases mutually hostile, styles. 'At the century's halfway mark,' complains one textbook, 'the historical strand that linked contemporary jazz to its roots suddenly began to fray. The cohesive thread had been pulled apart in the '40s by the bebop musicians, and now every fiber was bent at a slightly different angle' (Tirro [1977]: 291). Beginning with the 1950s and 1960s, the student of jazz history is confronted with a morass of terms – *cool jazz, hard bop, modal jazz, Third Stream, New Thing* – none of which convincingly represents a consensus.[3] For the most recent decades, the most that writers of textbooks can manage is to sketch out the contrasting directions pointed to by free jazz and jazz/rock fusion, implying to the impressionable student that an informed view embraces both, as it embraces all preceding styles, and that the future of jazz is bound up with a pluralism that somehow reconciles these apparently irreconcilable trends.[4] No one, apparently, has thought to ask whether the earlier 'cohesive thread' of narrative might mask similarly conflicting interpretations.

At the same time that jazz educators have struggled to bring order to jazz history, a controversy over the current state and future direction of jazz has become noisily evident in the popular media. The terms of this debate pit so-called *neoclassicists,* who insist on the priority of tradition and draw their inspiration and identity from a sense of connectedness with the historical past, against both the continuous revolution of the *avant-garde* and the commercial orientation of *fusion*. At stake, if the rhetoric is taken at face value, is nothing less than the music's survival. Some have argued, for example, that the neoclassicist movement, led by youthful celebrity Wynton Marsalis, has rescued jazz from extinction. 'Largely under his influence,' proclaimed a *Time* author in a recent cover story,

> a jazz renaissance is flowering on what was once barren soil. Straightahead jazz music almost died in the 1970s as record companies embraced the electronically enhanced jazz-pop amalgam known as fusion. Now a whole generation of prodigiously talented young musicians is going back to the roots, using acoustic instruments, playing recognizable tunes and studying the styles of earlier jazzmen. (Sancton [1990]: 66)

Other critics counter that the triumph of a retrospective aesthetic is in fact all the evidence one might need that jazz is dead; all that is left to the current generation is the custodial function of preserving and periodically reviving glorious moments from the past.[5]

The neoclassicists' nostalgia for a Golden Age located ambiguously some-where between the swing era and 1960s hard bop resonates curiously with issues that go back to the earliest days of jazz historiography. Marsalis and his followers have been called 'latter-day moldy figs' (Santoro [1988]: 17), a term that links them to critics of the 1930s and '40s who, by insisting on the priority of New Orleans-style jazz, earned themselves the reputation as defenders of an outdated and artificially static notion of what jazz is and can be. The countercharge that either (or both) avant-garde or fusion constitutes a 'wrong turn,' or a 'dead end,' in the development of jazz represents the opposing argument, of the same vintage: Any change that fails to preserve the essence of the music is a corruption that no longer deserves to be considered jazz.[6]

The difference in tone between these assessments – the rancor of the journalistic debate, and the platitudinous certainty of the classroom – disguises the extent to which certain underlying assumptions are shared. With the possible exception of those in the fusion camp (who are more often the targets of the debate than active participants in it), no one disputes the official version of the history. Its basic narrative shape and its value for a music that is routinely denied respect and institutional support are accepted virtually without question. The struggle is over *possession* of that history and the legitimacy that it confers. More precisely, the struggle is over the act of definition that is presumed to lie at the history's core; for it is an article of faith that some central essence named *jazz* remains constant throughout all the dramatic transforma-tions that have resulted in modern-day jazz.

That essence is ordinarily defined very vaguely; there is ample evidence from jazz folklore to suggest that musicians take a certain stubborn pride in the resistance of their art to critical exegesis. (To the question *What is jazz?* the apocryphal answer is: 'If you have to ask, you'll never know.') But in the heat of debate, definition is a powerful weapon; and more often than not, such definitions define through exclusion. Much as the concept of purity is made more concrete by the threat of contamination, what jazz is *not* is far more vivid rhetorically than what it is. Thus fusion is 'not jazz' because, in its pursuit of commercial success, it has embraced certain musical traits – the use of electric instruments, modern production techniques, and a rock- or funk-oriented rhythmic feeling – that violate the essential nature of jazz. The avant-garde, whatever its genetic connection to the modernism of 1940s bebop, is not jazz – or no longer jazz – because, in its pursuit of novelty, it has recklessly abandoned the basics of form and structure, even African-American principles like 'swing.' And the neoclassicist stance is irrelevant, and potentially harmful, to the growth of jazz because it makes a fetish of the past, failing to recognize that the essence of jazz is the process of change itself.

Defining jazz is a notoriously difficult proposition, but the task is easier if one bypasses the usual inventory of musical qualities or techniques, like improvisation or swing (since the more specific or comprehensive such a list attempts to be, the more likely it is that exceptions will overwhelm the rule). More relevant are the boundaries within which historians, critics, and musicians have consistently situated the music. One such boundary, certainly, is ethnicity. Jazz is strongly identified with African-American culture, both in the narrow sense that its particular techniques ultimately derive from black American folk traditions, and in the broader sense that it is expressive of, and uniquely rooted in, the experience of black Americans. This raises important questions at the edges – e.g., how the contributions of white musicians are to be treated and, at the other end of the spectrum, where the boundary between jazz and other African-American genres (such as blues, gospel, and R & B) ought to be drawn. But on the whole, ethnicity provides a core, a center of gravity for the narrative of jazz, and is one element that unites the several different kinds of narratives in use today.

An equally pervasive, if divisive, theme is economics – specifically, the relationship of jazz to capitalism. Here, the definition is negative: Whether conceived of as art music or folk music, jazz is consistently seen as something separate from the popular music industry. The stigmatization of 'commercialism' as a disruptive or corrupting influence, and in any case as something external to the tradition, has a long history in writings on jazz. In the words of Rudi Blesh (writing in 1946),

> Commercialism [is] a cheapening and deteriorative force, a species of murder perpetrated on a wonderful music by whites and by those misguided negroes who, for one or another reason, choose to be accomplices to the deed ... Commercialism is a thing not only hostile, but fatal to [jazz]. (11–12)

Such language was particularly popular with defenders of New Orleans-style jazz who, like Blesh, narrowly identified the music with a romanticized notion of folk culture. But the same condemnatory fervor could be heard from proponents of bebop in the 1940s:

> The story of bop, like that of swing before it, like the stories of jazz and ragtime before that, has been one of constant struggle against the restrictions imposed on all progressive thought in an art that has been commercialized to the point of prostitution. (Feather, *Inside* 45)

> Bebop is the music of revolt: revolt against big bands, arrangers ... Tin Pan Alley – against commercialized music in general. It reasserts the individuality of the jazz musician ... (Russell 202)

These attitudes survive with undiminished force in recent attacks on fusion, which imply a conception of jazz as a music independent of commercial demands that is in continuous conflict with the economic imperatives of twentieth-century America. *Agoraphobia,* fear of the marketplace, is problematic enough in artistic genres that have actually achieved, or inherited, some degree of economic autonomy. It is all the more remarkable for jazz – a music that has developed largely within the framework of modern mass market capitalism – to be construed within the inflexible dialectic of 'commercial' versus 'artistic,' with all virtue centered in the latter. The virulence with which these opinions are expressed gives a good idea how much energy was required to formulate this position in the first place, and how difficult it is to maintain. This is not to say that there is not an exploitative aspect to the relationship between capitalist institutions and jazz musicians, especially when the effects of racial discrimination on the ability of black musicians to compete fairly are factored in. But jazz is kept separate from the marketplace only by demonizing the economic system that allows musicians to survive – and from this demon there is no escape. Wynton Marsalis may pride himself on his refusal to 'sell out,' but that aura of artistic purity is an indisputable component of his commercial appeal.

Issues of ethnicity and economics define jazz as an oppositional discourse: the music of an oppressed minority culture, tainted by its association with commercial entertainment in a society that reserves its greatest respect for art that is carefully removed from daily life. The escape from marginalization comes only from a self-definition that emphasizes its universality and its autonomy. The 'jazz tradition' reifies the music, insisting that there *is* an overarching category called *jazz*, encompassing musics of divergent styles and sensibilities. These musics must be understood not as isolated expressions of particular times or places, but in an organic relationship, as branches of a tree to the trunk. The essence of jazz, in other words, lies not in any one style, or any one cultural or historical context, but in that which links all these things together into a seamless continuum. Jazz is what it is because it is a culmination of all that has come before. Without the sense of depth that only a narrative can provide, jazz would be literally rootless, indistinguishable from a variety of other 'popular' genres that combine virtuosity and craftsmanship with dance rhythms. Its claim to being not only distinct, but elevated above other indigenous forms ('America's classical music'), is in large part dependent on the idea of an evolutionary progression reaching back to the beginning of the century. Again and again, present-day musicians, whether neoclassicist or avant-garde, invoke the past, keeping before the public's eye the idea that musics as diverse as those of King Oliver and the Art Ensemble of Chicago are in some fundamental sense *the same music.*

Those who subscribe to an essentialist notion of jazz history (and there are few who do not) take all of this for granted. But even a glance at jazz historiography makes it clear that the idea of the 'jazz tradition' is a construction of relatively recent vintage, an overarching narrative that has crowded out other possible interpretations of the complicated and variegated cultural phenomena that we cluster under the umbrella *jazz*. Nor is this simply an academic complaint: The crisis of the current jazz scene is less a function of the state of the music (jazz has, in many ways, never been better supported or appreciated) than of an anxiety arising from the inadequacy of existing historical frameworks to explain it.

Notes (edited)

1   See, for example, Grover Sales's recent textbook *Jazz: America's Classical Music* (Englewood Cliffs: Prentice, 1984) and the address 'Jazz – America's Classical Music' delivered by Billy Taylor to the Black American Music Symposium at the University of Michigan in 1985 and subsequently reprinted in *Black Perspective in Music* 14.1 (1986): 21–25.

2   The language is that of House Concurrent Resolution 57, passed by the United States Senate on December 4, 1987.

3   A sampling from recent jazz textbooks gives some of the flavor of this loss of direction. Tanner and Gerow's *A Study of Jazz* follows neatly defined chapters on 'Early New Orleans Dixieland (1900–1920),' 'Chicago Style Dixieland (the 1920s),' 'Swing (1932–1942),' 'Bop (1940–1950),' 'Cool (1949–1955),' and 'Funky (c.1954–1963),' with a 'period' of over forty years called the 'Eclectic Era,' a 'potpourri of some eighty years of continuous development' (119). The 'Chronology of Jazz Styles Chart' in Mark Gridley's *Jazz Styles* begins with comfortingly concise periods for 'Early Jazz (1920s),' 'Swing (1930s),' 'Bop (1940s),' and 'West Coast (1950s),' but soon degenerates into 'Coexistence of Hard Bop, Free Jazz, and Modal Jazz (1960s),' 'Transition to Jazz-Rock (late 1960s),' and 'Coexistence of AACM, Jazz-Rock, and Modal Jazz (1970s)' (356–57). Billy Taylor's last chapter in *Piano Jazz* (after the terse chapters 'Bebop' and 'Cool') is entitled 'Abstract Jazz, Mainstream Jazz, Modal Jazz, Electronic Jazz, Fusion' (187).

4   This strategy is followed in textbooks by James McCalla, Donald Megill and Richard Demory, and James Lincoln Collier, among others. The persistence of earlier styles of jazz is sometimes counted as yet another direction. 'If we cannot predict where jazz is going ... we can at least discern certain trends,' wrote Collier in 1978, identifying three such trends: jazz-rock, free jazz, and what he called (anticipating the 'neoclassicism' of the 1980s) the 'neo-bop movement' (494–96).

5   See, for example, Henry Martin's recent textbook *Enjoying Jazz*. One of the basic hypotheses of the book is that contemporary jazz is facing a kind of stylistic dead end: 'By the 1970s and early 1980s, jazz was unlikely to undergo any further significant evolution because it lacked the popularity necessary for continued vitality. At that time all of its previous styles became recognized as artistic vehicles for performance. Indications are, therefore, that jazz will not undergo any further significant evolution' (204).

6   In a 1984 interview, Wynton Marsalis complained, 'I don't think the music moved along in the '70s. I think it went astray. Everybody was trying to be pop stars, and imitated people that were supposed to be imitating them ... What we have to do now is reclaim ...' (Mandel 18).

Works cited

Blesh, Rudi. *Shining Trumpets: A History of Jazz*. New York: Knopf, 1946.
Feather, Leonard. *Inside Be-Bop*. New York: Robbins, 1949.

Mandel, Howard. 'The Wynton Marsalis Interview.' *Down Beat*, July, 1984: 16–19, 67.

Russell, Ross. 'Bebop.' Williams, ed. *The Art of Jazz*. New York: Oxford University Press, 1959: 187–214.

Sancton, Thomas. 'Horns of Plenty.' *Time*, 22 October 1990: 64–71.

Santoro, Gene. 'Miles Davis the Enabler: Part II.' *Down Beat*, November 1988: 16–19.

Tirro, Frank. *Jazz: A History*. New York: Norton, 1977.

26 **Krin Gabbard** Writing the other history (1995)

Source: Krin Gabbard: 'Introduction: writing the other history,' in *Representing Jazz* (Durham: Duke University Press, 1995: 1–3) (excerpt).

At least until recently, jazz history has been based on an evolutionary model that emphasizes a handful of master improvisers and genius composers. Many of the essays in *Representing Jazz,* as well as in its companion volume, *Jazz Among the Discourses,* have radically called this model into question. Relying on various poststructuralisms as well as on discourses developed by cultural historians and literary theorists, many of the contributors have broken new ground by placing the music much more securely within specific cultural moments. Many also have undertaken the metacritical work of reading jazz histories within *their* own moments.

In another welcome anthology, *Reading Jazz,* David Meltzer has searched through eight decades of assorted texts to present a fascinating array of statements about the music. In his introductory 'Pre-ramble,' Meltzer goes so far as to argue that jazz was 'invented' by whites, who have created and maintained a discourse in order to 'colonize' the music. Meltzer is comparing the 'jazz' of the white critic – jazz as mythology and cultural commodity – with the extensive, elusive, often ignored musics that have been played, usually by African Americans, in various locales throughout the late nineteenth and early twentieth centuries. Until 1917, virtually all of this music was unrecorded. The word 'jazz' may not have been coined by whites, but dominant American culture has continued to accept it as the master term for certain kinds of musical practice in spite of the fact that many of that music's practitioners – Duke Ellington and Anthony Braxton are only two of the most prominent – have repeatedly rejected the term.

While Meltzer sees colonization as inevitable when whites write about jazz, he also argues that he has produced a 'source-book of permissible (intentional, accidental, unavoidable) racism.' Meltzer collects a large number of overtly racist writings about jazz, but he often juxtaposes them with nostalgic reveries on the glories of black culture. A central thesis of his book is that jazz has historically been configured to serve specific purposes for whites, who have associated it on the one hand with dark-browed primitivism and on the other with ecstatic freedom. But whether the music was demonized or romanticized, the result was the same: jazz was the safely contained world of the Other where whites knew they could find experiences unavailable to them at home.

Representing Jazz can be regarded as still more exercises in colonization and permissible racism, but I would argue that many of its contributors have examined racist and colonialist discourses with uncommon rigor. In this sense, the collected essays bring a new depth to the rapidly maturing discipline of jazz studies by concentrating on jazz myth and jazz culture rather than jazz *per se* (assuming for the moment that jazz can in fact be isolated from myth and culture). In spite of the new turn in jazz studies that this volume and its companion represent, we may still choose to embrace much of what has been written by traditional jazz writers, even those who are most out of date methodologically. Who can dispute, for example, the crucial importance of Louis Armstrong for early jazz? (There is, however, massive disagreement about Armstrong's stature and significance after 1929 or some other date – the *terminus ad quem* of Armstrong's great period is itself a subject of considerable debate.) But there is at least one, more subtle supposition within established jazz writing that we are not likely to question – the belief that jazz history ought to be written so that it can stand in opposition to popular misconceptions. The unspoken wisdom is that without jazz history our knowledge would depend on platitudes in the daily press as well as on trite movies and television dramas, lurid novels, sensationalizing photographs, and genre paintings. But over time, don't these artifacts begin to constitute a history of their own? Are there no reasons for looking at this other history, presumably inaccurate, presumably unavoidable? If the jazz historians are giving us a truth that is otherwise unavailable, does it necessarily follow that there is no truth in what we are told by authors, filmmakers, dancers, painters, photographers, and the rest? Can't the works of creative artists render the music as vividly as those of the critics? And even if we find these works to be flawed or even grossly inaccurate, can't we examine them critically to understand how American culture has actually received the music, with its volatile mix of black and white, high and low, sacred and profane? Isn't there value in writing this other history of jazz? The essays in *Representing Jazz* can be conceptualized as systematic assessments of what we know about jazz outside the official histories. Many of these contributions express a profound discomfort with the idea that an official jazz history *can* be written or that any representation of the music can transcend its own built-in limitations.

27 **Gary Tomlinson** The jazz canon as monological canon (1991)

Source: Gary Tomlinson, 'The jazz canon as monological canon,' in 'Cultural Dialogics and Jazz: A White Historian Signifies,' *Black Music Research Journal*, 11, 2 (1991: 245–9) (excerpt).

What ... happened [in antibebop criticism of the 1940s] was that even though the white middle-brow critic had known about Negro music for only about three decades, he was already trying to formalize and finally institutionalize it. It is a hideous idea. The music was already in danger of being forced into that junk pile of admirable objects and data the West knows as *culture.*

Recently [*ca.* 1963], the same attitudes have become more apparent in the face of a fresh redefinition of the form and content of Negro music. Such phrases as 'anti-jazz' have been used to describe the most exciting music produced in this country. But as critic A.B. Spellman asked, 'What does anti-jazz mean and who are these ofays who've appointed themselves guardians of last year's blues?' It is that simple, really. What does anti-jazz mean? And who coined the phrase? What is the definition of jazz? And who was authorized to make one?

Negro music is essentially the expression of an attitude, or a collection of attitudes, about the world, and only secondarily about the way music is made ...

Usually the critic's commitment was first to his *appreciation* of the music rather than to his understanding of the attitude which produced it.

Amiri Baraka [LeRoi Jones] (*Black Music* 1967, 18, 13)

In our thinking and writing about jazz and in our teaching of it we have not heeded Amiri Baraka's warnings. Jazz has been institutionalized, its works evaluated, and those judged to be the best enshrined in a glass case of cultural *admirabilia.* The jazz canon has been forged and maintained according to old strategies, according to what [Henry Louis] Gates identifies as Eurocentric, hierarchical notions, in which the limiting rules of aestheticism, transcendent-alism, and formalism are readily apparent. The institutionalized canon itself operates, in the hands of most writers, with little serious regard for the contexts in which canonic works were created and those in which their meaning and value are continually discovered and revised. It is a canon of the Same serving a history of the Same, and we have already all but lost sight of the partiality and impermanence of its structures of value.

Like the canon of European music, the jazz canon is a strategy for exclusion, a closed and elite collection of 'classic' works that together define what is and isn't jazz. The definition sets up walls, largely unbreachable, between 'true' or 'pure' jazz and varieties of music making outside it. These walls close out as 'nonjazz' whole realms of music that have resulted from the intersections of the critics' 'true' jazz with other idioms – popular balladry, crooners' song styles, rhythm and blues styles and the related Motown and funk, rock 'n' roll of various sorts, world beat syncretisms, New Age minimalism, and so on. But, we might ask with Baraka, who *are* the self-appointed guardians of the borderlines setting off jazz from such musics? Certainly not most jazz musicians themselves, who from Louis Armstrong on have more often than not been remarkably open to interaction with the varied musical environment around them. Indeed, if as Gates ([*The Signifying Monkey*] 1988, 63) has suggested, the jazz tradition is essentially a Signifyin(g) tradition – if 'there are so many examples of Signifyin(g) in jazz that one could write a formal history of its development on this basis alone' – it is also true that much of the jazz musician's Signification has played on musical works and styles from outside the jazz critics' mainstream. Jazz Signification is largely extracanonic.

The values behind the institutionalization of jazz are revealed particularly clearly in the jazz textbooks for college and university courses that have appeared in the last two decades. This is not surprising; textbooks and the survey courses they abet have an awkward habit of revealing our tacit structures of evaluation. A glance at four typical texts, Frank Tirro's *Jazz: A History* (1977), Mark C. Gridley's *Jazz Styles: History and Analysis* (1985), Donald D. Megill and Richard S. Demory's *Introduction to Jazz History* (1989), and James McCalla's *Jazz: A Listener's Guide* (1982), demonstrates some recurring patterns.

First of all, all four books rely on Martin Williams's *Smithsonian Collection of Classic Jazz* for many of their examples. The reliance is one of convenience, of course; recordings need to be easily available for students. But the effect of this surrender to convenience is to monumentalize Williams's choices, to magnify into a statement of transcendent artistic worth the personal canon of one insightful (but conservative) critic, constructed itself in a given time and place according to particular formative rules and limiting contingencies. In jazz courses around the country, Williams's 'classics' have come to function in precisely the same way as the classics of the European musical canons taught in the classrooms across the hall. They have come to stand as exemplars of timeless aesthetic value instead of being understood – as the European works next door should also be understood but too rarely are – as human utterances valued according to the dialogical situations in which they were created and are continually recreated. In this way the jazz canon embodies the aestheticism that continues to circumscribe our teaching of European canons and that short-circuits our archaeological understanding of the conditions in which they are made and remade.

In the service of this aestheticism, the makers of the jazz canon employ a resounding formalism. All four of the texts named above insist in their prefaces and their presentations on the priority of listening to and analyzing musical styles; their approach ranks musical above other kinds of understanding. Thus Megill and Demory (1989, ix) write that 'reading and discussion alone will not convey the essence of the various styles. Only listening does.' Tirro (1977, xv–xvi) notes that 'a critical evaluation of my opinions must certainly stand or fall upon the evidence: the sound recordings which document the history of jazz.' And McCalla (1982, vii) eschews 'the memorization of names, style periods, titles, dates, and other facts' – surely McCalla knows that this is a strawman caricature of extramusical historical understanding – in favor of listening to and analyzing particular pieces.

This listening orientation might at first glance seem unexceptionable. But Baraka's remarks on narrowly musical appreciation should sensitize us to its ideological basis. Behind it hides the view that meaning (and hence value, which only arises alongside meaning) inheres somehow in the notes themselves. Behind it lurks the absurd but hard-to-eradicate proposition that music alone, independent of the cultural matrices that individuals build around it, can *mean* – that a recording or transcription of a Charlie Parker solo, for example, or the score or performance of a Beethoven symphony, can convey *something* even in the hypothetical absence of the complex negotiations of meaning we each pursue with them. This is the internalist ideology that has led most writers on jazz, at least since André Hodeir, to seek its 'essence' primarily or exclusively in its musical features.

Instead of repeating such Western myths of the noncontingency of artworks, why not search for jazz meanings *behind* the music, in the life-shapes that gave rise to it and that continue to sustain it? Why not, in other words, scrutinize the interactions between our own rules of formation and those we impute to the makers of jazz as the source of our evaluations of it? Why not create a jazz pedagogy in which our construction of the varieties of black life experience takes priority, saving the music – intricately bound up with those experiences, after all – for last, construing it in light of them and resisting the aestheticizing tendency to exaggerate its differences from other manifestations of expressive culture? At least one writer, Amiri Baraka (1963), long ago attempted a history along such lines. His *Blues People* is a resonant example of vernacularism *avant la lettre,* but to judge by the textbooks named above it has had little influence on the developing pedagogy of jazz studies ...

Placing the music first will always distance it from the complex and largely extramusical negotiations that made it and that sustain it. It will always privilege the European bourgeois myths of aesthetic transcendency, artistic purity untouched by function and context, and the elite status of artistic expression. (Such myths concerning the composers of the European canon badly need to be exploded, so it is all the more troubling to see them neatly transferred to African-American composers and performers.) Emphasizing the musical appreciation of jazz only transfers to the study of African-American music the formalist view that remains debilitatingly dominant in Eurocentric musicology, with its continuing emphasis on internalist music analysis.

In their internalism, then, the jazz textbooks cited above reinforce rules that inform the European musical canon. Thus the worst results to be feared in Gates's formation of a canon of black literature have been anticipated in the making of the canon of black music. The laudable impulses, similar to Gates's, behind the crystallization of the jazz canon – jazz historians have worked hard to loosen the stranglehold of European 'art music' on college and university curricula – have certainly not protected it from retracing the limited trajectory of earlier European canons, musical or otherwise. The jazz canon now shares all the misguided pretensions to a contextual value and transcendent meaning that characterize those other canons.

Another way of putting this is to say that the musicological makers of the jazz canon have not Signified on the earlier European musical canon. To have done so would have necessitated a questioning, ironic distance from that canon. It would have called for the staking out of a rhetorical stance vis-à-vis that canon; and this stance would have provided a tropological lever, Signification itself, that jazz historians could have used to uncover the impermanent, selective rules of formation of the earlier canon and thus to discover also their own partiality and impermanence. Signifyin(g) on the European canon would have led to an archaeology of it and of the jazz canon as well. Instead, by not scrutinizing the postulates of earlier canons, jazz historians have engaged in a wholesale restatement of them. In the place of dialogical Signification they have offered monological Imitation.

The result is a brand of narrowly based value judgment that cannot do justice to the complex dialogues of self and other in which culture is created. Such evaluation is ill-equipped in the face of all expressive culture; but it is perhaps especially feeble in dealing with nondominant cultural strains, such as African-American traditions, that have developed in multivalent interaction with hegemonic cultures around them. The dialogical drama of such cultures is intensified by the marginalizing ploys of the dominant culture; white attempts to silence black voices make more strenuous the negotiations from which those voices arise in the first place. Thus the monological judgments that have appeared repeatedly in the brief history of jazz – the early, negative critiques of bebop, for example, or the cries of 'anti-jazz' that, as Baraka noted, greeted the free jazz innovations of Ornette Coleman and Don Cherry around 1960 – have often taken the form of white critics' attempts to silence or at least 'whiten' innovative black expression.

But this forfeiture of dialogue can cut both ways. Just as white writers have sometimes been intent on ignoring or minimizing the blackness of jazz innovations and of individual jazz voices, so black writers have sometimes proved just as intent on impoverishing the interethnic dialogues that stand behind jazz styles. Both positions fail to grasp the Signifyin(g) richness of the jazz tradition; both start from premises that drastically reduce the dialogics itself of cultural production.

28 **Amiri Baraka [LeRoi Jones]** Jazz and the white critic (1963)

Source: Amiri Baraka [LeRoi Jones], 'Jazz and the white critic,' in *Black Music* (New York: Morrow, 1967: 11–20). (Originally published in *Down Beat*, 15 August 1963: 16–17, 34.)

Most jazz critics have been white Americans, but most important jazz musicians have not been. This might seem a simple enough reality to most people, or at least a reality which can be readily explained in terms of the social and cultural history of American society. And it is obvious why there are only two or three fingers' worth of Negro critics or writers on jazz, say, if one understands that until relatively recently those Negroes who *could* become critics, who would largely have to come from the black middle class, have simply not been interested in the music. Or at least jazz, for the black middle class, has only comparatively recently lost some of its stigma (though by no means is it yet as popular among them as any vapid musical product that comes sanctioned by the taste of the white majority). Jazz was collected among the numerous skeletons the middle-class black man kept locked in the closet of his psyche, along with watermelons and gin, and whose rattling caused him no end of misery and self-hatred. As one Howard University philosophy professor said to me when I was an undergraduate, 'It's fantastic how much bad taste the blues contain!' But it is just this 'bad taste' that this Uncle spoke of that has been the one factor that has kept the best of Negro music from slipping sterilely into the echo chambers of middlebrow American culture. And to a great extent such 'bad taste' was kept extant in the music, blues or jazz because the Negroes who were responsible for the best of the music, were always aware of their identities as black Americans and really did not, themselves, desire to become vague, featureless Americans as is usually the case with the Negro middle class. (This is certainly not to say that there have not been very important Negro musicians from the middle class. Since the Henderson era, their number has increased enormously in jazz.)

Negroes played jazz as they had sung blues or, even earlier, as they had shouted and hollered in those anonymous fields, because it was one of the few areas of human expression available to them. Negroes who felt the blues, later jazz, impulse, as a specific means of expression, went naturally into the music itself. There were fewer social or extra-expressive considerations that could possibly disqualify any prospective Negro jazz musician than existed, say, for a Negro who thought he might like to become a writer (or even an elevator operator, for that matter). Any Negro who had some ambition towards literature, in the earlier part of this century, was likely to have developed so powerful an allegiance to the sacraments of middle-class American culture that he would be horrified by the very idea of writing about jazz.

There were few 'jazz critics' in America at all until the 30's and then they were influenced to a large extent by what Richard Hadlock has called 'the carefully documented gee-whiz attitude' of the first serious European jazz critics. They were also, as a matter of course, influenced more deeply by the social and cultural mores of their own society. And it is only natural that their criticism, whatever its intention, should be a product of that society, or should reflect at least some of the attitudes and thinking of that society, even if not directly related to the subject they were writing about, Negro music.

Jazz, as a Negro music, existed, up until the time of the big bands, on the same socio-cultural level as the sub-culture from which it was issued. The music and its sources were *secret* as far as the rest of America was concerned, in much the same sense that the actual life of the black man in America was secret to the white American. The first white critics were men who sought, whether consciously or not, to understand this secret, just as the first serious white jazz musicians (Original Dixieland Jazz Band, Bix, etc.) sought not only to understand the phenomenon of Negro music but to appropriate it as a means of expression which they themselves might utilize. The success of this 'appropriation' signaled the existence of an American music, where before there was a Negro music. But the white jazz musician had an advantage the white critic seldom had. The white musician's commitment to jazz, the *ultimate concern*, proposed that the sub-cultural attitudes that produced the music as a profound expression of human feelings, could be *learned* and need not be passed on as a secret blood rite. And Negro music is essentially the expression of an attitude, or a collection of attitudes, about the world, and only secondarily an attitude about the way music is made. The white jazz musician came to understand this attitude as a way of making music, and the intensity of his understanding produced the 'great' white jazz musicians, and is producing them now.

Usually the critic's commitment was first to his *appreciation* of the music rather than to his understanding of the attitude which produced it. This difference meant that the potential critic of jazz had only to appreciate the music, or what he thought was the music, and that he did not need to understand or even be concerned with the attitudes that produced it, except perhaps as a purely sociological consideration. This last idea is certainly what produced the reverse patronization that is known as Crow Jim. The disparaging 'all you folks got rhythm' is no less a stereotype, simply because it is proposed as a positive trait. But this Crow Jim attitude has not been as menacing or as evident a flaw in critical writing about jazz as has another manifestation of the white critic's failure to concentrate on the blues and jazz attitude rather than his conditioned appreciation of the music. The major flaw in this approach to Negro music is that it strips the music too ingenuously of its social and cultural intent. It seeks to define jazz as an art (or a folk art) that has come out of no intelligent body of socio-cultural philosophy.

We take for granted the social and cultural milieu and philosophy that produced Mozart. As western people, the socio-cultural thinking of eighteenth-century Europe comes to us as a history legacy that is a continuous and organic part of the twentieth-century West. The socio-cultural philosophy of the Negro in America (as a continuous historical phenomenon) is no less specific and no less important for any intelligent critical speculation about the music that came out of it. And again, this is not a plea for narrow sociological analysis of jazz, but rather that this music cannot be completely understood (in critical terms) without some attention to the attitudes which produced it. It is the philosophy of Negro music that is most important, and this philosophy is only partially the result of the sociological disposition of Negroes in America. There is, of course, much more to it than that.

Strict musicological analysis of jazz, which has come into favor recently, is also as limited as a means of jazz criticism as a strict sociological approach. The notator of any jazz solo, or blues, has no chance of capturing what in effect are the most important elements of the music. (Most transcriptions of blues lyrics are just as frustrating.) A printed musical example of an Armstrong solo, or of a Thelonious Monk solo, tells us almost nothing except the futility of formal musicology when dealing with jazz. Not only are the various jazz effects almost impossible to notate, but each note *means something* quite in adjunct to musical notation. The notes of a jazz solo exist in a notation strictly for musical reasons. The notes of a jazz solo, as they are coming into existence, exist as they do for reasons that are only concomitantly musical. Coltrane's cries are not 'musical,' but they *are* music and quite moving music. Ornette Coleman's screams and rants are only musical once one understands the music his emotional attitude seeks to create. This attitude is real, and perhaps the most singularly important aspect of his music. Mississippi Joe Williams, Snooks Eaglin, Lightnin' Hopkins have different emotional attitudes than Ornette Coleman, but all of these attitudes are continuous parts of the historical and cultural biography of the Negro as it has existed and developed since there was a Negro in America, and a music that could be associated with him that did not exist anywhere else in the world. The notes *mean something*; and the something is, regardless of its stylistic considerations, part of the black psyche as it dictates the various forms of Negro culture.

Another hopeless flaw in a great deal of the writing about jazz that has been done over the years is that in most cases the writers, the jazz critics, have been anything but intellectuals (in the most complete sense of that word). Most jazz critics began as hobbyists or boyishly brash members of the American petit bourgeoisie, whose only claim to any understanding about the music was that they knew it was *different*; or else they had once been brave enough to make a trip into a Negro slum to hear their favorite instrumentalist defame Western musical tradition. Most jazz critics were (and are) not only white middle-class Americans, but middle-brows as well. The irony here is that because the majority of jazz critics are white middle-brows, most jazz criticism tends to enforce white middle-brow standards of excellence as criteria for performance of a music that in its most profound manifestations is completely antithetical to such standards; in fact, quite often is in direct reaction against them. (As an analogy, suppose the great majority of the critics of Western formal music were poor, 'uneducated' Negroes?) A man can speak of the 'heresy of bebop' for instance, only if he is completely unaware of the psychological catalysts that made that music the exact registration of the social and cultural thinking of a whole generation of black Americans. The blues and jazz aesthetic, to be fully understood, must be seen in as nearly its complete human context as possible.

People made bebop. The question the critic must ask is: *why?* But it is just this *why* of Negro music that has been consistently ignored or misunderstood; and it is a question that cannot be adequately answered without first understanding the necessity of asking it. Contemporary jazz during the last few years has begun to take on again some of the anarchy and excitement of the bebop years. The cool and hard bop/funk movements since the 40's seem pitifully tame, even decadent, when compared to the music men like Ornette Coleman, Sonny Rollins, John Coltrane, Cecil Taylor and some others have been making recently. And of the bop pioneers, only Thelonious Monk has managed to maintain without question the vicious creativity with which he first entered the jazz scene back in the 40's. The music has changed again, for many of the same basic reasons it changed twenty years ago. Bop was, at a certain level of consideration, a reaction by young musicians against the sterility and formality of Swing as it moved to become a formal part of the mainstream American culture. The New Thing, as recent jazz has been called, is, to a large degree, a reaction to the hard bop-funk-groove-soul camp, which itself seemed to come into being in protest against the squelching of most of the blues elements in cool and progressive jazz. Funk (groove, soul) has become as formal and clichéd as cool or swing, and opportunities for imaginative expression within that form have dwindled almost to nothing.

The attitudes and emotional philosophy contained in 'the new music' must be isolated and understood by critics before any consideration of the *worth* of the music can be legitimately broached. Later on, of course, it becomes relatively easy to characterize the emotional penchants that informed earlier aesthetic statements. After the fact, is a much simpler way to work and think. For example, a writer who wrote liner notes for a John Coltrane record mentioned how difficult it had been for him to appreciate Coltrane earlier, just as it had been difficult for him to appreciate Charlie Parker when he first appeared. To quote: 'I wish I were one of those sages who can say, "Man, I dug Bird the first time I heard him." I didn't. The first time I heard Charlie Parker, I thought he was ridiculous ...' Well, that's a noble confession and all, but the responsibility is still the writer's and in no way involves Charlie Parker or what he was trying to do. When that writer first heard Parker he simply did not understand *why* Bird should play the way he did, nor could it have been very important to him. But now, of course, it becomes almost a form of reverse snobbery to say that one did not think Parker's music was worth much at first hearing, etc. etc. The point is, it seems to me, that if the music is worth something now, it must have been worth something then. Critics are supposed to be people in a position to tell what is of value and what is not, and, hopefully, at the time it first appears. If they are consistently mistaken, what is their value?

Jazz criticism, certainly as it has existed in the United States, has served in a great many instances merely to obfuscate what has actually been happening with the music itself – the pitiful harangues that raged during the 40's between two 'schools' of critics as to which was the 'real jazz,' the new or the traditional, provide some very ugly examples. A critic who praises Bunk Johnson at Dizzy Gillespie's expense is no critic at all; but, then neither is a man who turns it around and knocks Bunk to swell Dizzy. If such critics would (or could) reorganize their thinking so that they begin their concern for these musicians by trying to understand why each played the way he did, and in terms of the constantly evolving and redefined philosophy which has informed the most profound examples of Negro music throughout its history, then such thinking would be impossible.

It has never ceased to amaze and infuriate me that in the 40's a European critic could be arrogant and unthinking enough to inform serious young American musicians that what they were feeling (a consideration that exists before, and without, the music) was false. What had happened was that even though the white middle-brow critic had known about Negro music for only about three decades, he was already trying to formalize and finally institutionalize it. It is a hideous idea. The music was already in danger of being forced into that junk pile of admirable objects and data the West knows as *culture.*

Recently, the same attitudes have become more apparent in the face of a fresh redefinition of the form and content of Negro music. Such phrases as 'anti-jazz' have been used to describe musicians who are making the most exciting music produced in this country. But as critic A.B. Spellman asked, 'What does anti-jazz mean and who are these ofays who've appointed themselves guardians of last year's blues?' It is that simple, really. What does anti-jazz mean? And who coined the phrase? What is the definition of jazz? And who was authorized to make one?

Reading a great deal of old jazz criticism is usually like boning up on the social and cultural malaise that characterizes and delineates the bourgeois philistine in America. Even rereading someone as intelligent as Roger Pryor Dodge in the old *Record Changer* ('Jazz: its rise and decline,' 1955) usually makes me either very angry or very near hysterical. Here is a sample: '... let us say flatly that there is no future in preparation for jazz through Bop ...' or, 'The Boppists, Cools, and Progressives are surely stimulating a dissolution within the vagaries of a non-jazz world. The Revivalists, on the other hand, have made a start in the right direction.' It sounds almost like political theory. Here is Don C. Haynes in the April 22, 1946 issue of *Down Beat,* reviewing Charlie Parker's *Billie's Bounce* and *Now's The Time:* 'These two sides are bad taste and ill-advised fanaticism ...' and, 'This is the sort of stuff that has thrown innumerable impressionable young musicians out of stride, that has harmed many of them irreparably. This can be as harmful to jazz as Sammy Kaye.' It makes you blush.

Of course there have been a few very fine writers on jazz, even as there are today. Most of them have been historians. But the majority of popular jazz criticism has been on about the same level as the quoted examples. Nostalgia, lack of understanding or failure to see the validity of redefined emotional statements which reflect the changing psyche of the Negro in opposition to what the critic might think the Negro ought to feel; all these unfortunate failures have been built many times into a kind of critical stance or aesthetic. An aesthetic whose standards and measure are connected irrevocably to the continuous gloss most white Americans have always made over Negro life in America. Failure to understand, for instance, that Paul Desmond and John

Coltrane represent not only two very divergent ways of thinking about music, but more importantly two very different ways of viewing the world, is at the seat of most of the established misconceptions that are daily palmed off as intelligent commentary on jazz or jazz criticism. The catalysts and necessity of Coltrane's music must be understood as they exist even before they are expressed as music. The music is the result of the attitude, the stance. Just as Negroes made blues and other people did not because of the Negro's peculiar way of looking at the world. Once this attitude is delineated as a continuous though constantly evolving social philosophy directly attributable to the way the Negro responds to the psychological landscape that is his Western environment, criticism of Negro music will move closer to developing as consistent and valid an aesthetic as criticism in other fields of Western art.

There have been so far only two American playwrights, Eugene O'Neill and Tennessee Williams, who are as profound or as important to the history of ideas as Louis Armstrong, Bessie Smith, Duke Ellington, Charlie Parker or Ornette Coleman, yet there is a more valid and consistent body of dramatic criticism written in America than there is a body of criticism about Negro music. And this is simply because there is an intelligent tradition and body of dramatic criticism, though it has largely come from Europe, that any intelligent American drama critic can draw on. In jazz criticism, no reliance on European tradition or theory will help at all. Negro music, like the Negro himself, is strictly an American phenomenon, and we have got to set up standards of judgment and aesthetic excellence that depend on our native knowledge and understanding of the underlying philosophies and local cultural references that produced blues and jazz in order to produce valid critical writing or commentary about it. It might be that there is still time to start.

29 **Linda Dahl** Preface, *Stormy Weather* (1984)

Source: Linda Dahl, 'Preface,' *Stormy Weather: The Music and Lives of a Century of Jazzwomen* (London: Quartet Books, 1984: ix–xii).

To understand the experience of most women in jazz, we need to keep in mind that jazz is not only an art form but also a subculture. And arguably, even more than other art forms, the music we call jazz depends on its community, for the young jazz musician is trained on the job, really; the apprentice learns from the leader, the members of the group, the gig itself. The musician has thus been especially vulnerable to others' opinions and ideas, to peers and role models who train, explain, encourage, give job referrals, confer artistic recognition. The true lone genius of jazz – a Charlie Parker, say, or perhaps a Lester Young – is as rare in jazz as in any other creative endeavor. Most musicians strive for their own sound *after* having learned everything they can from the ones who went before. (This was true even for Bird and Prez and Monk, even as they developed their unique sounds.)

Jazz as art/subculture has apparently embraced paradoxical positions. It is, for example, a populist as well as a highly sophisticated music. It is both highly individualistic and communal; very competitive yet often very supportive; defensive but aggressive; artistically rich yet financially poor. So aspiring maverick soloists have to deal with the need to balance their drive toward self-expression against the constraints imposed by the group. And the jazz player generally can expect few rewards of the kind heaped on pop artists, since he or she shares the fate of many creative artists – in America, especially – which is to be misunderstood, ignored, underpaid. Still, the male jazz musician accepts and takes for granted that at every step he'll be dealing with other men – from club owners to booking agents to band-leaders, fellow players, reviewers and writers in the press: a male-dominated profession. The language that describes jazz, and jazz musicians, reflects this reality. Full of masculine metaphors, the sense of fraternity or of a male club is everywhere evoked. A fraternity that both offers a refuge from the hostile or square-seeming outside world and which also provides camaraderie-cum-healthy competitiveness. The actor in this world of music is with good reason commonly called the 'jazzman.'

For most of jazz history, until quite recently, it has appeared that few women were part of this community of musicians. The reasons for this are explored throughout *Stormy Weather,* but perhaps it is well to mention here a few factors that have tended to keep women from playing jazz. Clearly, the qualities needed to get ahead in the jazz world were held to be 'masculine' prerogatives: aggressive self-confidence on the bandstand, displaying one's 'chops,' or sheer blowing power; a single-minded attention to career moves, including frequent absences from home and family. Then too, there was the 'manly' ability to deal with funky and often dangerous playing atmospheres, nightclubs infested with vice and run by gangsters. These frequently went hand in hand with a tendency to drink vast quantities of hard liquor, or sometimes take hard drugs, while continuing to play coherently into the dawn. A woman musician determined not to be intimidated by such a tough, smoke-filled atmosphere (where one's peers were probably all men) often paid penalties designed to put her in her place – the loss of her respectability being high on the list, as well as disapproval, ridicule and sometimes ostracism. And sprinkle the sexist resistance to jazzwomen with a generous helping of male fear of increased economic competition, since jobs in jazz are highly prized and relatively scarce. For a black woman, there was also often heavy pressure not to compete with black men for jazz jobs, which at times came to represent both symbolic and concrete proof of the male's abilities in a culture that denigrated his manhood. The jazzman was – and is – an intellectual of music, a highly literate man in his way. His standing and prestige were not to be given up lightly. (And white players too were sometimes openly hostile to the notion of sharing the bandstand with white jazzwomen, especially during the swing era and the big-band days of the forties.)

Yet for all of that, the historian of women's music finds, as I did, a long and quite illustrious group of women who have participated in jazz from the beginning. Often they've been buried in footnotes, or in the memories of other musicians. A minority to be sure – and they probably will be for some time to come: women playing jazz, recording it, leading bands, writing, arranging, producing albums, managing groups, concertizing. Names of performers and songwriters appear from the latter part of the nineteenth century – notably, Mammy Lou, an ex-slave. Women who've been ignored almost completely in the articles, the reviews, in otherwise often excellent histories of the music. Under-recorded or, sadly, not recorded at all. Their slim oeuvre long out of print. A blanket of silence. From time to time, mention is made of women in the jazz press, as when they were played up as a gimmick by many promoters, a lucrative act during the swing era and beyond. But they were rarely taken seriously.

The assumption about women in jazz was that there weren't any, because jazz was by definition a male music. Therefore, women could not play it. Therefore, they did not do so. When confronted by women who belied the assumptions, women who competently played trumpets, saxophones, drums, a deaf ear was turned. Their achievements were explained away: 'It's only a woman – what can you expect?'; or, 'Wow, amazing for a woman!' These were the two horns of a dilemma on which many a female jazz career was impaled.

Researching many of the women's contributions to jazz is like what I imagine collecting butterflies to be – you go out with your net to many a remote, even secretive spot to track your shy and elusive quarry. Colorful, bright specimens, many of these women in jazz, far from the mainstream, and some of them downright eccentric. There are lots of them making music in small cities, pokey college towns, black neighborhoods, cheesy cocktail lounges – where record producers and jazz reviewers hardly venture. Ladies who have turned their backs on the business side of music, and who have validated themselves through their music. When I was putting together *Stormy Weather* over a period of several years, I was inspired by the personalities of the jazzwomen – the famous and the obscure, the white and the black, the old and the young. Their grit and determination and pride in their work often helped me keep going when I felt up to my ears in old newspaper dust. The struggles of these women in and out of music, their salty and witty views on life, work, men and the pursuit of happiness, lie at the heart of this book. I wanted not only to fill in the blanks of jazz history by citing their achievements, but also to capture some of the vividness of their lives. Because these are real foremothers, taboo-breakers, independent 'mamas.'

Who are the jazzwomen? They are the well-known, the stars of song. They are the blues 'royalty' of the twenties. Ma Rainey, Bessie Smith, Ida Cox. Scores of others. The well-known singers of today, most of whom started in the thirties, a few in the forties. Ella Fitzgerald, Sarah Vaughan, Carmen McRae. The ever-felt presence of Billie Holiday. Big-band singers, called 'canaries' or 'warblers' during the swing era. Helen Forrest, Helen O'Connell, Mildred Bailey, Peggy Lee and Anita O'Day – talented white band singers who became stars in their own right. And many, many more. Brazilian, Swedish, British, Japanese. Scat singers. Avant-garde. A whole section of *Stormy Weather* is devoted to women who sing; another chapter explores the vocal art of jazz improvisation in light of the statements of the instrumentalists.

And speaking of instrumentalists, we find there are dozens and dozens of women in jazz who have played or are playing every instrument. Their earliest work, seen in context of the social and cultural history from which they came, is examined in another section of this book. In New Orleans, piano was the instrument of choice of women in the teens and twenties, but there were women playing brass instruments in marching bands, and saxophones, upright bass, *before* the twentieth century. Early black traveling units, circus bands, family bands – like little Lester Young's aunts, and his sister Irma, all on sax. And there was lively activity elsewhere – composers and pianists Lil Hardin Armstrong and Lovie Austin in Chicago, for example, and a raft of women leading bands in New York and elsewhere on the East Coast. The piano players – a group of very swinging players who developed their own sound from the thirties on, around the nation – are here, led by the great Mary Lou Williams, player, composer, arranger. Here too are dozens of women instrumentalists who played from the twenties on. The famed trumpeter Valaida Snow; saxophonists L'Ana Webster Hyams and Vi Redd; trombonist Melba Liston; vibist Margie Hyams. These players of traditionally 'masculine' instruments often bucked nearly insuperable odds. We preface their stories with an essay about sex taboos and instruments – a glance at various attitudes about women playing horns, etc., at different times and places around the world. Bands and bandleaders deserve a special chapter to themselves, for women were so often excluded from men's bands, and from at least the 1800s in the U.S. they banded together in order to play. The swing era saw the rise of a number of interesting all-female units, especially the Melodears, and our featured orchestra, the International Sweethearts of Rhythm. The last chapter of the text discusses the reemergence of the all-woman band since the seventies and sums up the players and the happenings in jazz to the eighties. The jazzwomen, their music and their lives.

30 Nat Shapiro and Nat Hentoff
Introduction, *Hear Me Talkin' to Ya* (1955)

Source: Nat Shapiro and Nat Hentoff (eds), 'Introduction,' *Hear Me Talkin' to Ya: The Story of Jazz as Told by the Men Who Made It* (New York: Rinehart, 1955: x–xiii) (excerpt).

This is the story of jazz, as told by the musicians whose lives *are* that story. This book, therefore, is not an attempt to duplicate any of the formal histories of jazz that have appeared or are now in preparation. The academic histories are written by non-participants. This is the story – and the stories – that musicians tell.

From the remembrances of the musicians whose book this is, there emerges a portrait of the jazzman. This portrait is one of a skilled artist who takes his music seriously at the same time that he feels it joyously. This portrait, happily, is not anything like the caricatures of jazzmen too often found in the movies, daily press, and even in many otherwise accurate magazines and books. As you will hear in the voices to come, the musicians of jazz are citizens of a strong and original creativity, with deeply felt traditions of expression and a richly experienced way of life.

Our part in this book was solely to give these men and women their first collective opportunity to tell their story their own way. To do this, we talked to scores of jazzmen, from members of New Orleans brass bands to San Francisco polytonalists. The conversations took place in night clubs and bars, in offices, on the sidewalk between sets, and in homes. There were also letters, tape recordings, and telephone conversations. There were scrapbooks that have been saved for years by the families of musicians. Generous musicians even allowed us to look into material for books they themselves had been writing, or hoping, for a long time, to write.

We also looked through magazines and newspapers to find first-person accounts by jazz musicians that had been lost as the magazines went out of business and as newspapers settled into bound volumes in libraries. There were also articles that had appeared in specialized magazines that most readers would not ordinarily come by. And there were other articles and interviews in English and French publications to which even American jazz specialists do not often have access.

This book is told directly and in many voices. You will, therefore, find in it candor, conceit, warmth, contradictions, bitterness, nostalgia, fulfillment, and frustration. There are many incidents and personalities in these pages that cannot be found in the formal histories, for much comes out in informal conversation that does not usually get into the history books. Most of the material is used here with no editorial or grammatical interference. For example, Louis Armstrong's colorful reminiscences of Storyville are set down virtually as Louis himself typed them. [(See **VII/99**.]

We do not pretend that, even in its informal way, this volume is entirely comprehensive. The world of jazz is multi-layered and complex. To tell the really complete story of jazz – and some of it has already been lost with the deaths of musicians – would require many more volumes than this one ...

We did not, and could not, talk with all the jazz musicians now alive nor utilize all first-person accounts of jazzmen in print. We did not, and could not, try in one book to cover fully all periods and all aspects of jazz. We preferred to indicate the perspective of jazz evolution, as seen by the musicians themselves.

31 **Charles Mingus** I don't see nothin' over there but critics (1971)

Source: Charles Mingus (ed. Nel King), *Beneath the Underdog: His World As Composed by Mingus* (New York: Knopf, 1971: 294–5) (excerpt). (Editor's title)

'Good to see you here, Mingus. I often spoke to Miles as to why you didn't come sooner.'

'Oh, I'm not ready yet, Bird, just visiting. Going to come around and listen to all you cats.'

'You sit in anytime, Mingus.'

'Soon as I hear whatcha doing.'

'Mingus, who invited all those white folks?'

'I guess my white old lady, Dizzy.'

'I don't see nothin' over there but critics.'

'Man, that's a lot of talent, don't you dig it? I see Leonard Feather, he's a piano player. There's Bill Coss and Gene Lees – they sing, I heard. Barry Ulanov must play drums or something, dig, with that *Metronome* beat. Martin Williams can play everything, I can tell by the way he writes. Put Marshall Stearns on bass and let Whitney Balliett score and John Wilson conduct. Let all them other young up-and-coming critics dance. How would you like to review that schitt for the *Amsterdam News*?'

'Especially would I love to hear Gene Lees sing. Ka badga dougee! Sing, Gene Lees! Right on stage in New York City so I can be there at your grand opening and compliment you backstage, dig?'

'Thank God you didn't make him sing right now 'cause here's Art. Hey, Art!'

'Oh-oh! Ladies and gentlemen, your attention please! God is in the house. On your knees as Art Tatum walks by. That's what Fats Waller said, Mingus.'

'Yeah, some white man heard Fats say that. They always hear something else. What Fats said was, "Oh, my God, Art Tatum's in the house!" Fats had a left hand, too. He wouldn't be calling Art God.'

'Why not? Art's definitely related to The Man.'

'Yeah, Bird, but related don't make him *The*. But here's his baddest piano-playing son walking up right now. Remember the gardener in the New Testament, after the Crucifixion? In this century, the gardener is a piano player ... Hey, Art!'

'How're you doing there, Mingus? Can you still play, boy?'

'Yeah, Art, but I'd rather listen tonight, for future reference. I hear on this coast people pay attention ... Bird's taking his horn out.'

'Come on, Bird, let's see what you got to say tonight!'

'"Lover." One, two, one, two, three, four ...'

'Damn, Diz! You ever heard any schitt like that in your life?! Art backing up Bird with left-hand solos, playing a counterline with his right and somehow keeping the rhythm striding at the same time. Bird's laying out now, look at his big moonface smiling down at Art. Uh oh. Art looked up. There goes Bird. Art ain't comped him yet. Don't seem to be draggin' Bird none. Listen at them motherfuckers. Dig the critics over there still talking to each other. Don't hear a thing.'

Riff 3

The usual model in jazz history ... amalgamates evolution ... expansion ... and synthesis. (Barry Kernfeld, *What to Listen for in Jazz*, 1995)

The flags of convenience flown on the angry seas of criticism. Dixieland, traditional, Chicago style, hot, swing, Kansas City, bop, progressive, modern, cool, West Coast, East Coast, mainstream, hard bop, funky, soul, and Third Stream are some of the terms critics have employed through the years, in communicating with the public, as labor-saving reference tags ... To ... musicians, they represent divisions, ill-defined and indefensible, which tend to restrict the artist's prerogative of freedom. (Stanley Dance, 'The art is in the cooking,' *Down Beat*, 1962)

I don't play that way any more. I play different; I live different. This is later. That was then. We change, move on. (Lester Young, in Joachim Berendt, *The New Jazz Book*, 1962)

A jam session is a foregathering of jazzmen to engage in a musical free-for-all. Its locale is most frequently a nightclub, but musicians will jam in public halls, ballrooms, backstage at a theater, or even a hotel room. Their purpose is to play for the sheer fun of playing, without any commercial restrictions on what they are doing, to extend their ideas as far as they will reach by means of free improvisation, and to test their ability under competitive conditions. (Ross Russell, *Jazz Style in Kansas City and the Southwest*, 1971)

The best statements Negroes have made, of what their soul is, have been on tenor saxophone. (Ornette Coleman, in A.B. Spellman, *Four Lives in the Bebop Business*, 1966)

Improvisation is an intuitive process for me now, but in the way in which it's intuitive, I'm calling upon all the resources of all the years of my playing at once: my academic understanding of the music, my historical understanding of the music, and my technical understanding of the instrument that I'm playing. All these things are going into one concentrated effort to produce something that is indicative of what I'm feeling at the time I'm performing. (Arthur Rhames, in Paul Berliner, *Thinking in Jazz*, 1994)

Chorus III
The Sound of Surprise:
Jazz and style
(convention, repertoire, improvisation)

For some historians and musicians, the *style* of jazz is often seen as the true history of the music. Barry Kernfeld, in *What to Listen for in Jazz* (1995), concludes his study of technical concepts and procedures, as a way of understanding jazz history, with an 'Epilogue' on jazz style (ibid.: 184–99). Kernfeld's work is prompted by admitted frustration with the stylistic approach; he warns listeners of the need to learn the properties of jazz (e.g. form, rhythm, improvisation, composition) *before* trying to tie these up into 'assorted stylistic packages.' Nevertheless, Kernfeld feels impelled to offer a 'tour' through general styles, noting his outline follows the usual model in jazz history: 'it amalgamates *evolution* (new styles emerge from old styles), *expansion* (old styles remain viable instead of disappearing), and *synthesis* (jazz styles merge with other genres)' (ibid.: 185; my italics). **Chorus III** looks at styles in jazz, through formal appreciation, 'enacted criticism' (musicians' performances) and the conventions and repertoire which underlie improvisation; it also samples 'style wars' between opposing factions within the music, and jazz's synthesizing return to tradition.

Kernfeld's model is a fruitful way of viewing the jazz tradition and patterns of stylistic development and change, even if his survey falls into predictable types: New Orleans jazz, swing, bop, free jazz and fusion. This descriptive categorization certainly provides one version of jazz history, supporting those who insist that 'the real history of jazz is in the music itself' (Coker 1978: 4). The unified, linear and evolutionary model is early represented by Joachim **Berendt** (**32**). Berendt argues jazz styles reflect their particular historical times, a relation much more extensively explored by Burton Peretti, in *Jazz in American Culture* (1997) (**IV**). Included in Berendt's opening chapter (5) is one of the familiar charts (or 'trees'), purporting to illustrate the main stem (or 'backbone') of the 'entire evolution'; columnar versions of this have recurred in other jazz histories, e.g., Hodeir (1956: 24), Stearns (1956: 262–3), Gridley (1999: 327–3).

Where this comforting approach to style evolution breaks down is when jazz dissolves into a number of different, sometimes incompatible styles. Tirro (1993: 330) complains that in the 1940s, jazz's 'cohesive thread' was inconveniently 'pulled apart' by bebop. Certainly, attempts to preserve the linear history of style when describing post-bebop jazz have run into a morass of conflicting and overlapping terminology. 'Cool jazz,' 'hard bop,' 'modal jazz,'

'Third Stream,' and 'New Thing' hardly amount to a convincing consensus; and Billy Taylor's *Jazz Piano* (1982), for example, bewilderingly calls its last section 'Abstract Jazz, Mainstream Jazz, Modal Jazz, Electronic Jazz, Fusion' (DeVeaux 1991: 526–7, 553–4, n. 3). Gioia's recent jazz history freely admits a 'fragmentation' of styles (1997: 277) and settles for 'Freedom and Beyond' as its closing chapter (ibid.: 337).

Geoff **Dyer** examines the perspective afforded by style development and syntheses in jazz history in his 'Afterword' (**33**) to *But Beautiful: A Book About Jazz* (1991). The evolution of jazz styles – and work of individual musicians – is seen as an ongoing process of what Dyer calls 'imaginative criticism.' In this argument, the best exemplars of the jazz tradition are the musicians themselves, performing, drawing and commenting on the music at their feet. The evolutionary process expands the resources and possibilities of the form, a point made repeatedly by Martin Williams, in his analysis of jazz style in the work of master improvisers (e.g. 'Louis Armstrong: Style Beyond Style' [1993: Chapter 5]). In Dyer's projection, however, the culture of Williams' commentary would be decentred by the creators themselves: he instances Duke Ellington as an 'illustration of the way in which the music offers the best commentary on itself.' For Dyer, the accumulating 'catalogue' of jazz – tradition, repertoire, reputation, connection – is found in 'a constant network of cross-performances'; and, in jazz's ability to absorb and enact its own history. Jazz allows us access to black America and gives musicians a unique opportunity for self-expression. In this broader sense, Dyer persuasively argues that jazz's 'catalogue' becomes the medium representing not only a people but a century – 'a condition of history,' no less.

If the 'catalogue' of jazz is 'imaginative criticism' – a metamusic – the locus of this working process is the 'jam session,' which constitutes jazz's demonstration of its central, identifying characteristic: *improvisation*. Both Bruce **Lippincott** (**34**) and Ingrid **Monson** (**35**) describe the creative tension between collective group and individual solo performance, which is the essence of improvisational style and the social organization of musicians. The conventions, repertoire and structure of jazz playing – the organic process and etiquette – are conveniently outlined by saxophonist Lippincott to explain the 'mysterious business' (Gleason 1958: 168) of the 'open session.' The 'conversational' dynamic or tension at the moment of *making* or *speaking* jazz is, as Monson suggests, inherent in the interplay between ensemble and soloist. Such performance contexts affect composition and development of the music, and are a determinant of style.

The musical sociability of improvisation (Monson's 'grooving') is where the horn soloist 'speaks' or 'says something' to/over the rhythm section. This is illustrated not only in formal appreciation of style (*à la* Williams and Schuller), but actual jazz playing and performance. 'Writing' jazz playing – rather than writing *about* it – can become, to re-apply Whitney Balliett's famous phrase (1959), 'the sound of surprise.' The performance dynamic, the action of 'blowing,' is caught in (re)created 'moments,' where jazz's energy, invention, momentum and immediacy combine to express a distinct musical style.

In the selections following (**36–40**), Hayden **Carruth** (**36**) creates an improvisatory and acoustic evocation of a classic Milt Gabler (1944) recording session, where 'Sitting In' is transformed into 'a moment ecstatic/in the history/of creative mind *and* heart.' In an extract (**37**) from Ross **Russell**'s jazz novel, *The Sound* (1961), 'dark and primitive forces' are on aural display when bop trumpeter Red Travers (modelled on Charlie Parker) opens a frenetic set at the Hi De Ho club. 'We in B-flat now. Let's get off.' The sense of a momentary dynamic, surprising as it is levitating, is also well caught by the memories of musicians themselves. Pianist Mary Lou **Williams** (**38**) recollects a spectacular 'cutting contest' in Kansas City clubland, where Coleman Hawkins meets his unexpected match with half a dozen other tenor saxophonists. Art **Pepper**, as a coda (**39**) to his harrowing autobiography, *Straight Life* (1979), experiences the intensity of playing 'Cherokee' with fellow-jazzman Sonny Stitt – in spite of his wretched personal circumstances, a moment of sublime transcendence and confirmation: 'That's what it's all about.' The entire 'mystique' of strapping the horn to the body and blowing is personalized in J.C. **Thomas**'s portrait of Coltrane at practice (**40**). 'The music goes round and round inside John Coltrane's head, pouring forth from his horn as he continues his creative explorations, the only way any artist must if he is to be worthy of the name. Alone.' Equipped with a Selmer Mark VI six-pound weight tenor horn, it is an heroic moment.

Jazz musicians draw on an agreed repertoire and playing conventions to improvise and create distinctive styles – it is their way of interpreting and using the common currency of the music. In a study of regional style, an extract (**41**) from Nathan **Pearson**'s *Goin' to Kansas City* (1988) interviews musicians who explain the City's jazz style, with its characteristic 4/4 'swing' rhythm, extensive use of blues riffs, and blend of dance music with improvised jazz in informal jam sessions. The result is a distinctive sound, or style, and a 'shared musical sensibility' that typified K.C.'s major bands of the 1930s – Pearson instances Count Basie, Andy Kirk, Jay McShann and Bennie Moten. One celebrated instance of jazz's repertoire and performance conventions is a 1958 interview with Miles Davis (Hentoff 1958), which John Gennari describes as 'one of the most incisive statements ever made about jazz' (1991: 480).

The evolutionary model of jazz style has encountered notable periods when the assumptions of its progress have been challenged by the music's inherent eclecticism and divergence. Jazz has thus resisted any simple categorization or clear line of development. These challenges – or debates – illuminate both Kernfeld's three-part model and Dyer's interest in periods of stylistic synthesis. They also bear on the larger issue of who is authorized to define jazz and construct narratives of its stylistic history.

'To Be or Not to Bop' was the title of an article in *The Record Changer* in 1949, where bandleaders Dizzy Gillespie (bop) and Tex Beneke (swing) battled it out over the merits of bebop style; Bill Gottlieb, in anatomizing bebop, had already insisted it was replacing swing, as 'modern, progressive music, harmonically suited to the times' (1947). In the history of jazz styles, the bop revolution was born in the middle of one of the most divisive disputes in jazz, between followers of swing music and the 'dixieland' revivalists, proposing a return to the classic New Orleans style of the 1920s (Gendron 1994: 137). This opposition was fought out publicly in the pages of the 1940s musical press (e.g. *Down Beat, Metronome, The Record Changer*) – a 'style war.' The boppers disparaged the traditionalists as reactionary 'moldy figs,' and the latter pejoratively labelled the boppers 'progressives' or 'filthy modernists.' Barry **Ulanov**'s *Metronome* article (**42**) describes one such 'jazz joust' of that time, broadcast on Mutual radio.

David Stowe, who examines the polarized infighting of the post-war years in *Swing Changes* (1994: Chapter 6), points out this was not simply a response to bebop, but part of a longer struggle between critics and musicians over the authority of defining jazz. A more complex alignment is Stowe's suggestion that arguments over bop's validity took place in the larger context of the demise of popular swing in the 1940s: at the heart of anti-bop sentiment was the fear it was bringing about the demise of jazz itself (ibid.: 224). This was certainly the view of Louis Armstrong, leading black exponent of the older style, who was persuaded to deride bop as meaningless and unmelodic – 'all them weird chords which don't mean nothing' – and as 'modern malice' in its perceived threat to the commercial viability of jazz (Borneman 1948: 2).

If 'Pops' Armstrong could 'pop' his 'top' on 'sloppy bop,' as a *Metronome* headline had him doing (Feather 1949), the new style prevailed and even flourished as the form of early modern jazz, and was soon accommodated by the evolutionary model. Gillespie's advice, 'you've got to play bop if you want to make it' (1949), is amusingly deployed in a 1947 story by Martin **Gardner** (**43**). Flatbush Smith (*alias* Bunk Johnson), an inept, off-key New Orleans-style trumpeter, experiences a 'downfall' in being converted from lionized purism to bebopper on 52nd Street, where he plays 'wild, meaningless riffs that completely obliterated the melody.' His fateful success is to be hired by 'sweet' bandleader, Guy Lombardo. Flatbush buys up his early discs, all collectors' items, for his grandson, who smashes them to pieces . . . style conversion with a vengeance.

In more recent times, jazz modernism as a broad style has given way to a more postmodern sensibility, in which *all* jazz history has become 'grist for the mill' (Davis 1986: x). This eclecticism and an implicit assimilationist agenda have brought with it, in the 1980s and 1990s, a kind of cyclical return, or style renewal. If the term 'mainstream' is a compromise between conservatism and radicalism, 'neoclassicism' maintains a careful balance between 'continuous innovation and an insistence on the priority of tradition' (DeVeaux 1991: 550–1).

Gary **Giddins** (**44**) has been adversarial in urging the notion of a resurgence of jazz's older styles after a period of avant-garde extremism and experiment, and this has meant a renewed investigation of the music's past: in essence, 'an inventive reappraisal of the jazz repertory.' Giddins would place 'neoclassicism' – rightly, it seems – within the sub-genre of postmodernist style, and suggests the thesis of the 'new wave' is opposed by the antithesis of 'the jazz tradition.' The future of jazz, as with any art style, lies in a creative 'rapprochement' of these opposites.

Martin **Williams** also investigates this tension, in an essay (**45**) from *Jazz in Its Time* (1989). This draws attention, again, to 'stylistic retrenchment,' which represents a synthesis and summation of the elements comprising the jazz tradition. To Williams, an impediment to this renewal of process is jazz-fusion, largely associated with Miles Davis. In a working example of the restrictive 'monologic canon' (see Tomlinson: **II/27**), Williams deplores the inaccessibility of fusion and its rhythmic inertia. Contrastingly, he applauds the synthesis achieved by trumpeter Wynton Marsalis, a musician stylistically antithetical to Davis and the participant (with Davis) in one of the more public racial/musical feuds of the 1980s (e.g. see Davis 1986: 32–5; Gioia 1997: 388–9).

Marsalis himself has frequently voiced opinion on 'what jazz is – and isn't' (1988); his vehement proselytizing of the tradition has amounted to a crusading role. He has attributed his initial success to playing 'real music,' against then-current fashions of fusion, rock, funk and pop. 'Everybody was saying that jazz was dead because no young black musicians wanted to play it anymore, and because the established cats who should have been setting an example were *bull*shittin', wearing dresses [African robes] and trying to act like rock stars' (Davis 1986: 32). Marsalis has disparaged black pop music and called Davis' electronic experiments 'crap' (Peretti 1997: 167). In a 1990 *Down Beat* profile by Dave Helland, 'prophet' Marsalis provided a closing footnote on the Davis clash, and cumulatively defined jazz as 'group improvisation, vocalization, and a swinging optimism.' If these qualities sound like America itself, they are also the 'fundamentals' of the music and, for Marsalis, comprise jazz's valued artistic legacy. On all counts, he has been 'taking care of business' (Nicholson 1995: vi).

32 **Joachim Berendt** The styles of jazz (1959)

Source: Joachim Berendt, 'The styles of jazz,' in *The New Jazz Book: A History and Guide* (London: Peter Owen, 1962 [1959]: 3–4) (excerpt).

The most impressive thing about jazz – aside from its musical value – is in my opinion its stylistic development. The evolution of jazz shows the continuity, logic, unity, and inner necessity which characterize all true art. This development constitutes a whole – and those who single out one phase and view it as either uniquely valid or as an aberration, destroy that wholeness of conception. They unbalance that unity of large-scaled evolution without which one can speak only of fashions, but not of styles. It is my conviction that the styles of jazz are genuine, and reflect their own particular times in the same sense that classicism, baroque, romanticism, and impressionism reflect their periods in European concert music.

The untroubled joyousness of Dixieland corresponds with the times just prior to World War I. The restlessness of the 'roaring twenties' comes to life in Chicago style. Swing style embodies the security and massive standardization of life before World War II; perhaps, to quote Marshall Stearns, Swing 'was the answer to the American – and very human – love of bigness.' Bebop captures the nervous restlessness of the forties. Cool jazz often reflects the resignation of men who live well, yet know that H-bombs are being stockpiled. And in the hard bop of the late fifties and the early sixties, there is protest and hardness and dissatisfaction – directed first against racial discrimination, and then against the conformity of modern life in general.

33 **Geoff Dyer** Tradition, influence and innovation (1991)

Source: Geoff Dyer, 'Afterword: tradition, influence and innovation,' in *But Beautiful: A Book About Jazz* (London: Jonathan Cape, 1991: 165–170, 171–5) (excerpts).

In his book *Real Presences* George Steiner asks us to 'imagine a society in which all talk about the arts, music and literature is prohibited.'[1] In such a society there would be no more essays on whether Hamlet was mad or only pretending to be, no reviews of the latest exhibitions or novels, no profiles of writers or artists. There would be no secondary, or parasitic, discussion – let alone tertiary: commentary on commentary. We would have, instead, a 'republic for writers and readers' with no cushion of professional opinion-makers to come between creators and audience. While the Sunday papers presently serve as a substitute for the experiencing of the actual exhibition or book, in Steiner's imagined republic the Review pages would be turned into listings: catalogues and guides to what is about to open, be published or released.

What would this republic be like? Would the arts suffer from the obliteration of this ozone of comment? Certainly not, says Steiner, for each performance of a Mahler symphony (to stick for a moment to his own preferred terrain) is also a critique of that symphony. Unlike the reviewer, however, the performer 'invests his own being in the process of interpretation.'[2] Such interpretation is automatically *responsible* because the performer is answerable to the work in a way that even the most scrupulous reviewer is not.

Although, most obviously, it is not only the case for drama and music; all art is also criticism. This is most clearly so when a writer or composer quotes or re-works material from another writer or composer. All literature, music and art *'embody an expository reflection on, a value judgement of, the inheritance and context to which they pertain'* (my italics).[3] In other words it is not only in their letters, essays or conversation that writers like Henry James reveal themselves also to be the best critics; rather, *The Portrait of a Lady* is itself, among other things, a commentary on and a critique of *Middlemarch.* 'The best readings of art are art.'[4]

No sooner has Steiner summoned this imaginary republic into existence than he sighs, 'the fantasy I have sketched is only that.'[5] Well, it's not. It is a real place and for much of the century it has provided a global home for millions of people. It is a republic with a simple name: jazz.

Jazz, as everyone knows, grew out of the blues. From the beginning it developed through the shared participation of a community of audiences and performers. Those like Charlie Parker who went to hear Lester Young and Coleman Hawkins in Kansas City in the 30s got a chance to blow with them at after-hours jam sessions later the next morning. Miles Davis and Max Roach served their apprenticeship first by listening to and then by sitting in with Parker at Minton's and the 52nd Street clubs, learning as they went along. In their turn John Coltrane, Herbie Hancock, Jackie McLean and dozens of others who went on to school many of the leading players of the 70s and 80s learnt their trade, as McLean put it, 'in the university of Miles Davis.'[6]

Because jazz has continued evolving in this way, it has remained uniquely in touch with the animating force of its origins. From time to time in his solos a saxophonist may quote from other musicians, but every time he picks up his horn he cannot avoid commenting, automatically and implicitly, even if only through his own inadequacy, on the tradition that has laid this music at his feet. At its worst this involves simple repetition (those interminable Coltrane imitations); sometimes it involves exploring possibilities that were previously only touched upon. At its best it expands the possibilities of the form.

The focus of these endeavours is frequently one of a number of tunes which have served jazz, throughout its history, as springboards for improvisation. Often these tunes have inauspicious origins as light pop songs. Alternatively, original compositions become standards (in what other medium would a classic be a standard? Imagine Tolstoy published as a Penguin Standard.) Thelonious Monk's 'Round Midnight' has probably been played by every jazz musician on earth; each subsequent version tests it, finds out if there is still anything that can be done with it. Successive versions add up to what Steiner calls a 'syllabus of enacted criticism.'[7] No other art form more ravenously investigates T.S. Eliot's famous distinction between that which is dead and that which is already living.[8]

Ideally, a new version of an old song is virtually a recomposition and this labile relation between composition and improvisation is one of the sources of jazz's ability to constantly replenish itself. Writing on the 'Appassionata' piano sonata op. 57, Theodor Adorno notes, that 'it makes sense to think that what occurred to Beethoven first was not the main theme as it appears in the exposition but that all-important variant of it in the coda, and that he, as it were, retrospectively derived the primary theme from its variation.'[9] Something very similar happens frequently in jazz: in the course of a solo a musician touches momentarily and almost accidentally on a phrase which may become the basis for a new tune which will also be improvised on – and these solos may in turn yield another phrase to be developed into a composition. Duke Ellington's musicians frequently grumbled that some lick they'd played in a solo had been noted by Duke and built into a tune published under his name – though they were quick to concede that only someone with Duke's genius could have grasped the potential of that phrase and made as much out of it as he did.

Since he is the most fertile source, we can begin with Ellington in a more explicit illustration of the way in which the music offers the best commentary on itself. Ellington wrote 'Take the Coltrane' for the great tenor player; Charles Mingus's 'Open Letter to Duke' is a musical essay on Ellington; it has since been followed by the Art Ensemble of Chicago's 'Charlie M.' In years to come this chain will almost certainly be lengthened by a homage to Art Ensemble saxophonist 'Joseph J' or an 'Open Letter to Roscoe' (Mitchell).

This kind of party game could be continued indefinitely, taking various names as our starting point. Thelonious Monk or Louis Armstrong are especially fruitful places to begin but there are literally hundreds of musicians who have had one or two songs written for them. If we drew lines between all available songs in a kind of flow diagram of homages and tributes the paper would soon become impenetrably black, the meaning of the diagram obscured by the quantity of information it would have to convey.

A less explicit strand in the ongoing process of enacted criticism is at work in the evolution of jazz musicians' individual styles. To have a sound and style that are unmistakably your own is a prerequisite of greatness in jazz. Here, as is often the case in jazz, an apparent paradox is at work: to sound like themselves musicians begin by trying to sound like someone else. Looking back to his early years Dizzy Gillespie said: 'each musician is based on someone who went before, and eventually you get enough of your own things in your playing, and you get a style of your own.'[10] Miles Davis in turn tried to sound like Dizzy, and countless trumpeters after him – Wynton Marsalis most recently – have tried to sound like Miles. Often musicians arrive at their own sound by default. Dizzy again: 'All I ever did was try to play like [Roy Eldridge], but I never quite made it. I'd get all messed up 'cause I couldn't get it. So I tried something else. That has developed into what became known as bop.'[11] Miles's lonely, chillingly beautiful sound came about as a result of his inability to sustain the high register leaps that were Dizzy's trademark.

There are two apparently contradictory ways in which the antecedent's voice makes itself heard. Some musical personalities are so strong, so closely associated with a certain sound that they colonise a whole area of expression, and others can encroach on it only at the price of surrendering their individuality. The personality of one musician can so pervade a certain style that it only seems possible to imitate that style, never to adequately absorb or transcend it. It is now almost impossible for a trumpeter to play a ballad with a harmon mute and not sound as if he is imitating Miles Davis.

Alternatively, there are rare instances of musicians assimilating their predominant influences to such an extent that they seem at times, as Harold Bloom has said of some poets, to 'achieve a style that captures and oddly retains priority over their precursors, so that the tyranny of time almost is overturned, and one can believe for startled moments, that they are being *imitated by their ancestors*' (italics in original).[12] Lester Young frequently sounds as if he is indebted to those like Stan Getz who in fact owe their sound entirely to him. At times early Keith Jarrett makes us wonder if Bill Evans does not sound too much like Jarrett.[13]

By the nature of its style of performance jazz affords more opportunities for exactly this kind of comparison than any other art form. The distinction between a group performance and a jam session has always been hazy (a band for a studio date is often flung together at the last moment and even 'named' groups are temporary shifting units, rarely demanding the exclusive commitment of any members), and in the course of a year many different musicians will play together in many different formats: duets, trios, quartets, big bands. At its worst this involves a touring star player teaming up with a new pick-up rhythm section in each town he plays; alternatively a bassist gets a steady flow of work because he can be depended on to provide solid if uninspired support with minimum rehearsal time. The great advantage of this flexible style of employment, though, is that the individual voices of jazz are heard together in an almost infinite number of permutations, each giving rise to a new collective sound ...

One of the standard procedures of literary criticism is to juxtapose texts by different authors in order to bring out the particular qualities and relative merits of each. In jazz the constant network of cross-performances means that that task is implicit and inherent in the accumulating catalogue of the music. The performance of a given player simultaneously answers certain questions (about musicians he is playing with or who have come before, about his relation to the developing tradition) and raises other questions (about what he himself is doing, about his own worth, about the form he's working in); the musicians he works with and who come after him provide provisional answers but these answers are also questions – about the worth of *these* musicians, *their* relation to tradition. In an elaborate critical kind of circular breathing, the form is always simultaneously explaining and questioning itself.

With the music itself performing so many of the tasks normally left to commentators, it is not surprising that the contribution of critics to jazz has been relatively insignificant. Of course there are jazz critics and jazz journals. Historically, however, writing on jazz has been of such a low standard, has failed so signally to convey any sense of the animating dynamics of the music as to be irrelevant except – and this is just as Steiner would have it – insofar as it conveys facts: who played with whom, when a given album was recorded etc. To strip the Western literary or art-historical tradition of criticism would be to decimate our cultural capital (no Berger on Picasso, no Benjamin on Baudelaire). All that has ever been written about jazz, on the other hand, with the exception of musicians' memoirs and the odd jazz-inspired novel (Michael Ondaatje's *Coming through Slaughter* is a masterpiece), could be lost without doing any but the most superficial damage to the heritage of the music.[14]

Despite all that has been said above jazz is anything but an hermetic form. What makes it a vital art form is its astonishing ability to absorb the history of which it is a part. If no other evidence survived, some computer of the future could probably reconstruct the whole history of black America from the jazz catalogue. I am not even thinking of explicit works like Ellington's *Black, Brown and Beige,* conceived as a tone-parallel to the history of Afro-Americans; Archie Shepp's 'Attica Blues' or 'Malcom, Malcom, Semper Malcom'; Mingus's 'Prayer for Passive Resistance'; Pharoah Sanders's 'Soledad,' or Max Roach's *Freedom*

Now Suite. I intend something more general, along the lines suggested by Adorno's observation that 'it is not for nothing that the newly soulful tone of the violin counts among the great innovations of the age of Descartes.'[15] Elaborating on Adorno, Fredric Jameson comments that 'throughout its long ascendancy, indeed, the violin preserves this close identification with the emergence of individual subjectivity.'[16] Adorno was referring to the period from the seventeenth century onwards but his words are equally applicable to the trumpet's identification with the emergence of Black American consciousness in the twentieth century, from Louis Armstrong through to Miles Davis. From the 40s onwards that identification has been rivalled and complemented by the saxophone. According to Ornette Coleman, 'the best statements Negroes have made, of what their soul is, have been on tenor saxophone.'[17]

Although Coleman is here distinguishing primarily between the tenor and alto saxophones his claim also holds true for a larger distinction between the tenor and other means of expression: literature, painting. This is important, for hand in hand with jazz's capacity to absorb its surrounding history goes its capacity to raise to the level of genius those who would otherwise have lacked a medium to express themselves. Jazz, as Eric Hobsbawm observes, 'has been able to draw upon a wider reservoir of potential artists than any other art in our century.'[18] Ellington was a talented painter but many of the other giants of jazz were dependent, in their work, on exactly those qualities and idiosyncracies which would have hampered their progress in other arts All the traits that made Mingus's music the wild unpredictable thing it was made the writing in his autobiography, *Beneath the Underdog,* sloppy, foolish. He had nothing of the clerk in him and all writers need something of the pettiness of the clerk, the diligence of the proof-reader. 'Louis Armstrong without his trumpet is a rather limited man,' notes Hobsbawm. 'With it he speaks with the precision and compassion of the recording angel.'[19] In what other art form could a man like Art Pepper have achieved the beauty he did?

The mention of Pepper is apposite since it reminds us that although primarily, jazz is not exclusively a medium of expression for black experience (as the title of Ellington's *Black, Brown and Beige* indicates, the history of black Americans is inextricably tangled up with that of white America; the Black Nationalist movement was a negative proof of that). The white band-leader Stan Kenton extended the terms of debate still further, hearing in jazz the potential for expressing the anguished spirit of the age: 'I think the human race today may be going through things it never experienced before, types of nervous frustration and thwarted emotional development which traditional music is entirely incapable of not only satisfying but expressing. That's why I believe jazz is the new music that came along just in time.'[20]

If there is something a little self-serving about Kenton's words – a tacit advertisement for his own music – we can turn instead to a figure of considerable authority who had no vested interest in music. In 1964 Dr Martin Luther King gave the Opening Address to the Berlin Jazz Festival, his presence there serving as a reminder of how the black people's struggle for civil rights was paralleled by jazz musicians' struggle to have their art recognised as such. In his speech King noted the role played by music in articulating the suffering, hopes and joys of the black experience long before the task was undertaken by writers and poets. Not only was jazz central to the lived experience of negroes, he went on, but 'in the particular struggle of the negro in America there is something akin to the universal struggle of modern man.'

This is a vital connection; once it has been made jazz becomes a medium not only representative of a people but, implicitly, of a century, a medium that expresses not simply the condition of the black American but a condition of history.

Notes (edited)

1 George Steiner, *Real Presences,* London: Faber and Faber, 1989, p. 4.
2 Ibid. p. 8.
3 Ibid. p. 11.
4 Ibid. p. 17.
5 Ibid. p. 21.
6 Quoted by A. B. Spellman, *Four Lives in the Bebop Business,* New York: Limelight, 1985, p. 209.
7 Steiner, *Real Presences,* p. 20.
8 T. S. Eliot, 'Tradition and the Individual Talent,' *Selected Prose,* London: Faber and Faber, 1975, p. 44.
9 Theodor Adorno, *Aesthetic Theory,* London: Routledge and Kegan Paul, 1984, p. 249.
10 Quoted in Ira Gitler, *Swing to Bop: An Oral History of the Transition in Jazz in the 1940s,* New York: Oxford University Press, 1985, p. 56.
11 Quoted in Nat Shapiro and Nat Hentoff, *Hear Me Talkin' to Ya,* New York: Dover Press, 1955, p. 347.
12 Harold Bloom, *The Anxiety of Influence,* New York: Oxford University Press, 1973, p. 141.
13 Cf. Bloom on Wallace Stevens and John Ashbery, ibid. p. 142.
14 There may be little first-rate writing on jazz but few art-forms have been better served by photographers. Indeed, pictures of jazz musicians are virtually the only photographic evidence we have of people engaged in the actual creation of art. This is not to say that actors, singers or classical musicians are not artists but, however innovative or original, their work is essentially interpretive. Of course there are photographs of composers at their pianos, artists at their easels, writers at their desks, but these are almost always posed – desk, easel or piano serving as a prop rather than tool. A photograph of a jazz musician in full flight can bring us as close to the act – or vicarious essence – of artistic creation as a photograph of an athlete can to the act – or vicarious essence – of running.
15 Quoted by Fredric Jameson, *Marxism and Form,* Princeton: Princeton University Press, 1971, p. 14.
16 Ibid. p. 14.
17 Quoted in Spellman, *Four Lives in the Bebop Business,* p. 102.
18 Eric Hobsbawm, *The Jazz Scene,* London: Weidenfeld and Nicolson, 1989, p. 219.

19 Ibid.
20 Quoted in Shapiro and Hentoff, *Hear Me Talkin' to Ya*, p. 385.

34 **Bruce Lippincott** Aspects of the jam session (1958)

Source: Bruce Lippincott, 'Aspects of the jam session,' in Ralph Gleason (ed.), *Jam Session: An Anthology of Jazz* (New York: Putnam, 1958: 168–74).

This is an approximation of the way jazz is played in an open session:

Who plays with whom

Like-minded men try to play together. They know the same tunes, have similar vocabularies, communicate easier, produce a better group art. Thus, there may be considerable backstage lobbying when the set is being chosen. Some men are interdependent and have to play the same set together. If there is an *organizer* for the session, he may try to include a variety of instruments, telling a trumpeter, for instance, to wait till the next set if one already has been named to play. Sometimes, for comparisons, a trio of trumpets may all play on the same set. Or it may be a 'battle,' wherein two similar instruments show each other their strength, friendly or un-friendly. A loner-jazzman may never get a chance to unpack his horn unless he asks to play. Usually he is spotted and invited to sit in; if not, he should ask not the club owner but the musicians if he may sit in. 'Getting on the waiting list' is one way of asking. As the musicians take their places on the stand some men prefer to introduce themselves to the others, but more frequently the calling card is stated by one's horn, words later.

Choice of tune, key, tempo

The set made up, the assembled musicians try to reach an immediate agreement on some tune wherein they can improvise comfortably. Often as the men warm up their instruments, one will fall into some familiar theme which, if acceptable to the others, will be picked up by them, with no words needed. Theoretically, each performer has veto power over the tune. Squeeze-plays and freeze-outs usually occur between the pianoman (who is keeper of the tune, knowing its chords for the soloists to improvise on) and a hornman (any frontline instrument, e.g., sax, trumpet, trombone, clarinet). The drummer and bass player usually get no vote. Sometimes two or more hornmen try to insist on a tune in which they excel, and will go as far as to show the pianoman the changes; but generally everyone wants to relax on the first tune of a set. Each in-group or school of jazz has its standards and preferred warm-up tunes.

Knowing them is paramount to acceptance. The usual polite thing is to ask a stranger on the bandstand what he wants to play. Here, blues is the Universal Elixir. The key a familiar tune is to be played in is open to discussion. Many tunes are automatically in a specific key, e.g., 'I'll Remember April' in G; 'Tea for Two' in A-flat; but a tune like 'Just Friends' or 'I Remember You' may be in one of many often-played keys; a good musician should know his tunes in any key. Usually, if there is disagreement as to what key the tune should be played in, the pianoman has the final say. Likewise, the pianoman, unless someone else finger-clicks, chooses the tempo, which he usually confirms by nodding to the horns. Often, after a tune is decided, several men will snap their fingers, look at each other, tap their feet, trying to agree on the tempo.

Introduction

The tune settled, the key and tempo decided upon, the pianoman usually takes an 8-bar intro. In the old days it was 4 bars, perhaps 2. At best, the piano intro sets the mood for the ensuing piece, perhaps as community song piano players or church organists do when they play the last phrase of the song, leading to its beginning ensemble. The jazz intro is not sacred as far as its relation to the coming piece is concerned. Sometimes it should be played according to the record, but usually it is only to establish tempo and tonality. The drummer may take the intro on his highhat. Or the bass man may 'walk it in.' Rarely does a hornman play an intro by himself in grassroots jazz. Group-improvised intros, likewise, are rare, although sometimes the horns riff together contrapuntally for a chorus before they play the regular melody. In a pianoless group the band usually starts on a count of 4. If an intro is common knowledge, as in 'Walkin',' easy enough for all to play, someone counts four and they're off. (An organized group, one that has worked out intros and other special effects, is a different matter. They do the presentation that can't be done hit-and-miss with strangers.) It is generally quite a breach of session etiquette to try to organize any special arrangements or details. Music paper is out. Each man is getting ready to solo his best in open sessions, and to work out or explain anything would be disturbing to many musicians. Perhaps if it could be done *very* simply, with little word-talk, it would not interfere with their desire to collect their musical thoughts preparatory to speaking to each other in the language of music.

The first chorus

The ensemble chorus may be played loosely, with incidental harmonizing and individual interpretations of the melody. It is a chance to flex the muscles, correct faulty intonation, listen to the chord changes, get ready for the forthcoming improvisations. In some cases it is helpful to be able to play the jazz melody or 'chart' as it was on the record; paying homage to the creator; later more liberties can be taken. If there is a bridge with no prescribed melody in the middle of the first chorus, one or several horns may take it as a solo, or else the pianoman does.

Solo order

Near the end of the first chorus, one of the horns must prepare to take the usual two-bar break which separates the ensemble from the solo playing. This is often a touchy spot. It brings forth peculiar facial grimaces and contortions from the hornmen, who are all playing the melody and trying to signal with their eyes or eyebrows or by pointing of horn who will take the break and the first blowing chorus. The featured horn, the one with the most prestige or strength or popularity, will get the nod. The nod is in the form of a yes, or a twist of head or a pushing out of horn, or if someone has a free finger, an actual pointing. There may be a front-line director, the strongest horn, or the one who has most friends, who will nod toward someone else. Or all the hornmen may keep their heads down, eyes closed, and all jump into the break at once, the devil take the hindmost ... then it is an unfriendly session, less apt to produce a homogeneous group effort. Or the solo may be taken by instrument classification: with two tenors and a trumpet on the stand, one tenor would take the first solo, which would be followed by the trumpet, who thus separates the two similar instruments. (On the second tune of the set, a different horn takes the first solo; like going to the end of the line after your turn.) After the horns solo, the piano has his turn. Possibly this is because he can't play as loudly. Then the bass man gets a chorus or so, depending on whether he is playing melodic ideas or just walking around in 4/4. During the bass solo the piano usually tinkles, the drummer accents phrase-marks. Sometimes a drummer will take a solo. But usually the drum solo is tied in with the horns who, in solo order, alternate four bars with him. The framework of the tune is not changed. The bass, who usually solos last, is at the whim of the first horn soloist, whose function is then to come in accurately (at the beginning of a chorus). There is always the question 'what shall we do with it?' i.e., shall we play fours with the drummer or just play the melody out? This question is often decided by a hasty poll; it is polite to ask the drummer if he wants fours (or eights, or whatever). The hornman with most prestige, usually the first soloist, makes the decision and calls it out. If the tempo has decreased considerably, it is usually blamed on the drummer; then with some carefully disguised disdain, the hornmen may look at each other with long faces and a shrug not supposed to be seen by the drummer, and say, 'Let's take it out.' (Do drummers feel this? Maybe this is why they're sometimes so paranoid.) The ensemble chorus is played again, with the final bridge being taken by someone in the rhythm section, perhaps to compensate for the fact that they are not included in the fours which precedes the out-chorus.

Remaining tunes of the set

The next tunes are frequently decided in terms of a change in key ... It is more interesting to play in different keys, and psychologically it affects the listener better. Or the next tune may be chosen because of a different tempo. Traditionally, each man gets a choice, but this varies according to how sociable the performers feel. The general practice is to open with a medium tempo, then a slightly faster tune, then a slow one, perhaps a medley of ballads, followed by a fast tune.

General thoughts about sessions

Each instrument solos as long as he wants. Session hogs, who take an excessive number of choruses, tire the rhythm section, ruin the form of the piece, make the other men impatient. But if a man is really saying something, constantly developing his ideas rather than repeating a set of clichés, he is in order. It is an extreme discourtesy to cut a man's solo short by coming in while he is still playing. Bass men get trampled on this way most of all. A person cutting another short should have a great deal of support and a good reason for doing so. This is not to be confused with riffing behind a soloist. The men who are waiting their turn to solo may play some simple background patterns which orchestrate the framework of the tune for the soloist. The simple figure, perhaps in harmony, may help re-establish the tune for the soloist if he seems to be lost, or relieve or revitalize the rhythm section and break the monotony.

A man may stop and listen, his head cocked toward the piano, if he becomes lost, i.e., doesn't know exactly where he is in the tune as it flows by. Usually the drummer and the piano accent the beginnings of choruses or phrases to help the hornman. Sometimes a hornman gets lost because the piano goofs. No matter how good the extended idea or experimentalism is, a soloist is expected to keep his time straight; he may be able to get back in place by listening for a moment to the piano chords. But sometimes he will lose all the others, and then it is up to the drummer to snap it back, with a strong accent; then the drummer's punctuation is the final word. The drummer lets everyone know what time it is. A soloist is invariably discovered if he gets lost, stays lost, and won't admit it. When he stops playing he is expected to end at the chorus end, not in the middle of it. Probably the most embarrassing moment in a session, when all the musicians' faces fall, is when a man has been playing what to all outward respects is a very exciting solo; then he stops in the middle of his chorus and has on his face the expression of satisfaction, as though he had really made it ... Then he is either an amateur or a phony. The worst remark is when the guy standing next to you turns and asks, 'Man, what tune are we playing?'

Audience applause for an individual soloist as he finishes his solo is often disconcerting. It disrupts the continuity of the piece. (Jazz is like a relay race to most musicians, who hand the baton of melody from one soloist to the next.) Also, audience applause can create a great deal of self-consciousness among the musicians; they may worry to the point of compromising their solo if they don't get clapped for; playing for the crowd and not for the group is not good, unless the group itself is bad. Of course, when there has been an exceptional soloist, one who goes far beyond the group as a whole, then perhaps applause is in order. It also can give confidence to a man who is otherwise unsure of himself; but ultimately that confidence must come from his camaraderie with the group, not the audience. One of the greatest joys of jazz is this camaraderie, when everyone is attentive, economical, in good spirits; then the ensemble melody is played with no brazenness; the solos are related to the mood of the entire piece; each new soloist takes, without premeditation, the final phrase of the former soloist and tries to develop the ideas of it, then hands it on to the next man. When the piece is finished, each man feels glad he was part of the whole.

35 **Ingrid Monson** The ensemble and the soloist (1996)

Source: Ingrid Monson, 'Grooving and feeling,' in *Saying Something: Jazz Improvisation and Interaction* (Chicago: University of Chicago Press, 1996: 66–72 (excerpt). (Editor's title)

The ensemble as a whole: grooving as an aesthetic ideal

There is an inherent tension within the jazz ensemble between the individual and the group. On the one hand, the aesthetic of the music is centered on the inventiveness and uniqueness of individual solo expression; on the other, climactic moments of musical expression require the cohesiveness and participation of the entire ensemble. In an improvisational music, such as jazz, the interaction between group and individual greatly affects the ultimate composition and development of the music. Since the ensemble is divided into soloist and rhythm section, it should be noted that there are two levels on which this individual-versus-group tension operates: the relationship of the soloist (who may be a rhythm section member) to the rhythm section, and the relationship of each individual to the remainder of the rhythm section. Cecil McBee described how this tension arises in the context of a performance and how a musician must be prepared to face the uncertainty of the situation:

> We are all individuals ... When we approach the stage ... we are collectivized there. I mean history is about to take place, right? When ... the band begins to play, history is going to take place. This energy proceeds to that area and says, 'All right, I'm here, I will direct you and guide you. You as an individual must realize that I am here. You cannot control me; you can't come up here and say, "Well, I'm gonna play this,"' unless you're reading ... You can't go there and intellectually realize that you're going to play certain things. You're not going to play what you practiced ... Something else is going to happen ... so the individual himself must make contact with that and get out of the way. (McBee 1990)

Just as the ride cymbal provides stability and unity to the multiple rhythms played on the drum set, the notion of the groove supplies underlying solidity and cohesiveness to freely interacting, improvising musicians. We've already encountered *groove* as a noun when we talked about rhythmic feels – those particular sets of rhythm-section parts that combine to produce particular rhythmic patterns. Jerome Harris's description of a groove as a 'rhythm matrix' illustrates this usage. Harris's comments also remind us that although *groove* is most centrally a rhythmic term, the flow of harmony, rhythm, and timbre affects how a groove feels in a particular performance. Since a tune is played within a particular groove, the bass and piano fulfill their rhythmic function by playing harmonic and melodic parts appropriate to that groove or feel.

Groove is also an aesthetic term, and in this capacity it is usually used as a verb. It is synonymous with a number of other terms found with varying frequency in the jazz community: *swinging, burning, cooking, putting the pots on* (Davis 1989). When I asked musicians to define the term *groove*, I tried to phrase the question in a way that left it open to each musician to select the noun or verb meaning, but most musicians chose the latter. Most also described grooving as a rhythmic relation or feeling existing *between* two or more musical parts and/or individuals. Don Byron, for example, described grooving as 'a euphoria that comes from playing good time *with* somebody' (Byron 1989). Michael Weiss explained it as a type of personal and musical chemistry:

> Every bass player and drummer [and] piano player sort of feels the rhythm their own way, and some are more sensitive or flexible than others ... It's not ... different than when you meet somebody and you find a compatibility of personalities that's just there . And it's not something that you have to try to do. And sometimes it just isn't there and it's nobody's fault. (Weiss 1990)

The use of the term *feeling* as a synonym for *groove* underscores the emotional and interpersonal character of groove – something negotiated between musicians that is larger than themselves. Good time in this sense produces not only the physical patting of the feet but an emotional response as well. Phil Bowler called it a 'mutual feeling of agreement.' Both Richard Davis and Kenny Washington emphasized the interpersonal aspect of groove by comparing it to 'walking down the street' with someone. Davis's description likened groove to a romantic or familial relationship, Washington's to walking 'arm-in-arm' with someone.

Once established, there is something inexorable about groove as well. Kenny Washington talked of the feeling that the 'instrument is playing by itself.' Michael Carvin compared it to a 'trance' in which you experience 'being out of yourself.' He also spoke about musicians being 'so relaxed that they weren't forcing anything out.' The physical pleasure of being in a groove is captured in Carvin's image of soaking in a bathtub and feeling, 'Oh, that's what I needed,' as well as in Don Byron's comment that 'it's about feeling like time itself is pleasurable.'

Two more points deserve to be emphasized. Michael Weiss commented that 'a lot of times it's a matter of just hitting the right tempo.' Although other musicians did not state this explicitly, I doubt that they would disagree. Informally, I heard musicians comment that certain tunes or time feels just don't groove if they are played too quickly or too slowly. The association of tempo with swing or groove is long-standing. Count Basie's guitarist Freddie Green, for example, credited Basie's tempos for the achievements of the legendary rhythm section of Basie, Green, Jo Jones, and Walter Page: 'Basie was the greatest tempo setter ... that I ever ran into' (Green 1977). Second, musicians stressed that grooving is an aesthetic ideal that cannot be premeditated (Carvin 1990) and that in its fullest form is achieved only rarely (McBee 1990).

If the groove (in the nominative sense) is to the ensemble what the ride cymbal (or stable limb) is to the drum set, moments of deviation from the predictable flow of rhythmic energy are comparable to the functions of the drummer's other limbs. Continuing his familial imagery for the drum set, Michael Carvin told me to think of my ride cymbal and hi-hat (which I was playing on 2 and 4) as the 'father and mother' and my left hand and bass drum as the 'children.' I should 'let the children play,' while the mother and father kept time. At another time he told me that I should allow my snare and bass drum to 'have a conversation.' If for a moment we think of the jazz ensemble as a drum set writ large, the groove is a collectively produced sense of time against which the children play or the musicians converse. The fundamental sociability of improvisation as a musically creative process is underscored by this anthropomorphic imagery ...

The soloist

I have left the role of soloist for last to emphasize that it is in relation to this complex musical sociability that a musician organizes his or her improvised solo. The role of soloist is one that every member of the ensemble is expected to fulfill.

Trumpets, trombones, saxophones, flutes, and other instruments not generally used in the rhythm section are often referred to collectively as *horns* or *the front line*. The latter term derives from the typical spatial arrangement in jazz performance that places the reeds and brass instruments in front of the rhythm section. Using the term *horn* for any single-line melody instrument collapses instrumental differences into a particular musical role played by a soloist who is accompanied by the full rhythm section. The horn player is in a position to exploit most fully the accompanimental resources of the jazz ensemble, as he or she is not required to sustain the groove during the solos of other ensemble members. Unlike pianists, who as soloists frequently comp with their left hand while playing melodic lines with their right, horn players can devote their full attention to phrasing against the relatively fixed rhythmic environment created by the rhythm section. Even so, comments about horn soloists apply in a general sense to rhythm section soloists as well, although at least one accompanimental role is missing when the bass player or the drummer plays a solo.

If we return to the image of the drum set writ large, the soloist's phrasing functions analogously to the drummer's left hand in a general sense. The requirement that the soloist sustain melodic, harmonic, and rhythmic interest, however, creates significant differences between actual phrases occurring in the drummer's left hand and the horn player's solo. What the two have most in common is a rhythmic independence characterized by offbeat phrasing. The musical excitement of the phrasing derives from the juxtaposition of this independence with a relatively stable background.

The fact that some musicians describe a particular musician's style by reference to the character of the eighth note is germane here. Since the second half of a pair of eighth notes is particularly flexible, the way in which the second note is emphasized greatly affects the offbeat feeling of a musician's phrasing style. Clarinetist Don Byron noted:

> Different cats have different eighth note concepts, man. [Steve] Lacy, man, that's the closest thing to like a Monk eighth note on the piano ... It's like real punchy ... 'I play with my thumbs too much' type of thing like Monk plays. (Byron 1989)

We are now in a better position to understand the prioritization of rhythm ... The harmonic and melodic expertise of the soloist, which is essential to competent jazz improvisation, must be expressed against the rhythmic flow generated by the musically sociable rhythm section. Those who take for granted their competence in the harmonic and melodic dimension commonly discuss pitch selection in relationship to rhythm. Don Byron commented on tenor saxophonist Wayne Shorter in this manner:

> I mean, note choice is just the way you tend to color the rhythm ... I feel that when I hear Wayne. It's those groups of five and seven and thirteen notes. There's always some odd number. It's always starting on some odd offbeat ... And ... where you get his mind is [in] what color he's going to put on each note. The drama of his playing to me is which one of them notes that he's going to color it with is going to be right and which one is going to be wrong, cause he can place them all right ... it's obvious that he's got *that*. So *where* he's going to put the note that's a half-step away from where it ought to be, that's the drama in *his* playing. (Byron 1989)

An improviser's pitch choice during the course of a lengthy solo can augment and intensify rhythmic development as well, a point that underscores the interdependence of musical dimensions. Jerome Harris spoke about tenor saxophonist Sonny Rollins's abilities in this regard:

> You might be able to get the same mileage out of working in a restricted range harmonically ... Then when you bring in the alterations they have a context ... because what's gone before is different than what you're introducing ... Sonny's *real good* at this sort of thing. You won't really ... notice it, but he'll be hanging out in a certain pentatonic or six-note ... place ... through a substantial amount of a tune. *Then* he'll bring in ... some notes that aren't *in* that key ... which are more chromatic alterations and you really *feel* the change going to a new [place]. (Harris 1989)

If we return to the tension between the group and the individual, the role of horn soloist in some ways is both the most independent and the most dependent in the ensemble. The soloist's ability to float on top of the rhythmic energy generated by the rhythm section is an independence that the members of the rhythm section do not as fully share. This musical independence is perhaps a factor in the high prestige accorded to horn soloists in the jazz tradition. At the same time, the soloist's ability to be an effective voice requires considerable support from the rhythm section. The horn player, for example, cannot define a change in groove as clearly as a rhythm section member, nor can he or she as fully accompany another soloist. Nevertheless, the role of soloist is the most prestigious in the jazz ensemble. To be a jazz musician, one must be able to play solos as well as fulfill the ensemble responsibilities of one's instrument.

Note

Quoted passages and references are from Monson's interviews with jazz musicians.

36 **Hayden Carruth** Three paragraphs (1978)

Source: Hayden Carruth, 'Three paragraphs,' in *Sitting In: Selected Writings on Jazz, Blues, and Related Topics* (Iowa City: University of Iowa Press, 1986: 83–4).

> A day   very solid   February 12th, 1944
> cheerless in New York City
> > (while I kneedeep
> elsewhere in historical war
> was wrecking Beauty's sleep
> and her long dream)
> > a day (blank, gray) at four
> in the afternoon, overheated in the W.O.R.
> Recording Studios. Gum wrappers *and* dust
> *and* a stale smell. A day. The cast
> was Albert Ammons, Lips Page, Vic Dickenson,
> Don Byas, Israel
> Crosby, and Big Sid Catlett. (*And* it was Abe Linkhorn's
> birthday.) And Milt Gabler
> presided beyond the glass with a nod, a sign. Ammons
> counted off
> > a-waaaaan,,,   *tu!*

> > and went feeling
> his way on the keys gently,
> > while Catlett summoned

> the exact beat from –
> > say from the sounding depths, the universe ...
> When Dickenson came on it was all established,
> no guessing, and he started with a blur

as usual, smears, brays – Christ
the dirtiest noise imaginable
                              belches, farts
                                             curses
but it was music
                         music now
                              with Ammons trilling in counterpoise.
Byas next, meditative, soft/
                              then Page
with that tone like the torn edge
of reality:
                      and so the climax, long dying riffs –
groans, wild with pain –
and Crosby throbbing *and* Catlett riding stiff
yet it was music   music.
                                   (Man, doan
fall in that bag,
                      you caint describe it.)
                                   Piano & drum,
Ammons & Catlett drove the others. *And* it was done
and they listened *and* heard themselves
                      better than they were, for they had come

high above themselves.   Above everything, flux, ooze,
loss, need, shame, improbability/   the awfulness
of gut-wrong,   sex-wrack,   horse & booze,
the whole goddamn mess,
And Gabler said 'We'll press it'   *and* it was
     'Bottom Blues'
BOTTOM BLUES   five men knowing it well   blacks
     & jews
yet music, music   high
in the celebration of fear, strange joy
of pain: blown out, beaten out
                              a moment ecstatic
in the history
of creative mind *and* heart/   not singular, not the
     rarity
we think, but real and a glory
our human shining, shekinah ...   Ah,
                      holy spirit, ninefold
I druther've bin a-settin there, supernumerary
cockroach i' th' corner, a-listenin, a-listenin ,,,,,,,
              than be the Prazedint ov the Wuurld.

37 **Ross Russell** Seein' red (1961)

Source: Ross Russell, *The Sound* (London: Cassell, 1962 [1961]: 47, 48–52) (excerpts). (Editor's title)

Red slipped through the door. The crowd had spilled over from the main room into the corridors. The hipster ranks opened a way for him. The horn glinted in the catchy light. Recognizing not a single face, Red heard them saying, 'Ready like Teddy! Not dragged at all. Real happy – you can see it in his eyes. Just got the Word from upstairs. Ready to romp, man!' Red made his way through the strange room and vaulted onto the bandstand ...

Red turned his back on the house and faced the rhythm section ... He crouched and began bobbing to show the tempo he wanted. 'Seein' Red, men!'

Slim Cook and Bernie looked in dismay at Hassan. The drummer made a helpless gesture and flung back at Red. 'This the up blues?'

'No, no, man,' Red scolded. 'Seein' Red is the chords of I Got Rhythm.' He gave them a look as if to ask, three thousand miles for this? 'We in B-flat now. Let's get off.'

Chuey Figueroa, a fat musician with a round baby face, stood blandly aside, faintly amused by the whole thing, his alto saxophone cradled gently in the crook of one elbow. *He* knew the tune.

'Up, up, up!' Red urged. 'Come on, Hassan, bring it *up* to *me*!' He continued to bob, his lips quivering in a rage to get at the trumpet.

Hassan glared back, his wrist flying ever faster. Even he had forgotten those fearsome tempos of the Street, or how hard Red could come on, those times that he really wanted to, when he had an impression to make, or some interloping musician had to be cut down once and for all and shown who was boss. But the real problem was the piano. 'I Got Rhythm, Bernie. B-flat, man!' ...

Bernie Rich was conditioned to a more orderly type of performance. Of course, practically everybody knew the chords to I Got Rhythm. Bernie Rich knew them. Bleakly, they flashed through his mind's eye – B-flat, C-minor seventh, F seventh, B-flat, C-minor seventh, and so on. Except that he had not the faintest notion of the new riff based on these chords. It had not been among any of the Red Travers records to which he had listened again and again ... Nor had he the faintest idea of how a trumpet could be tongued at the insane tempo Hass was now setting up.

Hassan's ride cymbal began to vibrate, pumping its shimmering sound across the bandstand. He was playing six notes to the bar, And-One-TWO, And-Three-FOUR, but the notes seemed to run together so that the big cymbal, with light splashing off its gentle coolie-hat curves, had a musical pulse of its own. The stick flew in the drummer's wiry wrist and fell against the alloyed metal, hammered to paper thinness by the craftsman who had forged it. Hassan's fingers maintained the stick in a suspended motion, like a juggler with a stream of balls flying. The sound came in waves, one close behind the other, until all the air in the night club was dancing to its airy sound. To the backmost corner, where the curious cradled their highballs and the hip huddled over their glasses of iced coffee, past the velvet rope and out onto the street, the shimmery sound ghosted and gathered in its thrall. Hassan began to add little percussive figures, muffled thuds on the bass, pistol shots on the snares, jungly throbs on the tom-tom, puffs of air lightly caught between the surfaces of the high hat and charged with a bubbly froth of sound, truncated press rolls that were like thunder heard briefly and at a distance – his mosaic of skilled, subtle sounds.

The tempo was more of a quiver than a beat. Hassan sounded an admonitory rim shot and Red spun out of his crouch and came up, facing the crowd, dead on mike, with his mute inches away. Like the partner in a clever vaudeville act, Chuey Figueroa was right there at rendezvous with the alto saxophone. The two instruments almost touched. Nestling one another, they breathed into the microphone, softly and in unison, the subtle phrases of Seein' Red, a grim parody on the old Gershwin tune. Dead at the end of the 32-bar statement, Chuey let out a bubbling laugh and stepped away. Red flipped the mute out of the bell and dumped it down on the top of the piano with a clatter and turned the horn towards Bernie.

Red had him under direct fire. The bell of the trumpet shone like a great headlight. For Bernie it was like the first time when, as a child, he had ridden a roller coaster at a beach resort, and the free-rolling cars, released by the starter, had drifted to the foot of the first big incline. Then, all at once, from somewhere underneath, were seized up by a hook running on a conveyor mechanism which began hauling them forward and upward with terrifying and irresistible force. Everything that had a moment before seemed on the point of flying apart was now gathered together by a sure hand. The trumpet continued to hammer him down with its metal tones.

Red played an entire chorus with only the three notes of the triad. But he varied them infinitely; altered their intonation and attack, bent and fitted them into various positions of the bar structure, creating a whole series of rhythmic patterns and levels, each more complex than the other. Bernie's knees banged against the under side of the piano. He could feel the cross rhythms powerful inside himself. People had stopped talking and drinking, even the square waiters had downed trays. Dark and primitive forces were set loose in the room.

Red held the trumpet with one elbow wedged to his side, the other winged out and loose, so that his wrist was higher than the valves and he could fan them with his fingers. When he crouched, or turned, or leaned back to point the horn at the ceiling, he preserved exactly the same position, the same embouchure. Man and instrument moved in a solid block. In one piece. He blew with his cheeks hard packed from compressed air, a glazed look on his face, his throat distended like a bellows. Spewn forth from the trumpet's bell a festoon of notes, each perfectly in place and tied to the next, uncoiled and hung quivering over the tables and the crowd, the longest melodic line Bernie had ever heard, an entire thirty-two bars without a break in continuity, without a pause for breath. A complete unanimity existed between the fingers and lips, and the mind which moved with such breath-taking speed among the ancient bones of harmony of the old Gershwin standard. The technique in itself was prodigious, yet always subjected to a greater creativity. Never in the long solo did he suffer it to exist for itself. Not once did he embellish with a mechanical device or easy trumpet figuration. Every turn, triplet, arpeggio, grace note, smear, slur had its place in the final tonal and rhythmic fabric of the solo.

They played Seein' Red for almost fifteen minutes. During that time no one else took a solo. It was all trumpet, one chorus piled on to the next, variation upon variation, surprise topped by surprise. Bernie's wrist muscles had begun to lock on him and even Hassan looked a little desperate. Towards the end Chuey Figueroa came in for a series of chase choruses where eight bar sections were traded back and forth between trumpet and saxophone. Red took every phrase that Chuey played and rephrased it instantly. Chuey would shake a series of notes out of the gleaming cornucopia of his alto, then step back and cock his head, only to wag and smile in wondering disbelief as Red turned them all inside out. They finished the chase and Red took charge once more for a final dizzying ride into the upper register, pinching off high notes as easily as if he were playing a fife. He came diving out of that last flight dead on cue, and the group was back on rails, tracked dead in on the unison-and-out. The final note hung aloft, like a streamer, over the house, and the crowd, stunned into some moments of silence, suddenly broke loose and began yelling. The applause continued, deafening. Red chuckled, adjusted his mute, waited, quiet and easy. Then called a new tune.

38 Mary Lou Williams The battle of the tenor kings (1954)

Source: Mary Lou Williams, 'The battle of the tenor kings,' in 'Mary Lou Williams: a life story' ('My friends the kings of jazz'), *Melody Maker*, XXX (3 April–12 June, 1954): 1 May: 11 (excerpt).

Of course, we didn't have any closing hours in these spots [Kansas City jazz clubs]. We could play all morning and half through the day if we wished to, and in fact we often did. The music was so good that I seldom got to bed before midday.

It was just such a late morning session that once had Coleman Hawkins hung up. Fletcher Henderson came to town with Hawkins on tenor, and after the dance the band cruised round until they fell into the Cherry Blossom where Count Basie worked. The date must have been early 1934, because Prohibition had been lifted and whiskey was freely on sale. The Cherry Blossom was a new night club, richly decorated in Japanese style even to the beautiful little brown-skinned waitress. The word went round that Hawkins was in the Cherry Blossom, and within about half an hour there were Lester Young, Ben Webster, Herschel Evans, Herman Walder and one or two unknown tenors piling in the club to blow.

Bean didn't know the Kaycee tenormen were so terrific, and he couldn't get himself together though he played all morning. I happened to be nodding that night, and around 4 a.m. I awoke to hear someone pecking on my screen. I opened the window on Ben Webster. He was saying: 'Get up, pussycat, we're jammin' and all the pianists are tired out now. Hawkins has got his shirt off and is still blowing. You got to come down.'

Sure enough, when we got there Hawkins was in his singlet taking turns with the Kaycee men. It seems he had run into something he didn't expect. Lester's style was light and, as I said, it took him maybe five choruses to warm up. But then he would really blow; then you couldn't handle him on a cutting session. That was how Hawkins got hung up. The Henderson band was playing in St. Louis that evening, and Bean knew he ought to be on the way. But he kept trying to blow something to beat Ben and Herschel and Lester. When at last he gave up, he got straight in his car and drove to St. Louis. I heard he'd just bought a new Cadillac and that he burnt it out trying to make the job on time. Yes, Hawkins was king until he met those crazy Kansas City tenormen.

39 Art Pepper and Laurie Pepper
That's what it's all about (1979)

Source: Art Pepper and Laurie Pepper, 'Conclusion,' in *Straight Life: The Story of Art Pepper* (New York: Schirmer Books, 1979: 475–6). (Editor's title)

I was given a gift. I was given a gift in a lot of ways. I was given a gift of being able to endure things, to accept certain things, to be able to accept punishment for things that I did wrong against society, the things that society feels were wrong. And I was able to go to prison. I never informed on anyone. As for music, anything I've done has been something that I've done 'off the top.' I've never studied, never practiced. I'm one of those people, I knew it was there. All I had to do was reach for it, just do it.

I remember one time when I was playing at the Black Hawk in San Francisco. I forget the date, but Sonny Stitt was touring with Jazz At The Philharmonic. He came in, and he wanted to jam with me. He came in, and he says, 'Can I blow?' I said, 'Yeah, great.' We *both* play alto, which is ... It really makes it a contest. But Sonny is one of those guys, that's the *thing* with him. It's a communion. It's a battle. It's an ego trip. It's a testing ground. And that's the beautiful part of it. It's like two guys that play great pool wanting to play pool together or two great football teams or two magnificent basketball teams, and just the joy of playing with someone great, being with someone great ... I guess it's like James Joyce when he was a kid, you know. He hung out with all the great writers of the day, and he was a little kid, like, with tennis shoes on, and they said, 'Look at *this* lame!' They didn't use those words in those days. They said, 'God, here comes this nut.' And he told them, 'I'm great!' And he sat with them, and he loved to be with them, and it ended up that he *was* great. That's the way Sonny felt; that's the way I've always felt.

I said, 'What do you want to play?' Sonny says, 'Let's play "Cherokee."' That's a song jazz musicians used to play. The bridge, which is the middle part, has all kinds of chord changes in it. It's very difficult. If you can play that … If some kid came around, and he wanted to play, you'd say 'Let's play "Cherokee,"' and you'd count it off real fast. I said, 'Well, beat it off.' He went, 'One-two, one-two'; he was flying. We played the head, the melody, and then he took the first solo. He played, I don't know, about forty choruses. He played for an hour maybe, did everything that could be done on a saxophone, everything you could play, as much as Charlie Parker could have played if he'd been there. Then he stopped. And he looked at me. Gave me one of those looks, 'All right, suckah, your turn.' And it's *my* job; it's *my* gig. I was strung out. I was hooked. I was drunk. I was having a hassle with my wife, Diane, who'd threatened to kill herself in our hotel room next door. I had marks on my arm. I thought there were narcs in the club, and I all of a sudden realized that it was *me*. He'd done all those things, and now I had to put up or shut up or get off or forget it or quit or kill myself or do *something*.

I forgot everything, and everything came out. I played way over my head. I played completely different than he did. I searched and found my own way, and what I said reached the people. I played myself, and I knew I was right, and the people loved it, and they felt it. I blew and I blew, and when I finally finished I was shaking all over; my heart was pounding; I was soaked in sweat, and the people were screaming; the people were clapping, and I looked at Sonny, but I just kind of nodded, and he went, 'All *right*.' And that was it. That's what it's all about.

40 **J.C. Thomas** John Coltrane is practicing (1975)

Source: J.C. Thomas, *Chasin' the Trane: The Music and Mystique of John Coltrane* (New York: Doubleday, 1975: 101–3). (Editor's title)

John Coltrane is practicing.

He is in the bedroom of his apartment; the tape recorder is running and he is standing, feet slightly apart and toes pointing outward, posture erect, six pounds of tenor saxophone pulling at his neck. This is a 25 per cent increase in weight from the alto; for comparison, a Pentax camera weighs just a few ounces over two pounds, a Nikon four.

His horn is a Selmer Mark VI, equipped with a 5-star medium metal Otto Link mouthpiece and a #4 Rico reed. The soprano he'd later purchase would be the same model and reed, the mouthpiece would be a metal Selmer, size E.

The saxophone he is holding is the Paris model, though actually made in a small town, Mantes, about forty miles away. Special-formula brass is the material, and the work is handcrafted. The saxophone parts are cut out and smoothed on a lathe, then hand-hammered before being assembled and shipped to the Selmer factory in Elkhart, Indiana. There, the horn is then stripped down, buffed, and lacquered. The keys and pads are rejoined to the body again, and a mechanic tests each saxophone separately (the intonation adjustments were already made in France). The cost of the instrument at that time (1958) was close to $500, and to hear Trane's sound on his Selmer, it was well worth it.

He is practicing from a book by Sigurd Rascher, a German expatriate living in upstate New York and an exponent of the French school of saxophone technique: a limpid vibrato and an intonation as smooth (and sometimes as syrupy) as French cream. Nevertheless, Rascher is a technician who knows the horn well enough to devise 158 exercises with no key signatures, tempo markings, or bar lines to constrict the player. These exercises are written primarily in eighth notes, with a constant crescendo and diminuendo, a continuous rising and falling of scales; they are so complex that some of them resemble snowflake patterns as seen through a microscope.

Coltrane hears the sounds of the scales in his ear, feels his fingers flicking over the saxophone keys and his breath coming strong and full, almost choking the horn with a huge onrushing column of air. His embouchure is as tight as the mouthpiece and reed connections. But he still feels the occasional, sometimes frequent, stabbing pain in his increasingly disintegrating molars. More bridgework is now there, but still the pain continues, digging like a dentist's drill into his nerves. But he does not stop; nothing short of nuclear war can stop his incessant, compulsive practice sessions.

The exercise book lies on his bed as he reads the notes, playing them faster and faster until they begin to bunch against each other, each note crowding the next. The notes bounce off the walls and ceiling, seep into the carpeting, and are sucked into the whirring tape recorder in the corner.

Then he is finished. But not with practicing; only with the saxophone book.

He unstraps his tenor, placing it on the bed. He puts the saxophone book away, replacing it with another practice book, this one for piano. It is called the *Thesaurus of Scales and Melodic Patterns*, written by Nicolas Slonimsky, a piano and composition teacher who commands great respect from classical and other musicians.

Opening the book, Trane straps his horn to his body again and starts playing from, and by, the book. He begins with tritone progressions, intervals of augmented fourths that contain three whole tones. He continues with a series of scales that call for interpolation of four or more notes, constructed from a complex series of sixteenth notes and an amazing number of accidentals, for almost every other note seems to have a sharp or flat preceding it, indicating an immediate change of tone, either up or down a half step. These exercises are excellent for developing the lower register, as the tenor saxophone range extends to the first space in the bass clef.

Again, only the tape recorder and himself are present.

A few years ago, in Detroit, Paul Chambers had introduced Coltrane to pianist Barry Harris, a man with a formidable reputation as teacher and theorist who includes such Detroit musicians as pianist Hugh Lawson, trumpeter Lonnie Hillyer, and altoist Charles McPherson among his more diligent students. Coltrane and Harris often played tenor-piano duets at the latter's house. It was Harris who told him about the Slonimsky book, and the pianist would also pass on, to anyone who would listen, his particular music theory, which placed a stronger emphasis on scales than chords as a method of fostering improvisation, including the interrelationship of common or complementary notes between different scales and the ease of moving from one to another. He believed that the dominant rather than the tonic degree of the scale should do exactly what it says, dominate; he'd often hold court around the piano, playing exactly what he was talking about.

Trane continues his practicing.

The room is full of music now; so much music that it seems as if he is as engulfed in notes and chords as a fish swimming in deep water, so deep that the density of his music is putting pressure against every part of his body.

When he finishes with piano, he will switch to violin. A violin practice book, since the best classical music is written for the instruments that predominate in the symphony orchestra – the strings. His practice method for violin exercises is the same as with piano music; he plays it straight from the pages, without transposing. This is an extra obstacle course for the musician, certainly designed to improve his dexterity but damned abrasive on his patience.

Coltrane closes this practice session with a harp book.

Hugh Lawson explains, 'The harp has an extremely high range, more than six octaves, and you can hear some incredible chromatic runs when it's played properly. Saxophone music is not written high because the horn has a range of less than three octaves. But harp music is written for the very top notes on the treble clef, so I think Trane used this music for practicing to increase his range on tenor, to play as high as he could. It might have started him thinking about soprano, too, because he often said he was hearing things higher than he could play on tenor.'

The music goes round and round inside John Coltrane's head, pouring forth from his horn as he continues his creative explorations, the only way any artist must if he is to be worthy of the name.

Alone.

41 **Nathan W. Pearson** Kansas City jazz style (1988)

Source: Nathan W. Pearson, 'Kansas City jazz style,' in *Goin' to Kansas City* (London: Macmillan, 1988: 114–20).

The Kansas City style is most strongly identified with swing. K.C. swing is founded on a strong 4/4 rhythm, fluid soloists, and, most important, riffs. Although not unique to Kansas City, these brief, repetitive, harmonic passages played in strong rhythm became so important to K.C. jazz music that 'setting riffs' (creating the riff structure), building new compositions through riff-based improvisation, and using the base of swinging riffs for extended solos were all part of a musical ethos and were a splendidly effective way to blend dance music with improvisational jazz.

Dance music requires consistent and strong rhythm. Constant performance of even the most interesting dance music, however, often becomes boring for talented musicians who want to experiment, learn, create, and grow. Riffs became the Kansas City musician's primary release from potential artistic stagnation.

Background riffs set by rhythm, horn, and reed sections provided a foundation for both dancers and soloists. The persistence of the dance rhythm gave the soloist freedom to depart from it, to weave his musical concepts in relatively free time around this rhythmic core. Riffs are the device that gave such brilliant instrumentalists as Lester Young, Buster Smith, Charlie Christian, Ben Webster, Lips Page, Buck Clayton, and Charlie Parker opportunities to develop fresh concepts in music while still playing economically viable dance music.

Of course, the essence of Kansas City jazz style is found in more than just riffing. A strong feel for the blues was fundamental, as was an innate sense of showmanship. Many fine composers and arrangers also had key parts in producing the K.C. sound, but most acknowledged that their creative inspiration primarily came from their fellow musicians, who were creating new riffs in orchestras and during jam sessions, or stretching musical boundaries in solos emerging from swinging dance music.

The following descriptions of this sound are grouped by major elements – rhythm, riffs, and jam sessions – and conclude with observations on the overall sound that resulted. Most important, these comments also describe a foundation of shared musical sensibility that characterized Kansas City's major jazz orchestras of the thirties – Bennie Moten, Andy Kirk's Twelve Clouds of Joy, Count Basie, George E. Lee, Thamon Hayes's Kansas City Rockets, and Jay McShann.

Rhythm

Charles Goodwin: As far as Kansas City jazz was concerned ... it was just a beat, ... we called it the Kansas City beat, ... and I think the man responsible for this more than anyone else was Bennie Moten ... It was a simple, two-beat thing,

but it was such an effective thing that everybody was Bennie Moten-oriented ...
You could tell a Kansas City musician.

Booker Washington: Kansas City has a certain beat of music, and anybody plays
here knows that beat. If you're jamming, it's that same beat, you can feel it. And
people that knew that went wild. They would ... go up and down the street,
whistling 'Moten's Swing.'[1]

It's kind of a 4/4 beat backsway. Bennie [Moten] started that [with] his left
hand. That left hand, that drum, and the bass fiddle player can carry a solid
beat. If you hear Basie, you hear Kansas City. There wouldn't be no boogie-
woogie stuff, just straight beat, but he added little extras. I can't describe that,
but it's something like a backbeat.

Mary Lou Williams: The Kansas City style was a swinging left hand ... If a
pianist didn't have a strong left hand, well, he was not considered very good at
all. Nobody would play with him ... They had quite a number of good piano
players.

Gene Ramey: Let me give you my definition ... of the forms of jazz. New
Orleans, which is the original jazz, you know, was ... built off of marching
band, parade band [music]. The drums swung the band ...

You go to Chicago-style jazz, which was the same thing, but they put a little
organization in the front line. In other words, the three horns, instead of just
going for themselves ... would play some little old arrangement. One guy
played the lead, another played the tenor, another played the alto, but they
played organized.

Now comes Kansas City, which is like an old-time revival, ... like an old
camp meeting ... You hear the people shouting, you hear that in Basie's band,
you know. It's just a happy-go-lucky thing. The trumpets are going one way, the
saxophones another way, the trombones are still going a different way, and that
rhythm section is just straight ahead ...

[With a Kansas City band] the rhythm section is supposed to be free ... For
example, [in] the Basie band, the rhythm section never read the music after the
first time ... This is why Basie's band has always been famous, and it still
sounds the same. The rhythm section is not harnessed. And don't forget, the
rhythm section is the food [of a band] ... There never was a band that was great
unless it had a great rhythm section ...

The rhythm section [has to] sound together. In those days they didn't have
an amplifier for a piano or for a guitar. The drums were the loudest one in
there. Now all four of us got to play, and we've got to play so that the loudest
instrument is no louder than the softest instrument ...

The drummer's foot was never supposed to be so loud ... it's called a 'big
foot' drummer, ... anybody'd go crazy after a while, you know, jump out of
windows. The Kansas City rhythm sections got together.

Riffs

Jesse Stone: There was a different Kansas City style because the horns
themselves played with the rhythm section, like Count Basie's band plays
now [in the 1970s] ... They can play in rhythm without a drummer. They have

that sense of rhythm feeling and that's where the change [to a Kansas City style] happened. When we started transferring the rhythm power from the rhythm section into the brass and reed sections and then played. We practiced that sound.

Gene Ramey: We don't need any [written] music. What we play is on ... a riff ... Kansas City jazz is supposed to be more freedom ... But you didn't go too far with the solos ... [When] the McShann band went to New York we had the first chorus and the last chorus ... written. All in between was nothing but riffs ... It was [the same] with the Basie band, too. You're getting more to the people because you're going to play those little simple things that they can understand. The rhythm section's got to be swinging ...

The less piano you play and the more room you give the bass player to walk and the guitar player to play his chords [the better off you are] ... That's why Basie's just swinging. He stays out of the way ...

We'd have a jam session, this guy sets a riff over here and this one sets a riff over here and another one sets a riff, and the guys just go on swinging. Each chorus, they'd build it up.

Booker Washington: Riffing is just a pattern that builds from the type piece you're playing. You can play a certain number, and all it requires is [a] harmony background. You take a swing number; to give it more punch you got to add a riff. That's between you and various sections. Your trumpets get together, [and with] somebody else, just build it right from there ... But keep it as simple as possible so that you are free jamming ... The more simple it is, the better all of it [will] sound.

Buck Clayton: Kansas City music is mostly where they set riffs behind you. No matter who's playing a solo, the guys would get just as much kick out of setting a riff. Like Prez [Lester Young] ... or Joe Smith ... if you heard them playing behind somebody ... The first one that set the riff, we all had to follow. If you could think of a riff quicker than anybody else, then we'd all follow you. You play it first, then the whole group would play it with you underneath the soloist. And he's just blowing away ...

That's what used to make Kansas City music stand out. Nobody else did that. It's the solo playing and the moving background below it, and a strong rhythm section ... Swing music ... I'm sure it wasn't planned, but it just became the style in Kansas City.[2]

Jam sessions

Myra Taylor: [At the Sunset Club] musicians would come in and ... sit and talk with their friends. Their instrument would be down at their side. If ... they wanted to play, they would just pick up their instrument and play from where they were ... You might hear a trumpet from way over there, a trombone from way over here. But they always managed to play a background for whoever was playing a solo.

Sam Price: Jam sessions is just where ... guys get together and ... start playing ... I remember one night I went in the Subway about nine-thirty, Hot Lips Page was playing 'Am I Blue?' or ... something with Ben Webster or some other musicians, and I stayed there ... till about twelve or one o'clock and ... I went home and came back a couple of hours later. They were still playing the same song.

Herman Walder: [A jam session] will wear a drummer down and a piano player and a bass man ... I've seen Big [Walter] Page ... play so long one night ... [that] his bass just crumbled, looked like toothpicks.

William Saunders: One guy would take fourteen or fifteen choruses before he'd stop ... [and] you'd steal passages [from him] ... They might be trite to the guy that was playing them, but to you they were different things that you could relate to your playing.

Ernest Daniels. Born 1911, Little Rock, Arkansas. Drums. Moved to Kansas City in 1925. Played in local bands until joining Harry Dillard's WPA band in 1934. Active through the 1970s.

What the jam sessions did to a person was acquaint them with new ideas, and you got the chance to play with the best, and so by playing with the best some of that rubs off on you.

T. Holder: In [Kansas City] it seemed like all the boys was musically inclined, because they always had something going ... They always was working on some kind of job ... They had a whole lot of that [jamming] there. And I loved to jam. I loved to blow cats out. [I'd go down] to the Subway, the Yellow Front. I went to all the clubs, man. Most of them boys would go hide when I came to town. Even if they catch me drunk, they still won't get me.

Gene Ramey: Even to this day, I can ... tell you that Kansas City is the only place where the musician wants to battle each other with all guns blazing.

Buck Clayton: I remember the first time I went to Kansas City. The first time I took out my horn. There's a place called the Sunset Club, and all those ... trumpet players looked like they came from behind the walls; they came from under the rug; they came all the way from Kansas City, Kansas, because they knew I was going to be there that night and they all want to cut you.

Mary Lou Williams: [In a jam session] we'd improvise. Somebody'd say, 'Let's play "Georgia Brown."' You improvise, and I've heard arrangements that were sensational; an arranger couldn't do as good ... That's the type of band that Count Basie had ... You see, there's an awful lot of love in the music ... There was quite a bit of love [in Kansas City]. That's what made it so wonderful.

Buster Smith: There wasn't nothing but jamming then. There wasn't but one band that would come there and wouldn't jam, and that's Duke's boys [Duke Ellington]. But all them other fellows, Fletcher Henderson was the main one. He'd come there, Coleman Hawkins would come there, wouldn't be nothing but tenor players, and Lester Young and Dick Wilson, Ben Webster, Herschel Evans, all of 'em went down there and started jamming, jam all night long. Lester Young and Ben Webster would [come out on top]. See, 'Body and Soul' was the main tune [for jamming]. Wasn't but one man made it there and made it back out, that was Chu Berry, all the rest of 'em was run out of town ...

Kansas City had the big name, they reigned down here ... Some guys didn't think about nothing but Kansas City. All them bands hung out around there.

Jay McShann: Kansas City is at the center of the United States, so when ... musicians gathered here the styles evolved to ... the loose, relaxed ... improvised style.

William Saunders: We'd go down every day and ... have little sessions down at the union. And everybody knew every out chorus together.[3] ... We listened. We didn't have radios or television to interrupt us ... That developed the Kansas City style because you would hear in a cluster and the style just developed between your ideas coming in here from Texas and Oklahoma and possibly Nebraska and Colorado, and there's a fusion of all those ideas together, and over a period of years and a period of sessions it became obvious as the Kansas City style.

Notes (edited)

1 'Moten's Swing' was a 1931 composition by Eddie Durham based on 'You're Driving Me Crazy.' It became the theme song of the Moten band, and, eventually, of Kansas City jazz.
2 K.C. was not the only jazz center where riffing was popular. In somewhat different fashion riffs were also commonly used in New Orleans, and by other prominent 1930s swing bands elsewhere.
3 The 'out chorus,' or theme, of a tune was often used as the foundation for riffs. Shared knowledge of such basic musical building-blocks gave Kansas City musicians a common vocabulary of key musical phrases that in turn permitted the exuberant jamming that characterized the city.

42 **Barry Ulanov** Moldy figs vs. moderns! (1947)

Source: Barry Ulanov, 'Moldy figs vs. moderns!', *Metronome*, 63 (November 1947: 15, 23).

There has been so much shouting on both sides about the respective merits of New Orleans jazz and the modern school, there have been so many claims and counter-claims of distinction, but never a live comparison of the two styles, until September 13 and 20, when the oldtimers and the newcomers fought to a finish in the New York Mutual [radio] studios. It was my privilege to gather the modern clan which battled the fixed personnel of Rudi Blesh's *This Is Jazz* show on Larry Dorn's *Bands for Bonds* program on successive Saturday afternoons.

Rudi and I both felt that our positions, purist in the sense that neither leaves room for the commercial middle ground, had been sufficiently debated verbally. Now is the time for all good jazz fans to come to the aid of their music, we said in effect, and because Mutual's Wyn Goulden and Larry Dorn felt the same way, we went proudly on the Treasury Department's program to do musical battle. Wyn and Larry were enthusiastic and well over a hundred Mutual stations carried the show; unfortunately the powers-that-be at 'that power-full station, WOR,' the network's New York outlet, weren't convinced of the importance of the jazz joust; New Yorkers had to glue their ears to their radios to hear what they could of the remarkable hot hostilities over WICC, Bridgeport, Connecticut.

The first week, Rudi and I split the half-hour. After suitable introductions from the center of the ring, my side gave way to Rudi who promised 'real melody, American melody, always treated in a creative way by great artists. And we think that is modern. So we're going to dip right back into the past for a number which is just as new as when it was written in 1917, the famous *Sensation Rag*.' Rudi couldn't have stated the basic contradiction of his point-of-view more clearly: for the modern he was 'going to dip right back into the past.' Wild Bill Davison, Edmond Hall, Jimmy Archey (trombone), Ralph Sutton (on piano), Danny Barker (guitar), Pops Foster, and Baby Dodds continued to dip into the past for *Save It Pretty Mama* and *That's-a-Plenty*.

When we took over I promised 'the choicest of the moderns' and I think Dizzy Gillespie, Charlie Parker, Lennie Tristano, John LaPorta, Billy Bauer, Ray Brown and Max Roach proved to be just that. Lennie and Billy filled out *Hot House* with piano and guitar chords which punctuated and amplified the unison bebop line as never before. John LaPorta offered what I am convinced is the first really new clarinet style in jazz since the Dixie formulations of Johnny Dodds, Jimmie Noone and Benny Goodman in *Hot House* and the concluding *Fine and Dandy*. And Lennie and Billy showed once more their sensitivity to each other's musicianship and contrapuntal lines in *I Surrender Dear*, with rhythmic assistance from Ray Brown and Max Roach. We went off the air to a sustained shout of *Dandy*, with announcer Bruce Elliott screaming, 'If you can still hear me, this is the Mutual Broadcasting System,' and a promise of things to come next week.

Startling, stunning – choose your own weapon; the second broadcast was certainly a high-water mark on the levees of jazz. Here we alternated bands, playing the same three tunes, *On The Sunny Side of the Street, How Deep Is the Ocean* and *Tiger Rag*. Again, Dizzy promulgated Promethean blasts, Yardbird demonstrated a greater facility than ever before on the alto and Lennie, John and Billy smote the smirks from the banal melodies and their protesting adherents, as they altered chords and lengthened lines. What The Moderns did to *Tiger Rag*, entirely new to all of them as a piece to perform, surely must rank high in jazz history. Its remorseless progression from B flat to A flat to E flat was never accomplished with more ingenuity and less confinement.

At press-time, the mail on the show was large and promising. All of us, the musicians, Rudi, Wyn, Larry and myself, are enthusiastic about the possibilities of a regular network program presenting the embattled music and musicians in weekly scraps. We were warmed by words of praise from Frank Coniff in the New York *Journal-American* and determined to keep this kind of musical contest going. Notes are still better than words to settle differences of musical opinion. When they are blown by the greatest representatives of the warring sides, the schisms of the jazz community assume a dignity of which all of us are jealous, for which we intend to fight hard.

43 **Martin Gardner** The fall of Flatbush Smith (1947)

Source: Martin Gardner, 'The fall of Flatbush Smith,' *Esquire*, 28, 9 (September 1947: 44).

I'm the guy who discovered 'Flatbush' Smith. I discovered him in Flatbush. The subway had dropped me off sooner than I expected, and I had a half-hour to kill before showing up at Brooklyn College for a jam session sponsored by *Blue Beat* Magazine. I stopped into the nearest tavern partly to get a beer and partly because I heard jazz inside.

It was hard to tell which was worse – the beer or the jazz. Behind the long bar a small platform held up two Negroes and a white man who were making noises with musical instruments. The sounds coming from the colored drummer and piano player had a resemblance to jazz, but the blasts from the white trumpet player didn't resemble anything.

He was a fat, greasy man of fifty or sixty with a head as smooth as a bowling ball, and a row of crooked gold teeth. He needed a shave and a bath. His battered horn was patched in six spots with adhesive tape and one of the springs was broken so he had to keep raising the key with his finger. To save himself trouble, he played most of the time on the other two keys.

He had an amazing ability to hit the wrong note. His timing was bad. His tones were flat. A dozen standard riffs were repeated over and over, with accidental variations.

I called the bartender over. 'What's the name of the horn player?' I asked.

'Smith,' he said, 'but everybody calls him Flatbush.'

'Did you say Flatbush or Flatnote?' I said.

The bartender didn't laugh. He just looked sad and tired. 'Ain't it awful?' he sighed.

I stood it as long as I could, then drained my glass and left. I would have forgotten about Smith if it hadn't been for the *Blue Beat* party.

Blue Beat, as everyone knows, is the leading jazz magazine of the New Orleans cult. According to the editors, jazz reached its peak before the first World War, in New Orleans, and has been on the skids ever since.

I'd been invited to the jam session because I edit a rival magazine called *Hot Beat* – dedicated to be-bop and other modern heresies. The *Blue Beat* boys said they wanted me to hear the 'real thing.'

Actually, the session wasn't bad at all. I enjoy New Orleans jazz when it's played well. I like Bunk Johnson. I like Kid Ory. But after the session I got into a heated argument with the editor of *Blue Beat*. Before we finished it took six men to keep us apart.

In my apartment, later, cooling down, I remembered the horn player in Flatbush and a fiendish idea popped into my head. The next issue of *Hot Beat* carried the following paragraph:

'Some of my New Orleans pals [I wrote] have been urging me to listen to

Flatbush Smith, now blowing trumpet with a small combo at Blackie Ryan's, on the corner of Nostrand and Flatbush Avenues, in Brooklyn. Take it from me, he stinks. For one thing, he can't play on pitch. He claims, of course, he does this deliberately, for weird tonal effects. Don't believe it. How can you expect a musician to develop technical skill when he can't even read music?'

The *Blue Beat* boys fell for it like a ton of bricks. Their next issue had Smith's picture on the cover and a long biography inside. Flatbush, it turned out, in his youth had been a shipfitter in the Merchant Marine. At the age of 18 he bought a secondhand horn and taught himself how to play. His ship made frequent trips to Africa where, according to *Blue Beat*, he listened to native music and unconsciously absorbed the rhythms and off-key tones of the African diatonic scale.

Not only was Smith unable to read music – he couldn't read anything. With effort he could sign his name. This illiteracy, the editor pointed out, had been a major factor in isolating him from the world of modern jazz – permitting him to develop his own free, relaxed, uninhibited style.

Smith's rise was unprecedented. Every group of jazz purists in the East lionized him. He played exclusive little jam sessions in the Village. He made trips to Boston, Philadelphia, and Chicago. Finally, he was featured in a concert at Carnegie Hall.

'How do you know when to play a flat note and when not to play one?' I asked him at a press conference on the day before the concert.

He took a cigar stub out of his mouth and squinted at it. 'It's accordin' to how I feel at de time. I play de African system.'

The concert was a great success. Critics hailed him as the modern master of the off-key note. A dozen record companies began to bid for him. His waxing of *Flatbush Wobble* broke all sales records.

Then a remarkable thing happened. Smith began to improve. It was due I suppose to several reasons – he was getting lots of practice, he had a better horn, and he played constantly with top musicians.

The first hint I had of Smith's downfall was a paragraph in *Blue Beat*. It viewed with alarm the fact that he was beginning to 'go commercial.' Several weeks later the same magazine accused him of having abandoned New Orleans style altogether for wild, meaningless riffs that completely obliterated the melody. He was even indulging occasionally in suggestions of be-bop.

I went to hear him one night on Fifty-second Street, and it was true. His technique had improved enormously. His timing was excellent and he was playing squarely on the note. His musical ideas were fresh, vigorous, and original. He was wearing a flashy green suit and a dark brown toupee.

'How come you quit playin' those off-key blue notes?' I asked him between sessions.

He mopped his forehead with a sleeve and flashed a big grin of gold tooth at me. 'I got tired a' de African scale,' he said.

A few months later he disappeared suddenly from the Street. The following week Guy Lombardo hired him as a sideman.

The New Orleans crowd gave him up, of course, but they still collect his early platters. I heard one the other day at a party in the Village. At first I thought the turntable was warped, but it turned out to be an old Flatbush recording.

It was a collector's item. In fact most of the early Smith discs are collector's items. The reason they're scarce, I'm told, is that Flatbush buys them up for his three-year-old grandson.

The kid likes the noise they make when he bops them with his wooden mallet.

44 **Gary Giddins** Jazz turns neoclassical (1985)

Source: Gary Giddins, 'Introduction: jazz turns neoclassical,' in *Rhythm-a-ning: Jazz Tradition and Innovation in the '80s* (New York: Oxford University Press, 1985: xi–xv).

We hear frequent talk of a renaissance in jazz. Musically, the signs are unmistakable; nevertheless, jazz remains nearly subterranean, a thing apart, a private cultural zone. Its state of alienation is frequently blamed on the Hydra that is variously known as the avant-garde, the new thing, the new wave, and free jazz – that is, the contemporary post-modernist jazz of the past twenty-five years. Avant-gardists are depicted, not always inappropriately, as musical Jackson Pollocks spewing sounds into the air without benefit of formal or narrative guidelines. Their music is considered esoteric when it isn't impenetrable, and erstwhile jazz fans, now repulsed by the gladiatorial anarchy that used to attract them, ask accusatory questions: where's the beat, the melody, the beauty? Musicians and critics continue to wonder when free jazz (allowing the supposition that free jazz *is* jazz – the debate here is unceasing) will be assimilated into the mainstream. In other words, when will Joyce become Dickens, and Bartók Mozart?

As I see it, the avant-garde has been studiously aligning itself with mainstream jazz for some time. The resurgence of jazz means in large measure the resurgence of swing, melody, and beauty, as well as other vintage jazz qualities such as virtuosity, wit, and structure – not that they've ever been entirely absent. If jazz, like other fine arts, had to be relearned in a period of avant-garde extremism, it has long since – and with a vengeance – turned neoclassical. Musicians weaned on the free jazz of the '60s now sift '20s' classicism, '30s' swing, '40s' bop, and '50s' soul for repertoire and expressive wisdom. They are, in effect, going home again.

From 1960 to 1975, adventurous jazz often meant indulgences on the order of 20-minute solos, or freely improvised polyphony, or endlessly repeated ostinatos layered over a single scale. Though the great figures of that period – John Coltrane, Cecil Taylor, Ornette Coleman, Albert Ayler, and a few others –

141

could bring off the most demanding improvisational conceits, at least as far as the knowing, sympathetic, and determined listener was concerned, they spawned imitators who mistook freedom for license and justified excess with apocalyptic rhetoric. A backlash was inevitable. Not only were many listeners yearning for restraint but a younger generation of jazz musicians, many of them trained in conservatories, expressed horror that formalism appeared to be vanishing. Jazz has always been a dialectic between improviser and composer: when the improviser gets out of hand, the composer emerges with new guidelines, sometimes borrowed from the distant past.

A couple of years ago, while teaching at a university, I found – for the first time – a way to kindle students' interest in the new jazz players (they need only exposure to appreciate classic players). The course began with a survey of such jazz precursors as spirituals, marches, blues, and ragtime; I simply provided symmetry by concluding the course with treatments of those precursors by avant-garde musicians, including Arthur Blythe's version of 'Just a Closer Walk with Thee,' Anthony Braxton's march from *Creative Orchestra Music 1976*, 'Blues,' by Leroy Jenkins and Muhal Richard Abrams, and Air's arrangement of Scott Joplin's 'Weeping Willow Rag.' Nor was it necessary to stop there. Having traced the evolution of jazz from the beginnings to the present, I might have retraced it with modernistic but idiomatically satisfying interpretations – all recorded since 1975 – of nearly every school and style. Indeed, I might have brought the course full circle by playing the Art Ensemble of Chicago's avant-garde parodies of the avant-garde. Jazz is so eclectic these days that you can find in it almost anything you please.

Jazz modernists rarely investigated the music's past before the avant-garde blew the old jazz truths out of the water. The composers and players of the era immediately following World War II ignored the traditional repertory, and when they did pay homage to the ancients (ragtimers and New Orleans-style players), whatever regard they may have felt was often soured by condescension. Modernism, after all, was a rallying point, and a political movement – a transformation of mere entertainment into art. The genius-leaders of the movement – Charlie Parker, Dizzy Gillespie, and Thelonious Monk – knew better, of course; the traditions live in even their most volatile experiments, whereas their disciples, more obsessed with the propaganda of the new, were inclined to dismiss as passé the sweetness of Johnny Hodges or the showboating of Louis Armstrong. Still, what both the geniuses and their disciples propagated *was* new. By comparison, the neoclassicists of the '80s may seem to be offering, at worst, nothing more than half-baked historicism or, at best, an inventive reappraisal of the jazz repertory. In this regard, it's useful to remember that one saving grace of neoclassicism is its impatience with nostalgia. Whereas a modernist of 30 years ago might have used a plunger mute to demonstrate bemused affection for an outmoded style, a neoclassicist of today uses the mute because he knows that it can convey singular and immediate passions.

When all the post-modernist styles – expressionist and neoclassicist alike – are considered 'avant-garde' (as, rightly or wrongly, they often are), they constitute an enduring sub-genre in jazz, one that dates back over 25 years. It has its own thesis ('the new wave') and antithesis ('the jazz tradition'). The distinction was made frustratingly clear to me by my students, who were enchanted by the contemporary restatements of classic styles, but resisted the unsettling innovations (works by Taylor, Coleman, etc.) of the '60s. I'm almost resigned to this response. Maybe only in a period of national tumult are people willing to listen to music for the pleasure of being battered and tested. The avant-garde, by definition, has no right to an audience larger than its true believers. Besides, the violent expressionism of the '60s made the current wave of neoclassicism possible; it freed the present generation to look on the jazz tradition with agnostic curiosity. And this generation – virtuosic, ambitious, and disarmingly unpretentious – has no axes to grind about the claims of art over entertainment or of freedom over form, except for the conviction, apparently widespread, that the future of jazz lies in a rapprochement between those putative opposites.

Still, when we talk about a renaissance in jazz, we are talking about a wealth of interesting music, not a broad-scaled awakening of interest in that music. Most of the neoclassical ventures discussed in this book are unknown outside the small enclave of New York clubs and European festivals. For, as all but the most provincial fans know, American jazz musicians are largely invisible in their own country. Few educated Americans can name even five jazz musicians under the age of forty. Jazz is virtually banished from television and commerical radio, and is usually conflated with pop in the press, when acknowledged at all – *Time* runs a Christmas music wrap-up that lists the best in classical and rock, as though jazz didn't exist. In four decades of prize-giving, the Pulitzer Committee has never recognized a jazz composer (the jurors who voted unanimously to award Ellington, in 1965, were overruled by the Advisory Committee). Booking agencies and record companies no longer scout for serious young jazz musicians. Even colleges, which once provided a network of concert halls for the Modern Jazz Quartet or Gerry Mulligan, now house lab bands that perform standard orchestrations but fail to book active innovators. Most significant jazz recordings of recent years were made abroad for labels like Black Saint in Italy, Hat Hut in Switzerland, Trio in Japan, Enja in Germany, SteepleChase in Denmark, and BVHAAST in Holland, or by tiny American labels, some of them little more than vanities; they are distributed in only a few American cities.

Yet, despite what amounts to a media blackout, jazz somehow manages to replenish its audience and its musicians with every generation. Jazz festivals proliferate, at least in Europe, and so do independent labels and reissue series. Mail-order companies, from the Smithsonian Collection to Time/Life, have found a bonanza in jazz. The music may be in exile, but it isn't fading away. I intend to help spread the news of the increasing accessibility of swing and melody and beauty in the jazz of the '80s, but I'm fully aware that the bounding line between jazz and the mainstream of American life is a tradition unto itself. In 1965, Dwight Macdonald wrote an account of an arts fesival at Lyndon Johnson's White House that unwittingly embodied the problem. Macdonald, who was rarely unwitting about anything, complained that 'no composers of any note were present.' Several paragraphs later, he observed parenthetically that the 'best thing at the festival' and 'the only really happy-looking people, in fact were Duke Ellington and his bandsmen.' That's the way it is now, only more so. Nobody here but us happy-looking jazzmen, boss.

45 **Martin Williams** How long has this been going on? (1989)

Source: Martin Williams, 'How long has this been going on?' in *Jazz in Its Time* (Oxford: Oxford University Press, 1989: 45–50) (excerpt).

Wynton Marsalis is not the first jazz musician to perform classical music, but he is surely the most widely accepted and the most popular. Marsalis is also obviously one of the most musically outstanding young jazz musicians in over a decade. His work might be called a synthesis, a virtuoso summary of everything that jazz trumpet has ever achieved and ever been.

Marsalis is not the first about whom such a statement might be said. Almost a decade ago, it was obvious that Stanley Cowell (for one) was a comparable virtuoso for jazz piano and its history. Marsalis also has a counterpart in cornetist Warren Vaché, who in the past decade has explored the history of jazz cornet-trumpet tradition in public, and by now has learned bebop thoroughly. He has also explored the possible range of his instrument high and low, with commendable virtuosity.

All of which suggests that jazz is in a period of stylistic retrenchment or, if you will, a period of conservatism. And with Lester Bowie recording pieces that suggest nothing so much as the 1920s New Orleans style; with the presence of the O.T.B. group playing basically a late 1950s hard bop with all urgency and drive that almost suggests they invented the style; with the feasibility of jazz repertory orchestra on everybody's mind – with these and similar things – who could doubt that we are in a time of musical conservatism?

It is a conservatism of a sort that jazz has never experienced before, because, as is surely worth pointing out, the players and groups I have mentioned above, except for Vaché, are black, and that would mean that the most obviously outstanding young black players are (so far) doing nothing truly new. That has certainly never happened in jazz before: in the past, the kind of musical conservatism they represent has largely been the white man's burden.

To go back to Marsalis, however, and to be fair to him, there certainly is indication of growth in his work, and the signs are that the growth will come rhythmically – and that is something worth celebrating.

If I am correct about this state of affairs in the music, one might assume that jazz is in trouble, even that its future may be in jeopardy. I don't think so. Artistic retrenchment is not stagnation. It may be a necessary, even healthy state of affairs.

I have used words like *synthesis* and *summary* rather freely in the foregoing. If I applied the word *synthesis* to all jazz up to the 1960s, say, there would be a general understanding, a general agreement on what musical and stylistic elements, and whose accomplishments, were being brought together and synthesized – from New Orleans through early Monk, let's say. But for events from the mid-1960s onward there may not be a general knowledge of, or even a general agreement on, what went on, with whom, and with what results. So a bit of a review seems to be in order.

And if we are going to review the recent past, there is one phenomenon that seems to be standing in the way – fusion, jazz-rock, call it what you will. To go back to Wynton Marsalis, he has been quite outspoken on the subject – indeed, he, and some others, seem to see the whole fusion thing as a kind of commercial opportunism and artistic blind alley, maybe even a betrayal of the music, on the part of everyone involved, on the part of record companies, record producers, and the artists themselves. Marsalis wasn't the first to voice such disillusionments on fusion: several years ago, when he left CBS Records, Freddie Hubbard said some things which several observers had been feeling for some time, and they were the same sorts of things Marsalis has said. Nowadays, almost every month may find another musician voicing a disenchantment with fusion or quietly dropping the style.

Jazz-fusion (as though you didn't know) mostly finds its origins in Miles Davis's two-record album '*Bitches Brew*,' and '*Bitches Brew*' is indeed a witch's brew of jazz and every sort of then-popular pop style, black, white, and Latin, and the several participants in the various sessions that went into that album mostly moved into one or another of them as his own territory. Wayne Shorter, Joe Zawinul, and Weather Report chose jazz and electric rock. John McLaughlin and the Mahavishnu Orchestra, a version of rock that seems to have moved from acid trips to Eastern mysticism for its orientation. Herbie Hancock embraced a kind of jazz-r&b. Chick Corea, jazz and salsa. Keith Jarrett, on the other hand, mostly stayed on his own tracks.

Strictly on the fact of it, there is no reason why fusions might not have worked. Jazz has always been able to meet, absorb, and put to its own purposes almost everything in popular prospect – from the waltz and the tango through the works of the great popular songwriters and (for a brief moment) the *bossa nova*. And jazz has learned many lessons from the experience.

Furthermore, the idea of a contemporary fusion had already had its artistic successes. Thad Jones's jazz boogaloo, *Central Park North,* was surely one of his best pieces. Stanley Cowell's *Abscretions* is a dazzlingly cohesive piece made up of allusive fragments one could pick up listening to the local soul station. And with *In Front,* Keith Jarrett found something excellent in gospel impressions. (However Jarrett intended that piece, it comes off as a free-form impression of two kinds of gospel music.) Concurrently the Modern Jazz Quartet brought off a commendable jazz-reggae in *Walkin' Stomp* (did anybody notice?). For that matter, one might say that Ray Charles's band has (off and on) been playing a kind of fusion since the late 1950s. And I have a feeling that on a pop level Quincy Jones could fuse anything to anything with musicianship if he wanted to.

Nevertheless, I don't think jazz fusion worked very well, and I think my best way of explaining why not is to paraphrase something I heard Clark Terry say to a student band a few years ago: the beat in jazz moves forward; it is played so as to contribute to the all-but irresistible momentum of the music: jazz *goes* somewhere. The beat in most rock bobs and bounces away in one place – like the kids on the dance floor these days. Rock *stays* somewhere. And to be a bit technical about it, 'jazz eights,' the implied 'triplet feel' of jazz, is rarely heard in fusion, and can seem strangely out of place when it is.

'Jazz' eight notes, the 'jazz' triplet, are not the superficialities or the mere ornaments of a musical style; in jazz, they have always been among the fundamentals. One of the unwritten (and undiscussed) laws of jazz has been that each of the great players has found his own way of pronouncing the triplet, expressed or implied, and Roy Eldridge's triplet didn't sound like Louis Armstrong's; Miles Davis's didn't sound like Dizzy Gillespie's; Lester Young's triplet was unlike Coleman Hawkins's; and Stan Getz's is unlike Lester Young's. Nobody's triplet is exactly like anybody's. And developing a personally-articulated triplet not only has been an identifying mark for the great players, it has been an expression of the high individuality on which this music depends and which it celebrates. Also, swing is not simply a matter of musical momentum: that momentum is an aspect of the spontaneous, personal creativity which the music also celebrates. Swing encourages that creativity, makes it possible at the same time that it is an intricate part of it.

About Miles Davis and fusion, maybe I can be as blunt and outspoken as he usually is about everything and everybody. When I last heard Miles Davis he was stalking around a stage in what looked like a left-over Halloween fright-suit, emitting a scant handful of plaintive notes. A fast-fingered young tenor player, the piece being a B-flat drone, showed us how many ways he could run out of B-flat and back in again. A guitarist played with competence and little feeling. The whole thing reached the audience through speakers, each of which seemed bigger than the whole room I first heard Miles play in. And the music, like so much contemporary rock, seemed to get louder and louder in a desperate frustration over its inability to express anything.

Davis has always been one of those musicians who could come up with something so fresh, even on familiar material, as to make one forget, temporarily, all of his beautiful past. That evening everything I heard made me remember that beautiful past with pain. Soon I found that the booming of the speakers was producing a physical pain in my chest. I left, sad, and almost angry with the feeling that I had somehow been shut out by the music itself.

I am not going to tell you that all the efforts of a decade by such men as Wayne Shorter or Joe Zawinul, to name only two, have come to naught. There can be some nice houses even on a dead-end street. Those men and others are too talented as composers for that to have happened, and Shorter is too talented a player as well. But I do note that whenever I ask one of Weather Report's admirers to name a particularly favored piece, he will say, 'Oh, something from (naming one of their LPs).' I can't imagine an admirer of Louis Armstrong, or Duke Ellington, or Charlie Parker, or an earlier Miles Davis responding that way. He'd name you a piece or a solo, and then maybe tell you the LP it comes from.

Riff 4

Jazz reasserts the truth that the creation of art is a social function; that music should be made for people to use. (Sidney Finkelstein, *Jazz: A People's Music*, 1948)

We should view the music not simply as text but as social practice. (David W. Stowe, *Swing Changes: Big-Band Jazz in New Deal America*, 1994)

The nature and significance of the type of attention our society has paid to jazz reveal a great deal about our culture. (Lawrence Levine, 'Jazz and American Culture,' *Journal of American Folklore*, 1989)

The predominance of the jazz factor may make it the master trope of this century: the definitive sound of America in our time. The sound of the American twentieth century is the jazz line. (Robert G. O'Meally [ed.], *The Jazz Cadence of American Culture*, 1998)

I am saying that if the music [blues and jazz] of the Negro in America, in all its permutations, is subjected to a socio-anthropological as well as musical scrutiny, something about the essential nature of the Negro's existence in this country ought to be revealed, as well as something about the essential nature of this country, *i.e.*, society as a whole. (Amiri Baraka [LeRoi Jones], *Blues People*, 1963)

Beyond the prima facie feeling that a performance *is* jazz music, lurks the disquieting feeling that jazz, like all other forms of music, is not simply to be swallowed whole. It is subject to analysis. Jazz must be related to a number of vectors: first, its own antecedent and internal history; second, other contextual forms of musical expression; third, extra-musical connotations about jazz; and fourth, the technology and commerce of the jazz culture ... Any multivariate approach yields fertile sources for the sociological analysis of jazz. (Irving Horowitz, 'Authenticity and Originality in Jazz: Toward a Paradigm in the Sociology of Music,' *Journal of Jazz Studies*, 1973)

Chorus IV

A People's Music: Jazz and culture
(context, audience, social practice)

Stuart Nicholson has remarked, 'throughout its existence, jazz has been inexorably linked to the social fabric from which it emerged' (1995: v). Historically, jazz has received special notice as 'a people's music.' Sidney Finkelstein's Marxist advocacy of jazz's democratic utility – reflecting the social function of art – has been to suggest a cultural universality for jazz (1948). And, as 'America's classical music' (Sales 1984), the indigenous nature of jazz has also been often emphasized. Jazz's inherent nativeness and its capacity to reflect the socio-cultural milieu which has produced it have made it a valuable index of American life and culture. Burton Peretti, in a welcome attempt to examine the roles of jazz in American culture (1997), argues that through the music itself, its audience reactions, and the critical debates involving its nature, jazz can be placed within the contexts of American history and the development of American culture since 1900 (Introduction and Conclusion [**55**]). This contextual aesthetic, then, has employed social and cultural history to situate the music, and has been applied to jazz 'ages,' styles and activity. It has been supplemented by social science fieldwork, which has documented the professional circumstances of the jazz life and social organization of the jazz community. **Chorus IV** examines the social and cultural dimensions of jazz and, through specific contexts and perspectives, the factors of performance, production and reception so crucial to its understanding.

Viewed contextually, jazz has indubitably its *own* culture. A sociology of jazz would point especially to the relations between musicians and their performance contexts. These include a sub-cultural community, a specific public, and socio-economic conditions of professional livelihood; they also involve a degree of isolation, self-segregation and non-conformity. A social history of jazz involving two interrelated dynamics is suggested by Charles **Nanry**, in *The Jazz Text* (1979). In an introductory passage (**46**) he proposes a tension between (1) the *external*, popular conception of jazz history, which involves production and entertainment and is media-orientated, and (2) the *internal* understanding of jazz music, involving players, audience and the jazz community, and focused on performance and creativity. Put together, this dual, relational perspective offers a persuasive social history of jazz.

While sociologists have conducted field research into the nature of the jazz audience and community (see Merriam and Mack: **52**), data sources such as the US Census Bureau have provided information on the participation of Americans in cultural activities like jazz. For Harold **Horowitz**, insufficient attention or information has been accorded the audience for jazz, particularly its size and make-up. A paper of 1986 (**47**), drawing on the Census, shows the American jazz audience is fairly complex, and includes people from diverse categories like residence, age, gender, race, education and income. A description of the 'typical' jazz audience suggests it is quite large, mostly urban, young, white, well-educated, and from high-income backgrounds. But statistics actually show the black population's proportionally much higher participation rates, as well as a figure of just 3 per cent of adults being a highly dedicated jazz audience.

The study of jazz as social and historical process arguably stems from the early 1960s, and partly reflects growing dissatisfaction with a purely musicological approach. The year 1962 saw publication of Charters and Kunstadt's locally documented *Jazz: A History of the New York Scene* and Leonard's *Jazz and the White Americans* (see **50**), which examines the acceptance of a new art form from the perspective of 1920s America. More recent, full-length studies, by cultural historians like Ogren (1989), Kenney (1993) and Stowe (1994), have all sought to locate jazz activity and production – through researched factors such as performance, entertainment, and reception contexts – in American culture at times of resonant social change. As William Kenney writes in his cultural history of Chicago jazz (1904–30),

> a closer analysis of one particular time and place, widely recognized to have been important to the evolution of jazz, will help to re-create a clearer sense of the particular social and cultural circumstances ... within which jazz musicians molded their music. (1993: xi)

This analysis is at work in Stowe's *Swing Changes: Big-Band Jazz in New Deal America* (1994), whose title alone makes explicit the intention to relate a dominant musical taste and jazz style to a specific cultural context. Alluding to the popular idea that swing expressed 'a certain spirit of the age', David **Stowe** examines ways in which the music may be centrally linked to Depression and war years America: through its own cultural status, but also in contemporary politics and race relations, the mass culture industry and the role of women. In his 'Introduction' (**48**), he uses swing as 'historical source,' understanding the music 'not simply as text but as social practice.' As he initially remarks, 'the ways in which people thought about swing revealed new patterns of thinking about history, about racial and cultural difference, and about the nature of American society' (1994: 1). Swing's popular, jazz-oriented dance music in the decade ending 1945 offers sugggestive parallels with American culture. Embodying both utopian ideology and social practice, swing captures the dynamic of movement and change in an historically charged time. American culture, in the 1930s and 1940s, is 'swing-shaped.'

The argument that the music of jazz and the circumstances of its performance embody social change has been impressively demonstrated by Kathy **Ogren**. In *The Jazz Revolution: Twenties America and the Meaning of Jazz* (1989), she examines the controversy surrounding the music's popular advance, placing it in its historical context. Arguing that many of the performance characteristics of jazz – location, participation, improvisation, rhythmic vitality, expressive excitement – made it resonant of rapid social change, jazz centrally represented 'the transcience and transformations of modern American life' (**49**). The controversy concerning the new music is also reflected in historian Neil **Leonard**'s pioneering study of the acceptance of jazz in the period 1918–40. *Jazz and the White Americans* (1962) has two main purposes: to throw light on the questions raised by the jazz debate, and reveal the nature of the artist–audience gap. In both cases, the rejection–acceptance of jazz and dynamics of change in cultural taste and value are fundamental to Leonard's investigation. A section of Chapter 3 (**50**) describes the conduct and culture of a jazz fraternity of white musicians (the 'Chicagoans'), in revolt against traditional values – a revolt reflected in middle- and upper-class interest in the art and entertainment of subcultures like jazz. In Leonard's examination, the attractions of jazz become the arena of contest between traditionalists and modernists; jazz exercises strong appeal for the rebellious and independent. Drawing on the autobiographies of Mezz Mezzrow, Benny Goodman, Eddie Condon and Hoagy Carmichael, Leonard documents the Chicagoans' sense of cultural alienation from mainstream values, and identification with the music, practices and lifestyles of an art derived historically from black culture. He concludes (1962: 68) that the musicians' unconventional behaviour strengthened the brotherhood of the jazz fraternity, helping 'to protect the new music from the assaults of those who could not appreciate it.'

Social science studies have contributed substantially to the contextualization of jazz, not least in earlier research conducted by sociologists into the professional activity and behavioural patterns of jazz musicians. Broadly, sociological investigation of jazz has divided into two categories: (1) 'assimilationist,' placing jazz in the larger context of American society and socio-cultural changes (e.g. Leonard 1962; Berger 1947 [**51**]); and (2) 'sub-cultural,' investigating the music/musicians as part of a deviant, potentially rebellious 'outsider' group, and emphasizing those characteristics that set jazz musicians apart from others (e.g. Becker 1963; Stebbins 1968; Leonard 1975; Merriam and Mack 1960 [**52**]).

Leonard (1962: 3) reveals his book's starting point is an influential case study on resistance to the diffusion of jazz, by sociologist Morroe **Berger** (1947). Berger's opening summary of the opposition to jazz appears below (**51**). It proceeds from the hypothesis that 'in the diffusion process the prestige of the donors has considerable bearing on the way in which a borrowing group reacts to cultural traits of other groups,' and the fact that Negroes have a low social status (1962: 461, 491). Berger's ensuing review of evidence effectively documents the moral and racial repression of black jazz in white America. Another important sociological article, from Alan **Merriam** and Raymond **Mack** (**52**), describes the jazz community. In their analysis, it is characterized by a number of distinctive behaviour patterns, which focus on one central theme: 'the isolation of the group from society at large.' The authors attribute this isolation and self-segregation to the rejection of jazz and the jazz musician by the general public; the occupational isolation of jazz musicians; and the contradictory roles of commercial entertainer and creative artist. If the influence of some of these factors is now somewhat diminished, the sense remains of a jazz community which is culturally separate – even alienated – and of distinctly minority status.

Jazz's roots in black social experience and African-American aesthetics have given the music an expressive relationship with black sociocultural history (see **Chorus V**). Typically, Peretti (1997: 183) thinks it clear 'that jazz has been closely tied to the African-American struggle for equality.' Indeed, black Marxist critics like Baraka and Kofsky have insisted that:

> all forms of black music are an African-derived response to the endless oppression of black people in this country, and the development of the various strains of the music are best understood in light of the changing circumstances of these people. (Kofsky 1971: 410)

What interests Amiri **Baraka** in 'Where's the music going and why?' (1987) (**53**) is that music's correlation with 'the real aesthetic and emotional life' of African-Americans. Examining new and altered trends and recurrent patterns of black music in the United States, he finds the dollar-sign has invaded jazz and blues, to provide a corruption of style into formulaic fad (e.g. funk, fusion). Baraka sees signs of a reawakening, both in neo-bop and expression of the legacy of the new music revolution of the 1960s and early 1970s, but contexts for the developing music remain racially oppressive and exploitive. For combative Baraka, African-Americans must achieve political and economic self-determination before black music can escape being borrowed and co-opted by 'white racist monopoly capitalism.' The music is going 'wherever the masses of the African-American people are going or have gone.'

The treatment accorded jazz by American society, and the dialectic between jazz and culture, is the subject of an influential contribution from Lawrence **Levine**. He initially argues (**54**) – later amassing evidence to support his view – that until World War II, new, indigenous jazz and a Eurocentric, hierarchical culture expressed 'radically divergent impulses' in America, with routine denigration or condescension of the music, and appreciation largely by those at the margins of society. Thereafter, these attitudes were reversed, once the cultural significance and status of jazz could no longer be denied. Jazz has become a force that transforms art and culture – and in its specialness and inclusiveness has revolutionized the concept of culture. As an integral, vibrant part of American life, jazz has much to tell Americans about their history – and their *American-ness*.

Levine's argument is common with Burton **Peretti** (1997), who charts the ways in which jazz reflects cultural conditions and change in twentieth-century America. His 'Epilogue' (**55**) to *Jazz in American Culture* (1997) reviews this process and draws on an earlier proposition, that 'any study of a complex twentieth-century music in its rich social and cultural context will uncover different cultures of expression that vary by class, ethnicity and generation' (1997: 9). Peretti's imaginative, inter-disciplinary approach suggests how jazz has embodied the varied situations and hopes of Americans, served as a principal focus for debate over social change and cultural value, and reflected changing notions of popular taste. In these varied and vital ways, jazz speaks to American history and American culture. 'A people's music,' no less.

46 **Charles Nanry** Jazz as social history (1979)

Source: Charles Nanry, with Edward Berger, 'Jazz as social history,' in *The Jazz Text* (New York: Van Nostrand, 1979: 20–1).

The social history of jazz involves two interrelated, yet analytically separable, phenomena. One is the external dynamic of the form, in which the development of jazz has been shaped and even contained by the larger world of entertainment. (The tendency toward discrimination in studio hiring practices is an example of containment.) In this sense, jazz is a music shaped and molded by the mass media, in particular the worlds of radio broadcasting and the phonograph recording studio. Most Americans first hear something called jazz on a record or over the radio. While it is true that what they hear is probably not 'pure' jazz, it is a modified version of the real thing. Since the production of records and radio broadcasting is motivated by the desire for profit, the most widely disseminated jazz is closer to 'easy listening' and to rock than to modern chamber music. This pattern of cultural diffusion is not an unusual one in mass societies; any form that seeks a wide audience must have recognizable elements in order to be accepted. This process sets up a tension between the best jazz and the most easily understood elements of jazz.

Jazz also has an internal dynamic. Jazz musicians, like everyone else, have to make a living. While they are doing that, however, they are expected to extend and re-create the form itself. But there is risk involved in attempting to create art in a popular context, the risk of losing one's audience if the music goes beyond what the audience understands. This sets up a tension between the acts of performance and the act of creation. This tension is nowhere more evident than in jazz, because it is a music where creation (formally, musical composition) usually occurs during performance. One of the key elements of jazz – improvisation – demands that new melodic, harmonic, and rhythmic patterns emerge in the context of performance. But limits have to be imposed both by audiences and by performers. Performing jazz is not a random process. The narrow line between authenticity and creativity must be perceived and manipulated by the good jazz player.

I do not wish to suggest that there is a rigid dichotomy between the internal and external factors affecting jazz. Rather, there are large-scale, global factors constraining the development of jazz as well as small-scale, internal constraints on the music and the musicians who play it. The jazz community is only one community existing side-by-side with other cultural communities in the social world of the arts. The external history of jazz starts with the broadest popular conception of how jazz came to be. This conception is then susceptible to refinement in the same way as other historical and sociohistorical phenomena. The internal dynamic of jazz implies, alternatively, an understanding of the people and of the social organization of the jazz community.

47 **Harold Horowitz** The American jazz audience (1986)

Source: Harold Horowitz, 'The American jazz audience' (1986), in
D.N. Baker (ed.), *New Perspectives on Jazz* (Washington, Smithsonian
Institution Press, 1990: 1–8).

American jazz has been studied from many perspectives. The musical form
itself, its origins and evolution, and the artists who perform it have become
subjects for a large body of scholarly and critical literature. The audience for
jazz, however, has not attracted the same kind of intensive study, and little
information can be found in the open literature. Of course, the major
recording companies conduct surveys of potential record buyers and of
recorded music sales, and local radio stations have their surveys of listeners,
but the results of such sales development research have not become widely
available as an open literature. In the absence of reliable audience
information, anecdotes and personal observations have been used. Differing
viewpoints have been debated on such questions as the size and makeup of
the audience for jazz. But until recently, there has not been an acceptable data
source that might help to resolve some of the broad and widespread
differences of opinion.

A significant step toward improving the understanding of the American jazz
audience was taken when the National Endowment for the Arts commissioned
the U.S. Bureau of the Census to collect information on the participation of
adult Americans in a wide range of arts and cultural activities, including jazz.
Development work for a Survey of Public Participation in the Arts started in
1979, and the first of two national surveys was fielded in 1982. A report
containing a detailed statistical analysis of these data was first distributed at the
'New Perspectives on Jazz' conference. The following highlights from that
report take the form of questions that are frequently asked, and the answers
suggested by the data.

The statistical quality of this survey was high, and the probability sample of
American adults that was drawn by the Bureau of the Census is large by usual
standards. So it is possible to break down the information and reorganize it into
many different combinations. The analysis shows that the American jazz
audience is fairly complex and cannot be described simply in a few words
without blurring many of its important features. There are many patterns
within this audience, which includes people from diverse categories of
residence, age, sex, race, education, and household income.

A one-line answer might be that the jazz audience is quite large, and mostly
urban, young, white, well-educated, and from high income-level households.
This simple answer may be technically correct as a description of the
characteristics of the 'typical' jazz audience, but it fails to explain the diversity
in the patterns that showed up in the survey results. The readers of the
following questions and answers should also be aware that survey results of

samples of the population may vary somewhat from the results that would have been found if the entire population had been surveyed.

The question most often asked is, How large is the jazz audience? The answer is, quite large. When four kinds of participation are combined, the jazz audience in 1982 included about 54 million individuals, or nearly one-third of all American adults. The four types of jazz participation measured in the survey were: attending live performances, listening to recordings, listening to the radio, and watching television. Obviously, there can be big differences in the quality or in the seriousness of the participation in these four different activities. Attending a live performance is considerably more demanding, in requiring the effort to go out and give undivided attention to a performance, than is listening to music on your auto radio for background while driving to work.

But we shouldn't be too quick to make such simple distinctions. The survey data indicate that, in general, older Americans tend toward the types of participation that are less physically demanding than attending live performances, such as listening to radio and watching television. The survey data also show a clear difference in the age distribution patterns of persons who attend live jazz performances and those who participate by means of the electronic media.

There is also a sobering information item found in the answers to questions about the kinds of music the public likes. Only about 43 million respondents answered that they liked jazz, which suggests that some of the 'yes' responses to the participation questions were given by persons who do not actually like jazz, but may have caught some of it on a radio or television broadcast, perhaps inadvertently, or perhaps went along and did something that friends wanted to do while in a group or on a date. But even if we take the 43 million as our gross estimate rather than 54 million, the general conclusion remains the same: the jazz audience is quite large.

Question: How do the four different kinds of participation compare for their shares of the jazz audience? **Answer:** The largest jazz audience is for listening to recordings. Twenty percent of American adults (32 million) said they listened to jazz recordings at least once in the year preceding their survey interview. Following in size are the audiences for radio and for television, which are about 18 percent each (29 million each). The audience for live performances is the smallest, with 10 percent of adults (16 million). There is quite a bit of overlap in these four audiences, as is apparent by adding together the figures and comparing the sum to the gross audience size described in the preceding answer. When one examines the size of the audiences who participate in only one way, the television-only audience is the largest, with 5 percent of adults (8 million); the recording-listening-only audience second, with 3.5 percent (6 million); the radio-only audience next, with about 3 percent of adults (5 million); and the live-performance-only audience the smallest, with about 2 percent of adults (3 million). The highly dedicated jazz audience, which is the audience that participates in all four ways, has about 3 percent of adults (5 million).

Question: What does the survey show about the demographic characteristics of the jazz audience? **Answer:** The audiences for the four forms of participation display individual demographic patterns. There are certain similarities but there are also differences, so a complete description requires study of the statistical tables. Moreover, it is easy to become confused by the differences between the audience proportions of the publics in each subgroup or stratum (which are described in terms of concentrations or rates of participation), and the differences in terms of absolute numbers of persons in each subgroup or stratum. For example, as mentioned earlier, a simple answer regarding the racial makeup of the jazz audience is that it is mostly white. This answer obscures the black population's much higher rates of participation. [The] table shows more clearly than words by themselves that blacks, when considered in proportion to their numbers, are much more frequent participants in each of the four audiences than whites. It is only when one takes the participation average for the entire population that the greater number of white persons becomes dominant.

Of all the demographic characteristics that were considered in the survey, the level of educational attainment emerges as the most important predictor of jazz participation. When the population is stratified by levels of educational attainment, the corresponding rates of participation in each of the four audiences were found to increase with education. The jazz recording audience illustrates the ranges that were found in each of the four kinds of participation: only 5 percent of persons whose highest level of education was grade school said that they listened to jazz recordings, while 39 percent of the persons who had completed their first college degree and had also attended graduate school were listeners to jazz recordings. But educational attainment levels are not divided equally among the whole population, and most people have not attended graduate school. At the time of the survey, the highest educational attainment of nearly 40 percent of the adult population was graduation from high school, and another group of about 20 percent had completed some college but had not graduated. The majority of the jazz audiences come from these two large middle-education groups, even though the concentration or rates of participation are considerably greater for the smaller groups that have completed college and gone further with their educations.

Unlike educational attainment, the household income patterns for the four

Table Rates of jazz participation by race

Race	Number of adults	Attend live events (%)	Watch on TV (%)	Listen on radio (%)	Listen to recordings (%)
Black	17,470,000	15	28	36	36
White	143,355,000	9	17	16	18
Other	3,750,000	9	21	23	20

forms of participation are not consistent with each other. Jazz audience participation by means of attending live events and by listening to recordings follows patterns similar to those of educational attainment. For these, the concentration or rate of participation goes up with increasing household income, but the ranges are not as wide as for education. For the audience watching television, the differences are quite small as they ascend the income scale, and for respondents listening to the radio there are hardly any differences at all between the different income groups.

The characteristic of audience age generally shows a pattern of greater rates of participation by younger persons. This relationship is most striking for attenders of live performances, but the differences are much less for the other kinds of participation and, in the case of the audience watching television, the differences are quite small. Once again, one should pay attention to the numbers of persons in the various groups. In 1982 over 40 percent of the adult population was under 35 years of age, and the 35–44 age group included nearly 17 percent of the adult population. For these reasons, jazz audiences look fairly young, and the appeal of jazz to persons in the older age groups may be overlooked. Except for attendance at live performances, persons in the 45–74 age groups report substantial participation rates. Watching jazz performances on television and listening to jazz recordings are about as popular with persons in these older age groups as they are to persons in the younger age groups, and only slightly less so for listening to jazz on the radio.

When considered by the sex of the audience members, the patterns for the four kinds of participation are similar. The rates of participation by men are greater than for women in each of the four audiences, but the differences are small. On the other hand, there are more women in the adult population than there are men, so the numbers of persons of each sex work out to be nearly the same for each type of participation.

Question: Where do people go to hear live performances of jazz? **Answer:** The survey responses from people who only attend jazz performances differ quite a bit from the answers given by people who also attend other kinds of performing arts. The jazz-only attenders mentioned concert halls and auditoriums, nightclubs and coffeehouses, and parks and other open-air facilities as their most frequent places; each of these three categories was mentioned by at least 20 percent of the jazz-only attenders. The segment of the audience that attends other types of performing arts as well as jazz named two additional frequent performance places: college or university facilities, and theaters. Each of the five top performance places of the audience for multiple performing arts was cited by at least 30 percent of these attenders.

Question: Where does the jazz audience live? **Answer:** Again, a simple answer is not satisfying, because the distributions of the audiences for the four types of participation are not the same. The southern region has the largest number of attenders of live jazz performances, but the West, with the smallest population of the four regions, has the greatest rate of participation at live performances. Listeners to jazz recordings are found in about equal numbers in the four U.S. regions, while the number of live performance attenders varies substantially. The northeast region has the smallest number of attenders, but

New York City has the largest jazz audience of any single city. The one generalization that can be made about the locations of jazz audiences is that they are extremely urban. For example, 13 percent of the persons who live in the central cities of metropolitan areas attend live performances, compared with 6 percent of the population living outside of metropolitan areas and with 4 percent of the people who live on rural farms.

Question: Do jazz audiences cross over into other performing arts? **Answer:** Correlation studies using the survey data show some crossover between the audience for jazz and the audiences for each of the other performing arts. For example, out of the audience for live performances of jazz, 9 percent also attend performances of opera, 14 percent also attend ballet performances, 31 percent also attend performances of plays, 34 percent also attend classical music and chamber music performances, and 41 percent also attend performances of musical plays.

Question: Is there a demand for increased attendance opportunities? **Answer:** About twice as many persons want to attend jazz performances compared to the number already attending them. The reasons most often given for not attending were: not enough time, cost, not available, and too far to go. The last two distance-related reasons were cited by 22 percent and 13 percent, respectively, of the respondents who wanted to increase their attendance. Most of the attenders at live performances were in the youngest age groups; the survey also found that about 60 percent of the persons who want to attend more jazz performances are in the 18–24 age group, which suggests a participation demand that may persist for a long time.

48 **David W. Stowe** Understanding swing (1994)

Source: David W. Stowe, 'Introduction: understanding swing,' in Swing Changes: Big-Band Jazz in New Deal America (Cambridge, MA: Harvard University Press, 1994: 9–16) (excerpt).

Studying culture through music depends on the fundamental assumption that some kind of meaningful overlap or continuity exists between the cultural form, music, and the broader entity of society or culture. Certainly, reducing swing to its aural dimension, by focusing on surviving recordings or various bands' arrangements and styles, would commit the same violence to the lived experience of its consumption as would reducing an actual performance to its song lyrics. The problem with using a musical form like swing as a historical source lies not so much in the abstractness of music, but in the arbitrary reduction of the scope of what is meant by 'music.' The solution lies not in musicological positivism, which privileges the written score above the experience of 'sound-in-time' and elements of musical reference, but in broadening our conception of 'the music' to include social elements: audience, performance context, ideology, and mass media. Historians must regard the score or recording as merely the sign of a large field of social forces that provide the ground for those texts. In other words, the arbitrary distinction between a musical performance and its origin or source can be abolished. Swing would then be understood not as a collection of written arrangements or recordings but as the field that makes such texts possible. In short, we should view the music not simply as text but as social practice.[1]

As musicologists increasingly acknowledge, music's meaning is constructed; thus the contradictions and ironies present in swing reflect the work of different social groups in constructing their own assorted understandings of it. This is not to strip musical texts of their particularity, to claim that musical performances or texts are homogeneous. Indeed, the point is that the qualities of music that produce meaning in the audience are culturally and historically specific. Different audiences actually hear the same music differently, and take different meanings away. The social meanings 'read into' the music by contemporary listeners depended on how their ears and bodies were conditioned to respond, which in turn reflected the influence of family members, neighbors, ministers, magazine feature writers, and the like. In this sense swing was a cultural Rorschach test for its contemporaries.

Looking at music as a broad social field takes us closer to the idea of a swing-shaped culture ... Changes in the ways the music was arranged, produced, distributed, and enjoyed reflected larger social patterns. Compared to the polyphonic, collectively improvised music of New Orleans and Chicago, swing was tightly structured through written arrangements that allowed relatively little room for spontaneous improvisation (even solos tended be worked out in advance and performed with little variation). The twelve-bar blues and other, more complex forms that had provided the framework for much early jazz were largely supplanted in swing by popular songs written in the standard thirty-two-bar, AABA structure of Tin Pan Alley. As functional dance music, swing replaced the choppy two-beat 'bounce' characteristic of early jazz with a more flowing, streamlined four-beat rhythm, partly a result of the substitution of the more rhythmically flowing stringed bass for the tuba in the rhythm section. Swing bands were larger than the typical early jazz ensembles, and they shifted the counterpoint from individual lines played by trumpet, clarinet, and trombone to two sections or 'choirs,' reeds (saxophones and clarinet) and brass (trumpets and trombones).

The turn away from the loose, open-ended, and nonhierarchical playing of 1920s jazz toward the more regimented modes of swing registered the move toward larger, more bureaucratic, and more rationalized units of organization characteristic of American society during the 1930s. It was analogous to the arrangements worked out among business, unions, and the government under the New Deal, for example. Swing's much-noted quality of enabling the individual voice to contribute to the collective whole also accords well with the notion of a cooperative commonwealth central to Franklin Roosevelt's vision of America.

Swing's jazz-tradition successor, bebop, drastically reduced ensemble size, typically to five pieces, and reinstated extended improvisation, sequential rather than collective. Bebop 'arrangements' were not compositions in the sense in which swing arrangements had been; instead, they were open frameworks used to highlight the spontaneous creativity of the soloist. Bebop dramatically expanded the harmonic vocabulary and rhythmic idioms available for improvisation (and arrangements). Although most bebop compositions were derived from the repertoire of popular song on which swing drew, the familiar melodies were discarded in favor of the underlying harmonic structures. The sharp contraction of the ensemble in bebop, together with the emphasis on individual virtuosity and dissonant (to swing-attuned ears) sonorities, suggests the heroic alienation of the postwar individual cut loose from Depression-era modes of commitment, or the racial militancy taking root among African-Americans in the late 1940s.

Swing's trajectory can be linked to those of several other aspects of American culture in the same years. For example, both the regionalist paintings of Thomas Hart Benton and swing expressed the ideals of progressive reform and a populist producerist ideology through symbols that embodied the uniquely American values of energy and democracy. Both swing and regionalism depicted a utopian vision of an 'American way of life' that at once drew on and lent itself to Hollywood and advertising. Both clashed with the mores of the regional cultures in which they operated. And after the war both rapidly lost ground to styles that appeared abruptly discontinuous but were related through their defining artists; the abstract expressionist Jackson Pollock had studied with Benton, just as the jazz modernists had come up through the big bands. In its studied apoliticism, its emphasis on freedom, alienation, and the individual, its turn from society to self, from Marx to Freud, abstract expressionism was an apt reflection of the prevailing ideology of Cold War America. Bebop likewise was taken to express this cultural mood of alienation; it too was abstract in the sense that its solos were based not on melodies but on chord changes (a practice that in fact predated bebop).

Baseball during those years affords still another parallel to swing. Baseball games, ranging from pickup scrimmages played by bands whose buses happened to cross paths on a highway on the Great Plains, to regulation games played in team uniforms, were a constant feature of big-band life. Harry James in particular took the sport with deadly seriousness and compiled an impressive record. 'We made baseball fields out of cow pastures all over the eastern part of the country,' according to a sideman. 'We would practice all day, barely making it to that night's job.' The two vocations had much in common, as Gene Krupa pointed out: 'the living out of suitcases, the constant time pressures to get to another place so that you can perform on schedule, the working with the same people every day, being watched all the time by the public, trying to live up to a reputation, and, of course, all the mental and emotional intangibles that must affect ballplayers just the way they affect musicians.'[2]

Moreover, both inspired a similar devotion among fans. 'Hundreds of thousands of youngsters (and adults too, for it is a provocative diversion) know the personnels of the leading swing bands as a baseball enthusiast knows the roster of every major-league club,' wrote an observer. To reach these audiences, both big band jazz and baseball required the new technology of the twentieth century – namely automobiles and radio – to assume what was to be their central role in the new culture of leisure apparent by the 1920s. Both galvanized their respective audiences through the force of personality: Ruth and Goodman, Robinson and Armstrong.[3] And both embodied the new sense of a transnational mass culture that was displacing a more localized, homegrown variety of cultural participation.

The parallel extends to the formal, ideological, and economic planes. In its choreographed symmetry, its balance of routine anonymous play alternating with moments of individual self-expression, baseball has much in common with swing. Both were performances within performances, in which spectators paid to watch professionals play. Both involved contestation, more subtle in swing, as different 'choirs' (brass or reeds) played off one another, or a soloist played against the ensemble as a batter would face a defensive alignment. Both required teamwork at a high level of precision, and a balancing of the individual and the collective. Swing, like baseball, is regarded as quintessentially American. Both collected a bewildering range of political meanings, were championed at different times by both the Communist Party and the U.S. government. Baseball's 'great experiment' of integration in the late 1940s has been cited as a watershed event in American race relations; swing performed a similar function a decade earlier. As jazz critic George Simon observed in 1947, when Jackie Robinson was struggling for acceptance with the Brooklyn Dodgers, the athlete's talents lay 'in an unfortunate field'; as a jazz musician, he would have been immediately accepted. In both cases the legacy of integration was mixed. 'Since Robinson's debut, blacks have done the same thing in Major League Baseball that they have done in popular music: entertain, make large salaries, and generate money for businesses that funnel precious little of it back into the black community,' observes Nelson George.[4] The same argument was made about integrated big bands in the early 1940s.

The central cultural link, however, is the New Deal, understood not as a collection of legislative initiatives and alphabet agencies but as a broad-based cultural movement. Swing did more than symbolize this movement; it participated in it in direct, material ways. Swing was the preeminent musical expression of the New Deal: a cultural form of 'the people,' accessible, inclusive, distinctively democratic, and thus distinctively American. Like the politics of Franklin Roosevelt, swing provided the ideological terrain for ethnic and regional inclusiveness on a scale unprecedented in American history. It emerged in a culture defined by shocks amid dislocations, divided by competing impulses toward political radicalism and social conservatism. Swing reflected those shocks and, as it evolved through the late 1940s, helped assuage them, producing a different kind of American culture in the process. To its proponents, swing was both proof and cause of an American society growing ever more egalitarian and progressive.

Among its performers and their audiences, swing attracted a previously unrecognized constituency similar in many ways to Roosevelt's new Democratic coalition of organized labor, urban white ethnics, African-Americans, intellectuals, and farmers. Linking people across racial, ethnic, class, and regional lines, swing seemed to embody the American melting pot. Not since the heyday of blackface minstrelsy in the decades before the Civil War had America been forced to confront so directly its indebtedness to African-American culture, to acknowledge that its culture was unmistakably formed by a racial group systematically excluded from its society. And in its alliance with the politics of the Popular Front after 1935, a highly visible sector of the swing community took part in a broad-based leftist coalition that sought to root itself in the American past and thereby define Americanism in its own terms.

Like the New Deal, swing also represented different and sometimes incompatible things to participants and observers. It struck proponents as the domain of healthy fun, critics as the source of hedonism and mindless exhibitionism eerily akin to the social effects of fascism. To some observers swing expressed escapism, a fantasy relief from economic hardship. To others it suggested the down-to-earth embrace of a reality obscured by much of the popular music that preceded swing. Like the New Deal, swing served to bridge polarities of race, of ideology, and of high and low culture. And like the New Deal, swing sometimes failed to fulfill its apparent promise in terms of actual social practice.

It was no coincidence that the big bands struggled and ultimately failed in the same postwar years that witnessed the ultimate fragmentation of the New Deal coalition. These centrifugal forces were reflected in various sectors: in the crisis faced by labor as it struggled with the challenges of congressional hostility, Red-baiting, and the renewed determination of business leaders; and in the travail of the Democratic Party, torn between the southern Dixiecrats and the Wallace progressives. These cleavages reflected comparable forces of race, ethnicity, geography, economics, demography, and technology. That they occurred at the same time and for similar reasons points to swing's cultural centrality. Its jazz-tradition successor, bebop, absorbed some of these ideological currents, producing an oppositional subculture whose politics of style were also rooted in swing.

Several metaphors already vie for the attention of those studying the Depression and war years. The figure of Roosevelt continues to loom over the period, and the New Deal, once almost synonymous with 'the Thirties,' still serves as a focal point. Broadening the field of inquiry to recover the experiences of larger numbers of people, historians have looked to expressive culture, especially movies and radio, for clues. Mickey Mouse, suggests Warren Susman, has superseded FDR as the central figure of the age. For others, the aesthetic of the documentary, expressed in journalism, photography, social science writing, fiction, and other popular culture genres, has been the defining cultural impulse.[5] A by-product of this cultural history is the tendency to ascribe psychological qualities to the decade. Susman and Lawrence Levine, for example, have identified strong currents of fear, shame, and guilt in 1930s culture as a consequence of unprecedented economic calamity. The postwar years have been linked to a mood of anxiety or doubt stemming from the technological forces unleashed by the war and by the new role of the United

States in the world.[6] In these accounts, historical periods are identified above all as states of mind, collective and individual.

To propose the notion of swing-shaped culture is not to discard these or other suggestive attempts to characterize the culture of the 1930s and 1940s. Swing is only one of an unlimited number of maps that can be drawn from the culture of the period, none of which is reducible to any other. But because it operated in so many domains, swing offers a particularly suggestive map. A broad-based, unified but heterogeneous social practice with its own trajectory of rise and decline, swing captures the dynamic of change and movement in the period. Like other forms of expressive culture, it encompassed a variety of ideologies and touched the lives of people from a range of ethnic, class, and regional backgrounds. But it was also a national phenomenon, materially anchored in the complex mass culture industry. A unified but heterogenous area of social practice, swing complicates our understanding of a period that has frequently lent itself to reduction and oversimplification.

Finally, swing offers a useful way of periodizing the years that can only awkwardly be labeled 'the 1930s and 1940s.' It stresses the continuities between these two decades rather than the abrupt rupture caused by the beginning of the Second World War. The war in fact marked the culmination of the swing aesthetic just as it represented the climax of other cultural movements of the 1930s. By highlighting the ideals that swing was supposed to embody, the war revealed the contradictions implicit in swing as ideology and as social practice. If 1948 was 'the last year of the Thirties,' as Michael Harrington has written, 'the very last moment when the philosophical preoccupations of the Great Depression were still primary,' it is fitting that swing enjoyed a final surge of popular enthusiasm that year, in the appropriately deceptive guise of bebop.[7]

Notes (edited)

1   For a full discussion of problems raised by the historical interpretation, see David W. Stowe, 'Historians, Homologies, and Music as Cultural Text,' paper presented at the annual meeting of the American Studies Association, Boston, November 1993.

2   Krupa quoted in George T. Simon, *The Big Bands* (New York: Schirmer Books, 1981), p. 21. See also Ira Gitler, *Swing to Bop: An Oral History of the Transition in Jazz in the 1940s* (New York: Oxford University Press, 1985), pp. 239–40.

3   Irving Kolodin, 'Number One Swing Man,' *Harper's* 179 (Sept. 1939), p. 433. In a special fiftieth-birthday issue on Louis Armstrong, *Down Beat's* editors compared him to Babe Ruth. *Down Beat*, July 14, 1950, p. 10.

4   Jules Tygiel, *Baseball's Great Experiment: Jackie Robinson and His Legacy* (New York: Oxford University Press, 1983). Nelson George, *The Death of Rhythm & Blues* (New York: Pantheon, 1988), pp. 57–8.

5   Warren I. Susman, *Culture as History: The Transformation of American Society in the Twentieth Century* (New York: Pantheon, 1984), p. 197; Alan Lawson, 'The Cultural Legacy of the New Deal,' in Havard Sitkoff, ed., *Fifty Years Later: The New Deal Evaluated* (New York: Knopf, 1985), pp. 155–81;

William Stott, *Documentary Expression in Thirties America* (New York: Oxford University Press, 1973).

6   Lawrence W. Levine, 'American Culture and the Great Depression,' in *The Unpredictable Past: Explorations in American Cultural History* (New York: Oxford University Press, 1993), pp. 206–30; Susman, *Culture as History*, pp. 193–209; William Graebner, *The Age of Doubt: American Thought and Culture in the 1940s* (Boston: Twayne Publishers, 1991).

7   Michael Harrington, *Fragments of the Century* (New York: Saturday Review Press, 1973), p. 64.

49 **Kathy J. Ogren** The significance of the jazz controversy for twenties America (1989)

Source: Kathy J. Ogren, 'Introduction: the significance of the jazz controversy for twenties America,' in *The Jazz Revolution: Twenties America and the Meaning of Jazz* (New York: Oxford University Press, 1989: 3–10).

> The Salvation Army of Cincinnati obtained a temporary injunction today to prevent the erection of a moving picture theatre adjoining the Catherine Booth Home for Girls, on the ground that music emanating from the theatre would implant 'jazz emotions' in the babies born at the home. The plaintiffs realize that they live in a jazz age declared the suit, ... 'But we are loathe to believe that babies born in the maternity hospital are to be legally subjected to the implanting of jazz emotions by such enforced proximity to a theater and a jazz palace.' (*New York Times*, 1926)

Nineteen-twenties readers of the *New York Times* would not have been surprised by the above item from Cincinnati, Ohio. Throughout the decade, the *Times* as well as other newspapers, recorded a growing controversy concerning the influence of jazz. Reports came not only from American cities, but also from Europe. Most of the articles documented fears about the spread of this new form of popular music. As suggested in the Cincinnati Salvation Army complaint, jazz was both a popular craze and a music used to describe the ambience or mood of the decade.

One can plausibly argue that the debate over jazz was just one of many that characterized American social discourse in the 1920s. Dualistic descriptive schemes seem to characterize best the major economic and social changes of the post-war era, and histories of the decade typically characterize it as a battle of opposites. On the one hand it was a 'return to normalcy' after World War I, and on the other hand, youthful, exuberant, and 'roaring.'

Certainly the end of the Great War marked the beginning of a troubled peace. The acrimonious fight over ratification of the League of Nations Treaty concluded with defeat for Woodrow Wilson's plan, and the nation wearily drifted towards increased isolation. American class and ethnic tensions had already been unleashed by wartime jingoism, which culminated in the Palmer Raids and Red Scare of 1917–20. America's civil liberties record was permanently scarred when nonconformists were harassed, and in some cases deported, on the bases of ethnic background or political conviction.[1]

American leftists and radicals found their organizations on the defensive following the political repression at home, despite the fact that 900,000 Americans voted for Socialist party candidate Eugene Debs in 1920. Similarly, American labor began the decade with a wave of strike activity – including the Seattle General Strike in support of the Russian Revolution in 1918 – but by the end of the 1920s, labor union membership fell from about 5 million in 1921 to less than 3.5 million in 1929. Returning veterans joined the ranks of the unemployed as demobilization slowed down the economy immediately following the war.

American race relations exploded in a series of urban riots stretching from East St. Louis in July 1917 through Charleston, S.C., Longview, Texas, Washington, D.C., and Chicago, in the 'Red Summer' of 1919. In all cases, racial violence was fueled by the competition for jobs between returning war veterans and black workers who had replaced them during the war. A number of factors contributed to the Great Migration of 500,000 blacks out of the South before and after World War I, although most were looking for relief from rural poverty and political repression. Black migrants were often optimistic about starting new lives in rapidly growing northern cities like New York and Chicago, but they resented the appalling overcrowding that was the result of residential segregation. When white vigilantes invaded black neighborhoods in the 1919 race riots, blacks held their ground to defend their hard-fought gains in the new urban 'meccas.'

Jazz histories have typically portrayed the 1917 closing of New Orleans's Storyville red light district by military officials as the main impetus behind the movement of jazz musicians to new jobs and audiences in northern cities. In fact, musicians were part of the general migration and several of them witnessed the race riots since they made their living in the entertainment districts located in segregated black neighborhoods. The war itself most directly affected those musicians who were drafted or had enlisted in the army and performed in military bands.

For many Americans, these political, racial, and social conflicts appeared to wane with the growth of a strong economy – prompting some to point to the elections of Republicans Warren G. Harding and Calvin Coolidge as cause for celebration. Presumably, American voters who supported Coolidge also endorsed his philosophy: 'brains are wealth and wealth is the chief end of man' and the 'business of America is business,' when they gave the Republicans landslide victories in 1920 and 1924.

Many economic indicators did point to unprecedented prosperity. Industrial production boomed and the gross national product rose 40%. The expanded availability of consumer products like automobiles, electrical appliances, radios, and telephones indicated the importance of consumer spending in this 'second industrial revolution,' with affluent Americans receiving the greatest benefits. This revolution in consumption patterns directly affected blues and jazz musicians because their music was disseminated to a larger audience as a result of the expanded availability of their music on radio and phonograph recordings.

The audience for jazz was inadvertently stimulated when Congress passed the Volstead Act, which banned the manufacture and sale of alcoholic beverages, in 1919. Nightclub and entertainment venues that provided an escape from Prohibition were common locations for jazz performance. Clubs like Chicago's Club Alabam or Harlem's famed Cotton Club flourished when sophisticated urbanites consumed good music, food, and drink and danced to the latest musical fad. These establishments were often tied to bootlegging rings, like Al Capone's, and as a consequence many performers found themselves on a gangster's payroll. Jazz was immediately associated with the carnal pleasures of the cabaret.

Prohibition advocates often justified their campaign on the grounds that they were preserving 'traditional' American values. Religious fundamentalists joined the anti-saloon agitators in denouncing modernism, the growth of science, immigration, and urbanization as symbols of moral decay. The 1925 legal battle between William Jennings Bryan and Clarence Darrow over John Scopes's right to teach evolution in a Tennessee school turned the modernist versus fundamentalist clash into a national spectacle. The argument over jazz split down similar lines.[2]

Exhortations of fundamentalists fell on ears supposedly deafened by the exciting sounds and sights of the jazz band. The attractiveness of urban nightlife was embraced by American youth in revolt against what they saw as stuffy prewar society, and their critique joined that of young intellectual dissenters who published an alternative set of beliefs that they hoped would challenge the general confidence in commercial values. Writers and critics like Malcolm Cowley and Ernest Hemingway chose to exile themselves from America and eschew its materialism, gentility, and parochialism. Labeled the 'lost generation' by Gertrude Stein, these and other nonconformists registered their resistance to American society through artistic experimentation and the hedonistic pursuit of dancing, drinking, fast cars, and sexual freedom. For them, the newest musical sensation – jazz – became the specific symbol of rebellion and of what was new about the decade.[3]

The centrality of jazz in our historical memory is neither an accident nor a facile convention derived from the 'roaring twenties' stereotype. Jazz and its practitioners were directly affected by or participated themselves in major changes taking place in the teens and 1920s. Although the partisans in the jazz controversy sometimes drew on the other arguments that raged in the 1920s, the music itself and the circumstances under which it was performed embodied social change. The Cincinnati Salvation Army's injunction sounds comical today, but the debate over jazz should not be dismissed as trivial argument. Americans shared a common perception that jazz had transforming qualities that could last beyond the time of a song and the space of a cabaret act. For many Americans, to argue about jazz was to argue about the nature of change itself.

Jazz was indeed a powerful new music, characterized by syncopation, polyrhythms, improvisation, blue tonalities, and a strong beat. It rose to popularity amidst strident criticism and extravagant praise. Detractors criticized jazz's musical characteristics – unless they dismissed it as noise – and its origins in lower-class black culture. Jazz lovers hailed the same sounds as everything from exciting entertainment to an antidote for repressive industrial society.

Americans on all sides of the jazz debate found the music symbolic of fundamental – and provocative – changes they were experiencing in the maturing post-World War I urban and industrial society. The music represented the end of an earlier era and the transition to a modern one. The renowned conductor Leopold Stokowski predicted:

> Jazz has come to stay because it is an expression of the times, of the breathless, energetic, superactive times in which we are living, it is useless to fight against it ... America's contribution to the music of the past will have the same revivifying effect as the injection of new, and in the larger sense, vulgar blood into dying aristocracy ... The Negro musicians of America are playing a great part in this change. The jazz players make their instruments do entirely new things, things finished musicians are taught to avoid. They are pathfinders into new realms.[4]

Stokowski was joined by hundreds of thousands of other participants in jazz performance – all of whom found in the music a voice with which they acknowledged, celebrated and coped with change.

What is striking about the jazz controversy is that jazz communicated change across vast racial and cultural dividing lines, despite its development from a participatory and distinct black musical culture. Jazz performance in the twenties may well have played a role in what anthropologist Victor Turner describes as 'public reflexivity' in which a group 'communicates itself to itself.'[5] In the case of jazz, this process is particularly interesting since it was a music most closely identified with blacks and entertainers – two social groups often labeled marginal – yet it helped white Americans with diverse social backgrounds explain their world. 'Jazz emotions' did indeed seem to penetrate physical – and social – barriers.

The ability of jazz to represent change in the 1920s is best reconstructed through social and cultural analysis that locates jazz performance in its historical context. Jazz was related to several patterns of oral and musical performance particular to Afro-American culture. As such, it emerged from a cultural tradition that literary critic Houston Baker has called an Afro-American vernacular composed of the 'material conditions of slavery in the United States and the rhythms of Afro-American blues which combined and emerged from ... an ancestral matrix that has produced a forceful and indigenous American creativity.'[6]

When black audiences and performers migrated to urban centers they hastened the spread of blues and jazz. Black Americans found, in turn, new performance environments and commercial markets for electrically and mechanically reproduced jazz that catapulted the vernacular into a national rage. Beginning in the 1920s, many Americans identified jazz not only as a popular music they loved but also as a symbol of the nation's coming of 'jazz age' in a modern world.

Listening and dancing to jazz was not, therefore, merely, an entertaining pastime. Despite commercialization and exposure to new audiences, jazz maintained the participatory qualities of its origins. The rich exchange between performers and their audiences became a definitive feature of jazz entertainment and is the key to understanding the larger drama of the jazz controversy.

Although this study is aimed at improving our understanding of the jazz controversy – and our assessment of the cultural significance of jazz – I do not begin with the controversy. Instead, I first describe the social and cultural milieus in which jazz appeared, giving special attention to form and content in performance. My reasons for this approach are partly methodological – I am intrigued by the difficulties and rewards of trying to analyze the context and meaning of past performances. But I also have substantive reasons. It was the expressive quality of jazz that made it controversial. Although critics projected their own fears and values on it, they could not have done so had it not had striking social and musical characteristics, if, in other words, it had not been played in certain places and in certain ways. By themselves, those characteristics of jazz performance say something about cultural change. But they also lead to my end point, which is a remarkable debate about jazz and – ultimately – about America in the 1920s.

Reconstructing jazz performances in the early twentieth century poses several problems. Jazz music provides a valuable but elusive primary source because written scores reveal little about how a piece of music sounded to its audience. In the case of jazz, performances are often notated after they have been played and simply reflect what a transcriber thought the musicians actually did at any particular moment. Studio recordings from the twenties preserve some wonderful performances, but the recording technology was rudimentary and many performers were either never recorded or recorded inadequately. In any case, recordings usually cannot capture the excitement of live music. It is especially difficult to reconstruct the interaction between audience and performers without live recordings of the sort only possible with present-day technology.

Nevertheless, a performance history of early jazz can be reconstructed by combining the many fine musicological studies of classical jazz with an analysis of how the experiences of performers changed at the turn of the century, how the locations and settings of live performances influenced performers and musical entertainment. The experience of jazz performance can be reconstructed not only from print media, secondary sources, and jazz recordings but also from business and trade publications relevant to the broadcasting and recording industries. The perspective of performers is well documented in biographies, autobiographies, and a growing number of oral histories.

This study, which is based on both traditional and newly appreciated sources, treats the years in which the controversy emerged, 1890–1930. It focuses primarily on the cities most identified with jazz: New Orleans, Chicago, and New York, and secondarily on locations like Kansas City, Los Angeles, and San Francisco. Jazz was played in many other locales, but these were the leading urban centers for jazz performance.

Jazz virtuoso Sidney Bechet understood well the power of jazz performance to symbolize changing American life. 'My story goes a long way back,' wrote Bechet in his autobiography *Treat It Gentle*, 'It goes further back than I had anything to do with. My music is like that ... I got it from something inherited just like the stories my father gave down to me.' Bechet's music never belonged exclusively to him, and he described how the improvisational dynamic between an individual performer's skill and the community created a musical road open to many travelers:

> The music, it's that road. There's good things alongside it, and there's miseries. You stop by the way and you can't ever be sure what you're going to find waiting. But the music itself, the road itself – there's no stopping that. It goes on all the time. It's the thing that brings you to everything else. You have to trust that.'[7]

Jazz was controversial because it symbolized the changing and often contradictory character of American entertainment. Bechet's jazz road was paved with Afro-American participatory musical traditions, and in the 1920s that represented the transience and transformations of modern American life.

Notes (edited)

1   A standard interpretation of pre- and post-World War I changes in sensibility is Henry May, *The End of American Innocence: A Study of the First Years of Our Own Time, 1912–1917* (Chicago: Quadrangle Books, 1959). May is interested in establishing the context in the prewar years for postwar changes. His model of a battle between traditionalists and moderns also characterized Neil Leonard's fine study of the jazz controversy: *Jazz and the White Americans: The Acceptance of a New Art Form* (Chicago: University of Chicago Press, 1962). Leonard's new study, *Jazz: Myth and Religion* (New York: Oxford University Press, 1987), puts his earlier work in a larger and different context that sees jazz as part of a spiritual quest. Macdonald Smith Moore's study of the arguments over turn-of-the-century music, *Yankee Blues: Musical Culture and American Identity* (Bloomington: University of Indiana Press, 1985), likewise studies discussions by composers seeking to redeem American culture through genteel aesthetic standards. Entertainment histories by Lewis A. Erenberg, *Steppin' Out: New York Nightlife and the Transformation of American Culture* (Chicago: University of Chicago Press, 1981) and John Kasson,

Amusing the Million: Coney Island at the Turn of the Century (New York: Hill and Wang, 1978), both describe changes in leisure time activities that encouraged the relaxation of genteel Victorian moral codes prior to World War I. In jazz itself, many of the musical characteristics that made it sound novel were present in its precursors: ragtime and blues.

2   See William E. Leuchtenburg, *The Perils of Prosperity, 1914–1932* (Chicago: University of Chicago Press, 1958), 204–24, on the decade generally; and Neil Leonard, *Jazz and the White Americans,* on jazz specifically.

3   See Malcolm Cowley, *Exile's Return* (New York: Viking, 1956), on the lost generation.

4   Leopold Stokowski is quoted in J. A. Rogers, 'Jazz at Home,' in *The New Negro,* ed. Alain Locke (New York: Atheneum, 1975), 221–2. See also 'Stokowski Declares in Favor of Jazz,' *Musical Leader* 47 (April, 24, 1924).

5   See Victor Turner, 'Frame, Flow, and Reflection: Ritual and Drama as Public Liminality,' in Michael Benamou and Charles Caramello (eds), *Performers in Post-Modern Culture* (Madison, Wisc.: Coda Press, 1977), 33–5.

6   Houston Baker, *Blues, Ideology, and Afro-American Literature* (Chicago: University of Chicago Press, 1984), 2.

7   Sidney Bechet, *Treat It Gentle* (New York: Hill and Wang, 1980), 5.

50 **Neil Leonard** Acceptance of jazz in the twenties (1962)

Source: Neil Leonard, 'Acceptance of jazz in the twenties,' in *Jazz and the White Americans: The Acceptance of a New Art Form* (Chicago: University of Chicago Press, 1962: 55–64, 65) (excerpts).

Among those young whites of the twenties who either ignored or were in open revolt against traditional values, the new jazz musicians were the most rebellious. Take, for example, the best-known group of white midwestern jazz men whom we shall loosely call Chicagoans. Four of them have written autobiographies which reflect four gradations of repudiation of traditional norms. The most rebellious was clarinetist Milton (Mezz) Mezzrow. For him jazz was sacred, and his rejection of traditional standards was so vehement that he self-consciously gave up his ties with the white world and moved into a Negro community. At the other extreme was clarinetist Benny Goodman, who learned to play jazz in a poor section of town but at the same time mastered traditional musical techniques and disciplines and maintained an air of respectability. Between these two extremes were guitarist Eddie Condon and pianist Hoagy Carmichael. Goodman's book is largely anecdotal and deals only briefly with his early experiences in Chicago. But the books of Mezzrow,

Carmichael, and Condon,[1] in spite of naïveté, exaggeration, and occasional foolishness, clarify the thoughts and feelings of the white jazz men of the twenties.

For young white jazz men like the Chicagoans, jazz was a voice of rebellion. As Hoagy Carmichael explained, 'The first World War had been fought, and in the back-wash conventions had tumbled. There was rebellion then, against the accepted, and the proper and the old ... The shooting war was over but the rebellion was just getting started. And for us jazz articulated ... It said what we wanted to say though what that was we might not know.'[2] Members of the 'Austin High Gang,' who came from comfortable middle-class families in Chicago's West Side (all but one of them had discarded a violin for an instrument more appropriate in a jazz band), considered their music parallel to criticism they found in Mencken's *American Mercury*. Mezz Mezzrow, who frequently played with them, described their feelings as follows: 'Their jazz was ... collectively improvised nose-thumbing at all pillars of all communities, one big syncopated Bronx cheer for the righteous squares everywhere. Jazz was the only language they could find to preach their fire-eating message.'[3]

While the Chicagoans accorded composers of academic music – particularly modern ones – respectful silence or outright admiration, most of them rebelled against the formal techniques, procedures, and discipline they associated with traditional academic music. 'When you come right down to it,' argued Mezzrow extravagantly, 'what brought about the whole change in American music? What spread the gospel of jazz far and wide across the country, pulling at least one part of our native music free at last from European influences? It was the rebel in us. Our rebel instincts broke music away from what I'd call the handcuff-and-straitjacket discipline of the classical school, so creative artists could get up on the stand and speak out in their own honest and self-inspired language again.'[4] Although academic musical training did not necessarily ruin a jazz musician, it often did him no good. Jazz requires the ability to improvise, but many academic and commercial jazz men either could not improvise at all or failed to equal the accomplishments of the true jazz man when they tried. Benny Goodman showed the jazz man's disdain for traditionalists' inability to improvise and for the importance they gave to reading music: 'If a fellow happened to be a good legitimate [traditionally trained] trumpet man or a swell straight clarinet player, he might get credit for being a fine musician who could read a part upside down at sight, but we didn't pay much attention to them [sic].'[5] Other Chicagoans joked about traditional musical norms. When Eddie Condon was teaching himself to play the banjo, his father told him, 'You are terrible and you can't read music.' Condon replied, 'What's that got to do with being a musician?'[6] And when one member of a group of Chicagoans known as the 'Wolverines' (only two of their original eight members could read music) suggested that the band use written arrangements, another member disposed of the idea by asking, 'What would we do if the lights went out?'[7]

The Chicagoans first found jazz on records, and some of these men indiscriminately received the commercial outpourings of, say, Ted Lewis, with the same enthusiasm they did real jazz. But their preferences soon galvanized around bands such as the Original Dixieland Jazz Band or the New Orleans

Rhythm Kings, bands made up of whites whose style was close to that of the Negro jazz men. The trail eventually led to Negroes. The Chicagoans learned of colored artists through records and went to the South Side to hear or to play with them. Elsewhere, young musicians, who would later join the Chicagoans, also imbibed jazz and its esthetic values. In Indianapolis, having been expelled from high school, Hoagy Carmichael learned to play the piano by listening to a Negro pianist, Reggie Duval. Carmichael recalls the following conversation:

> What are you doing there?
> I bring my thumb down, like that, [explained Duval] I dunno it just makes it.
> You bring your thumb down on the chord right after you've hit it with your right hand [Carmichael said].
> Yeah, [answered Duval], I want that harmony to *holler* ... [Italics Carmichael's throughout].
> I want it so it sounds right to *me.* And that is the way it sounds rightest.
> It's wonderful [declared Carmichael].
> Naw but it's *right* [Duval answered]. Never play anything that ain't *right.* You may not make any money but you'll never get hostile with yourself.[8]

The young Chicago musicians and their future associates found in jazz not only a voice of rebellion but also a rich esthetic experience which helped fill the vacuum left by the rejection of traditional or other values inherited from their parents. Eddie Condon wrote of the first time he heard the Negro cornetists, King Oliver and Louis Armstrong, play together on Chicago's South Side: 'It was hypnosis at first hearing. Everyone was playing what he wanted to play and it was all mixed together as if someone had planned it with a set of micrometer calipers; notes I had never heard were peeling off the edges and dropping through the middle; there was a tone from the trumpets like warm rain on a cold day. Freeman and McPartland [two other Chicagoans] and I were immobilized; the music poured into us like daylight down a dark hole.'[9] Hoagy Carmichael recalls upon hearing Bix Beiderbecke and the Wolverines, 'Boy, he took it! Just four notes ... But he didn't blow them – he hit 'em like a mallet hits a chime – and his tone, the richness ... Whatever it was he ruined me. I got up from the piano and staggered over and fell on the davenport.'[10]

Such experiences created a strong fraternal understanding among young jazz men. They felt that they had something important that the rest of the world should recognize. Carmichael recalls the following reaction upon first hearing Louis Armstrong: ' "Why," I moaned, "why isn't everybody in the world here to hear that?" I meant it. Something as unutterably stirring as that should be heard by the world.'[11] But other Americans did not hear jazz this way. Some resisted its diffusion – sometimes vehemently – and others who had partially or half-heartedly strayed from orthodox norms accepted traditional popular music or the commercial dilutions of jazz but ignored or disliked jazz itself. It was, in short, a musician's music, which had only a handful of lay enthusiasts.

As a result of public scorn or lack of interest white jazz men took a pessimistic view of their audience. Cornetist Jimmy McPartland showed this pessimism in speaking about a recording session, 'We started kidding around and playing corny. Out comes the recording manager from his booth, and he says, "That's it. You gotta do that". So we sort of used the "St. Louis" chord progressions and blew all this cod [*sic*] Dixie, and we called the number "Shirt Tail Stomp." It sold more than any of the others; or I should say it sold the rest of the sides because it was corny. It shows the taste of people; still the same, I guess, the world over.'[12] Other Chicagoans were more disturbed. 'What's the use, Milton?' Mezzrow recalls clarinetist Frank Teschmacher saying, 'You knock yourself out making a great new music for the people, and they treat you like some kind of plague or blight, like you were offering them leprosy instead of art, and you wind up in the poor house or the asylum.'[13]

The fact that not only jazz but its practitioners were rejected or not recognized by the respectable world heightened their sense of brotherhood. 'The result of this [rejection],' explained Benny Goodman, 'was that musicians who played hot [real jazz] were pretty much of a clique by themselves. They hung around in the same places, made the same spots after work, drank together and worked together whenever they had the chance ... None of us had much use for what was known then, and probably always will be, as "commercial musicians." '[14] Mezzrow wrote, 'If you could catch a couple of cats [jazz musicians or enthusiasts] that just met each other talking about certain musicians they know or humming a riff or two to each other, before you could call a preacher they'd be practically married ... Jazz musicians were looked down on by the so-called respectable citizens as though they were toads that crawled out from under a rock, bent on doing evil. We could roam around town for weeks without digging [seeing] another human who even knew what we were talking about.'[15] And drummer Dave Tough said, 'We jazz players are supposed to be vulgarians beyond the moral as well as the musical pale; I guess we might as well live up to what is expected of us.'[16]

At the heart of the jazz musician's behavior was an absorption in esthetic experience which made the new music their main source of happiness and morality.[17] Speaking of the time he first heard Bix Beiderbecke, Hoagy Carmichael wrote, 'Those four notes that Bix played meant more to me than everything else in the books. When Bix opened his soul to me that day, I learned and experienced one of life's innermost secrets to happiness – pleasure that it had taken a whole lifetime of living and conduct to achieve in full.'[18] Mezzrow declared, 'Every time I got in trouble, it was because I strayed away from the music. Whenever I latched on solid to the music, I flew right. I was beginning to sense a heap of moral in all this.'[19]

Jazz men lived primarily for 'kicks' in music but by extension also in other activities. While the stereotype of the jazz man as a drunkard or dope addict was and is false, the incidence of indulgence in drink and drugs among jazz men was higher than among most Americans in their sex and age group.[20] For those who indulged, dope and liquor removed inhibitions and provided stimulation, confidence, and ease helpful to the creation of jazz. Carmichael describes the influence of marijuana and liquor on him while listening to Louis Armstrong: 'Then the muggles [marijuana] took effect and my body got light. Every note Louis hit was perfection. I ran to the piano and took the place of Louis's wife. They swung into "Royal Garden Blues." I had never heard the tune before but somehow I knew every note. I couldn't miss. I was floating in a strange deep-blue whirlpool of jazz. It wasn't the marijuana. The muggles and gin were, in a way, stage props. It was the music. The music took me and had me and it made me right.'[21] Mezzrow's first taste of marijuana affected him in much the same way. 'I found I was slurring much better and putting just the right feeling into my phrases – I was really coming on. All the notes came easing out of my horn like they'd already been made up, greased and stuffed into the bell, so all I had to do was blow a little and send them on their way ... I felt I could go on playing for years without running out of ideas and energy ... I began to feel very happy and sure of myself.'[22]

Autobiographies of white jazz men in the twenties are full of examples of living for 'kicks.' Sometimes kicks took the form of normal adolescent pranks. Benny Goodman tells about an incident in the Ben Pollack band: 'For a while ... we had been trying to cook up a gag on Ben, and finally somebody got the idea of smearing limburger cheese on the inside of Pollack's megaphone. Harry [Goodman] was delegated to do the job ... When the time came, Pollack picked up his megaphone and put it up to his face, then suddenly got a whiff of this stuff. He made a horrible face ... Everybody thought Harry had done a wonderful job, until we picked up our megaphones to sing, and discovered that he had given the same dose to us.'[23] Sometimes kicks went beyond this sort of horseplay as the following quotation from Mezzrow indicates:

> I brought the record [Louis Armstrong's 'Heebie Jeebies'] home to play for the gang, and man, they all fell through the ceiling. Bud, Dave and Tesch almost wore it out by playing it over and over until we knew the whole thing by heart. Suddenly, about two in the A.M., Tesch jumped to his feet, his sad pan all lit up for once, and yelled, 'Hey, listen you guys, I got an idea! This is something Bix should hear right away! Let's go out to Hudson Lake and give him the thrill of his life!'
>
> A scramble was on, and it was most mad, old man. Bix was fifty miles away, but we were all half-way down the stairs before Tesch's chops got together again. We drove every which-away in that green monster of mine (that's what the boys called my chariot) and started off like gangbusters for Hudson Lake, a summer resort where Bix, Pee Wee Russell and Frankie Trumbauer were playing with Gene Goldkette's Greystone Dance Orchestra. All the way there we kept chanting Louis' weird riffs, while I kept the car zigzagging like a roller-coaster to mark the explosions ...
>
> It was three in the morning when we busted into the yard-dog's stash that Bix and Pee Wee used for a cottage. Jim, the funk [stench] in that dommy was so thick you could cut it with a butterknife, and them cats had the whole insect population of Indiana for their roommates ...
>
> Pee Wee and Bix shared a small room off the kitchen that would have made any self-respecting porker turn up his snout and walk away. They slept in their clothes most of the time ... The first thing they did when they unglued their lamps each day was to reach for the gallon of corn that always leaned against the bedpost and wash out their mouths. Those cats used corn mash like it was Lavoris. Whenever you tipped into their room you had to pile through big stacks of empty sardine and baked-bean cans; those two canned delicacies made up the whole menu of this establishment. The backporch was loaded with thirty or forty quarts of milk, some of them over

a month old ...

That morning, as soon as we grabbed those cats out of their pads and played *Heebie Jeebies* for them, they all fractured their wigs. 'Ha! Hal Ha!' Bix kept chuckling as the record played over and over, and his long bony arms beat out the breaks, flailing through the air like the blades of a threshing machine. He never did get over Louis' masterpiece. Soon as it was over he grabbed it from the machine and tore out of the house, to wake up everybody he knew around Hudson Lake and make them listen to it ...

Anyhow, on this particular night, like all the other times we visited him, Bix sat at that beat-up piano for hours, sometimes making our kind of music and sometimes drifting off into queer harmony patterns that the rest of us couldn't dig. The rest of the world melted away; we were the last men left on earth, skidding on a giant billiard-ball across a green felt vacuum with no side-pockets, while Bix crouched over his keyboard in a trance, barleycorned and brooding, tickling bizarre music out of the ivories.[24]

Despite apparent exaggerations, this account illustrates the musician's single-minded interest in their music and their tendency to ignore or affront considerations that concerned traditionalists; it shows their habit of living for kicks both in music and in unusual experiences; and it demonstrates their willingness to tolerate almost anything in an environment that did not interfere with playing or listening to jazz. The sharing of all these inclinations helped to unify the jazz fraternity.

Jazz men's unconventional use of language further tended to bind them together and separate them from traditional values. They employed a private or semi-private slang in everyday speech. This included words or phrases like 'get off,' 'change,' 'lick,' 'cut,' 'ride,' 'sock,' 'solid,' 'jam,' 'fake' – all with unorthodox meanings.[25] Another unconventional type of language was scat vocal which contained nonsense syllables that had no meaning for people outside of the jazz fraternity. Take, for example, the second chorus of 'Heebie Jeebies' by Louis Armstrong.

> Eef, gaff, mmff, dee-bo, dee-la-bahm,
> Rip-rip, de-do-de-da-do, do-de-da-de-da-doe,
> Ba-dode-do-do, ba-ro-be-do-be-do,
> Geef-gaf, gee-bap-be-da-de-do, d-da-do,
> Rip-dip-do-dum, so come on down, do that dance,
> They call the heebie jeebies dance, sweet mammo,
> Poppa's got to do the heebie jeebies dance.[26]

Still another sort of language of the jazz men resembled Dada usage. For example, the following quatrain by Hoagy Carmichael's fellow-musician, Bill Moenkhaus:

> If castor oil removes a boil
> And Oscar rows a goat
> Don't use your feet on shredded wheat
> Inhale it through a boat.[27]

Or, the first lines of a story by the same author: 'Once upon a time, during an extra horse, Silo McRunt, age thirteen, tried to count up to his mother. His actions were noticed by his wet neighbor (a mere bacon fanner by trade) who had just defeated his breakfast.'[28]

While these utterances said little or nothing to most people, they held meaning for the initiated and played a part in the jazz men's rebellion against the traditional culture. Mezzrow considered the musician's slang a form of protest,[29] and Carmichael thought of Moenkhaus' Dada-like expressions as complaints against conventional society.[30] Moreover, unconventional language served as part of a ritual and a means of identification within the brotherhood ...

The jazz man was a specialist in one type of musical communication, but since he was usually untutored in traditional esthetics he was, as William Cameron suggests,[31] unable to translate his feelings into conventional symbols and he could communicate his musical, and to a lesser extent his verbal, sentiments only to persons who already understood his esthetic world. He resorted to unconventional language because he knew no other words to express his feelings. The language helped cement the unity of the jazz fraternity in the face of an indifferent or hostile world.

Notes

1   The books are: Benny Goodman and Irving Kolodin, *The Kingdom of Swing* (New York, 1939); Eddie Condon and Thomas Sugrue, *We Called It Music* (New York, 1947); Hoagy Carmichael, *The Stardust Road* (New York, 1946); Milton Mezzrow and Bernard Wolfe, *Really the Blues* (New York, 1946).

2   Carmichael, *Stardust Road,* pp. 7–8.

3   Mezzrow and Wolfe, *Really the Blues,* pp. 103–4.

4   *Ibid.,* pp. 125, 127.

5   Goodman and Kolodin, *Kingdom of Swing,* p. 101.

6   Condon and Sugrue, *We Called It Music,* p. 62.

7   E. J. Nichols, 'Bix Beiderbecke,' in Frederic Ramsey, Jr. and Charles Edward Smith (eds.), *Jazzmen* (New York, 1939), pp. 151–52, and insert at pp. 128–29.

8   Carmichael, *Stardust Road,* p. 17.

9   Condon and Sugrue, *We Called It Music,* p. 107.

10   Carmichael, *Stardust Road,* pp. 6–7.

11   *Ibid.,* p. 53.

12   Nat Shapiro and Nat Hentoff (eds.), *Hear Me Talkin' to Ya* (New York, 1955), p. 279.

13   Mezzrow and Wolfe, *Really the Blues,* p. 110.

14   Goodman and Kolodin, *Kingdom of Swing,* p. 101.

15   Mezzrow and Wolfe, *Really the Blues,* p. 61.

16   Condon and Sugrue, *We Called It Music,* p. 110.

17   This idea was suggested by William B. Cameron, 'Sociological Notes on the Jam Session,' *Social Forces,* XXXIII (1954), 181.

18   Barry Ulanov, *History of Jazz in America* (New York, 1952), pp. 130–31.

19   Mezzrow and Wolfe, *Really the Blues,* p. 182.

20   See Cameron, 'Sociological Notes on the Jam Session,' p. 181.

21   Carmichael, *Stardust Road,* p. 53.

22 Mezzrow and Wolfe, *Really the Blues,* pp. 72–73.
23 Goodman and Kolodin, *Kingdom of Swing,* p. 97.
24 Mezzrow and Wolfe, *Really the Blues,* pp. 120–24; Condon confirms Mezzrow's description of life at Hudson Lake in his own account of a visit there, Condon and Sugrue, *We Called It Music,* pp. 138–39.
25 H. Brook Webb, 'The Slang of Jazz,' *American Speech,* XII (1937), 179–84, contains a glossary of jazz slang; for another glossary and some questionable material on the subject see Mezzrow and Wolfe, *Really the Blues,* pp. 216–28, 354–60.
26 Okeh recording 8300.
27 Carmichael, *Stardust Road,* p. 40.
28 *Ibid.,* p. 105.
29 Mezzrow and Wolfe, *Really the Blues,* pp. 222–23.
30 Carmichael, *Stardust Road,* p. 143.
31 Cameron, 'Sociological Notes on the Jam Session,' pp. 179, 180.

51 **Morroe Berger** Jazz: Resistance to the diffusion of a culture-pattern (1947)

Source: Morroe Berger, 'Jazz: resistance to the diffusion of a culture-pattern,' *Journal of Negro History,* XXXII (January, 1947): 461 (excerpt). (Reprinted in Nanry, *American Music* [1971]: 11–43.)

The purpose of this paper is to examine the implications, for the diffusion of jazz, of the fact that the Negroes, with whom jazz is correctly associated, are a low-status group in the United States. The evidence to be presented will confirm the hypothesis that in the diffusion process the prestige of the donors has considerable bearing on the way in which a borrowing group reacts to cultural traits of other groups. Thus mere exposure to certain influences does not insure acceptance of them.

From this hypothesis and the fact of the Negroes' inferior status, the following facts may be expected to follow:

1 Leaders and representatives of the white community, especially those who concern themselves with 'public morality' and education, opposed the acceptance of jazz music and the dances accompanying it. The basic reason for this opposition is the identification of jazz with crime, vice and greater sexual freedom than is countenanced by the common rules of morality. Certain leaders among the Negroes could be expected to take a similar position.

2 The musicians (and those on the periphery of the profession) associated with 'classical' music and forms of popular music other than jazz, also

opposed the introduction of jazz, since it was produced by musicians who were not educated in the familiar tradition, and did not conform to rules of public conduct developed by centuries of the concert stage.

3 The white South did not accept jazz to the same degree as the white North, since in the South the Negro is in a lower status-position than in the North.

4 Throughout the United States, jazz was not so readily accepted as other forms of Negro music, especially spirituals, since they are associated with religious fervor and, in the eyes of white persons at least, show the Negro in a submissive rather than exuberant role.

A review of the relevant data will show that each of the four implications is correct.

52 Alan P. Merriam and Raymond W. Mack
The jazz community (1960)

Source: Alan P. Merriam and Raymond W. Mack, 'The jazz community,' *Social Forces*, 38, 3 (March, 1960: 211, 213, 218) (excerpts).

The literature on jazz, which has grown enormously in recent years, consists in the main of biographies of jazz musicians, record reviews, and analysis of the music itself. Relatively little attention has been devoted to the study of social groups in jazz and, with some exceptions, what literature exists is primarily descriptive and widely scattered. It is our intention ... to present a factual description of what we shall call the jazz community. The available literature, as well as our own empirical observation, suggests that this is organized along well-developed lines which reveal specific behavioral patterns. We are dealing, then, with a number of people who share an occupational ideology and participate in a set of expected behaviors. We use the term community here not to denote a group with a geographic locus, but in the sense of a community of interest; what is implied by the word is that the people described here share a set of norms which in turn define roles for them.

The community to be analyzed is that set of people who share an interest in jazz, and who share it at a level of intensity such that they participate to some extent in the occupational role and ideology of the professional jazz musician. They learn and accept at least some of the norms which are peculiar to the jazz musician: norms regarding proper and improper language, good and bad music, stylish and unstylish clothing, acceptable and unacceptable audience behavior, and so on.

One special feature of the jazz community is the extreme identification with and participation in the occupational ideology of the jazz musician by his public. Unlike the fans, buffs, or publics of other occupational groups, the jazz musician's public contains some huge, unknown proportion of members who are former professional musicians, or amateurs of varying levels of real or fancied competence. A man who can play one set of three chords in the key of C can linger at a ringside table and imagine himself sitting in with Count Basie's band. This possibility for empathy undoubtedly helps to account for the degree of identification which welds the jazz musician and his public together into a group.

The specific character which sets the jazz community apart from all other occupational groups, then, is that not only do the professionals constitute a group, but their public is included in it. This is not to say, of course, that there are not cliques and inner circles of hierarchical nature within this broad social grouping, but rather that the occupational professional people and their public are set off as a relatively closely-knit group which shares behaviors and the results of those behaviors in common and in contradistinction to people outside the group. More than this, these common behaviors are recognized by members of the community and provide a means of entrance to the jazz group wherever the individual finds himself. Thus, once oriented in a strange location, a member of the jazz community can always find other members who share his own behaviors as well as general tastes, attitudes, beliefs, pleasures, and values.

While the jazz community is characterized by a number of distinctive behavior patterns, almost without exception these tend to cluster around one central theme – the isolation of the group from society at large, an isolation which is at once psychological, social, and physical ... This sense of isolation and self-segregation ... marks the outlook of the jazz musician and that of his admirers as well; it is the primary characteristic of the jazz community.

The underlying causes of this attitude of rejection of the normal world can be summarized under three major headings: (1) the rejection of jazz and the jazz musician by the general public; (2) the fact that the jazz musician, whether by choice or not, is isolated from the public by the nature of his occupation, as is his group of admirers as well since it associates with the musician; and (3) by the nature of his occupation, the musician (and his public by association) is faced with a dilemma regarding the nature of his art and, in his own view, is expected to be both a creative artist and a commercial entertainer, contradictory roles which lead to confusion in respect to status ... [There follows a discussion of these three major 'problems' or 'factors.']

These three major points, then, summarize the basic causes for the rejection of the normal world, the self-segregation and isolation of the jazz musician: (1) the rejection of jazz and the jazz musician by the general public because of the connotations which have grown up in connection with it, as well as its potential threat, in psychological terms, to the white culture; (2) the nature of the profession of jazz which physically isolates the musician from society, which is uncertain, which usually involves early recruitment and thus lack of formal education, and which is associated with protest and revolt; and (3) the nature of the artistic product and the necessity for earning a living which are contradictory in themselves and which lead to confusion and, again, to isolation.

These general points apply to the jazz musician specifically, but in most respects they apply to his knowledgeable audience as well. If this audience cannot itself participate in the creation of music, it can, and does, accept the basic attitudes and behaviors which characterize the jazz musician's actions and take them for its own. Thus, while there must always be internal divisions, the jazz community is characterized by its general attitude of isolation from and rejection of the standards and behaviors of the public at large, and this dominating theme is shared by the musician and his public.

53 **Amiri Baraka** Where's the music going and why? (1987)

Source: Amiri Baraka, 'Where's the music going and why?', in Amiri Baraka and Amina Baraka, *The Music: Reflections on Jazz and Blues* (New York: William Morrow, 1987: 177–80).

A general answer to that question, if we're talking about African-American music, would be, 'Wherever the masses of the African-American people are going or have gone.' And I would hold that as an accurate and verifiable insight. But at the same time there is such a constant flow of new or altered trends or recurring patterns that sometimes it might seem that there are simply too many things happening to analyze.

Under the broad rubric of black music in the United States, in recent years we have seen the continued significance and endless stylistic variations of the Funk (on one level simply the restating or re-expression of the basic African-American blues impulse, in most cases the intensification, the speeding up, the re-instrumentation of the rhythm that be with the modern instrumental urban blues). This aspect of the music was sucked up immediately in its formula corporate form *Disco*, a commercial mostly mindless flattening of black urban rhythms into dollar-producing hypnosis. The popular Afro-American music of any period is the blues, and the most significant styles of the music are rooted in and connected to the blues. But when the heavy corporate hand is laid on the music, any aspect of it, blues included, can turn it into dead formulas which have much more significance in the corporation's financial records than in the real aesthetic and emotional life of the people.

The Funk explosion in the early seventies was also accompanied by a period of death and transformation of important trends in the sixties' avant-garde music. The deaths of innovators like Trane, Ayler, Dolphy created a vacuum that sometimes saw their disciples carrying those trends into dead ends of mysticism or commerce or both at the same time.

A trend arose that in much the same way as the fifties' cool development expressed emotionally and historically a change in the society (the letdown of a post-revolutionary age) in which now the funk bottom or rhythm was harnessed gently to the cooled-off top or melodic and harmonic lines, and the result was Fusion. A corporate composite in its worst incarnation, though like everything else there were all kinds of Fusion from the highly commercial to the highly experimental. But mostly it was dollar-sign music.

We could credit Miles Davis for the mainstream creation of Fusion as a jazzlike trend. His Bitches Brew bands and Post-Bitches Brew bands read like a who's who of Fusion (Corea, Hancock, Weather Report, Tony Williams, etc.). But like Cool, not only was the rhythm, blues, and improvisational fire cooled out in most Fusion, for the sake of formulas and commercial charts, but a whole royalty of performers, mostly non-African-American, was raised so that it was possible on the defunct WRVR to listen nonstop to a so-called Jazz Music, hour after hour, that made little reference to the greatest names and musical tradition of the African-American experience, except the obvious golden straw stuck into the ear and jabbed deep in the brain of that same tradition like an electric cord stuck in a wall socket.

But so trendy and faddish was the Fusion mini-epoch that it was possible to trace its ebb very clearly, and the morning that WRVR turned hillybilly right before our ears was simply evidence that the trend had risen and fallen on greenbacks. It is interesting in the face of this that Columbia would then urge Miles out of retirement, and his *Man with the Horn* is in one reading simply a further restatement of the Fusion trend.

There was by the downturn of the Fusion trend a reawakening, it would seem, of a neo-BeBop voice. In much the same way that Hard Bop, pushed by players like Horace Silver, Art Blakey and the Messengers, Sonny Rollins, Max Roach, reappeared to do battle with the Cool school in the early sixties, trying to restore the heart and soul to the music. So in the late seventies, BeBop had made a distinct comeback (not that it ever left among a lot of folks), and reissues of records and some new clubs indicated the artistic reinfusion as well as some commercial interest. To me this was a healthy sign, concrete evidence that Fusion, for all its great sweeping trendiness which saw a few of our greatest musicians turn out a couple of new-style mood-music albums and bands, could not erase the deeper mainstream traditions of the music.

But there was also, at the same time, a restatement, a new coming together or just an initial breakthrough of musicians who had heard the new music revolution of the sixties and early seventies, younger musicians in most cases, who had been turned around by the Coltranes and Ornette Colemans and Cecil Taylors and Albert Aylers and Sun Ras and Eric Dolphys and Pharoah Sanders and now were ready to make their own further statements. Their clarifications and refinings, their new expressions rooted in the profundity of the African-American musical tradition, which has always borrowed from whatever and wherever it wanted and at the same time remained itself.

The Art Ensemble of Chicago, Air, World Saxophone Quartet, Olu Dara's Okra Orchestra, David Murray's big bands and Octet and Henry Threadgill's sextets, the consummate artistry of Arthur Blythe are some of the obvious examples and pluses of this period which extends until today. This is like a second wave of Avant-gardists, coming out of Chicago and St. Louis and

California and other places to be sure, but a generation of players that not only sounds the most contemporary note of the music but brings a great deal of respect and knowledge about some of the oldest of black American musical traditions.

The present situation sees the newest black music developing within a social framework that is, as is also traditional, oppressive and exploitive. But at the same time there is an even broader range of influences and cross-currents in the music than ever. Advancing technology, especially in communications, makes it possible now to sample a whole crush of world cultures, and the movement and relationship of people in the United States and internationally add to this. There is a broadening of the palette created by a welter of different trends and influences (e.g., reggae, new wave, etc.) and also the corporate drummers whose general approach to art (and especially progressive art) is always, first ignore it, second coopt it, then water it down and formularize the weakest version. For the African-American artist and his art there is also the added opposition and ignore/coopt cycle set up by racism. So that in rhythm and blues it is Bill Haley, Elvis Presley, or for that matter the Beatles, Rolling Stones, or the various instant superstar white teenagers, rather than black blues players of any generation.

A neophyte listener to alleged jazz station WRVR a couple years ago would think Chuck Mangione, Weather Report, and Phoebe Snow were the High Art creators of the music. Somehow it always seems strange or untrue to some people, especially in corporate and media posts, that the major innovators in African-American music would be African-Americans.

No one would question that the major innovators in European concert music are European and that if the various non-Europeans who have played that music were somehow not talked about, it would not change the essential history of that music. (World influences would be more to the point, including African.) So too for African-American music; if the non-African-American who played the music had not played it, it would not change the essential history of African-American music.

The problem for the Creators of Black Music, the African-American people is that because they lack Self-Determination, i.e., political power and economic self-sufficiency, various peoples' borrowings and cooptation of the music can be disguised and the beneficiaries of such acts pretend they are creating out of the air.

The absence of African-American-owned concert spaces, theaters, clubs, recording companies, publishing companies, and periodicals means that black music, like black people generally, is then left to the tender mercies of white racist monopoly capitalism.

The creation of such institutions by any nationalities independent of monopoly capitalism is obviously important to most of us!

African-American music like the other profound expressions of that culture can only be strengthened by the whole people focusing in on the struggle for Self-Determination for the African-American Nation! – whether black artists or black businessmen, black workers or progressive people of any nationality. The only way for the music to achieve self-determination is for the people to.

54 **Lawrence W. Levine** Jazz and American culture (1989)

Source: Lawrence W. Levine, 'Jazz and American culture,' *Journal of American Folklore*, 102, 403 (January–March, 1989: 6–8) (excerpt).

The increasing scholarly interest in jazz symbolizes what I trust is an ongoing reversal of a long-standing neglect by historians and their colleagues in many other disciplines of a central element in American culture. The neglect, of course, has not been an aberration on the part of academics. In neglecting or ignoring jazz, scholars have merely reflected the values and predispositions of the larger society in which they operated. But even this simple statement belies the true complexity of the problem: American society has done far more than merely neglect jazz; it has pigeonholed it, stereotyped it, denigrated it, distorted its meaning and its character. The nature and significance of the type of attention our society has paid to jazz reveal a great deal about our culture.

Anthropologically, perhaps, my title – Jazz *and* American Culture – doesn't make a great deal of sense since jazz is an integral part of American culture. But it is not culture in the anthropological sense that I'm dealing with here, since in fact that's not what culture meant to the society at the time jazz came upon the scene as a recognizable entity. When jazz became an identifiable form of music to the larger society, it was held to be something quite distinct from *Culture* as that term was then understood. It is the dialectic between the two – between jazz and Culture – that forms the subject of this article.

One can debate at great length the specific origins of the music we have come to know as jazz: *when* it first appeared, *where* it first appeared, *how* it was diffused, *what* its relationships to other forms of American music were. For my purposes, it is sufficient to observe that roughly during those decades that spanned either side of the year 1900, that period we call the Turn of the Century, a music or musics that came to be known as jazz appeared in and were quickly diffused throughout the United States at the same time that a phenomenon known as Culture (with a capital C) made its appearance.

America emerged from the 19th century with most of the cultural structures that have become familiar to us in place, or in the process of being put into place. Adjectival categories were created to box and identify expressive culture: High, Low, Highbrow, Lowbrow, Popular. Though these terms lacked, and continue to lack, any genuine precision, they were utilized with some consistency though always with a degree of confusion since the terms themselves were confusing and deceptive. That is, Popular Culture, in spite of its name, did not have to be truly *popular* in order to win the title. It merely had to be considered to be of little worth aesthetically, for that became the chief criterion: the cultural categories that became fixed around the turn of the century were aesthetic and judgmental rather than descriptive terms. So pervasive did this system of adjectival boxes become, that from the early years of this century, if one used the word 'culture' by itself, it was *assumed* to carry the adjective 'high' with it. The notion of culture was lifted out of the surrounding world into the universe of gentility. The word 'culture' became equated with the word 'refinement' which in fact was precisely the definition it carried in the single-word definition pocket dictionaries popular at the turn of the century (Levine 1988: 224–225).

Thus at approximately the same time, two new words – or more accurately, two older words with new meanings – came into general usage. Their dual appearance is significant because the two – Culture and Jazz – helped to define one another. That is, they served as convenient polar points, as antitheses. One could understand what Culture was by looking at the characteristics of jazz and reversing them.

Jazz was, or at least seemed to be, the new product of a new age; Culture was, or at least seemed to be, traditional – the creation of centuries.

Jazz was raucous, discordant; Culture was harmonious, embodying order and reason.

Jazz was accessible, spontaneous; Culture was exclusive, complex, available only through hard study and training.

Jazz was openly an *interactive,* participatory music in which the audience played an important role, to the extent that the line between audience and performers was often obscured. Culture built those lines painstakingly, establishing boundaries that relegated the audience to a primarily passive role, listening to, or looking at the creations of true artists. Culture increased the gap between the creator and the audience, jazz narrowed that gap. Jazz was frequently played in the midst of noisy, hand-clapping, foot-stomping, dancing and gyrating audiences. Those who came to witness Culture in art museums, symphonic halls, opera houses, learned what Richard Sennett has called 'Silence in the face of Art' (Sennett 1978: 230, 261).

If jazz didn't obliterate the line between composer and performer, at the very least it rendered that line hazy. Culture upheld the differentiation between the composer and the performer and insisted that the performer take no liberties with the work of the creator who in Culture assumed a central, often a sacred, position. Jazz was a performer's art; Culture a composer's art.

Jazz seemed uniquely American, an artistic form that, if Frederick Jackson Turner and his followers had only known it, might have reinforced their notions of indigenous American development and divergence from the Old World. Culture was Eurocentric – convinced that the best and noblest were the products of the Old World which the United States had to learn to emulate.

These two very different entities were expressions of radically divergent impulses in America. Culture was the product of that side of ourselves that craved order, stability, definition. It was the expression of a colonial side of ourselves that we have not done nearly enough to understand. I am convinced that we would know ourselves better if we understood our past more firmly as the history of a people who attained political and economic independence long before we attained cultural independence. Culturally we remained, to a much larger extent than we have yet recognized, a colonized people attempting to define itself in the shadow of the former imperial power. Jazz was an expression of that other side of ourselves that strove to recognize the positive aspects of our newness and our heterogeneity; that learned to be comfortable with the fact that a significant part of our heritage derived from Africa and other non-European sources; and that recognized in the various syncretized cultures that became so characteristic of the United States, not an embarrassing weakness but a dynamic source of strength.

It is impossible, then, to understand the place jazz occupied in America – at least until the years after World War II – without understanding that its emergence as a distinct music in the larger culture paralleled the emergence of a hierarchized concept of Culture with its many neat but never precisely defined adjectival boxes and categories.

References

Levine, Lawrence W. 1988. *Highbrow/Lowbrow: The Emergence of Cultural Hierarchy in America*. Cambridge: Harvard University Press.
Sennett, Richard. 1978. *The Fall of Public Man*. New York: Knopf.

55 **Burton W. Peretti**: Epilogue: Jazz as American history (1997)

Source: Burton W. Peretti, 'Epilogue,' in *Jazz in American Culture* (Chicago: Ivan R. Dee, 1997: 177–84). (Editor's title)

The story of jazz tells us a great deal about the ideas, feelings, and activities of Americans in this century. It is hazardous to generalize about such aspects of the human experience, especially when the focus is on a relatively small feature of the national scene such as jazz music. Biography and experience teach us that individuals have special relationships with their culture and the music they hear. Americans pride themselves on their individualism, and as persons as dissimilar as Wynton Marsalis and Jimmy Carter have argued, jazz improvisation almost epitomizes the American ideal of individual expression. One of the supreme joys of listening to jazz is to acquaint oneself with the unique creative sensibilities of master soloists; it is equally satisfying to explore their life stories and to associate those stories with the music they produce. A 'culture,' though, gains its identity by providing behavior that is shared by the members of a society, and by creating a certain level of regularity in how they think, listen, and act. Even individualistic jazz can give us a sharp collective picture of cultural conditions and change in twentieth-century America.

Jazz's importance to American *musical* culture is perhaps most obvious. While minstrelsy, the blues, ragtime, and other forms preceded jazz, they belonged to earlier eras; minstrel songs, for example, gave voice to nineteenth-century Victorian morality and racism. Jazz was a blend of these and many other styles, the statement of a new generation of young people in the 1910s who had new emotions and experiences and developed new ways of expressing them. Ragtime inspired stride pianists in New York and musicians in New Orleans, and French music deeply influenced the latter; but jazz was something new, reflecting the players' accelerating style of life and urge to express their sense of difference from more sedate earlier generations. The body of new performance conventions, musicians' practices, jazz slang, instrumental techniques, touring habits, and training regimens translated their youthful perspectives into a coherent musical form. The rapid evolution of styles – from Dixieland to symphonic jazz to hot jazz to swing to bebop – showed the jazz 'guild' reinventing itself, testing, abandoning, and adopting musical ideas at a furious rate. The pace of experimentation ensured that jazz would eventually become an avant-garde art, evolving too quickly for most listeners to appreciate and holding the interest of only a small group of sophisticated enthusiasts. In this way the music of New Orleans longshoremen and hack drivers became the difficult *objet d'art* of a highly cultivated international elite. The twentieth century moved that quickly.

As a result, the jazz story raises some interesting questions about the role of the arts in recent history. As jazz musicians became more accomplished and began to create for themselves – rather than to satisfy audience tastes – did they become irresponsible 'elitists'? Should performers originally nurtured *by* the people continue to *serve* the people? Stan Kenton, the 'progressive' jazz bandleader, thought he was doing so, though many jazz fans rejected him. The players active in 1960s black communities tried to connect with average listeners by playing simple melodies and incorporating soul and funk elements into their sounds, but their complex styles kept them from gaining wide followings.

On the other hand, jazz's occasional mass popularity raises a separate set of concerns. Did the rages for 1920s 'happy' jazz, 1930s swing, and 1970s 'fusion' occur because players and promoters were simplifying jazz and pandering to the 'lowest common denominator' of public taste? Artie Shaw felt that way about swing, and in the 1940s more than once he 'retired' from bandleading in disgust. Even Duke Ellington, who straddled popular success and avant-garde innovation more successfully than any other figure in jazz, was accused at various times either of 'losing his audience' or shamelessly seeking the leisure dollars of the musically ignorant masses. Ironically jazz ultimately became a victim of the mass media and the worldwide promotion it had helped to create, as rhythm and blues and rock and roll overwhelmed it in the 1950s and 1960s. The American audience's tastes, in short, changed as rapidly as jazz music, but in noticeably different directions. As a result, jazz is now an honored, much studied, and widely known music, but only one of many 'niche' musics in a vast terrain of diverse popular tastes.

The division, uniting, and redivision of the popular audience into new 'taste cultures' over the years and decades alerts us to changes in modern American culture as a whole. Not just music but family life, gender roles, leisure habits, living arrangements, work, politics, spirituality, and other aspects of daily life have evolved rapidly. Industrialization, urbanization, world wars, and mass media – followed in turn by deindustrialization, suburbanization, the cold war, and the counterculture – have shaped and reshaped average Americans' lives and tastes. From its beginnings to the present, jazz has reflected the modernizing spirit in the lives of many Americans. In the 1920s youth and some elders used jazz to experiment with new sexual, gender, and leisure attitudes in urbanizing settings; in the thirties swing became a mouthpiece for the common-man liberalism of the New Deal; bop and progressive jazz illustrated post-World War II militancy and existentialism, respectively; fifties cool jazz expressed suburbanization; and sixties 'outside' experiments voiced the angry demands of Black Power.

Jazz's story furthermore shows how adolescent Americans have largely led the way for their elders, using music to explore their emotions and desires in the midst of constant social innovation. Beginning with ragtime, modern popular music has been a young person's domain, an art for energetic people with little to lose and brave (or reckless) enough to express their emotions with relentless honesty. Jazz's energy initially came from the wild children playing in the streets of New Orleans, Ferdinand Lemott and Jack Laine in the 1880s and 1890s, hungrily consuming French and ragtime sounds and regurgitating them as amateurish, vulgar 'noise' that captured their experience of youth and city life. The musical youth movement of the twentieth century first shone brightly during the Jazz Age of the 1920s. Less likely than their elders to revere tradition, teenagers in every decade built new music, and behavior that supplemented it, out of the novel aspects of life that kept rushing in to meet them. War, technology, money, cities, automobiles, 'strange' ethnic groups, radical college professors, and mood-altering chemicals fed new popular music and made rough-hewn amateurs such as Louis Armstrong, Charlie Parker, Elvis Presley, and John Lennon into improbable new leaders of world taste and opinion. Politics, clothing, philosophies, and social customs changed with the music.

As jazz's generational history indicates, youth rebellions rarely continue after the youths enter their late twenties. Still, each rebellion has allowed the next one to become even more daring, and as a result the America of 1900 that first created jazz is almost alien to us today. While jazz has been a victim of this change ever since youth embraced R and B and rock (and swing and bebop musicians and fans grew older), its 'hot' and 'cool' emotions and specific musical gestures remain embedded in our complex culture, which resembles a colorful, wild, and overgrown musical garden. In this way and others, jazz was the first, and perhaps the most important, cultural youth rebellion of twentieth-century mass society.

We should not view the jazz story too idealistically, though. Since 1900 promoters and commercializers of popular music – driven by the profit motive and often totally lacking in musical taste – have exploited the creativity of rebellious adolescents. Young musicians had to make a living, but while a few jazz players profited healthily and happily with the help of appreciative and capable promoters, most of them suffered economically or artistically at the hands of managers, record companies, and other hucksters.

The haphazard process of trying to bring honest musical expression to a large audience is a major aspect of twentieth-century music history in itself.

1930s swing declined largely because the music business broke into turf wars (between broadcasters, songwriters, and the union) over profits, overexposed the big-band sound, and then diluted it with totally alien popular styles. The 'race records' mentality of the major labels and discrimination in radio hid black musicians from most white listeners for decades. In the 1960s rock's overwhelming popularity encouraged all media virtually to ignore jazz and other traditional sounds. Fortunately jazz history also shows generations of resourceful 'independent' producers and promoters – from the Gennett label in the twenties to Black Saint in the seventies – coming to the rescue of jazz musicians and listeners, preserving the music and nurturing a small but dedicated audience. The revival of historic independent labels such as Impulse! and Blue Note was a pleasant 1990s development.

The tumult of cultural change and commerce hurt jazz in many ways, but many Americans' resistance to change may have stifled the music more deeply. Despite decades of general change, jazz has remained a symbol of modernization, city life, sexual freedom, and interracial activity, and for this reason culturally conservative whites and blacks continue to denounce it. Even within the jazz subculture itself, the Dixieland revival of the late thirties, the condemnation of bebop in the 1940s, and the popularity of the 'classicism' of Wynton Marsalis have shown some players' and fans' resistance to change and their nostalgia. Like the heroin that some bebop musicians took to escape the pain of the present, nostalgia has been a narcotic of choice for people terrified by the unfamiliarity of the ever-changing present. Almost regularly in the twentieth century, Americans have expressed disgust with the present and yearned for the imagined 'normalcy' of yesteryear.

While older jazz styles allowed veteran fans to reminisce about the good old days of their youth, jazz never really captured the general American imagination as the music of traditionalism. That mantle has been worn more successfully by country and western music, which became a popular sensation almost at the same time as jazz in the early 1920s, grew dramatically in later decades, and has now overtaken jazz in popularity. Despite the enormous ideological and stylistic diversity of country music, politicians, promoters, and some musicians have helped to make it a symbol of white America's resistance to cities, suburbs, political liberalism, racial integration, and women's liberation. It is remarkable how jazz and country, two Southern musics with common taproots, have symbolically diverged in recent American culture – even though both contributed directly to the sound of rock and roll, the most antinostalgic and radical musical innovation of them all. Perhaps we can only tentatively conclude that innovation and nostalgia are fundamentally interrelated in modern popular music and culture.

Much clearer is that jazz has been closely tied to the African-American struggle for equality. Ragtime and the blues expressed black subordination to white culture and white power, before World War I gave them hope; rhythm and blues, soul, funk, and rap gave voice to blacks' deferred dreams and angry sense of betrayal after World War II. Black jazz came between these two trends. It arose during the crucial 1910s and 1920s, when nationalism and civil rights activism took hold. Jazz was the music of the newly optimistic black masses that had fled Jim Crow. The urban black, like the jazz improviser, struggled with the present in order to achieve victory in the immediate future, and the spirit of Harlem and other communities rallied behind the individual's cause. That spirit was the essence of Garveyism, the Harlem Renaissance, King's civil rights movement, and Black Power – and it brought energy to jazz in nightclubs and dance halls. That energy, as well as growing bitterness and doubt, fueled the innovation of bebop, but the revitalized 'soul' spirit of the 1950s enlivened hard bop and free jazz. While the aptly named Paul Whiteman had begun the major white presence in jazz, the ghetto long supplied the creative core of the music; white innovators kept coming back to it to learn more.

Even though jazz critics and promoters have rarely been black, black musicians have defined the essence of jazz and many of its styles. The fragmentation of the African-American community after 1960 was reflected in the breakup of the jazz mainstream. Just as the civil rights movement broke into various conflicting groups, so did jazz – fragmented into modal, 'free,' and 'outside' styles – face a crisis of identity and lose its revolutionary fervor. Since 1970 black avant-gardists have thrived in healthy and vibrant oases, and they have benefited from the occasional spurts of black political and nationalistic rebellion that continue to remind the world of the existence of racism and the underclass. While these problems remain in the 1990s, the traditions of black activism and the jazz spirit also remain and thrive, waiting to be tapped by the next Martin Luther King or Malcolm X.

Black equality and nostalgia, cities and suburbs, art and commerce, mass culture and the avant-garde – jazz embodies all of these major qualities of the twentieth century, and many more. They are the elements out of which Americans – and those around the world who share American culture – will build new sounds, new leisure, and new concepts of community and social identification. In mysterious ways, music-making and listening bring all these complex cultural changes into focus and encourage publics to create forces of change and to preserve their heritages. This is one of the major lessons of jazz as history.

Riff 5

Learning a grief
That is racial,
Cached in the soul
From generations of suffering ...
                    (Cyrus Cassells, 'Strange Fruit', 1984)

You *own* the music and we *make* it. (Archie Shepp, quoted Kofsky, 'The Jazz Tradition,' *Journal of Black Studies*, 1971)

Black saxophone man
Carrying freedom in your mouth.
                    (Amiri Baraka, 'For Pharoah Sanders,'
                The Music: Reflections on Jazz and Blues, 1987)

Twenty years ago when jazz was finding an audience, it may have had more of a Negro character. The Negro element is still important. But jazz has become a part of America. There are as many white musicians playing it as Negro ... We are all working along more or less the same lines. We learn from each other. Jazz is American now. *American* is the big word. (Duke Ellington, interview, *PM*, 1945)

Every idiom of black music ... has declined in its negroidery and purpose. It became more whitified. It's not the white people's fault ... they do what they do to support the misconceptions that they started when they brought the brothers and sisters over here as slaves. We are, in effect, in a state of war.' (Wynton Marsalis, *Tony Brown's Journal*, TV talk show, quoted Gene Lees, *Cats of Any Color*, 1994)

I'm a spade and you're an ofay. We got the same soul – so let's blow. (Louis Armstrong, to Jack Teagarden, quoted Terry Teachout, 'The Color of Jazz,' *Commentary*, 1995)

CHORUS V
So Black and Blue: Jazz and race
(colour, identity, otherness)

One of the most notable aspects of jazz is the omnipresent relation of the music to the culture of race and racism. Charley Gerard's recent study, *Jazz in Black and White* (1998), examines racial attitudes in the jazz community and jazz as an integral part of African-American identity. Central to Gerard's purpose is the formulation of black musicians' identity in the face of racial difference, and the problematic situation of jazz musicians within black culture. For Gerard, black musicians may seek identity and expression – as well as certain socio-political goals – through involvement with jazz and the jazz community; and not least through what has been called 'the black aesthetic' (Gayle 1971). White musicians face the problem of creating 'an art form rooted in black culture and marked by the stylistic imprints of black innovators' (Gerard 1998: xix). Some of these different racial attitudes are reflected in the way musicians have understood their idiom and tradition – between jazz as competitive individualism and artistic self-expression (white), and ethnicity, collectivism and a search for culture (black) (e.g. see Panish 1997). Overall, jazz musicians seem eternally embroiled in issues like racial essentialism and nationalist ideology, in racism in jazz audiences and communities, and in the assimilation of jazz into the wider American culture. All of this creates a symbiotic relationship between jazz and race. **Chorus V** is concerned with the discourse and aesthetics of race; the 'otherness' of racial identity and difference, as reflected in jazz and musicians' own experiences; and the creation of a racial vernacular to 'signify' on the cultural meaning of the music.

Gerard's section on the 'battle' of black music ideology (**57**) illustrates the conventional division of jazz history and its practitioners according to race, and the challenge to describing jazz as a product of black culture. Such a challenge, as Gerard observes, reflects a claim for the universal artistry of jazz – transcendent of race. Yet the claims for ethnicity, black 'ownership' of jazz, persist. Amiri Baraka (LeRoi Jones) first emphatically demonstrated, in *Blues People* (1963), the critical idea that jazz must be closely related to changes of value and attitude within the African-American community: jazz expresses socio-cultural 'intent' and its aesthetic embodies black American experience (Baraka 1963: Introduction). These issues of racial difference and context were taken up by Ben Sidran's valuable study of the orality and social function of black music in *Black Talk* (1971), which argued jazz poses a radical challenge and alternative to the values of white, mainstream culture. The mode of black protest writing in America – a tradition of orally expressive racial polemic and linguistic 'signifyin'' – is strongly present in Amiri and Amina **Baraka**'s more recent collection, *The Music: Reflections on Jazz and Blues* (1987). In 'Masters in collaboration' (**58**), Baraka celebrates drummer Max Roach, 'master' of rhythmic sources, and saxophonist Archie Shepp (also **62**), 'master' of elaboration. These are proffered as two famed black musicians in a revolutionary tradition which expresses cultural consciousness, 'art to life,' the aesthetics of a struggle for black liberation. Baraka encapsulates (signifies) a minor history of black musical achievement here.

A contrary, white perspective on the ownership of jazz and the tradition is offered by James Lincoln **Collier**, whose views on the excesses of black music ideology were first presented in *The Reception of Jazz in America: A New View* (1988) and followed up in *Jazz: The American Theme Song* (1993). Collier poses the question of how reasonable it may be to describe jazz as black music (**59**). He sets out his considerable stall for the dominant presence of white audiences, consumers and even historians. In an argument that insists we can no longer talk of jazz being shaped exclusively by a black culture, Collier makes the case for a pluralist music of integration and internationalism. If jazz cannot ever be race-free, there is an ongoing dialectic, a proposal that the music 'has been modified by too many forces to assign it an ethnicity.' Gene **Lees** makes a similar case for jazz's musical transcendence in his collection, *Cats of Any Color* (1994), prefaced with Armstrong's assertion: 'it's no crime for cats of any color to get together and blow.' Lees' last section has anecdotal reflections and miscellaneous reports on the whole issue of racism ('Jazz black and white,' 1994: 187–246). In it (**60**), he includes considerable evidence of reversed, anti-white racism in jazz ('Crow Jim'), and concludes with the fervent hope that the music is a major art, capable of healing separation and difference. Both Collier and Lees undertake a long-overdue appraisal of race and culture. As Gerard observes, this seeks to present a corrective agenda to 'the black nationalist jazz-as-black-music perspective [which] dominated jazz criticism for years' (1998: xvii). This should not, however, disregard the dominant gift of black culture to jazz.

'They could be Eskimos for all I know.' Trumpeter Roy Eldridge's less-than-50 per cent accurate distinctions between white and black jazz musicians appear in one of Leonard **Feather**'s aural 'blindfold tests' (**61**) – first started in *Metronome* in 1946. They revealingly point up the difficulties of racial guesswork; and suggest, too, patterns of stylistic assimilation and cross-imitation which transcend divisions of race and blur the 'color bar.' Eldridge loses his bet.

Historically, jazz playing and the life experiences of musicians have articulated the nature of racial difference and identity. Some of this is 'voiced' in vernacular style, in interview, as in the 1968 encounter of Nat **Hentoff** with avant-garde saxophonist Archie Shepp (**62**) and Arthur **Taylor**'s extensive exchanges (**63**) with black musicians (1968–72). The latter, to a varying degree, see jazz as the expression or symbol of racial condition, whereby the music – in the language of a militant 1960s – can correlate 'Black Power' with 'Black Jazz,' and catch the emotional urgency of the moment in an act of self-expression. Taylor's homage-paying *Notes and Tones* (1993 [1977]) prides itself on reproducing 'the real voices of musicians as they saw themselves,' and offers a valuable record of informal, candid exchange in a particular period of raised consciousness (Foreword). In 'musician-to-musician' interviews with Charles Tolliver, Freddie Hubbard, Hazel Scott and Betty Carter (**63**), the burden of discussion revolves round topics like music, critics, drugs, racism and the word 'jazz.' Recurrently, interviewees are disinclined to accept or use 'jazz'; they prefer 'Afro-American music,' since it is the form of black experience, over the terminology of white nomenclature (Tolliver). Black musicians, too, are concerned with the issue of control over/ownership of the music, particularly in a time of heightened racial and political awareness. For Scott and Carter, this is linked to the need to restore black pride, a collective self-respect and re-discovery of identity.

Race 'is in everything,' asserts Langston **Hughes**'s disingenuous persona, Simple (**64**), anxious to instruct his listener on the merits of 'Bop'. 'The real thing like the colored boys play' contains a music and language of profound racial difference. For Hughes, the jazz of Dizzy, Thelonious, Tad and Charlie, and its onomatopoeic sound ('BOP! MOP! . . . BE-BOP! . . . MOP!'), is the music of oppression. 'Bop comes out of them dark days . . . not to be dug unless you've seen dark days, too.' In a different and later era, the 1960s, jazz's 'dark days' could especially evince political protest and slogan-like anthems in titles and recordings. This is notable in Charlie Mingus' 'Freedom' (1963), where lyrics articulate an assertive racial awareness and self-acceptance, and demand for change; and the often hostile material found in musicians like Archie Shepp ('Malcolm, Malcolm, Semper Malcolm,' *Attica Blues*, *Cry of My People*); Max Roach (*We Insist! Freedom Now Suite*); Rahsaan Roland Kirk ('The Seeker,' *Blacknuss*, *Volunteered Slavery*); and Pharoah Sanders (*Soledad*). (See Cayer 1974: especially 60–64, n. 65.)

The permeation of race and racism into jazz musicians' professional lives is recorded in personal reminiscence and memoirs of 'the jazz life,' particularly autobiography (**Chorus VII**). Here, musicians of both colour run the gauntlet of club and concert performance, experience playing in mixed-race bands, and suffer the indignities of touring in racially hostile environments. 'As long as I'm in America, I'll never in my life work with a white band again!' Roy Eldridge's vow, testifying to the frustrations of segregated working conditions, is representative enough (Shapiro and Hentoff 1955: 328–30). In 'Travelin' Light' (**65**), from *Lady Sings the Blues* (1956), Billie **Holiday** recounts pioneer touring in the West and mid-West of 1937. The blatant discrimination of 'white crackers' sorely tests the best intentions of white bandleader Artie Shaw's colour-blindness toward his 'good Negro singer.'

In a reversed situation, for some white jazz musicians the racial pressures to merge identity in a black world and espouse the creativity of African-American culture proved inescapable. 'The only real jazz [is] the colored man's music,' opined white clarinettist Mezz **Mezzrow**. His lively autobiography, *Really the Blues* (1946), famously records the author's near-total immersion in black culture and music, wanting 'to be a musician, a Negro musician, hipping the world about the blues the way only Negroes can' (1946: 18). Mezzrow's rather self-deluded tale of Jewish boy as 'wannabe black' finds apotheosis in 'Out of the Gallion [slave quarters]' (Chapter 17) (**66**). As 'the climax of all my born days . . . and locked in my conkhouse till the day I die,' he claims an ephiphanic crossing of 'the color line': it is the exultant playing of authentic jazz in the manner and spirit of his black masters.

The celebratory nature of black jazz style expresses racial difference and otherness, beyond the comprehension of 'folks who ain't suffered much' (Hughes). The fine poem, 'Here where Coltrane is' (1977), by Michael **Harper** (**67**), instances the tribulations of 'soul and race' – memories of Coltrane's 'modal/songs' in elegiac form which ultimately suggest a racial transcendence over sorrow and individual pain. This collective note and the spiritualized depth of the 'other,' black experience achieve memorable lyric expression in song – e.g. Hughes's poem 'The Weary Blues' (1926) with its 'drowsy' syncopations and blues-based form; in Armstrong's famous version of colour difference and exclusion, 'What did I do to be so black and blue?' (1929); and Ellington's 1943 'tone' poem, *Black, Brown, and Beige*, where 'The Blues' express the inclusive lamentation of an essentially black form and paradoxical capacity to 'sing' affirmatively about black heritage and identity.

'It is also about the also and also of signifying and qualifying.' Albert **Murray**'s seminal *Stomping the Blues* (1976) pointed the racial aesthetics of jazz criticism in the direction of African-American literary theory, as developed in the work of Houston Baker (1984) and Henry Louis Gates (1988) (**Chorus II**). Murray's book is a highly imaginative, almost improvised reworking of black cultural resources, exemplified in the aesthetic of the blues tradition. This kind of 'embodied' argument sees musical criticism joining literary analysis. It employs a distinctive racial discourse: 'signifyin(g)' through the practice of the black vernacular. In vitally creative terms, Murray's 'analysis' of the blues 'signifies' on its own cultural resources. These are the rituals of black social engagement: resilience and exuberant celebration, as in 'Epilogue' (**68**).

This organic accommodation of jazz's variety and difference is fluidly present in the cross-play/fire between modernist musicians in a 'set' (**69**) from Charles **Mingus**'s autobiography, *Beneath the Underdog* (1971). It epitomizes black culture, in its 'motherfucking' irreverence, badinage and inter-textual playfulness. This is the black vernacular aesthetic at its inventive ('as if,' 'also') work. Finally, Ross **Russell**, Charlie Parker's biographer, manager and Dial recorder, provides a strident summary of black 'minstrelsy' (**70**) – the progeny of race and racism in 'dungheap' America.

56 **Sascha Feinstein** Miss Brown to you (1915–1959) (2000)

Source: Sascha Feinstein, 'Miss Brown to you (1915–1959),' in *Misterioso* (Port Townsend, WA: Copper Canyon Press, 2000: 19–20).

Nobody, you once wrote, *really loves me.*
They just love my music. I'm listening
to the end of your life, sessions
from '58, and forgive me for thinking
That's all I have, Billie.
Because you were right. I'm not the woman
in this photo, signing autographs
behind the enormous letters
of your name. To your left,
one of the men checks to see
if you've spelled his right;
another watches your downcast
eyelashes. I wish I had a moment
like that to remember you by, though
with 'Don't Explain,' I'm sent to a blue room,
your scratched voice like winter wind
under the door, pushing forward.
There are days, Uncle Bob once told me,
I listen to Bach and it's so perfect
I can't hear anything else. Except Billie,
of course. You might have answered, *Honey,*
I'm flattered, but I ain't perfect.
If it were '58, you'd probably give a wink
to the rhythm section, sing
for everyone you thought didn't love you
and for people, I'd like to believe,
not yet born. But if it crossed your mind
later, you might think about perfection,
all the things you had to become
for others: 'restricted' diners flashing
the bus window pink, how even
Basie once asked you to wear
brown makeup, skin not dark enough,
the backstage mirror reflecting your white
gardenia as fingers slowly spread
the new color across your cheek,
red lips seeping into the darkening rouge.

57 **Charley Gerard** Battling the black music ideology (1998)

Source: Charley Gerard, 'Battling the black music ideology,' in *Jazz in Black and White: Race, Culture and Identity in the Jazz Community* (Westport, CONN: Praeger, 1998: 31–7).

One of two things is true. Either jazz has evolved into a major art form, and an international one, capable of exploring and inspiring the full range of human experience and emotion. Or it is a small, shriveled, crippled art useful only for the expression of the angers and resentments of an American minority. If the former is true, it is the greatest [artistic] gift of blacks to America, and America's greatest aesthetic gift to the world.

If the latter is true, it isn't dying. It's already dead.

Gene Lees, *Cats of Any Color*

The proponents of the black music ideology have written a revisionist history of jazz that overstates the impact of racism on African-American musicians and minimizes the influence of whites. Any books written by whites that stray from these views are subjected to charges of racism. Even the most benign statements are criticized as being racist. For instance, ethnomusicologist Helen Myers singles out the following sentence in Frank Tirro's textbook, *Jazz: A History,* as an example of the thinking of white writers who deny the achievements of African Americans: 'Contrary to popular belief, jazz does not owe its existence to any one race.'[1] Tirro was simply stating the obvious – that jazz did not spring from African-American culture without the influences of American band traditions and Western harmony, melody, and rhythm. Myers is wrong to accuse him of racism on the basis of one sentence taken out of context.

White musicians have, naturally, not taken kindly to the unflattering views of black music ideologists. Jim Hall responded with the following comment to charges that whites stole the music: 'I've always felt that the music started out as black but that it's as much mine now as anyone else's. I haven't stolen the music from anybody – I just bring something different to it.'[2]

Bill Evans was appalled by the notion that 'only black musicians can be innovative,' since he believed that creativity is an innately human characteristic that goes beyond race. He rationalized the black music ideology as the reaction of a group of people who 'haven't had much, so they want to make jazz one hundred percent black.' Evans wanted 'more responsibility among black people and black musicians to be more accurate and to be spiritually intelligent about humanity.' He believed that African Americans should consider the consequences of their statements before putting them in print. He warned them that 'to say only black people can play jazz is just as dangerous as saying only white people are intelligent or anything like that.'[3]

Trumpeter Ruby Braff finds ridiculous the notion that jazz could be called black music:

What is 'black music?' I never saw black music. What is black music? Would you mind telling me? What is black music? Are they referring to jazz? Jazz is an American product made up by all people in this country ... It just so happens that great pioneers of jazz, of improvised music, were the black people, the great black artists, who would turn over in their graves if they ever heard the way any of these guys are playing today. It's a horror show. It's terrible ...

For years and years black people wanted integration in this society and to get together, and they got all these people to help them – white people, black people. Now are they saying that they want to be separating now? Or do they want to be separating in music but not in housing, in industry, in politics? Where is it? Where is it?

I never in my life thought of music or anybody's color. We played with people. If you asked me if there was black cats in the band, I couldn't even tell you. I'd have to say, 'Who's black here, who's white[?]' That's how little any of us give a damn.[4]

There is an edge of disingenuousness to the ways these three white musicians – Bill Evans, Jim Hall, and Ruby Braff – responded to the black music ideology in interviews between 1974 and 1992. They spoke about jazz as if they were oblivious to the fact that 'white' has been a pejorative term among jazz musicians and critics for decades, going back at least as far as 1930, when the jazz critic Charles Edward Smith wrote that Louis Armstrong's playing 'succumbs more and more to the white man's notion of Harlem jazz.'[5] In a 1959 article, 'Race Prejudice in Jazz,' Nat Hentoff describes how he heard an African-American musician '[curse] one of his sidemen loudly for playing "too white." '[6] Jazz musicians, white and black, have been denigrating for decades the average white musician's ability to swing. Hentoff cites a white pianist who admitted that he preferred 'not to play in an all-white rhythm section, because there aren't that many white groups that can really swing.' Hentoff also noted that Europeans have developed a reputation for believing that 'a Negro musician must be superior to a white musician if only because he is a Negro.'[7] In fact, critic Gary Giddins was told by a few musicians that European jazz promoters in the 1960s insisted that black-led bands have all-black personnel. As a result of this quest for authenticity, some black musicians had to fire white sidemen.[8]

One of the leaders in this backlash against the extremes of black nationalism was Billy Taylor, a noted jazz pianist with a doctoral degree in education. Although he recognizes that jazz came out of African-American culture, he believes that the music is no longer solely black music, having transcended its ethnic boundaries. He calls jazz 'a unique American phenomenon, ... America's classical music.' Jazz artists have developed 'an American way of playing music' that reflects American values and contributes to the shaping of American culture. Jazz 'meets all the criteria for determining whether a music is classical: it is time-tested; it serves as a standard or model; it has value; and it is indigenous to the culture for which it speaks.'[9]

Pop music standards provide those who believe that jazz is an American classical music with their best argument. Written by both whites and African

Americans, it can only be viewed as American, neither white nor black. The importance of these songs as inspiration for jazz musicians is not often recognized by the musicians themselves or by jazz critics. Irving Louis Horowitz and Charles Nanry wrote in 'Ideologies and Theories about American Jazz' that universal recognition of the central role of the popular song repertoire 'would signify the end of most forms of racial and ideological disputation concerning the writing, nature and purpose of jazz.'[10]

In the last few years two jazz writers, James Lincoln Collier and Gene Lees, have taken upon themselves the task of battling the racist propaganda that has been written over the last thirty years. Collier's views on the excesses of black music ideology are laid out in *Jazz: The American Theme Song* (1993). Lees addresses the topic in *Cats of Any Color* (1994). It is only regrettable that their agenda appears to be not only to correct inaccuracies in the literature but to cast doubt on the premise that African Americans have a culture of their own, distinct from white American culture.

Collier believes that it is historically inaccurate to describe jazz as a product of 'black culture.' Jazz came into existence at a time when black Creoles, key figures in the birth of jazz, were regarded as culturally distinct from American blacks. The differences between the two groups – Creoles and American blacks – were real and substantial. Creoles were Catholics, blacks were Protestant. Creoles spoke French, blacks spoke English. Creoles had their own songs, American blacks had an entirely different repertoire consisting of work songs and spirituals. These profound cultural differences extended into the economic and social arenas as well.[11] In Collier's opinion, during the formative years of jazz, 'black' culture did not include Creole culture. He therefore concludes that 'jazz did not arise from some generalized "black culture" or "black experience." '[12]

Collier takes a different approach toward the jazz establishment's tacit acceptance of the black origins of jazz. He points out the disdain many African Americans have felt toward jazz. It was not an art form they were proud of, especially since some of its early development took place in brothels. But Collier ascribes too much significance to African-American antipathy toward jazz, as if the animus itself somehow proved that jazz could not be an integral part of black culture. The disdain jazz suffered was not unique: Popular music in general has always been regarded with negative feelings by many sectors of American society.

Collier's notions about black culture could not have been timed more poorly, for a wide range of African-American artists and intellectuals, cultural theorists and even television writers have been promoting the view that there are many ways of being African-American. Their views are more sophisticated than Collier's and allow for a more flexible conception of black culture that takes into account the diversity of the African-American experience.

Collier treats at length the history of the dance band in America and ties its development to such white musicians as Ferde Grofé and Art Hickman. It is a commendable addition to the literature on American popular music and adds a new dimension to our appreciation of swing. Because Collier's work is so well documented, jazz writers can no longer assume that African-American musicians invented the dance band and formulated the ways in which the ensemble came to be orchestrated. But despite Collier's contribution, the roles of Fletcher Henderson and Don Redman in making the dance band a jazz group remain unassailable.

While most writers divide jazz history according to race, Lees and Collier provide a view of jazz history as a unified stream. They show that jazz has not always been a one-sided affair, with African Americans creating the music and whites copying it. They emphasize that whites also influenced African Americans, a point that black music ideological literature often ignores. Lees points out that Lester Young was influenced by Frank Trumbauer, Rex Stewart was influenced by Bix Beiderbecke, and Henderson learned from Bill Challis. He also reminds us that Gil Evans and Bill Evans were major figures in the development of jazz.

Despite its shortsightedness, the black music ideology makes several valid points. In *Blues People* Baraka successfully proved that change in jazz is closely related to changes of attitude within the African-American community. That is, change is not the result of musical developments per se but of sociopolitical events affecting the African-American community. And black musicians have indeed determined the directions the music has taken over the years. It was New Orleans musicians who originally created jazz out of march music; Louis Armstrong who created the soloist's role in jazz; Fletcher Henderson and Don Redman who took the dance band and made it into a jazz group; James P. Johnson who created stride; Dizzy Gillespie, Charlie Parker, and Bud Powell who made bebop. After World War II, Miles Davis, Ornette Coleman, Cecil Taylor, and John Coltrane developed and brought to fruition free jazz, cool jazz, jazz-rock, and modal jazz. Even when African Americans have not been the first to create a new jazz style, they have invariably become its leading figures.

Black music ideologists are correct in their assessment of jazz as a language that black musicians understand in a different way than whites. For whites, jazz is a means of self-expression and a display of artistry. For African Americans, jazz is certainly that, but in addition it is an assertion of ethnic identity. The philosopher Kwame Anthony Appiah noted in the context of his study of African culture and philosophy that there was a profound difference between the respective goals of European and African writers that could be summarized as 'the difference between the search for the self and the search for a culture.'[13] The same words could be used to distinguish between white and African-American jazz musicians.

The exponents of 'jazz as American classical music' are happily free of the rancor that makes the 'jazz as black music' perspective such an off-putting experience. Theirs is an ecumenical vision of the jazz world, a place in which everyone is equal according to his or her ability and one's ethnic background is never a drawback. Yet the 'jazz as American classical music' ideology somehow manages to skirt the issue of black dominance in jazz. The blacks who have proclaimed jazz to be a universal language still pay homage to its African-American ethnicity. When Duke Ellington said in his autobiography that jazz was 'an international music' he also commended white musicians for growing close to the 'black soul.'[14] Billy Taylor, a popular exponent of the notion that jazz is American classical music, has some harsh words for white ethnomu-sicologists and jazz writers that reveal Taylor's mixed feelings about relinquish-ing the African-American culture's 'ownership' of jazz. According to Taylor, books by white authors 'are interpreting, from another cultural background, what they have heard from black people. Though they are excellent books, if one reads them all they show emphatically how a subject may be defined in part by what is left out as well as what is included.' If jazz is international music, it doesn't need to have a black soul or a white soul. But if jazz is not black music, why do students of the music need to know, as Taylor insists, about 'the value system of its creators?'[15]

Such racial paradoxes are what make the music so compelling as a cultural phenomenon. Jazz is somehow able to be both an African-American ethnic music and a universal music at the same time, both an expression of universal artistry and ethnicity. Black musicians lash out at whites, and yet invite them into their bands. Wynton Marsalis refuses to accept white accomplishments in jazz, but proclaims the genius of Beethoven. Amiri Baraka heaps scorn on the art of the white world, and in the next breath praises Roswell Rudd. There is no accounting for jazz. As Dexter Gordon once put it to jazz critic Gary Giddins, 'Jazz is the great octopus; it'll do anything; it'll use anything.'[16]

Notes (edited)

1 Cited in Helen Myers, 'African-American Music.' In Helen Myers (ed.), *Ethnomusicology: Historical and Regional Studies* (New York: W.W. Norton, 1993), pp. 427–28.

2 Cited in Whitney Balliett, *American Musicians: Fifty-Six Portraits in Jazz* (New York: O.U.P., 1986), pp. 342–43.

3 Len Lyons, *The Great Jazz Pianists: Speaking of Their Lives and Their Music* (New York: Quill, 1983), pp. 227–28.

4 Wayne Enstice and Paul Rubin, *Jazz Spoken Here: Conversations with Twenty-Two Musicians* (Baton Rouge: Louisiana State University, 1992. Reprint of New York: Da Capo, 1984), p. 39.

5 Cited in James Lincoln Collier, *Jazz: The American Theme Song* (New York: O.U.P., 1993), p. 90.

6 Nat Hentoff, 'Race Prejudice in Jazz: It Works, Both Ways,' *Harper's Magazine* (June 1959), pp. 74–76.

7 Ibid.

8 Gary Giddins, *Riding on a Blue Note* (Oxford: O.U.P., 1981), p. 256.

9 Billy Taylor, *Jazz Piano: A Jazz History* (Dubuque, Iowa: Wm. C. Brown, 1983), pp. 3, 8.

10 Irving Louis Horowitz and Charles Nanry, 'Ideologies and Theories About American Jazz,' *Journal of Jazz Studies* 2, No. 2 (June 1975), p. 33.

11 Bob Wilber, a protégé of the famous Creole musician Sidney Bechet, remembers that Bechet 'never thought of himself as a black man,' and sometimes made anti-black statements. *Music Was Not Enough* (New York: O.U.P., 1988), p. 48.

12 Collier, *Jazz: The American Theme Song*, p. 201.

13   Kwame Anthony Appiah, *In My Father's House: Africa in the Philosophy of Culture* (New York: O.U.P., 1992), p. 74.
14   Cited in Gene Lees, *Cats of Any Color* (New York: O.U.P., 1994), p. 241.
15   Taylor, *Jazz Piano*, p. 62.
16   Bert Primack, 'Critical Analysis: Jazz Critics Under the Microscope,' *Jazz Times* 24, No. 7 (September 1994), p. 39.

58 **Amiri Baraka** Masters in collaboration (1987)

Source: Amiri Baraka, 'Masters in collaboration,' in Amiri Baraka and Amina Baraka, *The Music: Reflections on Jazz and Blues* (New York: William Morrow, 1987: 207–13).

Everyone here to consciously get in on history. Years later the references to this event will let you know how heavy twas that you and we could get together like this, to hear this. Because, I'm sure, for most of us here, we have come to witness the collaboration of two masters. One, a master of source, the other, a master of elaboration. One who goes back further to the great crossing and extension of our collective historical lives (as America and as African-America), that crossing where the corporations had conspired to come up with the formula to turn our verbishness into quiet nouns of commerce – so that suddenly one day we would look up and swing would no longer mean the soul's uttering itself into music, the most sensitive among us transforming the seeming quiet air into what is always, *rhythm* – no, the fiends had conspired to turn fire notes of our human striving (and anguish) into bank notes of flattened sensibility and (un)sophisticated intention – suddenly there was ten Casa Lomas or twelve Kay Kaisers (as the market dictated); you see, they meant to inundate us in the death formula, which they, so confident in their infamy, dared call Swing.

It means as soon as the little money bums come up with the right stuff they canned it and shat it out everywhere at once to kill off the real, as the theory says that gold can be diminished in its life by cheaper metal pushed for that purpose. Corporation NonMusic to make profit from the black prophets and sound scientists who could not fully explore their own consciousnesses because of the national oppression of the African-Americans, so they had to settle for *genius,* while others had their works taught at universities or made millions imitating these exploited musical workers.

We understood that it was White Man (Paul, to be exact) who had created jazz, despite what Jelly Roll Morton might say or Duke Ellington might play! We was hipped that it was Good Man (full of Benny) who had founded that desperate brightness called Swing. But we still wondered (excuse us, yo' infamy) who we ourselves, excuse the expression, was!?

So involved did we become in this quest that we sent certain scientists and aesthetes of the real, some cultural workers, off to the side, after hours, so to speak, to check out if we were still we (even though we knew we had not got free). You see we had in mind those kinds of advanced artists who carried our whole history in their consciousness, who could conduct some sound experiments, so to speak, to obstruct and finally foil the demonic plan of suffocation the corporations had laid out to turn us all into furniture, as the only correct audience for the nonmusic they invented from watering down our own.

Thus, at certain laboratories and city *do*-tanks these artists gathered to explore the outside of the inside and recreate us for ourselves. Minton's, Monroe's Uptown were some of the in/sites. It was there that these heavy musical explorations took place. It was there that certain Birds, Monks, Kooks, and Dizzys gathered to reinvigorate the African, who alone among us did not come to these shores voluntarily, but trapped in slavery transported in the holds of bloody slave ships, had for all that, by the nineteenth century, involved his/her sensibility in America by means of English, Spanish, and French whips and chains, at the same time picking their brains, and then sometimes in flight, hanging out all night with certain Native Americans, so that by the time of the appearance of the Slave Narratives and the black conventions, there was a people a culture that could be called *African-American* (which later, them/ itselves became a Nation in the black-belt South). So that the African-American, its source and basic content African, wired up with English, French, Spanish, Native American language, culture, logic, and history comes to exist to be heard as grunts against the wind, for the picking of cotton. We made the work song. For the worship of the God (from the old African one in the storefront to the Jeeeee-zuz of AfroXtian design) we created the spiritual; and then to celebrate our real lives blues was willed into being, and to show we could hook our matrix upon these new instruments we encountered on our tour of the southern U.S. (loitering around New Orleans we spied these aesthetic weapons of European design), bands such as those Dessaline had wasted in Haiti, we heard also certain harmonies that were, after all, interesting. Yes. And so we thought we would introduce all these to our own heartbeat, there in Congo Square, Master Drum was allowed to infect us, and anybody calling themselves American once more.

And inside the ho houses – ho ho ho – whilst involved in jassing, did certain immortal journalists respond to the elegant wailing that accompanied the sliding up and down of their pants, to certify their profound understanding of these events and that time and place by saying, hey now, that noise is good for jassing. What do you call it, sir? (It was Jelly Roll so addressed, and he went off to the Library of Congress and responded to the question in twelve long-playing records, now out of print!)

We know that the music came up the river, the Mississippi, when the people did. How else would it get there? We know of the funeral stomps and the small group classics. How black blues got in them gold horns and set fire to foolishness. We know about King Oliver and Louis. And ragtime and boogie woogie. How the urban spaces where we showed up with our buckets in our hands trying to get some guts still had the shadow of the plantation chained to the streets. How blues came up, and that old blues and old jazz were carried up there wrapped carefully by certain Fletchers and even royal personages like Dukes and counts unfolded the gift and extended it in suites and riffs and tone poems of our historical, social, and artistic consciousness.

And each time, the same corporations that had got over exploiting the African's tragic willingness to sell off pieces of weself to anybody who had the necessary trinketry, these same villains would reappear to scoop out the insides of our hearts and sell them for super profits and then convince us that the scooped-out portions of ourselves existed as such because we had never been whole, never, we had only and always at any time in anybody's history been simply *Niggers.*

But to get back to this evening arumm let me see ... Yes, we had alerted these scientists to experiment, and they had, and their experiments were successful. And the results of these sound workings could be picked up by the sensitive. The drum master here, Brother Max, as a very young man was turned on by the fertile whispering rhythms set loose in the environment by these revolutionary cultural workers. The period the forties, the Second World War, brought a prosperity to Bloods, new jobs, a new higher consciousness in the cities, rebellions in Harlem and Detroit, the Black consciousness movement, 'Don't buy where you can't work,' the Negro National Congress, Margaret Walker and Theodore Ward and young Max Roach picket it all up in the throbbing of the rhythm.

Max Roach in a long line of masters of the art, in the African-American tradition. As an incredibly young man/boy working with Bird in 1946–8. I came up the street and my cousin mashed some Savoys and Dials on me. I heard also Max Roach's BeBop Boys. Later I understood what it all was, what they called *BeBop.* To restore us to ourselves, to restore the polyrhythms of Africa, the primacy of improvisation and the blues, and the fundamental AFRICAN-American reidentification of ourself back to ourselves as Industrialized Africans of the West.

And Max has never turned his back from the initial fire and attack of the original bop revolution. That was a fundamental rejection of the corporate values – values that included our own slavery. So the boppers were weird, America. They had dug that it was America that was fucked up, not we ourselves. Like most black people if you could dig it. Play advanced African-American music on the airwaves all day everyday and watch what this country will turn into!! I became a BeBopper (I didn't even think of it until my father asked me why I wanted to be one). It was like somebody asking you why you wanted to be conscious.

But that act of saving the music and removing it to yet higher planes of thought and action was revolutionary. That music sounds as fresh today as then. And Max was among the primary creators of that music even in his youth. He is the master of polyrhythmic construction. To speak of classic modern drumming is, of course, to speak of Max Roach.

Interesting also, and again to further make the point, when the music was attacked again (as it is always being) that is, when the corporations again gathered the antarctic renegades of dollarocracy to attack screaming as they came at us COOL COOL COOL (meaning, 'we mean to get rid of this *hotness* you niggers are stirring up' – we answered that hot shit with the cold war on one level, with McCarthyism on another level – hell we even indicted DuBois as agent of a foreign government, humiliated Langston at the HUAC hearings, sent Richard Wright into exile, and placed Paul Robeson under house arrest). So now we going to stomp those hot rhythms flat, we gonna banish the blues, we gonna create ubiquitous charts that sound like mechanical organ grinders – aha yes, to grind out the bux – we'll injure you niggers and our code word of attack is COOL COOL you want emotion we'll give you non-motion, want fire we'll give you ice – you want life we'll give you death. 'COOL COOL COOL,' pretending all the while to be admirers of Lester Young, not understanding that we had already heard *Taxi War Dance*!! And dug, that underneath Pres's distance he was very very hot.

But then among those of the next generation who saved the music once more was Max. When cool seemed like it would rule, here came Horace bringing the church in it. I guess he figured if they wanted to fight, we can go get some really spooky hot shit for ye to deal wid mister. Horace, Art Blakey from Messenger University, what they called hardbop, to bring back the real and oppose the steal. And amongst those groups called hardbop was perhaps the high mark of that, Max Roach-Clifford Brown-Sonny Rollins. On the high level, showing the direct vector from the sound scientists of the forties to raise it to another level for battle in the fifties. It was bad! bad! Another classic.

Throughout the years Max has always communicated high consciousness. Not just directly inside the music but in himself as African-American artist and man. Whether it was revolutionary music or revolutionary thought, it was joined together as a whole, as the whole the man is. When the cool fifties turned hotter and the African independence struggles came full up and the civil rights movement raised more open cries for democracy Max said WE INSIST – FREEDOM NOW. He told us about the 'Driva Man' and made us cry 'Tears for Johannesburg' even while we were loading our guns. He tells us 'Deeds Not Words.' 'It's Time.' 'Speak Brother Speak.' Or looking deep in our eyes he might know we need to be told to 'Stay Up' so he'll say 'Members Don't Get Weary.' Or tell us about the 'Long March.' Or very recently he made us weep with him about our children's murders in 'Atlanta-Chattahoochee Red!'

The percussion group MBeam is innovation on still a high level. Uniting some of the most impressive percussionists of the period to show us the extent to which percussion can be totally expressive. The totality of Max Roach's consciousness is what we hear when we listen to him. Everything that needs to be said is coming out, pointing at everything, always in motion, creative and transforming, aesthetically powerful, and politically revolutionary.

I came upon Archie Shepp in New York City in the early sixties. He was playing at the Living Theater in the play *The Connection* and I was startled by the newness trying to get through and organize itself. Archie was linked up to the same forces of tradition. Tradition in Transition. Was it Sonny Rollins who'd shaped him or Ben Webster or John Coltrane or was it the whole of that tradition trying to carry him with it through that horn?

Archie too comes from the revolutionary aspect of the tradition, like Max.

Archie emerged as a professional in the hot sixties. The music had already been restored by Max and Clifford and Sonny; its base had been reidentified and held aloft like a red flag. Archie came out when Trane had finished Miles Davis's prep and was about to enter Thelonious Monk University, then held at the Five Spot. When Ornette Coleman came to town with a plastic horn and Eisenhower jacket trying to send BeBop into outer space and cut it loose from the popular commercial song. When Pharoah Sanders was a youngster from Arkansas everybody called Little Rock and we used to get on both of them about who had the worst feet, him or Archie.

I think I first heard him with Cecil Taylor, who invented the Five Spot. Cecil was a revolutionary player as well. He had dashed through the conservatory screaming BUD POWELL IS WHAT'S HAPPENING, LAMES! So Cecil's intense pianistics, which made European concert form stand up and be counted as possibly hip if it could only be extended to include the fire and funk of the man who hipped Stravinsky and Gershwin to the blues, in combination with Archie's new raw snarling grumbling ultrablue wail made a sound of those times that seemed to be able to say what actually was happening in the streets and in people's heads and hearts.

It is critical that we understand that there is in Archie and Max the open link of art to life. That these are both revolutionary artists, who will not bite their tongues aesthetically or politically. And that is what makes their art so hot. So that their own collaborations like 'The Long March on Hat Hut' celebrating the triumph of revolutionary China and which includes Max's *South Africa Goddam* is simply among the near recent homages to the progressive spirit of world transformation. The piece 'Sweet Mao' made together after Mao's death is more essential contemporary world comment at a high level of aesthetic accomplishment. Yet, get to this, both the albums with this music have had to be produced in Europe, as the corporate villains of America continue to fight revolution all over the world, usually with our money!

Archie came out in a revolutionary period, a hot time, and so he was shaped in his deepest heart by that process, the liberating force of struggle, the ecstatic revelation of victory, and always as contradiction to the powerful forces of reaction that constantly threaten any of us with elimination. In his playing one can hear black tradition recalled and absorbed and set in motion at the next level. All those midnight urban horn men and dudes stomping on the bartops like Trane did can be heard in Archie's sound. All those solitary blues players creating a world by waving their fingers across strings. All that history and pain and beauty and meaning, it's the blues, quiet and loud as the world.

Archie and I were comrades in struggle during those early years. We were in organizations together whose focus was to destroy the system that had tried to destroy our people and most people. We were openly antiimperialist, and even discovered that hid off not too well, right up in the middle of the so-called art world, were some of the worst racists and running dogs of monopoly capitalism that we had ever checked, disguised as artists and what not.

We knew that our art had to be a weapon in the struggle for black liberation, if it was going to be worthy of our people's memory. We found out also that there were people like us struggling all over the planet against exploitation and oppression and we tried to organize people as well as make our art.

Throughout Archie's career, in the titles of his pieces and the public stance he has taken, one can see this commitment to struggle, this willingness to take chances. It's in the music clearly. The Malcolm pieces, the focus on older more traditional lynchings, crying out about contemporary mass lynchings like Attica. He has incorporated African liberation struggles, African-American contemporary battles for democracy, the cry of the old and the scream of the new. He is traditional and at the same time avant-garde. And for that reason the mainstream of the African-American aesthetic tradition. Archie was part of the Black Arts Movement, wherein we tried to make an art that was African-American rather than Euro-American, an art that was public and open that was intended to move and be moved by the people. It was an openly agitational art, meant to get people hot and make them do something about the ugliness of what is. It was meant to be a revolutionary art, a people's art, fuel for social transformation. As Mao said, Artistically Powerful and Politically Revolutionary. So Archie was among the artists who played at the Black Arts programs in the streets that hot summer of 1965, where thousands heard the new music and thought it as funky as the old music. The music for *Slave Ship*, my play about our original transportation problems, Archie did, and made that production perhaps the most memorable for me. So moving for us all that many stood in tears shaking hands to the strains of Archie's music for 'When We Gonna Rise/UP When We Gonna Rise.' Which is still a good question. At one point in the sixties Archie and I even made appearances in forums at local nightclubs showing that not only was our art connected with struggle but we ourselves were also. We wanted Malcolm poems and Malcolm music.

All this to say that you are in the presence of two great artists, two masters. I hope you can dig it!

59 **James Lincoln Collier** Black, white, and blue (1993)

Source: James Lincoln Collier, 'Black, white, and blue,' in *Jazz: The American Theme Song* (New York: Oxford University Press, 1993: 218–24) (excerpt).

To what extent is it reasonable to describe jazz as black music, and what does it mean to do so? Jazz was originally devised by blacks, albeit a very anomalous group of blacks, many of whom refused to admit they were in fact black; and the music bore a clear relationship to nineteenth century black folk music, which traced its roots back to both Africa and Europe. At that early stage it was certainly possible to say that jazz was, if not black music, at least the music of blacks. After the diaspora, from about 1925 to 1935, most of the leaders in the development of the music were black. True enough, by the late 1920s whites dominated in clarinet playing, and there existed very influential whites like Beiderbecke, Miff Mole, and Teagarden on other instruments. But Hines, Waller, and other stride players were the leaders on piano; Hawkins, Hodges, and others set the pace on saxophone; blacks like Jimmy Harrison, Benny Morton, and Dickie Wells – not Teagarden or Mole – were establishing the basic trombone style; the Duke Ellington Orchestra was charting new paths, and Louis Armstrong was supreme overall. Once again it could at minimum be said that blacks dominated the jazz world.

Furthermore, from time to time jazz continued to dip back into the black culture for refreshment: for example, when the Kansas City bands brought into swing the riff style, developed out of the black boogie-woogie system; and when the *white* players of the dixieland revival looked back to New Orleans jazz for a hot antidote to the well-groomed swing of the big bands. Thus, up until 1940, I should judge that jazz could be considered a black province more than a white one.

But today jazz has had a primarily white audience for perhaps seventy-five years. Jazz criticism was devised by whites and has been mainly in white hands ever since. Jazz education, since it began to have a real existence in the early 1950s, had been dominated by whites. And ever since jazz began to revive in the 1970s after the onslaught of rock, white players like Dave Liebman, John Scofield, Scott Hamilton, and others have done as much to give the music direction as blacks have.

Perhaps more critically, it is my hunch that today a white child from a middle-class suburb is as likely to encounter jazz growing up as is a black child from the ghetto. The audience for jazz today lies mainly in the white middle class: ... [a] N.E.A. study ... shows that the better educated any group is, the more likely it is to be interested in jazz[1] ... There is a surprising amount of jazz being played in mainly white suburbs. It may be true – although I can find no figures – that the black middle class is as interested in jazz as its white counterpart; but as their numbers are substantially smaller, they cannot constitute a major portion of the jazz audience.

For another, the commercial big-city radio stations play little or no jazz, and neither do the black oriented stations. The jazz programs are almost always found on small radio stations – college stations, publicly funded ones, and smaller suburban ones – which are by and large aimed at the better-educated middle-class market.

Finally, the market for jazz records is lodged primarily in the mainly white middle class. Most middle-class people who listen to recorded music at all will have at least a few jazz records of one kind or another on the shelf. It is a terrible irony that jazz has for most of its life got its main support from the very people the jazz world has seen as the enemy, quintessential squares – accountants, car salesmen, high school teachers, insurance brokers, advertising copywriters.

The consequence of all of this is that most white middle-class kids will encounter jazz in some form occasionally as they grow up; and some of them will hear a good deal of it in their homes or the homes of their friends, where somebody regularly listens to the music.

I do not think that that is the case any more in the majority of black homes – at least in such homes where the parents are under fifty. Recently a woman I know who teaches in a black high school – my wife, as it happens – out of curiosity asked her students if they knew who Louis Armstrong was. Only one student even dared to volunteer, and she suggested that he might have been an astronaut. These kids had been born in the mid-1970s when Armstrong was only recently dead. Their parents, who were themselves growing up when Armstrong was becoming the most celebrated American black in the world, could hardly have been unaware of him. And yet so little did Armstrong mean to them that they left no idea of him in the heads of their children. Jazz was simply not part of these children's heritage.

All of this is, of course, anecdotal and only suggestive. It may be that if careful studies were made, they would unearth greater interest in jazz among blacks than this indicates. But I doubt it: it is a simple fact that jazz clubs exist mainly in white, not black areas, that jazz is broadcast on radio aimed at affluent, not ghetto audiences, that jazz educators come mainly from white college-educated groups.

What this means is that if we are to understand how jazz was shaped, we have to stop focussing solely on black culture, however defined, and look as well at the middle-class whites who have provided the bulk of the jazz audience for decades. It is crucial to realize that in Harlem the incipient Ellington band was playing 'cocktail' music: when it moved to Broadway, Ellington reached out for the hot musicians Bechet and Miley; and when it went to the white Cotton Club, Ellington had to expand it and play the arranged hot music white audiences wanted. Fletcher Henderson, with the black-owned Black Swan label, was producing mainly pseudo-blues and pop records; when it moved into the white venues it rapidly evolved into a hot big band playing complex arrangements. In the late 1920s Armstrong had to abandon the blues-oriented small band style blacks preferred and front a big band. In sum, as it became clear that there was a large white audience for jazz, it was redesigned to suit white, not black, tastes. Later, it was whites, mainly middle class, who populated Birdland to hear Parker, bought those hundreds of thousands of copies of 'A Love Supreme' and 'My Favorite Things,' made Davis wealthy, and Marsalis a star. Jazz does not simply blossom from the black culture: it is shaped by an audience who will buy this and not buy that. Yet to my knowledge no jazz critic has ever looked at this group to see why they have chosen what they did. Almost universally they continue instead to look at jazz as if it were purely a product of 'the black experience.' As a consequence, we have a *Down Beat* writer denominating as 'African-American music' a record by white trumpeter Warren Vaché, accompanied by the Beaux-Arts String Quartet playing Tin Pan Alley tunes like 'With the Wind and the Rain in Your Hair.'[2] This is simply ludicrous.

Second, it does not do jazz any good – or jazz studies at any rate – when we by reflex turn to blacks as authorities on the music simply because they are black, as has been the case for example of Lincoln Center in New York. Nobody has racial knowledge of jazz history or the ability to analyze a jazz solo. Black scholars who are interested in black music usually choose some other form of it to study: gospel, the spirituals, black classical composers. Black jazz historians are extremely rare.

As a consequence, a jazz lecture program, repertory series, and the like must perforce depend on many whites. Any program that attempts to rule whites off the turf (as has happened) will be impoverished.[3] I am by no means saying that there are no blacks out there capable of running such jazz programs, or that they all ought to be turned over to whites. There are certainly qualified blacks available, and it is equally true ... that there are a lot of white jazz journalists running jazz programs of one kind or another who are not qualified to do so.

My point simply is that we ought to be choosing people to review jazz books, run jazz studies programs, sit on grants committees and so forth on the basis of their qualifications, rather than on skin color. And yet as obvious as this would seem, there remain a large number of people in the jazz world who continue to use race as a critical guidepost, as the cases of Schuller, Williams, Peretti, and others suggest.

The jazz world was the first area in American life to become reasonably well racially integrated, and it remains in the forefront today: in sports it is still difficult for blacks to get into the 'front office,' but they have been in the front offices in jazz for a long time. Do we really wish to polarize jazz into white and black camps? In the short term the insistence that jazz is black music and that blacks ought to run it may do a few blacks, who get jobs out of it, some good. I cannot see how it is going to be for the good of anybody, white or black, in the long run.

Bruce Boyd Raeburn has said:

> I have always found it ironic that many jazz adherents will make claims (usually with political implications) on behalf of 'jazz' that the originators of the music themselves would never have endorsed. The willingness to let talent or innovation serve as the standard (as opposed to 'race' or 'class') was a major breakthrough and helped to cement relations within the broader jazz community. Isn't the point of *contact* exactly where we should be focusing our efforts? Emphasis on a *black* or *white* ethos for heuristic purposes is fine, as long as we finally come to grips with the *American* ethos – what ties it all together – more than a composite of African and European.[4]

Gerald Early makes the same point: 'Where else, other than in the popular culture arenas of sports and music, have the races really come together, really syncretized their being? And has it not been, in many compelling ways, that society has experienced its greatest changes for the better through just these avenues of marginalized culture suddenly taking center stage in the culture for one crucial moment?'[5]

It is only human for people to feel proprietary about a cultural artifact they love. The English educated classes have always resented hearing Shakespeare played with American accents, and they think of English literature as *theirs*, something that Americans might do well to study, but surely should not offer any comment on. The French laugh viciously at foreigners who attempt to speak their language without doing so perfectly, and Americans have equally resented claims by the French that they appreciate jazz more than Americans do.

Yet can we really claim that a cultural artifact, like the plays of Shakespeare, the sculpture of classical antiquity, the music of Bach, 'belongs' to anybody? Can Italian opera be performed only by Italians, English literature written only by the English, Chinese painting criticized only by the Chinese? It seems to me that a cultural artifact belongs to anyone who brings to it passion and effort – that English literature, Italian opera, French painting, or African drumming belong to any of us who will cherish them.

How then can we conclude that jazz belongs to anyone? It is worth pointing out that today Europeans are beginning to insist that jazz, far from being black music, is not even American music, but an international form whose practitioners need not look to the United States for leadership. Jazz has been modified by too many forces to assign it an ethnicity. Surely it belongs to us all, and just as surely, the masterpieces of Armstrong, Coltrane, Beiderbecke, and the rest are as much the heritage of the kid from the suburban middle class as they are of the child from the ghetto.

Notes (edited)

1   Alvin E. Amos and William C. Smiley, 'An Investigation of Factors That Influence the Ability to Discriminate Jazz Music,' 1–13, *Proceedings of the National Association of Jazz Educators Research*, Vol. 2 (1982). According to his study, blacks were no better able to 'discriminate' jazz than whites. The critical factors were education, class status, family income, etc. See also Horowitz, *The American Jazz Audience* (Washington, DC: National Jazz Service Organization, 1986), 22–28.
2   Kevin Whitehead, *Down Beat*, Vol. 57, no. 3 (March, 1990), 43.
3   The recently installed jazz program at Lincoln Center, for example, has been criticized for the disproportionate number of blacks appearing as musicians and lecturers in its programs. See Whitney Balliett, 'Wynton Looks Back,' *The New Yorker* (October 14, 1991).
4   Bruce Boyd Raeburn, personal communication.
5   Gerald Early, *Tuxedo Junction* (New York: Ecco, 1989), 52.

60 **Gene Lees** Jazz black and white (1994)

Source: Gene Lees, 'Jazz black and white,' in *Cats of Any Color: Jazz Black and White* (New York: Oxford University Press, 1994: 187–90) (excerpt).

On April 12, 1991, a remarkable interview with Sonny Rollins appeared in the *New York Times,* remarkable because it was a highly visible public admission by a major black artist that there exists a substantial anti-white racism in jazz.

The occasion for the interview, with Peter Watrous, was a Carnegie Hall reunion concert with guitarist Jim Hall. Thirty years earlier, Rollins had made the album *The Bridge* with Hall.

Rollins told Watrous, 'In 1961 I had been off the music scene for a while, so in contemplating my return ... I thought it would be good to have a band without a piano to make an impression, get a little different sound. Jim had an incredible harmonic sense; he's such a sensitive player. So to me, he was the perfect guy to play with.'

Rollins continued: 'As I recall, we got very good response, it was a big story and the group was great. But there was some controversy about the fact that Jim was white. After *Freedom Suite*' – an album Rollins recorded in 1958 – 'some people expected me to behave in a certain way and wondered why I would hire a white musician. I took some heat for that. I thought it was a healing symbol, and I didn't have any qualms about doing it. Social issues didn't have anything to do with hiring white musicians who were qualified; it was that simple. And it was a great group.'

The job had a salutary effect on the career of Jim Hall. He had been patronized as a mere white west-coast player when that style of music was denigrated in New York as effete. Since Rollins was seen as a black militant, his approval opened doors for Hall, who was forthwith accepted as a major guitarist. The association with Rollins validated Hall, as the period with Miles Davis gave a sort of Good Housekeeping Seal of Approval to Bill Evans and other white musicians Miles hired, including Chick Corea, Dave Holland, Dave Liebman, John Scofield, John McLaughlin, and the saxophonist Bill Evans.

Quiet as it's kept, anti-white bias has existed in jazz for a long time. Oscar Peterson encountered opprobrium when in 1953 he hired Herb Ellis as the guitarist in his trio. 'We,' he said, meaning himself, Herb, and Ray Brown, 'really became a close-knit unit. Our friendship became even tighter, and we were criticized for having a white person in our group.

'I would get hate letters in Chicago about Herbie Ellis being in the group – from both races, by the way, just so everybody gets their rightful recognition. I'd get hate letters about, "What is that white cat doing in the band? He can't play nothin' – he's white." Whatever that had to do with it, I don't know.'

Another black musician who will talk openly of anti-white bias is Art Farmer.

'This whole racial thing,' Art said, 'is a lot of shit, from all the way down all the way to the top. And the closer you get to the top, the more it disappears. But I used to think that way too.

'After Miles Davis made that nonet record for Capitol, what they called *The Birth of the Cool,* he came out to Los Angeles. I'd known him for years. That was a great record, with Gerry Mulligan and Lee Konitz and the others. I said to Miles, "Man, why have you got those white guys on your gig?" Miles said, "I don't care what color they are. As long as they can play the music the way it's supposed to be played, that's what it's all about."

'It made me re-examine my thinking.

'Where I grew up, Arizona and California, you were damned sure that white people couldn't play jazz. The situation was so divided. Your ears would be closed right from the beginning. You just wouldn't listen to some white person playing jazz, just wouldn't give a damn. It went on and on and on and on and on. White people playing jazz, it didn't make any sense to me at all.

'I don't apologize for my ignorance; I was a young kid. But, man, look, if you were a black kid coming up in L.A. and went through all the shit out there, I didn't want to hear about no white people playing jazz. You'd go out and play in a club that drew a mixed audience, and the police would come in and close it down. That kind of thing closed my ears, man. I couldn't give credit where credit was due, because of the social scene.

'After I got away from that, and was able to be more objective about it, then I could hear what people were doing. And then it seemed to me the most stupid thing on earth to think that just because somebody is white they can't play, and vice versa – that just because somebody is black, they can play.

'Years ago, Dizzy Gillespie was on the Mike Wallace television show. Mike said something like, "Is it true that only black people can play jazz?"

'And Dizzy said, "No, it's not true. And if you accept that premise, well then what you're saying is that maybe black people can *only* play jazz. And black people, like anyone else, can be anything they want to be".'

Yet another black musician who will talk about the issue is Clark Terry. But first let me tell you a harrowing story that Clark told me some years ago.

Soon after high school, Clark traveled with Ida Cox and the Darktown Scandals in the Reuben and Cherry Carnival. After finishing a tour, the group went south from Pennsylvania to its winter quarters in Jacksonville, Florida. Clark said, 'I was hanging out with William Oval Austin. We called him Fats Austin. He was a bass player. We had no warm-weather clothes. We went to the five and ten cent store to buy some T-shirts. They cost about fifteen cents in those days.'

The store was crowded, and Austin accidentally bumped into an elderly white woman carrying a cane. She started screaming, 'That nigger tried to knock me down. Kill him, kill him!' Clark and his friend edged their way to the door, and, as soon as they were outside, ran. A screaming mob pursued them. The two musicians came to a site where an office building was being erected. Fortunately for them it was a Saturday and the site was deserted. They ran into it. Clark pulled Austin down into an excavation and the two young men covered themselves with mud and debris. They could hear the crowd running above them. At last a silence descended. 'But we stayed buried in that mud till dark,' Clark said. Then, cautiously, they crawled out of the excavation and left.

It is one of numberless incidents of that kind I have heard, variations on an ugly theme. But it remains especially vivid in my mind, and it is one reason Clark's magnanimity of spirit amazes me. It amazes me that men like Clark can even speak to whites, let alone rise far above racism. Clark despises racism both black and white.

Some years ago he formed a big band to teach music to boys in Harlem. 'I started that band out of my own pocket,' Clark said. 'It was the forerunner of what turned out to be the Jazzmobile. I got all those little kids together and bought instruments for them. One of those kids is now head of the jazz department at Boys High School in Brooklyn.

'We were rehearsing at this little cold-water walkup flat on 125th Street. There was a very talented kid named Fred Wayne, who wrote me about sixty charts. We had a full big band, and I was teaching these kids how to read.

'Don Stratton at the Manhattan School of Music made it possible for us to use the school. Here we've got kids coming off the corner, and for the first time they've got access to classrooms, to blackboards, to music books, to tapes – real college atmosphere.

'After a while I had to go out a lot. I had Don and a few other people to help me teach the kids while I was away. Attendance started falling off. I found out that one kid was a sort of ringleader in the hate-Whitey movement. He had instigated the kids to not pursue the program any more.

'I came back. Don Stratton said, "Things are not going too well, Clark. I kind of suspect what it is, but you'll find out."

'I called a little meeting and came to find that that's what it was. One of the little dudes had the nerve to say to me, "Man, we don't want Whitey teaching us about *our* music."

'There they were with university facilities, instead of climbing up those damned stairs, five flights to rehearse in a cold studio.

'I just gave it up. I just completely forgot about it, I got so disgusted.

'A long time ago, I had a problem with this when I had a big band at Club Baron. The band was about 50–50. I had people come up to me and say, "Man, what kind of shit is this, bringing Whitey up to Harlem?"

'I'd say, "Well, man, Harlem is known as the home of good jazz, and I thought it was up to somebody to bring good jazz back here. In doing so, I picked the best cats I can get, and I don't listen with my eyes."

'My theory is that a note doesn't give a fuck who plays it, as long as he plays it well.'

61 **Leonard Feather** The jazzman as critic: The blindfold test ('Riddle of the races') (1960)

Source: Leonard Feather, 'The jazzman as critic: the blindfold test ("Riddle of the races"),' in *The New Edition of The Encyclopedia of Jazz* (New York: Horizon, 1960: 477–8) (excerpt).

After a long stay in France, the land of Crow Jim, Roy Eldridge made a bet with me that he would be able to distinguish white musicians from Negroes. He did not even guess the 50% to which the law of averages entitled him. Following are racial guesses from Eldridge's ... [interview]:

George Shearing. *To Be or Not to Bop* (London). Shearing, piano; accompanied by white English musicians, Jack Fallon, bass; Norman Burns, drums.

Roy Eldridge: This could be three or four people I know ... On this kind of playing it's hard to tell white from colored. The piano player *might* be white; the bass player, I think – yes, I think he's colored. The drummer's colored, too. It's very well executed, doesn't kill me too much, but gets going nicely when he goes into the block-chords stuff. Two stars.

Miles Davis. *Venus de Milo* (Capitol). Gerry Mulligan, baritone and arranger.

Eldridge: Haven't the slightest idea who this is; it's a nice-sounding thing ... I couldn't tell whether this is white or colored. Most of these guys play with hardly any vibrato, and a sound without vibrato is an easier thing to capture than one with a distinctive vibrato. One minute I thought it might be Miles Davis, but it's not quite like his sound. The baritone I didn't care for. Arrangement very nice. Three stars.

Billy Taylor quartet. *All Ears* (Coral). All colored musicians.

Eldridge: This is a fair side, combining bop influences with boogie-woogie. Sounded nice on the first chorus. I liked the pianist. Couldn't tell who was colored and who was white. They could be Eskimos for all I know. Two stars.

Billy Strayhorn-Duke Ellington. *Tonk* (Mercer).

Eldridge: This is [a] nice little ditty. Let's see now, what two-piano teams are there? White or colored? It's impossible to tell. Two stars.

Afterthoughts by Roy Eldridge: I guess I'll have to go along with you, Leonard – you can't tell just from listening to records. But I still say that I could spot a white imitator of a colored musician immediately. A white musician trying to copy Hawkins, for instance. And, in the same way, I suppose I could recognize a colored cat trying to copy Bud Freeman. I can only talk about individual sounds that have made it, highly individual sounds. But you take a sound like Tommy Dorsey gets – any good musician could get that. Okay, you win the argument!

62 **Nat Hentoff** Archie Shepp: The way ahead (1968)

Source: Nat Hentoff, 'Archie Shepp: the way ahead,' in Pauline Rivelli and Robert Levin (eds), *Giants of Black Music* (New York: Da Capo, 1979 [*The Black Giants*, 1970]: 118–21).

I first saw and heard Archie Shepp in early 1959. Cecil Taylor brought him to a record date I was 'supervising.' Actually, with Cecil, the only 'supervising' to be done was to tell him how long each take was. He knew exactly what he wanted in his music. As I remember, my initial impression of Archie's playing was that it was very powerful – the kind of intensity that wasn't manufactured, that came from far inside a man with strong feelings and an urgent need to get them out. I also thought at the time that his playing wasn't quite together, but then I wasn't entirely together in my own mind about what was happening in the 'new jazz,' or however you want to describe what has since become part of the basic jazz language of the 1960s.

In the years following, I watched Archie's development – both as a musician and as a trenchantly articulate critic of the contradictions and hypocrisies in American society. He wrote articles and plays; and when a critic would write something about his music that Archie thought obtuse, Archie would usually respond with a stinging rebuttal to the magazine in question. I dug that. For too long most musicians had not answered back, but now critics were being held directly accountable by the musicians themselves for the accuracy of what they said.

Of course, as a result of his determination to speak his thoughts and feelings candidly, Archie came to be considered 'controversial' by some. I consider that term an honorable one, because without controversy, you may get order but you never get justice. Meanwhile he was also acquiring a larger and larger audience for his music. Not that work came easily or often in the States, but it did come from time to time, and his series of LPs for Impulse also added to his public.

In late 1967, Archie and his group toured Europe as part of a musical assembly organized by George Wein. He was heard in Denmark, Holland, Germany, France, Italy, Sweden, and England. There were some dissenters, but, in very large part, both audiences and critics were most impressed. Writing in the British *Jazz Journal*, Barry McRae described how Archie had brought a week in London of 'assorted jazz attractions' to a 'tremendous climax.'

When he returned home, Archie was still buoyant about the reaction of European audiences. 'I think,' he said, 'part of the reason for the success of the tour was the fact that it was imaginatively presented. There was a real diversity of groups. I'd been telling that to club owners in America for years. Diversify. Engage Cecil Taylor and Thelonious Monk together. Or Miles Davis and myself. Anyway, it certainly worked there. At Hammersmith on the British tour we sold out twice in one day.'

The band came off that European tour really together, and although there was no immediate club work for it, Archie did make another album for Impulse, a label with which he had just signed a new extended contract. I asked him what directions he felt his music was going to take in the next year or so. 'For one thing,' Archie answered, 'I'd like to work more and more with African rhythms. I'd like to take a trip to Africa soon, just look around, and absorb some of the contemporary folk material there as well as the older forms of music. It seems to me we have to keep developing a contemporary folk language. That's one of the reasons I listen very closely to rhythm and blues singers – the late Otis Redding, Wilson Pickett, James Brown. They exemplify what I mean by a contemporary folk language. We need more of that in jazz.'

As he spoke, I remembered that a couple of years ago Archie had emphasized his conviction that jazz could reach a wide audience among the young as it got down to basic emotions in a folklike language. And he was especially interested in reaching the black young. He still is. 'But,' he adds, 'we're kept out of communication with the black young. Look at those huge government expenditures for "culture" in poverty areas. They give the money to teach the kids Shakespeare, but why not some of those funds for black music so that kids – and not only black kids – can see how deep and rich the heritage of that music is?'

Archie's own jazz reflects his concern for the full scope and history of the music. How, I asked, would you define the base of the jazz tradition? 'Self-expression,' he answered. 'And a certain quality of human dignity despite all obstacles, despite the enslavement of the black man and then his oppression. And each of the great players has had so distinctive, so individual a voice. There is only one Bird, one Ben Webster, one Cootie Williams. That's jazz – the uniqueness of the individual. If he believes in himself, every person is not only different but valuably different.

'I think this uniqueness of the individual,' Archie added, 'is less operative in the so-called 'new jazz' because many of the younger players haven't had the chance to get enough experience relating to audiences. Nor has there been enough understanding by some of them of the whole jazz tradition. We all need deep relationships to the masters – Pres and Bird and the like – who led the way. That's one thing our group has, that sense of relationship. In Europe, we moved audiences even though we followed Miles Davis. And you know it's hard to follow Miles. But I'd spent a lot of time listening to Miles. I knew each of his periods, I know his tradition. So although we certainly played our own way, what we played showed our knowledge of what had preceded us – and an audience feels that.'

I mentioned to Archie that a British journalist had written, 'Shepp's playing has an immediacy that demands action,' and that, accordingly, when he played at Ronnie Scott's club, there were people who couldn't keep themselves from dancing. 'Yes,' said Archie, 'I'm always pleased when people dance. Jazz *ought* to be danced to. Don't forget music has always been a *performing* art – and that means in terms of the audience as well as the players. In the past, when people have felt jazz strongly, they've danced to it. There's no reason it shouldn't be that way now. And a player needs this added dimension of communication with an audience. It's a great feeling, a very graphic emotional sight, when an audience moves.'

A while ago, Archie recalled, he and his band had played at the wedding of the daughter of film maker Shirley Clarke. 'We'd been into a tune for forty-five minutes,' Archie said, 'when Jason, a man Shirley made a picture about, grabbed her and they started to dance. In a split second everyone was dancing. And you know, seeing and feeling them dance recharged us so that we played that tune for ninety minutes!

'That all makes sense to me,' Archie went on. 'It's part of the tradition I was talking about. I like it when people clap their hands and pat their feet to our music. And every once in a while we play in 4/4. Some of the so-called "avant-garde" guys don't do that. They think it's passé. I don't. It's absurd to throw out everything from the past in order to be "new." If things from the past fit, you use them.'

Thinking of the jazz past and of its future, I remembered what Archie had written about the present sounds of jazz in a *New York Times* article, 'Black Power and Black Jazz': 'This new statement has been accused of being "angry" by some, and if so, there is certainly some justification for that emotion. On the other hand, it does not proscribe on the basis of color. Its only prerequisites are honesty and an open mind. The breadth of this statement is as vast as America, its theme the din of the streets, its motive freedom.'

In our conversation, I asked him to elaborate. 'The underlying symbolism of jazz,' Archie said, 'has always been black, and so have been the great innovators. But jazz is accessible to all people, if they're honest enough to receive it. Roswell Rudd in our band is an example of that. It's an honesty that's necessary not only in jazz, but with regard to the most crucial problem in America – the racial problem. Most whites have allowed the relationship between the races to deteriorate, but there are some who are honest about what has to be done and who do see the need for profound and meaningful change in this country to end racism. But there's so much distance now between the white and black worlds, so much noncommunication. And yet if that problem isn't solved, the future is, to say the least, very bleak.'

And what of Archie's own future? 'As rough as it may be economically, I'm going to keep the band together as best I can. And we'll keep recording for Impulse.' Archie also remains active as a playwright, having recently completed two one-act works, *Skulls* and *69*. He had taught in the schools for a while. Would he ever do it again? 'Not in the schools as they are now,' Archie answered. 'The only kind of teaching I'd like to do is in a school I'd build myself with the kind of curriculum which allows for creative teaching and for learning in a natural environment.'

What of the future of jazz? 'It must return to the ghetto where it began,' Archie emphasized. 'We have to reach the kids and become part of the whole cultural experience, the whole history out of which jazz came. But again I wouldn't limit the experience of the music to ghetto children. White kids also need to know what jazz has to say if they're going to live in a real world.'

It is this sense of reality that particularly characterizes Archie's music. As in all the best jazz, the music is an extension of the man. And as a man, Archie addresses himself to the totality of experience in his life. He is an intellectual who does not shut off emotion. Quite the contrary. He is black, and proud of being black, and he is an increasingly important communicator – in his music, in his articles, in his plays – of black consciousness.

In writing about the change in the music of the American black man as he became more and more urbanized, Archie also writes about himself: 'As the tempo of life increased, all art reflected the change. People walked faster. Notes were played faster. New hopes were born and, like the tall buildings of cities, they seemed to reach to the sky. The children of the previous generation were now grown up and were challenging the democratic process to provide solutions instead of academic inquiries. They were not going to be put off with the same old lies, not about to be hacked to death on their knees.'

I don't know what's going to happen with regard to the black-white division in America. I do know that Archie Shepp is one man who is going to keep telling us what he feels – without dilution – in his music and in everything else he does. And you'll never see him on his knees. I also know that the music, like the man, will continue to grow and surprise and provoke listeners into further explorations of their own emotions, their own definitions of what life is about. Like all durable jazzmen in the tradition, Archie is unmistakably unique. But also like them, his basic concerns are universal and elemental – freedom, dignity, honesty. And that's why his music has such seizing force. It gives you no place to hide.

63 **Arthur Taylor** Interviews with Charles Tolliver, Freddie Hubbard, Hazel Scott and Betty Carter (1970–2)

Source: Arthur Taylor, Interviews with Charles Tolliver, Freddie Hubbard, Hazel Scott and Betty Carter, in *Notes and Tones: Musician-to-Musician Interviews* (New York: Da Capo, 1993 [1977]: 76–7, 78, 81, 198, 200–1, 263–4, 276–8) (excerpts).

Charles Tolliver

What about the word jazz?
It's a word which was given to the music we're playing by the people who control the music we're playing. It's just a nomenclature. I very rarely use it.
   Do you consider the music you play jazz?
I have to, because that's the given name for the music.
   Some people think it should be canceled.
Yeah, what it should be and what it isn't is a matter of who controls what. If you control the media you can change the dictionary and put in, 'Our form of music is a black experience. It was originated by black people and it should be called Afro-American music'; something like that would be cool. But how the hell are we going to print dictionaries to change the word *jazz*? You know what the definition of jazz is in Webster's dictionary. It's a matter of control. They made a lot of money off the music. That's what they wanted to call it, and that's what it is. Jazz is a derivative of music which was played in the brothels of New Orleans ...
   You have referred to control many times.
The reason we went immediately into that is because what we have now, what we are witnessing, what we are part of and what we are affected by is the result of lackadaisical attitudes in the twenties, the thirties and the forties, when this music became prominent, when people started listening to it and coming out

to hear the musicians they had been reading about. Many of the artists were lackadaisical about that. They were just interested in playing. I don't want to leave only a musical legacy but something material, a foundation for the youth to draw from. This is done in all other art forms except ours ...

Would you say that our form of music stems from black experience in a racist society?
Well, it stemmed from that. We certainly are the innovators of this particular type of music. The only thing for us to do now is to gain control over it – by doing what we've been doing for the last few years; by becoming more aware of ourselves socially, culturally, politically; by being aware of the fact that ownership carries a lot of weight in today's world. You have to own something. We own the musical value, but we don't own the music itself or the direction of the music.

Freddie Hubbard

What do you think of the word jazz?
This is something I encounter all the time when I'm on the road. That's the first thing a white cat will ask me. A disc jockey will say, 'What would you like to call the music: jazz or black music?' It has a stigma, but it's just a word to describe music which doesn't bother me at all. It's like classical music – if people really knew what that meant, they wouldn't judge it. Classical music is something that lasts through the years that people dig. They keep it. To me a Charlie Parker composition is a classic, it's a work of art!

Jazz is a label white people gave to the music. How do you know some black cat didn't say it? You know. 'Hey, baby, that's jazz.' That's usually what happens: White people will take up your phrases, use them and tell you that they're new.

Just like the word *jazz*, so what. Jazz has connotations of barrooms and prostitutes and having to play in those kind of conditions. That's why I'm trying to get into the colleges. If some professor asks me what jazz is, it's a music and it's a word that I heard describing the music and it's beautiful music regardless of what you think about it. It's just a word, just like your name. Somebody says Arthur Taylor, then looks at you as a black person: It's the same thing. It's a white name, it's a slave name. White people would like to create that kind of mystique about it. It's jazzy, it's black and it comes out of the underground, which it does ...

What do you think about the strife going on in America with our people?
It's good. The more strife, the more advancement we make. You as a black man living in another country are not confronted with all these problems, since there are not that many black people to cause problems. But the same conditions exist in Europe, too. I've been to Europe about nine or ten times, and I don't see that much more work, I don't see that many more business opportunities. I'm not talking about you as an individual, I'm talking about black people. So in fact the only problem Europe doesn't have is the racial thing; it's not as tense as it is in the States. But they use you in Europe, too, if they can.

It's just as tense in Europe as it is in the States, but a little bit more undercover.
I think revolution is good for the United States. Black people are beginning to
wake up and say wow, he's been doing this to me, he's been prostituting me
and using me ... There's always going to be strife in this country, because
they're white and we're black. They tried to teach us that they were better, but it
doesn't mean anything. I'm glad to see what's happening today. I think this will
eventually tune these white people in. If we can burn down a few houses, that's
good, because they've got to put up new ones. We as musicians – and black
people in general – should learn to trust each other and get out of this petty ego
trip thing. Once black people realize they're black and that white men have still
got the hammer, it will be better for all of us. I'm not totally blaming whitey. If
only you could get musicians to think on a business level ... but they won't
stick together ... If we could only get black people to dig themselves! I'm just
beginning to dig myself as a human being and to be proud that I can play the
trumpet. I'm proud of the fact I can do what I'm doing, and that's the message I
want to convey to all my black brothers.

Hazel Scott

What do you see in the future for us as black people?
Well, I don't intend to stop trying to help us get ourselves together. Every time I
see one of us doing something separative which will hurt us, I have to open my
mouth ... We need to love one another much more than we do. To help one
another, to look out for each other. To see that what has gone before us is
known to those who are coming along now. To give the children a sense of
pride which, thank God, black people have today ... I think we musicians are
emissaries. Every time we go before the public, we're there to make converts.
We can either be ugly and contemptuous in our behavior, which will turn
people off, or else we can carry ourselves with dignity and pride. We can't
expect anyone else to respect us if we don't respect ourselves.

Betty Carter

Betty, I am very impressed with your sons. They are very respectful.
... We expose them to all kinds of music, because we listen to everything ... all I
want is for young kids to be exposed to other music so they can make a choice
... Kids often come up to me and ask, 'Where have you been? I haven't heard of
you before; how long have you been singing?' I ask them how old they are, and
they say maybe twenty-two. Why have you got to be twenty-two before you
know anything about Miles Davis? Right now there are some black kids in high
school and college who know nothing at all about him. When it comes to
picking out something on one of those records that have been released lately,
you can't find anything to talk about because there's so much sound going on.
It's just sound. It hasn't got anything to do with music. New gimmicks coming
up, the wa-wa this and the wa-wa that, the synthesizer this and the Fender that.
And CBS needs more money? They don't need more money! They're making
plenty of money out of us.
    We can do things the white man could never do when it comes to swinging

consistently. We were steady. You remember in the fifties, when we had it sewed up? We made our marks then. We had plenty of giants during those years. What has happened in the last ten years?

Everybody wants a sound, even Miles Davis ... This is what's happening today. We're sticking it right into our own thing by playing sound and not music. Our young musicians are going to pay dues behind sound, because sound is all over the place, and we should learn our instruments. For instance, they don't know any songs or melodies. Forget the melodies, forget the roots, they don't even want to play ordinary blues. You hardly hear Charlie Parker's name mentioned anymore.

It's old-fashioned!

Right! So they do a play called *The Musical Tragedy of Billie Holiday,* and Archie Shepp writes the music. To me ... it was an insult to Billie Holiday, because he wrote rock music. I know she wouldn't have dug it, because that wasn't what she was all about. But they were influenced by the white media. They put up the money and hoped it would be another *Jesus Christ Superstar* or another *Hair,* with the story of Billie Holiday involved. No, no! What do you think this play could have done for the young individual who went to see it if only they had told the story the way it really was musically? It could have educated a lot of young kids. But they don't want to do that, they just want to make some money and distort the issue at the same time. I wouldn't even insult myself by going to see it. I heard the music and I know that Archie Shepp wasn't the man who should have written that music. Maybe the white people thought he could do it, but you can go uptown and ask ten people on the street who Archie Shepp is and they won't be able to tell you. Ninety percent of his audience is white.

I feel that if you're playing something black, black people should know about it. You shouldn't avoid them. You ought to go to them to get the stamp. Unless they give you the stamp, you're not doing anything worthwhile, because it's their culture.

64 **Langston Hughes** Bop (1961)

Source: Langston Hughes, 'Bop,' in *The Best of Simple* (New York: Hill and Wang, 1961: 117–19).

Somebody upstairs in Simple's house had the combination turned up loud with an old Dizzy Gillespie record spinning like mad filling the Sabbath with Bop as I passed.

'Set down here on the stoop with me and listen to the music,' said Simple.

'I've heard your landlady doesn't like tenants sitting on her stoop,' I said.

'Pay it no mind,' said Simple. 'Ool-ya-koo,' he sang. 'Hey Ba-Ba-Re-Bop! Be-Bop! Mop!'

'All that nonsense singing reminds me of Cab Calloway back in the old *scat* days,' I said, 'around 1930 when he was chanting, "Hi-de-*hie*-de-ho! Hee-de-*hee*-de-hee!"'

'Not at all,' said Simple, 'absolutely not at all.'

'Re-Bop certainly sounds like scat to me,' I insisted.

'No,' said Simple, 'Daddy-o, you are wrong. Besides, it was not *Re*-Bop. It is *Be*-Bop.'

'What's the difference,' I asked, 'between *Re* and *Be*?'

'A lot,' said Simple. 'Re-Bop was an imitation like most of the white boys play. Be-Bop is the real thing like the colored boys play.'

'You bring race into everything,' I said, 'even music.'

'It is in everything,' said Simple.

'Anyway, Be-Bop is passé, gone, finished.'

'It may be gone, but its riffs remain behind,' said Simple. 'Be-Bop music was certainly colored folks' music – which is why white folks found it so hard to imitate. But there are some few white boys that latched onto it right well. And no wonder, because they sat and listened to Dizzy, Thelonious, Tad Dameron, Charlie Parker, also Mary Lou, all night long every time they got a chance, and bought their records by the dozens to copy their riffs. The ones that sing tried to make up new Be-Bop words, but them white folks don't know what they are singing about, even yet.'

'It all sounds like pure nonsense syllables to me.'

'Nonsense, nothing!' cried Simple. 'Bop makes plenty of sense.'

'What kind of sense?'

'You must not know where Bop comes from,' said Simple, astonished at my ignorance.

'I do not know,' I said. 'Where?'

'From the police,' said Simple.

'What do you mean, from the police?'

'From the police beating Negroes' heads,' said Simple. 'Every time a cop hits a Negro with his billy club, that old club says, "BOP! BOP! ... BE-BOP! ... MOP! ... BOP!"'

'That Negro hollers, "Ooool-ya-koo! Ou-o-o!"'

'Old Cop just keeps on, "MOP! MOP! ... BE-BOP! ... MOP!" That's where Be-Bop came from, beaten right out of some Negro's head into them horns and saxophones and piano keys that plays it. Do you call that nonsense?'

'If it's true, I do not,' I said.

'That's why so many white folks don't dig Bop,' said Simple. 'White folks do not get their heads beat *just for being white*. But me – a cop is liable to grab me almost any time and beat my head – *just* for being colored.

'In some parts of this American country as soon as the police see me, they say, "Boy, what are you doing in this neighborhood?"'

'I say, "Coming from work, sir."'

'They say, "Where do you work?"'

'Then I have to go into my whole pedigree because I am a black man in a white neighborhood. And if my answers do not satisfy them, BOP! MOP! ... BE-BOP! ... MOP! If they do not hit me, they have already hurt my soul. *A dark man shall see dark days.* Bop comes out of them dark days. That's why real Bop is mad, wild, frantic, crazy – and not to be dug unless you've seen dark days, too. Folks who ain't suffered much cannot play Bop, neither appreciate it. They think Bop is nonsense – like you. They think it's just *crazy* crazy. They do not know Bop is also MAD crazy, SAD crazy, FRANTIC WILD CRAZY – beat out of somebody's head! That's what Bop is. Them young colored kids started it, they know what Bop is.'

'Your explanation depresses me,' I said.

'Your nonsense depresses me,' said Simple.

65 **Billie Holiday** Travelin' light (1956)

Source: Billie Holiday, with William Dufty, 'Travelin' light,' in *Lady Sings the Blues* (London: Penguin, 1984 [1956]: 70–3) (excerpt).

Don't tell me about those pioneer chicks hitting the trail in those slip-covered wagons with the hills full of redskins. I'm the girl who went West in 1937 with sixteen white cats, Artie Shaw and his Rolls-Royce – and the hills were full of white crackers.

It all began one night at Clarke Monroe's Uptown House.

Artie came in and got to talking and dreaming about his new band. He thought he needed something sensational to give it a shove.

'Something sensational? That's easy,' I told him. 'Hire a good Negro singer.'

That did it. Artie waited for me all night at the Uptown House and put me right in his car to take me to Boston for the opening. Georgie Auld, Tony Pastor, and Max Kaminsky were with him. Before we left, we drove over to Mom's and she fixed fried chicken for a 6:30 A.M. breakfast for the whole gang. The chicken knocked Artie out. He never ate anything like she fixed it. When the chicken was gone, we piled into his car and were off.

Boston was jumping then. We were booked in Roseland. Glenn Miller was working just around the corner, and a block away there was Chick Webb and his band with Ella Fitzgerald. Chick's group was the best known; but we were still better known than Miller.

The sight of sixteen men on a bandstand with a Negro girl singer had never been seen before – in Boston or anywhere. The question of how the public would take to it had to be faced opening night at Roseland. Naturally Sy Schribman, the owner of Roseland and a guy who did a lot for bands like Dorsey, Miller, and others, was worried.

But Artie was a guy who never thought in terms of white and colored. 'I can take care of the situation,' was his answer. 'And I know Lady can take care of herself.'

'As far as I'm concerned,' I told Artie, 'I don't care about sitting on the bandstand. When it comes time for me to sing a number, you introduce me, I sing, then I'm gone.'

Artie disagreed. 'No,' he insisted. 'I want you on the bandstand like Helen Forrest and Tony Pastor and everyone else.' So that's what I did. Everything up in Boston was straight – but the real test was coming up. We were heading for Kentucky.

Kentucky is like Baltimore – it's only on the border of being the South, which means the people there take their Dixie stuff more seriously than the crackers farther down.

Right off, we couldn't find a place that would rent me a room. Finally Artie got sore and picked out the biggest hotel in town. He was determined to crack it – or he was going to sue. I tried to stop him. 'Man,' I said, 'are you trying to get me killed?'

Artie had taken the band on the road for a good reason – he wanted to play to as many people as possible before risking a New York opening. The band had enough work to do without looking for lawsuits around every corner and doing a job for the NAACP.

But there was no moving Artie. He's a wild one; he has his own peculiarities but he's amazing and a good cat deep down. He's not one to go back on his word. Whatever he says, Jack, you can believe that's it. Whatever he'd set out to do, he would believe in it. He might find he was wrong, but rather than go back on his word, he'd suffer. That's the way he was and that's why I liked him, and that's why he wouldn't listen to me in Kentucky. He got eight cats out of the band and they escorted me to the registration desk at the biggest hotel in that little old Kentucky town.

I don't think anybody black had ever got a room there before, but the cats in the band acted like it was as natural as breathing. I think the man at the desk figured it couldn't be true what he thought he saw, and I couldn't be a Negro or nobody would act like that. I think they thought I was Spanish or something, so they gave me a nice room and no back talk.

The cats had a little taste of triumph, so they went on from there. All eight of them waltzed into the dining room, carrying me with them like I was the *Queen Mary* and they were a bunch of tugboats. We sat down, ordered food all around and champagne, acting up like we were a sensation. And we were.

After that scene I guess the management thought they were getting off easy in letting me have a room.

It was a one-man town. And the sheriff was the man. He ran things. He was on the scene that night when we opened in a real-life natural rock cave. The sheriff was haunting the place, letting kids in for half price. They were selling kids whisky right under his nose. But he didn't pay any mind to that. He was too busy dogging me.

When it came time to go on, I told Artie I didn't want any trouble and didn't want to sit on the bandstand.

'It just don't make sense,' I told him. 'This is the damn South.' But Artie didn't want to give in. He was unhappy. I was unhappy. Finally we compromised and agreed I would come out on the stand and sit just before my numbers.

I could smell this sheriff a mile off. I told the cats in the band he was looking for trouble.

'He wants to call me nigger so bad he's going to find a way,' I told them. And so I bet Tony Pastor, Georgie Auld and Max Kaminsky two bucks apiece he would make it.

He did.

When I came on, the sheriff walked up to the raised bandstand; Artie's back was to the dance floor, so he pulled Artie's pants leg and said, 'Hey you!' Artie turned around. 'Don't touch me,' he hollered over the music.

But the sheriff didn't give up so easy. I had money riding on what he would do, so I was watching him real close. So were the cats I had the bet with. They were keeping a free eye on him. He pulled Artie's leg again. 'Hey you,' he said.

Artie turned around. 'You want to get kicked?' he asked him.

Still the old cracker sheriff didn't give up. Back he came again. 'Hey you,' he said. Then he turned to me and, so loud everybody could hear, he said, 'What's Blackie going to sing?'

Artie looked like it was the end of the world – and the tour. I guess he thought I was going to break down and have a collapse or something. But I was laughing like hell. I turned to Georgie, Tony, and Max, put my hand out, and said, 'Come on now, give me the money.'

66 **Mezz Mezzrow** Out of the gallion (1946)

Source: Mezz Mezzrow, with Bernard Wolfe, 'Out of the gallion,' in *Really the Blues* (New York: Random House, 1946: 319, 321–4) (excerpts).

One afternoon things came to a head for me; in ten frantic minutes the formless mush of my life bubbled and seethed and then jelled, in a shape I could finally recognize ... It won't sound like anything much – we were just marching along in the band, playing the same old corny *Our Director*, and the professor stopped to talk with the warden but we continued on across the Island. I was captain of the band by this time, so I took over. Then we drew close to the powerhouse, where the all-colored Ninth Division was working, and all the guys came running out to hear us, like they always did ...

Well, as I stepped along, the rhythm of the march made me feel exhilarated and lightheaded, and when we got near to the power-house and I saw all our friends there, I decided to break all the chains off me and let myself go. I was so excited and tense, all of sudden, you would of thought I was about to rob a bank. I started to improvise the march on my clarinet, forgetting all the written music we'd rehearsed with the professor. And then, Jesus, I fell into a queer dreamy state, a kind of trance, where it seemed like I wasn't in control of myself any more, my body was running through its easy relaxed motions and my fingers were flying over the keys without any push or effort from me – somebody else had taken over and was directing all my moves, with me just drifting right along with it, feeling it was all fitting and good and proper. I got that serene, crazy kind of exaltation that you hear religious people sometimes talking about and think they're cracked. And it was exactly, down to a T, the same serene exaltation I'd sensed in New Orleans music as a kid, and that had haunted me all my life, that I'd always wanted to recapture for myself and couldn't. Frankie Ward was just behind me, and the spirit caught hold of him too and he fell right in, playing drums that suddenly weren't talking the beat-up language of Sousa but the ageless language of New Orleans, thumping it out loud and forceful. Right away the whole band stiffened up and began to sparkle, like they'd all got a heavy shot of thyroid extract. Travis, who was playing the lead on his horn, got carried away in the flood too and he began to swing out with a sudden husky vibrant tone, taking his breath at the natural intervals just where he felt them, and the whole band was suddenly marching and swaying to a new rhythm. And every beat Frankie pounded on his drums was in perfect time with every variation somebody picked out on my clarinet, and my clarinet and the trumpet melted together in one gigantic harmonic orgasm, and my fingers ran every whichaway, and the fellows in the Ninth Division began to grin and stomp and shout. 'Blow it Mezz!' they yelled. 'Yeah, I hear you!' 'Get away, poppa!' 'Put me in the alley!'

And all of a sudden, you know who I was? I was Jimmy Noone and Johnny Dodds and Sidney Bechet, swinging down Rampart Street and Basin Street and Perdido Street, down through Storyville, stepping high and handsome, blowing all the joy and bounce of life through my clarinet. While the guy on those powerful drums behind me was Tubby Hall and Baby Dodds and Zutty Singleton, all rolled up in one, and the boy on the trumpet that was playing melodious hide-and-seek with my clarinet was King Oliver and Tommy Ladnier, and yes, Louis too, the one and only Pops, the greatest of them all. And it was Mardi Gras time, and we were strutting on down at the head of the gay parade, blowing *High Society* and *Didn't He Ramble* and *Moose March* and *Dusty Rag* and *Muskrat Ramble* and *Milneburg Joys* and *When the Saints Go Marching In* and *We Shall Walk Through the Streets of the City*, back in the great days when jazz was born, back at the throbbing root and source of all jazz, making it all fresh and new. All of a sudden we were right smack in Gay New Orleans. Not the one out on Flushing Meadows, Long Island, the mecca of the summer tourists – the one down on the Mississippi delta, full of levees and cribs and red lights and barrelhouse joints and honkytonks, where the greatest music in the world first trembled and soared into being. I had been wandering for twenty years, looking for this fine fabled place, and suddenly I made it, I was home. I was solid home.

For the very first time in my life, you see, I had fallen all the way into the groove and I was playing real authentic jazz, and it was *right* – not Chicago, not Dixieland, not swing or jump or Debussy or Ravel, but *jazz*, primitive, solid, rocking and weaving. All my life I'd been yearning to play this way, and all my life I'd been so scared I couldn't do it (even during those Panassié recordings) that I'd kept running off into sidestreets and detours to avoid trying and failing – and all my misery and frustration and going tangent came from that fear and that running away. Now I was no more afraid. All the rambling years behind suddenly began to make sense, fitted into the picture: the prison days, the miss-meal blues, the hophead oblivion, the jangled nerves, the reefer flights, the underworld meemies. They were all part of my education, had gone into my make-up until I was battered and bruised enough to stumble into the New Orleans idiom and have something to say in it. Those twenty years of striving and failing had all gone down into my fingertips, so that now, all of a sudden, I could tickle the clarinet keys and squeeze out the only language in the whole wide world that would let me speak my piece.

And you know what my piece was? A very simple story: *Life is good, it's great to be alive!* No matter how many times you go hungry, how many times you get a boot in your backside and a club over your head – no matter how tough the scuffle is, it's great to be alive, brother! I had to get my knocks, plenty of them, before I could understand that. The colored people, fresh up out of three hundred years of slavery, still the despised pariahs of the country in spite of their 'liberation,' had understood it all along and finally, forty, fifty years ago, had roared out a revolutionary new music to shout that message to the world. That was what New Orleans was really saying – it was a celebration of life, of breathing, of muscle-flexing, of eye-blinking, of licking-the-chops, in spite of everything the world might do to you. It was a defiance of the undertaker. It was a refusal to go under, a stubborn hanging on, a shout of praise to the circulatory system, hosannas for the sweat-glands, hymns to the guts that ache when they're hollow. Glory be, brother! Hallelujah, the sun's shining! Praise be the almighty pulse! Ain't nobody going to wash us away. We here, and we going to stay put – don't recognize no eviction notices from the good green earth. Spirit's still in us, and it sure must got to jump. We going to tell 'bout all that in this fine music of ours ... I knew exactly what there was to say on my horn now; knew all the words in the New Orleans idiom, and how to express them. Jimmy Noone and Johnny Dodds and Sidney Bechet, they'd known all along, and now they were inside my skin, making my fingers work right so I could speak my piece.

Yes, right then and there I busted out of my spiritual gallion and came home, and my burden melted away. The rest of my life spread out in front of me smooth and serene, because I not only knew what I had to do, I knew I could do it. *I could do it.* I was with it Jim, really with it. The millennium was on me – a small-size, strictly one-man millennium, but still a millennium. It told this green man something.

67 **Michael Harper** Here where Coltrane is (1977)

Source: Michael Harper, 'Here where Coltrane is,' in *Images of Kin: New and Selected Poems* (Urbana: University of Illinois Press, 1977: 160).

Soul and race
are private dominions,
memories and modal
songs, a tenor blossoming,
which would paint suffering
a clear color but is not in
this Victorian house
without oil in zero degree
weather and a forty-mile-an-hour wind;
it is all a well-knit family:
a love supreme.
Oak leaves pile up on walkway
and steps, catholic as apples
in a special mist of clear white
children who love my children.
I play 'Alabama'
on a warped record player
skipping the scratches
on your faces over the fibrous
conical hairs of plastic
under the wooden floors.

Dreaming on a train from New York
to Philly, you hand out six
notes which become an anthem
to our memories of you:
oak, birch, maple,
apple, cocoa, rubber.
For this reason Martin is dead;
for this reason Malcolm is dead;
for this reason Coltrane is dead;
in the eyes of my first son are the browns
of these men and their music.

68 **Albert Murray** Epilogue, *Stomping the Blues* (1976)

Source: Albert Murray, 'Epilogue,' *Stomping the Blues* (New York: McGraw-Hill, 1976: 257–8).

The main thing that it is always about is the also and also of dragging, driving, jumping, kicking, swinging, or otherwise stomping away the blues as such and having a good time not only as a result but also in the meanwhile. Which is also why whatever else hearing it makes you remember you also remember being somewhere among people wearing fine clothes and eating and laughing and talking and shucking and stuffing and jiving and conniving and making love. So sometimes it is also about the also and also of signifying and qualifying. Because sometimes, especially when you are still only a very young beginner standing at the edge of the dance floor getting yourself together to go over to where the girls (whose prerogative it is to say no) stand waiting to be approached and asked, it is also as if the orchestra were woofing at you. Back in the heyday of big dance halls like the Savoy, when the orchestra used to break into, say, *Big John Special* (Fletcher Henderson, Decca DL 9228) or, say, *Cavernism* (Earl Hines, Decca DL 9221) or *Second Balcony Jump* (Earl Hines, Bandstand Records 7115) or *Wolverine Blues* (Louis Armstrong, Ace of Hearts AH 7) or *Miss Thing* (Count Basie, Columbia G 31224) or *Panassié Stomp* or *Shorty George, Every Tub* or *Dogging Around* (Count Basie, Decca DXSB 7170) or, say, *Cottontail* (Duke Ellington, RCA Victor LPM 1364), *Johnny Come Lately* (Duke Ellington, RCA Victor LPV 541), *Rockabye River*, erstwhile *Hop Skip Jump* (Duke Ellington, RCA Victor LPM 6009) it was as if you were being challenged (in a voice not unlike the rhapsodized thunder of a steam-snorting bluesteel express train highballing it hell for leather) to test your readiness, willingness, and nimbleness by escorting a girl of your choice around and up and down and across and crisscross the ballroom floor as if into and back again from the region of blue devils with all her finery intact, as if who else if not you were the storybook prince, as if whoever if not she were the fairytale princess.

Not that anybody has ever actually qualified once and for all. When the storybook hero is reported to have lived happily ever after his triumph over the dragon, it is not to be assumed that he is able to retire but rather that what he has been through should make him more insightful, more skillful, more resilient, and hence better prepared to cope with eventualities. Because there will always be other dragons, which after all are as much a part of the nature of things as is bad weather.

Nor has anybody ever been able to get rid of the blues forever either. You can only drive them away and keep them at bay for the time being. Because they are always there, as if always waiting and watching. So retirement is out of the question. But even so old pro that you have become, sometimes all you have to hear is the also and also of the drummer signifying on the high-hat cymbal, even in the distance (and it is as if it were the also and also of time itself whispering red alert as if in blue italics), and all you have to do to keep them in their proper place, which is deep in the dozens, is to pat your feet and snap your fingers.

69 **Charles Mingus** The final set for this afternoon (1971)

Source: Charles Mingus (ed. Nel King), *Beneath the Underdog: His World As Composed by Mingus* (New York: Knopf, 1971: 156–9) (excerpt). (Editor's title)

'And now, ladies and gentlemen, the final set for this afternoon. Stan Levy, drums, from Dizzy Gillespie's group. Dodo Marmarosa, piano. Lucky Thompson, tenor sax.'

'Who's he, Buddy?'

'Cat cut from Basie's.'

'Buddy Collette, alto sax. Charlie Parker, a gentleman from Dizzy's group also. And Charles Mingus on bass. And please will all you people give Miles Davis a hand – Miles is just in from New York. Come on now, everybody – Miles Davis! Give him a good California welcome!'

'Okay, Bird. Something everybody knows.'

' "Billy's Bounce"?'

'Don't know that, Bird.'

'It's just the blues in F. Buddy, gone ... Take four, Dodo ... Blow, Miles.'

'I done blew, motherfucker. Now you got it, cocksucker. Blow, Lucky.'

'... Miles, why's his head so swollen? ... He sounds like a sub-tone Don Byas.'

'What was that, country-boy bass-player? Cool it and keep some time behind me!'

'Keep your own time, Lucky, before I start playing your solos back at you.'

'What? Dig this cat! With a bass? Come on, I want to hear that.'

'Move over and share the mike, big head, so you won't be embarrassed. I'll ape you. Dodo, Stan, lay out. Stroll.'

'Whewhee! This motherfucker can play! What was that tag you added to my solo?'

'Kiddle lid.'

'How the hell you play that sound like you laughing and talking?'

'Bird, you hear this country boy?'

'Yeah, Lucky, did you? The same way we make dah ooh dah down on chromatics from your C to C sharp to B to C natural, B flat to B natural, and so forth. He just added a quarter tone glissando, put his heart in it.'

'The other night I heard a cat play bass the way Adolphus Allbrook used to. It don't supposed to be possible but they do it.'

'Bird, you putting me on? That's the second time I heard about Adolphus Allbrook. Jimmy Blanton told me he carved a wooden pick with one hand, kept playing with the other, finished his pick, and played more than a guitar with it.'

'Stone genius, Mingus.'

'I'd sure like to meet him.'

'Yeah, he's great. A scientist too – physics major. Teaches judo at the police department. Mastered the harp in two years.'

'When are you motherfuckers going to stop talking and start playing, instead of just Dodo and Stan over there jacking off?'

'Miles, you're so vulgar.'

'I want to hear Bird blow, not all this dumb-ass conversation.'

'So gone. One, two, one, two, three, four.'

'Yeah, Bird. Play, baby! Go, man!'

'Hooray!'

'Ladies and gentlemen, will you all shut up and just listen to this motherfucker blowing!'

'Miles! Careful, man, you can't say that.'

'Schitt, man, I put my hand over the mike on "motherfucker." Remember Monk calling the club owner in Detroit a motherfucker seven times on the mike 'cause he didn't have a good piano?'

'He had it next night though. If he'd called him "sir" he'd of had the same old clunker.'

'Who's this Buddy Collette, Mingus?'

'My best friend. He used to really play but Whitey scared him white inside. He likes to sound white. He can read fly-schitt scattered on a fly-swatter though.'

'And that ain't jazz.'

'So tell *him*, Lucky.'

'I will. First I'll cut him in his own bag.'

'Don't try, Lucky, you'll bleed to death. Everybody in the studio clique tried it. He plays flute, clarinet, everything – just like the white man says you're supposed to play and a little fuller.'

'Cat named Paul Desmond up in Frisco plays like that. You heard him?'

'Who's that little boy holding onto Bird's pants leg?'

'That's my son.'

'Duke Ellington, Daddy! Duke Ellington, Daddy!'

'What's he mean?'

'He's telling me he digs Bird. Look at old Bird smiling from cheek to cheek. He's sure a beautiful person.'

'Go on, Dodo! Man, that ofay sure can play! And that drummer too. What's his name?'

'Stan Levy. He's a Jew. You know them Jew boys got the soul and gone.'

'Gone. Take it out.'

'Hooray! Yeah!!'

'How about "April in Paris," Bird?'

'Sure thing. Sure thing.'

'Ming, listen to this!'

'*God dog!* Sounds like millions of souls all wrapped up in that old ragged horn of his. Scotch tape, rubber bands and chewing gum and they say he squeaks. Haw! Squeak, Bird! He's just holding it listening to it sing.'

70 **Ross Russell** Minstrelsy (1961)

Source: Ross Russell, *The Sound* (London: Cassell, 1962: 260–1). (Editor's title)

'I will tell you that jazz springs from a milieu where the Negro has had to struggle against poverty, hunger, disease, and your particular form of white colonialism. Not you personally, but your class, Bernie, although you still share some of the responsibility. You've forced him to live in a dungheap, made it clear that of the few avenues of employment open to his race, the most acceptable, and rewarding, is a form of minstrelsy, out of which has evolved his music. A music half European in origin, and half African, and, most curiously of all, possible only in America, in this vast, rich, dynamic, often monstrous country of yours, with its dollars and frightening machines. And in it the Negro has put all of the entertainment values that the white public accepts: animation, melody, rhythm, a certain verve. Underneath remains his own secret language of pathos and triumph, which makes this another music altogether, and a very great one. And if your minstrels resort to alcohol and narcotics, and even violent aggressions, or consort with prostitutes, don't blame them, blame the dungheap. It is your America that should be ashamed.'

Riff 6

With jazz we are yet not in the age of history, but linger in that of folklore. (Ralph Ellison, 'The Golden Age, Time Past,' *Esquire*, 1959)

The curse of jazz music is its hagiography, perhaps only to be expected in an art form possessing so much surface flamboyancy. (Benny Green, *The Reluctant Art: The Growth of Jazz*, 1962)

Two principal narrative forms have undergirded ... [jazz] history's telling: tragedy and romance. (Gary Carner (ed.), *Black American Literature Forum*, 1991)

The history of jazz has come to be read as fabulous, in fact as a kind of Romance; and that history shows how Romance can turn readily into cult, into the regular making of icons ... That the history of jazz has lent itself so readily to the making of myths explains much of its fascination, much of the power it has with us. (Frederick Garber, 'Fabulating Jazz,' in Krin Gabbard (ed.), *Representing Jazz*, 1995)

There are at least three different stories explaining the death of Charlie Parker ... Of course, each of these stories could have elements of the truth. (Carl Woideck, *Charlie Parker: His Music and Life*, 1996)

His whole style on horn changed ... He bombarded his emotions inward, into himself, and breathed out feelings on his horn like a sanctified soul shouting for salvation in a Baptist church and the blue note became his calling card ... His tone mellowed out huge as the soul of a bottomless wellspring pouring hot lava down an indifferent mountainside, and the word got around. (Herbert A. Simmons, *Man Walking on Eggshells*, 1962)

Chorus VI
Young Man with a Horn: Jazz and myth
(narrative, romance, fabulation)

One of the persistent myths of jazz is the music's autonomy. Earlier selections have suggested that standard jazz history texts rarely deal with the 'constructedness' of jazz history or the ways that extramusical forces affect the nature and understanding of the music. But if there is a myth constructed for the music's intrinsically self-contained nature, another myth is to create historical fictions about the musicians themselves and their jazz lives. 'Unofficial' histories of jazz have made narratives and plots from jazz chronology (e.g. biographies, autobiographies, legends, stories) and peopled them with characters (e.g. musicians, audiences, professional adherents). 'Jazz people' become valorized and elevated, sometimes to heroic, iconic status; in their fabulation, they achieve the level of myth. As Garber observes, this is part of the power and fascination which jazz holds for us (**Riff 6**).

This mythopoeic narrative is often constructed along hagiographic lines, involving extensive infusions of romance and tragedy. Indeed, DeVeaux (1991: 532–3) identifies these modes as the twin narrative forms that undergird jazz history's telling, and romance particularly as the dominant mode of the music's 'story.' The ready identification of jazz with biography is not in dispute, and narratives of jazz musicians' creative lives have served, as Frederick Ramsey and Charles Smith argue in *Jazzmen* (1939: Introduction), to counterbalance a musicological and critical appraisal of the music. Clearly, then, this mythobiographical dimension – as it might be termed – is experiential and democratically accessible. It has been popularly used by non-specialists as well as musicians themselves, by journalists, reviewers, oral historians, film-makers and writers of literary forms, all drawn to the 'world' and 'life' of jazz. **Chorus VI** focuses on this mythic dimension of the music, its prevailing narrative forms, and the comingling of romance, tragedy and heroism in the lives of representative jazz musicians: Bix Beiderbecke, Lester Young and Charlie Parker.

Sociologist Charles Nanry argues 'the jazz myth' has resulted in part from 'overly romantic and celebrationist notions' about jazz and musicians, and an insufficiently critical attitude toward the music (1979: 244). The biographical approach so conducive to myth-making is early demonstrated in the imagistic preface to *Jazzmen* (**72**). **Smith** and **Ramsey** create the requisite tone of adulation and awe (Gabbard 1995b: 82) as they establish the credentials for Buddy Bolden's heroic legacy: 'a whacky horn playing an uptown rag, way out and way off, filling out the tune. That would be King Bolden, calling his children.' This is the myth of time and place: the 'beginnings' of jazz in early-1900 New Orleans, 'a fantastic and wonderful city ... a city with a hundred faces,' with Bolden cutting his first cornet chorus on Congo Square, and the romance of homecoming linked to a jazz progeny – Louis, Joe, Bunk ... As Donald Marquis's de-mythologizing biography (1978: 1) observes, the accepted story of Bolden passed through trumpeter Bunk Johnson to authors Smith and Ramsey. Bolden was said to be an important early jazzman, 'blew a loud cornet, drank a lot, ran a barber-shop, edited a scandal sheet, and died in a mental institution.' Marquis's task is to sort and document this legend. The 'jazz hagiography' and 'gossip' surrounding Bolden's (lost) music is lovingly (re-) imagined by poet William **Matthews** in 'The Buddy Bolden cylinder' (**73**). And earlier, Robert **Sargent**'s gently nostalgic enquiry evokes the 'smiling' memory of Bolden, '*King, King* Bolden,' in 'Touching the past' (**71**).

While jazz has been heralded since its inception as a coming-of-age art music, the contrary impulse, of 'celebrating the down-and-out, subcultural appeal of a repressed art form' (Gabbard 1995a: 14), has enjoyed an enduring tradition. Neil Leonard (1975) has presented a socio-historical viewpoint of jazzmen as 'romantic outsiders,' examining both 1920s writers and musicians, and bop musicians of the 1940s. As a study of behavioural patterns and values, Leonard finds jazzmen conforming to the roles of 'legendary heroes' and 'secular saints' – evinced in an aesthetic conviction, a strong sense of fraternity, verbal language, unorthodox behaviour and a revolt against a hostile general culture. The issues raised here, of jazz as a romantic response to modern society and a music of spiritual, ritualized impulse at a time of religious decline, are taken further in Leonard's full-length study, *Jazz: Myth and Religion* (1987).

The general sense of charisma and those rituals and myths – social and musical – upholding the jazz mystique can be found in the lives of individual musicians, iconic figures elevated by association with legendary prowess and excess. DeVeaux (1991: 533) points out it is possible to configure jazz 'stories' as ones of success (romance), where musicians have not suffered decline and fall, but enjoyed admiration and triumph – he instances Armstrong, Ellington and Goodman. However, the prevailing mode to have caught attention and memory is, expectedly, the tragic one. The often-sordid tale of the doomed, self-destructive, early-death jazz musician has become almost *de rigueur* in jazz (auto)biography and versions of the jazz life. Bolden's 'chillun' might well also include Beiderbecke, Holiday, Young, Parker, Powell and Baker, among others.

For many, Bix Beiderbecke 'remains a being apart, an enigma' (Sudhalter 1999: 411). Krin Gabbard writes (1989: 13), 'as the mythologized progenitor of several generations of young whites aspiring to play jazz, Beiderbecke occupies a unique place in the history of the music.' Beiderbecke's early demise (of 'everything'), innocent, doomed and alcoholic, is foreshadowed in Dana **Gioia**'s poem (**74**), as Bix speeds across the small-town Iowa snowscape in 1926. His shimmering notes, that 'hovered in the air above the crowd,' are part of a lyricism, bell-like, vibrant tone and sure harmonic invention celebrated in journalist Otis **Ferguson**'s *New Republic* tribute (**75**) of 1936. Unlike many other accounts, the piece concentrates on Beiderbecke's music rather than brief life, analysing 'one of the fine natural resources of this American country.'

According to Ralph Gleason (1958: 38), Dorothy **Baker** later used Ferguson's title for her 1938 novel recounting the life of Rick Martin (Beiderbecke). Baker's romanticized 'story' of Martin's life draws attention to the self-destructive element in jazz, the 'nervous, crazy life that goes with it.' Hagiographically, in Martin's uncompromising devotion to Art, his Life 'goes to pieces ... so thoroughly that he kills himself doing it' ('Prologue'). The novel's final section (**76**) records in sentimental dramatics Rick's fight against alcohol and illness (Bix's lobar pneumonia) and expiry as 'jig-man.' Against this ending might be set Hoagy Carmichael's memory of Beiderbecke's own abrupt death:

> He was walking to catch a train that would take him to a job, his horn under his arm, a somber fellow clad in a tuxedo, the raiment of his trade, a golden horn under his arm, walking toward a train, walking toward a bandstand; he collapsed. It was pneumonia. As simple and as quick as that. And she [Bix's girlfriend] sent me his mouthpiece. A hunk of iron for a soul so sweet. (1946: 143)

Golden horns and sweet souls became the stuff of Beiderbecke's fabled life, as 'jazz's Number One Saint' (Green 1962: 19).

Lewis Porter prefaces *A Lester Young Reader* (1991) by observing the life and music of Young are legendary and notes there are 'Presophiles' the world over. Al **Young**'s poem, 'Lester leaps in' (**77**), contains the lineaments of the fabled style – angled horn, trademark porkpie, cool-smooth sound, the titles ('Lady Day') bestowed on fellow-musicians. Yet any glamour is more than balanced in Lester's vulnerability, his sensitivity to birth-life pain, the expression of 'heartbroken'-ness and 'leaping' into self-destruction. In an edited François **Postif** interview of 1959 (**78**), conducted shortly before Young's death, the saxophonist ranges laconically across musical starts, early influences, experiences with the Henderson and Basie bands – including the much-quoted pressure to adopt the style of Coleman Hawkins – modern saxophone, Uncle Tomism and survival: 'you fight for your life.' Within two months, Young was dead. His influence on modern jazz playing was, perhaps, only exceeded by a propensity for making life into the art of dying. Musician Willie Jones, interviewed in 1985 by biographer Frank **Büchmann-Møller** (**79**), talks of the start of Young's sojourn at the Alvin Hotel, Broadway, an ultimate reclusive state and withdrawal from the pain of illness, unemployment and dwindling recognition. Geoff **Dyer**, writing fictionalized accounts of jazz lives as 'imaginative criticism' in *But Beautiful*, frames these last days (**80**). Young floats and dissolves, sometimes wondering 'if he was just dozing, dreaming he was here, dying in a hotel room ...'. Sensitively written, Dyer's apt imagistic style perfectly captures Young's drink-sipping, suspended languor – drifting across the frontier of death into a snowy Broadway. William **Matthews** (**81**), 'listening' to Young in 1976, thinks back from a 'never born' language to 1958, and Young's tired-to-the-death quoting of himself, with remembered fingering and the reliable tone, 'slurring toward the center/of each note.' *Hey Pres*, hipster extraordinaire.

'Hipster, hustler, cocksman, junkie and songster ... [a] black urban-ghetto culture hero,' is how biographer Ross Russell describes bop saxophonist Charlie

Parker. Parker 'was the cool cat who could do anything. The Sepia Superman with all the plays and all the answers. He lived straight off the top' (1973: 366, 245). For another recorder of Parker's life, Robert Reisner, 'no one had such a love of life, and no one tried harder to kill himself' (1962: 15). If there was, as Russell maintains, a hunger for a mythic hero in 1940s' modern jazz, Parker fitted the bill. Musically, he was perceived to be 'the fountainhead' of the new music and the intense flow of musical ideas suggested 'mysterious, primal forces.' 'Yardbird' (Parker's nickname), shortened to 'Bird,' connoted elevation, flight, speed and horizons-ahead. Parker became an object of reverence and 'a genuine culture hero,' someone whose epic ingestion of drink and narcotics was only exceeded by the miracle of his dynamic music (Russell 1973: 180–1, 255–61).

The response of awe and homage to Parker's fabulous gifts as improviser is shown by pianist Hampton Hawes, describing the 1945 opening night at Billy Berg's club in Hollywood.

> Bird played an eight-bar channel on *Salt Peanuts* that was so strong, so revealing, that I was molded on the spot, like a piece of clay, stamped out. Bird never once in his lifetime played a single bar of bullshit. The vibrations he started are still moving across the world. He was like going to the moon thirty years ago ... A jazz musician makes a total commitment, which is himself, his attitude, his sound, his story, and the way he lives. Bird was like a god. (Russell 1973: 324)

The ultimate act of Parker veneration was performed by ace unauthorized recorder, Dean Benedetti, whose own mythic vocation was to capture every Parker solo on tape. The 'Obbligato' of **Russell**'s *Bird Lives!* recreates this recording context, with Parker in heroic portrait, preparing to play, and a description of his 'fantastical machine-gunner' performance of 'Cherokee' (**82**). 'The music of the jazz revolution reaches a new level of everything ... Bird on one of his great nights.' Benedetti, seated in the men's room, diligently inscribes the spool: Monday, December 10, 1945, Billy Berg's, Hollywood.

Amiri **Baraka**, in 'A tribute to Bird' (**83**), 'signifies' on Parker's contribution to jazz as African-American music, which speaks a contemporary language of sensitivity and beauty, but also racial survival and self-determination. Parker, as 'spirit catcher,' is 'spirit transferrer,' worthy of commemoration, and duly celebrated. The recurrent *'Blow Bird!'* of Michael **Harper**'s poem (**84**) conveys the life-enhancing qualities of Parker's music, expressive of his own life-scream and pain, of black oppression and racism, and the central paradox: Bird 'lives' most after his death. 'All the principals are dead, so we may never confirm any of the accounts of the death of Charlie Parker' (Woideck 1996: 50). The imperatives of the jazz myth are well served by Baroness Pannonica de **Koenigswarter**'s famous account (**85**) of Parker's expiry while laughing at a TV show in her hotel suite in 1955. According to Reisner, the end 'set off wild conjecture, lurid copy, and rampaging rumor' (1962: 131), as well as an alleged 'tremendous clap of thunder' at the moment of death. Tony **Scott**'s compact story, 'Destination K.C.' (**86**), is expressively ironic. It captures the final impact of Parker on a humble jazz worshipper and worker for Railway Express, unwittingly about to ship his idol's coffin off to its mid-west destination. 'Contents ... Charles Parker.' After Parker's death, Reisner records how for weeks he saw a crude legend written on New York sidewalks and fences: BIRD LIVES. Charles Mingus's contribution to Parker mythology is quoted almost as often as Reisner's obituary: 'Bird is not dead; he's hiding out somewhere, and he'll be back with some new shit that will scare everyone to death' (Reisner 1962: 26, 152). For John **Holmes** (**87**), the iconic jazz Horn still blows 'the truth,' new songs which sing of survival and self-renewal, even as the singers, one by one, are carried off.

71 **Robert Sargent** Touching the past (1987)

Source: Robert Sargent, 'Touching the past,' in *Aspects of a Southern Story* (Wasington, DC: The Word Works, Inc., 1987: 17).

Uptown New Orleans, 1940,
And here was a man of the right color,
Old enough to have been there,

Who maybe heard. So I enquired
From the old man doing his yard work,
'Ever hear Buddy Bolden play?'

'Ah me,' he said, stopping his work,
'Yes. But you mean *King, King* Bolden.
That's what we called him then.'

He leaned on his rake a while, resting.
'Used to play in Algiers, played so loud
We could hear him clear 'cross the river.'

He seemed listening. 'King Bolden, now,
There was a man could play.' We stood there,
Thinking about it, smiling.

72 Frederick Ramsey, Jr. and Charles Edward Smith New Orleans: Callin' our chillun home (1939)

Source: Frederick Ramsey, Jr. and Charles Edward Smith (eds), 'New Orleans: Callin' our chillun home', in *Jazzmen* (New York: Harcourt, Brace: 1939: 3–6).

A fantastic and wonderful city. A city with a hundred faces. The hard face for commerce and the soft face for making love. Scratching figures on the back of an envelope where the girl with the deep dark eyes waits on counter. Smell of burnt coffee and sound of ships. The deep face for a sad life and the pinched face for poverty. Marching, singing, laughing. The silver and copper laugh of the prostitute, and the toothless chuckle of the old man who remembers Buddy Bolden at Bogalusa.

Every writer makes his own city. The city of fine living and free spirit, woven into the dream of a poet. The city of brass bands and military marches, grand balls and rowdy lake-front parties. The city of Lulu White and Mahogany Hall, Josie Arlington and the palm tree growing crazily there in a vacant lot. The thin young man who drinks too much, looking at Congo Square, squeezing the last acrid sweetness out of sight and sound.

Come on and hear
Come on and hear

This is our city, not so far from Madame John's legacy but carrying with it another legacy, the dark human cargo of a Yankee slaver, the Marquis de Vaudreuil, raising a thin glass above a fringed cuff, drinking the drink and shattering the glass into tiny tinkling fragments. Bamboula and tinkling glass. Flat voices of invitation behind shuttered cribs. Canal Street murky yellow with night, her standards the Carnival colors, symbols of transient ownership, like a mistress smiling in turn at her lovers.

Up Rampart beyond Canal. That's Uptown. That's Bolden territory. Perdido by the gas works. Maybe there used to be a cypress swamp there but nobody remembers now. Everybody remembers Bolden and his barber shop and his scandal sheet and his ragtime band, playing a new music that didn't have a name of its own. (They say the word for it came from Chicago 'down around 22nd'; they say it came from an Elizabethan slang word meaning hit it hard and from an American slang word meaning it don't mean a thing but it costs real money around 22nd.)

Don't look for the eagle on the Eagle Saloon. And don't look for Masonic Hall because it's a vacant lot. But listen hard some night, listen hard at the corner of Rampart and Perdido and you'll hear a whacky horn playing an uptown rag, way out and way off, filling out the tune. That would be King Bolden, calling his children.

If you want to know why Ragtime (the first) wasn't jazz, and why uptown rags weren't just a new ragtime but had to wait for a trip up the river to get a name out of the barrel, well, listen to that horn. There's a little of it in Louis and in Joe Oliver and in Bunk. Maybe if you listen close there's a little of it here, between the covers of a book. Maybe if you listen hard (standing on the corner of Rampart and Perdido where the old Eagle sign blew down one night) you'll see what Bunk meant when he played that way, and what Louis meant when he played that way, and what Buddy Bolden meant when he said, 'You can't play without the king.'

Maybe you'd go down Perdido where there aren't any sidewalks, even today, and where the battered houses squat in patterns of poverty, with a hedge or a flower or a puny palm tree out front, trying to say what poverty can't say ...

I knows how to write!

And maybe you don't think this has much to do with jazz, or the city we'd like to build for you. But if you want to go with the saints to the funeral (to a slow march) you want to know where he lived and died, don't you, and what he was up against because his skin was black or white or maybe a shade between? You want to know why he came from the beat side of town (but wasn't beat) to play down in Storyville where they wanted the blues slow and mean and the rags fast and dirty, to play for a gangster out at Pontchartrain (the big shot from Chicago who threw the dough around), to play in the brass bands Carnival Day and on the wagons Sunday night.

Maybe you'll turn back, see the slave ships unload their flesh-and-blood cargo, see the trickle from the plantation country ... free bewildered black skin, coffee skin, saffron skin, coming to the hard city of commerce, soft city of song, martial city of music, dream city of silver and copper laughter. And you'll find the answer, you'll know why it began just there, not somewhere else.

You have to think of New Orleans the band city or it will be hard to understand why it couldn't have happened on the levee at Memphis, on the waterfront of Savannah, or on the Gulf Coast with the deep, sobbing blues. You think of the band city, the opera, the funerals and the balls, you think of the Creole Negroes:

> *'Jazz came from uptown.'*
> *'It was that raggedy uptown stuff.'*

Elsewhere they forgot the music that they had brought with them, and they forgot the words. In Carolina all that would be left would be the blues and a children's nonsense game with some words that might have come over in the hold of a Yankee clipper or might have been made up out of the sharp phonetics of children at play.

In New Orleans you could still hear the bamboula on Congo Square when Buddy Bolden cut his first chorus on cornet. You could still hear the bamboula and you couldn't see a note of written music. Whatever he learned he put away when he started off on the real tune. It was something like Bunk:

> *If you put down what Bunk played he would say,*
> *do you think I'm a fool, I can't play that!*

Cajun or Creole, black or white, the others heard. They heard because their lives were part of that life, and because the music didn't draw a color line. White or black or a shade between, they listened hard when the Bolden Band pointed its horns towards Lincoln Park, because that was the King.

Old Willy Cornish said the crowd would be over there, with Robichaux, and Bolden's Band would start right out like the killers they were. You could see a glow on his very dark cheek and the soft voice seemed to come from back there, wherever his eyes were. He said that was

callin' our chillun home.

73 **William Matthews** The Buddy Bolden cylinder (1991)

Source: William Matthews, 'The Buddy Bolden cylinder,' *Poetry,* CLIX, 1 (October 1991: 26).

It doesn't exist, I know, but I love
to think of it, wrapped in a shawl
or bridal veil, or, less dramatically,
in an old copy of the *Daily Picayune,*
and like an unstaled, unhatched egg
from which, at the right touch, like mine,
the legendary tone, sealed these long years
in the amber of neglect, would peal and re-
peal across the waters. What waters do
I have in mind? Nothing symbolic, mind you.
I meant the sinuous and filth-rich
Mississippi across which you could hear
him play from Gretna, his tone was so loud
and sweet, with a moan in it like you were
in church, and on those old, slow, low-down
blues Buddy could make the women jump
the way they liked. But it doesn't exist,
it never did, except as a relic
for a jazz hagiography, and all
we think we know about Bolden's music
is, really, a melancholy gossip
and none of it sown by Bolden, who
spent his last twenty-four years in Jackson
(Insane Asylum of Louisiana)
hearing the voices of people who spooked
him before he got there. There's more than one
kind of ghostly music in the air, all
of them like the wind: you can't see it
but you can see the leaves shiver in place
as if they'd like to turn their insides out.

74 **Dana Gioia** Bix Beiderbecke (1903–1931) (1986)

Source: Dana Gioia, 'Bix Beiderbecke (1903–1931),' in *Daily Horoscope* (St. Paul, MN.: Graywolf Press, 1986: 42).

January, 1926

China Boy. Lazy Daddy. Cryin' All Day.
He dreamed he played the notes so slowly that
they hovered in the air above the crowd
and shimmered like a neon sign. But no,
the club stayed dark, trays clattered in the kitchen,
people drank and went on talking. He watched
the smoke drift from a woman's cigarette
and slowly circle up across the room
until the ceiling fan blades chopped it up.
A face, a young girl's face, looked up at him,
the stupid face of small-town innocence.
He smiled her way and wondered who she was.
He looked again and saw the face was his.

He woke up then. His head still hurt from drinking,
Jimmy was driving. Tram was still asleep.
Where were they anyway? Near Davenport?
There was no distance in these open fields –
only time, time marked by a farmhouse
or a barn, a tin-topped silo or a tree,
some momentary silhouette against
the endless, empty fields of snow.
He lit a cigarette and closed his eyes.
The best years of his life! The Boring 'Twenties.
He watched the morning break across the snow.
Would heaven be as white as Iowa?

75 **Otis Ferguson** Young man with a horn (1936)

Source: Otis Ferguson, 'Young man with a horn,' *New Republic*, 87 (July, 1936: 354–5).

In the field of popular art ... the best thing at this time is the reminder that the brief obscure history of jazz music also has its great dead. And the greatest of these – the greatest of all, one is sometimes bound to think as some old scratched record is put on the machine and that vibrant tonal attack arches suddenly out over the band, unmistakable and perfect – the greatest of these was a young man from the corn belt, Leon (Bix) Beiderbecke, who played the horn.

The recent popularization of the best popular music has been tardy and responsible for much faddish nuisance: radio announcers with voices you might spread on a muffin suddenly trying to go barrel-house, young squirts all over the place in crew haircuts yelling Swing gate, send the cats! as though to do so were to do something very desirable and deep indeed. But the main results have been for the best and many things have been made possible. For instance, the Victor company has made several repressings of numbers that have long been cut out and now brings thoughtfully forward an album of twelve ten-inch sides from its back files. The album features Beiderbecke solos that up to now could not be had for love or money – which is such cheerful news that I can't help saying a few words to the folks.

Bix Beiderbecke lived very briefly and in what might be called the servants' entrance to art, dying in 1931 at the age of twenty-seven. His story is a good story, quite humble and right. He had a background of ragtime and riverboats and five and six-piece jazz bands, the changes and speeding up in America after the War. He seems to have been fooling around with music from the time he could walk, learning piano while he was still a kid in Davenport, later getting himself a cornet and learning to play it, turning by aptitude and instinct to music – especially to the raw spirits of music being distilled in the land around him.

For his talent there were no conservatories to get stuffy in, no high-trumpet didoes to be learned doggedly, note-perfect as written, because in his chosen form the only writing of any account was traced in the close shouting air of Royal Gardens, Grand Pavilions, honkeytonks, etc. And yet when Bix turned to the jazz cornet, he perfected a straight tone and absolute fluency which bow to no classical technique whatever, and which for that matter would be the despair of most brass sections to be found today.

An analysis of his music as a whole would amount to a statement of most of the best elements in jazz – which is a little too much for this spot. Briefly, he played a full easy tone, no forcing, faking or mute tricks, no glissando to cover unsure attack or vibrato to fuzz over imprecisions of pitch – it all had to be in the music. And the clear line of that music is something to wonder at. You see, this is the sort of thing that is almost wholly improvised, starting from a simple theme, taking off from that into a different and unpredictable melodic line, spontaneous, personal – almost a new tune but still shadowing the old one, anchored in its chord sequence. Obviously, without lyric invention and a perfect instinct for harmony, this is no go for a minute, let alone chorus after chorus, night after night. And yet here is this fantastic chap, skipping out from behind a bank of saxophones for eight measures in the clear and back again, driving up the tension with a three-note phrase as brash and gleeful as a kid with a prank, riding down the whole length of a chorus like a herd of mustangs – everywhere you find him there is always this miracle of constant on-the-spot invention, never faltering or repeating, every phrase as fresh and glistening as creation itself.

Just as characteristic was the driving rhythm against which he played, the subtle and incisive timing that could make even a low and lazy figure of syncopation explode like blows in the prize ring. Bix had a rhythmic invention that seemed inexhaustible, variety without straining; and in all his cross-rhythms and flights of phrasing, retarding the beat or flying on ahead of it, there was always the insistent implication of the steady one-two-three-four drive that usually has its base in the rhythm section, particularly in the riding beat of a solid swing drummer.

Still and all, these things were part of it, not the whole – something would have to be said about the spirit behind all this, the man in the music, before the music was explained: the candor, force, personal soundness, good humor and sheer love of the thing. Bix appears to have struck too fast a pace in the years after he was brought to New York by Jean Goldkette – an immigrant boy then burning up the East with the best big band of his time – drinking himself gradually out of the picture in the last years with Whiteman, becoming less and less productive and worrying his friends. But there is no evidence in his music that he ever got up-stage or did a small thing.

But talk about music is pretty generally doomed to be sterile and dull, because the only way to catch music is out of the air – to be listening to the heavy motion of the band as it comes down to the taking-off point in, say, 'Slow River' (one two three four *one* – stop) and hear those clear trumpet tones spring up over the iron of the banjo chords, boundless, exuberant of attack, as pure and easy as anything. They are there and then they are gone and the orchestra is back in its heavy stride. Patently, what is there to say about that? Or take another old one, 'After You've Gone,' where they get off with the expected wealth of arrangements and everything, and then as the violins are working them out of the vocal, and bad going at that, everything is suddenly an airy structure with trumpet notes falling down through it like showers, and Mr. Bix Beiderbecke is playing his fluent reckless little tune, this time with restraint and an instinctive sweet sadness, no doubt in deference to content: 'After you've gone, babe, after you've gone away.' Same thing in a recording Hoagy Carmichael made of his own tune 'Georgia,' where if you play it you will hear (directly following that beautiful eight-bar creation from Jack Teagarden's trombone) the Bix cornet still swinging free and bold, but sensitive now to the shadings of a foolish and eternally lovely tune about how 'just a little song keeps Georgia on my mind.'

And even these fragments and snatches are only side-issues, for Bix Beiderbecke is to be found at his highest and best in a few of the early Goldkette and Whiteman tunes ('Clementine,' 'San,' etc.) and especially in the small all-star outfits he and Trumbauer used to get together from larger personnels. Here he is irrepressible, with licks, full choruses, constant background work, all with the throttle wide open and devil take the highmost, but never a false move, never getting tired. The energy alone is something to marvel at, but when it comes to the complexities and lilt of music and rhythms, there is no way of describing it. If you would be patient with me I could mutter and whistle the general idea of the big full solo in 'Riverboat Shuffle,' which was on the back of 'Ostrich Walk,' which coupling just about represents the peak of a high and wonderful career – but why waste time with words and poor copies? One hears it, and is moved and made strangely proud; or one does not, and misses one of the fine natural resources of this American country.

76 **Dorothy Baker** from *Young Man With a Horn* (1938)

Source: Dorothy Baker, *Young Man with a Horn* (Boston: Houghton Mifflin, 1961 [1938]: 239–43) (excerpt).

He didn't show up anywhere for three weeks. The boys were laying bets he was dead. Smoke forced himself through the morgue twice, looked over the whole display, tags and all. Then he called up all the jails. Not the right Martin. But he wouldn't give it up. He kept trying everything he could think of, and then one morning an old woman gave him a tip and he found him and put him in a cure.

It was one of those cures where they saturate you with alcohol and then pump you full of a preparation that gives you an allergy to alcohol. It makes a conflict. The forces for good do battle with the forces of evil and the patient has a time of it. The patient is expected to remember the conflict as long as he lives, and the assumption is that he'll never take a chance on another. He'd just prefer not to.

Smoke came to get Rick the day he was supposed to be released. He'd had his suit cleaned and he brought it along for him to wear home. He rang a bell in the waiting-room, and a man in a surgeon's smock came in and said thank heavens he'd come, they'd been trying every place they knew to get in touch with him or somebody that knew the patient.

'What's wrong?' Smoke said, wide-eyed. 'Couldn't he take the cure?'

It wasn't that. He took the cure fine, at least they gave it to him, but he turned out not to be in such good shape in other respects. He had had a bad cold when he came in, and now it looked like either pneumonia or double pneumonia.

'You're a doctor, which do you think?' Smoke said, and the one in the smock said he was a special kind of doctor; he just gave alcohol and narcotics cures, and he wouldn't say anything for sure, but his guess was that that boy should be taken to a hospital; they had begun to think so two days before, but there wasn't anything to identify the patient, after Smoke took his suit, and they couldn't find anyone to give them an authorization.

'Why didn't you authorize yourself?' Smoke said. 'You didn't need to worry. I'd have paid you anyhow.'

'My own feeling is,' the cure doctor said, 'that we'd better get him out of here quick.'

He called an ambulance, and Smoke went in to see Rick.

It was a small room with white walls, one barred window, and a hospital bed. No other furniture, nothing to break. It was simply a cell, a place to suffer in while the conflict raged. The late sun poked through the bars. It was one of the first days of spring, a good day to ride on top of a bus, a rotten day for an ambulance.

Rick's head lay flat against the sheet; the covers were pinned close by his ears with huge safety pins, so that nothing but his head was outside.

His eyes flicked when Smoke came in. They stayed open for a moment and burned like lighted rum. He twisted violently and the sheet tore a little where it was pinned. Then he lay perfectly still and moaned low, but didn't speak.

Smoke tiptoed to the side of the bed and whispered: 'Take it easy, baby; I'm going to get you out of here. It's a quack joint, and the doctor doesn't know his business from a hole in the ground. He's not even a doctor.'

Rick's eyes came open halfway and the flames jumped out when they caught the draft.

He looked up at Smoke and said: 'I worked for him, but I couldn't get along. Can't get along in a band.'

Smoke couldn't make out the words. 'Sure,' he said. 'Just forget it.'

He closed his eyes again. He had a three weeks' beard, and there was a bright red circle on each cheek. His hair fell in rings over his forehead. The prophet in his homeland is not supposed to be taken seriously. Let him cut loose and go someplace else, or have done with prophesying. What do we know about this young man with the beard and the spots on his cheeks, this young man pinned down in a strange bed in a barred room, out of his head with a fever? What do we know except that he had a way of doing a thing, and that he had a love of the thing so strong that he never in his life compromised it, or let it down, or forgot it?

Rick twisted sharply against the sheet, but this time it didn't tear. His mouth was scarlet and he opened it and said: 'I don't see why we couldn't. Just call it the Memphis Ten or some name, same bunch all the time, do up a lot of good ones, all the ones we used to play.'

He said it, but the words he used didn't mean anything, and when Smoke bent down close to try to hear him he only heard sounds – sounds that should have meant: 'If I had been born into a different kind of world, at another place, in another time, everything changed, the name Martin might have lasted along with the names of the other devout ones, the ones who cared for music and put it down so that it's still good and always will be. But what chance has a jig-man got? He plays his little tune, and then it's over, and he alone can know what went into it. This is sad; but so is everything, and in the end there is another thing to say about it. The good thing, finally, is to lead a devoted life, even if it swings around and strikes you in the face.'

Smoke stayed there, close, trying to get anything he could, but the sounds just didn't mean anything.

The cure doctor came in with two ambulance men wearing white coats and carrying a stretcher between them. They took the pins out and turned back the covers and Rick lay quietly, his arms crossed unnaturally far over on his chest. The thing they had on him was a strait-jacket.

'Loosen it up and leave it on him,' one of the stretcher men said. 'This boy don't need restraining.'

They rolled him onto the stretcher and carried him to the ambulance. Smoke got in and sat beside him on a jump seat. They drove slowly between streets, but they put on a little speed at intersections and went across with the siren wide open.

The sun was in Rick's face. Smoke reached up and pulled down the blind. Then he settled back and said, 'I knew a guy once that took a cure and he said ...' But he stopped it there because he suddenly knew that it wasn't getting over. He looked down and saw Rick's face. He watched, stunned, and while he was watching, Rick died. He could tell when it happened. There was a difference.

77 **Al Young** Lester leaps in (1982)

Source: Al Young, 'Lester leaps in,' in *The Blues Don't Change: New and Selected Poems* (Baton Rouge: Louisiana State University Press, 1982: 130).

Nobody but Lester let Lester leap
into a spotlight that got too hot
for him to handle, much less keep
under control like thirst in a drought.

He had his sensitive side, he had
his hat, that glamorous porkpie whose
sweatband soaked up all that bad
leftover energy.

               How did he choose
those winning titles he'd lay on favorites
– Sweets Edison, Sir Charles, Lady Day?
Oooo and his sound! Once you savor its
flaming smooth aftertaste, what do you say?

Here lived a man so hard and softspoken
he had to be cool enough to hold his horn
at angles as sharp as he was heartbroken
in order to blow what it's like being born.

78 **François Postif** Lester Paris 59 (1959)

Source: François Postif, 'Lester Paris 59,' *The Jazz Review*, II, 8 (1959): 7–10. (Original version reprinted in Lewis Porter, *A Lester Young Reader* [1991]: 173–91.)

Although he wasn't free until five o'clock in the morning, I was determined to interview Lester. I knew he wasn't very talkative, but he wanted the interview to be taped, and that encouraged me. One afternoon at six o'clock I knocked at his door. Lester told me to come in: he had been waiting for me. When he saw my tape recorder he shouted happily. He asked me: 'Can I talk slang?' I agreed, and from then on he relaxed. I felt during the interview that he was pleased to be able to speak freely.

You weren't really born in New Orleans?
Uh, uh. Should I really tell you? I could tell a lie. I was born in Woodville, Mississippi, because my mother went back to the family; so after I was straight, you know, everything was cool, she took me back to New Orleans and we lived in Algiers, which is across the river.

I left when I was ten. They had trucks going around town advertising for all the dances, and this excited me, you know? So they gave me handbills and I was running all over the city until my tongue was hanging out. From there I went to Memphis and then to Minneapolis. I tried to go to school and all that ... I wasn't interested.

The only person I liked on those trucks in New Orleans was the drummer, you dig?
Drums now?
No eyes. I don't want to see them. Everytime I'd be in a nice little place, and I'd meet a nice little chick, dig, her mother'd say, 'Mary, come on, let's go.' Damn, I'd be trying to pack these drums, because I wanted this little chick, dig? She'd called her once and twice, and I'm trying to get straight, so I just said, I'm through with drums. All those other boys got clarinet cases, trumpet cases, trombone cases and I'm wiggling around with all that s–t, and Lady Francis, I could really play those drums. I'd been playing them for a whole year.
How did you get started on tenor?
I was playing alto and they had this evil old cat with a nice, beautiful background, you know, mother and father and a whole lot of bread and like that, you know, so everytime we'd get a job ... this was in Salinas, Kansas, so everytime we'd go see him, we'd be waiting ninety years to get us to work while he fixed his face, you know, so I told the bossman, his name was Art Bronson. So I said, 'Listen, why do we have to go through this? You go and buy me a tenor saxophone and I'll play the m-f and we'd be straight then.'

So he worked with this music store, and we got straight, and we split. That was it for me. The first time I heard it. Because the alto was a little too high.
When did you learn to read music?
When I first came up in my father's band I wasn't reading music; I was faking it,

but I was in the band. My father, got me an alto out of the pawnshop, and I just picked the m-f up and started playing it. My father played all the instruments and he read, so I had to get close to my sister, you dig, to learn the parts.

One day my father finally said to me, 'Kansas, play your part,' and he knew goddam well I couldn't read. So my sister played her part and then he said, 'Lester play your part,' and I couldn't read a m-f note, not a damn note. He said, 'Get up and learn some scales.' Now you know my heart was broke, you dig, and I went and cried my little teardrops, while they went on rehearsing. I went away and learned to read the music, and I came back in the band. All the time I was learning to read, I was playing the records and learning the music at the same time, so I could completely foul them up. I don't like to read music, just soul ... there you are.

I got a man in New York writing music for me right now, so when I get back it'll be for bass violin, two cellos, viola, French horn and three rhythm. I'll just take my time with it, if it don't come out right, I'll just say f–k it, no. This is the first time, and I always wanted to do that. Norman Granz would never let me make no records with no strings. Yardbird made million of records with strings. When I was over here the last time I played with strings, the first winners, I think they were. Germans. Anyway I played with them, and they treated me nice and played nice for me.

Who were your early influences?
I had a decision to make between Frankie Trumbauer and Jimmy Dorsey, you dig, and I wasn't sure which way I wanted to go. I'd buy me all those records and I'd play one by Jimmy and one by Trumbauer, you dig? I didn't know nothing about Hawk then, and they were the only ones telling a story I liked to hear. I had both of them made.

Was Bud Freeman an influence?
Bud Freeman??!! We're nice friends, I saw him just the other day down at the union, but influence, ladedehumptedorebebob ... s–t! Did you ever hear him [Trumbauer] play *Singing the Blues*? That tricked me right then and that's where I went.

How about Coleman Hawkins?
As far as I'm concerned, I think Coleman Hawkins was the President first, right? When I first heard him I thought that was some great jazz I was listening to. As far as myself, I think I'm the second one. Not braggadocious, you know I don't talk like that. There's only one way to go. If a guy plays tenor, he's got to sound like Hawk or like Lester. If he plays alto, he's got to be Bird or Johnny Hodges. There's another way, the way I hear all the guys playing in New York, running all over the place.

In Kansas City, when I was with Basie, they told me to go and see Coleman Hawkins, and how great he is; so I wanted to see how great he is, you know. So they shoved me up on the stand, and I grabbed his saxophone, played it, read his clarinet parts, everything! Now I got to run back to my job where there was 13 people and I got to run ten blocks. I don't think Hawk showed at all. Then I went to Little Rock with Count Basie, and I got this telegram from Fletcher Henderson saying come with me. So I was all excited because this was bigtime, and I showed it around to everyone and asked them what I should do. Count said he couldn't tell me, so I decided to split and went to Detroit. But it wasn't for me. The m-f's were whispering on me, everytime I played. I can't make that. I couldn't take that, those m-f's were whispering on me, Jesus! So I went up to Fletcher and asked him, 'Would you give me a nice recommendation? I'm going back to Kansas City.' He said, 'Oh, yeah' right quick. That bitch, she was Fletcher's wife, she took me down to the basement and played one of those old windup record players, and she'd say, 'Lester, can't you play like this?' Coleman Hawkins records. But I mean, can't you hear this? Can't you get with that? You dig? I split! Every morning that bitch would wake me up at nine o'clock to teach me to play like Coleman Hawkins. And she played trumpet herself ... circus trumpet! I'm gone!

How did you first go with Basie?

I used to hear this tenor player with Basie all the time. You see we'd get off at two in Minneapolis and it would be one in Kansas City, that kind of s–t, you dig. So I sent Basie this telegram telling him I couldn't stand to hear that m-f, and will you accept me for a job at any time? So he sent me a ticket and I left my madam here and came on.

How did you get along with Herschel?

We were nice friends and things, but some nights when we got on the stand it was like a duel, and other nights it would be nice music. He was a nice person, in fact I was the last to see him die. I even paid his doctor bills. I don't blame him; he loved his instrument, and I loved mine ...

Why did you leave the Basie band?

That's some deep question you're asking me now. Skip that one, but I sure could tell you that, but it wouldn't be sporting. I still have nice eyes. I can't go around thinking evil and all that. The thing is still cool with me, because I don't bother about nobody. But you take a person like me, I stay by myself, so how do you know anything about me? Some m-f walked up to me and said, 'Prez, I thought you were dead!' I'm probably more alive than he is, you dig, from that hearsay.

You've known Billie [Holiday] for a long time, haven't you?

When I first came to New York I lived with Billie. She was teaching me about the city, which way to go, you know? She's still my Lady Day.

What people do, man, it's so obvious, you know? If you want to speak like that, what do I care what you do? What he do, what he does, what nobody do, it's nobody's business! Man, they say he's an old junkie, he's old and funky, all that s–t, that's not nice. Whatever they do, let them do that and enjoy themselves, and you get your kicks yourself. All I do is smoke some New Orleans cigarettes, don't sniff nothing in my nose, nothing. I drink and I smoke and that's all. But a lot of people think I'm this way and I don't like that, I resent that. My business is the musical thing, all the way ...

Do you think you play modern today?

In my mind when I play, I try not to be a repeater pencil, you dig? Always leave some spaces – lay out. You won't catch me playing like *Lester Leaps In* and that s–t, but I always go back.

I can play all those reed instruments. I can play bass clarinet. If I brought that out, wouldn't it upset everything? I know both Coltrane and Rollins. I haven't heard Coltrane, but I played with Rollins once in Detroit. I just made some records for Norman with clarinet. I haven't played it for a long time, because one of my friends stole it. That's the way it goes. I made them in 1958, in the Hollywood Bowl. Oscar Peterson and his group.

I developed my tenor to sound like an alto, to sound like a tenor, to sound like a bass, and I'm not through with it yet. That's why they get all trapped up, they say 'Goddam, I never heard Prez play like this.' That's the way I want them to hear. That's *modern,* dig? F–k what you played back in '49 – it's what you play today, dig? A lot of them got lost and walked out.

Do you play the same thing every day?
Not unless you want to get henpecked.
What kind of group would you like to have?
Give me my little three rhythm and me – happiness … the four Mills Brothers, ha, ha. I can relax better, you dig. I don't like a whole lotta noise no goddam way. Trumpets and trombones, and all that – f–k it. I'm looking for something soft; I can't stand that loud noise. Those places, in New York, the trumpets screaming, and the chicks putting their fingers in their ears. It's got to be sweetness, you dig? Sweetness can be funky, filthy, or anything. Whatever you want!
The blues?
Great Big Eyes! Because if you play with a new band like I have and are just working around, and they don't know no blues, you can't play anything! Everybody has to play the blues and everybody has them too …
Am I independent?
Very much! I'd have taken off the other night if I had five hundred dollars. I just can't take that b–s, you dig? They want everybody who's a Negro to be an Uncle Tom, or Uncle Remus, or Uncle Sam, and I can't make it. It's the same all over, you fight for your life – until death do you part, and then you got it made …

Note

Translated Charles Delaunay. Transcribed from interview tapes.

79 **Frank Büchmann-Møller** He wanted to look down on Broadway (1990)

Source: Frank Büchmann-Møller, 'The last years (1956–1959)', in *You Just Fight for Your Life: The Story of Lester Young* (New York: Praeger, 1990: 202) (excerpt). (Editor's title)

He kept drinking because of the reputation and the attitude that they had towards him and the promoters had towards him, that it was difficult for him to get work because of this particular characterization. He became so hurt, and like I said, he kept drinking. He had so much to give and was so great an artist, so his wife – you know, notably to see one's husband just destroying himself and be upset of what's going on – she couldn't take it, and she tried to tell him.

One day in the spring of 1958 I received a telephone call from a lawyer, who was Miles Davis' lawyer by the name of Harold Lavette. Harold called me up and said: 'Lester Young wants to move into the Alvin Hotel,' and Lester wanted him to get in touch with me. The reason for this is, because we used to get jobs around Brooklyn and New York for Lester so he could work and play, because, you know, those guys had put that reputation on him. I said to myself, well, I didn't have that kind of money, so we'd bring him back and we'll do something.

Like I said earlier, Max was living in Brooklyn at the time, on Willoughby Avenue, and I called up Max and told him that Lester wanted to move into the Alvin Hotel, and that he should bring him by my house. Max said: 'As soon as we'd get to your house, you come over here,' so we went from my house to Max's house, and from Max's house we checked Prez into the Alvin Hotel, because he said he wanted to look down on Broadway and look at Birdland, so when we got there we tried to figure out what to do.

See, the people that really helped Lester Young up at the Alvin Hotel when he moved in there were Max Roach, Sonny Rollins, Miles Davis, 'Papa' Jo Jones, and I was assigned to be there to watch him and to do things, but these were the people that took care of the rent up there. Max never talks about it, but when we moved Lester in at the Alvin Hotel Max Roach put in the first money to pay the bill.

There was a funny thing that Lester was doing at the time. See, Lester Young was very, I'll only say, he used the word, very religious, because that could almost be contradictory to someone who would say: 'How can you be religious and drinking?' But he was a man that had deep belief in a supreme power that he used to term 'The Old Master.' When we first moved him into the Alvin Hotel, until I got a room there on the same floor, the first couple of days I stayed in the room with him. It was about a week or something. One of the things he would do before he'd take drink in the morning was to go to the bathroom. I mean, that was a ritual, and what he was doing in there I can't tell you, if he was on his knees or standing up or whatever he was doing. But he would go in there and close the door and had what he had to say to 'The Old Master,' and then come out and start his day, you know, take a drink or what he had to do. That's one of the things that I noticed about him.

80 **Geoff Dyer** Dying in a hotel room (1991)

Source: Geoff Dyer, *But Beautiful: A Book About Jazz* (London: Cape, 1991: 5–7, 9–10, 12–14, 23–4) (excerpts). (Editor's title)

It was the quiet time of the evening between the day-people heading home from work and the night-people arriving at Birdland. From his hotel window he watched Broadway grow dark and greasy with half-hearted rain. He poured a drink, piled a stack of Sinatra records on the turntable ... touched the unringing phone and drifted back to the window. Soon the view fogged over with his breath. Touching the hazy reflection like it was a painting, his finger traced wet lines around his eyes, mouth and head until he saw it turning into a drippy skull-shaped thing that he wiped clear with the heel of his hand.

He lay down on the bed, making only a slight dip in the soft mattress, convinced he could feel himself shrinking, fading to nothing. Scattered over the floor were plates of food he had pecked at and left. He'd take a bite of this, a little of that and then head back to the window. He ate almost nothing but he still had his preferences when it came to food: Chinese was his favourite, that was the food he didn't eat most of. For a long time he'd lived on buttermilk and crackerjacks but he'd even lost his taste for these. As he ate less he drank more: gin with a sherry chaser, Courvoisier and beer. He drank to dilute himself, to thin himself down even more. A few days ago he'd cut his finger on an edge of paper and was surprised how red and rich his blood was, expecting it to be silver as gin, flecked with red, or pale, pinkish. That same day he'd been fired from a gig in Harlem because he hadn't had the strength to stand. Now even lifting the horn exhausted him; it felt like it weighed more than him. Even his clothes did probably.

Coleman Hawkins went the same way eventually. It was Hawk who made the tenor into a jazz instrument, defined the way it had to sound: big-bellied, full-throated, huge. Either you sounded like him or you sounded like nothing – which is exactly how folks thought Lester sounded with his wispy skating-on-air tone. Everybody bullied him to sound like Hawk or swap over to alto but he just tapped his head and said,

– There's things going on up here, man. Some of you guys are all belly.

When they jammed together Hawk tried everything he knew to cut him but he never managed it. In Kansas in '34 they played right through the morning, Hawk stripped down to his singlet, trying to blow him down with that big hurricane tenor, and Lester slumped in a chair with that faraway look in his eyes, his tone still light as a breeze after eight hours' playing. The pair of them wore out pianists until there was no-one left and Hawk walked off the stand, threw his horn in the back of his car and gunned it all the way to St Louis for that night's gig.

Lester's sound was soft and lazy but there was always an edge in it somewhere. Sounding like he was always about to cut loose, knowing he never would: that was where the tension came from. He played with the sax tilted off to one side and as he got deeper into his solo the horn moved a few degrees further from the vertical until he was playing it horizontally, like a flute. You never got the impression he was lifting it up; it was more like the horn was getting lighter and lighter, floating away from him – and if that was what it wanted to do he wouldn't try to hold it down.

Soon it was a straight choice: Pres or Hawk, Lester Young or Coleman Hawkins – two approaches. They couldn't have sounded or looked more different but they ended up the same way: swilled out and fading away. Hawk lived on lentils, booze and Chinese food and wasted away, just like Pres was doing now ...

When he woke the room was filled with the green haze of a neon sign outside that had blinked to life while he slept. He slept so lightly it hardly even merited the name of sleep, just a change in the pace of things, everything floating away from everything else. When he was awake he sometimes wondered if he was just dozing, dreaming he was here, dying in a hotel room ...

His horn lay next to him on the bed. On a bedside cabinet were a picture of his parents, bottles of cologne and his porkpie hat. He'd seen a photograph of Victorian girls wearing hats like that, ribbons hanging down. Nice, pretty, he thought, and had worn one ever since. Herman Leonard had come to photograph him once but ended up leaving him out of the picture altogether, preferring a still-life of the hat, his sax-case and cigarette smoke ascending to Heaven. That was years ago but the photo was like a premonition that came closer to being fulfilled with each day that passed as he dissolved into the bits and pieces people remembered him by.

He cracked the seal of a new bottle and walked back to the window, one side of his face dyed green in the neon glow. It had stopped raining, the sky had cleared. A cold moon hung low over the street. Cats were turning up at Birdland, shaking hands and carrying instrument cases. Sometimes they looked up towards his window and he wondered if they saw him there, one hand waving condensation from the pane.

He went over to the wardrobe, empty except for a few suits and shirts and the jangle of hangers. He took off his trousers, hung them up carefully and lay back on the bed in his shorts, green-tinged walls crawling with the shadow angles of passing cars ...

In the morning he looked out at a sky colourless as a window-pane. A bird fluttered by and he strained his eyes to keep track of its flight before it disappeared over adjacent roofs. He'd once found a bird on a window-sill, wounded in some way he couldn't establish: something wrong with its wing. Cupping it in his hands he'd felt the flutter-warmth of its heart and nursed it back to health, keeping it warm and feeding it grains of rice. When it showed no sign of getting its strength back he filled a saucer with bourbon and that must have done the trick – after dipping its beak in the saucer for a few days it flew away. Now whenever he saw a bird he always hoped it would be the one he had taken care of.

How long ago was it that he'd found the bird? Two weeks? Two months? It seemed like he'd been here at the Alvin for ten years or more, ever since he got out of the stockade and out of the army. Everything had happened so gradually that it was difficult to establish the point at which this phase of his life had begun. He'd once said that there were three phases in his playing. First he'd concentrated on the upper range of the horn, what he called alto tenor. Then the middle range – tenor tenor – before moving down to baritone tenor. He remembered saying that but he couldn't fix in his mind when the various phases had been because the periods of his life they coincided with were also a blur. The baritone phase coincided with his withdrawal from the world but when had that begun? Gradually he'd stopped hanging out with the guys he played with, had taken to eating food in his room. Then he had stopped eating altogether, seeing practically no-one and hardly leaving his room unless he had to. With every word addressed to him he shrunk from the world a little further until the isolation went from being circumstantial to something he had internalised – but once that happened he realised it had always been there, the loneliness thing: in his playing it had always been there.

Nineteen fifty-seven, that was when he'd gone to pieces completely and ended up in King's County Hospital. After that he'd come here to the Alvin and abandoned interest in everything except gazing out of the window and thinking how the world was too dirty, hard, noisy and harsh for him. And booze, booze at least made the world glisten at the edges a little. He'd been in Bellevue in '55 for his drinking but he remembered little about either Bellevue or King's apart from a vague feeling that hospitals were like the army except you didn't have to do all the work. Even so there was something nice about lying around feeling weak and having no urge to get up. Oh yeah, and one other thing. It was in King's that a young doctor from Oxford, England, had read him a poem, 'The Lotos-Eaters', about some cats who roll up at this island and decide to stay there getting high and doing nothing. He'd dug its dreamy cadences, the slow and lazy feel it had, the river drifting like smoke. The guy who wrote it had the same sound that he had. He couldn't remember his name but if anybody had ever wanted to record it, he'd have dug playing on it, playing solos between the verses. He thought of it a lot, that poem, but couldn't remember the words, just the feel of it, like someone humming a song without really remembering how it went.

That was in 1957. He remembered the date but that got him nowhere. The problem was remembering how long ago 1957 was. Anyway, it was all very simple really: there was life before the army which was sweet, then there was the army, a nightmare from which he'd never woken up ...

He stacked records on the turntable and walked to the window, watching the low moon slip behind an abandoned building. The interior walls had been knocked down and within a few minutes he could see the moon clear through the broken windows at the front of the building. It was framed so perfectly by the window that it seemed as if the moon was actually in the building: a mottled silver planet trapped in a brick universe. As he continued watching it moved from the window as slowly as a fish – only to re-appear again in another window a few minutes later, roaming slowly round the empty house, gazing out of each window as it went.

A gust of wind hunted around the room for him, the curtains pointing in his direction. He walked across the creaking floor and emptied the rest of the bottle into his glass. He lay on the bed again, gazing at the cloud-coloured ceiling.

He waited for the phone to ring, expecting to hear someone break the news to him that he had died in his sleep. He woke with a jolt and snatched up the silent phone. The receiver swallowed his words in two gulps like a snake. The sheets were wet as seaweed, the room full of the ocean mist of green neon.

Daylight and then night again, each day a season. Had he gone to Paris yet or was that just his plan? Either it was next month or he'd already been there and come back. He thought back to a time in Paris, years ago, when he'd seen the Tomb of the Unknown Soldier at the Arc de Triomphe, the inscription 1914–18 – how sad it still made him feel, the thought of someone dying as young as that.

Death wasn't even a frontier any more, just something he drifted across in the course of walking from his bed to the window, something he did so often he didn't know which side of it he was on. Sometimes, like someone who pinches himself to see if he is dreaming, he felt his own pulse to see if he was still alive. Usually he couldn't find any pulse at all, not in his wrist, chest or neck; if he listened hard he thought he could hear a dull slow beat, like a muffled drum at a funeral in the distance or like someone buried underground, thumping the damp earth.

The colours were slipping from things, even the sign outside was a pale residue of green. Everything was turning white. Then he realised: it was snow, falling to the sidewalk in huge flakes, hugging the branches of trees, laying a white blanket over parked cars. There was no traffic, no-one out walking, no noise at all. Every city has silences like this, intervals of repose when – if only for one moment in a century – no-one is speaking, no telephones are ringing, when no TVs are on and no cars are moving.

As the hum of traffic resumed he played the same stack of records and returned to the window. Sinatra and Lady Day: his life was a song coming to an end. He pressed his face against the cold of the window-pane and shut his eyes. When he opened them again the street was a dark river, its banks lined with snow.

81 **William Matthews** Listening to Lester Young (1978)

Source: William Matthews, 'Listening to Lester Young,' in *Rising and Falling* (Boston: Little, Brown, 1978: 28–9).

For Reg Saner

It's 1958. Lester Young minces
out, spraddle-legged as if pain
were something he could step over
by raising his groin, and begins
to play. Soon he'll be dead.

It's all tone now and tone
slurring toward the center
of each note. The edges that used to be
exactly ragged as deckle
are already dead. His embouchure
is wobbly and he's so tired
from dying he quotes himself,
easy to remember the fingering.

It's 1958 and a jazz writer is coming home
from skating in Central Park. Who's that
ahead? It's Lester Young! *Hey Pres,*
he shouts and waves, letting his skates
clatter. *You dropped your shit,* Pres says.

It's 1976 and I'm listening
to Lester Young through stereo equipment
so good I can hear his breath rasp,
water from a dry pond –,
its bottom etched, like a palm,
with strange marks, a language
that was never born
and in which palmists therefore
can easily read the future.

82 **Ross Russell** At Billy Berg's (1973)

Source: Ross Russell, 'At Billy Berg's: an obbligato,' in *Bird Lives! The High Life and Hard Times of Charlie (Yardbird) Parker* (New York: Charterhouse, 1973: 14–15, 22–4) (excerpts).

Bird takes the saxophone. He is wearing the trousers to a pin-stripe suit and red web suspenders over a white shirt. The trousers are made of hard twill-like material, and the creases across the backs of the legs and knees look deep, almost pre-set, built into the garment. Bird opens the zipper at the waistband of the trousers to give himself breathing space. The soft flat fingers fall into place on the buttons of the saxophone as if the generations of craftsmen in France had custom-designed the entire mechanism to fit Bird's hands. The cheekbones become prominent. The lower jaw is firmly set. The mouthpiece slides into the teeth and is held there like an object set in concrete. Chest muscles rise against the white shirt and the red suspenders.

Bird splays out both legs, flexing them so that his upper body, balanced on the tilted dressing room chair, is braced three ways to the floor. Then the man and the instrument become one. The fingers fit on the keys. The saxophone itself is an extension of the voice. When the first sounds come they are colored with the vibrato of Bird's own husky baritone, but that quality is much refined and extended. In the upper register the notes are thin and haunting. The quality of the tone is broad, as if two tones were combined, a thin transparent tone and a fat thick tone, one on top of the other, all blended into a single textured fabric of sound.

As the notes bubble out of the bell of the saxophone they carry implications of Bird's own speech, its inflections and rhythms. Heard through the horn, Bird's speech is no longer broken and indirect. When Bird talks he never seems wholly at ease. When he is with people that he knows well, he is apt to be gruff, jolly, and direct, but sometimes he is also shy and withdrawn. With people that he does not know Bird acts out many little roles. Sometimes he is a gangster. He can also be a detective, a plainclothes operative attached to the narcotics squad of one of the large cities. He is also an Amos and Andy radio character, a stereotype like Kingfish, rigged out with cone-pone diction and a jawbreaking vocabulary. He is a Mississippi nigger who has just arrived in town from the Delta, he is a con man and a humble average fellow. The roles that he plays are carefully studied and put together, along with the gestures and turns of speech and inflections that they require, and are used to cope with situations that arise during his encounters with people in the music world. But now he is no longer acting. He is himself. He is the musician that he has struggled and woodshedded and connived to become. He has the saxophone in his mouth. He is ready ...

Dean Benedetti, struggling through the crowd now blocking the aisles, hears the first notes of the saxophone. The saxophone is somewhere in the distance, in the back of the club, moving out of the dressing room and down the passageway where the empty cases are stored. The notes are muffled, as if they were issuing from a tunnel, but they are becoming louder and stronger. Dean worms through the crowd and breaks free and runs without dignity for his toilet stall. Dean starts the portable tape machine as the first notes come over the wire.

The notes from the alto saxophone are more emphatic with each step taken by the player. The effect is like a band heard in the distance, a band in a parade that cannot yet be seen but is turning the corner and coming into view and suddenly getting louder. The saxophone moves slowly down the passageway until Bird stands framed in the main room of the night club, like a method actor making an entrance. His face is flushed and shining. The new suede jacket is flung open and the collar wrinkled. Underneath the flaring jacket can be seen the red suspenders. At his throat is the striped tie with its awkward knot.

Notes stream out of the horn, penetrating and multitudinous. The sound has its double edge, the two tones combined in one, the thin transparent tone and the fat thick tone, one on top of the other, blended into a single textured sound. It is at once veiled and clear, cloudy and incandescent. The saxophone is being played with the power of a trumpet, but the sound itself remains an extension of the human voice. The saxophone hums, purrs, sings, slides up and down the registers, talks, snarls, groans, exhorts, declaims, shouts, and cries out.

The notes funnel out of the curved end of the saxophone. When Bird moves the horn moves with him, both in one piece, like a statue turning on a pedestal. Notes rattle down the length of the bar, swing back across the back walls where the crowd is standing against the black velvet drapes, and walk in a broad sweep around the room.

Bird is a fantastical machine-gunner. He is attacking a crowded dugout with musical bullets.

Bird plays through the first sixty-four bars of *Cherokee*. He does not stop for breath. There is wind to spare. His belly muscles are feeding it up to him, and the number five reed is like a bird in his throat. The reed resists, stiffens, bends, flutters in the airstream. The column of air inside the saxophone is alive with song. Bird can feel the food in his gut and the fumes from the gin. He's cool. He's in control. Notes pop out of his fingers and go spinning away in skeins and clusters. The black velvet drapes and the low ceiling hold the sound so that notes pile up, one on top of another, until the entire room is packed and stuffed with sound. Bird can feel it feed back against the column of air inside the horn. The room is bigger than the one at the Three Deuces or any of the clubs on Fifty-second Street, and there are more people. The room of the night club is like a huge saxophone. When Bird strikes hard on a note the room quivers. All of the air inside the room vibrates. Bird bites down on the mouthpiece and plays through an odd scale that enters his head, something he remembers from one of the battles of music from his youth. It leads to the turnaround on *Cherokee – a new way to get there. As often happens when he is in full cry, he finds new ways to make the changes, new relationships between the sounds.*

Bird spots people in the crowd, young musicians he knows, and sees black faces mixed with the white faces. In the back of the club a young Negro, wearing horn-rimmed glasses and very correct in Oxford gray threads, has climbed to the top of a table so that he can see as well as hear, and yells out the only word that comes to mind and describes the emotion he feels, the good black superlative, '*Motherfucker!*'

Bird picks 'motherfucker' out of the air as if it were an 'amen' shouted at a revival meeting, and like a skillful evangelist works it into the second chorus of *Cherokee,* a rapid group of descending dactyls. Bird makes a final sweep of the room. A path opens for him through the crowded aisles. He plays his way onto the bandstand. He can feel the thrust and drive of the rhythm section. The bandstand is vibrating. Al Haig feeds him cues for the changes and turnarounds. Levey has two kinds of time going. Bird is on top of them. With a rhythm section like this anything is possible. Bird stares over the curved mouth-piece at the drummer. He feels the kick of Levey's drums. The brushes attached to Levey's hands sizzle. Bird rides up on top of everything.

Dizzy [Gillespie] zeroes in. With Dizzy, Bird trades eight-bar phrases. It's called a chase section. Dizzy is almost as fast as Bird and hard to lose. The eight-bar chase becomes a four-bar chase and involves the piano and the vibraphone. The band is moving in unison now. As good as it was before, it is now that much better. Everything is in focus. The music is stated with authority. The element missing has been fitted into place. It's all there, complete and irrevocable. The music of the jazz revolution reaches a new level of everything – concept, tonality, complexity, rhythmic energy.

83 **Amiri Baraka** A tribute to Bird (1987)

Source: Amiri Baraka, 'A tribute to Bird,' in Amiri Baraka and Amina Baraka, *The Music: Reflections on Jazz and Blues* (New York: William Morrow, 1987: 277–8).

Why do we commemorate and celebrate Charlie Parker? Because he helped create the contemporary language we still speak. As part of the yet developing African-American music called Jazz, really *Orgasm*; called that because it was a form of heat-transfer medium, the dancing coming from it, suggested that, the sudden ecstasy, the *Jism,* from the African *Jasm,* to mean a total epiphany, body-communicated revelation and psychological liberation. Come-Music!

But also in terms of our employment, like in New Orleans, it was music to Jazz By. HoHouse New Orleans was where all the cycles of culture had linked up, sweeping out the countryside from the plantations, the Native American villages, settlements of English, French, Spanish (Jelly Roll's Spanish tinge), Italian, Portuguese, all the various cultures, and the African base, African-American collective whatever-you-got-I-need-logic. In the city, the culture, and its art, was an urban, more elegant, slicker expression, still with the fire of Congo Square – and those sorrow songs express American tragedy, blind slavery, industrial savagery, the dawn of the twentieth century, and what was to come.

The early part of the twentieth century in the U.S. was called the Jazz Age, because by that time (the twenties) the music had come upriver as the people came, beat down by fake emancipation, destroyed reconstruction, black codes, boll weevils, the Klan, Republican betrayal.

Our modernism, the Harlem Renaissance, is contemporary with what's called the Age of Modernism. Langston Hughes went to Europe too, but came back, him and McKay. Zora Neale Hurston, Jean Toomer, along with the transformer of American music, Duke Ellington, the master American composer, who took the root and branch of African, African-American, peasant, city blue-black culture and raised it up to a sophistication that turned Europe on its ear. The most important composer in Europe by the thirties was Duke Ellington – or haven't you heard Stravinsky, Ravel? But the music had got to the Europeans befo dat – you haven't heard Debussy?

So that when the Eliots and Pounds, Hemingways, Carlos Williams, and Picassos and Ives were strutting what they were – the African-American Renaissance created a Jazz Age, for the whole world!

Bird took it upstairs another increment. Like Lenin said, Capitalism is the age of steam, socialism electricity, and as the nuclear age dawns, if we are not too primitive to harness it without destroying all life, communism is the nuclear age.

Bird blew a Nagasaki speed-up for us. He took it from the quarter note, as the main tongue, to the eighth note. As the new conversational form. The point being to make sense at higher and higher speeds! So then Trane came on the scene to make sense in long fabrics of sixteenth notes. Faster yet. Faster. Listen to the difference between earlier r & b and post-Stevie, you notice first the *speed.*

If you could speak the language of *Anthropology, Confirmation, Bloomdido, Klacktoveedesteen, Billies Bounce,* etc. you had entered the nuclear age, about the same time the Squares in their use of the same principle were destroying human life at Hiroshima. You see the different classes' directly opposite use of the same elements? Bird is nuclear, atomic; Trane, hydrogen. Duke was modern warfare, period.

Bird, Charles Parker, Bird, that name has been a spiritual symbol since before ancient Egypt. The hieroglyphic, bird, means *Spirit.* We used that symbol in Newark to indicate Spirit House. Ba. Bird. Soul. Ba. Bird's soaring lines, hip air calligraphy, the elegant sweeping dazzle of his line, the incredible speed. So he is also, this bird, the symbol of artist. The spirit catcher – spirit transferrer. From where he got it on over to us.

And his tragic death also must instruct us, that spirit can only be manifest through material life. That sensitivity and beauty can be destroyed easily by the gross thuggery of a primitive world. Record companies got big off Charlie Parker's wings – and thighs – and giblets, etc. Col. Sanders is smiling to let you know, you just a raw material, my man and sweet lady. Just a raw material. Until the bird consciousness also has its self-conscious entity of survival and self-determination.

Beauty without a self-created means of survival and development is what we mean by a chicken box! 'A couple of them chicken boxes to go, please?' We celebrate Bird's life because of his music, but also because of our own lives, and our own collective music, and because of our own determination to prevail! And still be hip and beautiful!

84 **Michael Harper** 'Bird Lives': Charles Parker (1977)

Source: Michael Harper, ' "Bird lives": Charles Parker,' in *Images of Kin: New and Selected Poems* (Urbana: University of Illinois Press, 1977: 173–4).

Last on legs, last on sax,
last in Indian wars, last on *smack,*
Bird is specious, *Bird* is alive,
horn, unplayable, before, after,
right now: it's heroin time:
smack, in the melody a trip;
smack, in the Mississippi;
smack, in the drug merchant trap;
smack, in St. Louis, Missouri.

We knew you were through –
trying to get out of town,
unpaid bills, connections
unmet, unwanted, unasked,
Bird's in the last arc
of his own light: *blow Bird!*
And you did –
screaming, screaming, baby,
for life, after it, around it,
screaming for life, *blow Bird!*

What is the meaning of music?
What is the meaning of war?
What is the meaning of oppression?
Blow Bird! Ripped up and down
into the interior of life, the pain,
Bird, the embraceable you,
how many brothers gone,
smacked out: blues and racism,
the hardest, longest penis
in the Mississippi urinal:
Blow Bird!

Taught more musicians, then forgot,
space loose, fouling the melodies,
the marching songs, the fine white
geese from the plantations,
syrup in this pork barrel,
Kansas City, the even teeth
of the mafia, the big band:
Blow Bird! Inside out Charlie's
guts, *Blow Bird!* get yourself killed.

In the first wave, the musicians,
out there, alone, in the first wave;
everywhere you went, Massey Hall,
Sweden, New Rochelle, *Birdland,*
nameless bird, Blue Note, Carnegie,
tuxedo junction, out of nowhere,
confirmation, confirmation, confirmation:
Bird Lives! Bird Lives! and you do:
Dead –

85 **Baroness Pannonica de Koenigswarter**
The death of Bird (1962)

Source: Robert George Reisner, *Bird: The Legend of Charlie Parker*
(New York: Citadel Press, 1962: 131–5). (Editor's title)

I'm sick of this 'shipped the body off to the morgue' business and 'laid unknown,' for how long, for that is ridiculous. The doctor was there within five minutes of his dying, and he had been there a half an hour beforehand. The medical examiner was there within an hour of the doctor; and the moment the medical examiner comes, he takes over everything, and you have nothing more to say about it. All the pertinent facts were given by myself and the doctor to the medical examiner, and I saw him take them down. He had Bird's name, Charles Parker, taken down absolutely correctly; so the story of the false name tag on Bird could not have been so. The doctor gave Bird's age as 53, because that was his impression, for some reason. I didn't say, because I didn't know.

The autopsy said he died of pneumonia, when, actually, he did not have pneumonia. The doctor said it was a heart attack that killed him, but he had terrible ulcers, and advanced cirrhosis of the liver; and he had been told by doctors for years previous that he might die at any moment.

He had stopped by that evening before leaving for Boston where he had a gig at Storyville. His horn and bags were downstairs in his car. The first thing that happened which was unusual was when I offered him a drink, and he said no. I took a look at him, and I noticed he appeared quite ill. A few minutes later he began to vomit blood. I sent for my doctor, who came right away. He said that Bird could not go on any trip, and Bird, who felt better momentarily, started to argue the point and said that he had a commitment to play this gig and that he had to go. We told him that he must go to the hospital. That, he said, was the last thing he was going to do. He said he hated hospitals, that he had had enough of them. I then said to the doctor, 'Let him stay here.' We agreed on that, and my daughter and I took shifts around the clock watching and waiting upon him and bringing ice water by the gallon, which he consumed. His thirst was incredible; it couldn't be quenched. Sometimes he would bring it up with some blood, and then he lay back and had to have more water. It went on like this for a day or two. When the doctor first came, he asked Bird the routine questions and some others. 'Do you drink?' he asked. This brought a sidelong wink from Bird. 'Sometimes,' he said ironically, 'I have a sherry before dinner.'

The doctor came three times a day and any other times we would call him. The doctor knew how serious it was. Before he left the first time, he told me, 'I have to warn you that this man may die at any moment. He has an advanced cirrhosis and stomach ulcers. He must not leave, except in an ambulance.'

The doctor liked Bird, and Bird, when he wasn't racked by seizures, was in wonderful spirits. He made me swear not to tell anybody where he was. The third day he was a lot better. Dr Freymann said he might be able to leave in a little while. At first, Charlie Parker was just a name to the doctor; he didn't know of Bird's genius, nor did he know of Bird's weaknesses. Bird wanted the doctor, who had been a musician, to listen to some of his records, and the doctor developed an interest in his patient and wanted to hear Bird's work. Bird and I spent considerable time mapping out a program. First we played the album with strings, 'Just Friends' and 'April in Paris.' The doctor was very impressed. Bird got a great charge out of that. That was on Saturday, about 7.30 p.m. Bird was so much better that the doctor agreed that he could get up and watch the Tommy Dorsey program on TV.

We braced him up in an easy chair, with pillows and wrapped in blankets. He was enjoying what he saw of the program. Bird was a fan of Dorsey's, and he didn't see anything strange in that. 'He's a wonderful trombonist,' he said. Then came part of the show consisting of jugglers who were throwing bricks around that were stuck together. My daughter was asking how they did it, and Bird and I were being very mysterious about it. Suddenly in the act, they dropped the bricks, and we all laughed. Bird was laughing uproariously, but then he began to choke. He rose from his chair and choked, perhaps twice, and sat back in the chair. I was on the phone immediately, calling the doctor. 'Don't worry, Mummy,' my daughter said. 'He's all right now.'

I went over and took his pulse. He had dropped back in the chair, with his head falling forward. He was unconscious. I could feel his pulse still there. Then his pulse stopped.

I didn't want to believe it. I could feel my own pulse. I tried to believe my pulse was his. But I really knew that Bird was dead.

At the moment of his going, there was a tremendous clap of thunder. I didn't think about it at the time, but I've thought about it often since; how strange it was.

It happened on a Saturday night. At one o'clock in the morning they took him away, and, from then on, it was out of my hands. I said nothing to the papers, because my first concern was for Chan, his wife. I did not want her to hear it over the radio or read it in the papers. I wanted to get to her first. I had attempted to find out where she was when Bird was at my place, but he said she had just moved into a new house, and he did not know the address.

Some people said that I had the body 'shipped to Bellevue where no one identified it for forty-eight hours.' Actually, Bird's name, Charlie (Yardbird) Parker, was entered on the death certificate that was made out in my apartment at the Hotel Stanhope. The one thing we couldn't find was Chan's address, who was known as Bird's wife. Also, somebody wrote that I was at the Open Door, your place, where you had those bop sessions in Greenwich Village, and that I was talking to Art Blakey and other friends of Bird and I didn't tell them of Bird's death. Actually, I wanted to find Chan before she got the news from the radio or the press, and I went to the Open Door to see if anybody there knew her address. Finally, I thought of Teddy Wilson, and his lawyer, it so happened, had the address of Chan's mother. Chan was finally contacted Monday evening and was told.

I did not know Bird too many years, but we did have a wonderful friendship going, nothing romantic. He always dropped in unexpectedly anytime during the day or night. He was a relaxed type of person, and you sometimes hardly knew he was around. He liked to play peggity with my daughter. That game actually superseded his love of chess. We'd talk about everything under the sun. Bird knew about everything, and then some.

I'd sit around and play him records. He loved Eddie Heywood's 'Begin the Beguine.' It fascinated him; he used to play it ten times around. Another thing he loved was Billie Holiday doing 'You're My Thrill.'

For all the adulation heaped upon him by fans and musicians, he was lonely. I saw him standing in front of Birdland in a pouring rain. I was horrified, and I asked him why, and he said he just had no place to go. He was wont to frequent a few of his friends' pads and just go to sleep in an armchair. This night he couldn't find anybody home. He said, when this happened, he would ride the subways all night. He would ride a train to the end of a line; then, when he was ordered out, he would go to another train and ride back.

Bird was a very trusting person with friends. He'd put himself completely in the hands of the people he loved. In sparing his wife the shock of a public announcement of his death, I felt I was carrying out something he would have wanted.

Following is a statement from Dr Freymann, who was attending Bird at the Baroness' apartment: I refused to sign the death certificate. He had been definitely off the drugs, I could see by his eyes. He had no veins left to inject anyway – all had been used up. To me he looked to be in his early 60's. When he died, the hotel wanted him taken away quickly. I saw him for three or four days. The second day he was in terrible pain. I gave him penicillin, and then he seemed to improve. No temperature. We begged him to go to hospital, but he would not have it.

86 **Tony Scott** Destination K.C. (1960)

Source: Tony Scott, 'Destination K.C.,' in Dom Cerulli, Burt Korall, and Mort Nasatir (eds), *The Jazz Word* (New York: Ballantine, 1960: 80–3).

'One night I went down to catch him at the Open Door and he didn't show. I heard he made it later, but I had to cut so's I could get up in time for my gig ... man, can't you just feature me comin' in late to this gig? Sheeit, Mr. Railway Express himself would swoop down on me ... this gig is dragging my butt. I'd like to take up a horn and learn to blow, man, all them fine chicks be chasin' me, all the cats be wantin' to buy me drinks, I'd stay high, hot damn, what a life ... sleep everyday till you feel like gettin' up, finish the gig at Birdland and go on up to an afterhour spot till squares like us is takin' off to make our daily bread with the daily news planted under our arms ... no wonder musicians call us squares.

'If I could hit the numbers one time, just one time, I'd take off from this slave an' cop me a tenor sax an' take a few lessons an' learn one note real good an' make record dates with some funky rhythm an' blues outfit just to get some experience an' after that I'd get me a gig in Brooklyn so's no one would recognize me, 'cause when I hit the jazz scene ev'rybody be sayin' you heard that new cat wailin', he's crowdin' Bird. Sheeit ... another time I went down to Birdland to catch him with strings an' he doesn't show up so Diz played with Bird's group and sounded the end ... I waited till next set an' still no Bird, so I cut out. Man, was I drug.

'If I could blow me a horn I'd show up on the gig all the time, man, that's be kicks, just blowin' all the time ... no worries, no boss watchin' over you ... sheeit, record companies after you all the time, get your name in the Downbeat, playin' with JATP all over the world, man, how could you ever get drug. Them cats ballin' all the time an' I'm hung up down here workin' for Railway Express pushin' around ev'rything from a live snake to this coffin with some cat who's headin' for Kansas City.

'Sheeit, man, this cat shouldna' waited till he died before he went to Kansas City. What a jump town, I don't mean *now*, 'bout twenty years ago when Basie was at the Reno an' the cats used to blow all night an' day. Sheeit ... that's where Bird came from, an' Pres, man, what a ball that musta been; that musta been sumpin' else, blowin', ballin', an' booze, the three B's –'

'Hey, Spody, give me a hand with this coffin.'

'Yeah, Joe, gotcha covered ... you got to watch you mouth when you goin' south.'

'Whadja say, Spody?'

'Nothin' man, just a little sayin' rhyme I picked up when I was young ... real young ... as I was sayin', that made two times I went to catch Bird an' he didn't show, so I'm pretty drug now 'cause I'm spendin' my hard-earned geets an' ain't catchin' my man in action, so three weeks ago I dug Bird comin' out'a Birdland an' I see the sign says Bird, Max, Mingus, Bud an' Blakey are cookin' together, so I follow Bird into the bar next door and told him how I was drug 'cause he didn't show two times I was down to catch him and he apologized an' said for me to wait and he'd take me in with him. I wouldn't have said nothin' did I know he was goin' to die. Man, that drug me.'

'Watch the end, lift it up a little higher ... straight up, baby.'

'So Bird says "What kinda gig you got?" ... so I told him ... I'm down the Railway Express, an' he says, "I'll be down to see you one day," so I told him, man, what would you be doin' down at the Railway Express an' he says, "I got friends ev'rywhere," so I told him, Bird, anytime you come by, I'll take care of you.'

'Easy does it, my man, lift up on your end real easy... that's it, my man, now slide it in, easy, easy ... that's got it.'

'But he never did show ... you know, I had a feelin' he meant it ... I was waitin' for him ... he'll never show no more, he died a week after I saw him, worn out and tired at thirty-four ... but the way he said it, I believed him. I don't know, I can't believe he's gone, nobody knew he was that tired, but man, a cat can only fight so long ... he laid down a strong message ... you know, I bet Bird woulda made it down to see me if he didn't die ...'

'Let's go, Spody, you're treatin' this crate like a newborn babe. This guy is dead as a doornail.'

'I know, Joe, but *this* cat is goin' back home to Kansas City and he deserves some special treatment, 'cause them Kansas City cats are liable to find out that we don't treat 'em right up here in New York and not send nobody up here no more; so take your time while I fix my man up here real comfortable like ... solid. Ride easy, my man, you'll be home soon.'

'Finished, Spody?'

'Yeah, Joe. Here comes Red with the check sheet ... I'll see you later.'

* * *

'Hey, Red, I'm checkin' in this coffin.'

'O.K., Joe. How's Spody doin'?'

'He's O.K., but all he talks about is his friend, Bert he calls him, since this coffin came in. He died a couple weeks ago.'

'Was he a close friend?'

'Naw, but he was very famous, one of those hotjive musicians.'

'My kids musta heard him, they're crazy about that stuff. Give me a check on this loading clip.'

'O.K ....'

'Destination: Brown's Funeral Home, 107 Van Dorn Street, Kansas City, Missouri ...'

'Check.'

'Contents ... Charles Parker.'

'Check.'

87 John Clellon Holmes The horn still blows (1958)

Source: John Clellon Holmes, *The Horn* (New York: Random House, 1958: 242–3) (excerpt). (Editor's title)

No, leave it there. I will go home, tonight, and chalk upon the unfeeling iron of the subway wall, 'The Horn still blows,' in grave, anonymous hand. And you will have another hero soon, America, to join the John Browns, Houstons, Poes. What matter that he was black in soul and skin and that sometimes he hated you and that, like all your heroes, he fell so far? A man is dead, the last fifth drained, the last girl loved, the last horn lost, and he is dead too young. You will have another hero, and it does not matter if the way you think of him is not the way he was. He will join the others who obsess us still: Bessie moaning in her blood as they carted her crosstown; King puttering away his days forgotten in Savannah; Bix coughing in his horn or glass; old Fats gone finally to sleep in the ultimate lower berth; young black Fats grown pale and thin; Wardell killed down hard in a snarling bar; Bunk finding he could still pick cotton; Tesche dead in an auto crash; Brownie dead in an auto crash; Bird dead, Horn dead – tuberculosis, narcosis, arteriosclerosis, neurosis – It does not matter what carried them off. Once they blew the truth.

No, leave it there. For somewhere at the suburb end of a subway line, where the wet streets glisten in the faint street lights, a gawky, awkward youth, black or white (or something in between), walks in a formless discontent, dreaming a new dream, hoping a new hope, loving a new love; and perhaps tomorrow he will begin his arduous woodshed, and (rank and living in armpit and in crotch) will give up his hoarded money, and go out carrying the horn, to fashion on it a new song – a further chorus of the one continuing song – as he, too, progresses inevitably down his own bleak street, toward his own blank wall, where all the music ends; for only the song goes on, continually creating the need to create it anew.

Riff 7

Within the burgeoning collection of autobiography there exists a significant alternative to 'mainstream' jazz history. (Christopher Harlos, 'Jazz autobiography: theory, practice, politics,' in Krin Gabbard (ed.), *Representing Jazz*, 1995)

'Extra, Extra, read all about it! Famed jazz musician tells all, bares breast in shocking disclosures! Hundreds implicated! Former bandleaders threaten damage suits! Club owners in hiding! Ex-wives vow vengeance!' (Richard Sudhalter, 'What's Your Story, Mornin' Glory: Reflections on Some Jazz Autobiographies,' *Annual Review of Jazz Studies*, 1991)

Many books came on the scene together with many falsehoods, lies and cooked-up stories. I read much of this crap and then I was told I should write some truth, and explanations of many jazz subjects that were not clearly explained. (Danny Barker, *A Life in Jazz*, 1986)

We knew from the beginning that it would not be the usual as-told-to life, in which the musician talks into a tape recorder and his collaborator edits the tapes into a coherent narrative ... We agreed, then, that while the raw materials would be Art's, I would do the editing and provide the transitions and the background and commentary needed to put the book together. (Art Hodes and Chadwick Hansen, *Hot Man: The Life of Art Hodes*, 1992)

My friend, Wingy Manone, has written a book ... entitled 'Trumpet On the Wing,' which is the story of his life. That Wingston should emerge as a literary, as well as musical figure of note, comes as no surprise to me. For the tales he has woven orally, have kept those of us who know him, in high humor for years on end. In fact, I have long looked forward to the day when Wingy should choose to put down in black and white, all the fantastic episodes, the humorous anecdotes, the tall tales with which he has regaled us, piecemeal ... Here in this book, Wingy has told the story of a jazzman ... his own story, in the inimitable language and style which has brought him fame. (Bing Crosby, Foreword to Wingy Manone and Paul Vandervoort II, *Trumpet on the Wing*, 1948)

Who talks about jazz better than the artists who created it? (Jacket blurb, Nat Shapiro and Nat Hentoff, *Hear Me Talkin' to Ya*, 1955)

Chorus VII

Hear Me Talkin' to Ya:
Jazz and the jazz life
(orality, autobiography, mediation)

'And the real story I've got to tell, it's right there. It's Jazz' (Bechet 1960: 1). The autobiographical or self-inscribed account of 'the jazz life' offers a humanized, inclusive and least specialised access to the music. Such access, too, is less likely to get caught up in the travails of dogma, formal analysis or theory. In case this may be an over-simplified approach to jazz autobiography, Christopher **Harlos**, examining the theory, practice and politics of the genre (Gabbard 1995a), reminds us of its problematical nature – especially the sometimes complicated ways it mediates its subjects. The earlier part of Harlos's article (**88**), remarking on the inundation of jazz literature with autobiographies, argues the genre offers not only a substantial body of new, primary material; it also raises important issues of literary and cultural interest, as jazz musicians move from a musical to literary subject and engage in the authoring of texts. For Harlos, jazz autobiography mediates oral, speech discourse – the subjectivity of jazz life – into a written, textual representation. This process is illustrated in (e.g.) Mingus's *Beneath the Underdog* (see **31**, **69**), Gillespie's *To Be or Not to Bop*, Pepper's *Straight Life* (see **39**) and Wells's *The Night People*; here, musician-authored texts raise issues like literary invention, self-discovery, collaboration, corroboration and authenticity (Gabbard 1995a: 158). The varieties of this mediation, particularly where dealing with socio-political issues like race and gender, mean that negotiating jazz autobiographies can be problematical for musician-writer and reader.

Qualified as they are, autobiographies can still offer (much like oral histories) useful, first-hand sources of information on jazz. Although highly subjective and personal accounts, often more colourful than veracious, they augment our understanding of the music and its contexts. In a sense – as Kathy Ogren has explained – autobiographies can offer textual performances where musicians, sometimes in concert with their collaborators and amanuenses, create personas and narrators 'equally as fascinating as those developed musically' (Ogren 1991: 112). Autobiographies, memoirs and personal accounts also provide a valuable supplement, even alternative to 'mainstream' jazz history, conveying the kind of authentic, lived experience ('payin' dues') of musicians themselves. **Chorus VII** selects material from this life, principally jazz autobiography and personal reminiscence, exemplifying the content and style of self-inscription, and ways in which jazz musicians have acted as author-historians and writing subjects.

In *Laughter from the Hip* (1963), bassist Whitey **Mitchell** constructs an *un*problematical prologue to the jazz life: an 'imaginary one-nighter' in West Virginia, where Claude Clyde and his Rhythm Rascals perform in the gym of the Kanawha State Teachers' College (**89**). This is the embryonic 'road' experience of gigs and stands which make up so much of musicians' itinerant existence – over-worked, under-paid and grossly over-travelled. Corollaries of the strenuous road life are occupational hazards like racism, sexism, violence, fatigue, boredom, alcohol dependency and drug abuse. If this kind of touring folklore is *de rigueur* for musicians' accounts, their stories read as a racy mix of humorous anecdote, low-life reportage and episodic narrative – which their collaborators and 'as-told-to' recorders interrogate and reproduce for readers.

Dicky **Wells**'s autobiographical 'Jazz Life,' *The Night People* (1991 [1971]), receives the mediation of Count Basie (Foreword), Stanley Dance (Preface), Martin Williams (Introduction), André Hodeir (essay), Chris Sheridan (disc-ography) and a glossary. Despite these 'institutional interventions' (Harlos, 1995: 155), Wells recounts (**90**) convincingly enough the 'hazardous road' of the segregated South, its endemic and unpredictable violence. Mary Lou **Williams** (**91**) narrates a much more unmediated itinerary of experience in 'ballin'' Kansas City and New York clubland and ballrooms, while pianist/composer with Andy Kirk's Clouds of Joy. Another 'payin' dues' account comes directly from trombonist Mike **Zwerin**. In a sophisticated and humorous narrative (**92**) from *Close Enough for Jazz* (1983), he recalls touring with the Claude Thornhill band in 1958. Vying for honours with the doomed and 'already dead' Thornhill is 'road-rat' and lead trumpeter, Squirms – affectionately known as 'Filthy McSwine' and existing outside organized society on 'powders and liquids in vials.' With his legendary 'switcheroo' of Tab and maximum codeine cough syrup, Squirms lives 'one long chemical Russian roulette game.' Zwerin ends with an interesting insight: 'road-rats,' alienated from society as 'losers,' may win out in a larger sense. Musicians like Squirms are inviolable survivors.

Two highly representative and lively autobiographies, penned in the 1940s with the assistance of collaborative writers, are Mezz Mezzrow's *Really the Blues* (1946) and Eddie Condon's *We Called it Music* (1947). Both these works, in their creation of incident and character, draw on the ingredients of fiction. Guitarist and tireless jazz publicist Condon's entertaining memoir rather presents its author as a protectively cynical, alcoholic *raconteur*, with journalist Thomas Sugrue providing historical 'narration' and a measure of narrative coherence. In one passage (**93**), **Condon** recounts the scuffling poverty of Dixieland musicians in New York, where, along with fellow-Chicagoans like Fred Teschemacher, Red McKenzie, Jimmy McPartland, Bud Freeman and Gene Krupa, he works briefly in a house band at the Palace Theatre – a group reviewed as 'the poorest 7-piece orchestra on earth.' Survival is attributed to a malnutrition diet of cocktail olives/cherries, and canned tomatoes, which 'feed the body and break the hangover.' Mezzrow's *Really the Blues* celebrates the 'real jazz' of black innovators, using the jazz idiom and vernacular with spirited effect and veneration. The autobiography was published with six appendices, including style, jive language, recordings, glossary and an Afterword by collaborator Bernard Wolfe. Here, Wolfe reprints essays on Negrophilia and Negrophobia, and alludes to his subject Mezzrow's own 'obsessive and unrelenting embrace of the pariah nether world.' In a selection (**94**), 'Them first kicks are a killer,' **Mezzrow** recounts how a 'flashy, sawed-off runt of a jockey ... whose onliest riding crop was a stick of marihuana,' turns him into a 'viper.' In the Martinique roadhouse, he describes the 'masterly' effects of playing his 'loaded horn,' which gave him 'a terrific lift from the richness of the music, the bigness of it. The notes eased out like lava running down a mountain, slow and sure and steaming. It was good.'

While the nature of many autobiographies is more impressionistic and folkloric than empirical, their concern with socio-political issues can make them useful documents of cultural history. Gary Giddins, introducing Hampton Hawes's *Raise Up Off Me* (1979 [1974]) – another co-authored insider's view – alludes to a number of musicians' 'as-told-to collaborations': Mezzrow (1946), Morton (1950), Armstrong (1954), Holiday (1956) and Bechet (1960). He suggests such autobiography provides insights into the music and practitioners, but also sheds light on race, sex, drugs, alienation, and 'the predicament of the black artist in America' (1979: vi). All of these matters are vividly present in Hawes's own lacerating account, and later self-examinatory autobiographies – notably Mingus's (ed. Nel King) *Beneath the Underdog* (1971) and Davis's (with Quincy Troupe) *Miles* (1989) – bring the vernacular style of black oral tradition to an acerbic insight into issues of culture, race and gender. Further substantial accounts, from Gillespie and Fraser and Pepper and Pepper, fill out similar areas of jazz life and sub-culture.

Alan Lomax provides interpretative and sometimes corrective 'Interludes' for *Mister Jelly Roll* (1950), where Ferdinand Morton narrates a life story spanning 'the whole of the "jazz age," from the street bands of New Orleans to the sweet bands of New York.' In fairness to Morton, Lomax has tried to give the narrative – an oral history recorded for the Library of Congress – 'as much inner consistency as possible'; otherwise, Morton and others tell the tale 'their own way' (Prelude). The latter is exemplified in **Morton**'s description of early performance environments encouraging participation in jazz: New Orleans street parades (**95**). Street activity of a differently violent kind – Watts, Los Angeles, 1965 – is recounted by another black musician, Hampton **Hawes**, in a chapter (**96**) from *Raise Up Off Me*. Giddins records collaborator Don Asher's struggle to arrive at a conversational tone, narrative flow and rhythmic immediacy in making Hawes's language 'ring true' (1979: v–vi). The achieved authenticity of Hawes's 'voice,' sardonic, vivacious and self-critical, makes the work a major contribution to the literature of jazz and a compelling record of jazz's early modernism.

Giddins sees jazz autobiographies performing a critical socio-political role within a broader context of American culture. Parallel with this, as Harlos observes, is the question of how jazz musicians 'use, challenge, or transform the institution of autobiography itself' (Gabbard 1995a: 134). This issue – one of methodology or strategy – is illustrated in what musicians reveal themselves of their motives in writing autobiography. Danny Barker's insistent correction of the 'crap' he has read (**Riff 7**) is echoed by Sidney Bechet's forthright opening to *Treat It Gentle* (1960): 'You know there's people, they got the wrong idea of Jazz' (ibid.: 1). The impulse to correct and authenticate partly explains the use made of corroborative voices and testimony in jazz autobiography, as if to buttress the credibility of the subject as witness and participant. Validation of the subject's 'story' lies behind the narrative strategy of Dizzy Gillespie and Al Fraser's *To Be or Not ... to Bop: Memoirs* (1979). The authors' Preface declares its aim of 'creating the best – the most complete, authentic, and authoritative autobiography of a musician ever published' (ibid.: xvii). Granted, this is admitted to be an 'ambitious goal' and the product 'imperfect.' Gillespie and Fraser attempt the task of writing Gillespie's 'personal memoirs' through using over 150 taped interviews with 'informants,' so that comparison and contrast may be made with 'Dizzy's own statements.' Together with the imperative of support and validation is Gillespie's own challenge to popular images – many media-created – of the jazz musician. In a central chapter, 'Beboppers ... the Cult' (**97**), **Gillespie** answers, point-by-point, the 'jive-ass stories' and 'bullshit' circulated by the press and music industry. These include the stereotypes, racial and cultural, of beboppers as degenerate, goateed, bereted, slang-ridden, licentious, unpatriotic drug-users ...

Laurie Pepper, who transcribed and edited the tape-recorded narrative of husband Art **Pepper**'s *Straight Life* (1979), claims it is 'a true story'; a frontispiece describes Pepper as jazz musician, innovator, junkie, convict. The autobiography employs a 'Cast of Characters,' supposedly as witnesses and corroborators for the subject's life and character, serving to augment the overall record. As 'authenticating textual voices' (Gabbard 1995a: 158), they serve little to enhance Pepper's own narrative and detract from the continuity and force of his relentless testimony. One such 'character' (Hersh Hamel) characterizes Pepper as 'big monstrous doper, outta control' (Pepper 1979: 468). It is a singular pathology, its extremity given credence in an extract from 'Heroin' (**98**). This conveys, with the honesty and intensity of Pepper's own saxophone playing, 'that moment' when he becomes what he will die as: 'a junkie.'

The distinction between jazz autobiography and oral history is a fine and even over-lapping one, both in content and method. Burton Peretti (Gabbard 1995a: 122) claims that jazz historians as a group have not made 'the methodological transition from journalistic interviewing to oral history.' Viewed in this light, so-called 'informal' or 'oral' histories have tended to be published *compendia*, their arrangement either biographical or chronological, with methodology relying on a *collage* of interviews. That they remain 'journalistic' may suggest an absence of the empirical rigour associated with *archival* oral histories, and account for their loose transcription of testimony and recall from jazz pioneers and memoirists. The most distinguished example of oral history is still Shapiro and Hentoff (1955; see also **30**) – though subsequent compilations, from (e.g.) Spellman (1966), Taylor (1977: see **63**), Gitler (1985), Stokes (1991) and Sidran (1992), have usefully extended the methodology to other jazz history and forms of autobiography. The Chorus closes (**99**) with Louis **Armstrong**'s early memories of New Orleans' Storyville. What is distinctive here, as in the more effective jazz autobiographies, is a sense of the authentic 'voice.' Editing and transcription mediate between spoken and written word, so that a mainly oral discourse is re-cast in textual form. *The real story I've got to tell ... Hear me talkin' to ya ...*

88 **Christopher Harlos** Jazz autobiography: Theory, practice, politics (1995)

Source: Christopher Harlos, 'Jazz autobiography: theory, practice, politics,' in Krin Gabbard (ed.), *Jazz Among the Discourses* (Durham, NC: Duke University Press, 1995: 131–7) (excerpt).

I remember one day being in a music history class and a white woman was the teacher. She was up in front of the class saying that the reason black people played the blues was because they were poor and had to pick cotton. So they were sad and that's where the blues came from, their sadness. My hand went up in a flash and I stood up and said, 'I'm from East St. Louis and my father is rich, he's a dentist, and I play the blues. My father didn't never pick no cotton and I didn't wake up this morning sad and start playing the blues. There's more to it than that.' Well, the bitch turned green and didn't say nothing after that. Man, she was teaching that shit from out of a book written by someone who didn't know what the fuck he was talking about. That's the kind of shit that was happening at Juilliard and after a while I got tired of it. (*Miles: The Autobiography*)

In the five decades since Miles Davis's brief encounter with institutionalized music history at Juilliard, the gradual acceptance of jazz studies on the American campus is indicative of a more general call for research in areas of popular culture previously considered beyond the purview of traditional scholarship. Lewis Porter spoke of jazz studies 'coming of age in the academic world' as late as 1988, and even more recently there is evidence of a genuine historiographical self-awareness, Scott DeVeaux's compelling critique of the jazz textbook macro-narrative, and Gary Tomlinson's related essay on the 'dialogics' of jazz discourse being two such signs. Both essays draw attention to a symptomatic and recurrent breakdown in the way jazz history has been commonly conceptualized: as a linear and altogether coherent progression, straightforward and logical in its development, and built on a well-established canon – rather than as a complex of musical forms and cultures in a perpetual state of collision, revolution, and redefinition. In contrast to Miles's succinct comment on the establishment version of black music history, such theorizing only serves as evidence that jazz historiography is just now catching up – some fifty years later – with the intuitive observation of an exasperated undergraduate that there is, simply, 'more to it than that.'

But the claim that jazz history is really much more complicated than the textbook version designed for the undergraduate curriculum should be neither surprising nor controversial. At issue is the means through which the experience of jazz musicians has been traditionally transformed into written prose – and in the wake of these recent historiographical stirrings are questions concerning the position from which any such *master narrative* might be constructed: its genealogy; the tacit goals it seeks to advance; and, perhaps most importantly, what voices, elements, or incidents that narrative might seek to suppress. Subject over the years to the pressures of economic interdependence in a highly volatile and ultimately shrinking market, the alliance between writers and jazz musicians has been fragile, producing a body of writing specifically tooled for a readership of supporting patrons. So it is no accident that such a dynamic tended to avoid specific reference to friction or even open animosity between the musicians and those wielding the substantial power of the press – much less toward promoters, club owners, or record companies. Obviously, for publishers to reveal contempt among musicians for the establishment would be to undermine the establishment's authority, and since the majority of jazz writing has sprung, until about 1991, from a few dozen industry-dependent critic/journalists, the accepted *mode* of *production* remained fairly stable by keeping acrimony in check.

Now, however, in two distinct but related movements, it is possible to observe a significant transformation in jazz writing's business-as-usual. The one movement, within which musicologists like Tomlinson, DeVeaux, and Porter could be cast, is discovered in the expansion of jazz titles among scholarly presses and academic journals – attributable to the growing acknowledgment that jazz has affected twentieth-century world culture in numerous ways not yet completely understood. The other movement in this transformation is manifested in the fact that since the early 1980s jazz literature has been inundated with autobiographies – especially as an entire generation of survivors rapidly dwindles. During the ten-year period from 1983 until 1993, dozens of book-length, first-person, nonfiction narratives published under the name of a jazz musician were added to an already sizable list of autobiographical works representing a wide spectrum of players from every generation and style: stories from leaders, headliners, and sidemen; stories about Chicago in the twenties, the road in the thirties, about the East Coast in the forties, the West Coast in the fifties, about expatriates in Europe; stories about long careers, short careers; about survival; about creating art – all of which also represent a wide range of approaches to the act of self-inscription.

One particular autobiography that points some new directions for jazz scholarship is Milt Hinton's *Bass Line* (written with David Berger). As one of the most recorded and respected musicians in jazz history, Hinton offers a carefully detailed, first-hand account of a remarkable career; one balanced between traveling with Cab Calloway's big band in the 1940s, and the greatly different demands of the New York studio scene in the fifties and sixties. But *Bass Line's* documentary value, beyond the interest and elegance of its narrative, is that Hinton includes more than two hundred photographs from his own collection – pictures of almost every major jazz figure in rehearsal and performance settings – taken over the course of forty years; and so vast is Hinton's reserve of photographs that he subsequently published a companion piece, *Over Time*. Hinton's one-of-a-kind legacy to jazz history provides a profoundly rich perspective on the life of one sensitive musician-historian; when juxtaposed with other books from the 1983–93 period, it is further evidence that despite the slight critical attention received so far, such a substantial body of primary material can have tremendous ramifications – both for jazz studies and for scholarly work on autobiography. So the fact that the growing academic interest in jazz would appear simultaneously with the plethora of autobiography, particularly as we approach the fin de siècle, seems more than merely coincidental – for not only are there new primary materials to be examined and considered, but surely, the synthesis of the jazz sensibility with 'the culture of autobiography' has produced texts whose literary and cultural interest parallels, or even surpasses, the biographical information made newly available in such works.

An early whispering of what the personal stories of jazz musicians – taken en bloc – might have to offer appears in Gary Giddins's brief introduction to pianist Hampton Hawes's *Raise Up Off Me*, a book from a cluster of late seventies' autobiographies, including Dizzy Gillespie's *To BE, or Not ... to BOP*, and Art Pepper's *Straight Life*. In his attempt to locate *Raise Up Off Me*, one of the first autobiographies by a postwar bebopper, Giddins quickly looks at a number of books by earlier musicians (Jelly Roll Morton, Sidney Bechet, Mezz Mezzrow and others), suggesting that the 'small, little-known genre of autobiographical works not only provides insight into the music and its makers, but also sheds light on race relations, Bohemian attitudes toward sex and drugs, alienation, and the predicament of the black artist in America.' Giddins perceptively foresees an expanded role for jazz autobiography within a broader reading of American music and popular culture, but his suggestion ultimately begs the question as to how one might go about extracting or interpreting any 'light' emanating from the works under consideration. Even to christen a given collection of texts a genre is to tacitly accept a number of literary conventions (in both writing and reading) that privilege features that may or may not be useful to a wholesale reading of jazz autobiographies. As a result, running parallel to the sociopolitical topics suggested by Giddins, there is the related question of how jazz musicians use, challenge, or transform the institution of autobiography itself.

With these questions in mind, the present essay proposes to examine the emerging body of jazz autobiography in terms that explicitly track the dynamic at work in a jazz player's transition from a musical to a literary subject. One motivation behind the jazz player's move to autobiography, for example, is signaled in the opening of *Treat It Gentle*, where Sidney Bechet states flatly, 'You know there's people, they got the wrong idea of Jazz,' and then a few pages later asserts that it was only 'a name white people have given to the music.' Likewise, in *Music Is My Mistress*, Duke Ellington makes a point of the fact that he was disinclined to use the term 'jazz' as a way of classifying his own musical endeavors. For Bechet and Ellington at least, one attraction to autobiography was the opportunity to deconstruct the label *jazz* (both denotatively and connotatively) as the binary other against which so-called 'serious' or 'legitimate' music was defined and subsequently marginalized (a project Ellington, for one, continued throughout his life). Implied in the terminological uneasiness expressed by Ellington and Bechet, however, is a deeper and more complicated set of conditions that informs the relationship between the jazz musician and jazz history; and for jazz musicians, the turn to autobiography is regarded as a genuine opportunity to seize narrative authority. So, to follow Giddins's suggestion, looking for possible insights to be gleaned from a collective reading of jazz autobiography quickly leads to the discovery that for many jazz musicians one source of the 'alienation' and 'predicament' to which Giddins refers is often previously written prose; that is, dissatisfaction with jazz writing is a theme that immediately surfaces in a number of autobiographical works.

In one of the handful of published essays to treat jazz autobiography as such, Kathy Ogren has already called attention to an annoyance with jazz writing expressed by two early musicians, pianist Willie 'The Lion' Smith and guitarist Danny Barker, in their personal narratives. Barker says of his motivation to turn to autobiography: 'Many books came on the scene together with many falsehoods, lies, and cooked up stories. I read much of this crap and then I was told I should write some truth and explanations of many jazz subjects that were not clearly explained' (120–21 [**Riff 7**]). Smith, a native New Yorker, complains bitterly about the early 'jazz books, most of them written by non-playing so-called critics,' that tended to discount musicians who came from anywhere but the Delta region. Though Ogren frames these passages in a somewhat different argument about storytelling and narrative performance from the one proposed here, it is hard to dismiss the contempt for jazz writing – particularly by nonmusicians – such works convey.

To take another example, in Charles Mingus's *Beneath the Underdog*, the critique is cast in slightly different terms when he lampoons a coterie of widely published jazz critics through an imagined New York jam session featuring *them* as performers: Leonard Feather on piano, Bill Coss and Gene Lees singing, Barry Ulanov on drums, Marshall Stearns on bass, Whitney Balliett as composer, John S. Wilson conducting, and Martin Williams, who can 'play everything,' the narrator quips, adding, 'I can tell by the way he writes' (294 [see **31**]). The dubious authority of the nonmusician writer is also depicted in an apocryphal story recounted in Art Hodes's *Hot Man* about an unnamed American jazz critic who, having recently published a book, is introduced to 'Ivan,' a Soviet jazz critic visiting New York. Hodes writes: 'After a bit the "Russian" says to the American critic, "what instrument do you play?" The critic replies, "Nothing." The "Russian" looks him over carefully. "You write on jazz and you don't play an instrument? In Russia we shoot you"' (108).

But the felt distrust for writers on the part of jazz musicians can take on a much more serious and acrimonious tone. In a more direct way, *To BE, or Not … to BOP* shows how Dizzy Gillespie came to regard the reaction of the American press to the bebop movement of the forties. At the core of the text, in possibly its finest chapter, 'Beboppers … the Cult' [see **97**], is a considered response to the popular image of the jazz musician – as a goateed, bereted, drug-using, nonpatriot – much of which was directed toward Gillespie himself. With specific reference to an article appearing in the March 25, 1946, issue of *Time*, warning of bebop's 'degenerative influence on youth,' he writes, 'Once it got inside the marketplace, our style was subverted by the press and the music industry.' 'I should've sued,' he continues a few lines later, 'even though the chances in winning in court were slim. It was all bullshit.' And for an even more explicit and sustained articulation of the contempt for jazz writing, we need only return to *Miles: The Autobiography*:

After bebop became the rage, white music critics tried to act like they discovered it – and us – down on 52nd Street. That kind of dishonest shit makes me sick to my stomach. And when you speak out on it or don't go along with this racist bullshit, then you become a radical, a black trouble-maker. (55)

I wasn't going to [grin] just so that some non-playing, racist, white motherfucker could write some nice things about me ... So a lot of critics didn't like me back then – still don't today – because they saw me as an arrogant little nigger. Maybe I was, I don't know, *but I do know that I wasn't going to have to write about what I played and if they couldn't or wouldn't do that, then fuck them* [emphasis added]. Anyway, Max [Roach] and [Thelonious] Monk felt like that, and J. J. [Johnson] and Bud Powell, too. So that's what brought us close together, this attitude about ourselves and our music. (83)

A lot of white critics kept talking about all these white jazz musicians, imitators of us, like they was some great motherfuckers and everything. Talking about Stan Getz, Dave Brubeck, Kai Winding, Lee Konitz, Lennie Tristano, and Gerry Mulligan like they was gods or something. *And some of them white guys were junkies like we were, but wasn't nobody writing about that like they was writing about us* [emphasis added]. They didn't start paying attention to white guys being junkies until Stan Getz got busted trying to break into a drugstore to cop some drugs. That shit made the headlines until people forgot and went back to just talking about black musicians being junkies. (156)

[Some] musicians had become victims of the critics, most of whom are lazy and don't want to work too hard to understand contemporary musical expression and language. That's too much like work for them, so they just put it down every time. *Dumb, insensitive critics have destroyed a lot of great music and musicians who weren't as strong as I was in having the ability* to say, 'Fuck y'all' [emphasis added]. (352)

Though anyone accustomed to Miles's scorching whisper would expect some level of invective to surface in *The Autobiography*, his attack against writers, when read on the heels of the others mentioned above, raises an important question about the extent to which such views are prevalent within a more general range of jazz autobiography. If there is an overarching sentiment that a good deal written about the music does not necessarily correspond with the sensibility or even lived experience of the musicians themselves, then it seems reasonable to conclude that within the burgeoning collection of autobiography there exists a significant alternative to 'mainstream' jazz history. So the expansion of jazz autobiography has, among other things, brought the discursive (i.e., nonmusical) voice of the jazz musician in direct contact and dialogue with history, and by consequence, the ethos of the musician-as-historian has risen exponentially. Moreover, to approach the body of jazz autobiography as a *reaction against* previous writing on jazz, to see *that* as one of its primary motivations will obviously lead to a different reading from one that would take the musician-writer relationship as being unproblematic. But lest this initial sketch seem inordinately polarized – particularly as it draws extensively upon the reported experience of one notoriously truculent trumpeter – we can hastily note many counterexamples that indicate a more positive relationship to jazz writing within musician-authored texts – some even in *Miles: The Autobiography.*

Works cited (edited)

Barker, Danny. *A Life in Jazz.* Ed. Alyn Shipton. New York: Oxford UP, 1986.

Davis, Miles, with Quincy Troupe. *Miles: The Autobiography.* New York: Simon, 1989.

Hinton, Milt, and David Berger. *Bass Line: The Stories and Photographs of Milt Hinton.* Philadelphia: Temple UP, 1988.

Hodes, Art, and Chadwick Hansen. *Hot Man.* Urbana: University of Illinois Press, 1992.

Mingus, Charles. *Beneath the Underdog: His World According to Mingus.* Ed. Nel King. New York: Vintage, 1991.

Ogren, Kathy. '"Jazz Isn't Just Me": Jazz Autobiographies as Performance Personas,' *Jazz in Mind.* Ed. Reginald T. Buckner and Steven Weiland. Detroit: Wayne State UP, 1991. 112–27.

89 **Whitey Mitchell** Getting there is half the fun (1963)

Source: Whitey Mitchell, 'Getting there is half the fun,' in Leonard Feather and Jack Tracy, *Laughter from the Hip* (New York: Horizon, 1963: 66–8).

I may be nuts, but I still enjoy one-nighters. The fact that I never do more than one in a row may have something to do with it; nevertheless, it's fun to play with a big band, and there are still a few left.

If you're not independently wealthy, it's a good idea to save your money before becoming involved with some of these groups, because big bands are no longer big business. But people still like dance bands, and the booking agencies furnish their clients with long lists of famous bandless bandleaders. Then when the contracts are signed, the bandless bandleader who gets the nod calls his contractor, who books fifteen or sixteen men for that particular date, making sure that at least four of the men have usable cars, and away they go.

It's not really a swindle for the people who attend the dance, for sure enough, there's their famous bandleader standing in front of his band, playing the music that made him famous. What they don't know is that no matter which famous bandleader they might have selected, they would probably have gotten more or less the same band; that is, the guys who do the big band one-nighters. Of course, there are a few big bands around that work enough to keep the same men together for long periods, have their own uniforms, library, arrangers and high musical standards; but this doesn't seem to cut any ice with either the public or the booking agents. This type of band nowadays is the exception, rather than the rule.

Now, let's go on an imaginary one-nighter with Claude Clyde and his Rhythm Rascals. You're told to be at the Capitol Hotel at 9:30 Saturday morning, complete with your dark suit and your toothbrush (assuming you're relatively fastidious) and your horn. You know from experience that there is no longer any Capitol Hotel, and that the band won't actually leave until 10:15, but you show up at 9:30 where the Capitol used to be because you're a good guy.

You're the first one there. The rest of the sidemen and a few of the cars begin to straggle in at 9:50, and you're assigned to the drummer's car. He's not a great drummer, but he has this big station wagon. You are a trifle dismayed when you have to sit in the back with the jackets, library, bass, drums, and Claude's golf clubs.

You notice that the drummer is poring over maps of West Virginia, but then you remember the contractor's assurance that it's only a short hop, 150 miles or so. You're pleased to notice that the girl vocalist is also assigned to your car; this indicates that, females being what they are, there will be many rest stops.

You rearrange the vocalist's gowns so that you can once again see out the window, and the car majestically pulls out into the Eighth Avenue traffic at precisely 10:17. A wonderful feeling of camaraderie exists in the station wagon, because you're all sharing this adventure together. You tell all the jokes that you can think of to tell, and so does everyone else; however, because of the presence of the girl vocalist, this becomes a rather limited category. Then there is a short discussion of world affairs and the state of the music business. Then, as everyone runs out of conversation, the long silence sets in. This happens about the time you reach the Lincoln Tunnel, and lasts until you reach your destination, Noshe, West Virginia, eight and a half hours later.

Of course, there were some wonderful sights and smells along the way. The oil refineries, the garbage incinerators, the auto graveyards, the acres of manure. And the trip was broken up by four rest stops, two gas stops, three Howard Johnson stops, and a Dairy Queen stop. And, oh yes, one liquor stop for those with enough foresight to be concerned with the return trip.

You arrive at Noshe and have no trouble locating the center of town. You have the table d'hôte dinner at the Noshe Hilton, and drive straight out to the gymnasium of the Kanawha State Teachers' College. You go to the men's locker room, find a vacant sink, and do the best you can with liquid antiseptic soap, paper towels, and your own shaving lotion. Then you just have time to get to the bandstand, look over the music, and warm up your horn. While you're doing this, you answer to the best of your ability the following questions, put to you by several eager early arrivals:

1) Is this the *real* Claude Clyde band, or just some boys he picked up in Clarksburg? You show them your 802 card.
2) How long have you been with Claude? You tell them you've been with him about 12 hours. They laugh.
3) Where do you go from here? You tell them back to New York.

4) You mean right after the job tonight? You tell them yes, it's all in the day's work. They don't believe you.

5) Does the drummer take dope? You tell them the drummer *is* a dope. They are disappointed. They go away.

Claude Clyde arrives by cab from the airport. He will check into the Noshe Hilton after the job and fly back to New York the next day. He calls out the first set of tunes, waves to the people, and gives the down beat. For the next four hours you play with Claude Clyde and his Rhythm Rascals, except for a twenty-five minute period when the past Prom Queen crowns the present Prom Queen, and eighteen brothers from Tau Upsilon (or is it Throw Upsilon?) entertain with their version of *Bloody Mary*.

It is eleven a.m. the following day when your red-rimmed eyes spot what used to be the Capitol Hotel. You know everyone in the station wagon so intimately that you hope you never see any of them again. You didn't sleep much on the way back, especially after that narrow squeak on the Jersey Turnpike, and your mouth tastes like the bottom of a birdcage, and the bottom of your bird-cage doesn't feel so good either. You look in your wallet and discover that you have spent about seventeen dollars. Your pay check will probably total $32.50 after deductions, leaving you with $15.50, which is better than one dollar per hour.

As you trudge home to your well-earned rest, you start thinking about next week's gig in Providence. Shouldn't be as tough as this one was, and after all, the contractor said it was only a hundred miles or so.

90 **Dicky Wells** The hazardous road (1971)

Source: Dicky Wells, as told to Stanley Dance, 'The hazardous road,' in *The Night People: The Jazz Life of Dicky Wells* (Washington, DC: Smithsonian Institution Press, 1991 [1971]: 47–8, 49–50, 52) (excerpts).

We used to travel the best way we could in the early days. When we were with Cecil Scott we had an old, twelve-cylinder Packard. We used to fill that thing up with gas paid for out of our own pockets. The tank would be leaking. About twenty miles – it would be empty again! We would be going up the Cotton Top Mountain, seven miles, right out of Ohio on the way to Pittsburgh, and we'd have to push the rascal halfway up that mountain and then ride down the other side. We'd all sleep in the car and everything – about ten of us. We had a bass player called Mike who used to drink a lot. He would put his fiddle case up on top of the car. We left Springfield once, got to Pittsburgh, opened up, and no fiddle! Mike was high and had left it in Springfield. All he had was the case.

We very seldom went by train, because we couldn't ride on tab. We took this raggedy old Packard up to the car lot once and asked the man how much he would give us, because we had eyes for a bus – about three-thousand dollars. The man said:

'I'll give you about fifteen seconds to get out of here!'

We had that idea because cats who rode in a bus then were something. Few had buses. Nearly all the bands traveled in private cars.

We had a Ford for traveling when we played with Tapp, an old-time Ford with these little window blinds. We had about six pieces. So we were going from Terre Haute, Indiana, back to Louisville, and the roads were covered with ice, and the windshield frosted up so we couldn't drive. This same bass player, who drank a lot, always kept his whiskey sticking out of his pocket, and he was asleep. So we had to take his whiskey and pour it on the windshield.

'For God's sake, don't tell him!' one of the guys said.

It was a wonder it didn't break the windshield. It was that bad corn. But when this cat woke up, we had to chain him. He called everybody everything.

We played a dance with Ferman Tapp when Bill Beason was in the band, about twenty-five miles out of Knoxville – the first time I ever had any trouble. So a guy brought us some corn whiskey, a gallon. He came back after a while and said:

'Everybody drinking the whiskey? I'll bring you another one.'

'Okay,' the cats say.

So he comes back with another gallon. An hour later, here he comes again, and we hadn't finished the whiskey.

'Drink up this whiskey,' he says.

He was under the impression you could play louder or something when you were drunk, and we weren't drinking fast enough for him.

'Why, you black b– s– .'

The usual thing to make you angry. I looked back, and Bill Beason had picked up a chair, to hit this man in the head, and us at nothing but an ofay dance, and we're twenty-five miles from Knoxville, Tennessee. A couple of cats had their rods then, but they couldn't pull them out, for what were you going to do at a dance with six hundred people? Bill's hotheadedness almost got us messed up there ...

In those days, when we were traveling in the South, most cats had firearms somewhere, somehow. Because you used to run up against a lot of frightful people, drunken people, and whatnot. The ofays would try to frighten you if somebody got out of line and want to beat up the band or shoot somebody. If you pull a gun, there's two chances to one the cat is going to cool down. It's a fool who's going to keep messing with you after he sees this gun. As a rule, all the bands, white and colored, used to have a stash someplace, because there'd always be some crank who wanted to mess with you. Somebody always seems to think a musician on a bandstand is woman's man, and he just hates you for that, so the best you can do is rub him down or fan him. You don't have time to make love to everybody! Or maybe you're a friendly guy, just going around shaking hands, trying to look neat and your best, as the public wants you to. You'd be surprised how a lot of guys figure you're acting cute and trying to be something else.

There was that incident in Florida some years ago. It happened to a band called, I think, the Whispering Serenaders of Gold, out of Columbus, Ohio. It was when the Charleston first came out. They had a drummer, a very nice-looking fellow with long black hair. They went to Miami, and some girls there wanted to learn to dance, and they asked their partners, and these ofays said to the band:

'Okay, go ahead. Learn 'em how to do this dance.'

So they danced around, and the drummer tried to learn them how to do it, although he probably didn't want to. But nobody bothered them.

Afterwards, some cars came to take them all to a party, and they asked for this drummer in particular:

'We're going to have a party and some drinks for you guys.'

They carried them out, and they cut him up, that drummer, castrated him, and he swelled up and died in the hospital. We heard about that in Louisville, and that's one of the reasons the cats started to carry firearms, because if we were traveling around and ran into something like that, we'd all have to die for nothing.

Later, when I was with Fletcher Henderson, I found he never approved of it, but the guys would say:

'We're going South, man! We've got to have our artillery.'

Now, Fletcher had good transportation – five or six cars, new ones mostly. They had a lot of wrecks, too, but Big Green was telling me something before he died that was funny.

'Man, you don't have fun like we used to,' he said. 'We'd be coming to a small town with all these big cars, and outside of town we'd start speeding up to around seventy, eighty miles an hour and start shooting at chickens, cats, and dogs as we went through town – anything but people! The chickens would be flying and running, dogs barking, and people screaming – it was like the Wild West!' . . .

In Baltimore, there was a Chinese restaurant next door to the hotel, and there was a Chinaman peeling potatoes at an open window. So someone bet Bobby Stark he couldn't shoot the dish out of this fellow's hands.

'Wham!'

The potatoes flew in the air, and the Chinaman split down the street yelling and carrying on. He got a cop and came back searching everybody.

Bobby did something like that to me in Kansas City. We had been drinking and were lying around in the hotel.

'Come on Wells-O,' he said. 'Let's get up and go to the show.'

'Bobby, I don't want to see no show,' I said. 'I'm supposed to see a chick tonight.'

'Man, if I shoot you in your ass you'll get up and go to the show!'

'You'll shoot what, man?'

'I will. I'll shoot you, you – .'

'Oh, go on, man,' and I turned over in the bed.

Bam!

He missed me, but he hit the bed railing about an inch away. He ran out the door to hide the gun or something, and I was dressed and waiting for him to go to the show in nothing flat. Well, he had been drinking, but I didn't know whether he was a hell of a marksman or not.

The next day, a couple of big cats came over from the Cherry Blossom, where Basie was playing, and they said:

'We hear you've got a bad man over here with a gun. We'd like to see him.'

'We ain't got nobody around here with a gun.'

'Yes, you have. His name is Bobby Stark.'

So they came on up to see Bobby.

'We've come to take you for a ride,' they say. 'We don't allow anything like that in our territory.'

Bobby was getting all sincere and frightened – the only time I ever saw him frightened. Then the guys – a colored fellow and a white fellow – winked and said:

'Okay, watch it around here. Don't let anybody catch you with that thing.'

So that cooled it, but it was a pretty close call for me.

91 **Mary Lou Williams** Music everywhere (1954)

Source: Mary Lou Williams, 'Mary Lou Williams: a life story' ['My friends the kings of jazz'], *Melody Maker*, XXX (3 April–12 June,1954): 24 April, 5. (Editor's title)

I found Kansas City to be a heavenly city – music everywhere in the Negro section of town, and 50 or more cabarets rocking on Twelfth and Eighteenth Streets. [Andy] Kirk's band was drawing them into the handsome Pla-mor Ballroom when my husband, John Williams, had me return to him in Kaycee. This was my first visit to Missouri's jazz metropolis, a city that was to have a big influence on my career.

With two sisters, Lucille and Louise, who knew every speakeasy in town, I began to make the rounds from 'Hell's Kitchen' on Fifth Avenue to a club on Eighteenth where I met Sam Price. Sammy was playing an unusual type of blues piano which I thought could hardly be improved on. I had the luck to hear him again when we were both in New York during 1934.

One night, we ran into a place where Ben Pollack had a combo which included Jack Teagarden and, I think, Benny Goodman. The girls introduced me to the Texas trombonist, and right away we felt like friends. After work, he and a couple of the musicians asked us to go out, and we visited most of the speaks downtown. One I remember particularly, because it was decorated to resemble the inside of a penitentiary, with bars on the windows and waiters in striped uniforms like down-South convicts. In these weird surroundings, I played for the boys and Jack got up and sang some blues. I thought he was more than wonderful. While they stayed in Kaycee, Jack and some of Pollack's men came round every night, and I was very happy to see them.

Now at this time, which was still Prohibition, Kansas City was under Tom Pendergast's control. Most of the night spots were run by politicians and hoodlums, and the town was wide open for drinking, gambling and pretty much every form of vice. Naturally, work was plentiful for musicians, though some of the employers were tough people. For instance, when Kirk moved from the Pla-mor, the orchestra went to work for a nationally feared gangster. He was real bad: people used to run when you just mentioned his name. At that time, Andy was playing tuba, and the band was conducted by our singer, Billy Massey. Billy was a man not easily scared, and one day at the new job he ran off his mouth to the boss. The hood concluded he was crazy (which was not far wrong), and told all the band to pack and leave – but fast. The rest of the guys were too nice, he said, for him to think about killing Billy. I heard that Count Basie later worked for the same dracula, and also had a slight misunderstanding. As a result, Basie had to work two weeks without pay.

So for the Clouds of Joy it was more one-nighters. After a few, short trips, we headed east to New York to open in the Roseland Ballroom, that spot made famous by Fletcher Henderson. Kirk was on his way up. By now, I had graduated to composer, arranger, and first-class chauffeur for the organization. I was not playing in the band but was doing their recordings for Brunswick, and sometimes sitting in to try things I had written.

In Kansas City, Kirk had liked my ideas, though I could not set them down on paper. He would sit up as long as 12 hours at a stretch, taking down my ideas for arrangements, and I got so sick of the method that I began putting them down myself. I hadn't studied theory, but asked Kirk about chords and the voicing register. In about 15 minutes I had memorised what I wanted. That's how I started writing. My first attempt, 'Messa Stomp,' was beyond the range of half the instruments. But the boys gave me a chance and each time I did better, until I found myself doing five and six arrangements per week. Later on, I learned more theory from people like the great Don Redman, Edgar Sampson, Milton Orent, and Will Bradley.

The Clouds of Joy had a long run at the Roseland, playing opposite a bunch named the Vagabonds, then opposite the Casa Loma Band (later led by Glen Gray). From the Roseland, they moved to the celebrated Savoy Ballroom, where they faced Chick Webb's orchestra. The Savoy was a place of tremendous enthusiasm, a home of fantastic dancing. And Webb was acknowledged king of the Savoy. Any visiting band could depend on catching hell from little Chick, for he was a crazy drummer and shrewd to boot. The way I made it out, Chick would wait until the opposition had blown its hottest numbers and then – during a so-so set – would unexpectedly bring his band fresh to the stand and wham into a fine arrangement, like Benny Carter's 'Liza,' that was hard to beat. Few visiting bands could stand up to this.

Kirk must have stayed a couple of months at the Savoy, during which time I often sat in, playing either 'Mary's Idea' or 'Froggy Bottom,' and doing quite well with the kids who liked a good beat for their dancing. From there, we toured Pennsylvania and the Eastern States, and after what seemed like a year of one-nighters, returned to Kansas City.

Kaycee was really jumping now – so many great bands having sprung up there or moved in from over the river. I should explain that Kansas City, Missouri, wasn't too prejudiced for a Mid-western town. It was a ballin' town, and it attracted musicians from all over the South and South-west, and especially from Kansas.

Kansas City, Kansas, was right across the viaduct, just about five or six miles distant. But on the Kansas side they were much snootier. A lot of their musicians were from good families who frowned on jazz, so the musicians and kids would come across to Kaycee to blast. In Kaycee, nothing mattered.

I've known musicians so enthused about playing that they would walk all the way from the Kansas side to attend a jam session. Even bass players, caught without street-car fare, would hump their bass on their back and come running. That was how music stood in Kansas City in those years around 1930.

At the head of the bands was Bennie Moten's, led by pianist Bennie, and featuring his brother, Buster, on accordion. Then there was George E. Lee, whose sister, Julia, played piano in George's band and took care of the vocals.

From Oklahoma came Walter Page, with a terrific combo named the Blue Devils. Page, known as 'Big One,' was one of the very first to use the string bass as well as tuba, and he also doubled on bass saxophone. For a while he had Bill Basie on piano. Count had come to Kansas City with the Gonzale White touring show, and dropped out of it to join Page. Later, Basie returned to the roadshow, again leaving it in Kaycee to go into Moten's band on second piano.

Singing with Moten then was the lovable Jimmy Rushing, 'Mr. Five by Five.' Unlike the run of blues shouters, Jimmy could read music, and he could be heard ten blocks away without a microphone (they used megaphones then, anyway). Jimmy was big brother to me, and some of the other band wives. I remember him playing piano and singing wonderful ballads to us; other times he would keep us laughing with his *risqué* stories, getting a kick out of seeing us blush.

Yes, Kaycee was a place to be enjoyed, even if you were without funds. People would make you a loan without you asking for it, would look at you and tell if you were hungry and put things right. There was the best food to be had: the finest barbecue, crawdads, and other seafood. There were the races, and swimming, and the beautiful Swope Park and zoo to amuse you. There were jam sessions all the time, and big dances such as the union dance given every year by our local. As many as 10 or 12 bands participated in this event, and you were sure to hear at least eight original styles there, as well as one or two outfits trying to imitate Duke.

For private entertainment we had our hot corn club every Monday, at which the musicians and wives would drink and play bridge, 'tonk' or 'hearts.' At these meetings the boys drank corn whisky and home brew – in fact, most anything with a high alcohol content – and they got laughs out of giving me rough liquor so strong it would almost blow the top of one's head off.

One of the regulars was Herman Walder, brilliant tenor player with Moten and brother of saxophonist Woodie Walder. Herman asked me if I'd like a cool drink one night, and not knowing the taste of corn I gulped down a large glassful. The next thing I remember was people putting cold towels on my head. Being stubborn, I thought: If they can take it, so can I. So each Monday I tried to drink, with much the same result. The boys took to betting that I'd be high within ten minutes of entering – and they always won.

92 **Mike Zwerin** Claude Thornhill: The square on the lawn (1983)

Source: Mike Zwerin, 'Claude Thornhill: The square on the lawn,' in *Close Enough for Jazz* (London: Quartet Books, 1983: 23–6, 27–9, 30–1, 32–4) (excerpts).

Claude Thornhill loved confusion. It seemed to be his only remaining pleasure. He never called out the number or the name of the next arrangement. Each started with a piano introduction and we had to recognize it. He tried tricking us with oriental, Flamenco or atonal disguises. He could be pretty clever about it. We would wait for Squirms, the lead trumpet-player who had been with Claude so long he could hear through him, to shout 'Lover Man' or 'Witchcraft' and then we scrambled to pull out the chart.

When we were ready, Claude modulated with grace and musicality into another introduction and watched our confusion. Eventually Squirms screamed another title and we scrambled again. It could go on three or four times. In the meantime, Squirms might grab a fast blast from the portable leather bar he always carried – 'my band aid' he called it – and groan: 'This band should disband.'

Claude adored the confusion setting up. Combination french horn-player and bandboy, Nooch would be unpacking while musicians ran scales and stage hands fussed. Once Claude grabbed a microphone, announced: 'Testing, testing onetwothree,' and then, looking totally revolted by the results, began shouting firm and completely unintelligible instructions to nobody in particular. He looked up, pointing with horror: 'What the blirdy spidle restitrew?'

'You're putting me on,' said the drummer.

'Are you kidding? Who'd want to wear a drummer?' Claude laughed to beat the band.

'Put on' is originally jazz slang. It is at the root of the irony of jazz humour. We would laugh at what was not supposed to be funny. Being put on was passing a test. We'd tell 'sick' cancer-, multiple sclerosis- and elephantitis-jokes just because they were not supposed to be funny. This expressed our anarchistic life-view. Lenny Bruce and Lord Buckley took 'hip' humour out of the closet so perhaps we should drop it here.

Though one more example serves. The writer Terry Southern (*Candy, The Magic Christian*) could carry sick humour to new lows. He called me for a period of months seriously suggesting we form what he called 'the Alltime

Allstar Fuckup Band'. It would include Allen Eager, Squirms, Tony Fruscella, Phil Seaman, Jimmy Ford, Chet Baker and all those outrageous fucked-up heroes. Laughing at them is like laughing at spastics, acceptable 'hip' humour it's true. Perhaps I wasn't hip enough. Sometimes Terry would call in the middle of the night: 'What about Junior Collins? Gotta have Junior Collins.' He thought it pretty funny to assemble these nodding-out, throwing-up, nose-scratching wasted souls on one bandstand. Terry was writing for *Esquire* magazine at the time and he was sure they'd go for an article about the Alltime Allstar Fuckups.

Considering the context of sick humour jazz musicians exist in, it was odd that I could not laugh at Claude Thornhill's sick jokes. One time he went down in the diving bell they used to have in Atlantic City, off the Steel Pier. There was nothing much to it – you just went down under the pier and right back up again. There was a microphone in there and the people on the pier could hear the 'oohs' and 'ahs' of that incredible experience. We heard Claude's voice among the others, getting louder and louder, until it became a scream drowning out everything: 'Look, look, water, water. There's a leak. Oh my God! Help! Please somebody help me. We're all going to drown like rats in a trap. HEEEELLLPPP ...'

That might have been an amusing little number had it not been for the fact that he sounded like he thought he was really drowning. He could see the water coming to drown him. He really did need help.

Claude died a few years later, but he was already dead musically by the fall of 1958 when I toured with his band for six weeks in Texas, Oklahoma, Louisiana and states like that.

Claude had been a pioneer, the first commercial dance band to play bebop arrangements and Charlie Parker tunes as early as the late forties. They were good, too, by Gerry Mulligan and Gil Evans. They were still in the book in my days but rarely pulled out. Claude was highly amused when we played 'Walter Winchell Rhumba' instead. He saw it as a huge joke on the public. But when he was drunk, nostalgic, or we pestered him enough, he sometimes launched into an introduction even Squirms couldn't remember, until he'd finally yell: 'Anthropology' or 'Yardbird Suite' and we'd find those yellow, fading, stained parts; but this was not often.

He was then a small, shrunken man with a W.C. Fields nose and there was quite a bit of Fields in him in general. His hair was combed straight back and the hairline was receding. His waistline was expanding. His eyes were often glazed, which I attributed to excessive alcohol but Squirms told me that Claude once suffered a nervous breakdown and had had electro-shock therapy, although he drank enough too.

The band's basic style was built around a soft, smooth sound obtained by a french horn playing the melody with harmonized saxophones. Glenn Miller with brains. Claude had been on top for a while with that sound, playing the best theatres, clubs and hotels. His theme song 'Snowfall' was on juke boxes and Fran Warren and Gene Williams were popular when they sang with him. But by my time his fortunes had taken a decided and, as it turned out, permanent turn for the worse.

Arrangements written for full sections were being played by only one trombone, two trumpets, four saxophones, a now guitarless rhythm section plus the essential french horn. We worked country clubs, American Legion halls and high-school gymnasiums in provincial towns where Claude Thornhill was still a name. Referring to more successful 'ghost bands' – Sam Donahue and the Tommy Dorsey Orchestra, Ray McKinley and the Glenn Miller Orchestra – Claude once said to me after a particularly grungy affair: 'I guess you have to be dead to make it these days.'

All twelve of us travelled in two cars and a supply truck, which was driven by Nooch. Claude's road manager, Kurt, who also played saxophone, was a fat nervous type who kept trying unsuccessfully to look cool. We started to tour one wet November night at the Nevada Hotel, a dive which many musicians called home, on Broadway and 68th Street. Kurt sipped coffee, sneaking looks at his watch and out the luncheonette's foggy window. 'Jeezus H. Keerist, where the hell is Claude?' he muttered. Squirms pulled me aside and said he had just grabbed a double in a little bar across the street and, look, Claude was there. We could see him peeking out the window, a pixyish smile on his face watching Kurt freak.

I learned about the day sheet. In those days, if you checked into a hotel at 7 a.m. you could check out as late as four the following afternoon and pay for only one night. With a little planning and a missed night's sleep here and there, it was possible to check in only three times a week. And ghosting. Ghosting is when two guys check into a double room and some time later four more wander through the lobby looking as though they are checked in somewhere else. By staggering their entrance into the elevator, they could usually get to the room without detection. Then they slept on a couch or the floor and the cost of the room got split six ways instead of two.

After a three-day drive interrupted only once by some boss ghosting we arrived in Port Arthur Texas just in time for the day sheet. Squirms and I were wary of ghosts, so we decided to room together alone, cost notwithstanding. We went to sleep, leaving a 5 p.m. wake-up call. I unpacked my horn beforehand. The hardest part about practising is taking the monster out of the case; it is often an unsurmountable psychological block. By 5.30 I was warming up ...

I fastened the slide to the bell at varying angles until it fit my hand, lubricated the stockings, put vaseline on the tuning crook so it would move easily but only when desired, passed a brush through the tubing, polished the balance-weight and made sure the spit-valve was properly corked. I shined the bell inside and out with a chamoix cloth, caressed it and might have even kissed it had not Squirms finished throwing up in the toilet and emerged groaning: 'I'm sick and tired of waking up tired and sick.'

Now here was a hero. My roomie, Squirms's definition of a square was someone who doesn't like to throw up. A funky road-rat with bleary eyes and a green complexion testifying to a dedicated pursuit of happiness, Squirms was laying low from the day. Daytime was not his friend. Under cover of darkness, he consumed small packages of powders and liquids in vials. He almost never ate and yet he was overweight. If the gin people had added vitamins to their product he would not have eaten at all. He ate out of a sense of duty. His idea of a meal was one Drake's Cake.

Squirms poured himself a libation from his band-aid, a quadruple. Four fingers, no fucking around. The smell of alcohol joined that of codeine syrup and the dyspeptic cloud which surrounded Squirms at all times. Even a ten-foot pole was not enough to escape its touch. The fact that the lead trumpet-player sits in the middle of the brass section made playing a brass instrument hazardous with Squirms, who would joke: 'My mouth feels like dinosaurs are walking around in it.' (Trombone-players have been known to bribe bandboys not to set their chairs directly in front of Squirms. Trombones sit in front of trumpets.) Squirms smelled like catfood. He even looked like catfood, the yuckie kind that comes out of a can. My roomie. And I'm allergic to cats – you figure it out.

Squirms won farting contests, which involve big-league farts with road-rats. And road managers have used the threat of riding in the same car with him to keep unruly players in line. 'Not that, Kurt, anything but *that.*'

Affectionately called 'Filthy McSwine', Squirms believed that playing a saxophone held together by rubber bands and chewing gum was *essential* to Charlie Parker's genius. He thought that the new brand of educated, punctual, well-mannered and responsible jazz musicians would be the death of the music. He considered himself to be preserving tradition, upholding true values. Everybody was too *clean,* that's why jazz was in trouble. His theory was that soap is bad for the skin, that it contains chemical impurities that interfere with natural body juices. 'Look at cats,' he'd say, 'they wash with their own spit.'

His fierce and dependable lead trumpet playing was a miracle. The lead trumpet-player of a big band must be a concertmaster and quarterback in one. He must be clear-headed with fast reflexes and great strength. The chair requires a unique and demanding combination of physical conditioning, tact, leadership and intelligence. Lead trumpet-players often lift weights. A heart attack is the occupational disease. There was controversy over Squirms in the band business, much like over fast-living quarterbacks such as Joe Namath in the sports world. Is it possible that dissipation can help not hinder performance? In certain cases involving genius, this may be true; one element of genius is excess, after all. Geniuses by definition are abnormal. How can they be expected to conform to norms? Physically, however, geniuses are mortal and, in addition to his not being a genius, the wonder was how Squirms's heart could take it. Kurt suggested he leave his heart to science.

'Are you kidding?' Squirms laughed. 'I have to jerk off to get it started in the morning.'

I have neglected to mention Squirms's legendary 'cough syrup switcheroo'. It went like this. Place a can of Tab on a table next to a bottle of maximum codeine cough syrup. Bury your head in the sports page. Read for a while and then absent-mindedly reach for the Tab. This avoids the awful anticipation of the syrup's sweet and sickening consistency. Pick up the syrup by 'mistake' and 'discover' the 'error' after it's all down. Act surprised. Swear. Burp. Wash it down with the Tab.

It went like this three times a day when Squirms could not score anything harder (sometimes even if he could). After only one day sheet, empty syrup bottles would be rolling around under the bed and in dresser drawers. Chambermaids gave him knowing winks: 'Cough any better?'

This did not embarrass him, on the contrary. He was proud of his excess. He gloated and joked about it: 'My stomach may be a mess, but I haven't had a cough in three years.' ...

Some context is necessary. Squirms is an exception, not the rule. He was both larger and smaller than real life. Most jazz musicians are somewhere in between. They are for the most part more or less normal blokes who take no more drugs than advertising agency executives. They might drink a bit because the road is tough, but so do truck-drivers. They have neither the courage nor the desperation it takes to live like Squirms, one long chemical Russian roulette game. Obviously I am not speaking about the great names, but by far the majority of jazz musicians are normal guys who found a way to live outside organized society – to avoid work in banks, record company offices or music stores. This takes a certain amount of sanity. Writing about Squirms is like telling a multiple sclerosis joke. Squirms was one big sick joke, and thus of some interest. But it's past interest, this type basically plays rock today. Rock stole our excess like our licks. So here we are preserving some exotic folklore about an endangered species. I felt pleased being finally part of that folklore, even only to observe it.

Claude Thornhill was not interested in how his band sounded in the autumn of 1958. He never gave any instructions about vibratos, phrasing or dynamics, if he ever even thought about such details. When someone was out of tune – not unusual – Claude would pound an 'A' on the piano. Over and over, two and sometimes four octaves. The customers usually looked perplexed, as if they did not understand modern music. At no time would he say or do something to improve the intonation, just pounded those notes and laughed. Once it got so bad he stopped pounding and rose from the piano bench waving a white handkerchief in unconditional surrender.

We were protected by a thick coat of provincial ignorance. Once in a while, a group of local musicians came to hear the famous Claude Thornhill orchestra, and then he went out of his way to play the dumbest arrangements in the book, which was pretty dumb. We did have our moments, and some nights for four or five minutes we could come close to a reasonable facsimile of the Claude Thornhill of yore. We were like an expansion team, over-the-hill veterans, rookies, and a few like myself who had other things on their minds. Bill's drumming varied with the quality of the girls on the dance floor. If they excited him the time would speed up, if pickings were lean it would be like walking through thick mud. The bassist was a nineteen-year-old hippy (and I use the word in the failed hipster sense) from the Bronx who was also on his first name band. He flew over all sorts of marvellous notes, few of which had any relation to the relevant chord.

I was loafing by the bandstand on a break between sets at the Fort Worth Country Club when Claude, looking elegant in his tuxedo and giggling into the palm of his hand, walked up to me and pointed to a pale, blue-haired little old lady at a nearby table. She had a carnation in her white gown and eyeglasses with fake jewels on the rim. He said she had just requested 'Chloe'. Claude said he politely answered that we had no arrangement for this composition and thus could not play it for her. She looked disappointed for a minute, but then cheered up, snapped her fingers and said: 'Fuck it. Play "Anthropology".' He looked into my eyes unblinking: 'Do you believe *that*?'

'Sure I do,' I answered. 'I believe it.'

The next set we played 'Anthropology'.

We bought an arsenal of cherry bombs in one of those southern counties where they were legal and tossed them out the window with lit fuses on lonely roads. Outside Holdenville, Oklahoma, we spotted Claude's car behind us and tried timing the fuses to explode under it. In Holdenville he jumped out, did a little dance and said: 'Hey fellows, you can't beat fun now can you?' ...

Copping out of straight society is central to the 'hip' ethic and playing with a road band is as good a way as any. All you have to do is show up on time and sober and not all that much of either at that. Alienation is no longer a problem; no need to worry, you are alien everywhere. You travel thousands of miles from Bangor to Baton Rouge (or Berlin to Barcelona) and end up in a hotel exactly like the one you just left. You speak to and play for people exactly like the people you just left. You cannot be reached, mail does not catch up. You skim more than read, pass out rather than fall asleep. You work when everybody else is off, breakfast in the evening dinner at dawn. Disorder is the order, physical alienation is so powerful, so omnipresent, that no treatment seems too extreme. Nobody can even question the need for treatment. Playing chess will not do the trick. You've got to find a familiar internal place to hang on to, it's a matter of survival. And there is one place, a warm corner called stoned.

I shiver remembering one hop we made with Squirms at the wheel. 'Wake me up when we get there,' he'd said starting out. His band-aid was empty by the time we reached the outskirts of Dallas, and he was complaining about the absence of coke to tone up his smack.

'Look at that fucking square,' he snarled, pointing to a man in an undershirt watering one in a line of small lawns. He looked square all right, watering his lawn at seven in the morning. He did not look like he had been up all night. Battling heartburn, I put on shades. The square stooped to smell a flower. His better half was probably cooking ham and eggs, maybe waffles. I could smell them blend with the odour of perking coffee in a sparkling kitchen, flooded with morning sun. It did not seem as square as it would have a few weeks earlier, and I did not feel as hip as I would have liked. Wouldn't it be hip, I thought, if 'hip' turned out to be square?

We pulled up at a light on the corner of 'Shoe City' and 'Hamburgerville.' American commercial enterprises often take names which hopefully put them on a larger map. Shoe Village, Bargaintown, Foam Rubber City, Disneyland, Miss Universe. This sort of geographical exaggeration is all over our culture. An adjective can cover square miles – Dullsville, Fat City.

Squirms extended it to cosmic proportions with a game he called 'Wordgrad'. After a gig he'd kick it off by saying something like 'Tired Hollow, man', or, seeing a beautiful woman, 'Stacked Junction'. As we started driving towards the last date, even Squirms squirmed with the ultimate Wordgrad:

'New York City *City*, baby'. It wasn't so absurd at all if you consider the real-life 'Roseland Dance City', two Wordgrads in one. Spooky Landing.

The last hop was from Dallas to Midland, Texas. We checked out of the White Plaza Hotel late in the afternoon planning to drive at night after the gig to open the day sheet in Midland. Claude passed out in the back seat at two when we finally left. He stayed that way the entire drive. We had to shake him awake in Midland. Eventually he flopped out of the car, entered the hotel and staggered towards the elevators. In the middle of the lobby he stopped, seemed to remember something, and approached the desk. 'Let me have my key,' he stuttered. The clerk looked puzzled and asked his name. Standing nearby, Kurt explained that this was Mr Thornhill who was expected. The clerk asked what kind of room Mr Thornhill would like. 'Look just let me have my key,' Claude repeated, getting red in the face. 'I like my room, I don't want to change it.' Claude had not checked out of the White Plaza and did not realize he was now in Midland, 300 miles west.

I was reminded of how old and tired Claude looked that morning in Midland when I recently purchased a record called *The Billie Holiday Story* and saw his picture in the enclosed booklet. He had accompanied her on a number of recordings and the photo shows a clean-cut cherubic face with a winner's smile. The contrast between those two images tells the Claude Thornhill Story.

But he kept his dignity as his audience dwindled. His hair was always combed, his suits pressed, his face shaven, his bow-tie straight. I marvel at how much control that must have involved, considering the skid he was on. He knew he had been something special. It had taken imagination, taste, talent and courage to play Charlie Parker's 'Anthropology' at fancy hotels and supper clubs when people had paid to hear a band that had won two *Billboard* magazine polls in the 'sweet band' category. The distinctive, softly dissonant swing he had pioneered anticipated 'cool' jazz by several years. In fact Claude Thornhill not Miles Davis had given birth to the cool.

His closest friends were the most alienated guys on the band. He loved Squirms, for example. Claude was attracted to people who were defeated, cynical, dissipated – who were, like himself, victims of changing public taste and their own inability to adapt to it. Road-rats, they appeal to me too. Losers appeal to me. Perhaps it can be explained by paraphrasing R.D. Laing – if an alienating society calls those who cannot adapt to it 'losers', does this not make them winners in a larger sense? In any case road-rats were to become so alienated that they were not even aware of the fact that some square folkie named Bob Dylan was singing about them: 'How does it feel to be without a home, like a rolling stone.'

93 **Eddie Condon** The poorest 7-piece orchestra on Earth (1947)

Source: Eddie Condon, with Thomas Sugrue, 'The poorest 7-piece orchestra on Earth,' in *We Called It Music: A Generation of Jazz* (New York: Da Capo, 1992 [1947]: 174–9) (excerpt).

Back in New York our money ran out. Musicians came to see us and brought liquor but never food. It was then I discovered a simple truth about modern society; you can drink yourself to death on your friends except for one thing – you'll die of malnutrition first. When you're broke you can get all the whiskey you want almost anywhere you go, but don't ask for a sandwich; it lowers the social tone of friendship. The important thing is to have enough money to buy a can of tomatoes the next morning; they feed the body and break the hangover.

We discovered the automat. We walked up and down Broadway, listening to the music coming from commercial bands in dime-a-dance halls. We went to see more agents. We lived on the olives from Martinis and cherries from Manhattans at the cocktail parties to which we were invited. We opened a charge account at a delicatessen for canned tomatoes, to be kept on ice until we called for them in the morning – or in the afternoon. We heard from Pancho again. Barbara Bennett had just left Maurice, her dancing partner, and was forming a new team with Charles Sabin. Sabin was from society; his mother was fighting prohibition. The team was scheduled to go into the Palace, and Pancho recommended us for background music. We auditioned for Barbara and she offered us the job. 'Are you sure you know what you're doing?' I asked. 'Is this the kind of music you want for your class act?'

'It will be something new,' she said. 'I'm delighted. We'll start rehearsals tomorrow at Steinway Hall.'

By then it was July. We rehearsed for ten days in heat that melted everything but our hunger. One of the dance numbers, a waltz, required a fiddle in the orchestra. Tesch had begun his career on the violin; we borrowed an instrument from Joe Venuti and handed it to him. After one rehearsal we took it away from him and gave it back to Venuti. We got a violinist from the Meyer Davis office, a nice guy named Charlie Miller. Then MacPartland and Freeman were offered a job on the *Ile de France*. They considered taking it.

'You mean you would rather play on a frog ferry than at the Palace?' McKenzie said. He was incredulous. 'Thousands of men and women have died of old age on the road trying to make the Palace, and you guys want to sell your chance for a doily and a *crêpe suzette!*' he roared.

MacPartland fidgeted. 'I was only thinking about it,' he said. 'I'll stay.'

'So will I,' Freeman said, but he looked unhappy. Bud loved culture.

We opened at the Palace on the 16th of July. We were nervous and hot; the fiddle sounded strange and embarrassed in the middle of our mob. When Barbara and Charles ended their waltz they stepped back and bowed; Barbara's legs were shaking worse than mine. Here we go, I thought, she's going to fall on her face – what are we doing here anyhow? While the team was changing costumes we played *I Must Have That Man*. When we finished there was silence. Then two, three, and finally four people applauded. 'Musicians,' Tesch whispered. At the end of the act the dancers got a good hand.

Barbara and Charles waited impatiently for the reviews to appear in *Variety* and *Billboard*. We didn't care if we never saw them. When they appeared Barbara was ecstatic. In *Variety* she was chosen as the 'best dressed woman of the week' by The Skirt, Jr. The Skirt described in detail the clothes worn during the act. Barbara read the piece to us … 'She appears again in a stunning orange chiffon gown with ragged hem reaching to the floor on one side with a huge spray of coque feathers on the other side and on one shoulder. This is for a weak blackbottom. After a pause in which their rather dreadful orchestra plays an off-key selection …'

She stopped. 'Don't mind us,' I said. 'Go right ahead.'

'I'm sure that's just meanness,' she said. 'There's a review here of the show itself, not of my clothes. Let's see what it says.'

It was bad for all of us: 'The class act was Charles Sabin and Barbara Bennett, nite club dancers. The nite club they were in may have had a steady trade of 750 people. Of these 600 are now out of town. And of the 600 not 50 would care to see either of the dancers anywhere other than at their homes or in a club ballroom … The couple are no stage dancers of any kind, with the poorest 7-piece orchestra on earth … As a side remark, Mr. Sabin and Miss Bennett neglected to bow to their musicians when exiting. No one could blame them, but it is customary.'

'That does it,' Tesch said.

'Local boys make good in big city in large way,' Joe Sullivan said. 'I can see the headlines in the *Chicago Tribune*.'

'Well, at last I've played the Palace,' I said. 'Now I owe Cliff for my banjo.'

The next day Krupa turned up with a copy of *Billboard*.

'Look at this,' he said. 'Maybe we're not as much a failure as we think.'

The review said: 'Charles Sabin and Barbara Bennett closed the first half in an exhibition of ballroom dancing, assisted by a commendable 7-piece musical unit … the act was heavily applauded but the hurrahs were not for the terpsichorean talents. They are both graceful, but far removed from being world beaters.'

'Who wrote that?' Tesch asked. 'The man is a genius.' Krupa read out the name – Elias E. Sugarman. 'He'll go down in history,' Tesch said.

At least the musicians were with us. Johnny Powell, the drummer, went twice a day every day during the week; in the general applause we spotted isolated patches of enthusiasm for our numbers. But we were about as far from being a popular success as it was possible to be. Jazz was still a special taste.

In the middle of the week Bud announced that he was going to take the job on the *Ile de France*. It was sailing the next day. McKenzie was in favor of violence. I told Bud that if he went we would collect his pay at the end of the week and split it among ourselves.

'I don't care,' he said. 'I'm going to France.'

'I will also not pay you that fifty dollars I owe you,' I said.

'I still don't care,' he said, and he went.

When we finished the run Sabin refused to pay us for Freeman, contending that Bud had forfeited his salary by deserting the act.

'I have had enough trouble, Charles,' McKenzie said, 'but if necessary I will make some more, all by myself, and give it to you. If you don't pay Freeman's salary I will really louse you up at the union – remember we rehearsed with you for ten days without pay.'

'Oh, Charles, shut up!' Barbara said. 'Let's not quarrel about trifles.' She reached into her stocking, took out a roll of bills, and handed McKenzie Bud's money. We used it to cut down the bill at the Cumberland. McKenzie went to St. Louis to see his family again.

There were five of us now in the two rooms; Mezzrow and Josh Billings, a jazz fan, had come in from Chicago. Very quickly we were back on the olive and cherry diet, with canned tomatoes for breakfast. One day the clerk handed me our bill and added a meaningful look. We owed an interesting sum, ninety-nine dollars. We had to do something.

The Jimmy Noone records were out under Brunswick's Vocalian label and were selling well. I took one of them and went to see Tommy Rockwell at Okeh.

'See how you like this small ensemble group,' I said. 'I can get you one like it – Teschmaker, Krupa, and Sullivan.'

Rockwell listened to the record and nodded agreeably. 'Let's make a date,' he said.

'Let's make it for tomorrow morning,' I said.

'I think we ought to have a vocal on one side,' Rockwell said.

I swallowed hard. 'I'll sing,' I said.

We were at the studio ahead of time. We set up and made *Oh Baby*, from 'Rain or Shine.' The second side was *Back Home In Indiana*, and I sang a chorus. Before the wax was cool on the master I was in Rockwell's office.

'Tommy,' I said, 'do something about this.'

I gave him the hotel bill.

'Why didn't you say something about it before?' he said.

He took a wallet from his pocket and handed me two fifty dollar bills.

'There will be fifty dollars more,' he said. 'I'll send it to you.'

I walked out of the room eighty pounds lighter than when I went in. Back at the hotel I paid the bill. The clerk gave me a dollar.

'What shall we buy with it?' I asked the boys. The vote was unanimous – canned tomatoes.

94 **Mezz Mezzrow** Them first kicks are a killer (1946)

Source: Mezz Mezzrow, with Bernard Wolfe, 'Them first kicks are a killer,' in *Really the Blues* (New York: Random House, 1946: 71–3, 76–7) (excerpts).

It was that flashy, sawed-off runt of a jockey named Patrick who made a viper out of me ... Back in the Arrowhead Inn, where I first met Patrick, he told me he was going to New Orleans and would be back one day with some marihuana, real golden-leaf. He asked me did I want some of the stuff, and coming up tough I said sure, bring me some, I'd like to try it. When Patrick marched into the Martinique one night I began to look for the nearest exit, but it was too late. 'Hi ya, boy,' he said with a grin bigger than he was hisself, 'let's you and me go to the can, I got something for you.' That men's room might have been a death-house, the way I kept curving away from it, but this muta-mad Tom Thumb latched on to me like a ball-and-chain and steered me straight inside.

As soon as we were alone he pulled out a gang of cigarettes and handed them to me. They were as fat as ordinary cigarettes but were rolled in brown wheatstraw paper. We both lit up and I got halfway through mine, hoping they would break the news to mother gently, before he stopped me. 'Hey,' he said, 'take it easy, kid. You want to knock yourself out?'

I didn't feel a thing and I told him so. 'Do you know one thing?' he said. 'You ain't even smokin' it right. You got to hold that muggle so that it barely touches your lips, see, then draw in air around it. Say *tfff, tfff*, only breathe in when you say it. Then don't blow it out right away, you got to give the stuff a chance.' He had a tricky look in his eye that I didn't go for at all. The last time I saw that kind of look it was on a district attorney's mug, and it caused me a lot of inconvenience.

After I finished the weed I went back to the bandstand. Everything seemed normal and I began to play as usual. I passed a stick of gauge around for the other boys to smoke, and we started a set.

The first thing I noticed was that I began to hear my saxophone as though it was inside my head, but I couldn't hear much of the band in back of me, although I knew they were there. All the other instruments sounded like they were way off in the distance; I got the same sensation you'd get if you stuffed your ears with cotton and talked out loud. Then I began to feel the vibrations of the reed much more pronounced against my lip, and my head buzzed like a loudspeaker. I found I was slurring much better and putting just the right feeling into my phrases – I was really coming on. All the notes came easing out of my horn like they'd already been made up, greased and stuffed into the bell, so all I had to do was blow a little and send them on their way, one right after the other, never missing, never behind time, all without an ounce of effort. The phrases seemed to have more continuity to them and I was sticking to the theme without ever going tangent. I felt I could go on playing for years without running out of ideas and energy. There wasn't any struggle; it was all made-to-order and suddenly there wasn't a sour note or a discord in the world that could bother me. I began to feel very happy and sure of myself. With my loaded horn I could take all the fist-swinging, evil things in the world and bring them together in perfect harmony, spreading peace and joy and relaxation to all the keyed-up and punchy people everywhere. I began to preach my millenniums on my horn, leading all the sinners on to glory.

The other guys in the band were giggling and making cracks, but I couldn't talk with my mouthpiece between my lips, so I closed my eyes and drifted out to the audience with my music. The people were going crazy over the subtle changes in our playing; they couldn't dig what was happening but some kind of electricity was crackling in the air and it made them all glow and jump . . .

It's a funny thing about marihuana – when you first begin smoking it you see things in a wonderful soothing, easygoing new light. All of a sudden the world is stripped of its dirty gray shrouds and becomes one big bellyful of giggles, a spherical laugh, bathed in brilliant, sparkling colors that hit you like a heatwave. Nothing leaves you cold any more; there's a humorous tickle and great meaning in the least little thing, the twitch of somebody's little finger or the click of a beer glass. All your pores open like funnels, your nerve-ends stretch their mouths wide, hungry and thirsty for new sights and sounds and sensations; and every sensation, when it comes, is the most exciting one you've ever had. You can't get enough of anything – you want to gobble up the whole goddamned universe just for an appetizer. Them first kicks are a killer, Jim . . .

The bandstand was only a foot high but when I went to step down it took me a year to find the floor, it seemed so far away. I was sailing through the clouds, flapping my free-wheeling wings, and leaving the stand was like stepping off into space. Twelve months later my foot struck solid ground with a jolt, but the other one stayed up there on those lovely soft clouds, and I almost fell flat on my face. There was a roar of laughter from Patrick's table and I began to feel self-conscious and nauseous at the same time. I flew to the men's room and got there just in time. Patrick came in and started to laugh at me.

'What's the matter, kid?' he said. 'You not feeling so good?' At that moment I was up in a plane, soaring around the sky, with a buzz-saw in my head. Up and around we went, saying nuts to Newton and all his fancy laws of gravitation, but suddenly we went into a nosedive and I came down to earth, sock. Ouch. My head went spattering off in more directions than a hand grenade. Patrick put a cold towel to my temples and I snapped out of it. After sitting down for a while I was all right.

When I went back to the stand I still heard all my music amplified, as though my ear was built right into the horn. The evening rolled away before I knew it. When the entertainers sang I accompanied them on the piano, and from the way they kept glancing up at me I could tell they felt the harmonies I was inventing behind them without any effort at all. The notes kept sliding out of my horn like bubbles in seltzer water. My control over the vibrations of my tones was perfect, and I got a terrific lift from the richness of the music, the bigness of it. The notes eased out like lava running down a mountain, slow and sure and steaming. It was good.

95 **Ferdinand 'Jelly Roll' Morton** Street parades (1950)

Source: Alan Lomax, *Mister Jelly Roll: The Fortunes of Jelly Roll Morton, New Orleans Creole and 'Inventor of Jazz'* (Berkeley, CA: University of California Press, 1973 [1950]: 12–14) (excerpt). (Editor's title)

Those parades were really tremendous things. The drums would start off, the trumpets and trombones rolling into something like *Stars and Stripes* or *The National Anthem* and everybody would strut off down the street, the bass-drum player twirling his beater in the air, the snare drummer throwing his sticks up and bouncing them off the ground, the kids jumping and hollering, the grand marshall and his aides in their expensive uniforms moving along dignified, women on top of women strutting along back of the aides and out in front of everybody – the second line, armed with sticks and bottles and baseball bats and all forms of ammunition ready to fight the foe when they reached the dividing line.

It's a funny thing that the *second line* marched at the head of the parade, but that's the way it had to be in New Orleans. They were our protection. You see, whenever a parade would get to another district the enemy would be waiting at the dividing line [between two wards]. If the parade crossed that line, it meant a fight, a terrible fight. The first day I marched a fellow was cut, must have been a hundred times. Blood was gushing out of him same as from one of the gushers in Yellowstone Park, but he never did stop fighting.

They had a tough little guy in the Broadway Swells named Black Benny. Benny hung around the charcoal schooners at the head of the New Basin, but on Sundays he'd get his broomstick and march as grand marshall of the second-line gang. He was a really tough egg and terrible to get along with, always in some argument.

Some of the enemy would say, 'Listen, don't cross this line.'

'Why not?' Benny would say.

'If you cross it, it will be your ass.'

'Whose ass?'

'Your ass.'

'Well, lemme tell you something. I don't give a damn about you and your whole family.'

'If I hit you, your old double grandfather will feel it.'

And about that time the broomsticks and brick-bats would start to fly, the razors would come into play and the seven shooters – which was a little bit of a .22 that shot seven times – would begin popping. I've seen one case when a fellow shot seven times and every bullet hit the other party and none of them even went into his skin. But, anyhow, everybody would move on out the way, because nobody wanted to take a chance with a pistol, because they'd known many of them to die that way. Myself, a razor was something I always moved from if I saw one in the fight. I knew what a razor was, my uncle being a barber. A razor is a very, very tough thing to come up against.

Well, if they'd have ten fights one Sunday, they didn't have many. Sometimes it would require a couple of ambulances to come around and pick up the people that was maybe cut or shot occasionally. This didn't happen all the time, but very seldom it didn't. The fact of it is, there was no parade at no time you couldn't find a knot on somebody's head where somebody had got hit with a stick or something. And always plenty to eat and drink, especially for the men in the band, and with bands like Happy Galloway's, Manuel Perez's and Buddy Bolden's we had the best ragtime music in the world. There was so many jobs for musicians in these parades that musicians didn't ever like to leave New Orleans. They used to say, 'This is the best town in the world. What's the use for me to go any other place?'

96 **Hampton Hawes** Watts burning (1974)

Source: Hampton Hawes and Don Asher, 'Watts burning,' in *Raise Up Off Me: A Portrait of Hampton Hawes* (New York: Da Capo Press, 1979 [1974]: 138–42).

The clubs were beginning to hurt. The kids were jamming the rock halls and the older people were staying home watching TV. Maybe they found they couldn't pat their feet to our music anymore. Big-drawing names like Miles and John Coltrane were breaking out of the thirty-two-bar chord-oriented structure and into free expression – or 'avant-garde' or 'outside,' whatever tag you want to stick on it – charging the owners so much they had to raise the covers and minimums. The players who were ace sight readers (which didn't include me) were going into the studios. In the late forties and fifties our music was called 'bebop' or 'cool jazz' or 'funk,' and we were neatly tucked into one of those compartments. I don't know why the people who write about music feel they have to slap labels on everything. It's the same watermelon mentality that says niggers can fuck and play boogiewoogie better than whites, Jews are rich, Irish are drunkards, Germans are mean, Japanese are mysterious, and Chinese smoke opium. Who cares? There are only two kinds of music – good and bad. The worst thing that can happen to old good music is that it might become dated for a while, but watch out, in ten to twenty years it will come drifting back like bell-bottoms and W. C. Fields movies. A critic once wrote that I was 'the key figure in the current crisis surrounding the funky school of jazz piano.' Shit, there wasn't no crisis. All he meant was that I can get down and I can swing. And if he could have looked deep into my life he would have learned that the reason I play the way I do is that I'm taking the years of being pushed off laps, denied love and holding in my natural instincts when I was a kid, of listening to the beautiful spirituals in my father's church and going in the back doors of clubs to play for white audiences, of getting strung and burned in the streets and locked up in dungeons when I tried to find my way – taking all that natural bitterness and suppressed animal feeling out on the piano. That's why I can swing. There really ain't no secret.

When I first heard the new sounds and saw those young kids – most of them not able to do much more than twirl some dials, look weird and play a few stereotyped licks or some far-out unmusical shit that if you ask them what they're doing they say, 'Well, I'm out there' – saw them making $15–$20,000 a concert while turning your brains to jelly with the volume, I thought along with the other cats I came up with, How dare they steal my stuff, play it so bad and make all that bread? Running up my banners just the way the older musicians did when Bird got all that fame and glory in the forties. But we all pick up from the players who came before us. In a way I was making the same mistake the critics make: sticking labels on music, putting down a particular style of playing, instead of just judging it good music or bad.

* * *

It was the summer of 1965. I was working Mitchell's Studio Club, getting a good thing going with Red Mitchell (no relation) on bass and Donald Bailey on drums (one of those reassuring gigs where everything works, acoustics just right, the audience responsive and enjoying itself – proof that you don't necessarily have to turn handsprings or run chimps on roller skates into the act to attract attention) when some brothers decided to tear it up along 103rd, Rosecrans, and surrounding blocks.

I was coming home late from a party in Hollywood after the gig, wheeling down Harbor Freeway, when off to the left I saw what at first looked like a heavy blanket of fog till I noticed the flames spurting through. Decided I'd get off and check it out. I took the Gage Avenue exit and a little while later said to myself, Either a couple of 707's have collided and crashed or else a war has started. Whole blocks were crackling with flames. Must have been the way Rome looked back then, except that these citizens were all a funny color and none of them were wearing togas ... Never saw so many people on the street at one time in my life – and this is five in the morning. Old people, little people, fat people, kids – looked like they'd just come swarming up out of the ground, waving torches and pistols, firing stores, carrying stuff out, cars screeching up to corners, picking up cats and shooting off again, and the police with their guns standing around at a kind of lazy, bewildered parade rest: shit, can't shoot a whole community. Didn't take me long to check things out and decide to get my ass home before the bazookas and armored trucks arrived. I made it back to the freeway – some nervous firemen trying to direct me the wrong way down one-way streets – shot home and told Jackie, 'Watts just declared war on the city of Los Angeles, and as many motherfuckers as I saw out there tonight they may win.'

Next day I called Sonny Criss who lived at 103rd and Central, in the heart of it, and asked him what happened. He said, 'I took a fifth of whiskey out to my lawn, sat down and started drinking and laughing. Felt like Nero. Wanted to get out my horn and blow. When I finished the bottle it was dawn, everything was down to the ground and smoking like when you were a kid watching the mist come off a lake.'

We didn't go to work the next two nights. No point trying to drive anywhere with the National Guard moving in their armor and brothers firing from the overpasses. I'd missed one Korea and wasn't looking to voluntarily involve myself in another.

The funny thing was that the town grew at the same time it was burning down. It had been a fairly small and compact area as southern California towns go, but after that week everyplace where there had been flames and fighting, from Central to Crenshaw, became Watts.

I wondered what the cats at Fort Worth who used to call me Watts thought when the shit hit the papers. *Hampton said there were some bad motherfuckers around there but not bad enough to burn the place down.*

Watts changed a lot of things. You don't see as many revolving red lights along Central Avenue as you used to. Slap a person around often enough one day he's going to slap back, so you think: Damn, that hurt, better try something different. Niggers have been fucked over for two hundred years and finally some ofays are beginning to feel nervous and guilty. But the only ones who should feel guilty are the ones who fucked over us, not the young girls today who were taught fear of niggers 'cause their mamas might have got raped by a nigger, or *said* she was raped, and the nigger got hung. What we got to remember is to be militant against ignorance, not race, get the shit on right, because the day might come when blacks will no longer be able to use the color they came into the world with as a badge of injustice or a crutch to lean on and help them get ahead. And that's the thing niggers got to watch out for.

Reading the aftermath in the papers, the ruin and desolation, dried blood mixing with the ashes in the streets, I thought of another day in Watts ten years earlier. A hot, sunny summer day on Central Avenue, Bird and Miles and me sitting on the hood of Chuck Thompson's old Deusenberg, while Chuck – who I'd last seen in a white bathrobe in a Rochester, New York hospital ward – squatted in the street shooting pictures of us eating watermelon, trying to look funny.

97 **Dizzy Gillespie** Beboppers ... the cult (1979)

Source: Dizzy Gillespie, with Al Fraser, 'Beboppers ... the cult,' in *To Be or Not ... to Bop: Memoirs* (New York: Doubleday, 1979: 278–81) (excerpt).

Around 1946, jive-ass stories about 'beboppers' circulated and began popping up in the news. Generally, I felt happy for the publicity, but I found it disturbing to have modern jazz musicians and their followers characterized in a way that was often sinister and downright vicious. This image wasn't altogether the fault of the press because many followers, trying to be 'in,' were actually doing some of the things the press accused beboppers of – and worse. I wondered whether all the 'weird' publicity actually drew some of these way-out elements to us and did the music more harm than good. Stereotypes, which exploited whatever our weaknesses might be, emerged. Suable things were said, but nothing about the good we were doing and our contributions to music.

Time magazine, March 25, 1946, remarked: 'As such things usually do, it began on Manhattan's 52nd Street. A bandleader named John (Dizzy) Gillespie, looking for a way to emphasize the more beautiful notes in 'Swing,' explained: "When you hum it, you just naturally say bebop, be-de-bop ..."'

'Today, the bigwig of bebop is a scat named Harry (the Hipster) Gibson, who in moments of supreme pianistic ecstasy throws his feet on the keyboard. No. 2 man is Bulee (Slim) Gaillard, a skyscraping zooty Negro guitarist. Gibson and Gaillard have recorded such hip numbers as "Cement Mixer," which has sold more than 20,000 discs in Los Angeles alone; "Yeproc Heresay," "Dreisix Cents," and "Who Put the Benzedrine in Mrs. Murphy's Ovaltine?"'

The article discussed a ban on radio broadcasts of bebop records in Los Angeles where station KMPC considered it a 'degenerative influence on youth' and described how the 'nightclub where Gibson and Gaillard played' was 'more crowded than ever' with teen-agers who wanted to be bebopped. 'What bebop amounts to: hot jazz overheated, with overdone lyrics full of bawdiness, references to narcotics and doubletalk.'

Once it got inside the marketplace, our style was subverted by the press and music industry. First, the personalities and weaknesses of the in people started becoming more important, in the public eye, than the music itself. Then they diluted the music. They took what were otherwise blues and pop tunes, added 'mop, mop' accents and lyrics about abusing drugs wherever they could and called the noise that resulted bebop. Labeled bebop like our music, this synthetic sound was played heavily on commercial radio everywhere, giving bebop a bad name. No matter how bad the imitation sounded, youngsters, and people who were musically untrained liked it, and it sold well because it maintained a very danceable beat. The accusations in the press pointed to me as one of the prime movers behind this. I should've sued, even though the chances of winning in court were slim. It was all bullshit.

Keeping in mind that a well-told lie usually contains a germ of truth, let's examine the charges and see how many of those stereotypes actually applied to me.

Lie number one was that beboppers wore wild clothes and dark glasses at night. Watch the fashions of the forties on the late show, long coats, almost down to your knees and full trousers. I wore drape suits like everyone else and dressed no differently from the average leading man of the day. It was beautiful. I became pretty dandified, I guess, later during the bebop era when my pants were pegged slightly at the bottom, but not unlike the modestly flared bottoms on the slacks of the smart set today.

We had costumes for the stage – uniforms with wide lapels and belts – given to us by a tailor in Chicago who designed them, but we didn't wear them offstage. Later, we removed the wide lapels and sported little tan cashmere jackets with no lapels. This was a trendsetting innovation because it made no sense at all to pay for a wide lapel. *Esquire* magazine, 1943, America's leading influence on men's fashions, considered us elegant, though bold, and printed our photographs.

Perhaps I remembered France and started wearing the beret. But I used it as headgear I could stuff into my pocket and keep moving. I used to lose my hat a lot. I liked to wear a hat like most of the guys then, and the hats I kept losing cost five dollars apiece. At a few recording sessions when I couldn't lay my hands on a mute, I covered the bell of the trumpet with the beret. Since I'd been designated their 'leader,' cats just picked up the style.

My first pair of eyeglasses, some rimless eyeglasses, came from Maurice Guilden, an optometrist at the Theresa Hotel, but they'd get broken all the time, so I picked up a pair of horn rims. I never wore glasses until 1940. As a child, I had some minor problems with vision. When I'd wake up in the morning, I couldn't open my eyelids – they'd stick together. My mother gave me a piece of cotton, someone told her that urine would help. Every time I urinated, I took a piece of cotton and dabbed my eyes with it. It cured me. I read now without glasses and only use glasses for distance. Someone coming in from the night who saw me wearing dark glasses onstage to shield my eyes from the glare of the spotlights might misinterpret their meaning. Wearing dark glasses at night could only worsen my eyesight. I never wore dark glasses at night. I had to be careful about my eyes because I needed them to read music.

Lie number two was that only beboppers wore beards, goatees, and other facial hair and adornments.

I used to shave under my lip. That spot prickled and itched with scraping. The hair growing back felt uncomfortable under my mouthpiece, so I let the hair grow into a goatee during my days with Cab Calloway. Now a trademark, that tuft of hair cushions my mouthpiece and is quite useful to me as a player; at least I've always thought it allowed me to play more effectively. Girls like my goatee too.

I used to wear a mustache, thinking you couldn't play well without one. One day I cut it off accidentally and had to play, and I've been playing without a mustache ever since. Some guy called me 'weird' because he looked at me and thought he saw only half a mustache. The dark spot above my upper lip is actually a callus that formed because of my embouchure. The right side of my upper lip curls down into the mouthpiece when I form my embouchure to play.

Many modern jazz musicians wore no facial hair at all. Anyway, we weren't the only ones during those days with hair on our faces. What about Clark Gable?

Number three: that beboppers spoke mostly in slang or tried to talk like Negroes is not so untrue. We used a few 'pig Latin' words like 'ofay.' Pig Latin as a way of speaking emerged among blacks long before our time as a secret language for keeping children and the uninitiated from listening to adult conversations. Also, blacks had a lot of words they brought with them from Africa, some of which crept over into general usage, like 'yum-yum.'

Most bebop language came about because some guy said something and it stuck. Another guy started using it, then another one, and before you knew it, we had a whole language. 'Mezz' meant 'pot,' because Mezz Mezzrow was selling the best pot. When's the 'eagle gonna' fly, the American eagle, meant payday. A 'razor' implied the draft from a window in winter with cold air coming in, since it cut like a razor. We added some colorful and creative concepts to the English language, but I can't think of any word besides bebop that I actually invented. Daddy-O Daylie, a disc jockey in Chicago, originated much more of the hip language during our era than I did.

We didn't have to try; as black people we just naturally spoke that way. People who wished to communicate with us had to consider our manner of speech, and sometimes they adopted it. As we played with musical notes, bending them into new and different meanings that constantly changed, we played with words. Say sumpn' hip Daddy-O.

98 Art Pepper and Laurie Pepper Heroin (1979)

Source: Art Pepper and Laurie Pepper, 'Heroin,' in Straight Life: The Story of Art Pepper (New York: Schirmer Books, 1979: 82–9) (excerpt).

In 1950 I was in Chicago at the Croyden Hotel. That was the hotel all the musicians stayed at. I was rooming with Sammy Curtis. He was a tall guy with a roundish face, rosy cheeks, blonde, curly hair, and he had this lopsided grin; he played the little boy bit. He thought it was charming. He was very talented.

I think we played the Civic Opera House that night. I was featured. I got all the praise and applause, and it was great while it was happening, but after everybody left, there I was alone. I wandered around the town. I went to all the bars. I ended up back at the hotel and went into the bar there. I just had to continue getting loaded; it was a compulsion; I had demons chasing me. The only way I ever got loaded enough, so I could be cool, was when I passed out, fell out someplace, which is what I used to do almost every night. They kicked me out of the bar at about four o'clock in the morning, and I didn't know what to do. There was no place I could get a drink. It was getting daylight, and I couldn't peep in any windows. There was no one on the streets.

I went back up to the room. Sammy was there and Roy King, a tenor player, and Sheila Harris, who's a singer, and some piano player. They were all using heroin. Sammy had been using stuff for a long time, and I knew it, but I never would try it because I knew that the minute I did it would be all over for me. I asked them if they had anything other than stuff, and they didn't. I was so unhappy, and Patti was two thousand miles away, and there was nothing I could do. I had to have something.

Sheila came over to me. She was a good singer who worked with another band. She was about five foot, two, and a little on the chubby side – what they call pleasingly plump. She had nice breasts, large, but nice, and although I've never liked chubby women she was one of the few that turned me on. She had long eyelashes and large eyes, bluish-green. Her face was oval and full, and she had full lips, and her eyebrows were full. Most women in those days plucked their eyebrows, but she had let hers grow, and I liked that. She had long fingers and nice nails. And she was a nymphomaniac. When she looked at a man she was thinking of sucking his cock; that was her thought and she turned you on because you could feel that; everyone could. And you were turned on by the stories. She was a legend among musicians. Whether they had ever made it with her or not they'd all tell stories about balling her. She was purely sensual, but only in a sexual way, no other. No warmth, no love, no beauty. When you looked at her you just saw your cock in her mouth.

She came over to me and offered me some stuff, just to horn it, sniff it. She said, 'Why don't you hang up that jive and get in a different groove? Why don't you come in the bathroom with me? I'll show you a new way to go.' I was at my wit's end. The only thing I could have done other than what I did was to jump out of the window of the hotel. I think we were on the fourteenth floor. I started to go into the bathroom with her, and Sammy saw what was happening and flipped out. He caused a big scene. He said, 'I won't be responsible for you starting to use stuff!' But Roy said, 'Man, anything would be better than that jive booze scene he's into now. What could be worse? That's really a bringdown.' We cooled Sammy out, and me and Sheila walked into the bathroom and locked the door.

When we got in there she started playing with my joint. She said, 'Do you want me to say hello to him?' She was marvelous, and she really turned me on, but I said, 'Wait a minute. Let's get into this other thing and then we'll get back to that.' I was all excited about something new, the heroin. I had made up my mind.

She had a little glass vial filled with white powder, and she poured some out onto the porcelain top of the toilet, chopped it up with a razor blade, and separated it into little piles, little lines. She asked me if I had a dollar bill. She told me to get the newest one I had. I had one, very clean and very stiff. I took it out of my pocket and she said, 'Roll it up.' I started to roll it but she said, 'No, not that way.' She made a tube with a small opening at the bottom and a larger opening at the top. Then she went over to the heroin and she said, 'Now watch what I do and do this.' She put one finger on her left nostril and she stuck the larger end of the dollar bill into her right nostril. She put the tube at the beginning of one pile, made a little noise, and the pile disappeared. She said, 'Now you do that.' I closed my nostril. I even remember it was my left nostril. I sniffed it, and a long, thin pile of heroin disappeared. She told me to do the same with the other nostril. I did six little lines and then she said 'Okay, wait a few minutes.' While I'm waiting she's rubbing my joint and playing with me. I felt a tingly, burning sensation up in my sinuses, and I tasted a bitter taste in my throat, and all of a sudden, all of a sudden, all that feeling – wanting something but having no idea what it was, thinking it was sex and then when I had a chance to ball a chick not wanting to ball her because I was afraid of some disease and because of the guilt; that wandering and wandering like some

311

derelict; that agony of drinking and drinking and nothing ever being resolved; and ... no peace at all except when I was playing, and then the minute that I stopped playing there was nothing; that continual, insane search just to pass out somewhere and then to wake up in the morning and think, 'Oh, my God,' to wake up and think, 'Oh God, here we go again,' to drink a bottle of warm beer so I could vomit, so I could start all over again, so I could start that ridiculous, sickening, horrible, horrible life again – all of a sudden, all of a sudden, the demons and the devils and the wandering and wondering and all the frustrations just vanished and they didn't exist at all anymore because I'd finally found peace.

I felt this peace like a kind of warmth. I could feel it start in my stomach. From the whole inside of my body I felt the tranquility. It was so relaxing. It was so gorgeous. Sheila said, 'Look at yourself in the mirror! Look in the mirror!' And that's what I'd always done: I'd stood and looked at myself in the mirror and I'd talk to myself and say how rotten I was – 'Why do people hate you? Why are you alone? Why are you so miserable?' I thought, 'Oh, no! I don't want to do that! I don't want to spoil this feeling that's coming up in me!' I was afraid that if I looked in the mirror I would see it, my whole past life, and this wonderful feeling would end, but she kept saying, 'Look at yourself! Look how beautiful you are! Look at your eyes! Look at your pupils!' I looked in the mirror and I looked like an angel. I looked at my pupils and they were pinpoints; they were tiny, little dots. It was like looking into a whole universe of joy and happiness and contentment.

I thought of my grandmother always talking about God and inner happiness and peace of mind, being content within yourself not needing anybody else, not worrying about whether anybody loves you, if your father doesn't love you, if your mother took a coathanger and stuck it up her cunt to try to destroy you because she didn't want you, because you were an unclean, filthy, dirty, rotten, slimy being that no one wanted, that no one ever wanted, that no one has still ever wanted. I looked at myself and I said, 'God, no, I am not that. I'm beautiful. I am the whole, complete thing. There's nothing more, nothing more that I care about. I don't care about anybody. I don't care about Patti. I don't need to worry about anything at all.' I'd found God.

I loved myself, everything about myself. I loved my talent. I had lost the sour taste of the filthy alcohol that made me vomit and the feeling of the bennies and the strips that put chills up and down my spine. I looked at myself in the mirror and I looked at Sheila and I looked at the few remaining lines of heroin and I took the dollar bill and horned the rest of them down. I said, 'This is it. This is the only answer for me. If this is what it takes, then this is what I'm going to do, whatever dues I have to pay ...' And I *knew* that I would get busted and I *knew* that I would go to prison and that I wouldn't be weak; I wouldn't be an informer like all the phonies, the no-account, the nonreal, the zero people that roam around, the scum that slither out from under rocks, the people that destroyed music, that destroyed this country, that destroyed the world, the rotten, fucking, lousy people that for their own little ends – the black power people, the sickening, stinking motherfuckers that play on the fact that they're black, and all this fucking shit that happened later on – the rotten, no-account, filthy women that have no feeling for anything; they have no love for anyone; they don't know what love is; they are shallow hulls of nothingness – the whole group of rotten people that have nothing to offer, that are nothing, never will be anything, were never intended to be anything.

All I can say is, at that moment I saw that I'd found peace of mind. Synthetically produced, but after what I'd been through and all the things I'd done, to trade that misery for total happiness – that was it, you know, that was it. I realized it. I realized that from that moment on I would be, if you want to use the word, a junkie. That's the word they used. That's the word they still use. That is what I became at that moment. That's what I practiced; and that's what I still am. And that's what I will die as – a junkie.

99 **Louis Armstrong** Storyville (1955)

Source: Nat Shapiro and Nat Hentoff (eds), *Hear Me Talkin' to Ya: The Story of Jazz As Told by the Men Who Made It* (New York: Rinehart, 1955: 43–5) (excerpt). (Editor's title)

Storyville had a lot of different characters ... People from all over the world made special trips to see what it looked like ... There were amusement for any type of person ... Regardless of some of the biggest pimps who lived there at that time Storyville had its nice spots also ... There were night clubs with all of that good music that came from the horns of the great King Joe Oliver (my my whatta man) ... How he used to blow that cornet of his down in Storyville for Pete Lala ... I was just a youngster who loved that horn of King Oliver's ... I would delight delivering an order of stone coal to the prostitute who used to hustle in her crib right next to Pete Lala's cabaret ... Just so's I could hear King Oliver play ... I was too young to go into Pete Lala's at the time ... And I'd just stand there in that lady's crib listening to King Oliver ... And I'm all in a daze ... That was the only way we kids could go into The District – I mean Storyville ... I'd stand there listening to King Oliver beat out one of those good ol good-ones like *Panama* or *High Society* ... My, whatta punch that man had ... And could he shout a tune ... Ump ... All of a sudden it would dawn on the lady that I was still in her crib very silent while she hustle those tricks – and she'd say – 'What's the matter with you, boy? ... Why are you still there standing so quiet?' And there I'd have to explain to her that I was being inspired by *the* King Oliver and his orchestra ... And then she handed me a cute one by saying – 'Well, this is no place to daydream ... I've got my work to do.' So I'd go home very pleased and happy that I did at least hear my idol blow at least a couple of numbers that really *gassed* me no end ...

King Oliver was full of jokes in those days ... Also the days before he passed away (bless his heart). He had a good heart.

Whatta band he had at Pete Lala's ... Oh that music sounded so good. In that band he had Buddy Christian on the piano – Professor Nicholson on the clarinet – Zue Robertson on the trombone – himself on cornet and Henry Zeno on drums ... ahh – there was a drummer for ya ... He had a press roll that one very seldom hear nowadays ... And was he popular ... With everyone ... With all the prostitutes – pimps – gamblers – hustlers and everybody ... Of course they called gamblers 'hustlers' in those days ... Most of the pimps were good gamblers also ... And Henry Zeno was in there with them ... He even had several prostitutes on his staff working for him ... By that he would handle more cash than the average musician ... And he was a little short dark sharp cat – and knew all the answers ... He even was great in a street parade ... He also played in the Onward Brass Band which was made up of the top-notched musicians and featuring on the cornets Manuel Perez and King Oliver ... And you never heard a brass band swing in your whole life like those boys ... Ump Ump Ump ... I'll never be able to explain how they would swing like mad – coming from the cemetery – after playing funeral marches to the cemetery with the body and after the Preacher sez – ashes to ashes and dust – et cetera – Henry Zeno would take his handkerchief off of the snare under the bottom of his snare drum so's every member could get in his place and get ready to march back to the hall with some of the finest swing music pushing them ... And with Black Benny on the bass drum and Henry Zeno laying that press roll on the cats (the second line) that was a musical treat in itself ... P.S. the second line (cats) was consisted of raggidy guys who hung around poolrooms and et cetera.

Henry Zeno died a natural death ... He lived up in Carrolton – a section of the city that's miles away from Storyville ... Yet – still – when he died everybody all over the city including Storyville were very sad ... The day of his funeral – there were so many people that gathered from all sections of the town until you couldn't get within ten blocks of the house where Henry Zeno was laid out ... There were as many white people there to pay their last respect for a great drummer man and his comrades, and the people who just loves to go to funerals no matter who dies ... Although I was only a youngster – I was right in there amongst them ... I had the advantage of the other kids – by meeting great men as Henry Zeno and King Oliver, et cetera ... So it broke my heart too.

Riff 8

Far-Out Words for Cats. (Title, glossary of terms, *Life*, 1954)

Hiya cat, wipe ya feet on the mat, let's slap on the fat and dish out some scat. You're a prisoner of wov, W-O-V, 1280 on the dial, New York, and you're picking up the hard spiel and good deal of Fred Robbins, dispensing seven score and ten ticks of ecstatic static and spectacular vernacular from 6:30 to 9 every black on the 1280 Club ... We got stacks of lacquer crackers on the fire, so hang out your hearing flap while His Majesty salivates a neat reed. (D.J. Fred Robbins, quoted 'Prisoners of WOV,' *Time*, 1947)

Hip is an uncrackable code ... a hang-loose ironic cool (Roy Carr, Brian Case and Fred Dellar, *The Hip: Hipsters, Jazz and the Beat Generation*, 1986)

The hipster's lingo is a private kind of folk-poetry, meant for the ears of the brethren alone. (Mezz Mezzrow, *Really the Blues*, 1946)

More than any other aspect of ... [the black] experience the language of the black musician has had the greatest total effect on the informal language Americans speak. (Clarence Major [ed.], *Dictionary of Afro-American Slang*, 1970)

Poppa's got the heebie jeebies bad ... ay! eeff, gaff, mmmm, de-boy, a deddle-la-bahm; rip bib ee-doo-dee-doo-doo ... (Bill Gottlieb, 'From Heebie Jeebies to Bebop,' *Saturday Review of Literature*, 1948)

Chorus VIII
Reetie Vouties with a Little Hot Sauce: Jazz and language
(vernacular, argot, hipness)

Oop-shoo-be-do-be, Oo-Oo. Gimme some skin! The language of any music necessarily involves technical codes that 'speak' to musicians and listeners alike. Composition, performance, communication, interpretation – all use notation, sign systems and symbols as 'texts,' or auditory conventions that direct reception for listeners. To this musicology, jazz adds codes involving improvisation, so its language is voiced and received as a particular kind of musical idiom, involving significantly different linguistic mastery. The titles of two studies of jazz improvisation, Paul Berliner's *Thinking in Jazz* (1994) and Ingrid Monson's *Saying Something* (1996), are suggestive of this expertise with idiom and familiarity with a special language.

In addition to technical terminology, the language of jazz may be most obviously approached from the perspective of socio-linguistics, where much of its vocabulary is derived from sociological and cultural contexts. Jazz language appears in spoken and written form as a particular vernacular, argot or code. In many instances – especially racial contexts – it is a language, a lingo, which signals and expresses difference. It often emphasizes the separateness, if not alienation, of jazz musicians from the dominant culture. Any study of the vernacular of the jazz world, as Robert Gold maintains, involves examining the sociology of jazz musicians in conjunction with their linguistic usage. Jazz language is inseparable from the growth of jazz, the identity of its creators, and the kinds of lives they have led (Gold 1957: 271). **Chorus VIII** selects studies of jazz lingo, 'hip' parlance and musicians' vernacular; gives examples of jazz language 'at work' in non-conventional, subversive and vocalized texts; and offers sample terminology from specialist jazz glossaries and dictionaries. Material is largely drawn from the 1940s–1950s, arguably the period of most prolific invention and interest for jazz language, and one which has left a permanent legacy.

Linguist-lexicographer Robert Gold has demonstrated the profound relationship of jazz language to the larger perspective of the jazz life (1957; 1975). What emerges from his extensive citation of 'jazz talk' and Neil Leonard's survey of jazz musicians' 'verbal usage,' (**100, 101**) is the strong affinity of jazz language and African-American culture. Jazz talk has been highly eclectic, essentially combining black folk idiom and argot of the underworld. This coalescence was strengthened by migratory black urban experience in the 1930s–1940s, and the emergence of a racial sub-culture, focused on jazz. Historically, too, black cultural rebellion in America has expressed itself musically through the medium of jazz, and linguistically through speech and coded language (Gold 1957: 273).

The fusion of jazz and speech, and its racial provenance, is exhibited in Gold's *Jazz Talk* (1975), still the best, most comprehensive dictionary, providing definitions and etymology, and selecting examples used in specific contexts. **Gold**'s 'Introduction' (**100**) overviews jazz's specialized vocabulary, drawing attention to locutions which register 'feelings, behavior, and moral and esthetic judgments,' since they especially reflect the philosophy and 'style' of jazz speakers. Of note are: (1) the characteristic semantic reversals, reflecting distrust of conventional white morality and standards (e.g., 'bad,' 'shit,' 'crazy' all carry favourable connotations); (2) terminology derived from struggles for professional survival and jazz's basic affirmation as music; and (3) the narrow range and multi-meaning of terms, especially verbs. Aside from noting the prolific inventiveness of jazz slang, and its vulnerability to change, Gold emphasizes the durability of staple terms, e.g., words like *bop, cool, crazy, gig, groove, hip, jive, scat, square, swing* and many more have survived.

Gold's observation of the 'coterie value' of jazz slang and its identification with the music and life it reflects make it a creative, vital language of appreciable social significance. Neil **Leonard** (**101**), drawing on Gold's researches, concludes jazz talk celebrates community separateness and solidarity, and demonstrates 'credentials in its elite fellowship.' But if successive argots started as semi-secret codes, they are not entirely explained by 'separatist impulses.' Some jazz jargon obviously derives from speakers' inarticulateness and the inexpressiveness of standard language; other, from the rituals of the black/jazz community's word play, verbal games of wit and invention – sometimes translated into vocal style (e.g. 'scat') or providing a source for 'kicks.' Leonard explains the attraction of jazz argot: novelty and curiosity value enhance the mystery of jazz and its life – often one of racial difference – giving it a 'demimondial glamor.'

The appeal to novelty and fashion is demonstrated in the social phenomenon and posture of the hipster. To be 'hip' is to be informed and in the know. Neil Powell's dictionary entry (1997: 61) finds 'hip' evasive, resisting definition, but suggests the 'cachet of its minority, cognoscenti appeal'– and its classic embodiment in the figure of Lester Young. Long a central concept in the jazz lexicon, 'hip' (*c*. 1900?) suggests sophistication and 'silent knowingness' (Collier 1978: 360), announcing its relation to the later coinage: 'hipster' (*c*. 1940). The hipster is one who is 'knowledgeable and resourceful' (Gold 1975: 130). Either as jazz musician or follower, he expressed the values of a subculture with a 'recondite social philosophy': 'squares' were the 'true outsiders,' and hipsters knew 'where it was at' (Sidran 1971: 114). The 'hip ethic' articulated the social style and musical stance of 1940s black bop musicians; the emergence of bop as a newly adversarial and experimental idiom accentuated the accompanying linguistic process of alienation and separation. Anatole **Broyard** (**102**), in a highly stylized and theoretical 'portrait,' reflects an existential interest in the social philosophy and conduct of the hipster. 'Jive' music (bop) and 'tea' (marijuana) are the basic components of hipster life and, along with an equally reductive and indirect vocabulary, correspond to the hipster's social refusal and incapacitation.

In the primer 'The parlance of hip' (1960), compiler Robert **Reisner** records eight meanings for the word 'cool' (**103**), demonstrating its flexible and nuanced utility. Along with the durable 'hip,' its survival as a tool of varied meaning is found in many examples. For Amiri **Baraka** (LeRoi Jones), the transfer of 'cool' from verb to musical noun, like its counterpart 'swing,' involves a value change from racial agency and reaction dynamic to white commodification and appropriation (**104**). Others proffer fashionable advice on 'how to speak hip,' with guards against 'uncool'-ness (Meltzer 1993: 230); or parody the very 'hipness' of knowing about HIP (Carr *et al.* 1986: 11).

The fashion of hipsterdom and association with the language of jazz, drugs and dress was reflected in a *Time* 'Radio' column of 1946, reported in Dizzy Gillespie's autobiography, *To Be or Not ... to Bop* (**VII/97**). This ignores the sociology of bop, and concentrates on the novelty value of the new music, the capacity of its anti-lyrics and leading devotees (Harry 'The Hipster' Gibson and Bulee 'Slim' Gaillard) to offend public taste. Bop is accused of making young listeners 'degenerate,' and Gaillard and Gibson records were banned on an L.A. station (sample lyrics from *Who Put the Benzedrine in Mrs. Murphy's Ovaltine?*). Gaillard's notoriety as hipster *supremo* is well-founded. Closely connected with earlier bop and its recordings (he participated in a 1945 session with Gillespie and Parker), the 'zooty Negro guitarist' is best known for his invention of a private, jazz-influenced language, 'vout.' His 'reet-a-voutie' routines appeared in dictionary form, and he is briefly but reverently featured as the divine nightclub hipster in Jack **Kerouac**'s novel, *On the Road* (**105**).

The cultural separation of jazz language, its oppositional stance, and increasing fashionability are all demonstrated in a number of representative texts of the 1940–1950s. This was a period of accelerated linguistic expansion and semantic change, given the advent of modern jazz (bebop), its burgeoning urban sub-culture, and increased post-war racial self-awareness. These texts (**106–110**) may be described as non-conventional, and potentially subversive in intention; they exemplify jazz lingo at work. Dissociation from dominant values and the orthodoxy of popular forms is marked by parody, linguistic and cultural transcription, and invasion of humorous and mocking argot into common speech. Much of this usage is an overlapping combination of the two vocabularies of black (Harlem) and jazz slang – as Gold demonstrates in a comparison of glossaries (1957: 277–8).

Harlem 'racial talk' and the sub-world of pushing 'gauge' is part of everyday activity recorded in Mezz Mezzrow's 1946 autobiography, *Really the Blues* (see also **V/66**, **VII/94**). In a feature review (**106**), *Newsweek* reproduces a specimen 'jive' exchange and warns coyly of the *risqué* appeal of 'Vipers, tea and jazz.' Sociologically, the magazine sees Mezzrow's downward life as reversed Horatio Alger. Zora Neale **Hurston** (**107**) assembles authentic 1942 street Harlemese in a story involving competition between two impecunious, failed hustlers, zoot-suited and 'airing out on the Avenue.' This has the feel of loosely improvised conversation – fluid, vernacular speech – and is not without a narrative turn on the Harlem (and Northern) seductions of 'wealth and splendor.' The penetration of jazz parlance into traditional material is evinced in Steve **Allen**'s 'bop fable' of 'Crazy Red Riding Hood' (**108**). 'Hip' embellishment turns the story locale into 'the Land of Oobopshebam,' and the heroine as 'lovely little girl' into a 'fine chick.' In the book's original illustration, the wolf appears in beret, shades and zoot suit, sporting a bent trumpet, and looking rather like jazzman Dizzy Gillespie. The craze for bop vocals – often wordless 'scat' or onomatopoeic jive which mock the conventions of lyric song – appears in Mary Lou **Williams** and Milton **Orent**'s 'The land of Oo-Bla-Dee,' in a version recorded by Gillespie's orchestra and vocalist Joe Carroll in 1949 (**109**). This subverts the content of fairy tale – the speaker discovers a 'switcheroo' bride and hops a freighter – and enjoys its three-eyed princess and internal translations of riffy nonsense syllables. The genre degenerated into faddism, but was bop's ironic rejoinder to the orthodoxy of the popular song, on whose structure it was so dependent. Finally, Lawrence **Ferlinghetti** (**110**) converts the familiar story of Christ evidence into an irreverent 'beat' poem. Metaphor and diction ('combo,' 'cat,' 'blow,' 'cool') are derived from jazz lingo, and the entire languorous style might come from any 1950s hipster. Indubitably, Christ is 'real dead.'

The expansive period of jazz slang in the 1940s also encouraged appearance of glossaries and dictionaries designed to inform the uninitiated and otherwise attract the curious 'square.' Two of the most important compilations came from bandleader Cab Calloway and journalist Dan Burley. **Calloway** had already popularized the 'jive' vocal as alternative lyric. His band–audience exchange as 'Hi-de-ho-man' became a personal signature, and its song source, 'Minnie the Moocher/She was a low-down hoochy-coocher' (1931), an example of earlier jive/ scat singing. *The New Cab Calloway's Hepster's Dictionary* (**111**), of 1944, had achieved five editions since 1938; its reissue claims that jive talk is now 'an everyday part of the English language,' though the derivation was originally Harlem patois. Stanley Frank, writing in a *Negro Digest* feature on Dan **Burley**, termed him 'the nation's poobah of spiels' and 'perhaps the most extensively quoted man in America' (1944: 11–15). In his *Original Handbook of Harlem Jive* (1944), Burley's speciality is Harlem-originated black speech idiom. In one section, 'The technique of jive,' he offers thirteen 'lessons' of instruction in the principles and nature of the language. This concludes with 'Advanced reading' (**112**) in jive soliloquy, and after-comments on the new language as a dynamic and democratic argot, 'a defense mechanism,' whose slang essence is 'gleaned from all nations ... cities, hamlets, and villages.' Harlemese is the universal *lingua franca*.

Vocal styles in jazz language include not only 'scat' and bebop lyrics, but 'vocalese' and, extensively, a host of poems which are jazz-inflected verse. 'Scat,' as a vocal strategy, is the sound of the voice approximating to an instrument. It allegedly derives from Louis Armstrong dropping his sheet music in 'Heebie Jeebies' (1926), and improvising 'a mess of nonsense syllables which he sang as if he were blowing them through his horn' (Gottlieb 1948: 50; **Riff 8**). In vocalese, newly invented texts (lyrics) are set to already recorded jazz improvisations, so that jazz solos are reproduced in melodic and linguistic terms. The best-known early practitioners were Leo Watson, Eddie Jefferson and King **Pleasure** [Clarence Beeks], whose 1953 vocalese, 'Parker's mood' (**113**), used Charlie Parker's blues improvisation (1948) of the same title. Barry Grant – in an appreciation of vocalese's aesthetic – rightly describes Pleasure's words as 'a lyrical pastiche of evocative conventional blues images,' with

Pleasure reportedly saying he saw instrumental solos as narratives – 'stories' (Gabbard 1995b: 292, 294).

Jazz-related poems, in drawing on the history and nature of jazz, evoke analogues between musical and linguistic structures, both in their content and/or stylistic features **(IX)**. One such poem is Angela **Jackson**'s 'Make/n My Music' (**114**), imbued with vernacular vigour and the proximity of 'run/n jazz rhythms' to black speech utterance. Here, orthography, diction, metre, spacing, slashes, lineation – all contribute to a syncopated voicing of narrative, the progress from 'colored child/hood' to 'Black woman/hood'. Only the discovery of Billie Holiday clouds the music's 'sooo/good!' feeling.

100 **Robert S. Gold** Introduction, *Jazz Talk* (1975)

Source: Robert S. Gold, 'Introduction,' *Jazz Talk* (New York: Bobbs-Merrill, 1975: ix–xii).

Taking the stand one night at a West Coast jazz concert a quarter of a century ago, jazz's premier tenor saxophonist, Lester Young, turned to his drummer, Louis Bellson, and said, 'Lady Bellson, don't drop no bombs behind me, baby, just give me that *titty-boom, titty-boom* all night on the cymbal, and I'm cool.' The uninitiated might have been mystified by the instruction, but the drummer wasn't: 'bombs' are the sudden bass-drum explosions which had come into vogue a few years earlier and which Lester's Kansas City swing style was uncomfortable with; 'cool,' in context, means contented; 'baby' is a popular term of address among jazzmen; the double 'titty-boom' is simply Lester's onomatopoeic rendering of the desired rhythmic pattern; and 'Lady' is what Lester aristocratically called everyone, an ironic-respectful term of address.

What's missing from the above transcription and exegesis is Lester's speaking style – the nuances achieved by phrasing, tone and pitch variation, which are also aspects of Lester's musical style. (Proposition: Transcribed speech is to speech as transcribed music is to actual performance.)

A slang dictionary can provide definitions (and, sometimes, word origins), but no mere glossary will inflame the reader's auditory imagination; if jazz slang's spirit of rich musicality and existential wit is to be captured, there must also be examples of the terms as they are used in specific contexts.

Jazz Talk offers selective citations from an admittedly sketchy written record (it's unfortunate that those who most use slang are least likely to express themselves in writing). The thousands of quotations in this volume will serve to encapsulate jazz language within the larger perspective of the jazz life, spanning its 80-year-or-so history. As jazz has evolved from its funeral-march, brass-band and piano-rag beginnings to small-band New Orleans and Chicago style, big-band swing (or Kansas City) style, bop and post-bop, its special argot has undergone many changes, sometimes though not always parallel to changes in the music.

Slang – *any* slang – is the creation and property of people lacking formal education, and the blacks who created jazz in the first two decades of our century brought into the musical life a colorful rural and ghetto vocabulary that had resisted the standardization of language which typifies educated urban centers. As the new music became grist for the commercial mill, black folk idiom was infused with terms deriving from new conditions of musical performance and, most important, with underworld argot. Always close (though hardly by choice) to the most sordid aspects of big-city life, urban blacks had early assimilated the jargon of the rackets – dope peddling, prostitution, larceny and gambling; but now even the gin mills, brothels and nightclubs which housed jazz were owned by racketeers, most of them white.

As the jazz community coalesced, understandably an entire sub-vocabulary emerged – terms for musical styles, devices and effects; for instruments; for dances and dancers. Later, a critical vocabulary arose as writers struggled to describe freshly the quality of jazz art. These purely musical terms constitute a jargon such as exists in all occupations, and is perhaps the least interesting part of any specialized vocabulary.

It's the locutions that flow out from the center, registering feelings, behavior, and moral and esthetic judgments, that are most interesting, because they most crucially reflect the philosophy and 'style' of the speakers. For example, *mean, dirty, low-down* and *nasty* (all current *c.* 1900), and *bad, tough, hard* and *terrible* all carry favorable connotations in jazz speech, while *sweet, pretty, square* and *straight* are usually unfavorable; it requires no cultural historian to detect the basic black distrust of white moral and esthetic standards lying behind such semantic reversals. If one is 'bad' or 'tough,' he might just be bad enough or tough enough for the society not to ignore (an old habit of white officialdom when it comes to blacks). If one is 'square,' on the other hand, he might well enjoy *Mickey Mouse* or *ricky-tick* music or a *businessman's bounce* and not understand that many blacks still *feel a draft.*

The distrust of conventional white morality is also evident in the practice of assigning favorable connotations to terms of mental derangement (*crazy, insane, nutty*); there is also an implied antipathy to the bleak realities of twentieth-century existence in such transcendent superlatives as *out of this world, far out, gas(sed), gone, out of sight* and *something else.*

The travails of survival can lead a musician (black *or* white) to feel *beat, brought down, bugged, drugged, hung up, strung out, hassled* or *up tight,* so that he must *scuffle* and *pay dues* in order to survive, and ease his way by being *hip, fly, down, booted* and *ready.*

Problems and solemnity aside, jazz slang most often reflects the basic affirmation of the music, its joy and ebullience: *jump, ride, rock, roll, romp, swing, stomp, jitterbug* and *boogie-woogie*; its fire and intensity: *hot, burning, cooking* and *smoking*; its colorful settings: *honkytonk, barrelhouse* and *gutbucket*; its people: *cats, chicks, studs, foxes* and *dudes*; its clothing: *togs, drapes, threads* and *vines*; and its good times: *jamming, balling, grooving,* and *getting one's kicks.*

In opting for color and incisiveness, slang necessarily sacrifices the standard vocabulary's finer distinctions and exactitude of expression. Jazz slang gets plenty of mileage from its narrow range of locutions, particularly from its verbs. *Pick up,* for example, covers a lot of waterfront: to get, take, learn, find, understand, appreciate, etc. Most jazz slang verbs are multiple-meaning action verbs (*blow, broom, cook, cop, dig, jump, knock, latch on, make,* and *put down*), a linguistic image of jazz's playfulness and vitality.

Obviously most slang is metaphoric, but less obvious is why metaphors tend to be elaborately decorative in one period and severely functional in another, though World War II is a divider between the easy-going, loose hyperbole of the Louis Armstrong–Cab Calloway generation (*collar the jive; like the bear, I ain't nowhere; plant you now and dig you later*) and the unsmiling incisiveness of the boppers (*dig it; ax; cool*). The always prevailing tendency, however, is the movement toward simplicity, of pruning away as much of a phrase as seems extraneous: *split the scene* becomes simply *split; dig you later* simply *later.*

The high casualty rate of emotionally charged slang terms (especially superlatives, which sometimes have only a three- or five-year vogue) has led some students of language to regard the entire slang vocabulary as ephemeral. Not so. Some staples of jazz slang have been around for a long time: *dig, jive, cop, gig, scarf, hip, jazz* itself and dozens more have survived the ravages of linguistic fickleness.

The slang casualty rate, however, does exceed that of the standard language. Sometimes the fatality is caused by the spontaneous discovery of a fresher or wittier metaphor or image (*stud* with its macho connotation, for example, yielding to the more humorous tenderfoot image of *dude*), and sometimes by the coterie value of a term's being destroyed by the general public's adoption of it (these days even DAR members may be heard intoning that someone 'tells it like it is' or assuring a host that they've 'had a ball'). Jazzmen are not especially flattered by imitation, particularly when their language is aped by people with no appreciation of the life that produces it. The media's tendency to caricature jazz slang is not very different from Hollywood's antique and dishonorable practice of using jazz on a sound-track to suggest tawdriness or sleaziness.

In the 1960s there were copious borrowings from jazz slang by the rock-youth culture, and many of these terms were further disseminated among the general public by TV dramas, ads and talk shows; the upshot of all the media attention was to blur the already fuzzy distinctions among the various specialized slangs (jazz, black, rock, narcotics, hot rod, underworld, etc.). For its part the jazz world seems to have resisted the rock-youth linguistic impact: jazzmen will only occasionally be heard using terms like 'rap,' 'rip off,' 'where (someone) is coming from,' 'bummer,' 'trip,' 'let it all hang out,' 'good (or bad) vibes' and 'right on!' (the jazz equivalent remains *straight ahead!*).

There is evidence lately, for better or worse, of a rapprochement between jazz and rock: many young musicians play both; some of the middle-generation of established jazzmen (e.g. Freddie Hubbard, Herbie Hancock and McCoy Tyner) have converted to the rock practice of using heavily amplified rhythm sections; jazz publication *Down Beat* now gives considerable coverage to rock.

Add one more heavy fact – the inevitable dying out of the older generation of jazzmen – and it's plain to see that the future of jazz slang is in question.

Whether its identity as a separate vocabulary is preserved, or the behavioral segment of it continues to be absorbed into the amalgam of general slang available to a Madison Avenue plugged-in public, historically jazz slang is a triumph (albeit a minor one set beside the music). To be sure, there are egregious lapses of taste in the usage: jazzmen can be as corny as American Legionnaires in matters of money, intoxication and – God help us! – women (those appalling blues lyrics!). But overall, jazz slang is like the music and the musical life it reflects, a vital, creative and socially significant form of human expression.

101 **Neil Leonard** The jazzman's verbal usage (1986)

Source: Neil Leonard, 'The jazzman's verbal usage,' *Black American Literature Forum*, 20 (1986: 151–60).

Jazz talk has been highly eclectic, combining black English with the jargons of gambling, prostitution, larceny, music, and dance.[1] Successive versions of this rapidly changing parlance started as semisecret codes, vocational idioms which were proud symbols of the jazz community's identity and separateness. As Louis Armstrong explained in the thirties, 'Jazzmen have a language of their own, and I don't think anything could better show how much they are apart from the regular musicians and have their own world that they believe in and that most people have not understood' (78).

But the incomprehensibility of this speech did not necessarily limit its appeal, even among those who understood it only fractionally. For fringe followers and outsiders, intrigued by the jazz life (if not always by its music), the novelty of its argot served to enhance its demimondial glamor. And its words spread to the outside world in a pattern of imitation and replacement analogous to that of fashion in dress, with elitists finding new words for those debased by general use. In 1946 clarinetist Mezz Mezzrow said that the term 'swing ... was cooked up after the unhip public took over the expression "hot" and made it corny by getting up in front of a band and snapping their fingers in a childish way, yelling, "Get hot! Yeah man, get hot." ... This happened all the time ... It used to grate on our nerves because it was usually slung in our faces when we were playing our hottest numbers ... That's the reason we hot musicians are always making up new lingo for ourselves' (Mezzrow and Wolfe: 142). New terms for marijuana seemed to emerge hourly: 'muggles,' 'weed,' 'tea,' 'grass,' 'reefer,' 'muta,' 'hemp,' 'gay,' 'pod,' 'pot,' 'golden leaf,' 'cool green,' 'stuff,' 'gauge,' and so on. Similarly, boppers coined many words for being in the know: 'hip,' 'fly,' 'booted,' 'down,' 'ready,' and so forth.

Although a few in-words remained fashionable over relatively long periods – for instance, 'dig,' 'jive,' and 'gig' – there was usually a turnover in usage when musical styles changed, as in the forties when the loose, overblown argot of pre-World-War-II jazz was contracted into the economies of bop talk. To be 'on drugs' was shortened to 'on'; 'split the scene' became 'split'; and 'flip one's wig' became 'wig' (Gold: x–xi).

Although successive jazz argots started out as more or less secret idioms among insiders, they were not entirely the outgrowth of separatist impulses. Their unconventionality stemmed in part from speakers' inarticulateness or the incapacity of ordinary language to express extraordinary feelings. Unable to convey his deepest emotions in the received idiom, the jazzman invented terms of his own. 'Jazzmen come to grips with emotions so strong,' wrote Robert Reisner in 1960, 'that they are unable to cope with them in ordinary adjectives. They are gassed, fractured, killed, tore up. A wonderful instrument is too much, the end, gone' (179). Such words held proper meaning only for those already aware of the intended referents, those who knew about the music's evocations.

Verbal expression of his feelings led the jazzman to 'the edges of language,' according to Paul van Buren, far from the rule-governed center of the standard idiom with its emphasis on clarity and precision (4–5, 98). Here, however unconsciously, like the poet and prophet, the jazzman probed the unknown or unexpressed with metaphor, oxymoron, and synecdoche in ways puzzling to unattuned ears. Yet every insider knew what Lester Young meant when he said he 'felt a draft' or when he told an unfamiliar drummer, 'Don't drop no bombs behind me, baby. Just give me that *titty-boom titty-boom* all night on the cymbal and I'm cool' (Gold: ix). Nor was the aficionado puzzled when Charlie Parker declared, 'I lit my fire. I greased my skillet and I cooked' (Shapiro and Hentoff: 232). And he knew about the rhyming slang in which 'jack the bear' meant 'nowhere,' which in turn meant off the 'scene' or out of it. He also knew that 'bread' referred to dough (money), and about the reversals in which words like 'mean,' 'bad,' 'dirty,' 'lowdown,' and 'crazy' conferred status, while others like 'sweet,' 'pretty,' 'square,' and 'straight' were pejorative. The ecstatic areas on experiential frontiers were 'out of this world' or 'far out.' To 'swing' was to 'jump,' 'rock,' 'ride,' or 'stomp'; and words like 'hot,' 'burn,' and 'cook' (all suggesting shamanistic 'heat') referred to ecstatic performance. The meanings or shadings of most of these expressions were heavily contextual. Nowhere is this more obvious than in the uses of 'cool' and 'like,' the latter employed as almost every part of speech and as a punctuation mark (Reisner: 179). To exclaim 'Like!' was to express the otherwise unsayable, comprehensible only to those who already knew the message.

Jazz talk not only meant, it *created*. As I. A. Richards, Kenneth Burke, and others have pointed out, language is a form of 'symbolic action' which both expresses and formulates, imposing order and significance on experience.[2] This was notably evident in the jazz world's use of nicknames. Ned E. Williams notes in Shapiro and Hentoff's *Hear Me Talkin' to Ya* that Duke Ellington had

a penchant for pinning nicknames on those most closely associated with him, usually nicknames that st[u]ck. Thus Freddy Jenkins, the little trumpet player, ... became Posey, Johnny Hodges ... is called Rabbit by those closest to him.

The late Richard Jones, Duke's valet for years, jumped only to the call of Bowden, and Jack Boyd, erstwhile manager of the band, whose given name is Charles, for no explainable reason was always just Elmer to Duke. It was Elmer in turn who dubbed Ellington as Dumpy, and I can't remember when I've called him anything else in direct communication. It may be a signal honor, but Duke went into a big corporation routine for me, never refers to me except by my first initials, N. E. Another leader while playing trumpet for Ellington, won the name which he still uses professionally, Cootie Williams, and there are many other instances. (236)

Such bynames stimulated and evoked as well as described. Call a man 'King,' 'Duke,' 'Count,' 'Pops,' 'Satchelmouth,' 'Rabbit,' 'Dumpy,' or 'Elmer,' and you create not just an image but an attitude of affection, respect, derision, or whatever, and encourage the behavior that goes with it. Accordingly, the wordplay of nicknames helped to establish identity and to shape perceptions, expectations, and social relationships. When used tactfully, bynames could indicate things which could not be said directly. To call someone 'Dizzy,' 'Muggsy,' or 'Mousey' in some contexts was to court open offense, but in the rituals of nickname usage these terms were socially sanctioned outlets for aggression absorbed in friendly banter.[3]

There were times, however, when the jazzman's talk was not all that amicable. The jazz community, like other groups, had language intended to sting, as in the ridicule of squares, naive followers, or fledgling musicians. The story of music abounds with tales of veteran performers 'putting on' the uninitiated in ways that provided safety valves for aggression and a means of social control. The butts of such jokes were disinclined to repeat their errors, although the message did not always sink in right away. During the twenties a cocky, fifteen-year-old clarinet prodigy, Artie Shaw, was gradually cut down to size by persistent ridicule of older bandsmen in New Haven, ridicule which did not necessarily center on music. 'It took me quite a while to learn to keep my mouth shut and never ask questions about anything that did not directly and immediately concern me,' Shaw writes. His colleagues, for example, once started to talk excitedly about an upcoming job at a marvelous place called Webb Inn. He had never heard of it and, since he was pointedly not included in the discussion, began to fear that he had been left out of the booking. Finally, he asked, 'Where *is* Webb Inn?' Whereupon everybody else broke 'into a loud chorus, "Up the spider's ass!"' Gradually, the message got through: '... I began,' Shaw recalls, 'to learn a little about what was what' (180–1).

Other uses of verbal humor were more benign. Dizzy Gillespie consciously followed the lead of Fats Waller in using banter to reach listeners. It was especially helpful in breaking the ice at the beginning of performances. 'Comedy is important,' Gillespie feels. 'As a performer, when you're trying to establish audience control, the best thing is to make them laugh if you can. That relaxes you more than anything. A laugh relaxes the muscles; it relaxes the muscles all over the body. When you get people relaxed, they're more receptive to what you're trying to get them to do. Sometimes, when you're laying on something over their heads, they'll go along with it if they're relaxed. Sometimes I get up on the bandstand and say, "I'd like to introduce the men in the band," and then introduce the guys to one another. There's a reason for that. I just don't come out with it to get a laugh' (303–04). Gillespie worked this routine virtually to death, but no matter how well-worn, it continued to have the desired effect, helping the performers to stay loose in intense performance conditions and at the same time establishing audience control. Verbal humor or foolishness also helped musicians to 'role distance' themselves between sets. Pianist Art Hodes recounts going backstage during the interval of a Louis Armstrong appearance: 'There'd be a lot of good feeling in the room. And somebody would say something funny, and that would give Louis an opening, and you couldn't beat Louis at being funny … And we'd laugh through the whole intermission, and then walk Louis back to the stand … Man, the guy could really blow then' (18). No matter how manic, such joking allowed the musicians temporarily to escape the pressure and return to the bandstand refreshed.

Jazz talk, then, was not just denotative. At times, it worked mainly to 'engender feelings' (a term Charles Keil uses in connection with jazz itself) in a cumulative process resting heavily on associational linkages.[4] In this process what you said might matter less than *how* you said it, with semantics depending largely on spontaneous integration of appropriate linguistic, kinesic, proximal, and other codes. Performance here,[5] as in music, had its share of rituals, for instance in the jazz community's verbal games, which sometimes resembled musical cutting sessions. Among American blacks in general, speech duels take the form of 'playing the dozens,' 'signifying,' 'rapping,' 'chopping,' and 'capping.'[6] Akin to these, the jazzman's verbal jousts could occur in brief moments of kidding, needling, or good-natured horseplay, but usually they were episodes in serious, ongoing rivalries over music, women, and other things. This competitive play might go on for months, even years, particularly in successful, big bands where sidemen were together day in and day out for long periods. Fletcher Henderson's wife Leora recalls that the musical and verbal duels of her husband's sidemen overflowed into rehearsals in the twenties: 'Charlie Green (we called him Big Green) would be playing something wonderful and then Jimmy Harrison [the band's other star trombonist] would say, "Huh, you think *you* done something!" and then try to cut him,' provoking further banter and fueling another round in the ongoing encounter (Shapiro and Hentoff: 219).

Such wordplay was less prevalent among whites than blacks, who had grown up in a tradition which rewards prowess in verbal games – the black community granting special recognition to the skillful talker who in the white world might be discounted as a backyard lawyer, conman, or fabricator.[7] For this or other reasons, many whites could not hold their own in black-rooted jive talk. They knew the right words, but not how to use them. Registering admiration at the way his black acquaintances on Central Avenue in Los Angeles traded words, saxophonist Art Pepper observes: 'I used to stand around and marvel at the way they talked. Having really nothing to say, they were able to play those little verbal games back and forth. I envied it but was too self-conscious to do it. What I wouldn't give to just jump in and say those things. I could when I was joking to myself, raving to myself in front of the mirror at home, but when it came time to do it with people, I couldn't' (44). Raised in a repressive, white family and naturally shy, he knew the content but could not perform comfortably, at least among native speakers.

Pepper is right to call such banter a game, because it has all the attributes of play as defined by Huizinga, Caillois, and others: its own special time, place, rules, flow, competition, chance, imitation, ecstasy, and balance of formality and spontaneity.[8] It also evidences play's proclivity to promote separatist and secretive social groupings. Beyond this, it sharpens wits and ears. Participants in these verbal jousts have to 'get' the fast-moving messages with all of their shadings quickly and send appropriate replies almost without thinking, according to a complicated set of rules demanding, among other things, inversions of conventional proprieties. Ralph Ellison recalls standing on an Oklahoma City street corner with his 'hep' young friends and responding to the music of the Count Basie band playing in a nearby dance hall:

'Now that's the Right Reverend Jimmy Rushing preaching now, man,' someone would say. And rising to the cue another would answer, 'Yeah, and that's old Elder "Hot Lips" signifying along with him; urging him on, man.' And, keeping it building, 'Huh, but though you can't hear him out this far, Ole Deacon Big-un [the late Walter Page] is up there patting his foot and slapping on his big belly [the bass viol] to keep those fools in line.' And we might go on to name all the members of the band as though they were the Biblical four-and-twenty elders, while laughing at the impious wit of applying church titles to a form of music which all the preachers assured us was the devil's potent tool. (234)

Other speech play crossed conventional syntactical and morphological borderlines, twisting words into new significances and concocting new terms. 'As we played with musical notes,' explains Dizzy Gillespie, 'bending them into new and different meanings that constantly changed, we played with words. Say sumpn' hip Daddio' (281).

Jazz vocalists were especially adept at such games. Many of them could scarcely utter the banalities of popular lyrics straight. Through assorted gestures and verbal manipulations singers reworked vacuous lines for new significances. An interjected blue note or raised eyebrow of Fats Waller could make the sober hilarious or the ridiculous serious. With altered accents and phrasing, hornlike intonation, and omitted words Billie Holiday breathed new life into dead stanzas. Louis Armstrong elicited double takes when he casually changed the penultimate line of 'Just a Gigolo' (OK 41468) from 'When the end comes I know they'll say just another gigolo' to 'When the end comes I know they'll say just another jig I know.'

Sometimes the alterations introduced just enough nonsense to throw the old lyrics into fresh perspective. At other times, they crossed the lines of sense altogether, as in scat singing and scat talk, which helped to develop acute musical discrimination. To singer Betty Carter, 'Scat singing is good training. It trains your ear to be in tune and to hear different changes' (Dahl: 45). In the scat idiom are all of the characteristics of extreme, verbal ritual: special styles and registers, fast delivery, high pitches, broken rhythms, grunts, anomalous mumbo jumbo words, and prosaically pleasing repetitions (Samarin, 'The Language of Religion': 8–9). We can hear a good deal of this in the reet-a-voutee routines of Slim Gaillard and the bop utterances of Dizzy Gillespie in songs like 'Oop-Bop-Sha-Bam' and 'Oop-Sho-Be-Do-Bee.' And the same qualities are evident in the early singing of Louis Armstrong, most notably in 'Heebie Jeebies' (OK 0300), which inaugurated the scat craze of the twenties. After a perfectly comprehensible rendition of the Tin-Pan-Alley doggerel, first chorus, he departed from the lyrics entirely with 'Eef, gaff, mmf, dee-bo, dee-la-bhm' and so forth. These lines made an overwhelming impression upon his followers. 'I brought the record home to play for the gang,' recalled Mezz Mezzrow, 'and man, they almost fell through the ceiling' (120). They and others soon learned the words, and before long the lines became a form of street greeting among the initiated.

Like other such nonsense, this language, while intended to conceal or exclude, depended on the transformation of, or contrast with, a commonly used source language, and was readily decipherable to insiders. Attuned listeners responded to it as to other systems of signs, and took pleasure in its defiance of the seemingly tyrannical order of standard English with its respectable associations. As one youngster told Jablow and Withers, 'We like nonsense because all the squares think something has to *mean* something all the time' (255).[9]

Aside from being an outlet for complaint, nonsensical wordplay was a source of kicks. Pianist Hoagy Carmichael declared that Louis Armstrong's 'blubbering, cannibalistic sounds tickled me to the marrow' (40). At a college dance in the twenties he and his friends, including Bix Beiderbecke, went into hysterics when another vocalist performed scat routines with what Carmichael called 'off color inanities in staccato [that] baffled the chaperones.' After the dance the group repaired to a local hangout where Monk Moenkhaus, a dadaistically inclined would-be musician and writer, 'composed one of his greatest lines for Bix, "*One by one a cow goes by.*"' At this, according to Carmichael, 'Bix's eyes popped, he turned his head a little to the side as he did on the bandstand when great things were coming from his horn, and murmured once again his entire vocabulary of praise and admiration. "I am not a swan"' (116–17). Twenty years later singer Ella Fitzgerald found related kicks in the nonsense of Dizzy Gillespie, particularly the verbal games he played with his friends after hours. 'It was quite an experience,' she recalled, 'and he used to always tell me, "Come up and do it with fellas." ... That to me was my education in learning how to really bop. We used to do "Ooo-Bop-Sha-Bam-Klook-a-Mop" ... and "She-bop-da-ool-ya... She-bop-da-ool-ya ..." and that fascinated me. When I felt like I could sing like that, then I felt that I was in, in. And I followed him everywhere they went' (Gillespie and Fraser: 272). Such nonsense was autotelic: It followed its own rules and ends and existed in and of itself, with semantics resting almost entirely on process. It *did* what it meant.[10] And like other 'incomprehensible' ritual language it had its own magic, implying another reality.[11]

To use jazz talk was to participate in the kicks, celebrate the separateness and solidarity of the community, demonstrate credentials in its elite fellowship, and touch upon mysteries which implied supernatural sanction.

Notes

1 'The best material on this subject is in Robert S. Gold's *Jazz Talk* (ix and passim). Other jazz dictionaries have appeared in recent decades, particularly in the forties when bop talk spread contagiously into common speech, and all of them have been out-of-date before their ink dried because of the rapid development of the argot. They include, among others, Lou Shelly's *Hepcats Jive Talk Dictionary*, Elliot Horne's *Hiptionary*, the *New Cab Calloway's Hepster's Dictionary*, and *Dan Burley's Original Handbook of Harlem Jive*.

2 See Richards' *The Philosophy of Rhetoric* and Burke's *Language As Symbolic Action* (44–84, 391).

3 For a review of the scholarship on nicknames see Barbara Kirshenblatt-Gimblett's *Speech Play* (198–201) and Alan P. Merriam and Raymond W. Mack's 'The Jazz Community' (218).

4 See Charles Keil's 'Emotion and Feeling through Music,' Richard Bauman's *Verbal Art as Performance* (10–11), and Ray L. Birdwhistell's *Introduction to Kinesics*.

5 In connection with linguistic performance see, among other things, Bauman's *Verbal Art as Performance*, Dell Hymes's 'The Breakthrough into Performance' (18–20), and Erving Goffman's *Forms of Talk*.

6 See Roger D. Abrahams' *Deep Down in the Jungle*, and Kirshenblatt-Gimblett for an excellent survey of the writing on agonistic wordplay (5–7, 184–7).

7 Abrahams, *Deep Down in the Jungle* (39–60); see also his 'Patterns of Performance in the West Indies' (164–65).

8 See Johan Huizinga's *Homo Ludens* (9, 13, 34, 50, 63–73); see also Roger Caillois' extension and qualification of Huizinga's hypothesis in *Man, Play, and Games* (4–5, 11–36). David L. Miller's *Gods and Games* includes a good review of the scholarship of play through the late sixties. The concept of flow is examined in Mihaly Csikszentmihalyi's *Beyond Boredom and Anxiety*.

9 See also Kirshenblatt-Gimblett (10–11), Michael Holquist's 'What Is a Boojum?', and Elizabeth Sewell's *The Field of Nonsense*.

10 Here I paraphrase Holquist (159, 161).

11 See Kirshenblatt-Gimblett (11) and William J. Samarin's *Tongues of Men and Angels*.

Works cited

Abrahams, Roger D. *Deep Down in the Jungle: Negro Narrative Folklore from the Streets of Philadelphia*. Rev. ed. Chicago: Aldine, 1970.
————. 'Patterns of Performance in the West Indies.' *Afro-American Anthropology: Contemporary Perspectives*. Ed. Norman E. Whitten, Jr., and John F. Szwed. New York: Free Press, 1970. 163–78.
Armstrong, Louis. *Swing That Music*. New York: Longmans, Green, 1935.
Bauman, Richard. *Verbal Art as Performance*. Rowley: Newbury, 1977.
Birdwhistell, Ray L. *Introduction to Kinesics*. Louisville: University of Louisville, 1952.

Burke, Kenneth. *Language As Symbolic Action: Essays on Life, Literature, and Method*. Berkeley: University of California Press, 1966.

Burley, Dan. *Dan Burley's Original Handbook of Harlem Jive*. New York: Burley, 1944.

Caillois, Roger. *Man, Play, and Games*. Trans. Meyer Barash. Glencoe: Free Press, 1961.

Calloway, Cab. *New Cab Calloway's Hepster's Dictionary*. New York: Calloway, 1944.

Carmichael, Hoagy. *The Stardust Road*. New York: Rinehart, 1946.

Csikszentmihalyi, Mihaly. *Beyond Boredom and Anxiety: The Experience of Play in Work and Games*. San Francisco: Jossey-Bass, 1975.

Dahl, Linda. *Stormy Weather: The Music and Lives of a Century of Jazzwomen*. New York: Pantheon, 1984.

Ellison, Ralph. *Shadow and Act*. New York: Random House, 1964.

Gillespie, Dizzy, and Al Fraser. *To Be, or Not ... To Bop: Memoirs*. Garden City: Doubleday, 1979.

Goffman, Erving. *Forms of Talk*. Philadelphia: University of Pennsylvania Press, 1981.

Gold, Robert S. *Jazz Talk*. Indianapolis: Bobbs-Merrill, 1975.

Hodes, Art, and Chadwick Hanson, eds. *Selections from the Gutter: Jazz Portraits from 'The Jazz Record'*. Berkeley: University of California Press, 1977.

Holquist, Michael. 'What Is a Boojum? Nonsense and Modernism.' *The Child's Part*. Ed. Peter Brooks. Boston: Beacon, 1972. 145–64.

Horne, Elliot. *Hiptionary*. New York: Simon and Schuster, 1963.

Huizinga, Johan. *Homo Ludens: A Study of the Play Element in Culture*. Boston: Beacon, 1955.

Hymes, Dell. 'The Breakthrough into Performance.' *Folklore: Performance and Communication*. Eds. Dan Ben-Amos and Kenneth S. Goldstein. The Hague: Mouton, 1975. 11–74.

Jablow, Alta, and Carl Withers. 'Social Sense and Verbal Nonsense in Urban Children's Folklore.' *New York Folklore Quarterly* 21(1965): 243–57.

Keil, Charles. 'Emotion and Feeling through Music.' *Rappin' and Stylin' Out: Communication in Urban Black America*. Ed. Thomas Kochman. Urbana: University of Illinois Press, 1972. 83–100.

Kirshenblatt-Gimblett, Barbara, ed. *Speech Play: Research and Resources for Studying Linguistic Creativity*. Philadelphia: University of Pennsylvania Press, 1976.

Merriam, Alan P., and Raymond W. Mack. 'The Jazz Community.' *Social Forces* 38 (1960): 211–22.

Mezzrow, Mezz, and Bernard Wolfe. *Really the Blues*. New York: Random House, 1946.

Miller, David L. *Gods and Games: Toward a Theology of Play*. Cleveland: World, 1969.

Pepper, Art and Laurie Pepper. *Straight Life: The Story of Art Pepper*. New York: Schirmer, 1979.

Reisner, Robert G. *The Jazz Titans*. Garden City: Doubleday, 1960.

Richards, I. A. *The Philosophy of Rhetoric.* New York: Oxford University Press, 1936.

Samarin, William J. 'The Language of Religion.' *Language in Religious Practice.* Ed. William J. Samarin. Rowley: Newbury, 1976. 3–13.

——. Tongues of Men and Angels: The Religious Language of Pentecostalism. New York: Macmillan, 1972.

Sewell, Elizabeth. *The Field of Nonsense.* London: Folcroft, 1970.

Shapiro, Nat, and Nat Hentoff. *Hear Me Talkin' to Ya: The Story of Jazz as Told by the Men Who Made It.* New York: Dover, 1966.

Shaw, Artie. *The Trouble with Cinderella: An Outline of Identity.* New York: Da Capo, 1979.

Shelly, Lou, ed. *Hepcats Jive Talk Dictionary.* Derby: T. W. O. Charles, 1945.

van Buren, Paul. *The Edges of Language: An Essay on the Logic of a Religion.* New York: Macmillan, 1972.

102 **Anatole Broyard** A portrait of the hipster (1948)

Source: Anatole Broyard, 'A portrait of the hipster,' *Partisan Review*, XV, 6 (June, 1948: 723–7) (excerpt).

Jive music and tea were the two most important components of the hipster's life. Music was not, as has often been supposed, a stimulus to dancing. For the hipster rarely danced; he was beyond the reach of stimuli. If he did dance, it was half parody – 'second removism' – and he danced only to the off-beat, in a morganatic one to two ratio with the music.

Actually, jive music was the hipster's autobiography, a score to which his life was the text. The first intimations of jive could be heard in the Blues. Jive's Blue Period was very much like Picasso's: it dealt with lives that were sad, stark, and isolated. It represented a relatively realistic or naturalistic stage of development.

Blues turned to jazz. In jazz, as in early, analytical cubism, things were sharpened and accentuated, thrown into bolder relief. Words were used somewhat less frequently than in Blues; the instruments talked instead. The solo instrument became the narrator. Sometimes (e.g., Cootie Williams) it came very close to literally talking. Usually it spoke passionately, violently, complainingly, against a background of excitedly pulsating drums and guitar, ruminating bass, and assenting orchestration. But, in spite of its passion, jazz was almost always coherent and its intent clear and unequivocal.

Bebop, the third stage in jive music, was analogous in some respects to synthetic cubism. Specific situations, or referents, had largely disappeared; only their 'essences' remained. By this time the hipster was no longer willing to be regarded as a primitive; bebop, therefore, was 'cerebral' music, expressing the hipster's pretensions, his desire for an imposing, full-dress body of doctrine.

Surprise, 'second-removism,' and extended virtuosity were the chief characteristics of the bebopper's style. He often achieved surprise by using a tried and true tactic of his favorite comic strip heroes:

> The 'enemy' is waiting in a room with drawn gun. The hero kicks open the door and bursts in – *not upright, in the line of fire* – but cleverly lying on the floor, from which position he triumphantly blasts away, while the enemy still aims, ineffectually, at his own expectations.

Borrowing this stratagem, the bebop soloist often entered at an unexpected altitude, came in on an unexpected note, thereby catching the listener off guard and conquering him before he recovered from his surprise.

'Second-removism' – *capping* the *squares* – was the dogma of initiation. It established the hipster as keeper of enigmas, ironical pedagogue, a self-appointed exegete. Using his *shrewd* Socratic method, he discovered the world to the naive, who still tilted with the windmills of one-level meaning. That which you heard in bebop was always *something else, not* the thing you expected; it was always negatively derived, abstraction *from,* not *to.*

The virtuosity of the bebopper resembled that of the street-corner evangelist who revels in his unbroken delivery. The remarkable run-on quality of bebop solos suggested the infinite resources of the hipster, who could improvise indefinitely, whose invention knew no end, who was, in fact, omniscient.

All the best qualities of jazz – tension, élan, sincerity, violence, immediacy— were toned down in bebop. Bebop's style seemed to consist, to a great extent, in *evading* tension, in connecting, by extreme dexterity, each phrase with another, so that nothing remained, everything was lost in a shuffle of decapitated cadences. This corresponded to the hipster's social behavior as jester, jongleur, or prestidigitator. But it was his own fate he had caused to disappear for the audience, and now the only trick he had left was the monotonous gag of pulling himself – by his own ears, grinning and gratuitous – up out of the hat.

The élan of jazz was weeded out of bebop because all enthusiasm was naive, nowhere, too simple. Bebop was the hipster's seven types of ambiguity, his Laocoön, illustrating his struggle with his own defensive deviousness. It was the disintegrated symbol, the shards, of his attitude toward himself and the world. It presented the hipster as performer, retreated to an abstract stage of *tea* and pretension, losing himself in the multiple mirrors of his fugitive chords. This conception was borne out by the surprising mediocrity of bebop orchestrations, which often had the perfunctory quality of vaudeville music, played only to announce the coming spectacle, the soloist, the great Houdini.

Bebop rarely used words, and, when it did, they were only nonsense syllables, significantly paralleling a contemporaneous loss of vitality in jive language itself. Blues and jazz were documentary in a social sense; bebop was the hipster's Emancipation Proclamation in double talk. It showed the hipster as the victim of his own system, volubly tongue-tied, spitting out his own teeth, running between the raindrops of his spattering chords, never getting wet, washed clean, baptized, or quenching his thirst. He no longer had anything relevant to himself to say – in both his musical and linguistic expression he had finally abstracted himself from his real position in society.

His next step was to abstract himself in action. *Tea* made this possible. Tea (marihuana) and other drugs supplied the hipster with an indispensable outlet. His situation was too extreme, too tense, to be satisfied with mere fantasy or animistic domination of the environment. Tea provided him with a free world to expatiate in. It had the same function as trance in Bali, where the unbearable flatness and de-emotionalization of 'waking' life is compensated for by trance ecstasy. The hipster's life, like the Balinese's, became schizoid; whenever possible, he escaped into the richer world of tea, where, for the helpless and humiliating image of a beetle on its back, he could substitute one of himself floating or flying, 'high' in spirits, dreamily dissociated, in contrast to the ceaseless pressure exerted on him in real life. Getting high was a form of artificially induced dream catharsis. It differed from *lush* (whisky) in that it didn't encourage aggression. It fostered, rather, the sentimental values so deeply lacking in the hipster's life. It became a *raison d'être*, a calling, an experience shared with fellow believers, a respite, a heaven or haven.

Under jive the external world was greatly simplified for the hipster, but his own role in it grew considerably more complicated. The function of his simplification had been to reduce the world to schematic proportions which could easily be manipulated in actual, symbolical, or ritual relationships; to provide him with a manageable mythology. Now, moving in this mythology, this tense fantasy of somewhereness, the hipster supported a completely solipsistic system. His every word and gesture now had a history and a burden of implication.

Sometimes he took his own solipsism too seriously and slipped into criminal assertions of his will. Unconsciously, he still wanted terribly to take part in the cause and effect that determined the real world. Because he had not been allowed to conceive of himself functionally or socially, he had conceived of himself *dramatically,* and, taken in by his own art, he often enacted it in actual defiance, self-assertion, impulse, or crime.

That he was a direct expression of his culture was immediately apparent in its reaction to him. The less sensitive elements dismissed him as they dismissed everything. The intellectuals *manqués,* however, the desperate barometers of society, took him into their bosom. Ransacking everything for meaning, admiring insurgence, they attributed every heroism to the hipster. He became their 'there but for the grip of my superego go I.' He was received in the Village as an oracle; his language was *the revolution of the word, the personal idiom.* He was the great instinctual man, an ambassador from the Id. He was asked to read things, look at things, feel things, taste things, and report. What was it? Was it *in there?* Was it *gone?* Was it *fine?* He was an interpreter for the blind, the deaf, the dumb, the insensible, the impotent.

With such an audience, nothing was too much. The hipster promptly became, in his own eyes, a poet, a seer, a hero. He laid claims to apocalyptic visions and heuristic discoveries when he *picked up;* he was Lazarus, come back from the dead, come back to tell them all, he would tell them all. He conspicuously consumed himself in a high flame. He cared nothing for catabolic consequences; he was so prodigal as to be invulnerable.

And here he was ruined. The frantic praise of the impotent meant recognition – *actual somewhereness* – to the hipster. He got what he wanted; he stopped protesting, reacting. He began to bureaucratize jive as a machinery for securing the actual – really the *false* – somewhereness. Jive, which had originally been a critical system, a kind of Surrealism, a personal revision of existing disparities, now grew moribundly self-conscious, smug, encapsulated, isolated from its source, from the sickness which spawned it. It grew more rigid than the institutions it had set out to defy. It became a boring routine. The hipster – once an unregenerate individualist, an underground poet, a guerrilla – had become a pretentious poet laureate. His old subversiveness, his ferocity, was now so manifestly rhetorical as to be obviously harmless. He was bought and placed in the zoo. He was *somewhere* at last – comfortably ensconced in the 52nd Street clip joints, in Carnegie Hall, and *Life*. He was *in there* ... he was back in the American womb. And it was just as unhygienic as ever.

103 **Robert G. Reisner** Cool (1959)

Source: Robert G. Reisner, 'The parlance of hip,' in *The Jazz Titans* (New York: Doubleday, 1960: 148–9) (excerpt). (Editor's title.) (First published in shorter form, *Esquire*, November, 1959.)

The entire vocabulary of hip consists of perhaps three hundred words and phrases, but one word can be used in many ways. A good example is the word 'cool.' Besides its adjectival and musical meaning, there are others. Following is an imaginary conversation between A, using King's English, and B, a Cool Cat.

A   I am moved to censure X strongly for stealing my fiancée.
B   Be cool, man. (In stopping a fight or cautioning a person against losing his temper or of the approach of the policeman, one can also say, 'Cool it.')
A   You're right. I'll forget it ... Do you want to go to the movies?
B   It's cool with me (acquiescence).
A   Do you have enough money?
B   I'm cool (in good financial condition).
A   But aren't you supposed to play with that orchestra with which you have been rehearsing?
B   I'm cooling tonight (not playing).
A   Shall I call on X and take him with us?
B   I'm cooling on him (ignoring a person or subtly snubbing him).
A   You used to have a terrible addiction to ice cream. Shall we buy some at the next corner?

B   No, I'm cooling (tapering off).
A   Then you must be feeling lean and strong?
B   I'm cool (in good shape).
A   All right, let's go.
B   Cool.

104 Amiri Baraka [LeRoi Jones] Be cool (1963)

Source: Amiri Baraka [LeRoi Jones] *Blues People: Negro Music in White America* (New York: Morrow, 1963: 212–13) (excerpt). (Editor's title)

There are many important analogies that can be made between the cool style and big-band swing, even about the evolution of the terms. *Swing*, the verb, meant a simple reaction to the music (and as it developed in verb usage, a way of reacting to anything in life). As it was formalized, and the term and the music taken further out of context, *swing* became a noun that meant a commercial popular music in cheap imitation of a kind of Afro-American music. The term *cool* in its original context meant a specific reaction to the world, a specific relationship to one's environment. It defined an attitude that actually existed. To be *cool* was, in its most accessible meaning, to be calm, even unimpressed, by what horror the world might daily propose. As a term used by Negroes, the horror, etc., might be simply the deadeningly predictable mind of white America. In a sense this calm, or stoical, repression of suffering is as old as the Negro's entrance into the slave society or the captured African's pragmatic acceptance of the gods of the captor. It is perhaps the flexibility of the Negro that has let him survive; his ability to 'be cool' – to be calm, unimpressed, detached, perhaps to make failure as secret a phenomenon as possible. In a world that is basically irrational, the most legitimate relationship to it is nonparticipation. Given this term as a consistent attitude of the Negro, in varying degrees, throughout his life in America, certain stereotypes might suddenly be reversed. The 'Steppin-fechit' rubric can perhaps be reversed if one but realizes that given his constant position at the bottom of the American social hierarchy, there was not one reason for any Negro, ever, to hurry.

The essential irony here is that, like *swing*, when the term *cool* could be applied generally to a vague body of music, that music seemed to represent almost exactly the opposite of what *cool* as a term of social philosophy had been given to mean. The term was never meant to connote the tepid new popular music of the white middle-brow middle class. On the contrary, it was exactly this America that one was supposed to 'be cool' in the face of.

105 **Jack Kerouac** Just one big orooni (1957)

Source: Jack Kerouac, *On the Road* (New York: Viking, 1959 [1957]: 166–7) (excerpt). (Editor's title)

One night we suddenly went mad together again; we went to see Slim Gaillard in a little Frisco nightclub. Slim Gaillard is a tall, thin Negro with big sad eyes who's always saying, 'Right-orooni' and 'How 'bout a little bourbon-orooni.' In Frisco great eager crowds of young semi-intellectuals sat at his feet and listened to him on the piano, guitar, and bongo drums. When he gets warmed up he takes off his shirt and undershirt and really goes. He does and says anything that comes into his head. He'll sing 'Cement Mixer, Put-ti Put-ti' and suddenly slow down the beat and brood over his bongos with fingertips barely tapping the skin as everybody leans forward breathlessly to hear; you think he'll do this for a minute or so, but he goes right on, for as long as an hour, making an imperceptible little noise with the tips of his fingernails, smaller and smaller all the time till you can't hear it any more and sounds of traffic come in the open door. Then he slowly gets up and takes the mike and says, very slowly, 'Great-orooni ... fine-ovauti ... hello-orooni ... bourbon-orooni ... all-orooni ... how are the boys in the front row making out with their girls-orooni ... orooni ... vauti ... oroonirooni ...' He keeps this up for fifteen minutes, his voice getting softer and softer till you can't hear. His great sad eyes scan the audience.

Dean stands in the back, saying, 'God! Yes!' – and clasping his hands in prayer and sweating. 'Sal, Slim knows time, he knows time.' Slim sits down at the piano and hits two notes, two Cs, then two more, then one, then two, and suddenly the big burly bass-player wakes up from a reverie and realizes Slim is playing 'C-Jam Blues' and he slugs in his big forefinger on the string and the big booming beat begins and everybody starts rocking and Slim looks just as sad as ever, and they blow jazz for half an hour, and the Slim goes mad and grabs the bongos and plays tremendous rapid Cubana beats and yells crazy things in Spanish, in Arabic, in Peruvian dialect, in Egyptian, in every language he knows, and he knows innumerable languages. Finally the set is over; each set takes two hours. Slim Gaillard goes and stands against a post, looking sadly over everybody's head as people come to talk to him. A bourbon is slipped into his hand. 'Bourbon-orooni – thank-you-ovauti ...' Nobody knows where Slim Gaillard is. Dean once had a dream that he was having a baby and his belly was all bloated up blue as he lay on the grass of a California hospital. Under a tree, with a group of coloured men, sat Slim Gaillard. Dean turned despairing eyes of a mother to him. Slim said, 'There you go-orooni.' Now Dean approached him, he approached his God; he thought Slim was God; he shuffled and bowed in front of him and asked him to join us. 'Right-orooni,' says Slim; he'll join anybody but he won't guarantee to be there with you in spirit. Dean got a table, bought drinks, and sat stiffly in front of Slim. Slim dreamed over his head. Every time Slim said, 'Orooni,' Dean said, 'Yes!' I sat there with these two madmen. Nothing happened. To Slim Gaillard the whole world was just one big orooni.

106 **Anonymous** Vipers, tea, and jazz (1946)

Source: Anonymous, 'Vipers, tea, and jazz,' *Newsweek*, 28 October 1946: 88–9.

It's 1929, and Mezz Mezzrow is standing up on The Corner – 131st Street and Seventh Avenue, Harlem. He's pushing his gauge, and the vipers are coming up, one by one:

> *First Cat:* Hey there Poppa Mezz, is you anywhere?
> *Mezz:* Man I'm down with it, stickin' like a honky.
> *First Cat:* Lay a trey on me, ole man.
> *Mezz:* Got to do it, slot.
> *First Cat:* ... Jim, this jive you got is a gasser, I'm goin' up to my dommy and

dig that new mess Pops laid down for Okeh ...

This was Harlem talk, in a time when jazz and marijuana were cutting a new pattern of life. Mezzrow, a jazz musician, born in Chicago of Russian-Jewish parents, had come to New York full of fire for New Orleans music and the Negroes who made it, was selling marijuana ('gauge') to his reefer-smoking customers ('vipers'). In plain English, this is what they said:

> *First Cat:* Hello Mezz, have you got any marijuana?
> *Mezz:* Plenty, old man, my pockets are as full as a factory hand's on payday.
> *First Cat:* Let me have three cigarettes [50 cents' worth].
> *Mezz:* I sure will, slotmouth [racial talk for big mouth] ...
> *First Cat:* Friend, this marijuana of yours is terrific, I'm going home and

listen to that new record Louis Armstrong made for the Okeh company ...

Pretty or not, this is just a sample of the life Mezzrow led from the time he learned to play the saxophone at Pontiac Reformatory when he was 16 years old. With the collaboration of Bernard Wolfe, a jazz fan and free-lance writer, Mezz, now 46, has written a book about that life and the music and marijuana and opium which colored his days and haunted his nights. 'Really the Blues' is what he calls it, and what Thomas De Quincey did in 'The Confessions of an English Opium Eater' in the early nineteenth century, Mezzrow has most certainly brought up to date.

Because of its clinical frankness and brutal honesty, 'Really the Blues' may not sit well with a great many people. For a small thing, the style is so heavily peppered with jive talk that it sometimes sounds forced. But the biggest cause for alarm could be that kids are obsessed by jazz, and if this is how jazz was born, parents may wish the world had stayed with madrigals. If the jazz era as Mezzrow describes it actually is dead, then 'Really the Blues' is an American documentary. If it is still with us, nobody can read the book and claim ignorance.

Alger Upside Down: Mezzrow grew up with almost all of jazz's legendary great. He learned his music from men like Joe (King) Oliver, Sidney Bechet, Clarence Williams, Jimmy Noone, and Louis Armstrong. He was around when Bix Beiderbecke was at his greatest. The trouble with Bix, he thinks, is that the great cornetist strayed away from the pure idiom and got too conscious of 'serious' modern music. 'He should have kept his dirty socks on,' Mezz says, 'and never started sleeping between sheets.' Of Bessie Smith, the greatest blues singer of them all, he remembers that 'when she was in a room her vitality flowed out like a cloud and stuffed the air till the walls bulged.'

Mezz learned to smoke marijuana from a 'flashy, sawed-off runt of a jockey named Patrick. The first thing I noticed was that I began to hear my saxophone as though it was inside my head ... All the notes came easing out of my horn like they'd already been made up, greased and stuffed into the bell.' (Medical experiments have shown that marijuana addicts get no real help from their 'tea.' They merely imagine they are playing better.)

There is one point Mezzrow wants to make, however. 'I never advocated that anybody should use marijuana, and I sure don't mean to start now ... I laid off five years ago ... I know of one very bad thing the tea can do to you – it can put you in jail.' As for Mezzrow's four years in a Harlem opium den, they nearly cost him his life. And nobody who reads his racking account of the cure he took would ever want to taste the dubious joys of the poppy pipe and hop-pad.

For one thing or another, Mezzrow did one term in the reformatory and two in jail. 'Every time I got in trouble, it was because I strayed away from the music. Whenever I latched on solid to the music, I flew right.' And that is the moral to 'Really the Blues,' the confessions of a 'real American success story, upside down: Horatio Alger standing on his head.'

107 **Zora Neale Hurston** Story in Harlem slang (1942)

Source: Zora Neale Hurston, 'Story in Harlem slang', in Henry Louis Gates and Sieglinde Lemke (eds), *The Complete Stories* (New York: HarperCollins, 1995: 127–38). (First published in *The American Mercury*, July, 1942.)

Wait till I light up my coal-pot and I'll tell you about this Zigaboo called Jelly. Well, all right now. He was a sealskin brown and papa-tree-top-tall. Skinny in the hips and solid built for speed. He was born with this rough-dried hair, but when he laid on the grease and pressed it down overnight with his stocking-cap, it looked just like that righteous mass, and had so many waves you got seasick from looking. Solid, man, solid!

His mama named him Marvel, but after a month on Lenox Avenue, he changed all that to Jelly. How come? Well, he put it in the street that when it came to filling that long-felt need, sugar-curing the ladies' feelings, he was in a class by himself and nobody knew his name, so he had to tell 'em. 'It must be Jelly, ''cause jam don't shake.' Therefore, his name was Jelly. That was what was on his sign. The stuff was there and it was mellow. Whenever he was challenged by a hard-head or a frail eel on the right of his title he would eye-ball the idol-breaker with a slice of ice and put on his ugly-laugh, made up of scorn and pity, and say: 'Youse just dumb to the fact, baby. If you don't know what you talking 'bout, you better ask Granny Grunt. I wouldn't mislead you, baby. I don't need to – not with the help I got.' Then he would give the pimp's sign, and percolate on down the Avenue. You can't go behind a fact like that.

So this day he was airing out on the Avenue. It had to be late afternoon, or he would not have been out of bed. All you did by rolling out early was to stir your stomach up. That made you hunt for more dishes to dirty. The longer you slept, the less you had to eat. But you can't collar nods all day. No matter how long you stay in bed, and how quiet you keep, sooner or later that big gut is going to reach over and grab that little one and start to gnaw. That's confidential right from the Bible. You got to get out on the beat and collar yourself a hot.

So Jelly got into his zoot suit with the reet pleats and got out to skivver around and do himself some good. At 132nd Street, he spied one of his colleagues on the opposite sidewalk, standing in front of a café. Jelly figured that if he bull-skated just right, he might confidence Sweet Back out of a thousand on a plate. Maybe a shot of scrap-iron or a reefer. Therefore, Jelly took a quick backward look at his shoe soles to see how his leather was holding out. The way he figured it after the peep was that he had plenty to get across and maybe do a little more cruising besides. So he stanched out into the street and made the crossing.

'Hi there, Sweet Back!' he exploded cheerfully. 'Gimme some skin!'

'Lay de skin on me, pal!' Sweet Back grabbed Jelly's outstretched hand and shook hard. 'Ain't seen you since the last time, Jelly. What's cookin'?'

'Oh, just like de bear – I ain't nowhere. Like de bear's brother, I ain't no further. Like de bear's daughter – ain't got a quarter.'

Right away, he wished he had not been so honest. Sweet Back gave him a top-superior, cut-eye look. Looked at Jelly just like a showman looks at an ape. Just as far above Jelly as fried chicken is over branch water.

'Cold in hand, hunh?' He talked down to Jelly. 'A red hot pimp like you *say* you is, ain't got no business in the barrel. Last night when I left you, you was beating up your gums and broadcasting about how hot you was. Just as hot as July-jam, you told me. What you doing cold in hand?'

'Aw, man, can't you take a joke? I was just beating up my gums when I said I was broke. How can I be broke when I got de best woman in Harlem? If I ask her for a dime, she'll give me a ten dollar bill; ask her for drink of likker, and she'll buy me a whiskey still. If I'm lying, I'm flying!'

'Gar, don't hang out dat dirty washing in my back yard! Didn't I see you last night with dat beat chick, scoffing a hot dog? Dat chick you had was beat to de heels. Boy, you ain't no good for what you live.'

'If you ain't lying now, you flying. You ain't got de first thin. You ain't got nickel one.'

Jelly threw back the long skirt of his coat and rammed his hand down into his pants pocket. 'Put your money where your mouth is!' he challenged, as he mock-struggled to haul out a huge roll. 'Back your crap with your money. I bet you five dollars!'

Sweet Back made the same gesture of hauling out non-existent money.

'I been raised in the church. I don't bet, but I'll doubt you. Five rocks!'

'I thought so!' Jelly crowed, and hurriedly pulled his empty hand out of his pocket. 'I knowed you'd back up when I drawed my roll on you.'

'You ain't drawed no roll on me, Jelly. You ain't drawed nothing but your pocket. You better stop dat boogerbooing. Next time I'm liable to make you do it.' There was a splinter of regret in his voice. If Jelly really had had some money, he might have staked him, Sweet Back, to a hot. Good Southern cornbread with a piano on a platter. Oh, well! The right broad would, or might, come along.

'Who boogerbooing?' Jelly snorted. 'Jig, I don't have to. Talking about *me* with a beat chick scoffing a hot dog! You must of not seen me, 'cause last night I was riding round in a Yellow Cab, with a yellow gal, drinking yellow likker and spending yellow money. Tell 'em 'bout me, tell 'em!'

'Git out of my face, Jelly! Dat broad I seen you with wasn't no pe-ola. She was one of them coal-scuttle blondes with hair just as close to her head as ninety-nine is to a hundred. She look-ted like she had seventy-five pounds of clear bosom, guts in her feet, and she look-ted like six months in front and nine months behind. Buy you a whiskey still! Dat broad couldn't make the down payment on a pair of sox.'

'Sweet Back, you fixing to talk out of place.' Jelly stiffened.

'If you trying to jump salty, Jelly, that's your mammy.'

'Don't play in de family, Sweet Back. I don't play de dozens. I done told you.'

'Who playing de dozens? You trying to get your hips up on your shoulders 'cause I said you was with a beat broad. One of them lam blacks.'

'Who? Me? Long as you been knowing me, Sweet Back, you ain't never seen me with nothing but pe-olas. I can get any frail eel I wants to. How come I'm up here in New York? You don't know, do you? Since youse dumb to the fact, I reckon I'll have to make you hep. I had to leave from down south 'cause Miss Anne used to worry me so bad to go with me. Who, me? Man, I don't deal in no coal. Know what I tell 'em? If they's white, they's right! If they's yellow, they's mellow. If they's brown, they can stick around. But if they come black, they better git way back! Tell 'em bout me!'

'Aw, man, you trying to show your grandma how to milk ducks. Best you can do is to confidence some kitchen-mechanic out of a dime or two. Me, I knocks de pad with them cack-broads up on Sugar Hill, and fills 'em full of melody. Man, I'm quick death and easy judgment. Youse just a home-boy, Jelly. Don't try to follow me.'

'Me follow *you*! Man, I come on like the Gang Busters, and go off like The March of Time! If dat ain't so, God is gone to Jersey City and you know. He wouldn't be messing 'round a place like that. Know what my woman done? We hauled off and went to church last Sunday, and when they passed 'round the plate for the *penny* collection, I throwed in a dollar. De man looked at me real hard for dat. Dat made my woman mad, so she called him back and throwed in a twenty dollar bill! Told him to take dat and go! Dat's what he got for looking at me 'cause I throwed in a dollar.'

'Jelly, de wind may blow and de door may slam; dat what you shooting ain't worth a damn!'

Jelly slammed his hand in his bosom as if to draw a gun. Sweet Back did the same.

'If you wants to fight, Sweet Back, the favor is in me.'

'I was deep-thinking then, Jelly. It's a good thing I ain't short-tempered. 'T'aint nothing to you, nohow. You ain't hit me yet.'

Both burst into a laugh and changed from fighting to lounging poses.

'Don't get too yaller on me, Jelly. You liable to get hurt some day.'

'You over-sports your hand your ownself. Too blamed astorperious. I just don't pay you no mind. Lay de skin on me!'

They broke their handshake hurriedly, because both of them looked up the Avenue and saw the same thing. It was a girl and they both remembered that it was Wednesday afternoon. All of the domestics off for the afternoon with their pay in their pockets. Some of them bound to be hungry for love. That meant a dinner, a shot of scrap-iron, maybe room rent and a reefer or two. Both went into the pose and put on the look.

'Big stars falling!' Jelly said out loud when she was in hearing distance. 'It must be just before day!'

'Yeah, man!' Sweet Back agreed. 'Must be a recess in Heaven – pretty angel like that out on the ground.'

The girl drew abreast of them, reeling and rocking her hips.

'I'd walk clear to Diddy-Wah-Diddy to get a chance to speak to a pretty lil' ground-angel like that,' Jelly went on.

'Aw, man, you ain't willing to go very far. Me, I'd go slap to Ginny-Gall, where they eat cow-rump, skin and all.'

The girl smiled, so Jelly set his hat and took the plunge.

'Baby,' he crooned, 'what's on de rail for de lizard?'

The girl halted and braced her hips with her hands. 'A Zigaboo down in Georgy, where I come from, asked a woman that one time and the judge told him "ninety days." '

'Georgy!' Sweet Back pretended to be elated. 'Where 'bouts in Georgy is you from? Delaware?'

'Delaware?' Jelly snorted. 'My people! My people! Free schools and dumb jigs! Man, how you going to put Delaware in Georgy? You ought to know dat's in Maryland.'

'Oh, don't try to make out youse no northerner, you! Youse from right down in 'Bam your ownself!' The girl turned on Jelly.

'Yeah, I'm *from* there and I aims to stay from there.'

'One of them Russians, eh?' the girl retorted. 'Rushed up here to get away from a job of work.'

That kind of talk was not leading towards the dinner table.

'But baby!' Jelly gasped. 'Dat shape you got on you! I bet the Coca Cola Company is paying you good money for the patent!'

The girl smiled with pleasure at this, so Sweet Back jumped in.

'I know youse somebody swell to know. Youse real people. You grins like a regular fellow.' He gave her his most killing look and let it simmer in. 'These dicky jigs round here tries to smile. S'pose you and me go inside the café here and grab a hot?'

'You got any money?' the girl asked, and stiffened like a ramrod. 'Nobody ain't pimping on me. You dig me?'

'Aw, now, baby!'

'I seen you two mullet-heads before. I was uptown when Joe Brown had you all in the go-long last night. Dat cop sure hates a pimp! All he needs to see is the pimps' salute, and he'll out with his night-stick and whip your head to the red. Beat your head just as flat as a dime!' She went off into a great blow of laughter.

'Oh, let's us don't talk about the law. Let's talk about us,' Sweet Back persisted. 'You going inside with me to holler "let one come flopping! One come grunting! Snatch one from de rear!" '

'Naw indeed!' the girl laughed harshly. 'You skillets is trying to promote a meal on me. But it'll never happen, brother. You barking up the wrong tree. I wouldn't give you air if you was stopped up in a jug. I'm not putting out a thing. I'm just like the cemetery – I'm not putting out, I'm taking in! Dig?'

'I'll tell you like the farmer told the potato – plant you now and dig you later.'

The girl made a movement to switch on off. Sweet Back had not dirtied a plate since the day before. He made a weak but desperate gesture.

'Trying to snatch my pocketbook, eh?' she blazed. Instead of running, she grabbed hold of Sweet Back's draping coat-tail and made a slashing gesture. 'How much split you want back here? If your feets don't hurry up and take you 'way from here, you'll *ride* away. I'll spread my lungs all over New York and call the law. Go ahead. Bedbug! Touch me! And I'll holler like a pretty white woman!'

The boys were ready to flee, but she turned suddenly and rocked on off with her ear-rings snapping and her heels popping.

'My people! My people!' Sweet Back sighed.

'I know you feel chewed,' Jelly said, in an effort to make it appear that he had had no part in the fiasco.

'Oh, let her go,' Sweet Back said magnanimously. 'When I see people without the periodical principles they's supposed to have, I just don't fool with 'em. What I want to steal her old pocketbook with all the money I got? I could buy a beat chick like her and give her away. I got money's mammy and Grandma change. One of my women, and not the best one I got neither, is buying me ten shag suits at one time.'

He glanced sidewise at Jelly to see if he was convincing. But Jelly's thoughts were far away. He was remembering those full, hot meals he had left back in Alabama to seek wealth and splendor in Harlem without working. He had even forgotten to look cocky and rich.

Glossary of Harlem slang

Air out – leave, flee, stroll
Astorperious – haughty, biggity
Aunt Hagar – Negro race (also Aunt Hagar's chillun)
Bad hair – Negro type hair
Balling – having fun
'Bam, and down in 'Bam – down South
Battle-hammed – badly formed about the hips

Beating up your gums – talking to no purpose

Bèluthahatchie – next station beyond Hell

Big boy – stout fellow. But in the South, it means fool and is a prime insult.

Blowing your top – getting very angry; occasionally used to mean, 'He's doing fine!'

Boogie woogie – type of dancing and rhythm. For years, in the South, it meant secondary syphilis.

Brother-in black – Negro

Bull-skating – bragging

Butt sprung – a suit or a skirt out of shape in the rear

Coal scuttle blonde – black woman

Cold – exceeding, well, etc., as in 'He was cold on that trumpet!'

Collar a hot – eat a meal

Collar a nod – sleep

Color scale – high yaller, yaller, high brown, vaseline brown, seal brown, low brown, dark black

Conk buster – cheap liquor; also an intellectual Negro

Cruising – parading down the Avenue Variations: *oozing, percolating* and *free-wheeling*. The latter implies more briskness.

Cut – doing something well

Dark black – a casually black person. Superlatives: *low black*, a blacker person; *lam black*, still blacker; and *damn black*, blackest man, of whom it is said: 'Why, lightning bugs follow him at 12 o'clock in the day, thinking it's midnight.'

Dat thing – sex of either sex

Dat's your mammy – same as, 'So is your old man.'

Diddy-Wah-Diddy – a far place, a measure of distance. (2) another suburb of Hell, built since way before Hell wasn't no bigger than Baltimore. The folks in Hell go there for a big time.

Dig – understand. 'Dig me?' means, 'Do you get me? Do you collar the jive?'

Draped down – dressed in the height of Harlem fashion; also *togged down*.

Dumb to the fact – 'You don't know what you're talking about.'

Dusty butt – cheap prostitute

Eight-rock – very black person

Every postman on his beat – kinky hair

First thing smoking – a train. 'I'm through with this town. I mean to grab the first thing smoking.'

Frail eel – pretty girl

Free schools – a shortened expression of deprecation derived from 'free schools and dumb Negroes,' sometimes embellished with 'free schools, pretty yellow teachers and dumb Negroes.'

Function – a small, unventilated dance, full of people too casually bathed

Gator-faced – long, black face with big mouth

Getting on some stiff time – really doing well with your racket

Get you to go – power, physical or otherwise, to force the opponent to run

Ginny Gall – a suburb of Hell, a long way off

Git up off of me – quit talking about me, leave me alone

Go when the wagon comes – another way of saying, 'You may be acting biggity now, but you'll cool down when enough power gets behind you.'
Good hair – Caucasian-type hair
Granny Grunt – a mythical character to whom most questions may be referred
Ground rations – sex, also *under rations*
Gum beater – a blowhard, a braggart, idle talker in general
Gut-bucket – low dive, type of music, or expression from same
Gut foot – bad case of fallen arches
Handkerchief-head – sycophant type of Negro; also an *Uncle Tom*
Hauling – fleeing on foot. 'Man! He cold hauled it!'
I don't deal in coal – 'I don't keep company with black women.'
I shot him lightly and he died politely – 'I completely outdid him.'
I'm cracking but I'm facking – 'I'm wisecracking, but I'm telling the truth'
Inky dink – very black person
Jar head – Negro man
Jelly – sex
Jig – Negro, a corrupted shortening of Zigaboo
Jook – a pleasure house, in the class of gut-bucket; now common all over the South
Jooking – playing the piano, guitar, or any musical instrument in the manner of the Jooks (pronounced like 'took'). (2) Dancing and 'scronching', ditto.
Juice – liquor
July jam – something very hot
Jump salty – get angry
Kitchen mechanic – a domestic
Knock yourself out – have a good time
Lightly, slightly and politely – doing things perfectly
Little sister – measure of hotness: 'Hot as little sister!'
Liver-lip – pendulous, thick, purple lips
Made hair – hair that has been straightened
Mammy – a term of insult. Never used in any other way by Negroes.
Miss Anne – a white woman
Mister Charlie – a white man
Monkey chaser – a West Indian
Mug man – small-time thug or gangster
My people! My people! – Sad and satiric expression in the Negro language; sad when a Negro comments on the backwardness of some members of his race; at other times, used for satiric or comic effect
Naps – kinky hair
Nearer my God to Thee – good hair
Nothing to the bear but his curly hair – 'I call your bluff,' or 'Don't be afraid of him; he won't fight.'
Now you cookin' with gas – now you're talking, in the groove, etc.
Ofay – white person
Old cuffee – Negro (genuine African word for the same thing)
Palmer House – walking flat-footed, as from fallen arches
Pancake – a humble type of Negro

Park ape – an ugly, underprivileged Negro
Peckerwood – poor and unloved class of Southern whites
Peeping through my likkers – carrying on even though drunk
Pe-ola – a very white Negro girl
Piano – spare ribs (white rib-bones suggest piano keys)
Pig meat – young girl
Pilch – house or apartment; residence
Pink toes – yellow girl
Playing the dozens – low-rating the ancestors of your opponent
Red neck – poor Southern white man
Reefer – marijuana cigaret, also *a drag*
Righteous mass or *grass* – good hair
Righteous rags – the components of a Harlem-style suit
Rug-cutter – originally a person frequenting house-rent parties, cutting up the rugs of the host with his feet; a person too cheap or poor to patronize regular dance halls; now means a good dancer.
Russian – a Southern Negro up north. 'Rushed up here,' hence a Russian.
Scrap iron – cheap liquor
Sell out – run in fear
Sender – he or she who can get you to go, i.e., has what it takes. Used often as a compliment: 'He's a solid sender!'
Smoking, or *smoking over* – looking someone over
Solid – perfect
Sooner – anything cheap and mongrel, now applied to cheap clothes, or a shabby person.
Stanch, or *stanch out* – to begin, commence, step out
Stomp – low dance, but hot man!
Stormbuzzard – shiftless, homeless character
Stroll – doing something well
Sugar Hill – northwest corner of Harlem, near Washington Heights, site of the newest apartment houses, mostly occupied by professional people. (The expression has been distorted in the South to mean a Negro red light district.)
The bear – confession of poverty
The big apple, also *the big red apple* – New York City
The man – the law, or powerful boss
Thousand on a plate – beans
Tight head – one with kinky hair
Trucking – strolling. (2) dance step from the strolling motif
V and X – five-and-ten-cent store
West Hell – another suburb of Hell, worse than the original
What's on the rail for the lizard? – suggestion for moral turpitude
Whip it to the red – beat your head until it is bloody
Woofing – aimless talk, as a dog barks on a moonlight night
Young suit – ill-fitting, too small. Observers pretend to believe you're breaking in your little brother's suit for him.
Your likker told you – misguided behavior

Zigaboo – a Negro

Zoot suit with the reet pleat – Harlem style suit, padded shoulders, 43-inch trousers at the knee with cuff so small it needs a zipper to get into, high waistline, fancy lapels, bushels of buttons, etc.

108 **Steve Allen** Crazy Red Riding Hood (1954)

Source: Steve Allen, 'Crazy Red Riding Hood,' in *Bop Fables* (New York: Simon and Schuster, 1954: 35–49).

Gather 'round, kiddies, and your old Uncle Steve will tell you another story.

Once upon a time, many, many years ago, in the Land of Oobopshebam, there lived a lovely little girl named Red Riding Hood.

To give you an idea of what a sweet thing she was, children, I'll just say that she was not only a *lovely little girl;* she was a *fine chick.*

One day Red Riding Hood's mother called her into the kitchen and said, 'Honey, your grandma is feeling the least.'

'What a drag!' said Red. 'What's the bit?'

'Hangoversville, for all I know,' said her mother. 'At any rate, I've fixed up a real wild basket of ribs and a bottle of juice. I'd like you to fall by grandma's joint this afternoon and lay the stuff on her.'

'Crazy,' said Red, and, picking up the basket, she took off for her grandmother's cottage, going by way of the deep woods.

Little did Red Riding Hood know that a big bad wolf lurked in the heart of the forest.

She had traveled but a short distance when the wolf leaped out from behind a bush and confronted her.

'Baby,' he said, grinning affably, 'gimme some skin!'

'Sorry, Daddy-o,' said Red. 'Some other time. Right now I have to make it over to my grandmother's place.'

'Square-time,' said the wolf. 'Why don't you blow your grandmother and we'll have some laughs.'

'Man,' said Red, 'Cootie left the Duke and I'm leavin' you. For the time being we've had it.'

'Mama, I'm hip,' said the wolf. 'Dig you later.'

So saying, the wolf bounded off through the forest and was soon lost to sight. But his evil mind was at work. Unbeknownst to Red Riding Hood, he took a short cut through the trees and in a few minutes stood panting before the helpless old grandmother's cottage.

Quietly he knocked at the door.

'That's a familiar beat,' said Red Riding Hood's grandmother. 'Who's out there?'

'Western Union,' lied the wolf. 'I have a special invitation to Dizzy's opening at Birdland.'

'Wild,' said the grandmother, hobbling across the room.

Imagine her horror when, on opening the door, she perceived the wolf! In an instant he had leaped into the house, gobbled her up and disguised himself in her night clothes.

Hearing Red Riding Hood's footsteps on the stones of the garden path, he leaped into the poor old lady's bed, pulled the covers up to his chin and smiled toward the door in a grandmotherly way.

When little Red Riding Hood knocked he said, 'Hit me again. Who goes?'

'It's me, Gram,' said Red Riding Hood. 'Mother heard you were feeling pretty beat. She thought you might like to pick up on some ribs.'

'Nutty,' said the wolf. 'Fall in.'

Red Riding Hood opened the door, stepped inside and looked around the room. 'Wowie,' she said. 'What a crazy pad!'

'Sorry I didn't have time to straighten the joint up before you got here,' said the wolf. 'But you know how it is. What's in the basket?'

'Oh, the same old jazz,' said Red.

'Baby,' said the wolf, 'don't put it down.'

'I have to,' said Red. 'It's getting heavy.'

'I didn't come here to play straight,' said the wolf. 'Let's open the basket. I've got eyes.'

'I'm hip,' said Red, 'not to mention the fact that you can say that again. Grandma, what frantic eyes you have!'

'The better to dig you with, my dear,' said the wolf.

'And, Grandma,' said Red, 'I don't want to sound rude, but what a long nose you have!'

'Yeah,' said the wolf. 'It's a gasser.'

'And, Grandma,' said Red, 'your ears are the most, to say the least.'

'What is this,' snapped the wolf, 'face inspection? I know my ears aren't the greatest, but whadda ya gonna do? Let's just say somebody goofed!'

'You know something?' little Red Riding Hood said, squinting suspiciously at the furry head on the pillow. 'I don't want to sound square or anything, but you don't look like my grandmother at all. You look like some other cat.'

'Baby,' said the wolf, 'you're flippin'!'

'No, man,' insisted Red. 'I just dug your nose again and it's too much. I don't want to come right out and ask to see your card, you understand, but where's my grandma?'

The wolf stared at Red Riding Hood for a long, terrible moment. 'Your grandma,' he said, 'is gone.'

'I'm hip,' said Red. 'She *is* the swingin'est, but let's take it from the top again. Where is she?'

'She cut out,' said the wolf.

'Don't hand me that jazz,' said Red, whereupon the wolf, being at the end of his patience, leaped out of bed and began to chase poor Red Riding Hood about the room.

Little did he know that the wolf season had opened that very day and that a passing hunter could hear little Red Riding Hood's frantic cry for help. Rushing into the cottage, the brave hunter dispatched the wolf with one bullet. 'Buster,' said Red gratefully, 'your timing was like the end, ya know?' And so it was.

109 Mary Lou Williams and Milton Orent In the Land of Oo-Bla-Dee (1949)

Source: Mary Lou Williams and Milton Orent, 'In the Land of Oo-Bla-Dee.' Lyrics (slightly variant) as sung and recorded by Joe Carroll, with Dizzy Gillespie Orchestra, 1949 (RCA Victor RD-7827 [1967]).

I met a beautiful princess
In the Land of Oo-Bla-Dee.
She smiled and said, 'Oo-ba-del-ia,'
Meaning, 'You appeal to me.'
I said, 'Oo-bo-del-ia la-bin-doo,' with pride
Oo-oo-del-ia la-bin-doo, let's take a ride,'
In the land of Oo-Bla-Dee, Oo-Bla-Dee.

She drove me right to her castle,
In the Land of Oo-Bla-Dee.
And there I met her two sisters,
Bloo-ey-Da and Doo-ey-Blee.
Bloo-ey-Da without a doubt was twice my size,
Doo-ey-Blee, the other sister, had three eyes.
And the two had eyes for me,
Oo-Bla-Dee.

They led me right to the altar
In the Land of Oo-Bla-Dee.
I had a very bad feeling,
Things did not look right to me.
So before I said 'I do' I looked aside,
They had pulled a switcheroo,
They changed the bride.
Oh, they can't do that to me,
Oo-Bla-Dee ... [Dizzy Gillespie: trumpet solo]

I hopped the western bound freighter,
From the Land of Oo-Bla-Dee.
I jumped when I saw the princess,
Who was waiting there for me.
Now we say, 'O-del-ia la-bee-doo blee-oo,'
Meaning, 'I will always be in love with you.'
Oh, it happened in Bla-Dee, Oo-Bla-Dee.

110 **Lawrence Ferlinghetti** Sometime during eternity (1958)

Source: Lawrence Ferlinghetti, 'Sometime during eternity,' in *A Coney Island of the Mind* (New York: New Directions, 1958: 15–16).

Sometime during eternity
$\qquad\qquad$ some guys show up
and one of them
$\qquad$ who shows up real late
$\qquad\qquad$ is a kind of carpenter
from some square-type place
$\qquad\qquad$ like Galilee
and he starts wailing
$\qquad\qquad$ and claiming he is hip
to who made heaven
$\qquad$ and earth
$\qquad\qquad$ and that the cat
who really laid it on us
$\qquad$ is his Dad

And moreover
$\quad$ he adds
$\qquad$ It's all writ down
$\qquad\qquad$ on some scroll-type parchments
which some henchmen
$\qquad$ leave lying around the Dead Sea somewheres
$\qquad$ a long time ago
$\qquad\qquad$ and which you won't even find
for a coupla thousand years or so
$\qquad\qquad$ or at least for
nineteen hundred and fortyseven
$\qquad\qquad$ of them
$\qquad$ to be exact
$\qquad\qquad$ and even then
nobody really believes them
$\qquad\qquad$ or me
$\qquad\qquad$ for that matter

You're hot
$\qquad$ they tell him
And they cool him
They stretch him on the Tree to cool
$\qquad$ And everybody after that
$\qquad\qquad$ is always making models
$\qquad$ of this Tree
$\qquad\qquad$ with Him hung up
and always crooning His name
$\qquad\qquad$ and calling Him to come down

and sit in
on their combo
as if he is *the* king cat
who's got to blow
or they can't quite make it
Only he don't come down
from His Tree
Him just hang there
on His Tree
looking real Petered out
and real cool
and also
according to a roundup
of late world news
from the usual unreliable sources
real dead

111 Cab Calloway *The New Cab Calloway's Hepster's Dictionary: Language of Jive* (1944)

Source: Cab Calloway, *The New Cab Calloway's Hepster's Dictionary: Language of Jive* (1944), in Cab Calloway and Bryant Rollins, *Of Minnie the Moocher & Me* (New York: Thomas Crowell, 1976: 252–61).

A

A HUMMER (n.): exceptionally good. Ex., 'Man, that boy is a hummer.'

AIN'T COMING ON THAT TAB (v.): won't accept the proposition. Usually abbr. to 'I ain't coming.'

ALLIGATOR (n.): jitterbug.

APPLE (n.): the big town, the main stem, Harlem.

ARMSTRONGS (n.): musical notes in the upper register, high trumpet notes.

B

BARBECUE (n.): the girl friend, a beauty.

BARRELHOUSE (adj.): free and easy.

BATTLE (n.): a very homely girl, a crone.

BEAT (adj.): (1) tired, exhausted. Ex., 'You look beat' or 'I feel beat.' (2) lacking anything. Ex., 'I am beat for my cash'; 'I am beat to my socks' (lacking everything).

BEAT IT OUT (v.): play it hot, emphasize the rhythm.

BEAT UP (adj.): sad, uncomplimentary, tired.

BEAT UP THE CHOPS (or the gums) (v.): to talk, converse, be loquacious.

BEEF (v.): to say, to state. Ex., 'He beefed to me that, etc.'

BIBLE (n.): the gospel truth. Ex., 'It's the bible!'

BLACK (n.): night.

BLACK AND TAN (n.): dark and light colored folks. Not colored and white folks as erroneously assumed.

BLEW THEIR WIGS (adj.): excited with enthusiasm, gone crazy.

BLIP (n.): something very good. Ex., 'That's a blip'; 'She's a blip.'

BLOW THE TOP (v.): to be overcome with emotion (delight). Ex., 'You'll blow your top when you hear this one.'
BOOGIE-WOOGIE (n.): harmony with accented bass.
BOOT (v.): to give. Ex., 'Boot me that glove.'
BREAK IT UP (v.): to win applause, to stop the show.
BREE (n.): girl.
BRIGHT (n.): day.
BRIGHTNIN' (n.): daybreak.
BRING DOWN: (1) (n.), something depressing. Ex., 'That's a bring down.' (2) (v.). Ex., 'That brings me down.'
BUDDY GHEE (n.): fellow.
BUST YOUR CONK (v.): apply yourself diligently, break your neck.

C

CANARY (n.): girl vocalist.
CAPPED (v.): outdone, surpassed.
CAT (n.): musician in swing band.
CHICK (n.): girl.
CHIME (n.): hour. Ex., 'I got in at six chimes.'
CLAMBAKE (n.): ad lib session, every man for himself, a jam session not in the groove.
CHIRP (n.): female singer.
COGS (n.): sun glasses.
COLLAR (v.): to get, to obtain, to comprehend. Ex., 'I gotta collar me some food'; 'Do you collar this jive?'
COME AGAIN (v.): try it over, do better than you are doing, I don't understand you.
COMES ON LIKE GANGBUSTERS (or like test pilot) (v.): plays, sings, or dances in a terrific manner, par excellence in any department. Sometimes abbr. to 'That singer really comes on!'
COP (v.): to get, to obtain (see collar; knock).
CORNY (adj.): old-fashioned, stale.
CREEPS OUT LIKE THE SHADOW (v.): 'comes on,' but in smooth, suave, sophisticated manner.
CRUMB CRUSHERS (n.): teeth.
CUBBY (n.): room, flat, home.

CUPS (n.): sleep. Ex., 'I gotta catch some cups.'
CUT OUT (v.): to leave, to depart. Ex., 'It's time to cut out'; 'I cut out from the joint in the early bright.'
CUT RATE (n.): a low, cheap person. Ex., 'Don't play me cut rate, Jack!'

D

DICTY (adj.): high-class, nifty, smart.
DIG (v.): (1) meet. Ex., 'I'll plant you now and dig you later.' (2) look, see. Ex., 'Dig the chick on your left duke.' (3) comprehend, understand. Ex., 'Do you dig this jive?'
DIM (n.): evening.
DIME NOTE (n.): ten-dollar bill.
DOGHOUSE (n.): bass fiddle.
DOMI (n.): ordinary place to live in. Ex., 'I live in a righteous domi.'
DOSS (n.): sleep. Ex., 'I'm a little beat for my doss.'
DOWN WITH IT (adj.): through with it.
DRAPE (n.): suit of clothes, dress, costume.
DREAMERS (n.): bed covers, blankets.
DRY-GOODS (n.): same as drape.
DUKE (n.): hand, mitt.
DUTCHESS (n.): girl.

E

EARLY BLACK (n.): evening.
EARLY BRIGHT (n.): morning.
EVIL (adj.): in ill humor, in a nasty temper.

F

FALL OUT (v.): to be overcome with emotion. Ex., 'The cats fell out when he took that solo.'
FEWS AND TWO (n.): money or cash in small quantity.
FINAL (v.): to leave, to go home. Ex., 'I finaled to my pad' (went to bed); 'We copped a final' (went home).
FINE DINNER (n.): a good-looking girl.
FOCUS (v.): to look, to see.
FOXY (v.): shrewd.
FRAME (n.): the body.
FRAUGHTY ISSUE (n.): a very sad message, a deplorable state of affairs.

FREEBY (n.): no charge, gratis. Ex., 'The meal was a freeby.'

FRISKING THE WHISKERS (v.): what the cats do when they are warming up for a swing session.

FROLIC PAD (n.): place of entertainment, theater, nightclub.

FROMPY (adj.): a frompy queen is a battle or faust.

FRONT (n.): a suit of clothes.

FRUITING (v.): fickle, fooling around with no particular object.

FRY (v.): to go to get hair straightened.

G

GABRIELS (n.): trumpet players.

GAMMIN' (adj.): showing off, flirtatious.

GASSER (n., adj.): sensational. Ex., 'When it comes to dancing, she's a gasser.'

GATE (n.): a male person (a salutation), abbr. for 'gate-mouth.'

GET IN THERE (an exclamation): go to work, get busy, make it hot, give all you've got.

GIMME SOME SKIN (v.): shake hands.

GLIMS (n.): the eyes.

GOT YOUR BOOTS ON: you know what it is all about, you are a hep cat, you are wise.

GOT YOUR GLASSES ON: you are ritzy or snooty, you fail to recognize your friends, you are up-stage.

GRAVY (n.): profits.

GREASE (v.): to eat.

GROOVY (adj.): fine. Ex., 'I feel groovy.'

GROUND GRIPPERS (n.): new shoes.

GROWL (n.): vibrant notes from a trumpet.

GUT BUCKET (adj.): low-down music

GUZZLIN' FOAM (v.): drinking beer.

H

HARD (adj.): fine, good. Ex., 'That's a hard tie you're wearing.'

HARD SPIEL (n.): interesting line of talk.

HAVE A BALL (v.): to enjoy yourself, stage a celebration. Ex., 'I had myself a ball last night.'

HEP CAT (n.): a guy who knows all the answers, understands jive.

HIDE-BEATER (n.): a drummer (see skin-beater).

HINCTY (adj.): conceited, snooty.

HIP (adj.): wise, sophisticated, anyone with boots on. Ex., 'She's a hip chick.'

HOME-COOKING (n.): something very nice (see fine dinner).

HOT (adj.): musically torrid; before swing, tunes were hot or bands were hot.

HYPE (n., v.): build up for a loan, wooing a girl, persuasive talk.

I

ICKY (n.): one who is not hip, a stupid person, can't collar the jive.

IGG (v.): to ignore someone. Ex., 'Don't igg me!'

IN THE GROOVE (adj.): perfect, no deviation, down the alley.

J

JACK (n.): name for all male friends (see gate; pops).

JAM: (1) (n.): improvised swing music. Ex., 'That's swell jam.' (2) (v.): to play such music. Ex., 'That cat surely can jam.'

JEFF (n.): a pest, a bore, an icky.

JELLY (n.): anything free, on the house.

JITTERBUG (n.): a swing fan.

JIVE (n.): Harlemese speech.

JOINT IS JUMPING: the place is lively, the club is leaping with fun.

JUMPED IN PORT (v.): arrived in town.

K

KICK (n.): a pocket. Ex., 'I've got five bucks in my kick.'

KILL ME (v.): show me a good time, send me.

KILLER-DILLER (n.): a great thrill.

KNOCK (v.): give. Ex., 'Knock me a kiss.'

KOPASETIC (adj.): absolutely okay, the tops.

L

LAMP (v.): to see, to look at.

LAND O'DARKNESS (n.): Harlem.

LANE (n.): a male, usually a nonprofessional.

LATCH ON (v.): grab, take hold, get wise to.

LAY SOME IRON (v.): to tap dance. Ex., 'Jack, you really laid some iron that last show!'

LAY YOUR RACKET (v.): to jive, to sell an idea, to promote a proposition.

LEAD SHEET (n.): a topcoat.

LEFT RAISE (n.): left side. Ex., 'Dig the chick on your left raise.'

LICKING THE CHOPS (v.): see frisking the whiskers.

LICKS (n.): hot musical phrases.

LILY WHITES (n.): bed sheets.

LINE (n.): cost, price, money. Ex., 'What is the line on this drape' (how much does this suit cost)? 'Have you got the line in the mouse' (do you have the cash in your pocket)? (Also, in replying, all figures are doubled. Ex., 'This drape is line forty' (this suit costs twenty dollars).)

LOCK UP (v.): to acquire something exclusively. Ex., 'He's got that chick locked up'; 'I'm gonna lock up that deal.'

M

MAIN KICK (n.): the stage.

MAIN ON THE HITCH (n.): husband.

MAIN QUEEN (n.): favorite girl friend, sweetheart.

MAN IN GRAY (n.): the postman.

MASH ME A FIN (command): Give me $5.

MELLOW (adj.): all right, fine. Ex., 'That's mellow, Jack.'

MELTED OUT (adj.): broke.

MESS (n.): something good. Ex., 'That last drink was a mess.'

METER (n.): quarter, twenty-five cents.

MEZZ (n.): anything supreme, genuine. Ex., 'This is really the mezz.'

MITT POUNDING (n.): applause.

MOO JUICE (n.): milk.

MOUSE (n.): pocket. Ex., 'I've got a meter in the mouse.'

MUGGIN' (v.): making 'em laugh, putting on the jive. 'Muggin' lightly,' light staccato swing; 'muggin' heavy,' heavy staccato swing.

MURDER (n.): something excellent or terrific. Ex., 'That's solid murder, gate!'

N

NEIGHO, POPS: Nothing doing, pal.

NICKEL NOTE (n.): five-dollar bill.

NICKLETTE (n.): automatic phonograph, music box.

NIX OUT (v.): to eliminate, get rid of. Ex., 'I nixed that chick out last week'; 'I nixed my garments' (undressed).

NOD (n.): sleep. Ex., 'I think I'll cop a nod.'

O

OFAY (n.): white person.

OFF THE COB (adj.): corny, out of date.

OFF-TIME JIVE (n.): a sorry excuse, saying the wrong thing.

ORCHESTRATION (n.): an overcoat.

OUT OF THE WORLD (adj.): perfect rendition. Ex., 'That sax chorus was out of the world.'

OW! an exclamation with varied meaning. When a beautiful chick passes by, it's 'Ow!'; and when someone pulls an awful pun, it also is 'Ow!'

P

PAD (n.): bed.

PECKING (n.): a dance introduced at the Cotton Club in 1937.

PEOLA (n.): a light person, almost white.

PIGEON (n.): a young girl.

POPS (n.): salutation for all males (see gate; Jack).

POUNDERS (n.): policemen.

Q

QUEEN (n.): a beautiful girl.

R

RANK (v.): to lower.

READY (adj.): 100 per cent in every way. Ex., 'That fried chicken was ready.'

RIDE (v.): to swing, to keep perfect tempo in playing or singing.

RIFF (n.): hot lick, musical phrase.

RIGHTEOUS (adj.): splendid, okay. Ex., 'That was a righteous queen I dug you with last black.'

ROCK ME (v.): send me, kill me, move me with rhythm.

RUFF (n.): quarter, twenty-five cents.

RUG CUFFER (n.): a very good dancer, an active jitterbug.

S

SAD (adj.): very bad. Ex., 'That was the saddest meal I ever collared.'

SADDER THAN A MAP (adj.): terrible. Ex., 'That man is sadder than a map.'

SALTY (adj.): angry, ill-tempered.

SAM GOT YOU: you've been drafted into the army.

SEND (v.): to arouse the emotions (joyful). Ex., 'That sends me!'

SET OF SEVEN BRIGHTS (n.): one week.

SHARP (adj.): neat, smart, tricky. Ex., 'That hat is sharp as a tack.'

SIGNIFY (v.): to declare yourself, to brag, to boast.

SKIN-BEATER (n.): drummer (see hide-beater).

SKINS (n.): drums.

SKY PIECE (n.): hat.

SLAVE (v.): to work, whether arduous labor or not.

SLIDE YOUR JIB (v.): to talk freely.

SNATCHER (n.): detective.

SO HELP ME: it's the truth, that's a fact.

SOLID (adj.): great, swell, okay.

SOUNDED OFF (v.): began a program or conversation.

SPOUTIN' (v.): talking too much.

SQUARE (n.): an unhep person (see icky; Jeff).

STACHE (v.): to file, to hide away, to secrete.

STAND ONE UP (v.): to play one cheap, to assume one is a cut-rate.

TO BE STASHED (v.): to stand or remain.

SUSIE-Q (n.): a dance introduced at the Cotton Club in 1936.

T

TAKE IT SLOW (v.): be careful.

TAKE OFF (v.): play a solo.

THE MAN (n.): the law.

THREADS (n.): suit, dress or costume (see drape; dry-goods).

TICK (n.): minute, moment. Ex., 'I'll dig you in a few ticks.' Also, ticks are doubled in accounting time, just as money is doubled in giving 'line.' Ex., 'I finaled to the pad this early bright at tick twenty' (I got to bed this morning at ten o'clock).

TIMBER (n.): toothpick.

TO DRIBBLE (v.): to stutter. Ex., 'He talked in dribbles.'

TOGGED TO THE BRICKS: dressed to kill, from head to toe.

TOO MUCH (adj.): term of highest praise. Ex., 'You are too much!'

TRICKERATION (n.): struttin' your stuff, muggin' lightly and politely.

TRILLY (v.): to leave, to depart. Ex., 'Well, I guess I'll trilly.'

TRUCK (v.): to go somewhere. Ex., 'I think I'll truck on down to the ginmill (bar).'

TRUCKING (n.): a dance introduced at the Cotton Club in 1933.

TWISTER TO THE SLAMMER (n.): the key to the door.

TWO CENTS (n.): two dollars.

U

UNHEP (adj.): not wise to the jive, said of an icky, a Jeff, a square.

V

VINE (n.): a suit of clothes.

V-8 (n.): a chick who spurns company, is independent, is not amenable.

W

WHAT'S YOUR STORY? What do you want? What have you got to say for yourself? How are tricks? What excuse can you offer? Ex., 'I don't know what his story is.'

WHIPPED UP (adj.): worn out, exhausted, beat for your everything.

WREN (n.): a chick, a queen.

WRONG RIFF: the wrong thing said or

done. Ex., 'You're coming up on the wrong riff.'

Y

YARDDOG (n.): uncouth, badly attired, unattractive male or female.
YEAH, MAN: an exclamation of assent.

Z

ZOOT (adj.): overexaggerated as applied to clothes.
ZOOT SUIT (n.): overexaggerated clothes.

112 **Dan Burley** Advanced reading in jive – Sam D. Home's soliloquy (1944)

Source: from Dan Burley, 'The technique of jive,' in *Dan Burley's Original Handbook of Harlem Jive* (1944). Reprinted Alan Dundes (ed.), *Mother Wit from the Laughing Barrel: Readings in the Interpretation of Afro-American Folklore* (Englewood Cliffs, NJ: Prentice-Hall, 1973: 219–21).

A Square ain't nothing but a Lane, and a Lane ain't nothing but a Rum, and a Rum ain't nothing but a Perfect Lamb; and a Perfect Lamb comes on like the Goodwill Hour – and tips away, Jackson, like the Widder Brown. If I was booted, truly booted, I'd lay a solid beg on my righteous scribe, and knock a scoff on the zoom on Turkey Day. In fact, I'd cop a trot to her frantic dommy, lay a mellow ring on the heavy buzz, give her Poppa Stoppa the groovy bend; and then lay my trill into the scoff-pad, hitch one of those most anxious lilywhites around my stretcher; cop a mellow squat and start forking. But my thinkpad is a drag, when it comes to a triple-quick-click; and that's why I'm out here eating fish-heads and scrambling for the gills, instead of being a round-tripper, good for a double-deuce of bags every play.

Every time I shoot for the side-pocket, I scratch. I hunch the pinball layout, Jack, and it's an unhipped tilt. I'm a true Rum: A Perfect Lamb that ain't been clipped. Instead of my groundpads being spread under my bantam's heavy oak, scarfing down some solid scarf, I'm out here with Mister Hawkins, wringling and twisting, ducking and dodging, and skulking close to the buildings: jumping to knock a stool in the greasy spoon and slice my chops on a bowl of beef and shinny beans with the deuce of demons I knocked on that last beg on the stem. Lawd! Who shall it be? Peace, Father, it's truly wonderful, or Uncle Sam Here I Come?

Picking up from the sentence following the one about the Goodwill Hour, Sam D. Home, in his soliloquy, really said:

'If I understood things and was really smart, I'd have asked my girl friend to invite me to dinner on Thanksgiving Day. In fact, right now, I'd run to her comfortable home, ring the bell, bow to her father, and walk into the dining room, where I'd put a napkin around my neck, take a seat and start eating. But my thinking is faulty when it comes to quick thinking, that is why I'm out on the street trying to promote a free dinner, instead of hitting home runs like good ballplayers do. Every time I put forth an effort, I fail to achieve my purpose. Everything I do turns out wrong. I'm really a simple fellow playing in hard luck. Instead of having my feet under my girl friend's dinner table eating a good dinner, I'm out here in the wintry gale, trying to make my way without freezing to death to the lunch wagon for a bowl of chili for 20 cents I just borrowed from somebody on the Avenue. What shall it be, Father Divine's Restaurant and Heavenly Kingdom, or do I join the United States Army?'

So contagious is the inclination to talk in this jive lingo that already certain aspects of it have and are emerging in the commercial world, in the movies, the daily comic sheets, over the radio and on popular recordings. Orson Welles, the playwright-actor, told the author one of his plays will have a jive theme. The movie hit, 'Second Chorus' with Fred Astaire and Artie Shaw, featured an overdose of jive talk and jive dancing, freshly imported from Harlem. Popular comic strip characters in 'Terry and the Pirates' were found talking in a really 'hipped' manner to escape from a dire predicament.

Some high-brow psychiatrist might say that jive is the language of the 'infantile-extrovert,' but be that as it may, one can wander up Harlem way, night or day; pause for a bus or a cab, and one's ears are suddenly assailed by a bombardment of 'Whatcha know, ole man?' 'I'm like the bear, just ain't nowhere, but here to dig for Miss St. Clair' ... 'An' she laid the twister to her slammer on me, ole man, understand, and I dug the jive straight up an' down, three ways, sides and flats' ... Or: 'Gimme some skin, ole man. That's righteous. Jackson, truly reecheous. In fact, it's roacheous. I'm gonna put that right in my pocket so it won't get wet' ... 'I'm playing the dozens with my uncle's cousins; eatin' onions an' wiping my eyes' ... 'The heavy sugar I'm laying down, ole man, understand, is harder than Norwegian lard. Lay a little of that fine skin on me, studhoss.'

Such jargon is reminiscent of Tibet, Afghanistan, as unintelligible to the uninitiate as listening to a foreign dictator's harangue over a shortwave broadcast. One is confused and bewildered over this seemingly incomprehensible idiom. You forget about taking a cab or bus, and, lured by a sense of the occult and exotic, edge in closer to hear more, completely enchanted by the scene which greets your eyes – fellows in wide-brimmed fuzzy hats, pistol-cuffed trousers with balloon-like knees and frock-like coats the length of a clergyman's; you listen in breathless fascination as they exchange verbal bombshells, rhymed and lyrical, and although you do not know it, you are listening to the new poetry of the proletariat.

You glance about you in dismay. What has happened to the Harlem you thought you knew so well, or about which you read so much? Where are the poets, the high-brow intellectuals, the doctor-writers, and musicians, who spoke Harlem's language in the days of the Black Renaissance – that period ushered in by Carl Van Vechten and his 'Nigger Heaven'? Harlem, apparently, has side-tracked her intellectuals. So, although you are unaware of it as yet, they have invented this picturesque new language, *the language of action,* which comes from the bars, the dance-halls, the prisons, honkey-tonks, gin mills, etc., wherever people are busy living, loving, fighting, working or conniving to get the better of one another.

You tap your nearest companion, a serious-looking man in the crowd, on the shoulder and ask him, 'What kind of colored folk are these? What are they talking about?'

His answer is this, 'They're talking the new jive language, my friend.' As you listen to further parlance on the part of the zoot-suiters, gradually it dawns upon you that you are listening to the essence of slang gleaned from all nations, the cities, hamlets, and villages. You're listening to a purifying process in which expressions are tried and discarded, accepted or rejected, as the case may be. They are discussing politics, religion, science, war, dancing, business, love, economics, and the occult. They're talking of these things in a manner that those, orthodox in education and culture, cannot understand. This jive language may be a defense mechanism, or it may only be a method of deriving pleasure from something the uninitiated cannot understand. Little of it appears in print.

In a thousand and one places – poolrooms, night-clubs, dressing-rooms, back stage, kitchens, ballrooms, theatre lobbies, gymnasiums, jail cells, buffet flats, cafés, bars and grills – on a thousand and one street corners, when the sun shines warmly and they have a half-hour to kill, creators of the new Harlemese are busily adding words and expressions to their rapidly growing vocabulary of Jive. No aerial gunner ever had more ammunition for emergency use than a jiver's repertoire when encountering his gang. Each new phrase, each rhyme is received with delight. Like copyreaders and editorial writers on newspapers, jive addicts take infinite care of their latest brain-child. They trim and polish, rearrange, revise, reshuffle and recast certain phrases until they have the best and most concise expression that can be devised. Reputations as 'jivers' are eagerly sought, and advanced apostles, real masters of the jargon, are looked up to with awe and admiration by their less accomplished disciples.

113 **King Pleasure [Clarence Beeks]** Parker's mood (1953)

Source: King Pleasure [Clarence Beeks], 'Parker's Mood' (1953). Song lyrics written by singer King Pleasure [Clarence Beeks], recorded 1953 (Prestige 880), using Charlie Parker blues improvisation (1948) of same title.

Come with me,
If you want to go to Kansas City.

I'm feeling lowdown and blue,
My heart's full of sorrow.

Don't hardly know what to do.
Where will I be tomorrow?

Going to Kansas City.
Want to go too?
No, you can't make it with me.
Going to Kansas City,
Sorry that I can't take you.

When you see me coming,
Raise your window high.
When you see me leaving, baby,
Hang your head and cry.

I'm afraid there's nothing in this cream, this dreamy town
A honky-tonky monkey-woman can do.
She'd only bring herself down.

So long everybody!
The time has come
And I must leave you
So if I don't ever see your smiling face again:
Make a promise you'll remember
Like a Christmas Day in December
That I told you
All through thick and thin
On up until the end
Parker's been your friend.

Don't hang your head
When you see, when you see those six pretty horses pulling me.
Put a twenty dollar silver-piece on my watchchain,
Look at the smile on my face,
And sing a little song
To let the world know I'm really free.
Don't cry for me,
'Cause I'm going to Kansas City. [John Lewis: piano solo]

Come with me,
If you want to go to Kansas City.

114 **Angela Jackson** Make/n my music (1973)

Source: Angela Jackson, 'Make/n my music,' in *Voo Doo/Love Magic* (Chicago: Third World Press, 1973: 8–9).

my colored child / hood wuz mostly music
   celebrate / n be / n young an Black (but we din know it)

scream / n up the wide alleys
an holler / n afta the walla-mellon-man.

sun-rest time
my mama she wuz yell / n
  (all ova the block
       sang / n fa us
  ta git our butts in
                side.

we grew up run / n jazz rhythms
      an watch / n mr. wiggins downstairs
       knock the blues up side   his woman's
                 head
we rocked.   an the big boys they snuck
an rolled   dice /   in the hallways   at nite.

i mean. we laughed love.   an the teen
    agers they jus slow dragged thru smokey
                tunes.
    life wuz a ordinary miracle   an
    have / n fun wuzn no temptation

    we jus dun it.
an   u know
i think we grew.   thru them spirit-uals
    the saint-tified folks wud git happy off
    of even if we *wuz* jus clown / n
    when we danced the grizzly bear an
    felt good when the reverend
    wid the black cadillac   said:

    let the holy ghost come in
    side you

that music make you / feel sooo / good!

any how   i wuz a little colored girl
          then...

so far
my Black woman / hood ain't been noth / n but music

     i found billie
        holiday   an learned
              how
              to cry.

Riff 9

Blow as deep as you want ... tap from yourself the song of yourself, *blow! – now! – your* way. (Jack Kerouac, 'Essentials of Spontaneous Prose,' *Evergreen Review*, 1958)

When Lester came out he played very melodic ... He was always telling a story and Bird did the same thing. That kind of musical philosophy is what I try to do because telling a story is, I think, where it's at. (Dexter Gordon, quoted in Marcela Breton [ed.], *Hot and Cool: Jazz Short Stories*, 1991)

Most novels about jazz read as though their writers deliberately took pains to annoy their poor readers ... Somehow, most fiction with jazz as its theme just doesn't ring true. (Eddie Condon and Richard Gehman [eds], *Eddie Condon's Treasury of Jazz*, 1956)

A profane and powerful novel of life and love in the frantic world of jazz ... [with] the unbridled passions of ... uninhibited musicians, whose world is clouded by lust and marijuana smoke. (Edwin Gilbert, *The Hot and the Cool*, 1953)

A jazz poem is any poem that has been informed by jazz music. The influence can be in the subject of the poem or in the rhythms, but one should not necessarily exclude the other. (Sascha Feinstein, *Jazz Poetry: From the 1920s to the Present*, 1997)

> Making jazz swing in
> Seventeen syllables AIN'T
> No square poet's job.

(Etheridge Knight, 'Haiku,' in *The Essential Etheridge Knight*, 1986)

Chorus IX
Spontaneous Bop Prosody: Jazz and literature
(word, text, performance)

In *Drifting on a Read* (1999: ix), Michael Jarrett describes 'jazzography' as 'all writing that finds a referent or inspiration in jazz.' Within this broader definition, the relation between jazz and writing can usefully focus on the presence/effect of a jazz aesthetic in *literature*, or the *literary* dimensions of jazz. This synergism – a conjunction of music, text, word and performance – is best examined in literary forms with the closest proximity to jazz: autobiography (**Chorus VII**), fiction and poetry. **Chorus IX** selects texts from short fiction and poetry, where a distinct affinity with jazz is demonstrated through descriptive and referential content, and/or forms whose aesthetic allies them to their jazz counterpart: performance. Examining the relationship and cross-fertilization of jazz and creative literature illustrates the larger relevance of the music to American culture, and again supports a contextual approach to jazz.

Most literary writing about jazz attempts to describe the music, often at the moment of performance. Literature's jazz aesthetic creates a verbal semblance of jazz's sound, using what Marcela Breton calls 'the full arsenal of poetic, rhythmic and metaphorical language' (1991: 8). Fiction and poetry are the most appropriate forms for impressionistic description of the music; they possess techniques for reproducing or imitating what the music does and the way it affects players and listeners. Yet, as Leland **Chambers** explains in his analysis (**115**) of Eudora Welty's story, 'Powerhouse,' referential, descriptive language employed by narrative is ultimately inadequate for reporting/reproducing the sounds of jazz and activity of improvisation. Literary texture cannot become musical texture: the unique acoustic quality of music can only be indirectly approximated by literary technique (Albert 1996: xvi). Chambers identifies three categories of technique which describe music: (1) affective and impressionistic; (2) technically precise, but lifeless; (3) reliance on metaphors taken from other areas of experience. Most jazz fiction falls into the first category – indulging in much romantic posturing and stylistic exaggeration, both in creating ambience and attempts to transmit the actual sounds of the music. The third category, however, has been more successful in dealing with the themes and nature of jazz, being less confined to direct description and conveying or interrogating the music in alternative ways. Here, too, African-Americans' interest in jazz performance can serve as a powerful metaphor for larger issues – historical experience of racism, group solidarity, emotional expression and cultural development. (See Panish 1997: 96.)

The metaphorical equivalence achieved by Eudora Welty in 'Powerhouse' – described by Whitney Balliett (**120**) as 'may be the best fiction ever written about jazz' – is a prime example.* What Welty does, Chambers later demonstrates, is provide a substitute process for the activity of jazz improvisation. This lies in Powerhouse's capacity for myth-making, embodied in the story's narrative form. Powerhouse's formidable pianistic skills (based on jazzman Fats Waller) are replicated in a series of improvised stories concerning the reported death of his wife by a certain Uranus Knockwood. The nature of jazz improvisation is exemplified and clarified in Powerhouse's correlative oral narrative – the musician as alternative or dual creator/performer. Chambers' analysis confirms that the twin processes of improvising and myth-making, involving similar elements of theme-and-variation and collective activity, are clearly deployed in Welty's story. Ultimately, both stories and music humanize the earlier grotesqueness of Powerhouse, serving as 'a mechanism for resolving fears and anxieties.'

This linguistic interpretation of music through controlling metaphors is achieved in several other jazz stories, some reprinted in Breton's anthology, *Hot and Cool*. Breton herself notes the circular nature of such stories and their 'degree of extemporization,' the decoding and extension of jazz's musical idiom (Introduction). These flexible and indirect ways of interpreting jazz are present in the metaphorical displacement of the music into literary techniques and forms. In Ann **Petry**'s 'Solo on the drums' (**116**), the rhythmic and emotive resources of jazz performance provide an expressive vehicle: drummer Kid Jones's great, climactic solo embodies his 'blue' personal narrative, *becomes* his entire life. 'This is the story of my love, this is the story of my hate, this is all there is left of me.' Jazz embodies collective racial metaphor in Frank London **Brown**'s 'McDougal' (**117**), where a white trumpeter's suffering validates his blues playing and qualifies him for membership of an otherwise black group. McDougal is married to a pregnant, 'brownskin woman,' with three 'crumb-crushers,' and experiences discrimination from white landlords. No Harry James, says a fellow-musician, 'he's out to blow the real thing ... The man's been burnt ... Listen to that somitch – listen to him!' The contrary impulses of staying 'high pretty much all the time' and 'trying to make it' are announced in the opening of Al **Young**'s compact story, 'Chicken Hawk's dream' (**118**). A drug addict's deluded attempt to play jazz saxophone is an oblique metaphor for professional self-discipline and payin' dues in 'real life.' Donald **Barthelme**'s 'The king of jazz' (**119**) exhibits the literary equivalent of its subject, jazz 'cutting contests,' on which it 'performs' with a string of comic conceits and satiric invention, a stylistic *tour de force*.

The task of 'imagining music' is taken up by Whitney **Balliett** (**120**), in a review of jazz fiction which concentrates on Breton's selections. He observes the writing's idolatrous nature, and the difficulty it has in catching the moment of invention in such ephemeral music. This is exemplified in the jazz aesthetic adopted by Beat Generation writers, and especially other, often inferior fiction using impressionistic description. Here, the myth-making inclinations of biography persist. Characters are, Miles Davis-like, 'walking on eggshells'

---

* Copyright charges prohibit reprinting.

(Simmons 1962) and 'The Tarzan of the Trumpet' (Gilbert 1953), or modelled on Lester Young and 'Bird' Parker, as spent but eagle-soaring saxophonists (Williams 1961) – Parker being an inspiring legend for jazz fiction in its most prolific period, the 1950s–1960s (Albert 1996: x–xiii). Balliett, reviewing elsewhere John Holmes's *The Horn* (1958), complains of 'the countless drooping, bleary novels and stories ... in which jazz musicians, postured in various awkward attitudes, like bad statuary, produce a homely, cathartic, semi-divine music' (1959: 36). In fact, most writing suffers from what an early survey called 'a consistently romantic treatment of jazz subject matter' (Smith 1958: 467). These excesses are typified in an excerpt from Jack **Baird**'s confected novel, *Hot, Sweet and Blue* (1956). Club patrons – who include 'Fairies, Lesbians and ... shady ladies' – are 'restless souls'; musicians with names like Spades play 'vibrant' chords and a 'gone horn'; and available 'chicks' are abruptly sampled as 'hamburger' when male tastes are for 'T-bone' (**121**).

The 'spontaneous bop prosody' of 1950s Beat Generation writing is a more self-conscious attempt to develop an analogy with the jazz model, notably in Jack Kerouac's experiments with composition and creation of a referential jazz fiction. The Beats' 'action' style – the long, confessional line, full of the cadence and additive structures of extended 'flow' – comes close to the performance text. Kerouac's own literary aesthetic compares writer to jazz musician in searching for a 'sketching language' as 'undisturbed flow from the mind' – 'blowing' (1958; 1959). Alignment between improvised jazz solo and 'spontaneous' jazz description is attempted in material which later appeared in *On the Road* (1957). In 'Jazz of the Beat Generation' (1955) (**122**), **Kerouac** creates the ambience and style of performing musicians in San Francisco jazz clubs. In its inventive pace and 'open,' headlong prose, this conveys affectively the energy and excitement of jazz performance/reception and the momentary rapture of the Kerouac epiphany: 'IT.' However, the process remains resolutely *literary*, for all the attempts to suggest Kerouac 'writes' jazz music.

Charles Hartman, in *Jazz Text* (1991), argues that 'voice and improvisation constitute a common ground for jazz and poetry' (ibid.: 4). Certainly, modern American poetry has been vitally influenced by the example of jazz musicians and their practice of personal sound and spontaneous composition. Barry Wallenstein, surveying the twentieth-century 'wedding' of poetry and jazz (1991), has suggested the two forms are united by tone, rhythm, cadence and lyricism, and identifies three ways of approaching 'the jazz-poetry connection.' First, poetry may be embedded in jazz lyrics, where the performance of jazz is not unlike the performing language of poetry; second, jazz-influenced diction and other effects may be found in poetry (Wallenstein instances O'Hara's 'The Day Lady Died,' and Harper's 'Brother John' [**129**], below]); third, the two arts may combine more fully, in performance, so that language and music merge 'into a highly personalized synergism.' Wallenstein focuses on this last category, through jazz talk and 'raps' of (e.g.) Armstrong, Calloway, Gillespie, Gaillard, and Mingus; the pioneering influence of Hughes; more 'conscious collaboration' of formal poetry and jazz in the 1950s (see below); and recent fusions from contemporary black poets (e.g. Redmond, Cortez).

The synthesis of the two forms was most fully achieved in the 'jazz-and-poetry' movement of the mid-to-late 1950s (**123–6**). Larry Smith emphasizes how modern jazz music and open-form poetry readily evolved from forms 'based on intuitive improvisation and emotional flow,' both fostering free and uninhibited expression (1977: 89). For Smith and others (e.g. Gleason 1958a), the three principal figures in the movement were Kenneth Rexroth, Kenneth Patchen and Lawrence Ferlinghetti, all associated with San Francisco poetry of the 1950s. If jazz and open-form poetry have certain affinities in their methods of creation and structure, then 'jazzman and poet create an affective form through rhythmic suspensions and-or contrapuntal effects' (Smith 1977: 95). Accordingly, attempts at fusing poetry reading to jazz playing amount, if successful, to an integrated performance art. As Rexroth claimed (1958), 'jazz poetry' is the recitation of suitable poetry to jazz music – emphatically, not to 'background music,' though in most performances parallelism or alternation prevail. Poetry enriches jazz's verbal content, expands musical meaning and provides more flexible material. While the use of open-form verse may suggest approximation to jazz improvisation and chorus structures, Rexroth stresses that poetry is rarely actually improvised, and follows accepted patterns and conventions, much as jazz improvisation does (see **Chorus III**).

Poetry written with the intention of being recited or performed to jazz provides the most successful example of fusion and synergy. **Rexroth**'s 'Married blues' (**123**), recited to up-tempo blues improvisation (Fantasy 7008 [1958]), aims for a spontaneous interplay between word and music, rather than uttering words to musical notes (Wallenstein 1991: 609). Less parallel in effect, and written as neither speech nor thought but in musical phrase groups, is 'Lonesome boy blues' (**124**), by **Patchen**. The reading (Folkways 9718 [1959]), to a Parker blues, makes rhythmic use of jazz suspensions and may be heard as a 'verbal performance to a moving jazz beat' (Smith 1977: 96). **Patchen**'s prose-poem, ' Opening the window' (**125**), is a surrealistic, free-form narrative, with speech spaced to invite musical intervention (Folkways 9718). The practice of poetry as 'oral message' is advanced by **Ferlinghetti**, in readings of work like 'Autobiography' (**126**), described by Gleason as 'perhaps the first poem in the English language written specifically to be read with a jazz accompaniment' (Fantasy 7002 [1957]). This is less synthesis than traded statements between voice and improvising horns, but remains an accomplished performance of poetry-and-jazz.

In addition to this performance alliance are poems which have been directly influenced by jazz – in subject, content and technique. Sascha Feinstein, overviewing the cultural and aesthetic developments of 'jazz-*related*' verse, claims the history of jazz poetry 'comprises an enormous range of poems' (1997: 2, 10). This canon is assembled by Feinstein and Yusef Komunyakaa in two fine, comprehensive anthologies (1991, 1996). The editors aim to explore 'the broad responses to jazz as poetic inspiration' (1991: xvii), and note the verse's emotional complexity and rhythmic drive, where poets 'have listened to jazz and assimilated certain relationships between the two arts – not merely the issue of language but also the connection between jazz improvisations and poetic narratives as journeys' (1996: xi). Jazz poems essentially respond to the musical language of jazz – lines of speech, dialogue and talk, a kind of pulsed, syncopated narration, with cadence and inflection. They also respond to figures and periods in jazz as inspirational sources, creating readings of jazz history.

Sascha Feinstein's *Jazz Poetry* (1997: 3–7) uses 'For Eric Dolphy' (**127**), by Etheridge **Knight**, to introduce the nature of the form. In Feinstein's analysis, the poem addresses a jazz musician and his music, and suggests Dolphy's improvisatory sound, the phrasing of his flute-playing style: short, staccato lines (breath pauses), unclosed parenthesis, repetition ('spinning'), and phonetic and vertical spelling ('doing'). Etheridge transcribes Dolphy's sound into personal narrative: the abstractions of 'spinning,' 'love,' and 'universe' express violence, racial and family conflict. The musical lines of jazz playing are associated with personal experience: 'i/ know/ exactly/ whut chew mean/ man.' **Feinstein**'s own 'Blues villanelle for Sonny Criss' (**128**) offers an unusual fusion of precise literary form and jazz subject. The poem observes the villanelle's fixed rhyme and stanza scheme, yet within these structures movingly recalls the memory and legacy of its addressee – altoist Criss, dead, by suicide, aged fifty. In 'Brother John' (**129**), which opens Michael **Harper**'s tribute, *Dear John, Dear Coltrane* (1970), the rich patterning of repeated word sounds projects both white racism and black pride and has the effect of direct, rhythmic utterance. The poem insists on its aural/oral nature, a formulaic nomenclature (Bird, Miles, Trane, John) which returns over and over, riff-like, to the 'I am-ness' of *black*. Music-making from a word text is both described and enacted by Harryette **Mullen**'s 'Playing the invisible saxophone *en el Combo de las Estrellas*' (**130**). As a 'real performance poem' which becomes a 'magical musical instrument,' Mullen energizes her voice – 'scoring' the poem into melodic flight, giving it the energy of hard-blowing improvisation, a jumping rhythm and kinetic force which will turn the whole page into dance. Larry **Neal**'s 'Don't say goodbye to the porkpie hat' (**131**) refers to Charles Mingus's musical elegy to Lester Young, 'Goodbye Porkpie Hat.' Dedicated to '*Mingus, Bird, Prez, Langston, and them,*' the poem narrates details of Young's biography, recreates his long-lined, 'caressive' saxophone style, and ends with a listed, climactic appeal to remember ('dig') those musicians whose 'SPIRIT ! ! ! SWHEEEEEEEEEEEEEEEETTT ! ! !' lives on. 'Take it again/ this time from the top.'

115 **Leland H. Chambers** Improvising and mythmaking in Eudora Welty's 'Powerhouse' (1995)

Source: Leland H. Chambers, 'Improvising and mythmaking in Eudora Welty's "Powerhouse",' in Krin Gabbard (ed.), *Representing Jazz* (Durham: Duke University Press, 1995: 131–7) (excerpt).

I don't know much about words, but there are just a few words that describe exactly what something is. Music has suffered from that. People read something and get an idea in their minds. The only thing you can do for music is feel it and hear it. (Ornette Coleman)

When Lester came out he played very melodic ... He was always telling a story and Bird did the same thing. That kind of musical philosophy is what I try to do because telling a story is, I think, where it's at. (Dexter Gordon)

And who could ever remember any of the things he says? They are just inspired remarks that roll out of his mouth like smoke. ('Powerhouse')

Eudora Welty's 'Powerhouse,' originally published when 'swing' was the popular buzzword for what we now understand as an evolutionary step in the history of jazz, is a twice-unique story. For one thing, she never wrote another like it – that is, no other story with even a remotely similar focus. Moreover, no other story by any author I know of has been as successful in dealing with improvisation, one of the essential ingredients of jazz.

It seems to me a special act of the creative instinct that a white writer of southern background coming to maturity during the 1920s and 1930s should be able to approach a particularly salient aspect of black culture with the sensitivity and understanding shown in 'Powerhouse.' Welty was not even especially close to the music scene, not like Kenneth Rexroth had been as far back as the twenties, nor Hayden Carruth today. Yet at one moment of her life she was capable of transposing a New York exposure to Fats Waller's music to her own rural Mississippi milieu and finding a language capable of penetrating to the heart of that quality of jazz which most distinguished it from both the pop music of the day and the European-derived symphonic and chamber music tradition.

To recap, Powerhouse is the name of a renowned black piano player, famous recording artist, and bandleader, playing a dance for a sparse white crowd in a Mississippi town on a rainy night. The time is the late 1930s. In the course of the evening's entertainment the band plays dance tunes largely acceptable to a white audience; they even include a detestable waltz. In the midst of performing this tune Powerhouse begins to talk to the musicians closest to him, telling of having received a telegram with the news that his wife is dead.

The telegram was signed by a certain Uranus Knockwood. During the intermission, he and those three musicians go out to a small juke joint, the World Café, in what the narrator calls Negrotown, where Powerhouse continues the story of Gypsy and Uranus Knockwood. He tells it in three versions, each one different in its details. The story astonishes and delights the crowd of local blacks who, having recognized Powerhouse, stand around in awe. Having worked his way through all the versions, Powerhouse composes a telegram in response to the one he claimed to have received. The musicians go back to the bandstand again and play some more.

The music Powerhouse plays and the stories he tells demonstrate fundamental similarities. The two activities derive from impulses that are very close to each other but are displayed in different modes that appear to be incompatible – the inchoate but often pleasing sounds of music and the referential sense (always relative) of language. In comparison to music, language seems clear and exact. Yet language is an inadequate means of describing what music does. In 'Powerhouse,' though, the mediation of jazz improvisation through mythmaking turns out to be an overwhelmingly successful strategy, because since the descriptive language of narrative cannot adequately report the sounds of music and consequently the activity of improvisation, Welty substitutes a process that is in narrative form. The result is that the nature of jazz improvising becomes exemplified and clarified in the stories Powerhouse tells about the death of his wife. The analogies between the two processes of improvising and mythmaking (at least, as they appear in 'Powerhouse') are based on the fact that they employ similar basic elements. The most important of these are (1) theme-and-variation and (2) collective activity. These basic elements make it possible not only to communicate successfully the sense of the music in the language of narrative, but they permit each to become a metaphor for the other, thus enabling a reciprocal means of understanding and interpretation.

Using linguistic means (words) to convey affectively what happens in music has always led to distortions of one kind or another. Only a limited number of suitable onomatopoetic words exist, and these quickly lose their capacity for a sensitive approximation of the sounds they are intended to imitate, especially since they have to be experienced within the syntax of language rather than music. Consequently, the description of music most usually becomes impressionistic (focusing on how the listener reacts while listening or else what the player feels while playing), or it is technically precise but lifeless (at least for the purposes of fiction), or else it leans on metaphors from other areas of human experience.

This analysis is complicated by the purposes that motivate every attempt to explain any aspect of music. LP liner notes for most jazz record albums were sometimes designed as much to encourage buyer interest in a specific performance as they were to explain anything about the music in a general way, especially since the potential audience for a given jazz album already enjoys a sense of what jazz is, no matter how fragmentary or misguided their understanding. Jazz historians and critics appeal to a similar audience of jazz-oriented listeners, but again with differing purposes. André Hodeir's six-and-one-half-page analysis of Fats Waller's 'Keepin' Out Of Mischief Now' – a solo performance on a recording lasting three minutes and ten seconds – seeks to illustrate the continuity of musical thought possible in improvised jazz solos (169–76), and thus it is clearly addressed to those already well-informed about jazz. Martin Williams's much less technical remarks on Coleman Hawkins's tenor saxophone solo on the 1940 recording of 'The Sheik of Araby' are designed to introduce basic tenets of improvisation to beginning students of jazz (Where's The Melody? 38–40), while his remarks on the same solo in The Jazz Tradition are designed to make it fit into the context of Hawkins's development as a soloist/improviser (79), this time for an audience of more experienced students of jazz. And one could go on.

Perhaps such technically precise analyses do not fall into the abyss of impressionistic writing bemoaned by the poet Hayden Carruth, who, while conceding that 'technical criticism can be moderately helpful,' says:

> What I know for a fact is that the kind of impressionistic writing about jazz that has been foisted on us in superabundance during the past three or four decades is utterly useless; the kind of thing done by Whitney Baliett, Martin Williams, and sometimes Nat Hentoff. It exploits the musicians as romantic, not to say psychoneurotic, personalities, and it exploits the reader by promising what it cannot deliver, an explanation or at least a description of the expressiveness of jazz, which every fully engaged listener longs for. (48–49)

Fiction is perhaps a more appropriate place for the impressionistic description of music, but the pitfalls broached by Carruth apply equally here, especially when the stories use the description of jazz playing to go beyond the music to other concerns. In a typical complaint of the Beat Generation, John Clellon Holmes at one point in his novel The Horn egregiously links the playing of two performers involved in a cutting contest to certain depressing aspects of the American experience:

> Edgar ... blew four bars of a demented cackle, and for an instant they were almost shoulder to shoulder, horn to horn, in the terrible equality of art, pouring into each wild break (it felt) the substance of their separated lives – crazy, profound Americans, both! ... America had laid its hand on both of them. In Edgar's furious scornful bleat sounded the moronic horn of every merciless Cadillac shrieking down the highway with a wet-mouthed, giggling boy at the wheel, turning the American prairie into a graveyard of rusting chrome junk; the idiot-snarl that filled the jails and madhouses and legislatures; some final dead-wall impact. (19)

In Langston Hughes's 1934 story 'The Blues I'm Playing,' the piano playing of Hughes's protagonist Oceola is said to express something absolutely universal: 'In the blues she made the bass note throb like tomtoms, the trebles cry like little flutes, so deep in the earth and so high in the sky that they understood everything' (Breton 71). But throughout the story, jazz is depicted as directly interwoven with the everyday lives of Oceola's people, a situation that upper-middle-class white Americans are unable to grasp or appreciate because they are so narrowly fixed on a conception of art as an expression of the highest spirituality, as exemplified in the great composers of Europe, and therefore far above the mundane. J. F. Powers ('He Don't Plant Cotton') appears to show that the satisfaction of playing jazz as one feels it is able to compensate for the bitter sting of racial denigration, as a jazz pianist gets inside her own music while ignoring the insensitive requests of a white patron:

> And Libby was pleased, watching Baby. And then, somehow, he vanished for her into the blue drum. The sticks still danced at an oblique angle on the snare, but there were no hands to them and Libby could not see Baby on the chair. She could only feel him somewhere in the blue glow. Abandoning herself, she lost herself in the piano. Now, still without seeing him, she could feel him with a clarity and warmth beyond vision. Miniature bell notes, mostly blue, blossomed ecstatically, perished *affetuoso*, weaving themselves down into the dark beauty of the lower keys, because it was closer to the drum, and multiplied. (Breton 87)

James Baldwin's narrator in 'Sonny's Blues' is a jazz pianist's elder brother who has never really understood either the younger man's hurt or the nature of jazz, until everything becomes clear to him at the high point of the story:

> Sonny's fingers filled the air with life, his life. But that life contained so many others. And Sonny went all the way back, he really began with the spare, flat statement of the opening phrase of the song. Then he began to make it his. It was very beautiful because it wasn't hurried and it was no longer a lament. I seemed to hear with what burning he had made it his, with what burning we had yet to make it ours, how we could cease lamenting. Freedom lurked around us and I understood, at last, that he could help us to be free if we would listen, that he would never be free until we did ... And I was yet aware that this was only a moment, that the world waited outside, as hungry as a tiger, and that trouble stretched above us, longer than the sky. (Breton 129–30)

Sonny's performance, then, is also made to convey the often stated position that the freedom of jazz improvisation is the icon of an intellectual and emotional freedom that transcends any amount of social and political repression.

In fiction about jazz, then, one often finds the music interpreted to support nonmusical ideas or experiences. This is one effect of applying the referential aspects of language to the nonreferential sounds of music. Welty's story is no exception. It belongs to the third category mentioned, that which employs a controlling metaphor to permit the linguistic interpretation of music. Perhaps the nature of improvisation – at the heart of the music itself – is a more difficult concept for fiction to get at, or at least a concept less likely to produce an affective response in the reader. In any case, Powerhouse's use of theme-and-variation as he builds his successive stories about Gypsy's death and Uranus Knockwood's menacing presence, together with the collective activity of his friends and even the onlookers at the World Café, show that the process of mythmaking lies so close to that of jazz improvising that it can easily and unobtrusively be substituted for it.

Works Cited (edited)

Breton, Marcela. *Hot and Cool: Jazz Stories*. New York: Penguin, 1990.
Carruth, Hayden. *Sitting In: Selected Writings on Jazz, Blues, and Related Topics*. Iowa City: University of Iowa Press, 1986.
Hodier, André. *Jazz: Its Evolution and Essence*. New York: Grove, 1979.
Holmes, John Clellon. *The Horn*. 1958. New York: Thunder's Mouth, 1988.
Williams, Martin. *The Jazz Tradition*. New York: Oxford University Press, 1983.
————. *Where's the Melody? A Listener's Introduction to Jazz*. 1966. New York: Da Capo, 1983.

116 **Ann Petry** Solo on the drums (1947)

Source: Ann Petry, 'Solo on the drums,' in *Miss Muriel and Other Stories* (New York: Houghton Mifflin, 1971: 235–42). (Originally published in *The Magazine of the Year*, 1947.)

The orchestra had a week's engagement at the Randlert Theater at Broadway and Forty-second Street. His name was picked out in lights on the marquee. The name of the orchestra and then his name underneath by itself.

There had been a time when he would have been excited by it. And stopped to let his mind and his eyes linger over it lovingly. Kid Jones. The name – his name – up there in lights that danced and winked in the brassy sunlight. And at night his name glittered up there on the marquee as though it had been sprinkled with diamonds. The people who pushed their way through the crowded street looked up at it and recognized it and smiled.

He used to eat it up. But not today. Not after what had happened this morning. He just looked at the sign with his name on it. There it was. Then he noticed that the sun had come out, and he shrugged and went on inside the theater to put on one of the cream-colored suits and get his music together.

After he had finished changing his clothes, he glanced in the long mirror in his dressing room. He hadn't changed any. Same face. No fatter and no thinner. No gray hair. Nothing. He frowned. Because he felt that the things that were eating him up inside ought to show. But they didn't.

When it was time to go out on the stage, he took his place behind the drums, not talking, just sitting there. The orchestra started playing softly. He made a mental note of the fact that the boys were working together as smoothly as though each one had been oiled.

The long gray curtains parted. One moment they were closed. And then they were open. Silently. Almost like magic. The high-powered spots flooded the stage with light. He could see specks of dust gliding down the wide beams of light. Under the bands of light the great space out front was all shadow. Faces slowly emerged out of it – disembodied heads and shoulders that slanted up and back, almost to the roof.

He hits the drums lightly. Regularly. A soft, barely discernible rhythm. A background. A repeated emphasis for the horns and the piano. The man with the trumpet stood up and the first notes came out sweet and clear and high.

Kid Jones kept up the drum accompaniment. Slow. Careful. Soft. And he felt his left eyebrow lift itself and start to twitch as the man played the trumpet. It happened whenever he heard the trumpet. The notes crept up, higher, higher, higher. So high that his stomach sucked in against itself. Then a little lower and stronger. A sound sustained. The rhythm of it beating against his ears until he was filled with it and sighing with it.

He wanted to cover his ears with his hands because he kept hearing a voice that whispered the same thing over and over again. The voice was trapped somewhere under the roof – caught and held there by the trumpet. 'I'm leaving I'm leaving I'm leaving.'

The sound took him straight back to the rain, the rain that had come with the morning. He could see the beginning of the day – raw and cold. He was at home. But he was warm because he was close to her, holding her in his arms. The rain and the wind cried softly outside the window.

And now – well, he felt as though he were floating up and up and up on that long blue note of the trumpet. He half closed his eyes and rode up on it. It had stopped being music. It was that whispering voice, making him shiver. Hating it and not being able to do anything about it. 'I'm leaving it's the guy who plays the piano I'm in love with him and I'm leaving now today.' Rain in the streets. Heat gone. Food gone. Everything gone because a woman's gone. It's everything you ever wanted, he thought. It's everything you never got. Everything you ever had, everything you ever lost. It's all there in the trumpet – pain and hate and trouble and peace and quiet and love.

The last note stayed up in the ceiling. Hanging on and on. The man with the trumpet had stopped playing, but Kid Jones could still hear that last note. In his ears. In his mind.

The spotlight shifted and landed on Kid Jones – the man behind the drums. The long beam of white light struck the top of his head and turned him into a pattern of light and shadow. Because of the cream-colored suit and shirt, his body seemed to be encased in light. But there was a shadow over his face so that his features blended and disappeared. His hairline receded so far back that he looked like a man with a face that never ended. A man with a high, long face and dark, dark skin.

He caressed the drums with the brushes in his hands. They responded with a whisper of sound. The rhythm came over but it had to be listened for. It stayed that way for a long time. Low, insidious, repeated. Then he made the big bass drum growl and pick up the same rhythm.

The Marquis of Brund, pianist with the band, turned to the piano. The drums and the piano talked the same rhythm. The piano high. A little more insistent than the drums. The Marquis was turned sideways on the piano bench. His left foot tapped out the rhythm. His cream-colored suit sharply outlined the bulkiness of his body against the dark gleam of the piano. The drummer and the pianist were silhouetted in two separate brilliant shafts of light. The drums slowly dominated the piano.

The rhythm changed. It was faster. Kid Jones looked out over the crowded theater as he hit the drums. He began to feel as though he were the drums and the drums were he.

The theater throbbed with the excitement of the drums. A man, sitting near the front, shivered and his head jerked to the rhythm. A sailor put his arm around the girl sitting beside him, took his hand and held her face still and pressed his mouth close over hers. Close. Close. Close. Until their faces seemed to melt together. Her hat fell off and neither of them moved. His hand dug deep into her shoulder and still they didn't move.

A kid sneaked in through a side door and slid into an aisle seat. His mouth was wide open and he clutched his cap with both hands, tight and hard against his chest as he listened.

The drummer forgot he was in the theater. There was only him and the drums and they were far away. Long gone. He was holding Lulu, Helen, Susie, Mamie close in his arms. And all of them – all those girls blended into that one girl who was his wife. The one who said, 'I'm leaving.' She had said it over and over again, this morning, while rain dripped down the windowpanes.

When he hit the drums again it was with the thought that he was fighting with the piano player. He was choking the Marquis of Brund. He was putting a knife in clean between his ribs. He was slitting his throat with a long straight blade. Take my woman. Take your life.

The drums leaped with the fury that was in him. The men in the band turned their heads toward him – a faint astonishment showed in their faces.

He ignored them. The drums took him away from them, took him back, and back, and back, in time and space. He built up an illusion. He was sending out the news. Grandma died. The foreigner in the litter has an old disease and will not recover. The man from across the big water is sleeping with the chief's daughter. Kill. Kill. Kill. The war goes well with the men with the bad smell and the loud laugh. It goes badly with the chiefs with the round heads and the peacock's walk.

It is cool in the deep track in the forest. Cool and quiet. The trees talk softly. They speak of the dance tonight. The young girl from across the lake will be there. Her waist is slender and her thighs are rounded. Then the words he wanted to forget were all around Kid Jones again. 'I'm leaving I'm leaving I'm leaving.'

He couldn't help himself. He stopped hitting the drums and stared at the Marquis of Brund – a long malevolent look, filled with hate.

There was a restless, uneasy movement in the theater. He remembered where he was. He started playing again. The horn played a phrase. Soft and short. The drums answered. The horn said the same thing all over again. The drums repeated it. The next time it was more intricate. The phrase was turned around, it went back and forth and up and down. And the drums said it over, exactly the same.

He knew a moment of panic. This was where he had to solo again and he wasn't sure he could do it. He touched the drums lightly. They quivered and answered him.

And then it was almost as though the drums were talking about his own life. The woman in Chicago who hated him. The girl with the round, soft body who had been his wife and who had walked out on him, this morning, in the rain. The old woman who was his mother, the same woman who lived in Chicago, and who hated him because he looked like his father, his father who had seduced her and left her, years ago.

He forgot the theater, forgot everything but the drums. He was welded to the drums, sucked inside them. All of him. His pulse beat. His heart beat. He had become part of the drums. They had become part of him.

He made the big drum rumble and reverberate. He went a little mad on the big drum. Again and again he filled the theater with a sound like thunder. The sound seemed to come not from the drums but from deep inside himself; it was a sound that was being wrenched out of him – a violent, raging, roaring sound. As it issued from him he thought, This is the story of my love, this is the story of my hate, this is all there is left of me. And the sound echoed and reechoed far up under the roof of the theater.

When he finally stopped playing, he was trembling; his body was wet with sweat. He was surprised to see that the drums were sitting there in front of him. He hadn't become part of them. He was still himself. Kid Jones. Master of the drums. Greatest drummer in the world. Selling himself a little piece at a time. Every afternoon. Twice every evening. Only this time he had topped all his other performances. This time, playing like this after what had happened in the morning, he had sold all of himself – not just a little piece.

Someone kicked his foot. 'Bow, you ape. Whassamatter with you?'

He bowed from the waist and the spotlight slid away from him, down his pants legs. The light landed on the Marquis of Brund, the piano player. The Marquis' skin glistened like a piece of black seaweed. Then the light was back on Kid Jones.

He felt hot and he thought, I stink of sweat. The talcum he had dabbed on his face after he shaved felt like a constricting layer of cement. A thin layer but definitely cement. No air could get through to his skin. He reached for his handkerchief and felt the powder and the sweat mix as he mopped his face.

Then he bowed again. And again. Like a – like one of those things you pull the string and it jerks, goes through the motion of dancing. Pull it again and it kicks. Yeah, he thought, you were hot all right. The go-go gals ate you up and you haven't anyplace to go. Since this morning you haven't had anyplace to go. 'I'm leaving it's the guy who plays the piano I'm in love with the Marquis of Brund he plays such sweet piano I'm leaving leaving leaving –'

He stared at the Marquis of Brund for a long moment. Then he stood up and bowed again. And again.

117 **Frank London Brown** McDougal (1961)

Source: Frank London Brown, 'McDougal,' *Phoenix Magazine*, Fall, 1961: 32–3.

The bass was walking. Nothing but the bass. And the rhythm section waited, counting time with the tap of a foot or the tip of a finger against the piano top. Pro had just finished his solo and the blood in his neck was pumping so hard it made his head hurt. Sweat shone upon the brown backs of his fingers and the moisture stained the bright brass of his tenor where he held it. Jake, young eyeglass-wearing boy from Dallas, had stopped playing the drums, and he too was sweating, and slight stains were beginning to appear upon his thin cotton coat, and his dark skin caught the purple haze from the overhead spotlight and the sweat that gathered on his flat cheekbones seemed purple. Percy R. Brookins bent over the piano tapping the black keys but not hard enough to make a sound.

Everybody seemed to be waiting.

And the bass was walking. Doom-de-doom-doom-doom-doom-doom!

A tall thin white man whose black hair shone with sweat stood beside the tenorman, lanky, ginger-brown Pro.

Pro had wailed – had blown choruses that dripped with the smell of cornbread and cabbage and had roared like a late 'L' and had cried like a blues singer on the last night of a good gig.

Now it was the white man's turn, right after the bass solo was over … and he waited and Pro waited and so did Jake the drummer, and Percy R. Brookins. Little Jug was going into his eighth chorus and showed no sign of letting up.

DOOM-DE-DOOM-DOOM-DOOM-DOOM-DOOM!

Jake looked out into the audience. And the shadowy faces were hard to see behind the bright colored lights that ringed the bandstand. Yet he felt that they too waited … Pro had laid down some righteous sound – he had told so much truth – told it so plainly, so passionately that it had scared everybody in the place, even Pro, and now he waited for the affirming bass to finish so that he could hear what the white man had to say.

McDougal was his name. And his young face had many wrinkles and his young body slouched and his shoulders hung round and loose. He was listening to Little Jug's bass yet he also seemed to be listening to something else, almost as if he were still listening to the truth Pro had told.

And the bass walked.

Jake leaned over his drums and whispered to Percy R. Brookins.

'That cat sure looks beat don't he?'

Percy R. Brookins nodded, and then put his hand to the side of his mouth, and whispered back.

'His old lady's pregnant again.'

'Again?! What's that? Number three?'

'Number four,' Percy R. Brookins answered.

'Hell I'd look sad too … Is he still living on Forty Seventh Street?'

The drums slid in underneath the bass and the bass dropped out amid strong applause and a few 'Yeahs!' And Jake, not having realized it, cut in where McDougal was to begin his solo. He smiled sheepishly at Percy R. Brookins and the piano player hunched his shoulders and smiled.

McDougal didn't look around, he didn't move from his slouched one-sided stance, he didn't stop staring beyond the audience and beyond the room itself. Yet his left foot kept time with the light bombs the drummer dropped and the husky soft scrape of the brushes.

Little Jug pulled a handkerchief from his back pocket and wiped his cheeks and around the back of his neck, then he stared at the black, glistening back of McDougal's head and then leaned down and whispered to Percy R. Brookins.

'Your boy sure could stand a haircut. He looks as bad as Ol' Theo.' And they both knew how bad Ol' Theo looked and they both frowned and laughed.

Percy R. Brookins touched a chord lightly to give some color to Jake's solo and then he said.

'Man, that cat has suffered for that brownskin woman.'

Little Jug added.

'And those ... three little brownskin crumb-crushers.'

Percy R. Brookins hit another chord and then.

'Do you know none of the white folks'll rent to him now?'

Little Jug laughed.

'Why hell yes ... will they rent to me?'

'Sure they will, down on Forty Seventh Street.'

Little Jug nodded at Jake and Jake made a couple of breaks that meant that he was about to give in to McDougal.

Percy R. Brookins turned to face his piano and then he got an idea and he turned to Little Jug and spoke with a serious look behind the curious smile on his face.

'You know that cat's after us? I mean he's out to blow the real thing. You know what I mean? Like he's no Harry James? Do you know that?'

Little Jug ran into some triplets and skipped a couple of beats and brought McDougal in right on time.

At the same time McDougal rode in on a long, hollow, gut bucket note that made Percy R. Brookins laugh, and caused Pro to cock his head and rub his cheek. The tall worried-looking white man bent his trumpet to the floor and hunched his shoulders and closed his eyes and blew.

Little Jug answered Percy R. Brookins' question about McDougal.

'I been knowing that ... he knows the happenings ... I mean about where we get it, you dig? I mean like with Leola and those kids and Forty Seventh Street and those jive land-lords, you dig? The man's been burnt, Percy. Listen to that somitch – listen to him!'

McDougal's eyes were closed and he did not see the dark woman with the dark cotton suit that ballooned away from the great bulge of her stomach. He didn't see her ease into a chair at the back of the dark smoky room. He didn't see the smile on her face or the sweat upon her flat nose.

118 **Al Young** Chicken Hawk's dream (1966)

Source: Al Young, 'Chicken Hawk's dream,' *Spero*, 1,2 (1966: 19–21).

Chicken Hawk stayed high pretty much all the time he was 19 years old limping down academic corridors trying to make it to the 12th grade. Unlike his good sidekick Wine, whose big reason for putting up with school was to please his mother, Chicken Hawk just loved the public school system and all advantages that came with it. He could go on boarding at home, didn't have to work and could mess over a whole year and not feel he'd lost anything.

He sat behind me in Homeroom, sportshirt, creased pants, shiny black pointy-toed stetsons, jacket, processed hair. He'd look around him on lean days and say: 'Say, man, why don't you buy this joint off me so I can be straight for lunch, I'd really appreciate it.'

One morning he showed up acting funnier than usual. Turns out he was half-smashed and half-drunk because he'd smoked some dope when he got up that morning, then on the way to school he'd met up with Wine and the two of them did up a 5th of Nature Boy, a brand of sweet wine well-known around Detroit. Wine wasn't called Wine for nothin'. Between Thunderbird and Nature Boy he didn't know what to do with himself. Wine was a jokey kind of cat who drank heavily as a matter of form – his form. 'I like to juice on general principle,' is the way he put it.

That morning Chicken Hawk eased up to me and says: 'Al, I had this dream, the grooviest dream I had in a long time. You wanna know how it went?'

By that time I thought I could anticipate anything Chicken Hawk was going to say but to tell a dream was something else, something new. Never thought he'd come up with anything that private. 'What'd you dream, man?'

'Dreamed I was walkin' 'round New York, walkin' 'round all the places where Bird walked and seen all the shit he seen and all thru this dream I'm playin' the background music to my own dream, dig, and it's on alto, man, and I'm cookin' away somethin' terrible and what surprises me is I can do the fingerin' and all that jive – I can blow that horn, I know I can blow it in real life, I *know* I can! You know somebody got a horn I can borrow, I'll show everybody what I can do.'

'Drew's got an alto and he lives up the street from me. Maybe you can get your chops together on his horn. It don't belong to him tho, it's his brother's and Drew don't hardly touch it, he too busy woodsheddin' his drums. I'll ask him if you can come over after school and play some.'

'Aw, baby, yeah, nice, that's beautiful, Al, that sure would be beautiful if you could arrange all that. Think maybe Drew'd lemme borrow it for a few days?'

'Well, I don't know about that, you could ask him.'

'Yeah, unh-hunh, know what tune I wanna blow first? – Listen to this ...' – and he broke into whistling something off a very old J.J. Johnson LP on Prestige.

Wellsir – Drew said OK, to bring Chicken Hawk on over and we'd see what he could do, 'But if you ask me the dude ain't nothin' but another pothead with a lotta nerve' – Drew speaking – 'On the other hand he might just up and shake us all up.'

Six of us, mostly from band, went over to Drew's house after school to find out what Chicken Hawk could do with a saxophone. As we went stomping thru the snow old Wine was passing a bottle – 'Just a little taste, fellas, to brace ourself against the cold, dig it?'

Drew's mother, a gym teacher, took one look at us at the frontdoor and said: 'Now I know all you hoodlums is friendsa Drew's but you are not comin' up in here trackin' mud all over my nice rugs, so go on round the back way and wipe your feet good before you go down in the basement.'

We got down there where Drew had his drums set up and Drew got out his brother's old horn. 'Be careful with it, Chicken Hawk, it ain't mine and Bruh gon need it when he get back from out the Service.'

We all sat around and watched.

Chicken Hawk took the horn and said: 'Show me how you hold this thing, just show me how you hold it and I'll do the rest.'

One of the reed players, a lightskin fellow called Butter, leaned over Chicken Hawk and showed him where to place his fingers on the keys. Chicken Hawk looked at Butter like he was insane. 'Man, give me a little credit for knowin' somethin' about the thing, you ain't got to treat me like I'm some little baby.'

'Then go ahead and blow it, baby!'

'Damn, I shoulda turned on first, I'd do more better if I was high. Anybody got a joint they can lay on me?'

Everybody started to get mad and restless. Drew said: 'Mister Chicken Hawk sir, blow somethin' on the horn and shut up!'

'Shit, you dudes don't think I can blow this thing but I'll show you.'

'Then show us!'

Poor Chicken Hawk, he took a deep breath and huffed and puffed but not a sound could he make. 'You sure this horn work?'

'Don't worry 'bout the horn, man,' Drew told him, 'just go head and play somethin'.'

Chicken Hawk slobbered all over the mouthpiece and blew on it and worked the keys till we could all hear them clicking but still no sound. He wiped his lips on his coatsleeve and called his boy Wine over. 'Now, Wine, you see me playin' on this thing, don't you?'

'Yes, I am quite aware of that, C. H.'

'You see me scufflin' with it and it still don't make a sound?'

'Yes, I ain't heard anything, C. H., my man.'

'Then, Wine, would you say – just off hand – that it could be Drew's brother's horn ain't no damn good?'

Old Wine looked around the room at each of us and rubbed his hands together and grinned. 'Well, uh, now I don't know about that, C. H. Would you care for a little taste to maybe loosen you up?'

Chicken Hawk screwed his face up, blew into the instrument and pumped the keys till he turned colors but all that came out were feeble little squeaks and some pitiful honks. 'Well gentlemen, I've had it with this axe. It don't work. It just ain't no good. I can blow it all right, O yeah, I could blow it but how you expect me to get into anything on a jive horn?'

Drew packed the saxophone back in its case. Wine passed Chicken Hawk the

Nature Boy and we all started talking about something else. There were no jokes about what had happened, no See-Didn't-I-Tell-You. Drew got to showing us new things he'd worked out on drums for a Rock & Roll dance he was playing. After everybody got absorbed in that, Chicken Hawk and Wine, well-juiced, eased quietly up the back-steps.

Last time I saw Chicken Hawk was on 12th Street in Detroit. He was out of his mind – heroin – standing smack on the corner in the wind watching the light turn green, yellow, red back to green, scratching his chin and he smiled.

'Hey, Chicken Hawk!'

'Hey now, what's goin' on?'

'You got it.'

'And don't I know it, I'm takin' off for New York next week.'

'Whatcha gonna do in New York?'

'See if I can get me a band together and cut some albums.'

'Well – hope you make it, Chicken Hawk. Keep pushin.'

'Gotta get my instrument out the pawnshop first, mmmm – you know how it is.'

'Yeah, well, all right, take care yourself, man.'

119 **Donald Barthelme** The king of jazz (1977)

Source: Donald Barthelme, 'The king of jazz,' in *Sixty Stories* (New York: Putnam, 1981: 354–8). (Originally published in *The New Yorker*, 7 February 1977.)

Well I'm the king of jazz now, thought Hokie Mokie to himself as he oiled the slide on his trombone. Hasn't been a 'bone man been king of jazz for many years. But now that Spicy MacLammermoor, the old king, is dead, I guess I'm it. Maybe I better play a few notes out of this window here, to reassure myself.

'Wow!' said somebody standing on the sidewalk. 'Did you hear that?'

'I did,' said his companion.

'Can you distinguish our great homemade American jazz performers, each from the other?'

'Used to could.'

'Then who was that playing?'

'Sounds like Hokie Mokie to me. Those few but perfectly selected notes have the real epiphanic glow.'

'The what?'

'The real epiphanic glow, such as is obtained only by artists of the caliber of Hokie Mokie, who's from Pass Christian, Mississippi. He's the king of jazz, now that Spicy MacLammermoor is gone.'

Hokie Mokie put his trombone in its trombone case and went to a gig. At the gig everyone fell back before him, bowing.

'Hi Bucky! Hi Zoot! Hi Freddie! Hi George! Hi Thad! Hi Roy! Hi Dexter! Hi Jo! Hi Willie! Hi Greens!'

'What we gonna play, Hokie? You the king of jazz now, you gotta decide.'

'How 'bout "Smoke"?'

'Wow!' everybody said. 'Did you hear that? Hokie Mokie can just knock a fella out, just the way he pronounces a word. What a intonation on that boy! God Almighty!'

'I don't want to play "Smoke,"' somebody said.

'Would you repeat that, stranger?'

'I don't want to play "Smoke." "Smoke" is dull. I don't like the changes. I refuse to play "Smoke."'

'He refuses to play "Smoke"! But Hokie Mokie is the king of jazz and he says "Smoke"!'

'Man, you from outa town or something? What do you mean you refuse to play "Smoke"? How'd you get on this gig anyhow? Who hired you?'

'I am Hideo Yamaguchi, from Tokyo, Japan.'

'Oh, you're one of those Japanese cats, eh?'

'Yes I'm the top trombone man in all of Japan.'

'Well you're welcome here until we hear you play. Tell me, is the Tennessee Tea Room still the top jazz place in Tokyo?'

'No, the top jazz place in Tokyo is the Square Box now.'

'That's nice. OK, now we gonna play "Smoke" just like Hokie said. You ready, Hokie? OK, give you four for nothin'. One! Two! Three! Four!'

The two men who had been standing under Hokie's window had followed him into the club. Now they said:

'Good God!'

'Yes, that's Hokie's famous "English sunrise" way of playing. Playing with lots of rays coming out of it, some red rays, some blue rays, some green rays, some green stemming from a violet center, some olive stemming from a tan center – '

'That young Japanese fellow is pretty good, too.'

'Yes, he is pretty good. And he holds his horn in a peculiar way. That's frequently the mark of a superior player.'

'Bent over like that with his head between his knees – good God, he's sensational!'

He's sensational, Hokie thought. Maybe I ought to kill him.

But at that moment somebody came in the door pushing in front of him a four-and-one-half-octave marimba. Yes, it was Fat Man Jones, and he began to play even before he was fully in the door.

'What're we playing?'

'"Billie's Bounce."'

'That's what I thought it was. What're we in?'

'F.'

'That's what I thought we were in. Didn't you use to play with Maynard?'

'Yeah I was on that band for a while until I was in the hospital.'

'What for?'

'I was tired.'

'What can we add to Hokie's fantastic playing?'

'How 'bout some rain or stars?'

'Maybe that's presumptuous?'

'Ask him if he'd mind.'

'You ask him, I'm scared. You don't fool around with the king of jazz. That young Japanese guy's pretty good, too.'

'He's sensational.'

'You think he's playing in Japanese?'

'Well I don't think it's English.'

This trombone's been makin' my neck green for thirty-five years, Hokie thought. How come I got to stand up to yet another challenge, this late in life?

'Well, Hideo –'

'Yes, Mr. Mokie?'

'You did well on both "Smoke" and "Billie's Bounce." You're just about as good as me, I regret to say. In fact, I've decided you're *better* than me. It's a hideous thing to contemplate, but there it is. I have only been the king of jazz for twenty-four hours, but the unforgiving logic of this art demands we bow to Truth, when we hear it.'

'Maybe you're mistaken?'

'No, I got ears. I'm not mistaken. Hideo Yamaguchi is the new king of jazz.'

'You want to be king emeritus?'

'No, I'm just going to fold up my horn and steal away. This gig is yours, Hideo. You can pick the next tune.'

'How 'bout "Cream"?'

'OK, you heard what Hideo said, it's "Cream." You ready, Hideo?'

'Hokie, you don't have to leave. You can play too. Just move a little over to the side there – '

'Thank you, Hideo, that's very gracious of you. I guess I will play a little, since I'm still here. Sotto voce, of course.'

'Hideo is wonderful on "Cream"!'

'Yes, I imagine it's his best tune.'

'What's that sound coming in from the side there?'

'Which side?'

'The left.'

'You mean that sound that sounds like the cutting edge of life? That sounds like polar bears crossing Arctic ice pans? That sounds like a herd of musk ox in full flight? That sounds like male walruses diving to the bottom of the sea? That sounds like fumaroles smoking on the slopes of Mt. Katmai? That sounds like the wild turkey walking through the deep, soft forest? That sounds like beavers chewing trees in an Appalachian marsh? That sounds like an oyster fungus growing on an aspen trunk? That sounds like a mule deer wandering a montane of the Sierra Nevada? That sounds like prairie dogs kissing? That sounds like witchgrass tumbling or a river meandering? That sounds like manatees munching seaweed at Cape Sable? That sounds like coatimundis moving in packs across the face of Arkansas? That sounds like – '

'Good God, it's Hokie! Even with a cup mute on, he's blowing Hideo right off the stand!'

'Hideo's playing on his knees now! Good God, he's reaching into his belt for a large steel sword – Stop him!'

'Wow! That was the most exciting "Cream" ever played! Is Hideo all right?'

'Yes, somebody is getting him a glass of water.'

'You're my man, Hokie! That was the dadblangedest thing I ever saw!'

'You're the king of jazz once again!'

'Hokie Mokie is the most happening thing there is!'

'Yes, Mr. Hokie sir, I have to admit it, you blew me right off the stand. I see I have many years of work and study before me still.'

'That's OK, son. Don't think a thing about it. It happens to the best of us. Or it almost happens to the best of us. Now I want everybody to have a good time because we're gonna play "Flats." "Flats" is next.'

'With your permission, sir, I will return to my hotel and pack. I am most grateful for everything I have learned here.'

'That's OK, Hideo. Have a nice day. He-he. Now, "Flats." '

120 **Whitney Balliett** Imagining music (1990)

Source: Whitney Balliett, 'Imagining music,' in *Goodbyes and Other Messages*: *A Journal of Jazz, 1981–1990*. (Oxford: Oxford University Press, 1992: 281–6).

For a long time, jazz fans were idolaters, who enshrined their Louis Armstrongs and Billie Holidays and Charlie Parkers. This defensive zealotry was particularly apparent when the music was still regarded as mean and primitive. Early jazz writers were even more protective. They made such troubled heroes as King Oliver (down and out in Savannah in 1938, aged sixty), Bix Beiderbecke (dead of drink in 1931, aged twenty-eight), and Bunk Johnson (toothless and hornless in New Iberia, Louisiana, aged forty-five) into tragic figures and wrote about them with an 'O lost, and by the wind grieved, ghost' sentimentality. This sentimentality leaked into the first full-length jazz movies in the fifties, and it's still in evidence, despite such heavy lumber as '*Round Midnight* and *Bird.* (The best feature film about jazz is the little-known, low-budget *The Gig*, written and directed in the mid-eighties by the playwright Frank Gilroy. It deals with a group of white amateur musicians – and a black professional singer – who play a summer gig in the Catskills, and it explains for the first time the blue-collar ethos of the average jazz musician.) The same myth-making has also affected most of the fiction written about jazz since 1938, when Dorothy Baker published *Young Man with a Horn,* a pioneering, worshipful novel based on Beiderbecke.

But how *do* you write fiction (or poetry, for that matter) about painters and dancers and writers and musicians? The jazz fan's idol-making is common to all the arts. Perhaps there are three ways to write about Picasso or Balanchine or Horowitz: ennoble him; reduce him to life-size; try to show him as the obsessed, gifted drudge most artists are. Laboriously spinning their works out of themselves, artists are desperate more often than exultant. They take no vacations: one invention leads to another, and the iron must never be allowed to cool. All camouflage themselves. Writers pretend to be inarticulate, painters speak in symbols or hyperbole, musicians gossip and tell jokes, dancers talk about their bodies and about food. There is an added difficulty in writing fiction about jazz: The music is ephemeral. A novelist can describe the 'Appassionata' and tell you exactly how his pianist hero plays it, but a jazz novelist must describe a music that is gone the instant it is played. Nowhere else does invention turn into memory so quickly. (Playwrights have an edge in writing about jazz: plays are a performer's art, like jazz. Witness Jack Gelber's *The Connection* and August Wilson's *Ma Rainey's Black Bottom*; both even have onstage bands.)

Marcela Breton clearly kept these difficulties in mind when she put together the anthology of jazz short stories she calls *Hot and Cool* (Plume). There are nineteen stories, arranged in rough chronological order. The earliest, by Rudolph Fisher, a novelist of the Harlem Renaissance, was published in 1930, and the most recent, by Martin Gardner, in 1987. Five of the stories deal directly with jazz. Six are largely taken up by racial matters, and six are about drugs and drinking. One is about a jazz fan, and one is a love story. The quality of the stories varies a good deal. 'Mending Wall,' by Willard Marsh, is set in Mexico and reads like an inept translation from the Spanish. Fisher's story, 'Common Meter,' is an engaging antique that is full of dated black slang and anthropomorphic musical descriptions: 'Clarinets wailed, saxophones moaned, trumpets wept wretchedly, trombones laughed bitterly, even the great bass horn sobbed dismally from the depths.' In Ann Petry's 'Solo on the Drums,' a jilted drummer makes his 'big bass drum growl,' and in 'The Screamers' LeRoi Jones, using an arty epigrammatic prose, converts the music into Message: 'The repeated rhythmic figure, a screamed riff, pushed in its insistence past music. It was hatred and frustration, secrecy and despair. It spurted out of the diphthong culture, and reinforced the black cults of emotion. There was no compromise, no dreary sophistication, only the elegance of something that is too ugly to be described.'

These various excesses are nicely balanced by Terry Southern and Richard Yates and Langston Hughes. Southern writes with great subtlety about a white jazz lover who unwittingly becomes, in a black musician's disparaging words, a 'professional nigger lover.' Yates tells us of a black pianist who enrages two white admirers by Uncle Tomming with an important nightclub owner. Hughes, in his best jess-lissen style, deals with a rich white matron, Mrs. Ellsworth, who underwrites the classical training of a black woman pianist, Oceola Jones; in the end, Oceola marries and goes back to playing blues. ('Is this what I spent thousands of dollars to teach you?' Mrs. Ellsworth asks as Oceola makes 'the bass notes throb like tom-toms deep in the earth.')

There are several funny stories in the book. In Peter De Vries' 'Jam Today,' which first appeared in *The New Yorker,* the narrator goes to a forties 'platter party,' at which each guest is asked to play his favorite 78-r.p.m. record. The party turns out to be made up of moldy figs who believe that no good jazz has been played since 1930, but the narrator brings a Benny Goodman big-band record. Embarrassed, he breaks the record and stuffs it into his overcoat pocket, then discovers when he leaves that he has put it in his host's pocket. Martin Gardner's 'The Devil and the Trombone' deals with a professor returning home from a wearying evening meeting who stops in at a church to rest his mind and listen to the organ music he hears inside. The organist, dressed in a white robe, has wings folded at his sides, and he is playing unearthly music. Out of the blackness behind him comes a tall, hairy figure with swarthy skin and a forked-tail, who begins playing raucous tailgate trombone. The two jam together, and their music is so empyrean that the professor finds he suddenly understands the meaning of life – when the music stops, and the angelic figure tells him to go back to his pew and wake himself up. Donald Barthelme's ingenious 'The King of Jazz,' which also appeared in *The New Yorker,* is about the perfervid way that jazz has progressed in its ninety years, today's heroes trampling on yesterday's myths. It also attempts to solve the problem of how to describe the music – a problem that many writers have attacked with a metaphor in each hand. He gives us thirteen hilarious examples of how to approximate the sounds of jazz. Here are four: 'That sounds like polar bears crossing Arctic ice pans? That sounds like a herd of musk ox in full flight? That sounds like male walruses diving to the bottom of the sea? That sounds like fumaroles smoking on the slopes of Mt. Katmai?'

Toni Cade Bambara's 'Medley' is a dialect story told by a black beautician who walks out on the bass player she lives with. She describes him:

> Larry Landers looked more like a bass player than ole Mingus himself. Got these long arms that drape down over the bass like they were grown special for that purpose. Fine, strong hands with long fingers and muscular knuckles, the dimples deep black at the joints. His calluses so other-colored and hard, looked like Larry had swiped his grandmother's tarnished thimbles to play with. He'd move in on that bass like he was going to hump it or something, slide up behind it as he lifted it from the rug, all slinky. He'd become one with the wood. Head dipped down sideways bobbing out the rhythm, feet tapping, legs jiggling, he'd look good. Thing about it, though, ole Larry couldn't play for shit.

Al Young's 'Chicken Hawk's Dream' is short and nearly perfect. It begins: 'Chicken Hawk stayed high pretty much all the time and he was nineteen years old limping down academic corridors trying to make it to the twelfth grade.' Chicken Hawk is a drug addict who lives in Detroit and dreams that he is walking around New York playing fantastic alto saxophone. He is so sure that the dream is true that he borrows a horn to practice on. But he can only make it squeak. He blames the horn, and drifts away with his friend Wine. Later, the narrator runs into Chicken Hawk on the street, and Chicken Hawk tells him that he is about to leave for New York to put together a band and make some records, as soon as he gets his horn out of hock.

Three stories in *Hot and Cool* move close to the heart of jazz. The longest, at sixty-three pages, is 'The Pursuer,' by the Argentine novelist Julio Cortázar. It was published in the late sixties, and is a thinly disguised account of the last months in the life of Charlie Parker, here called Johnny Carter. Cortázar moves inside Carter's complex, duplicitous, crazy head. Carter tells his Boswell, a critic named Bruno, about how he has been remembering his past: 'It wasn't thinking, it seems to me I told you a lot of times, I never think; I'm like standing on a corner watching what I think go by, but I'm not thinking what I see. You dig?' Bruno decides not to alter the second edition of his biography of Carter, despite Carter's having told him that the book was fine except that he had been left out of it. Bruno explains with infuriating cool, 'I decided not to touch the second edition, to go on putting Johnny forth as he was at bottom: a poor sonofabitch with barely mediocre intelligence, endowed like so many musicians, so many chess players and poets, with the gift of creating incredible things without the slightest consciousness (at most, the pride of a boxer who knows how strong he is) of the dimensions of his work.'

Far more famous is James Baldwin's 'Sonny's Blues,' published in the late fifties. Baldwin was an exceptional essayist, but his fiction was often heated and clumsy. 'Sonny's Blues' is about a drug addict who finds salvation – apparent salvation – by becoming a jazz pianist. The narrator, who is Sonny's straight older brother, goes to a club to hear him and, after the first set, sends a drink up to the bandstand for Sonny. (There are a number of gaffes in the stories, and this is one. Musicians rarely stay on the bandstand between sets.) Baldwin ends the story with a disastrous sentence: 'For me, then, as they began to play again, [the drink] glowed and shook above my brother's head like the very cup of trembling.'

In its handmade, assiduous way, Eudora Welty's 'Powerhouse' may be the best fiction ever written about jazz. It first appeared in *The Atlantic*, in 1941, when she was a new writer, and it seems to be based on her having heard Fats Waller on the road in the South. (The central figure, Powerhouse, *is* Waller, and not 'a pianist in the style of Albert Ammons and Meade Lux Lewis,' as Marcela Breton claims in her introduction.) The story is an extraordinary mixture of surrealism and truth. It has a jittering comic surface, like Waller himself, that hides, as Waller's did, the heaviness and sadness most blacks carried around in this country fifty years ago – particularly if they were musicians from New York doing a string of one-night stands in the Deep South. The musicians play, have a beer at a nearby black café between sets, and play again. Here is some of Welty's exotic description of Waller: 'You can't tell what he is. "Nigger man"? – he looks more Asiatic, monkey, Jewish, Babylonian, Peruvian, fanatic, devil. He has pale gray eyes, heavy lids, maybe horny, like a lizard.' Powerhouse tells his musicians that he has got a telegram from one Uranus Knockwood, saying that his wife is dead. He had talked to his wife on the telephone the night before, and she said she might jump out of the window. But no one knows who Uranus Knockwood is (a Welty conundrum, in which the despotic Greek god Uranus is guarded by Lady Luck), and the musicians begin to understand that perhaps Powerhouse is fantasizing and that his fantasy rests on the hope that expecting the worst might bring the opposite. Eudora Welty makes the reader see *and* hear Powerhouse. He is outsize in the story, but he is utterly human – a huge man, like Waller.

121 **Jack Baird** A jazzman's heaven (1956)

Source: Jack Baird, *Hot, Sweet and Blue* (New York: Fawcett, 1956: 92–6) (excerpt). (Editor's title)

Johnny came back to the hotel in the early hours of the morning and found that Spades had packed and gone, drums and all. He stared at the empty spot where the traps had been gathering dust. The guy played a mess of skins. He would have been a good man in any rhythm section.

He undressed and crawled into bed ...

He was awakened the next morning by a heavy pounding on his door. He threw on his robe, plodding sleepily to open it. It was Spades, hollow-eyed, a bit shaky, but completely sober.

'Forget something?'

The drummer gave him a sour glim.

'Yeah – you.'

'Me? I thought I was on your no-good list?'

Spades came into the room. 'You are. Right at the top. But I got nothin' against your horn.'

Johnny fished a cigarette out of the pocket of his robe. Spades wobbled over to the bed and stretched out.

'I'm beat. Up all night.'

'Where's your drums?'

'Left them at the Union, where I ran into Milt Gaynor. That's why I'm here.'

Johnny waited for him to make some sense.

'Gaynor's fine piano. He's got a fine combo, and he's got a job. But he needs a horn like yours and a drummer like me.'

'Sounds good.'

'It is. We're gonna see him tonight.'

A job with a combo. Already anticipation and a flock of questions whirled in his mind. But Spades couldn't give him any answers. He was fast asleep.

It was a seven-piece combo, and a good one. Tenor, clarinet, trombone, drums, piano, bass and Johnny's cornet. It was his kind of jazz, and he had himself a ball at the first get-together.

'You're it, Johnny boy,' Gaynor said. 'On the job you make the front, with your looks and gone horn. I'll just play piano.'

The chance to make the front and be heard was there and knocking. And it hadn't taken too long.

Gaynor had latched onto a spot in the Village of the Big Town. He had come up with a six-week contract, and there were no commercial ties.

'We play the real stuff. Lew Monaco is willing to gamble on it in his place. He caters to an artistic, Bohemian group that goes for jazz; and they haven't been getting it ...'

They got into New York the first week of November, the day before the engagement was to start. They all went down to Monaco's that night to size up the joint and catch the combo moving out. A technical bunch, playing mechanically, grinding out colorless medleys of pop tunes. Their music left Johnny cold. Gaynor knew the guitar man, Jed Martin, and brought him over to the table for a drink at intermission.

'What kind of response will we get?' Gaynor asked Martin.

'Good. They like jazz and ask for it. We're either too commercial or too normal for them.'

'Characters,' Spades said, gazing about.

'Reet – and a motley group of them. Actors, agents, long-haired painters and their babes and models ... Fairies, Lesbians, and the usual shady ladies who scream and scratch if you call them whores, but they collect for all biological experiments – and the cats. Damned if they don't all dig.'

They found that Jed Martin had the right slant on the joint. Loudmouthed radical poets and artists, well-stacked models, call girls and homos, gathered nightly, each searching for something exciting to satisfy their restless natures. And the first time Johnny lifted the horn, he knew he had reached them.

'We'll make it something warm and friendly and familiar,' Gaynor said. '*Sweet Georgia Brown*. It'll make us or break us. Up-tempo!' He hammered his foot, four to the bar.

Johnny set the pace, blasting out a soaring, rhythmic eight-bar intro that brought half the patrons up to pack around the stand. He blew the first chorus straight, giving each note its full value, playing full and round. Spades went into sixteen-bar leeway, taking his drums down to a whisper and building back up to launch his sticks into the rim with a spine-tickling machine gun roll of four bars. Jeff Riggs, the tenor man, came in, deep in the lower register, hanging onto his first lick in a series of repeat measures as though loathe to let it go, then breaking it loose to whip it up above the staff, to come tumbling into the middle register. He romped it along at an even pace, his notes bubbling buoyantly. Johnny caught it on the last measure thrown at him, spiraling it up dizzily above the staff. Staccato notes peppered out from between his lips, caught and tied over at the end of each four bars. Spades, catching the mood of it, set the tempo at a terrific rock.

They found a nice rhythmic pattern for the final thirty-two bars and they brought it to a frenzied finish. Appreciative applause came from the restless souls who had been listening. Then Gaynor's searching fingers wandered over the keys, finding a thread of chords. Sounding them deep in a somewhat pleasing erratic manner, before he settled upon a vibrant chord that formed the basic foundation for the haunting melody he stabbed out with his right hand, single notes that quavered sweetly through the sonority of the bass harmonics. Johnny brought the silver mouthpiece against his lips, lifting the lament of his horn to the furthermost corners of Monaco's, and he knew he touched them by their listening silence ...

Jeff Riggs twisted the mouthpiece from off the horn. Gaynor light-fingered a final arpeggio and got up from his place at the piano. Johnny shoved the worn cornet into the sack and Spades came slowly down from his drums.

'Y'know, redhead, hearin' that lovely horn has made me fall in love with it all over again.'

'Enough to forget a punch on the jaw?'

'Yeah – I was sorta outa bounds, anyway.'

Johnny meandered out to the bar. He lost Spades somewhere in the short distance. Must have been the encouraging glance from the creamy-skinned blonde near the bar entrance.

He pulled himself up to the bar beside Gaynor. Monaco set a drink down in front of him. Lew Monaco was a short, fat guy with a grin that split his broad, red face, revealing a broken line of teeth.

'You play the good jazz,' he said, 'and they like you. That's all I ask.'

It sounded good. No restrictions on volume or style or tempo. Just play your music and as long as they liked you, you stayed. Jobs like this were a jazzman's heaven, scarce as a hot lick in a sweet-music band.

Monaco had played clarinet in the early days of jazz and the righteous music acted as a stimulation to his cooling blood and rusty lip. He was quite pleased. Riggs and the clarinet man, Gage, joined them and Lew kept pouring drinks for all of them, keeping up a running line of jive. The love of it was still in him, and the sound of it once more within his walls made him mellow.

Spades stuck his nose over Johnny's shoulder.

'I got a couple of live ones lined up.'

'Male or female?' Johnny asked blandly.

'My tendencies are normal, buster. Females – and class besides.'

Johnny revealed a lack of enthusiasm. He was tired and slightly on the tight side. He didn't want to fuss with some dame that slept all day and played all night.

'Yours is a brunette,' Spades informed him. 'She's as phony as her eyelashes, but she ought to be okay, once you get her undressed.'

'Count me out.'

'Aw, Johnny, I'll lose the blonde if you don't take her girl friend. You know how some babes are.'

'These two sound queer.'

'Don't be nasty.'

He went to the table with Spades. The brunette was a tall, languid job named Daphne; Spades's was called Carlotta. The dark-haired chick sat with carefully poised hands and eyed Johnny sideways from her almond-shaped green glims.

'This is the first time I've had a chance to see what you really look like. The horn was between us.'

'It's stood between me and a lot of trouble.'

She leaned close to him.

'Do I look like trouble?'

His eyes dropped to the dip in her gown and back to her face.

'I'd say about a hundred and twenty-five pounds of it all told.'

She gave an affected laugh, her eyes taking a full appraisal of him.

'Men who do things well interest me. You play that horn better than anyone I've ever heard.'

His blue eyes pierced deep, trying to find the real goods. It was a thin veneer and he didn't find it too hard. He wondered what she would sound like if he jolted her out of that boarding-school accent ...

She was a disappointment. It was really hamburger and his taste had drifted to T-bone. He waited until she had fallen asleep and then made his way back to his own hotel.

122 'Jean–Louis' [Jack Kerouac] Jazz of the Beat Generation (1955)

Source: 'Jean-Louis' [Jack Kerouac], 'Jazz of the Beat Generation,' in *New World Writing: Seventh Mentor Selection* (New York: New American Library, 1955: 7–9) (excerpt).

Out we jumped in the warm mad night hearing a wild tenorman's bawling horn across the way going 'EE-YAH! EE-YAH!' and hands clapping to the beat and folks yelling 'Go, go, go!' Far from escorting the girls into the place, Dean was already racing across the Street with his huge bandaged thumb in the air yelling 'Blow, man, blow!' A bunch of colored men in Saturday night suits were whooping it up in front. It was a sawdust saloon, all wood, with a small bandstand near the john on which the fellows huddled with their hats on blowing over people's heads, a crazy place, not far from Market Street, in the dingy skid-row rear of it, near Harrison and the big bridge causeway; crazy floppy women wandered around sometimes in their bathrobes, bottles clanked in alleys. In back of the joint in a dark corridor beyond the splattered toilets, scores of men and women stood against the wall drinking wine-spodi-odi and spitting at the stars ... wine, whiskey and beer. The behatted tenorman was blowing at the peak of a wonderfully satisfactory free idea, a rising and falling riff that went from 'EE-yah!' to a crazier 'EE-de-lee-yah!' and blasted along to the rolling crash of butt-scarred drums hammered by a big brutal-looking curl-sconced Negro with a bullneck who didn't give a damn about anything but punishing his tubs, crash, rattle-ti-boom crash. Uproars of music and the tenorman *had it* and everybody knew he had it. Dean was clutching his head in the crowd and it was a mad crowd. They were all urging that tenorman to hold it and keep it with cries and wild eyes; he was raising himself from a crouch and going down again with his horn, looping it up in a clear cry above the furor. A six-foot skinny Negro woman was rolling her bones at the man's hornbell, and he just jabbed it at her, 'Ee! ee! ee!' He had a foghorn tone; his horn was taped; he was a shipyard worker and he didn't care. Everybody was rocking and roaring; Galatea and Alice with beers in their hands were standing on their chairs shaking and jumping. Groups of colored studs stumbled in from the street falling over one another to get there. 'Stay with it man!' roared a man with a foghorn voice, and let out a big groan that must have been heard clear to Sacramento, 'Ah-haa!' – 'Whoo!' said Dean. He was rubbing his chest, his belly, his T-shirt was out, the sweat splashed from his face. Boom, kick, that drummer was kicking his drums down the cellar and rolling the beat upstairs with his murderous sticks, rattlety-boom! A big fat man was jumping on the platform making it sag and creak. 'Yoo!' The pianist was only pounding the keys with spread-eagled fingers, chords only, at intervals when the great tenorman was drawing breath for another blast of phrase, Chinese chords, they shuddered the piano in every timber, chink and wire, *boing!* The tenorman jumped down from the platform and just stood buried in the crowd blowing around; his hat was over his eyes; somebody pushed it back for him. He just hauled back and stamped his foot and blew down a hoarse baughing blast, and drew breath, and raised the horn and blew high wide and screaming in the air. Dean was directly in front of him with his face glued to the bell of the horn, clapping his hands, pouring sweat on the man's keys; and the man noticed and laughed in his horn a long quivering crazy mule's hee-haw and everybody else laughed and they rocked and rocked; and finally the tenorman decided to blow his top and crouched down and held a note in high C for a long time as everything else crashed along skittely-boom and the cries increased and I thought the cops would come swarming from the nearest precinct.

It was just a usual Saturday night goodtime, nothing else; the bebop winos were wailing away, the workingman tenors, the cats who worked and got their horns out of hock and blew and had their women troubles, and came on in their horns with a will, saying things, a lot to say, talkative horns, you could almost hear the words and better than that the harmony, made you hear the way to fill up blank spaces of time with the tune and very consequence of your hands and breath and dead soul; summer, August 1949, and Frisco blowing mad, the dew on the muscat in the interior fields of Joaquin and down in Watsonville the lettuce blowing, the money flowing for Frisco so seasonal and mad, the railroads rolling, extraboards roaring, crates of melons on sidewalks, bananas coming off elevators, tarantulas suffocating in the new crazy air, chipped ice and the cool interior smells of grape tanks, cool bop hepcats standing slumped with horn and no lapels and blowing like Wardell, like Brew Moore softly ... all of it insane, sad, sweeter than the love of mothers yet harsher than the murder of fathers. The clock on the wall quivered and shook; nobody cared about that thing. Dean was in a trance. The tenorman's eyes were fixed straight on him; he had found a madman who not only understood but cared and wanted to understand more and much more than there was, and they began duelling for this; everything came out of the horn, no more phrases, just cries, cries, 'Baugh' and down to 'Beep!' and up to 'EEEEE!' and down to clinkers and over to sideways echoing horn-sounds and horselaughs and he tried everything, up, down, sideways, upside down, dog fashion, horizontal, thirty degrees, forty degrees and finally he fell back in somebody's arms and gave up and everybody pushed around and yelled 'Yes, yes, he done blowed that one!'

123 **Kenneth Rexroth** Married blues (1966)

Source: Kenneth Rexroth, 'Married blues,' in *The Collected Shorter Poems* (New York: New Directions, 1966: 337).

I didn't want it, you wanted it.
Now you've got it you don't like it.
You can't get out of it now.

Pork and beans, diapers to wash,
Too poor for the movies, too tired to love.
There's nothing we can do.

Hot stenographers on the subway.
The grocery boy's got a big one.
We can't do anything about it.

You're only young once.
You've got to go when your time comes.
That's how it is. Nobody can change it.

Guys in big cars whistle.
Freight trains moan in the night.
We can't get away with it.

That's the way life is.
Everybody's in the same fix.
It will never be any different.

124 **Kenneth Patchen** Lonesome boy blues (1957)

Source: Kenneth Patchen, 'Lonesome boy blues,' in *Selected Poems by Kenneth Patchen* (New York: New Directions, 1957: 106).

Oh nobody's a long time
Nowhere's a big pocket
To put little
Pieces of nice things that

Have never really happened

To anyone except

Those people who were lucky enough
Not to get born
Oh lonesome's a bad place

To get crowded into

With only
Yourself riding back and forth
On
A blind white horse
Along an empty road meeting
All your
Pals face to face

Nobody's a long time

125 **Kenneth Patchen** Opening the window (1957)

Source: Kenneth Patchen, 'Opening the window,' in *Selected Poems by Kenneth Patchen* (New York: New Directions, 1957: 125–6).

They called across to ask me to get some beer and come up and cut a few touches.

I'd already gone to bed but I got some clothes on and went down to the store for the beer and some of that nice dry kind of salami.

When I got up there were two old women and a tall skinny man sitting half dressed holding musical instruments.

By half dressed I mean the old women were in their birthday suits and the skinny fellow had a couple heavy overcoats on over his regular duds.

And speaking of musical instruments, I refer to the fact that each of them was holding a full-blown mermaid in formfitting tights that was sort of crooning-like in a Greek accent.

As I commenced to set my parcels on the bed another old lady came barging out of the closet on zebraback.

After I lifted her off she said she had herself a sore behind from riding all the way from Boston and would I mind holding her for a while. Pretty soon they wanted I should fetch some more beer and I found out the only way I could manage her up and down the narrow stairs was to go backwards and to squeeze like all hell on her long legs and even then those bony knees of hers sounded like somebody having a fit with a snaredrum on either side of us. And every trip I went to a different store and they kept getting farther and farther away. I took the next day off and moved into a YMCA.

126 **Lawrence Ferlinghetti** from 'Autobiography' (1958)

Source: Lawrence Ferlinghetti, 'Autobiography,' in *A Coney Island of the Mind* (New York: New Directions, 1958: 60–3) (excerpt).

I am leading a quiet life
in Mike's place every day
watching the champs
of the Dante Billiard Parlor
and the French pinball addicts.
I am leading a quiet life
on lower East Broadway.
I am an American.
I was an American boy.
I read the American Boy Magazine
and became a boy scout
in the suburbs.
I thought I was Tom Sawyer
catching crayfish in the Bronx River
and imagining the Mississippi.
I had a baseball mit
and an American Flyer bike.
I delivered the Woman's Home Companion
at five in the afternoon
or the Herald Trib
at five in the morning.
I still can hear the paper thump
on lost porches.
I had an unhappy childhood.
I saw Lindberg land.
I looked homeward
and saw no angel.
I got caught stealing pencils
from the Five and Ten Cent Store
the same month I made Eagle Scout.

I chopped trees for the CCC
and sat on them.
I landed in Normandy
in a rowboat that turned over.
I have seen the educated armies
on the beach at Dover.
I have seen Egyptian pilots in purple clouds
shopkeepers rolling up their blinds
at midday
potato salad and dandelions
at anarchist picnics.
I am reading 'Lorna Doone'
and a life of John Most
terror of the industrialist
a bomb on his desk at all times.
I have seen the garbagemen parade
in the Columbus Day Parade
behind the glib
farting trumpeters.
I have not been out to the Cloisters
in a long time
nor to the Tuileries
but I still keep thinking
of going.
I have seen the garbagemen parade
when it was snowing.
I have eaten hotdogs in ballparks.
I have heard the Gettysburg Address
and the Ginsberg Address.
I like it here
and I won't go back
where I came from.
I too have ridden boxcars boxcars boxcars.
I have travelled among unknown men.
I have been in Asia
with Noah in the Ark.
I was in India
when Rome was built.
I have been in the Manger
with an Ass.
I have seen the Eternal Distributor
from a White Hill
in South San Francisco
and the Laughing Woman at Loona Park
outside the Fun House
in a great rainstorm
still laughing.
I have heard the sound of revelry
by night.
I have wandered lonely
as a crowd.

I am leading a quiet life
outside of Mike's Place every day
watching the world walk by
in its curious shoes.
I once started out
to walk around the world
but ended up in Brooklyn.
That Bridge was too much for me.
I have engaged in silence
exile and cunning.
I flew too near the sun
and my wax wings fell off.
I am looking for my Old Man
whom I never knew.
I am looking for the Lost Leader
with whom I flew.
Young men should be explorers.
Home is where one starts from.
But Mother never told me
there'd be scenes like this.
Womb-weary
I rest
I have travelled.
I have seen goof city.
I have seen the mass mess.
I have heard Kid Ory cry.
I have heard a trombone preach.
I have heard Debussy
strained thru a sheet.
I have slept in a hundred islands
where books were trees.
I have heard the birds
that sound like bells.
I have worn grey flannel trousers
and walked upon the beach of hell.
I have dwelt in a hundred cities
where trees were books.
What subways what taxis what cafés!
What women with blind breasts
limbs lost among skyscrapers!
I have seen the statues of heroes
at carrefours.
Danton weeping at a metro entrance
Columbus in Barcelona
pointing Westward up the Ramblas
toward the American Express
Lincoln in his stony chair
And a great Stone Face
in North Dakota.
I know that Columbus
did not invent America.

I have heard a hundred housebroken Ezra Pounds.
They should all be freed.
It is long since I was a herdsman.
I am leading a quiet life
in Mike's Place every day
reading the Classified columns.
I have read the Reader's Digest
from cover to cover
and noted the close identification
of the United States and the Promised Land
where every coin is marked
In God We Trust
but the dollar bills do not have it
being gods unto themselves.
I read the Want Ads daily
looking for a stone a leaf
an unfound door.
I hear America singing
in the Yellow Pages.
One could never tell
The soul has its rages.
I read the papers every day
and hear humanity amiss
in the sad plethora of print.
I see where Walden Pond has been drained
to make an amusement park.
I see they're making Melville eat his whale.
I see another war is coming
but I won't be there to fight it.
I have read the writing
On the outhouse wall.
I helped Kilroy write it.

127 **Etheridge Knight** For Eric Dolphy (1980)

Source: Etheridge Knight, 'For Eric Dolphy,' in *Born of a Woman: New and Selected Poems* (Boston: Houghton Mifflin, 1980: 31).

on flute
spinning   spinning   spinning
love
thru / out
the universe

```
i
know
exactly
whut chew mean
man

you like
tittee
my sister
who never expressed LOVE
in words (like the white folks always        d
she would sit in the corner                  o
and cry                                       i
everytime                                     n
I                                            g
got a whuppin
```

128 Sascha Feinstein Blues villanelle for Sonny Criss (2000)

Source: Sascha Feinstein, 'Blues villanelle for Sonny Criss,' in *Misterioso* (Port Townsend, WA: Copper Canyon Press, 2000: 15).

A lunar eclipse, and your solos spread
across wild clover as I exhale
and try not to think of the gun at your head,
how we say but rarely believe, 'You can't be dead

if you're on record.' Your alto wails
to the moon's elision, the solo spread
against the splintering woodshed.
It's '57, one year before jail,

twenty before the gun's at your head
and you're my age playing 'Calidad,'
'Willow Weep for Me,' 'Love for Sale,'
as the brief clips from your solo spread

the graying moon like cigarettes
in walnut-paneled dives, overpriced cocktails
cold as the gun you'll hold to your head.
But I'm trying not to see that, trying instead

to let the bass and chromatic scales
eclipse you, solo, outspread.
I'm trying not to think. The gun's at your head.

129 Michael Harper Brother John (1970)

Source: Michael Harper, 'Brother John,' in *Images of Kin: New and Selected Poems* (Urbana: University of Illinois Press, 1977: 181–2).

Black man:
I'm a black man;
I'm black; I am –
A black man; black –
I'm a black man;
I'm a black man;
I'm a man; black –
I am –

Bird, buttermilk bird –
smack, booze and bitches
I am Bird
baddest nightdreamer
on sax in the ornithology-world
I can fly – higher, high, higher –
I'm a black man;
I am; I'm a black man –

Miles, blue haze,
Miles high, another bird,
more Miles, mute,
Mute Miles, clean,
bug-eyed, unspeakable,
Miles, sweet Mute,
sweat Miles, black Miles;
I'm a black man;
I'm black; I am;
I'm a black man –

Trane, Coltrane; John Coltrane;
it's tranetime; chase the Trane;
it's a slow dance;
it's the Trane
in Alabama; acknowledgement,
a love supreme,
it's black Trane; black;

I'm a black man; I'm black;
I am; I'm a black man –

Brother John, Brother John
plays no instrument;
he's a black man; black;
he's a black man; he is
Brother John; Brother John –

I'm a black man; I am;
black; I am; I'm a black
man; I am; I am;
I'm a black man;
I'm a black man;
I am; I'm a black man;
I am:

for John O. Stewart

130 **Harryette Mullen** Playing the invisible saxophone *en el Combo de las Estrellas* (1981)

Source: Harryette Mullen, 'Playing the invisible saxophone *en el Combo de las Estrellas* (Galveston, TX: Energy Earth, 1981: 5–6).

for Vangie

One of these days I'm gonna write a real performance poem.
A poem that can grab the microphone and sing
till voice becomes music, and music dance.
A boogie poem sparkled with star presence.

The way I'll score it, poem gonna dance into melody.
(Let me tell you, this poem can move!)
And the way I'll choreograph the words,
each sound be a musical note
that flies off the page like some crazy blackbird.

Yeah, gonna have words turning into dance,
bodymoving music,
a get-down poem so kinetically energetic
it sure put disco to shame.
Make it a snazzy jazzy poem extravaganza, with pizzazz.
Poem be going solo,
flying high on improbable improvisational innovation.
Poem be blowing hard!

Want to speak a wordsong that moves folks' minds
and gets em up dancing to their own heartbeats.
Poem, say some words that jump into the blood
and tapdance in the pulse like rainfall.
Gonna let the rhythm of this poem
soak through the skin like rain into earth.

Let me play musician magician,
growing out my sleeve a poem that raises cane,
Poem so sweet, be my magical musical instrument,
flashing back the spotlight's spectrum as meteoric shower.
And poem, shoot off sparks like comets with tails of fire
as I play the invisible saxophone *en el combo de las estrellas.*

131 **Larry Neal** Don't say goodbye to the porkpie hat (1969)

Source: Larry Neal, 'Don't say goodbye to the porkpie hat,' in *Visions of a Liberated Future: Black Arts Movement Writings* (New York: Thunder's Mouth Press, 1989: 178–82). (Originally published in *Black Boogaloo*, 1969.)

Mingus, Bird, Prez, Langston, and them

Don't say goodbye to the Porkpie Hat that rolled
along on nodded shoulders
that swang bebop phrases
in Minton's jelly roll dreams
Don't say goodbye to hip hats tilted in the style of a soulful era;
the Porkpie Hat that Lester dug
swirling in the sound of sax blown suns
phrase on phrase, repeating bluely
tripping in and under crashing
hi-hat cymbals, a fickle girl
getting sassy on the rhythms.
Musicians heavy with memories
move in and out of this gloom;
the Porkpie Hat reigns supreme
smell of collard greens
and cotton madness
commingled in the nigger elegance of the style.
The Porkpie Hat sees tonal memories
of salt peanuts and hot house birds
the Porkpie Hat sees . . .

Cross riffing square kingdoms, riding midnight Scottsboro
trains. We are haunted by the lynched limbs.
On the road:
It would be some hoodoo town
It would be some cracker place
you might meet redneck lynchers
face to face
but mostly you meet mean horn blowers
running obscene riffs
Jelly Roll spoke of such places:
the man with the mojo hand
the dyke with the .38
the yaller girls
and the knifings.

Stop-time Buddy and Creole Sydney
wailed in here. Stop time.
chorus repeats, stop and shuffle.
stop and stomp.
listen to the horns, ain't they mean?
now ain't they mean
in blue
in blue
in blue streaks of mellow wisdom
blue notes
coiling around
the Porkpie Hat
and ghosts of dead musicians drifting through
here on riffs that smack
of one-leg trumpet players
and daddy glory piano ticklers
who
twisted arpeggios
with diamond-flashed fingers.
There was Jelly Roll Morton, the sweet mackdaddy,
hollering Waller, and Willie The Lion Smith –
some mean showstoppers.

Ghosts of dead holy rollers ricocheted in the air funky
with white lightnin' and sweat.
Emerald bitches shot shit in a kitchen smelling
of funerals and fried chicken.
Each city had a different sound:
there was Mambo, Rheba, Jeanne;
holy the voice of these righteous sisters.

Shape to shape, horn to horn
the Porkpie Hat resurrected himself
night to night, from note to note
skimming the horizons, flashing bluegreenyellow lights
and blowing black stars

and weird looneymoon changes; chords coiled about him
and he was flying
fast
zipping
past
sound
into cosmic silences.
And yes
and caresses flowed from the voice in the horn in the blue
of the yellow whiskey room where bad hustlers with big
coats moved, digging the fly sister, fingerpopping while
tearing at chicken and waffles.

The Porkpie Hat loomed specter like, a vision for the world;
shiny, the knob toe shoes,
sporting hip camel coats
and righteous pin stripes –
pants pressed razor shape;
and caressing his horn, baby like.

So we pick up our axes and prepare
to blast the white dream;
we pick up our axes
re-create ourselves and the universe,
sounds splintering the deepest regions
of spiritual space
crisp and moaning voices
leaping in the horns of destruction,
blowing death and doom to all who have no use for the spirit.

So we cook out of sight
into cascading motions of joy delight
shooflies the Bird lollygagging
and laughing for days,
and the rhythms way up in there
wailing, sending scarlet rays, luminescent,
spattering bone and lie.
we go on cool lords
wailing on into star nights,
rocking whole worlds, unfurling song on song
into long stretches of green spectral shimmerings,
blasting on, fucking the moon with the blunt edge
of a lover's tune, out there now, joy riffing
for days and do
railriding and do
talking some lovely shit and do
to the Blues God who blesses us.

No, don't say goodbye to the Porkpie Hat –
he lives, oh yes.

Lester lives and leaps
Delancey's dilemma is over
Bird lives
Lady lives
Eric stands next to me
while I finger the Afro-horn
Bird lives
Lady lives
Lester leaps in every night
Tad's delight
is mine now
Dinah knows
Richie knows
that Bud is Buddha
that Jelly Roll dug juju
and Lester lives
in Ornette's leapings
the Blues God lives
we live
live
spirit lives
and sound lives
bluebird lives
lives and leaps
dig the mellow voices
dig the Porkpie Hat
dig the spirit in Sun Ra's sound
dig the cosmic Trane
dig be
dig be
dig be
spirit lives in sound
dig be
sound lives in spirit
dig be
yeah! ! !

spirit lives
spirit lives
spirit lives
SPIRIT ! ! !

SWHEEEEEEEEEEEEEEETTT!!!

take it again
this time from the top

Riff 10

Black Music, White Movies. (Thomas Cripps, *Slow Fade to Black: The Negro in American Film, 1900–1942*, 1977)

The filming of a jazz solo is always as much about films, their requisite otherness, their built-in historicity, as about the solo itself. (Frederick Garber, 'Fabulating Jazz,' in Krin Gabbard [ed.], *Representing Jazz*, 1995)

The history of jazz in the movies (entertainment films, not documentaries) has been a long, sorry tale that reads like one of cultural displacement or arrested development. (Donald Bogle, on 'Jazz Films,' in Spike Lee, *Mo' Better Blues*, 1990)

The Story goes like this: a musician of genius, frustrated by the discrepancy between what he can achieve and the crummy life musicians lead (because of racial discrimination, or the demand that the music be made commercial, or because he has a potential he can't reach), goes mad, or destroys himself with alcohol and drugs. The Story might be a romance, but it is a valid one. (Vance Bourjaily, 'In and Out of Storyville: Jazz and Fiction,' *New York Times Book Review*, 1987)

Cheap melodrama set partly in jazz clubs where the characters are all lost, derelict or unreal and where the action is lurid and largely incomprehensible. (David Meeker, *Jazz in the Movies*, 1981; item 3640, *The Wild Party* [1956])

1. Commercial shorts.
2. The use of jazz musicians in cameo performances within the basic framework of film musicals.
3. The dramatic feature film with a jazz theme including 'biographies' of famous musicians.
4. The jazz documentary presenting its subject in a straightforward or possibly 'arty' way.
5. The all-black film – made with an all-star cast either for the general audience or for the black audience exclusively.
6. The films using jazz music and musicians on the background score with little or no jazz aspects in their subject content.

(Broad categories of jazz–film relationship, Donald Kennington and Danny Read, *The Literature of Jazz: A Critical Guide*, 1980)

Chorus X
All the Usual Pitfalls: Jazz and film
(cliché, stereotype, ambience)

'Most jazz films aren't really about jazz' (Gabbard 1996: 1). It is often remarked that jazz and film came of age at the same time and both are spoken of as America's major contribution to twentieth-century arts. The intersection between them, however, has often been a troubled one. Brian Priestley, in a radio review of jazz in film (1997), finds 'jazz in the movies equals bad news.' Certainly, for the most part, jazz has been used to serve the needs and demands of *film*, its relationship a subordinate, often marginal one. David Meeker's comprehensive listing, *Jazz in the Movies* (1981), is full of terms which suggest this: jazz is governed by the need to provide a 'vehicle' or 'background,' musicians make 'appearances' in 'sequences' or 'numbers,' and jazz appears as an 'item' – quite often relegated to commercial 'shorts,' 'featurettes,' or 'soundies.' There are, then – as Meeker's compilation amply demonstrates – plenty of films which *use* jazz, but few which give it a respectful or considerate role, or even a decent hearing. Too often, jazz is demeaningly equated with sleaze – an underworld of addiction, intemperance and degradation.

This subordination and devaluation are compounded by the agendas and ideologies which films follow in their use and representation of jazz. Krin Gabbard's study of jazz and the American cinema (1996) shows how jazz films need to be read within their historical-ideological 'moments': a canonical discourse which maintains white hegemony is as discernible in jazz film as in accounts of the music itself (see **Chorus II**). What is evident here – not least in the Hollywood genre of 'biopic' – is a discourse concerning jazz's elevation as art, and negotiation of issues like race, class and gender between makers of film and viewing public. **Chorus X** presents these contexts of canon, ideology and discourse through the typologies of jazz film and its reception. It concentrates on the stereotypical and 'public' narratives of film biographies, but also considers documentary-performance vehicles which have enjoyed some success in bringing value and respect to jazz music.

In the history of film, the biopic genre was hugely popular with major studios in the period 1927–60, and responsible for a Hollywood construction of 'public' history (Custen 1992). Here, an organized culture of production uses a highly conventionalized view of fame, profession, gender and family role to create Hollywood's dominant 'world view' for its viewers. Kenneth **Spence** (1988), in a lively 'digest' of jazz film (**132**), overviews this sanitizing effect – Hollywood's 'cleansing' of issues, its homiletic and nostalgic treatment of race, dream and heroism in jazz lives, its simplistic and 'troubling [racial] omissions.' Spence wants to argue jazz's very creativity and undefinedness still enable it to 'flie free' of the demeaning cage of film confinement. However, the constraints and prescriptions of Hollywood formulas surely create tension with potential racial politics, which sees the erasure of black hope and promise in films like *Birth of the Blues* (1941), *Syncopation* (1942), and *New Orleans* (1947). Stories lapse into conventional, safe romance and black music is interpolated into a white idiom. Also, African-American issues revolving round racial conflict and inter-racialism are largely side-stepped in films such as *St. Louis Blues* (1958) and *Paris Blues* (1961). (See Cripps 1993: 12–14, 208–9, 283–5.)

Hollywood's construction of a value system which maintains white hegemony and at the same time advances the cause of jazz as art is surveyed in Krin **Gabbard**'s section on 'the white jazz biopic.' Gabbard (**133**) argues jazz is consistently elevated in 'stories' about white musician-subjects. What biopic narratives construct is the legitimation of white-played jazz as it perfects the music from primitive black roots into high art. Gabbard illustrates this process from popular biopics like *The Fabulous Dorseys* (1947), *Young Man with a Horn* (1949), *The Glenn Miller Story* (1953), *The Benny Goodman Story* (1955) and *Pete Kelly's Blues* (1955). In all these – and other – films, says Gabbard, Hollywood introduced black characters so that white musician heroes could surpass them in terms of success and advance of their art. White subjectivity is thus protected 'from the overwhelmingly black presence in jazz.'

Donald **Bogle**'s study of black racial stereotypes in American film (1994) – 'toms,' 'coons,' 'mulattoes,' 'mammies' and 'bucks' – usefully prepares for his reading of Louis Armstrong's film roles in a study of the jazz trumpeter's cultural legacy (**134**). Here, Armstrong's appearances create a contradiction between his obsequious 'stepin fetchit' figure of the clowning routines and comic servant roles and his superb trumpet playing – hambone entertainer vs. musical artist. Armstrong can stand, in *A Rhapsody in Black and Blue* (1932), in demeaning leopard skins and soap suds, yet his trumpet is transformative. Interestingly, Bogle concludes that Armstrong gets lifted out of his black cultural context – the sly ethnic humour, satire and highly stylized, minstrel-like entertainment – and crosses over into more reductive contexts of white reception. If anything, such roles help confirm notions of unthreatened, white racial superiority – *except* for Armstrong as virtuoso jazz soloist.

The pre-eminence of African-Americans in more recent decades has been reflected in important black-subject biopics – notably *Lady Sings the Blues* (1972), *Round Midnight* (1986) and *Bird* (1988). Their milieu, inescapably, may still make them concerned with the 'sleaze' factor and 'underbelly of society,' so renowned of the jazz film (Priestley 1997); there are problems, too, with those residual elements of myth and melodrama – clichés – which belong to formulaic convention. Overall, such films, whatever their respectful provenance and sympathy, follow 'The Story' outlined by Vance Bourjaily (1987: 44; **Riff 10**). Yet, paradoxically, for all their lurid and over-coloured quality, such narratives may still mirror real jazz lives. 'The Musician's Tragedy,' no less.

'It took a damn Frenchman to finally make a serious movie about us!' (Ron Carter) Jean-Pierre **Coursodon** previews his interview with *Round Midnight*'s director, Bertrand Tavernier (**135**), by emphasizing the unprecedented empathy and respect the film shows to jazz and applauding its decision to cast an actual jazz musician (Dexter Gordon) in the lead role. Calling it 'the best fiction film ever made on the subject,' Coursodon notes Tavernier's quality of 'tenderness.' *Round Midnight*, as a tribute to the life struggles of Bud Powell and Lester Young, is a work of homage, 'a huge act of kindness.' Tavernier himself reveals a ready identification with the plight of American jazz musicians – and expatriate artists – and his determination to make a film about a jazz saxophonist, using a real life musician. Francis **Davis** (136) expands this generic role in suggesting Dale Turner is 'Everycat,' a composite musical figure of 'fact and lore' who appeals to musicians and validates their lonely endeavours. For all its clichés, and Gordon's lack-lustre playing (though this may reflect Turner's own decline), Davis can acknowledge *Round Midnight*'s undoubtedly sympathetic, compassionate account of the jazz life. In a study of films about jazz artists, Frederick Garber considers Tavernier's achievement 'the most satisfying exercise in rendering the complexities of jazz' (Gabbard 1995b: 4).

An interview conducted by Nat Hentoff (1988) confirms Clint Eastwood's *Bird* is rooted in his long interest in jazz and alleged knowledge of the black experience. While Eastwood disavows any political import, he agrees *Bird* may be understood in a context of individual versus the system – 'the basic theme' in making a portrait of Parker. In a rather sketchy view of his film, fan Eastwood emphasizes its concern with the 'story' musicians tell and, in Parker's case, the enjoyment of playing 'hot' bebop. Eastwood's relaxed responses contrast with the forthright views of commentators, which tend to divide on racial grounds. Support for *Bird* is proffered by Parker biographer Gary **Giddins** (137), who in an appreciative, detailed interview-review argues the slogan 'Bird Lives' is a promise fulfilled by the film. Where 'jazz movies as a rule are so farcically rotten,' *Bird* is a serious, adult, European-style film about a black artist – rare enough – which refuses to mute or romanticize Parker. Particularly impressive is Eastwood's recreation of 1940s period detail and careful handling of music and soundtrack. Giddins' claim for the film's inventive truth is countered by opposing voices, who have vociferously insisted on *Bird*'s unrelatedness to African-American culture (Crouch 1989), criticized its mistakenly doctored music, and even alleged Eastwood has insulted and degraded black artist-musicians (R. Porter 1991). Bogle, introducing Spike Lee's *Mo' Better Blues* (1990: 26–9), is one of several to have found *Bird* an 'overextended elegy,' sombre and lifeless, without serious attempt to examine Parker's black cultural context and the racial experiences that defined Parker and his music. Some of the very virtues argued by Giddins – *Bird*'s authenticity, its sure poise and invention – are overturned in Francis **Davis**'s dismissive review, 'Birdland, mon amor' (138). Davis finds Forest Whitaker's Parker unconvincing – torment, but neither hedonism nor genius – the film's treatment of the Parker history and context 'hooey,' the flashback structure 'a mess,' its music 'phoney.' It is damning, indeed, to conclude that *Bird*, supposedly a labour of love, is 'a jazz fan's movie in the worst possible sense.'

A filmography of jazz, then, includes many examples of the biopic, whose making and reception have proved a fruitful ground of cultural and racial debate – raising questions about what is authentic and historical in such a resolutely mythological genre. But another major jazz film genre, the documentary and performance vehicle, has perhaps provided a more objective, successful treatment, able to present jazz on something closer to its own musical terms and privileging the roles and performances of practitioners.

'This is a jam session. Quite often these great artists gather and play – ad lib – hot music. It could be called a midnight symphony.' An early, classic example of the jazz performance film is the ten-minute short, *Jammin' the Blues*, made by *Life* photographer Gjon Mili in 1944. Arthur Knight (Gabbard 1995b: 11–53), in a detailed study, reveals how mediations of art and race determine the film's reformulation of conventions used to represent jazz. In terms of the comprehensive credits, voice-over introduction, photographic strategy, and aural–visual techniques, Mili succeeds in envisioning the jazz process in ways different from Hollywood convention. Above all, he transforms viewers into insiders, 'acknowledged audience members and possible participants.' James **Agee** (**139**) sees less art in *Jammin'* than pretense and middle-browed artiness. Most reviewers of the time, however, like Charles **Emge** (**140**) and Jackie **Lopez** (**141**), applaud the film – for its hopeful depiction of black Americans, their creativeness and humanity, and a fine, skilful salute to the 'Negro' art of making jazz. Knight reproduces the coded headline of a 1945 *Ebony* magazine review: 'Jamming Jumps the Color Line.'

David Meeker (1981: 3025) describes Jack Smight and Robert Herridge's *The Sound of Jazz* (1957) as 'a great musical package.' Featuring groups led by Count Basie, Henry Allen, Thelonious Monk, Mal Waldron, Jimmy Giuffre, and vocalists Jimmy Rushing and Billie Holiday, this famous CBS television programme is unpacked by Whitney **Balliett** (**142**) – a retrieval job on an 'underground classic,' which sets right the film's process. With unequalled camera work and picture selection, *The Sound of Jazz* exemplifies the unambitious aim of such performance vehicles: 'to offer the best there was in the simplest and most direct way – no history, no apologetics, no furbelows.' Other historic studio-made jazz presentations to have followed this format include Smight and Herridge's own *The Sound of Miles Davis* (1959) and Shepherd Traube's *After Hours* (1961) – both of which eschew talk and concentrate on jazz performance. Bert Stern's record of the 1958 Newport Jazz Festival, *Jazz on a Summer's Day* (1960), is billed as 'the definitive jazz film' (video blurb). Claim apart, the film is really a pictorial documentary, with parallel images from the festival and its environs – principally footage of the 1958 America's Cup Yacht Race – that may suggest the unwelcome intrusions and pretensions of film art on the music's actuality. Yet, unarguably, typical notices of the film remark on its perceptive documentation of time and place.

It is indeed the jazz documentary which has proved to be an enduring and valuable vehicle for presenting the music and practitioners. The number of distinguished films made of individual musicians and contexts include those on Mingus (1968); Punch Miller (1971); jazz's 'religion' (1972); Basie (1973); Kansas City jazz (1979); Beiderbecke (1981); Coltrane (1985); Rollins (1986); Webster (1986); and Monk (1988) (see **Suggested reading**). Two other, more recent documentaries have worked in contrary directions and attracted considerable attention. Bruce Weber's homoerotic *Let's Get Lost* (1988) presents

410

a mythic yet unflattering portrait of hapless trumpeter Chet Baker, 'nowhere man' and once called the James Dean of jazz. Hal **Hinson**'s newspaper review (**143**) rightly sees Weber's film as rapturous homage, a working out of his infatuation with a subject and mystique which says as much about Weber as Baker. Conversely, Jean Bach's *A Great Day in Harlem* (1994), moves away from the personal and idiosyncratic to the collective and historical in a carefully synchronized evocation. The source of memory is an iconic 1958 photograph taken by Art Kane (for an *Esquire* special jazz issue) on the steps of a New York Harlem brownstone. From a group portrait that included three generations of jazz artists and 57 varieties of musician, Bach travels through still and moving footage, interview, music and affectionately voiced memory into the lives of many of the participants. James **Berardinelli** (**144**) salutes the remarkable good fortune, affection and joy of this acclaimed film – 'a magical documentary.' At the end of it all, Dizzy Gillespie asks the interviewer, 'What time is it? I gotta go call my wife.' Readers: he may have a point …

132 **Kenneth C. Spence** Jazz digest (1988)

Source: Kenneth C. Spence, 'Jazz digest,' *Film Comment* 24, 6 (1988: 38–43).

Consider four modest examples: 1) Idea's eureka light flashes for an instant across Jimmy Stewart's face: 'Wait a minute … a clarinet lead!' And so was born one of this century's more distinctive musical sounds – Glenn Miller's orchestra is instantly recognizable. But, of course, we knew that sound even before we had seen Stewart play the lead in *The Glenn Miller Story* (1953). Perhaps during this short scene the audience was meant to prompt poor struggling Jimmy, 'Come on, Jimmy, dump the trumpet, try the clarinet.' Jimmy (well, Glenn) was searching for ways to express himself. He played jazz; we see him join in a jam session with Louis Armstrong and Gene Krupa. The movie Miller has this deep-felt need to get that passage just right, announcing that the only way to express himself was through an *arrangement.*

2) Despite everyone telling him in the film, 'Don't be that way!' (not so co-incidentally the name of one of his hit songs), Benny Goodman just *is* that way, and that's how Steve Allen plays the title role in *The Benny Goodman Story* (1955) – stubbornly needing to play 'his kind of music.' Goodman/Allen pointedly eschews attempts by others to have him play in a more commercial (hence lucrative) manner.

3) Sal Mineo starred in *The Gene Krupa Story* (1959), quite ably mimicking the real drummer's rudiments on the soundtrack, expressing his need to play *his* kind of music.

4) As did Robert De Niro as the fictional Jimmy Doyle in *New York, New York*

411

(1977), spurning the commercial road to success while choosing the purer-intentioned road to artistic expression.

The filmic conventions illustrated here are fairly prominent: Set up the creative artistic genius as a cultural icon in as simple a manner as possible. Let the new musical 'discoveries' be that of an individual effort, found in isolation. Avoid talking about social conditions (much less depict them), and for the most part, wrap up the film with a happy marriage or at least some nice lighting effects. Hollywood has worked hard at expressing *its* need to explain how jazz is 'created' and how ultimately successful one can be in that creation, providing it is the 'right' kind of jazz.

Jazz, however, is not one but many forms of music ... Hollywood consistently has asked the question [of what jazz is] through the decades but has also answered it audaciously as well. There has always been an association between film and jazz, both developing simultaneously. The transition by musicians from silent film accompanists to soundtrack performers inevitably crossed paths with the medium's venturing into nooks and crannies for story and slice-of-life sidetrips.

Duke Ellington's band starred in Dudley Murphy's *Black and Tan Fantasy* (1929), a short film with a slight story, not much more than a filmed Cotton Club revue but packed with absolutely stunning music. This is a vital historical record. John Murray Anderson's *The King of Jazz* (1930) is less so despite it being an early technicolor amalgamation of sketches and musical perfor-mances. Paul Whiteman was hailed as the 'King of Jazz,' a preposterous idea so early in the development of film and jazz. That same year, however, Ellington returned in a feature film, *Check and Double Check,* an outrageous Amos 'n' Andy film. In 1934 he made another short, *Symphony in Black* (providing one of Duke's earliest extended compositions and introducing Billie Holiday), as well as two other features, *Murder at the Vanities* and *Belle of the Nineties,* as well as a film short and a newsreel.

As the bands' popularity grew, theaters began featuring them not in the pit but onstage as standardly as the lines of exultant teen-agers snaking around city blocks waiting for the 10 P.M. show. Not only did the kids dance in the aisles when Benny Goodman played the Paramount, but often the stage show was more popular than the film.

Unlike the rock films of the Fifties where the male rock star (Frankie Avalon, Elvis, etc.) was the central character – or of the Sixties where the decade began with films that incorporated the antics of a band into a storyline (*Help, A Hard Day's Night*) and then shifted into rockumentary (*Don't Look Back, Gimme Shelter,* etc.) because reality began outstripping fiction for interest – when a musician or a band was featured in a Thirties or Forties film, jazz fans tolerated the dismal plot for only a two- or three-minute glimpse of their idols. In some films it paid off with a dividend; in others it was an embarrassment.

Goodman's band and racially integrated quartet played powerhouse music in *Hollywood Hotel,* directed by Busby Berkeley (1937). The story was transparent: Dick Powell goes to Hollywood to seek fame and fortune and gets to sing a few numbers along the way – yet it is Goodman's band and its energy that are memorable. Rather forgettable is the 1941 *Birth of the Blues,* a melodrama that fancifully details the birth of jazz in New Orleans. The reward is Jack Teagarden playing some excellent trombone, but the effort is almost unbearable, however. As a form of penance for denying the role of blacks in the birth of jazz, the film concludes with brief homages to the Dorsey brothers, Louis Armstrong, Duke Ellington, Benny Goodman, and Paul Whiteman.

Several films featured major band leaders and soloists in better light. *Some Like It Hot,* a 1939 Bob Hope comedy, showcased Gene Krupa and recorded a few production numbers usually reserved for personal appearances. Glenn Miller's band was well-featured in the two films they made, *Sun Valley Serenade* (1941), a romantic comedy, and *Orchestra Wives* (1942), a comedy on the big-band business that preserves many of Miller's most popular recordings. The Nicholas brothers, however, stole both the films with their extraordinary precision tap dancing, and 'Chattanooga Choo-Choo,' one of Miller's major hit records, no longer seemed his property alone after Harold and Fayard Nicholas put their stamp on it.

Harry James, Count Basie, Artie Shaw, Tommy Dorsey and a host of others continued to make feature films and short subjects, and by 1948 *A Song Is Born* boasted a stellar roster: Lionel Hampton, Tommy Dorsey, Benny Goodman, Charlie Barnet, and Louis Armstrong all playing together. Despite the antics of Danny Kaye, these first-rate jazz musicians do manage a few tunes, yet Goodman is reduced for some idiotic reason to wearing a mustache and playing a character named 'Professor Magenbruch.'

Jazz fans did not see film as art; they were used to seeing musical artists treated poorly. Similarly, filmmakers did not look upon jazz as art. The big bands of the swing era had reigned supreme for more than a decade, but musical tastes and society kept shifting. During the Depression the big bands, with their insistent beat, brought a nation to its feet dancing. The Second World War, with all of its tensions, fears, anticipations, and anxieties set the stage for personal melodrama: Replacing the big bands postwar, vocalists stole the show and the kids swooned.

Modern harmonies fit the restlessness of the nation. William Wyler's 1946 *The Best Years of Our Lives* featured Hoagy Carmichael in a major role, playing some piano, too. His was a friendly voice – old reliable banging out the tunes in the corner bar. But the changed lives of the film's returning servicemen, who no longer fit in easily stateside, were underscored by the harmonic dissonance of the soundtrack. New lives needed to be newly lived, new sounds needed to be heard.

Modern music grew out of the big-band response to the social climate. Assembly lines for war production had been integrated racially and sexually. Nightclubs featured racially integrated musical groups routinely. Their audiences, too, reflected the change. Bebop, which began as small group musical expression, soon developed into large-scale format. Some big band musicians began experimenting with the new harmonics, and several embraced the new music. Stan Kenton, Charlie Barnet, Woody Herman, Gene Krupa, Dizzy Gillespie, Billy Eckstine, and Claude Thornhill fronted large bands that continued to play theaters, tour the country, and make films. Short films. Feature films did not present modern jazz to a large audience. Its importance as an art form was overlooked.

Yet not completely. The new music was more apt to turn up in some form as thematic underscoring in films. Employment of jazz musicians began to increase behind the camera while it steadily decreased in front of it. Many musicians unwittingly supported films that communicated mixed messages at best, clearly adversarial at worst.

Elia Kazan's *Panic in the Streets* (1950), set in New Orleans, perks with Dixieland (and the threat of bubonic plague.) Fritz Lang's 1952 *They Clash by Night* featured Benny Carter's band, while Don Siegel's *Private Hell 36* (1954) sported a full class of the West Coast 'cool school.'

The startling quality of the new music seemed fit for *film noir*, characterized by its brooding, somber, anxious nature. The war won, doubt floated up through the sea of tranquility, love, and happiness that was supposed to flow after victory.

A plethora of films alloyed psychological friction and neurosis with modern jazz. The zenith may have been reached in 1953 with *The Wild One*. Thematically and on the jukebox, Shorty Rogers' music supports the image of Marlon Brando and Lee Marvin as avenging angels. The Fifties hysteria induced by Joe McCarthy caused aliens from Mars and Metaphor to invade theaters. It seemed to be a war of the worlds with danger residing not in the unknown but in the known. The most devastating menace came from each town, each home – if they weren't Commies, they were teen-age rebels.

Zoot suits had already been banned in some cities after rioting between servicemen and teen-agers broke out, ostensibly over the threads. But the clothes simply dressed the music, and both reflected a shift in the social current. The zoot suiters preferred the Afro-Cuban elements of Bebop, which was banned from radio stations for being the cause of degeneracy among youth.

Teenagers were depicted as un-manageable (uncontrollable), perverted, twisted, 'out for kicks,' violent, unpredictable. *The Wild One* depicted youths as vagabond bikers, spoiling for a fight, disrupting a quiet town. And enjoying Shorty Rogers music. Obviously, modern jazz, motorcycles, and mashed potatoes (oh, what the hell) were responsible for all those who ran amok.

Movies mostly muddied jazz's image in the Fifties, and not unlike the benefits that accrued to black artists during the blaxploitation Seventies, the consolations were jobs and exposure. The chance to play, to create an audience, and to cash a check were far too tempting to resist. Jazz fans, again, overlooked the vehicle and came for the motion.

And so we see Frank Sinatra in *The Man With the Golden Arm* (1955) portraying a modern jazz drummer and junkie. Chico Hamilton's score sounded the alarm about America's trading authenticity for glitz in the 1957 *Sweet Smell of Success,* a tale of power and corruption. Susan Hayward won dramatic honors for her 1958 portrayal of a murderer who has a liking for modern jazz in *I Want to Live*. The film opens with a rush of modern jazz from the spectacular onscreen combo of Art Farmer, Gerry Mulligan, and Shelly Manne. Released later, the soundtrack became a hit, as did *The Wild One's*. Otto Preminger, who had done *Golden Arm*, directed the 1959 mystery *Anatomy of a Murder,* starring Jimmy Stewart but including Duke Ellington in a speaking and playing role. Duke had composed the soundtrack, and that, too, became a hit record.

Hollywood, then, became a kind of cleansing agent, at first introducing jazz into the mainstream the way it did sex – as titillating for the mystery of loss of control and status, then as reassuring of 'family' values (read 'white'). And so came a string of saccharine biographies of major jazz musicians during the late Forties and throughout the Fifties. Plots were devoid of real issues, and the central character possessed an idealistic heroism – usually in service to the American dream. The compression of time and events could only distort history. Nostalgia became pandemic; difficulties of life and time were forgotten; all was well.

In some cases there were troubling omissions. How account for the absence of black musicians or arrangers or songwriters in the story of Glenn Miller's life? How see the great band leader and arranger, Fletcher Henderson, who worked for both Miller and Benny Goodman, relegated to holding the latter's clarinet in one scene as if he were a valet? Not to mention Lionel Hampton serving as a waiter in the film at a waterfront dive in California? When Goodman hired him, in fact, as a member of the quartet, Hampton was fronting a band at the Paradise Café, a large nightclub in Los Angeles, and had been a recognized star for almost a decade. How else can we account for the absence of Lester Young, Teddy Wilson, or Buck Clayton in Billie Holiday's *Lady Sings the Blues,* when their important voices were integral to success? How else understand the inclusion of *fictional* characters created for 'stars' in order to bolster the box-office and somebody else's career? How else explain that films dealing with jazz musicians usually became homilies about violence or drugs? Perhaps the filmmakers knew that they could not adequately explain jazz and settled for the opportunity to explain it away.

Society can rarely account for genius. Film is no worse off. Talent, real talent, is a difference that cannot be accommodated in a world that has been so artificially created. The genius of the jazz musician subjects of the bio-films became a masquerade of diluted passions that had to fit the normative mold of white society. There was as little room in the world referred to onscreen for real genius, or real rebels, as there was offscreen for either.

The musical bio-pictures (and this may serve Michelangelo as well as Mozart, Liszt as well as Lautrec) portray genius as present not elusive, simple not complex. It seems easy. Yet jazz is struggle, and the creation of a jazz piece is not positioning a series of notes in some modal harmony but getting in touch with that struggle. Jazz has always been a fringe culture, always on the edge of society or of the soul, always an avant-garde music that resists reduction to Muzak. Jazz has become its own metaphor for the slippery self sliding around social constraints.

Too often we have been given portraits of jazz musicians that are mired in a wallow of nostalgia, rendering their creativity mundane. Yet their music lives. That is testament to the real power of their creativity. The music can speak to us from beyond time and place. It transcends to our inner being.

We come to it with our inner selves. In the words of a friend: 'I never liked jazz until I got to the point where my soul was tormented, until I experienced real pain. Then it spoke to me.' Jazz is the 'melody that haunts my reverie,' to borrow a line from Hoagy Carmichael's 'Stardust' ... Despite Hollywood, jazz cannot be adequately portrayed nor adequately described. For to describe it contains it and it cannot be contained. Certainly not by the four sides of a picture's frame. Jazz cannot be caged. It flies free.

133 **Krin Gabbard** Questions of influence in the white jazz biopic (1996)

Source: Krin Gabbard, 'Questions of influence in the white jazz biopic,' in *Jammin' at the Margins: Jazz and the American Cinema* (Chicago: University of Chicago Press, 1996: 76–82).

The cycle of films about actual jazz musicians probably begins with Al Jolson playing a character very much like himself in *The Jazz Singer* (1927). We might also include the cartoon that narrates how Paul Whiteman was 'crowned' at the beginning of *The King of Jazz* in 1930. At the beginning of the 1940s, Bing Crosby starred in *Birth of the Blues* (1941), based loosely on the rise of the Original Dixieland Jazz Band, the group that recorded the first widely known jazz records in 1917 and changed the life of the teenage Bix Beiderbecke. Another film that ought to be mentioned in the early history of the genre is the Ted Lewis biopic, *Is Everybody Happy?* (1943). Lewis led an extremely popular dance band from the 1920s through the 1940s. He did in fact record with a handful of canonical jazzmen such as Benny Goodman, Fats Waller, and Muggsy Spanier, but his success was primarily based on his image as 'The High-Hat Tragedian of Song' (Simon 1981: 497). On many levels, especially the Oedipal tension between father and son, the film is still another remake of the 1927 *Jazz Singer*. Although *Rhapsody in Blue* (1945) strives to carve George Gershwin's career to fit the European paradigm of the classical composer, even manufacturing for him a Viennese piano teacher who believes that Gershwin can become another Schubert, the film devotes a few scenes to his appropriations of blues and jazz ...

The white jazz biopic did not become well established until Columbia Pictures scored a sizable hit with *The Jolson Story* (1946), directed by Alfred E. Green (Custen 1992: 84). The film inspired a sequel, *Jolson Sings Again* (1949), and may also have been responsible for the decision to film the lives of Tommy and Jimmy Dorsey in *The Fabulous Dorseys* (1947), also directed by Green. After the abrupt demise of many big bands and the rise of the pop vocalists at the end of the 1940s, the cycle of white jazz biopics took an elegiac turn with most of the subsequent films building their appeal primarily on nostalgia. *The Glenn Miller Story* (1954) ends naturally with the trombonist's death in 1944, but the diegesis of *The Benny Goodman Story* (1955) concludes with Goodman's 1938 performance at Carnegie Hall, even though Goodman was still an active performer. The success of *The Glenn Miller Story* led to the Goodman biopic as well as to films such as *St. Louis Blues* (1958), *The Gene Krupa Story* (1959), and *The Five Pennies* (1959), the story of the pre-modern jazz cornetist Red Nichols.

For most audiences in the 1950s, what I am calling 'the white jazz biopic' was probably indistinguishable from films about entertainers with only marginal jazz associations, such as *The Eddy Duchin Story* (1956), *The Helen Morgan Story* (1957), and *I'll See You in My Dreams* (1951), in which Danny Thomas played songwriter Gus Kahn. As George Custen (1992) points out, most of these films rely on the same conventions that dominated the white jazz biopics. Much the same can be said of a number of fictional films about jazz musicians, including *Pete Kelly's Blues* (1955), *All the Fine Young Cannibals* (1960), and Michael Curtiz's 1953 remake of *The Jazz Singer*. After 1960 the cycle of white jazz biopics definitively came to an end. Black artists have dominated jazz biopics in more recent years, including Billie Holiday (*Lady Sings the Blues* [1972]) and Charlie Parker (*Bird* [1988]). In France, Bertrand Tavernier contributed to the cycle with *Round Midnight* (1986), in which a figure based on Bud Powell and Lester Young is assisted by a French admirer. The stories of white jazz artists are occasionally told today in documentary films such as *Let's Get Lost* (1988) and *Talmadge Farlow* (1981), although here, too, the vast majority of jazz documentaries have dealt with black artists. After 1960, when jazz had ceased to be a popular music and the nostalgia for swing had played itself out, Hollywood had no real use for white jazz biopics, especially as jazz became reconfigured as an art music practiced most expertly by African Americans.

Before the preeminence of African Americans in jazz became received wisdom, the white jazz biopic presented Hollywood with a dilemma concerning the place of blacks in the lives of the white subjects. Because blacks could not entirely be denied their role in the genesis of jazz and swing, filmmakers had to acknowledge their importance without departing from the entrenched practice of denying black subjectivity. *Pete Kelly's Blues* dispensed with the problem early by showing an all-black funeral behind the opening credits. While a choir sings, the cornet of a recently deceased jazz musician is placed on the coffin on its way to the cemetery. When the instrument falls off the wagon, a small child picks it up. Cut to close-ups of hands exchanging the horn, first in a pawn shop and then in a poker game. The camera then draws back to reveal that the last hands to hold the cornet belong to Pete Kelly (Jack Webb), who goes on to be one of the few unambiguously macho males to play jazz trumpet in the history of the American cinema. Although black instrumentalists are absent from the film after the prologue, the film has effectively solved the problem of acknowledging black influence without actually incorporating it into the plot.

Before *Pete Kelly's Blues*, Hollywood developed less adroit methods for dealing with the problem, most commonly the stigmatization of black jazz as a primitive, undeveloped form perfected by whites. This strategy was already operative in 1941 in *Birth of the Blues*, in which the white child who grows up to become Bing Crosby can already improvise on his clarinet more expertly than the folk artists who provide music for cakewalking blacks on the levee at the end of Basin Street. Surreptitiously accompanying the band from behind a wall of cotton bales, the white boy plays elaborate contrapuntal lines while a black cornetist, trombonist, and clarinetist simply play the melody to 'Georgia Camp Meeting.' The black clarinet player cannot understand how 'his own hot licks' can be emerging from his horn even after he has stopped playing. But as soon becomes apparent, the child is not simply copying the black musician's licks. When he is discovered behind the bales, he is asked where he learned to play. 'Oh, I just picked it up hanging around Basin Street.' The black clarinetist then tells him, 'White boy, come set beside me. There's a few things I want to pick up.' Just by listening, the white child has acquired enough musical knowledge to surpass his mentors.

The idea that whites are more accomplished than blacks in the performance of jazz becomes explicit in *The Jolson Story* when the hero decides to inject black music into blackface performance practice. By contrast, the film has shown Dockstader's performers singing in an unsyncopated style more reminiscent of Stephen Foster than King Oliver. Jolson is portrayed as a visionary who understood the appeal that 'jazz' could hold for a large white audience. He has also *improved* on a music that was naïvely made up 'out of the air' by unsophisticated blacks. An even more elaborate version of this same narrative appears in *The Benny Goodman Story* (1955) when young Benny hears Kid Ory. Ory, playing himself and speaking words he probably would never have spoken on his own, tells the young hero that the band simply plays 'New Orleans style.' 'It's nothing special. All the guys down in New Orleans play this way ... Most of these guys can't read music. They just swing on out and play the way they feel.' As in *Birth of the Blues,* a young white clarinetist can hold his own with mature blacks. In *The Benny Goodman Story,* however, the young white musician actually plays with as much expertise as a professional jazz musician.

The Benny Goodman Story does go out of its way to acknowledge the role of black artists in Goodman's career. Still, young Benny's easily acquired jazz competence in the scene with Kid Ory is only one of several racist fabrications in this early portion of the film. Most of the musicians in Ory's band did in fact read music, and viewers with some musical sophistication can tell from the scene that Ory and his band are playing music that has been carefully worked out ahead of time – it's not just 'swinging on out.' And even if members of the band are in fact improvising some of what they are playing, a child does not learn the art of improvisation simply by being told to 'play what you feel.' More importantly, the film shows how the child grows up to be much more than a mere improviser. Like Jolson, he is a visionary who understands what Americans need to hear, and he is sufficiently dedicated to keep a band together until the public catches up with his vision. Again, Hollywood suggests that it takes a white person to bring substance to something that anyone – black or white – can do simply by instinct.

Often films in the white jazz biopic genre wait until the end to elevate white music over black music. *The Fabulous Dorseys* (1947) makes no reference to African Americans until the film is approximately half over and one of the battling brothers says that he is off to a nightclub to hear some 'real jazz.' This real jazz turns out to be a performance by Art Tatum, the revered black pianist. The one scene with an African American artist takes place in a dark, basement-like club, where Tatum is eventually surrounded by white players who have clustered around his piano with their horns. Tatum's dark, claustrophobic domain is in stark contrast to the film's finale in which both Dorseys play on a mammoth stage behind a string orchestra. The marks of Eurocentric high art are recruited to lift white jazz out of its degraded roots. That same year, in *New Orleans* (1947), several scenes with black artists take place in a backroom while the finale, in which a white opera singer performs a song that she learned from her black maid (played by Billie Holiday), is set in a concert hall with a symphony orchestra. *The Benny Goodman Story* also ends with the clarinetist playing in Carnegie Hall before a sold-out audience of well-dressed white concertgoers. Even the black jazz biopic *St. Louis Blues* ends in a concert hall with W. C. Handy (Nat King Cole) singing with a symphony orchestra.

The most memorable moments toward the end of *The Glenn Miller Story* (1954) also function to elevate the bandleader's music, this time by associating it with America's military might and the all-important morale of her fighting men. In one scene the men in Miller's band, looking sharp in their crisp uniforms, continue playing fearlessly while the English audience ducks at the sound of a rocket falling from the sky. The men in Miller's band are clearly soldiers and not mere jazz musicians. Later, Miller is equally fearless in instructing his band to play 'St. Louis Blues' at march tempo while a general is reviewing the troops. As his commanding officer upbraids Miller for violating the military's rules of decorum, the visiting general arrives to congratulate the bandleader for doing so much to elevate morale.

Like Goodman and the Dorseys, the Miller of *The Glenn Miller Story* plays with black musicians in an early and crucial scene: the open spaces of the parade ground, like the dignified stage of the concert hall, contrast with the cramped jazz clubs to which black artists are invariably relegated. When the trombonist sits in with Louis Armstrong and an all-star group, Gene Krupa is also present, playing himself. The archetypal white Negro, Krupa was the subject of a biopic a few years later in which he would be portrayed by Sal Mineo, thus adding a homoerotic subtext to the many subtexts already associated with his character. The luridly colorful lights that wash over Krupa in the nightclub sequence in *The Glenn Miller Story* suggest these subtexts, especially his reputation as a user of marijuana, presented in *The Gene Krupa Story* in a manner reminiscent of *Reefer Madness* (1936). A more revealing example of how black and white jazz musicians must exist in different spaces takes place in a studio where Glenn Miller and the band record 'Tuxedo Junction' while a pair of black dancers are marginalized as black-and-white images projected onto a screen.

Young Man with a Horn is especially interesting in terms of how it handles the question of a black man's impact on the playing of a white artist. Nick LaRocca, the trumpeter with the all-white ODJB and the first jazz trumpet player that Bix Beiderbecke would have heard, undoubtedly developed a portion of his style from listening to black musicians in New Orleans. LaRocca's own playing does not sound much like the canonical black New Orleans trumpeters such as Armstrong, Freddie Keppard, and King Oliver. Beiderbecke was also influenced to some degree by Paul Mares, the cornetist with the New Orleans Rhythm Kings, another white group that toured and recorded extensively. NORK's first records date to 1922, but Beiderbecke heard the group live the previous year in Chicago when he was playing hooky from the Lake Forest Academy (Sudhalter 1974: 67). Basing his early style on white trumpeters like LaRocca and Mares, Beiderbecke sounds even less like a black jazz artist from New Orleans. If Hollywood was interested in erasing blacks from the history of jazz, the industry could have found no better subject than Bix Beiderbecke. A film about Beiderbecke could have moved seamlessly from Bix listening to records of white musicians to his encounter with the New Orleans Rhythm Kings in Chicago and then to his recording sessions with Hoagy Carmichael, Paul Whiteman, and other white groups. Such a film would have overlooked Beiderbecke's high regard for black performers such as Armstrong, with whom he probably played in Chicago clubs in 1923, but it would not have been a complete misrepresentation of his stylistic development. In 1950, with Hoagy Carmichael available as a highly knowledgeable resource on Beiderbecke, *Young Man with a Horn* could have been tilted in this direction.

A film made in 1990 did in fact tell Beiderbecke's story without bringing a black musician before the camera. *Bix: An Interpretation of a Legend* was shot on many of the original locations in Iowa, Illinois and Wisconsin by an Italian unit. Written by Antonio Avati and Lino Patruno and directed by Pupi Avati, the film starred Bryant Weeks as Beiderbecke. Although the film took a few small liberties with Beiderbecke's life, the music, supervised by Bob Wilber, was extraordinarily accurate in recreating the music of Beiderbecke and several of the ensembles with which he recorded. Told in a series of flashbacks, the diegesis never ventures back before 1921, so no mention is made of the ODJB or of Beiderbecke's early encounters with their records. *Bix: An Interpretation of a Legend* does depict the cornetist's exposure to Paul Mares in Chicago, his meeting with Carmichael, an early performance of the Wolverines at a dance at Indiana University, and numerous sessions with Paul Whiteman, Jean Goldkette, and other all-white groups. In a scene at the Cinderella Ballroom in the New York of 1924 a house musician brags that the Cinderella is always packed, even though 'Henderson's orchestra' has been filling Roseland every night since the addition of 'that kid who was with Oliver's band.' A voice off screen gives the name: 'Armstrong.' The house musician continues, 'Everybody's going nuts over him. He's pretty tough to beat.' End of conversation. Although numerous black servants and laborers appear throughout the film, there are no black musicians, and this one bit of dialogue is the only time that even the name of an African American artist is introduced.

Young Man with a Horn could have, with some justification, adopted this same approach to excising the black musical presence from Beiderbecke's life. And yet the film takes the black Art Hazard out of Dorothy Baker's novel and makes him into Rick Martin's father, mother, teacher, and musical inspiration. As with Kid Ory in *The Benny Goodman Story*, the black mentor eventually delivers the obligatory speech in which the white student is congratulated for outclassing the mentor. *Young Man with a Horn* demonstrates that Hollywood had a genuine need to bring forth black characters so that white musician/ heroes could surpass them. This was the case even when, as in the case of Beiderbecke's life, it was not actually necessary.

134 **Donald Bogle** Louis Armstrong: The films (1994)

Source: Donald Bogle, 'Louis Armstrong: the films,' in Marc H. Miller (ed.), *Louis Armstrong: A Cultural Legacy* (Seattle: University of Washington Press, 1994: 147–9, 153–9) (excerpts).

The 1947 film *New Orleans* is a dreary pedestrian mess. Although this story is supposedly about jazz's rise to mainstream acceptance, the real jazz innovators – Louis Armstrong and Billie Holiday – are neatly relegated to the sidelines while the plot follows the lives of the lead white characters, who are uniformly bland. Armstrong comes on for musical sequences and some playful comic dialogue, and Holiday is cast as a dippy maid named Endie who likes tinkering around at the piano and, so we are to believe, just happens to sing.

In a few key sequences in *New Orleans,* the nonsense ends and everything suddenly comes alive. In one, Holiday discards her maid's uniform and stands by a piano with a group of musicians, including Armstrong on trumpet, to perform 'Do You Know What It Means To Miss New Orleans.' Later the two reappear to perform 'The Blues Are Brewing.' These are sweetly rapturous moments. When they are free simply to do the thing they are best at – perform their music – Armstrong and Holiday are splendid together: an elegant, assured, luminous pair. And, of course, whenever Armstrong does take to his horn, backed by his orchestra, he's in top form.

Louis Armstrong's fine musical sequences in *New Orleans* may well redeem his checkered film career. While Holiday appeared only in this one feature film (and in the 1935 musical short *Symphony in Black*), Armstrong appeared in twenty-four American films from 1931 to 1969. In the 1950s and 1960s, he also performed on numerous television programs. Movies broadened his fame and enabled him to reach a huge audience that otherwise might have known nothing about either him or jazz. These films preserve some invaluable glimpses of his live performance. Although he was the most successful jazz musician ever to work in movies, Hollywood often did not serve Louis Armstrong well; his film work distorted his accomplishments and his place in cultural history.

For the mass audience, especially a later generation of African-Americans who did not experience Armstrong as a brilliant musical innovator during the

1920s and 1930s, his films and later television work have formed a deep impression and an image that still rankles sensibilities and remains a source of criticism and controversy. For many, his movie and television image is an all-grinning, all-mugging, ever-cheerful minstrel-like figure who with unabashed glee performs corny, knuckle-headed routines – singing 'Jeepers Creepers' to a horse or playing a character who can barely add two and two.

The screen image of that other jazz master Duke Ellington was a composed, controlled sophisticate, whereas the movies often seemed to have turned Armstrong into a misunderstood clown icon. Looking at his films today, it is sometimes hard to see the artist within the entertainer.

Yet audiences remain intrigued by Armstrong perhaps because each of his appearances is distinguished by his superb musicianship and killer energy, which when fused with his unwavering commitment to his work and one-of-a-kind enthusiasm, endow him with an almost mythic power and resonance. Love him or hate him, he is unfailingly mesmerizing.

Armstrong's movie work falls into various categories. For the most part, he performed specialty acts: musical segments in feature films. He might unexpectedly appear in a nightclub setting where he would perform a number or two and then vanish as the plot proceeded. Such films were less damaging to Armstrong because he simply played the music that made him famous.

In others, Armstrong was cast in settings and situations that conformed to then-accepted notions (reassuring perhaps to white audiences) of the Negro as a nonthreatening, childlike figure or that otherwise distorted African-American culture and experiences. In such features as *Pennies From Heaven* (1936) and *Going Places* (1938), Armstrong was saddled with dim-witted dialogue and played stereotyped characters: easygoing, ever-helpful, rather naive, and genial fellows at the beck and call of a white hero.

In such short films as *A Rhapsody in Black and Blue* (1932), Armstrong the star performed his hits but again was sometimes entangled in stereotyped conceptions about African-American life ... Armstrong's above-the-title billing in the opening credits certified his stardom. The film's mix of domestic harangue, lively popular music, and a rigidly stereotyped set of images are, however, an unfortunate setting for his talents.

A Rhapsody in Black and *Blue* opens with a record spinning on a Victrola while a man taps to the beat with drumsticks, clearly too caught up, so we soon realize, in the giddy excitement of listening to Louis Armstrong to be aware of anything else. That is, until his moment of musical bliss is interrupted by his wife – heavyset, dowdy, quarrelsome, and ready for a fight – who, upon entering the room, immediately berates him. She calls him a 'great big hunk of unemploy-ment' and warns 'Looka here, it's the last time I'm going to tell you to kick your ear from that jazz box and jazz that mop around the floor.' With little other choice, the husband soaks the mop in a pail of sudsy water, then begins mopping the floor. But once his wife leaves the room, he's back listening to the record.

The sequence conforms to the traditional stereotypes of African-Americans in films: the hardworking, long-suffering, crankily domineering black woman in conflict with her triflin', good-for-nothing, lazy man. This scene was played out repeatedly in movies of the time: *Judge Priest* (1934), in which the industrious

Hattie McDaniel goes about her kitchen work while Stepin Fetchit sits around playing his harmonica, and perhaps most notably in *Show Boat* (1936) with McDaniel and Paul Robeson. The music itself is cast as both solace and something of the devil's doings: in *Show Boat,* after McDaniel scolds Robeson as 'the laziest man that ever lived on this river,' he wants merely to whittle but finds real relief from domestic tensions and obligations by singing 'Ol' Man River.'

In *A Rhapsody in Black and Blue,* Armstrong's music prevents the husband from fulfilling his responsibilities, but it also transports him away from it all. When the man persists in listening to the jazz box, the wife hits him over the head with the mop, and the poor guy passes out. Unconscious, he dreams of the court of Jazzmania where he emerges dressed as an emperor with an attendant. In this world, any wish or pleasure is immediately gratified. There to perform for the new monarch is the one and only Louis Armstrong, dressed in a leopard cloth and standing in a floor of suds, with his orchestra in the background. Grinning throughout and sometimes widening his eyes, mugging it up almost shamelessly, Armstrong performs 'I'll Be Glad When You're Dead, You Rascal, You' and 'Shine.'

For contemporary audiences, some of the exaggerated expressions and movements seem a carryover from the nineteenth-century minstrel tradition, in which white males, made up in blackface with broad grins painted on their faces, mocked and cruelly caricatured the antics, movements, language, attitudes, and very rhythm of African-Americans. Some lyrics, too – 'When you're laying six feet deep/No more chicken will you eat' (from 'I'll Be Glad When You're Dead, You Rascal, You') – reinforce long-held stereotyped images of the Negro. In *A Rhapsody in Black and Blue,* Armstrong seems too obviously to be performing, almost as if he were on stage, without the subtlety and fluidity that film demands. But with undaunted energy and enthusiasm and a very knowing and shrewd manner that seems part-parody, he carries the material off.

He playfully works the lyrics. 'I brought you in my home/ You wouldn't leave my wife alone/ I'll be glad when you're dead, you rascal, you,' he sings in this tale of a man whose wife has taken a fancy to another, presumably a friend of his. Then he turns up some heat with the double entendre, 'You bought my wife a bottle of Coca-Cola/ So you could play on her Victrola/ You old dog, you.' It is a funny and surprisingly sexy song, performed with vigor and insight in an age when black male sexuality was far too great a threat to be presented on screen. In one respect, his humor neutralizes any fears about black sexuality, but Armstrong's rendering creates a sly man of the world, far more knowledgeable than he may first appear, from what could have been a simple stereotype.

The lyrics of his second number, 'Shine,' repeat the image of the stoic, happy-go-lucky darky, unphased by problems and very much satisfied with his lot in life. 'Just because my hair is curly/ Just because my teeth are pearly/ Just because I wear a smile,' he sings, later adding, 'Just because I'm glad I'm living/ I takes all my troubles with a smile ... That's why they call me Shine.'

When he puts the lyrics aside to take up his trumpet, he is transformed right before our eyes. For now his communication – intense, personal, demanding, imaginative, honest – is with his horn. His eyes close, and he's at one with his instrument. Part of Armstrong has forgotten the audience. In these moments, there is something so real, so pure, so sublime that he takes us with him as he transcends the sequence, the very nature and concept of the film itself, and makes us forget the hackneyed setting. Indeed, he has left it behind and takes the viewer into his world where he is the true emperor.

The type of material, setting, and performance seen in *A Rhapsody in Black and Blue* – so jarring to audiences today – was a staple of old-style black theatre and ethnic comedy. (Maybe that's why the film was not greatly criticized when first released.) The early Williams and Walker all-black productions, Sissle and Blake's and Miller and Lyles' *Shuffle Along* as well as *Runnin' Wild, Chocolate Dandies* all made use of similar exaggerations. As did later such race movies – all black cast films independently produced outside of Hollywood and made especially for African-American audiences – as *Killer Diller* (1948), *Boarding House Blues* (1948), *Juke Joint* (1947) and *Boy! What A Girl* (1946). So, too, did such comics as Moms Mabley (1897–1975), Pigmeat Markham (1906–1981), and Dusty Fletcher when they carried on at the Apollo or some club on the old chitlin circuit. This fast-moving, rambunctious, sometimes raucous and rowdy style, characterized by eye pops, thick dialects, broad gestures, and stylized theatrical mugging, is far different in spirit from the uninformed and sometimes vicious mockery of the white minstrels who understood nothing about black cultural experience.

Black performers' intonations, inflections, double takes were pitched to a black audience (even when the audience was integrated) that understood and enjoyed the performances as entertaining social comment, far-flung parody, and on occasion pointed satire. When this material was transferred to mainstream movies, it was lifted out of its cultural context and lost a distinct set of cultural references as well as the recognition by the audience that these shenanigans were but *one* comment on but *one* aspect of the African-American experience.

Because this type of comic exaggeration (via the comic servants) was just about the only depiction in Hollywood films of the black experience, shown without any counterbalancing image and without its cultural context, such antics made a shocking and inaccurate statement on black America. This aspect of black performers' work was no longer viewed as satire but perceived as a truth.

In some respects, Armstrong himself, as an early crossover star, was lifted out of a cultural context. At the start of his career, Armstrong's following was solely African-American. For that audience, he had talent to burn. An innovative musician, he could also get laughs with his highly personalized clownery. In the early years of Armstrong's career, black audiences did not greatly object to his mugging and the stylized persona he projected. After all, Armstrong's favorite comic Bert Williams went onstage in blackface and spoke with an exaggerated dialect. While Armstrong objected to the blackface tradition, he saw nothing wrong with ethnic humor and old-style ethnic images. Once his fame grew to the point where he was a favorite of integrated and finally white audiences, Armstrong remained true to the type of entertainment he had grown up with.

Perhaps Armstrong did not give enough serious thought to how another culture perceived him. For a large segment of the white audience, he was not simply entertaining and jiving it up (as he had initially been perceived by a black audience); instead, he represented an ever-enthusiastic, nonthreatening, friendly figure who did not challenge their assumptions on race or racial superiority – except when he played his instrument.

135 Jean-Pierre Coursodon *Round Midnight*: An interview with Bertrand Tavernier (1986)

Source: Jean-Pierre Coursodon, '*Round Midnight*: An interview with Bertrand Tavernier,' *Cinéaste*, 15, 2 (1986: 19–22, 23) (excerpts).

Cinéaste: *Critics have called you 'the most French' of your generation of film directors. At the same time, you've always had a passion for various aspects of American culture, from movies, to literature to jazz.* Round Midnight *reconciles your 'Frenchness' and this fascination for America for the first time in your work, at least in a fiction film.*
Bertrand Tavernier: It isn't quite the first time. My first film, *L'Horloger de Saint Paul* (*The Clockmaker*), was based on a Simenon novel that took place in the United States, and *Coup de Torchon* was adapted from Jim Thompson's novel *Pop. 1280*.
C: *They were thoroughly transposed, however, the audience couldn't detect their American origin.*
B. T.: I was faithful to the spirit, though. One of the reactions to *Coup de Torchon* that pleased me most was from someone who had been a close friend of Thompson's, and who said the film constantly reminded him of Jim, even though it was a thoroughly French movie. Actually, there has always been some kind of American influence on my films. My inspiration often comes from American sources, then a lot of work goes into 'making them French,' filtering them through a French sensibility and experience. I am very concerned not to lose my own roots. I am upset by French filmmakers who imitate American movies and make films that have no connection with any French reality.
C: Round Midnight *deals with the plight of the jazz musician, especially the black musician. This is a specifically American issue.*
B. T.: I have a love-hate relationship with America, because I admire so many of its artists and reject so many of its values. I have always been attracted to those creators America ignores, underrates or rejects, people like Jim Thompson, or the blacklisted writers and directors of the McCarthy era, and, of course, many of the great jazz musicians. The French angle that made it possible for me to develop *Round Midnight* as a personal statement was the character of Francis,

the young French jazz buff who befriends and helps the American musician.

C: *You had been thinking of a film about jazz musicians for many years. How did the project finally materialize?*

B.T.: I feel I would have made the film sooner or later, somehow, in spite of all the difficulties involved, but *Round Midnight* actually happened quite simply, almost by accident. I was having dinner with Martin Scorsese, who had brought along producer Irwin Winkler, and Martin and I started talking about our 'dream movies,' the ones we would like to make if we had complete freedom. I said mine would be about a jazz musician, a black American, living in Paris in the late Fifties. A photograph of Lester Young taken in Paris, at the Hotel Louisiane, around that time had stuck in my mind. I think it was that particular image that was at the root of my desire to make such a film. Two days later, Winkler called saying he was interested in the idea and offering a contract. It was that simple.

C: *Did you work with David Rayfiel from the start?*

B.T.: Yes, David and I had already discussed the problems of how to deal with jazz and jazz musicians in a fiction film. I knew exactly what I did *not* want the film to be like. As I put it at the time, it should be the exact opposite of *Paris Blues*. I don't want to sound disrespectful to Martin Ritt, who later directed several pictures I like a lot, such as *The Molly Maguires, Sounder* and *Conrack*, or Walter Bernstein, a screenwriter I admire, but one has to admit that in *Paris Blues* they were completely out of their depth.

C: *Superficially, it deals with the same issues* Round Midnight *does, but it's a compendium of Hollywood conventions and clichés.*

B.T.: Perhaps the most annoying of those conventions was a musical one: it was never clear what style of jazz those musicians were supposed to play, because, I suspect, neither director nor writer had any idea themselves. From their attitudes and speech they seemed to be modern musicians, from the be-bop generation, yet they worked with Louis Armstrong and Duke Ellington. There was total musical confusion, and that reflected on the characters' credibility as individuals.

C: *How did you develop a story that presented your characters in a credible way, both as musicians and individuals?*

B.T.: The writing was a long, painful process, especially in the early stages. Trying to develop a story line and dramatic structure we realized we had very special problems, because of the bizarre, enigmatic way jazz musicians relate to each other. They make Pinter's characters sound like introspective over-explainers. It was a musician who told us that if we wanted to be able to develop relationships, we needed a non-musician character to play opposite our protagonist. I tried to think of Americans who lived in Paris in the Fifties and had known jazz musicians. It occurred to me that we might use a blacklisted Hollywood writer or director. John Berry, for example, had spent a lot of time in jazz clubs in those days. We wrote a few scenes, but it soon became clear that the blacklist theme was taking over the picture.

C: *You had material for two different films, both about American expatriates, artists who have been forced to leave their country, abandon their roots ...*

B.T.: Yes, the two characters were too close to each other, it was the same theme. But I *would* like to make a film about the blacklist some day. I was discussing this with Steven Tesich recently, and after seeing *Round Midnight* he told me: 'You've already made your blacklist film; it's *Round Midnight*.' Still, there are important differences. The jazz musicians who came to Europe were well-known and still successful. They had a small but faithful following. The blacklisted writers and directors, on the other hand, had a hard time finding work. They even had to use pseudonyms in fear of reprisal. But it's true that if I made a film on the subject right after *Round Midnight* I would seem to be repeating myself; I should make two or three other pictures before tackling it.

Anyway, after we gave up the blacklist angle, we were stuck for a while. At the time we were researching musicians' lives in Paris. I met Francis Paudras, a Parisian jazz buff who had befriended be-bop pianist Bud Powell and helped him get over difficult times. He had a passion for Powell's music and became totally involved with his playing, and eventually his life. He told me how, when he didn't have the money to get into the club, he would crouch on the sidewalk and listen to the music through an air vent. He spoke of checking Bud in and out of hospitals, taking care of him, getting him ready for his return to New York, a 'comeback' that actually was to kill him. This was an inspiration. There was the relationship we had been looking for. From then on it became possible to develop the two characters along fictional lines. Paudras helped with a wealth of material, reminiscences, home movies he had made of Powell and other musicians. The only problem with him was to make him accept the fact that our character was not going to be Bud Powell, but a fictional composite. For one thing, I was determined from the start that the musician should be a tenor saxophonist, because the tenor sax is the quintessential jazz instrument, and I've always liked the way tenor men look playing their instrument.

C: *At what point did you decide to use an actual jazz musician for the part, and how did you come to cast Dexter Gordon?*

B.T.: I never seriously considered using anybody but an actual musician. It had to be someone who not only could play the part, but also had the appropriate musical style for the period. We screened a lot of footage of jazz performances, and narrowed the possibilities to three or four. Sonny Rollins and Frank Foster had qualities that were right for the part, but they looked the picture of health and vigor, which didn't at all fit the character we had devised. Finally, Francis tentatively suggested Dexter Gordon. He *would* be perfect for the part, but he hadn't been heard from in several years; no one seemed to know his whereabouts. When I saw Dexter on film I immediately wanted him and no one else, but it remained a big 'if' until one day I got a call from Henri Renaud announcing he had located Gordon, back in New York from an extended stay in Mexico. I flew to New York to interview him and was tremendously impressed by the man. The moment he walked into the room I knew he was the character. He was interested and we did a screen test, in which his screen presence proved fantastic.

C: *Did you have a completed script at the time?*

B.T.: Only a first draft, with which I was far from pleased. I had many discussions of the script with Dexter – unlike David, who, for some reason, preferred not to meet him – and he influenced me enormously. Even before he made actual contributions to the script, just seeing him, listening to him talk, suggested changes. His physical presence, the way he moved, made some scenes we had written impossible. We wrote two more versions of the script before even showing it to Dexter. I would drop by, have coffee with him, spend a couple of hours just chatting, absorbing everything about him – his gestures, his silences, his stubborn moments (he is a hard person to convince), the protective wall of elusiveness he surrounds himself with – it all went into the script. But Dexter's input was most crucial during production. He needs to mull things over for a long time. Often he would come up with a suggestion, or an objection, minutes before shooting a scene, and I hated him for it, but after a while I and the crew adjusted to his style so that we could use his suggestions. They ranged from lines of dialogue to bits of business to deletion of details or whole scenes he didn't feel were right.

C: *Some of his dialogue seems largely improvised.*

B.T.: Actually, most of it was written, but the scene with the psychiatrist *is* entirely improvised. We simply discussed what he would like to talk about, then we started shooting and I let him talk for five minutes. And there are extemporized bits throughout the film, such as when he comes home with the money paid him by the jazz club owner and proudly says, 'Direct!' This shows how involved in the part he was, for we had shot the scene in which he insists on being paid directly two weeks earlier.

C: *What kind of dialogue changes did he introduce?*

B.T.: Most of them had to do not so much with content as with vocabulary, rhythm, pace. Some, however, were very shrewd psychologically. A good example is the scene in which Dale and Francis are having dinner at Francis's place. Dale asks him if he has put water in the wine – which he did, as he is trying to control his friend's drinking. In the script as written Francis denied it, but Gordon objected that the friendship could only be based on honesty and Francis should tell the truth. François Cluzet was delighted; he thought it was a great idea and felt much more comfortable playing the scene that way.

C: *What about Gordon's musical input?*

B.T.: Here again, he made many useful suggestions. For the scenes at the Paris Blue Note I had thought of a rhythm section composed of Herbie Hancock, Ron Carter and Tony Williams. Dexter pointed out that an all-American rhythm section was unheard of in Europe in the Fifties; visiting players, like Gordon himself, were always backed by at least one, often two local musicians. So we substituted French bassist Pierre Michelot for Ron Carter. Originally, a rather complex arrangement had been written for Dexter's first number on his opening night at the Blue Note, but he objected that wouldn't sound credible, since he hadn't met the musicians before, so the arrangement was dropped, and Dexter plays a ballad with a simple rhythm backing.

C: *The character he plays is based, essentially, on two musicians, Lester Young and Bud Powell, whom he knew and admired. He even played and recorded with Powell in Paris. At the same time, he was, to a certain extent, playing himself. Did this ambiguity create any identity problems?*

B.T.: He was very anxious to distance himself from Powell's personality. 'I'm not Bud,' he said, 'I'm the opposite of him.' He was reluctant to do anything he felt he wouldn't do himself in real life. He objected to a scene in which he was supposed to beg for money. 'I'd never do that,' he said, 'I would steal, but never beg.' We rewrote the scene accordingly. On the other hand, he felt very close to Lester Young's personality. His general attitude to life, his sense of humor, his language even, are reminiscent of Lester's, and, of course, the fact that they play the same instrument and Lester was a major influence on his own style enhanced the compatibility. He also felt that Lester's experience was representative – more so than Powell's – of what many musicians have had to go through, so that he welcomed everything in the script that recalled Lester, including the painful episodes, such as the reminiscences about his time in the Army.

C: *Dale and Francis might seem to have almost nothing in common, beside the music, yet there are similarities in their respective situations: both are separated from a woman, both have a young daughter, both live a very isolated life. How deliberate was the parallelism?*

B.T.: The family reunion is a crucial scene, the turning point in the film. That's when Dale decides to go back to the United States. Francis takes him to visit his parents in a gesture to take him out of his isolation, and during the family affair, a birthday dinner for Francis's daughter, Dale realizes how estranged from his own roots he has become. I have recently come to realize the importance of families in my work. I don't seem to be able to make a film without a family in it – or else it's the *lack* of a family, family ties, that plays a major role.

C: *From* The Clockmaker *to* A Sunday in the Country *there are many fathers and father images in your films. The relation to the father is obviously a major theme. In* Round Midnight, *each of the two central characters serves as a sort of father image to the other.*

B.T.: It may sound like a paradox, but to me *A Sunday in the Country* and *Round Midnight* deal with exactly the same thing. Doing *Midnight* I had a feeling I was remaking *Sunday.*

C: *In both films the central character is an aging artist who lives in isolation and has doubts about his own work, although the self-questioning is much more emphasized in* A Sunday in the Country.

B.T.: That's because a jazz musician is much less likely to express such doubts directly. Dale's self-destructive behavior is his way to act out his doubts and frustrations.

C: *He puts it into words only once in the entire film, when he says: 'I wonder if I still have something to give.'*

B.T.: The remark was actually provided by one of the musicians. I asked him why Dexter at times seemed bent on destroying himself, and he answered, 'Maybe he's afraid he no longer has anything to give.' There's another line on the subject that came from a musician in the cast, Bobby Hutcherson: 'When you have to explore every night, even the most beautiful things become the most painful.'

C: *The self-destructiveness of the character was echoed by the performer's, or vice-versa. This must have created tensions and difficulties.*

B.T.: There were moments when life and fiction came very close to each other. The role was hard to play for Dexter precisely because it must have brought back many painful memories, so the temptation to ease the pain by drinking was great. His wife was very supportive. She told me, in his presence, that my relationship to him should be the same as Francis's to Dale in the film. Other musicians also helped a lot. But there *were* serious problems. Several times, in the early stages of filming, we had to stop because Gordon was in no condition to work. At one point I told him, with Winkler's approval: 'If I have to destroy a man to make a film, I'd rather give up. I'll call it off if things don't improve.' It made an impression, because after that we had very few problems.

C: *The character's drinking problem is central to the story, yet it's neither discussed nor even used dramatically, at least not in any traditional fashion: there are no binges, no D.T.'s, no drunken fights.*

B.T.: I wanted all this to be kept off screen. I still keep wondering whether I shouldn't cut the one scene in which he goes to a bar and orders wine.

C: *This oblique approach is typical of the whole film, and quite different from earlier films of yours, in which you tended to be at times very didactic.*

B.T.: ... I feel more and more like making plotless films, films that deal with emotions rather than stories; I'm attracted to looser dramatic structures ... Increasingly, I strive for a loose, musical construction. As far as *Round Midnight* was concerned, it seemed to be the only valid approach not only because the film deals with music, but because the way the musicians behave is itself oblique and non-dramatic, and I had to respect that in order to show them the way they are. This may require an effort from audiences who are used to simple conflicts, but the effort should be part of the pleasure. I didn't want to program audience reactions. I am upset to see how manipulative so many movies are these days ...

C: *The camera work is particularly fluid and musical.*

B.T.: In the musical sequences, the camera work *had* to adapt to the music constantly because the music was improvised, and all of it was recorded directly while filming – which no one thought we could manage to do. We never knew in advance what the musicians were to do, how many choruses they were going to take. A number that went on for four minutes in one take might go on for seven in the next. I was lucky to get a wonderful camera operator who is a musician himself and who patterned his camera moves after the harmonic structure of the compositions, so that he could smoothly track along a musician playing a solo and move past him just as he completed it. He did Lonette McKee's entire number, with all the tracking back and forth between her and Gordon, in one single take – although in editing I intercut the shot with footage from a second camera ...

136 **Francis Davis** At the movies: Everycat (1986)

Source: Francis Davis, 'At the movies: Everycat,' in *Outcats: Jazz Composers, Instrumentalists, and Singers* (New York: Oxford University Press, 1990: 211–13). (Originally published 1986.)

In jazz circles, the early word on '*Round Midnight,* the French director Bertrand Tavernier's nicotine-stained valentine to bebop in European exile in the late fifties, went roughly as follows: critics would loathe the movie for its trivialization of jazz history, but musicians – flattered to see one of their own on the big screen – would adore it for validating their existence (the 'I'm in Technicolor, therefore I am' impulse that made longhairs embrace *Easy Rider* in the late sixties, and black urban audiences embrace *Shaft* and *Superfly* a few years later). Musicians for, critics against, is indeed the way the sides are lining up, now that '*Round Midnight* has opened. You can probably guess which side I'm on, but I'm not saying that musicians are wrong.

'*Round Midnight* – starring the tenor saxophonist Dexter Gordon as Dale Turner, a fictional composite of Lester Young and Bud Powell – is about jazz as a religious experience, with all the stigmata and stations of the cross presented in jumbled, vaguely sacrilegious fashion. Gordon's Dale Turner is a tortured black innovator who, like Young, memorizes the lyrics to songs before interpreting them instrumentally, addresses even male acquaintances as 'Lady,' and spent time in the stockade during World War II for carrying a photograph of his white wife. Like Bud Powell, Turner was once beaten repeatedly on the head with billy clubs, and like many musicians of Powell's generation, he is easy prey for obsequious drug pushers and sleazeball promoters (typified here by Martin Scorsese, in a distracting cameo). He has an old sidekick nicknamed Hersch (presumably Herschel Evans, Young's sparring partner in the Count Basie Orchestra), a daughter named Chan (after Chan Richardson, Charlie Parker's common-law wife), a lady friend called Buttercup (just like Powell's widow), and another who sings with a white gardenia pinned in her hair (just like you-know-who, though the buppie princess Lonette McKee is unlikely to remind you of Billie Holiday). When the man standing next to Dale at the bar passes out, Dale says 'I'll have what he's been drinking,' just as legend has it Young once did. And like Young, he calls someone shorter than himself 'half-a-motherfucker'; the only problem is that Lester was talking to Pee-wee Marquette, the midget master of ceremonies at Birdland, whereas Dale is addressing the normal-sized Bobby Hutcherson.

You get the point: Turner is Everycat, less a character than an accumulation of fact and lore. Despite this, '*Round Midnight,* in its meandering middle stretches, is less a jazz film than another buddy-buddy flick, replete with unacknowledged homoerotic undertones (one scene in which Turner is writing music at the opposite end of the table from his French graphic-designer roommate and benefactor – played by François Cluzet and faithfully modeled on Powell's keeper, Francis Paudras – plays like an inadvertent parody of the successful two-career marriage). The only difference is that one of the buddies is a black, dypsomaniacal, six-foot-seven *down beat* Hall-of-Famer.

Even so, it's easy to understand why musicians are pleased with '*Round Midnight*. Clichés and all, it's as sympathetic an account of the jazz life as has ever been presented in a feature film, erring on the side of compassion rather than exploitation, guilty of sentimentality but not sensationalism. The uncertainty of Gordon's line readings betrays that he's no actor and that he was given no real character to work with. But his presence and dignity – his paunch-first stagger, his big-man's daintiness, his rasped expletives, and his vanquished Clark Gable good looks – rescue the movie from banality. A former alcoholic, drug abuser, and longtime expatriate himself, he's obviously drawn from personal experience to give a performance that one suspects would have been beyond the ability of a more experienced actor. His peers will recognize themselves in him, and they can be proud of what they see.

Oddly, the drawback to casting Gordon in the lead role was musical. When he's in peak form, Gordon's tone is as bracing and aromatic as freshly perked coffee. But he was recovering from assorted illnesses and an extended period of inactivity during filming, and as a result, his solos have a spent, desultory air. In dramatic terms, this may be just as well, inasmuch as we are given to understand that Dale Turner is a man slowly snuffing himself out, capable of summoning up his former brilliance only in flashes, convinced that death is nature's way of telling him to take five. (You wonder what Francis is using for ears when he says that Turner is playing 'like a god.') But a sub-par Gordon makes the soundtrack album (Columbia SC–40464) pretty tough going. Gordon isn't the only culprit; the soundtrack's supporting cast is made up of musicians ten to twenty years his junior, for whom bebop is little more than a formal exercise, and Herbie Hancock's incidental music is flat and uninvolving when divorced from the film's imagery. Gordon deserves the plaudits he's winning as an actor, but it would be a pity if the lay audience now discovering him accepts the music from '*Round Midnight* as characteristic.

Although '*Round Midnight* is the only recent movie to star a jazz musician, it's not the only one with a jazz soundtrack. Spike Lee's sleeper hit *She's Gotta Have It* boasts a fine soundtrack by his father, the bassist Bill Lee, which has just been released on Island 7 90528–1. The elder Lee's modest, by turns moody and frolicsome small-band score goes awry only once, exactly where the black-and-white movie does: in the too-sweet Ronnie Dyson vocal accompanying an oversaturated Technicolor ballet. But in its mix of disciplined composition and footloose improvisation, Lee's music recalls earlier film scores by such jazz composers as Duke Ellington (*Anatomy of a Murder*), Miles Davis (*Frantic!*), Sonny Rollins (*Alfie*), John Lewis (*Odds Against Tomorrow*) and Gato Barbieri (*Last Tango in Paris*). It also brings to mind Henry Pleasants's conjecture that the collaborations between composers and film directors have the potential to become the modern equivalent of lyric theater. Writing before the corporate takeovers of both film and record companies, and before the success of *Easy Rider*, *The Graduate*, and *Saturday Night Fever* made soundtrack albums little more than K-Tel greatest-hits collections in disguise, Pleasants had no way of knowing that film composers would eventually rank lower than the music-acquisitions lawyers in the overall scheme of things. It's becoming more and more unusual to hear a score like Bill Lee's, brashly original and homogenetic to the film it serenades. If Dexter Gordon's haunting portrayal in '*Round Midnight* suggests that jazz musicians can be riveting onscreen subjects, Lee's score confirms that they also have plenty to offer behind the scenes. Here's hoping that more film producers take them up on the offer.

137 **Gary Giddins** Birdman of Hollywood (1988)

Source: Gary Giddins, 'Birdman of Hollywood,' in *Faces in the Crowd: Players and Writers. Essays on Music, Movies and Books*. (New York: Oxford University Press, 1992: 39, 42, 43–4, 44–8) (excerpts).

There's never been a movie like *Bird* – a cinematic pasticcio based on the life of the great jazz saxophonist Charlie ('Bird') Parker. Lurching back and forth in time, it mirrors in its dark intensity Parker's own frenetic vitality and casual mastery, his outlaw irreverence and brazen charm. Seizing energy from his music, *Bird* probes its bigger-than-life hero and draws a bead on themes that American movies usually shun or, worse, patronize: black urban culture, miscegenation, drugs, the vagaries of art. In refusing to mute or romanticize Parker, or to pontificate about the evils that brought him down, *Bird* is remarkably adult and manifestly European in style. Parker's genius is depicted offhandedly – the movie proceeds from the foolhardy presumption that the audience knows him, or should. His life and art are addressed with such poise and affection you'd think Hollywood had been making serious movies about black artists for years. But no, it's taken Clint Eastwood to make that leap ...

Jazz and film are about the same age, and each is spoken of (often as if the other didn't exist) as America's sole contribution to the arts. In the 1930s, they defined popular culture; in the 1950s, they accrued intellectual pretensions. Each is a product of industrial life. Technology made movies possible and ensured the permanence of musical improvisation. Subsequent technological advances governed their growth – the introduction of tape and long-playing records no less than sound on film. Each has struggled for cultural status and received major boosts from Europe. Each is a collaborative art. The fundamental differences are symbolized by the addresses of their most acclaimed artists. Hollywood is the Valhalla of American fantasy; jazz lives on the outskirts of town. They represent the two sides of America's self-image, opulent vanity vs. scuffling hipness.

Although the impact of black American music around the world has been no less profound than that of cinema, its heroes – with the arguable exception of the blues singer Leadbelly, the subject of an underexhibited Gordon Parks film of the same name (1976) – have not been favored with much cinematic flair. A few Hollywood-produced jazz features are redeemed by the presence of Louis Armstrong, whose roles are often incongruous or condescending, and other performers. The contexts remain no more convincing than, say, those of Biblical epics. Even Anthony Mann's *The Glenn Miller Story* (1954), a nostalgic if distorted recounting of a pop musician tangentially related to jazz, expresses its contempt for the music it pretends to memorialize by slowing it down a hair so that it doesn't swing and by occasionally replacing the distinctive sound of Miller's orchestra with an indifferent ocean of strings. The lowest point was *Lady Sings the Blues* (1972), an appalling desecration of the life and music of Billie Holiday, who worked in Hollywood once – as a maid in *New Orleans* (1947). The urban jazz world, with its countless anecdotes of hipster transcendence and artistic triumph, its jam sessions and battles of the bands, has remained practically virgin territory. Until *Bird* ...

Eastwood's film focuses on the decade between Bird's debut on New York's 52nd Street in 1945 and his death 10 years later. Through a complex structure of flashbacks, flashbacks-within-flashbacks, and flashforwards, he gives us a Parker whose triumph and tragedy are intertwined and inescapable. A notorious heroin addict, Bird unwittingly attracted dozens of musicians to their doom, much to his horror. Eastwood punctuates the early scenes with a symbol – actually a cymbal, flying through the air and crashing with jarring finality. A flashback details a Kansas City jam session at which the cymbal was hurled at Bird's feet by a contemptuous drummer. The scene is loosely based on fact, and the effect, an idea of [scriptwriter] Oliansky's that is nonetheless reminiscent of the ominous flashbacks in Eastwood's surreal western, *High Plains Drifter*, ties Parker's humiliating apprenticeship to the hopelessness of his future. It also embodies his achievement, the adversity he overcame.

Eastwood was wary of relating the cymbal, which is the last sound his Parker hears before dying, to rejection metaphors in his other films or to personal experience, but said, 'Adversity makes you struggle a little harder. I think everyone is the product of some sort of setback or something – that thing where you snap and say, I don't give a crap what they say, I'm going to overcome this. Adversity pushes you. I don't know if I identify with Bird, I just like him very much' ...

Bird is filled with the kind of invention that mines truths barred to the documentarian. A composite character named Buster Franklin, for example, is a rather sinister musician who haunts Parker's musical progress. He presides over the humiliating jam session in Kansas City, quits playing in disgust after hearing Parker's mature brilliance, and winds up as a successful rock and roll honker making more bread than Bird ever dreamed. A more piquant episode, also fictional, conveys Parker's love of modern music, specifically Stravinsky, and the barrier between two cultures. Learning that his California lover and the transplanted Russian composer see the same dentist, Bird has her drive into the area where the famous expatriates live – Huxley, Thomas Mann, Schoenberg, Stravinsky. While *The Firebird* swells on the soundtrack, he rings the bell at Stravinsky's gate. The door opens, and the composer in his smoking jacket peers out; for one moment they stare at each other across the abyss, then the door is shut. As Bird climbs back into the car, Eastwood brings them together on the soundtrack. The opening phrase of 'Parker's Mood' floats over *The Firebird*. 'What that does to Stravinsky, I don't know,' Eastwood says, smiling with pleasure at the conceit. 'But here's two different guys from two different worlds, and I thought they should meet.'

Some of the liberties taken with history are irksome – not least because they are trite, therefore unnecessary. Bird's childhood doctor calls him Charles Christopher Parker, Jr., though Christopher was his father's middle name, not Bird's. In later years, Bird might have used it to stress his ties to the drifter who abandoned his mother and him – but his family doctor would never have made that mistake. The *New York Daily News* did not flag Bird's suicide attempt on the front page; it didn't even print much of an obit. The jam session in Kansas City is a tad too boppish for the mid-1930s. Bird rode a horse to Chan's door a few years *after* her eldest daughter was born, to impress the daughter, not before, as shown in the film. Bird figured out his style rehearsing with a guitarist, not a pianist. His West Coast lover, a mysterious sculptress, was nothing like the svelte blonde played by Anna Levine. Red Rodney met Parker in New York, not Los Angeles. And Rodney didn't play nearly as large a role in Parker's life as the picture suggests. Similarly, Chan's role is amplified at the expense of another common-law wife, Doris Sydnor, whom many musicians remember being on the scene more than Chan was.

None of this matters much. The scenes in which Rodney arranges for Parker to play a Hassidic wedding (a true story: the other musicians were Thelonious Monk and Art Blakey) and travels with him in the south pretending to be an albino blues singer (true in part, but much overstated) are so forcible and funny that it's impossible to mind the elaboration of his character. Eastwood avoids the cliché of having Rodney serve as a white filtering agent for Parker's black experience. The makeshift marriage between Bird and Chan works as a wholly credible love story, unmarred by the kind of didactic dialogue that turns each participant into a billboard for liberal cant. The quotidian detail that marks their scenes together gives their love a depth and credibility rarely seen in Hollywood movies, most especially in the depiction of an interracial couple.

Eastwood heard Parker three times while growing up in Oakland. The first time was in 1946, when Parker made his debut at the all-star theatrical jam sessions known as Jazz at the Philharmonic. 'I had gone to see Lester Young, who was God to me, and suddenly this guy in a pinstripe suit steps forward playing, and I'm not sure what it's all about, but there's a lot of things going on here. It's unexplainable – there was nobody like him. At the Jazz at the Phil, he was standing there with real heavyweights – Coleman Hawkins, who was still playing well, and Lester Young, and the more show business guys like Flip Phillips. I didn't even know who Bird was. But there was something about his music that was just unbelievably well played. They were great, they were giants, but here was somebody different. It was like four Joe Smiths and Gary Cooper or Clark Gable. Just something about the guy.'

One of the chief pleasures of *Bird* is the attention to period detail. Parker died in 1955, while watching the Tommy Dorsey show on television in the hotel apartment of Baroness Nica de Koenigswarter. Eastwood managed to find a kinescope of the actual show. After talking with the Baroness, he located the precise segment – a juggling act – that Bird was laughing at when he keeled over. 'I sent her the pages of the script about his death. She said, it wasn't quite like that, it was like this. She told me about how he stood up and started laughing, and so I took it down and did it like she said. I told her, if you don't mind, I'll just portray it like that.' He took equal care with the distraught telegrams Bird sent Chan when he learned their infant daughter had died. 'We even reshot one because the spelling wasn't exactly as on the original wires.'

Perhaps the most impressive attempt at recreation is the facsimile of 52nd Street, a block-long bazaar of nightclubs and bars, reproduced from a famous photograph and brought to life with the teeming energy of musicians, milling servicemen, and the phony doorman, Pincus, a fixture of the street, who pretended to work for all the clubs and would take tips for opening the door or pointing out a parking place ... We drove over to see the set where the 52nd Street scene was shot ... [and] reached a street of dour brownstones, false fronts for the most part. 'This is called the Annie Street, because it was built for *Annie*. We had the Deuces over here with the big long dolly shot, and then all down the street. We backlit the street so that it would have depth, and we had the awnings on and the neon and all that kind of stuff. Did it all in one shot. We picked up a high shot – an establishing shot – of Chan lighting a cigarette as she walked by a fruitstand, and backed up to reveal the whole street.'

Eastwood's New York of the 1940s is new to movies. You realize you've never seen it before, never seen wartime New York pulse with as much life – never seen it racially integrated. Not in wartime movies, at any rate, though Vincente Minnelli took care to place occasional black extras in crowd scenes in *The Clock*. Most location shots used in films of that period suggest the absence of all blacks other than an occasional doorman, shineboy, or porter. Even the independent black films failed to portray the interracial boisterousness that was part of the allure of 52nd Street, Harlem, and Greenwich Village. If Eastwood recreated New York on a soundstage, he did venture slightly beyond the studio for other locations. The scenes set in Kansas City were filmed in bars and theaters in old sections of Los Angeles and Pasadena. He persuasively simulated the deep south in the Sacramento Valley.

Equal care was spent on the music and soundtrack. Indeed, the movie's claim to innovation lies in its use of original Charlie Parker broadcast recordings. 'The first question a lot of jazz fans asked when they heard about *Bird* was, "Is this going to be another one of those films where they play a two-bar intro and then people talk over all the music?" And I said, "Well, I don't think so. You're talking to a fellow aficionado".' Instead of using Parker's famous records, Eastwood purchased rights to the relatively little known cache of concert recordings, most of them privately taped by Chan on a machine Bird bought her for her birthday. That decision makes perfect musical sense, since Bird's live performances have a vivacity and expansiveness lacking in his often punctilious studio recordings. The problem was poor sound and abrupt editing: Chan would turn off the machine as soon as Bird finished his solo.

To build up the sound of the recordings, Eastwood's technicians cleaned up the tracks, separating the alto from the accompanying instruments, which were then wiped away. Musicians were brought in to overdub drums, bass, piano, and trumpet. The results were laid out in stereo. 'We brought in Monty Alexander, Ray Brown, John Guerin, Walter Brown, Barry Harris, and Ron Carter and others. Dizzy wasn't available, so we had Jon Faddis play Dizzy's solos and a pretty good imitation of Howard McGhee, too, I thought. What is a guy like Ray Brown going to think? But they had a ball, they were all misty-eyed. Ray said he felt like he was 19 again. Red Rodney played his own solos and coached Michael Zelniker. For the incidental music, we had James Rivers, who played the title tune in *Tightrope*, and Charles McPherson. For the scene when Bird sends the telegrams, I had McPherson just stand there and watch the screen to try and get into Bird's head and play something, using "Parker's Mood" as a theme.' Lennie Niehaus, himself a formidable saxophonist, taught the instrument to Forest Whitaker, who, his hairline shaved back and a false plate on his teeth, reproduced Parker's playing stance down to the hunched shoulders, though the pistonlike activity of his fingers is exaggerated.

Eastwood decided that Bird, who traveled with a small ensemble of strings in the early '50s, would have enjoyed playing with a fuller complement of strings, and had Niehaus score 'April in Paris' for 20 violins and cellos. Bird is shown playing it during a triumphant tour of France, in an especially deft sequence. While Parker's solo continues on the soundtrack, the film cuts to the end of the performance, as Bird bows and a cheering audience pelts him with flowers. Then, viewed from the rear of the stage, Bird lifts a rose to his lips and consumes a petal. That night an expatriate musician, loosely based on the New Orleans-born Sidney Bechet, who became a national hero in France, tries to convince Parker to leave the United States for good. 'I'm not running from my own country,' Bird says. 'Your country?' 'Mine! whether they like it or not, mine.'

138 **Francis Davis** Birdland, Mon Amor (1988)

Source: Francis Davis, 'Birdland, Mon Amor,' in *Outcats: Jazz Composers, Instrumentalists, and Singers* (New York: Oxford University Press, 1990: 215–20) (excerpt). (Originally published 1988.)

Forest Whitaker plays Parker in *Bird,* a film produced and directed by Clint Eastwood and written by Joel Oliansky. Miming to Parker's actual solos, with his eyes wide open and his shoulders slightly hunched and flapping, Whitaker captures the look we recognize from Parker's photographs and the one surviving television kinescope of him (a 1952 appearance on Earl Wilson's *Stage Entrance,* which is featured in the excellent jazz documentaries *The Last of the Blue Devils* and *Celebrating Bird: The Triumph of Charlie Parker*). Unfortunately, even though he's been outfitted with a gold cap over one incisor to make his smile shine like Parker's, Whitaker is less convincing offstage, where most of *Bird* takes place. On the basis of his brief but effective turn as the young, possibly psychotic pool shark who spooks the master hustler played by Paul Newman in Martin Scorsese's *The Color of Money*, Whitaker was the right choice to play Parker – a master con, among other things. But Whitaker's performance is too tense and pent-up to bring Parker to life, and by the end of the movie, the actor seems as much the victim of heavy-handed writing and direction as the character does.

Why is it always raining in jazz films, and why are the vices that kill musicians always presented as side effects of a terminal case of the blues? It merely drizzled throughout 'Round Midnight, and though the movie was false in other ways, the mist was in keeping with the slow-motion music performed by the ailing Dexter Gordon. The music in *Bird* is supposed to be defiant and ebullient, but the *mise en scène* is downbeat, with rain gushing against the windows of melodramatically underlit interiors. (You come out of the theater squinting, just like Eastwood.) Like Milton's Lucifer, whither this Bird flies is hell. He brings rain and darkness with him wherever he goes. His unconscious is haunted by symbols – or, to be more specific about it, by a literal cymbal that flies across the screen and lands with a resounding thud every time he drifts off or nods out. The vision is based on a (perhaps apocryphal) incident to which Eastwood and Oliansky have given too much interpretive spin. As an untutored seventeen-year-old in Kansas City, Parker is supposed to have forgotten the chord changes to 'I Got Rhythm' while playing at a jam session with the drummer Jo Jones, who, legend has it, threw one of his cymbals to the floor as a way of gonging the teenager off the stage. Except for overwrought conjecture by Ross Russell in a purple passage toward the end of *Bird Lives!*, there is nothing in the voluminous literature about Parker to suggest that this public humiliation haunted him for the rest of his life. To the contrary, it's usually cited as the incident that strengthened his resolve to become a virtuoso. But in *Bird's* retelling, the echo of that cymbal deprives Parker of all pleasure in his accomplishments. *Bird's* Parker wants to rage but can only snivel, even when hurling his horn through a control-room window in abject frustration. You don't believe for a second that this frightened sparrow could have summoned up the self-confidence to make a name for himself in the competitive world of jazz in the 1940s, much less set that world on its ear with 'Ko Ko.' Parker was a compulsive, which is another way of saying that he was a junkie, but he was also obsessive, which is another way of saying that he was an artist. Parker's torment is here, but not his hedonism or his genius or the hint of any connection between them.

Much of what *Bird* tells us about Parker is hooey, and at least one of its inventions is an abomination – a character, a slightly older saxophonist who knew Parker as an upstart in Kansas City, who becomes jealous when he finds out that Parker is the talk of New York. A final encounter with this saxophonist seals Parker's doom. Parker stumbles down Fifty-second Street, dazed to find that the jazz clubs that were the settings for his early triumphs have given way to strip joints. (The excuse for his surprise is his having been holed up in the country with Chan for a few months, but anyone who knows anything about jazz during this period has to wonder if he's been on the moon – articles in the national press were bemoaning the departure of jazz from 'The Street' as early as 1948, and this is supposed to be 1955.) Told by another acquaintance that he hasn't seen anything yet, Parker wanders into a theater where his old Kansas City rival is knocking 'em dead with a greasy rhythm 'n' blues à la King Curtis. This triggers Parker's final breakdown. Even assuming that it was necessary to invent a fictional nemesis for Parker, why name that character 'Buster,' which the filmmakers should have known was the name of one of Parker's real-life Kansas City mentors, the alto saxophonist Buster Smith? And why pretend that Parker, who reportedly found good in all kinds of music, would have been shocked into a fatal tailspin by the advent of rock 'n' roll?

Jazz fans appalled by the fraudulent portrayal of Parker won't be the only moviegoers displeased with *Bird*. It's a mess. Even at the epic length of two hours and forty-five minutes, the narrative feels hurried and absentminded, with more flashbacks within flashbacks than any movie since Jacques Tourneur's 1947 *noir, Out of the Past*. You're never sure who's remembering what, what year it is, how famous Parker has become, or how long he has to live – Whitaker has the same puppy-dog look no matter how far gone he's supposed to be, so the only way of telling is by the hair style on Diane Venora, the actress who plays Chan Richardson (she gives up her bohemian bangs and braids after becoming a mother). In terms of explaining to an audience that knows nothing about jazz (most moviegoers, in other words) what made Parker's music so revolutionary, *Bird* is about as much help as *The Ten Commandments* was in explaining the foundations of Judeo-Christian law – you almost expect someone to point to Parker and proclaim, like Yul Brynner as Pharaoh, 'His jazz *is* jazz.' The script primes us for ironic payoffs it never delivers; as when, for example, Parker hears his blues 'Parker's Mood' sung by King Pleasure, whose lyrics envision six white horses carrying Parker to his grave in Kansas City [**see IX/113**]; he makes Chan promise not to let his body be shipped back to K.C. for burial. What we're *not* told is that, against Chan's wishes, that's exactly what happened – to tell us this would require acknowledging that Parker was separated from Chan at the time of his death, and still legally wed to Doris Snydor [Sydnor], who is conveniently never mentioned in *Bird*. This movie is probably going to be praised in some quarters for its 'unsensational' depiction of an interracial relationship. But the relationship between Whitaker and Venora could stand some sensationalizing. The only sparks that fly between them are acrimonious; they bicker from the word go. Although the script makes Chan an awful scold, Diane Venora brings unexpected shadings to the role: you believe in her as a thrill-seeking hipster who's just as glad when motherhood forces her into a more conventional way of life. Venora's is the film's only convincing performance. Michael Zelniker is affectless as Red Rodney, the white trumpeter who sang the blues in order to pass as a black albino while on tour with Parker in the segregated South in the late forties. Zelniker wouldn't have had to worry about white sheriffs; black audiences of the period would have hooted this yuppie off the stage. (He and Parker play a Jewish wedding, and when the cute little rabbi says about Parker and the other sidemen, 'These boys are not Jewish, but they are good musicians,' you feel as though you've witnessed this scene in a hundred other movies. Eastwood and Oliansky are delivering a sermon on the need for unity among oppressed minorities, and what's unbearable about it is that they think they're being subtle.) As the young Dizzy Gillespie, Sam Wright is sanctimonious and old before his time, and (as the jazz critic Bob Blumenthal has pointed out) the audience that knows nothing about the real-life Dizzy is going to wonder how he ever got that nickname. The first time we see Diane Salinger as the Baroness Nica, she's wearing her beret at a tilt that casts half of her face in shadow, and she watches Parker with predatory eyes. She's a shady lady from Grand Guignol. Why this visual insinuation about a woman who made her apartment into a salon for black musicians with whom she maintained platonic relationships, and whose only possible 'crime' was that of dilettantism? She had no responsibility – symbolic or otherwise – for Parker's death.

The music in *Bird* has a phoney ring to it, even though Parker's recordings were used for most of the soundtrack. There were fans who used to follow Parker around the country, sneaking cumbersome wire recorders into night-clubs to preserve his work and shutting them off when his sidemen improvised. Eastwood and music supervisor Lennie Niehaus go these ornithologists one better (or one worse) by filtering out Parker's sidemen altogether in favor of new instrumental backing. In addition to being unfair to Parker's sidemen, many of whom were indeed capable of keeping pace with him, this removes him from his creative context and gives no sense that bebop was a movement.

But Parker is out of context throughout *Bird*. The movie would have us believe that he had little curiosity about the world beyond jazz, which in turn showed only oppositional interest in him. In reality, the musicians who worshiped Parker remember him as well-read, with a consuming interest in twentieth-century classical composition. And black jazz musicians of Parker's era had a direct influence on those white artists from other disciplines – the nascent hipsters and beats who people such early fifties novels as Chandler Brossard's *Who Walk in Darkness* and John Clellon Holmes's *Go*. Parker was a source of fascination to these poets, novelists, and abstract impressionists who were beginning to define themselves as outlaws from middle-class convention. They recognized his artistic drive and suicidal self-indulgence as the *yin* and *yang* of a compulsive nature pushing against physical limitations and societal restraints. In *Bird,* few white characters, except those from the jazz under-ground, seem to know or care who Parker is, and he isn't sure himself.

The pity of all this is that Clint Eastwood is a jazz fan, and *Bird* is supposed to have been a labor of love. In 1982, Eastwood directed and starred in *Honkytonk Man*, the gentle, admirably straightforward story of a Depression-era Okie troubadour called Red Sovine, who succumbs to tuberculosis before realizing his dream of performing at the Grand Ole Opry. Among its other virtues, that film managed to suggest the succor that music can give both performers and audiences. Perhaps believing that Parker was subjected to a harsher reality than the fictional Sovine by virtue of being black and a drug addict, Eastwood's tried to find a more insistent rhythm for *Bird,* but the one he's come up with feels choppy, disconnected, and pointlessly arty, with dated experiments in time and point of view forcing him against his best natural instincts as a storytelling director.

Charlie Parker first appeared on screen in the guise of Eagle, a heroin-addicted saxophonist played by Dick Gregory in the forgotten *Sweet Love Bitter* (1967), which was based on John A. Williams's novel *Night Song*. Although Gregory's performance was surprisingly effective, Eagle was a peripheral figure in a civil-rights-era melodrama about a white liberal college professor on the run from his conscience. In the late 1970s, Richard Pryor was supposed to star in a film about Parker that never got made – which is probably just as well, because Pryor brings so much of his own persona to the screen that Charlie Parker would have gotten lost. That leaves us with *Bird*, a jazz fan's movie in the worst possible sense – a movie with the blues, a *Birdland, Mon Amor* that wants to shout 'Bird lives!' but winds up whispering 'Jazz is dead.' *Bird* communicates the melancholy that every jazz fan feels as a result of the music's banishment from mainstream culture. In projecting this melancholy on Charlie Parker – whose music still leaps out at you with its reckless abandon, and whose triumph should finally count for more than his tragedy – Eastwood has made another of those movies that make jazz fans despair that mainstream culture will ever do right by them or their musical heroes.

139 **James Agee** Films (1944)

Source: James Agee, 'Films,' *Nation*, 16 December 1944: 753 (excerpt).

'Jamming the Blues,' a hot-jazz short by the *Life* photographer Gjon Mili, is exciting quite a few people around Hollywood, and has some right to, for it is one of the few musical shorts I have ever got even fair pleasure out of hearing, and the only one, barring the jam scene in 'Phantom Lady,' which was not a killing bore to watch except as a heartsick attempt on the part of the makers to act as if this were the gayest, most provocative film assignment in the world. Yet I don't really care much for the picture. It is too full of the hot, moist, boozy breath of the unqualified jazz addict, of which I once had more than enough in my own mouth; and I thought the two effects which wholly compose it – chiaroscuro and virtual silhouette – too pretentious and borrowed and arty, despite their occasional good service, to be taken in a wholly friendly spirit, let alone an enthusiastic one. There are few things in any art or art-industry more discouraging to think of, more inimical to the furtherance of good work or to the chance to attempt it, than the middle-brow highbrows. Half a brow is worse than no head.

140 **Charles Emge** On the beat in Hollywood (1944)

Source: Charles Emge, 'On the beat in Hollywood,' *Down Beat*, 1 December 1944: 6 (excerpt).

Now that we have seen *Jammin' the Blues* we can unreservedly rate it, despite obvious faults, as the most notable jazz treatment to come out of Hollywood to date. The credit goes not to Warner Brothers but to Norman Granz, who is largely responsible for what went into it in the way of music; and to Gjon Mili (who had never directed a picture before) for the original photographic treatment. They had to battle Mr. Studio to accomplish every notable advance over trite studio formula methods.

What they accomplished can be judged from some of the difficulties encountered. One of the main problems in a picture of this kind is mechanical. Musical sound-track is recorded before a picture is photographed (except the underscoring of dramatic pictures). When a musical performance is photographed, the musician or singer *pretends* to play or sing *exactly* the same notes recorded, meantime guided by a play-back of the sound track.

Anyone who is familiar with jazz will understand why it is difficult to synchronize a good jazz performance, the essence of which is an improvised, spontaneously created solo. In this case the musicians were attempting to synchronize to improvised solos recorded a *full month previously*. Granz had phonograph recordings made of the solos so that the boys could take them home and memorize them. The idea worked very well except in the case of Illinois Jacquet and Lester Young. Lester, it's our opinion, didn't try very hard.

Drum solos are especially difficult to synchronize. Good results were obtained by Granz by recording some of the more complicated passages, such as 'rolls,' on the set during shooting and dubbing these sections into the track. However, we have a suspicion that some of the drumming that Sid appears to do was recorded by Jo, and vice versa.

Mr. Studio objected to the appearance of a white musician with Negroes. Of course, he didn't object personally, but it just wouldn't go with Southern audiences. Granz was asked to eliminate Barney Kessel or to get a Negro guitarist to 'fake' his playing in the picture. Granz refused but had to be satisfied with photography that hides the fact that Kessel is white from all but the most discerning eyes.

Mr. Studio wanted 'hundreds of jitterbug dancers in a gigantic spectacle of rhythm.' Mili and Granz managed to get it down to the Archie Savage-Marie Bryant routine, a formalized thing that smacks of the Katherine Dunham influence and adds nothing but doesn't detract too much. Marie Bryant's vocal on *Sunny Side of the Street* isn't hard to take.

The music in *Jammin' the Blues* is not notable considering the calibre of the musicians. It is not their best, but it is still the best of its kind ever heard in a picture. The names of the boys are given on the main title (that we should live to see this day!), but here they are again, for the benefit of the record: Lester Young, Illinois Jacquet, Harry Edison, Jo Jones, Sidney Catlett, Red Callender, John Simmons, Marlowe Morris, Barney Kessel.

141 **Jackie Lopez** Is Hollywood yielding? (1945)

Source: Jackie Lopez, 'Is Hollywood yielding?', *Chicago Defender*, 24 March 1945: 20.

The stiff lipped complaining we've been tossing Hollywood way may have some bearing on the fact that the movie town is viewing the race with new eyes. Every now and then we get the delightful little shock of seeing our own portrayed as interesting human beings, rather than as the lowest of the low. I'm thinking of the late rage, 'To Have and Have Not' now playing State and Lake. Did you see all those beautiful black faces drifting in and out of the café in which most of the story takes place? Did you see them drinking at the bar, sitting at the tables, shifting in and out among the whites, talking, laughing, dancing – like anyone else? The story takes place in Martinique, true. But as I remember, Hollywood has, in the past, stuck to her white-man-super tales even if the story had only one white man in it. If he drank at a bar and there were no other white men to drink with him, he drank alone. I believe, anyway, that this honest to goodness reality made 'To Have and Have Not' that much finer a picture.

Another delight shocker on the State and Lake bill was the 'Jammin' the Blues' short photographed by Gjon Mili. I mention the photographer because the use of the camera was a unique contribution to the effectiveness of the ten-minute short. For those ten minutes you held on to the arm rests of your seat, and you were saying to yourself over and over again: 'This is art.' This is art. Just a ten minute dose of pure, unadulterated, really fine jazz given in two numbers: 'Sunny Side of the Street,' with vocals by Marie Bryant, and improvisations on an unpublished piece called 'Jam Session.' The group was a get-together thing, but it did more than all-right for itself.

Hollywood has potentialities – it's about time they start showing.

142 **Whitney Balliett** *The Sound of Jazz* (1983)

Source: Whitney Balliett, '*The Sound of Jazz*,' in *Goodbyes and Other Messages: A Journal of Jazz, 1981–1990* (New York: Oxford University Press, 1992: 86–90). (Originally published 1983.)

The confusion about the soundtrack of 'The Sound of Jazz,' the celebrated hour-long program broadcast live on CBS television on December 8, 1957, began a minute or so before the program ended, when an announcer said, 'Columbia Records has cut a long-playing record of today's program, which will be called "The Sound of Jazz." It'll be released early next year.' A Columbia recording by that name and bearing the CBS television logotype *was* issued early in 1958, but it was not the soundtrack of the show. It was a recording made on December 4th in Columbia's Thirtieth Street studio as a kind of rehearsal for the television production. It included many of the musicians who did appear on December 8th, and except for one number the materials were the same. Columbia probably made the recording as a precaution: a live jazz television program lasting a full hour (then, as it is now, the basic unit of television time was the minute) and built around thirty-odd (unpredictable) jazz musicians might easily turn into a shambles. It didn't. The soundtrack, which is at last available in its entirety – as 'The Real Sound of Jazz,' on Pumpkin Records – is superior to the Columbia record in almost every way, sound included.

'The Sound of Jazz' has long been an underground classic, and a lot of cotton wool has accumulated around it. So here, allowing for vagaries of memory, is how the program came to be. In the spring of 1957, Robert Goldman asked me if I would be interested in helping put together a show on jazz for John Houseman's new 'Seven Lively Arts' series, scheduled to be broadcast on CBS in the winter of 1957–58. I submitted an outline, and it was accepted. I invited Nat Hentoff to join me as co-advisor, and we began discussing personnel and what should be played. Our wish was to offer the best jazz there was in the simplest and most direct way – no history, no apologetics, no furbelows. But John Crosby, the television columnist of the *Herald Tribune,* had been hired as master of ceremonies for the 'Seven Lively Arts,' and we feared that he would do just what we wanted to avoid – talk about the music. We suggested listing the musicians and the tunes on tel-ops (now common practice), but Crosby was under contract for the whole series, and that was that. Crosby, it turned out, pretty much agreed with us, and what he did say was to the point. For the brilliant visual side of the show, CBS chose the late Robert Herridge as the producer and Jack Smight as the director. The excitement of the camera-work and of Smight's picture selection – he had five cameramen – has never been equalled on any program of this kind.

Here is the form the program finally took: A big band, built around the nucleus of the old Count Basie band, was the first group to be heard, and it included Roy Eldridge, Doc Cheatham, Joe Newman, Joe Wilder, and Emmett Berry on trumpets; Earle Warren, Ben Webster, Coleman Hawkins, and Gerry Mulligan on reeds; Vic Dickenson, Benny Morton, and Dicky Wells on trombones; and a rhythm section of Basie, Freddie Green, Eddie Jones, and Jo Jones. This utopian band, which Basie seemed immensely pleased to front, played a fast blues, 'Open All Night,' written and arranged by Nat Pierce, who did all the arranging on the show. Then a smaller band, made up of Red Allen and Rex Stewart on trumpet and cornet, Pee Wee Russell on clarinet, Hawkins, Dickenson, Pierce, Danny Barker on guitar, Milt Hinton on bass, and Jo Jones, did the old Jelly Roll Morton-Louis Armstrong 'Wild Man Blues' and Earl Hines' 'Rosetta.' The group was a distillation of the various historic associations, on recordings, of Allen and Russell, of Allen and Hawkins, and of Stewart and Hawkins, with Dickenson's adaptability holding everything together. The rhythm section was all-purpose and somewhat in the Basie mode. Thelonious Monk, accompanied by Ahmed Abdul-Malik on bass and Osie Johnson on drums, did his 'Blue Monk.' The big band returned for a slow blues, 'I Left My Baby,' with Jimmy Rushing on the vocal, and for a fast thirty-two-bar number by Lester Young called 'Dickie's Dream.' Billie Holiday sang her blues 'Fine and Mellow,' accompanied by Mal Waldron on piano and by Eldridge, Cheatham, Young, Hawkins, Webster, Mulligan, Dickenson, Barker, Hinton, and Osie Johnson. The Jimmy Giuffre Three, with Giuffre on reeds, Jim Hall on guitar, and Jim Atlas on bass, did Giuffre's 'The Train and the River,' and the show was closed by a slow blues, in which Giuffre and Pee Wee Russell played a duet, accompanied by Barker, Hinton, and Jo Jones. Crosby introduced each group, and there were pre-recorded statements about the blues from Red Allen, Rushing, Billie Holiday, and Guiffre. (I found these intrusive, but Hentoff and Herridge liked them.) The show was held in a big, bare two-story studio at Ninth Avenue and Fifty-sixth Street, and the musicians were told to wear what they wanted. Many wore hats, as jazz musicians are wont to do at recording sessions. Some had on suits and ties, some were in sports shirts and tweed jackets. Monk wore a cap and dark glasses with bamboo side pieces. Billie Holiday arrived with an evening gown she had got specially for the show, and was upset when she found that we wanted her in what she was wearing – a pony tail, a short-sleeved white sweater, and plaid pants. There was cigarette smoke in the air, and there were cables on the floor. A ladder leaned against a wall. Television cameras moved like skaters, sometimes photographing each other. The musicians were allowed to move around: Basie ended up watching Monk, and later Billie Holiday went over and stood beside Basie.

The atmosphere at the Columbia recording session was similar. Many of the musicians had not been together in a long time, and a rare early-December blizzard, which began just before the session and left as much as a foot of snow on the ground, intensified everything. It also caused problems. Our plan had been to reunite the All-American rhythm section of Basie, Freddie Green, Walter Page on bass, and Jo Jones, but Page called and said that he was sick and that, anyway, he couldn't find a cab. (He didn't make the television show, either, and he died two weeks later.) Eddie Jones, Basie's current bassist, replaced him. Thelonious Monk didn't turn up, and that is why Mal Waldron recorded a four-minute piano solo, aptly titled 'Nervous.' There were various other differences between the recording and the show. Frank Rehak took Benny Morton's place on the recording, because Morton was busy. Harry Carney, a man of infinite graciousness, filled in for Gerry Mulligan, a man of infinite ego, because Mulligan insisted he be paid double scale, and was refused. Doc Cheatham solos on the Columbia session but only plays obbligatos behind Billie Holiday on the television show; he had asked to be excused from all soloing, claiming that it would ruin his lip for his regular gig with a Latin band. Lester Young provides obbligatos behind Jimmy Rushing on 'I Left My Baby' on the Columbia record, and he also solos twice. He was particularly ethereal that day, walking on his toes and talking incomprehensibly, and most of the musicians avoided him. But he was intractable on Sunday during the first of the two run-throughs that preceded the television show. He refused to read his parts, and he soloed poorly. He was removed from the big-band reed section and was replaced by Ben Webster, and his only solo is his famous twelve bars on 'Fine and Mellow' – famous because this sequence had been used so many times on other television shows and because of Billie Holiday's expression as she listens to her old friend, an expression somewhere between laughter and tears. Billie Holiday came close to not being on the show. A week or so before, word of her difficulties with drugs and the law had reached the upper levels at CBS, and it was suggested that she be replaced by someone wholesome, like Ella Fitzgerald. We refused, and were backed by Herridge, and she stayed.

It is astonishing how good the music is on 'The Real Sound of Jazz.' Billie Holiday and Red Allen and Jimmy Rushing are in fine voice. The big-band ensembles are generally dazzling. The solos are almost always first-rate. (Giuffre is dull, and Roy Eldridge is overexcited.) Listen to Dickenson's boiling, shouting statement on 'Dickie's Dream,' wisely taken at a slightly slower tempo than on the Columbia record, and to his easy, rocking solo on 'Wild Man Blues.' And listen to Rex Stewart, sly and cool, on 'Wild Man' (he had recently emerged from a long semi-retirement) and to the way Jo Jones frames its breaks – suspending time, shaping melody, italicizing emotion. Some of the music on the show has not weathered well. Monk, surprisingly, sounds hurried and the Giuffre trio, which was extremely popular at the time, is thin and synthetic. And Pee Wee Russell swallows Giuffre in their duet. CBS never ran the program again, but it was shown at the Museum of Modern Art in the sixties, and there is now a copy at the Museum of Broadcasting.

143 **Hal Hinson** *Let's Get Lost*: Baker as icon (1989)

Source: Hal Hinson, '*Let's Get Lost:* Baker as icon,' *Washington Post*, 2 June 1989: Style (D2).

In *Let's Get Lost*, Bruce Weber's enigmatic, hypnotic film portrait of Chet Baker, the director returns periodically to an ecstatic, romantic image of the jazz musician wedged in the back seat of a Cadillac convertible, the wind in his thinning hair, as the big car plunges into the night. Captured from the angle of myth, these shots of Baker hold the key to *Let's Get Lost*'s entrancing, poetic appeal. Filmed in star-caressing black and white, they borrow from the pop style of '50s Hollywood teen movies, with Baker cast in the role of the antiheroic loner. But there's an even more primal, Dionysian quality about them, too. His eyes half-closed, Baker is visibly enthralled, tending to inner visions. If he's heading anywhere in particular, or if he cares, nothing in his face shows it. He's drifting, far away, lost.

The focal point of these shots – and the focus of the movie as a whole – is Baker's ravaged, iconic face. Once movie-idol handsome, now scarred by age and hard living, Baker has the sort of dramatic features that immediately inspire interpretation – his face speaks volumes. It also evokes a deluge of contradictions. As a young man, he carried the cool, world-weary allure of James Dean and Montgomery Clift. As an older man – he was 57 in 1987 when the film was shot – he looks, at some moments, like one of Edward S. Curtis's noble Indians; at others, like a common drifter. Weber's mission is to try to piece all these impressions – plus the film footage, photos and the testimony of family, lovers and friends – into a dramatic, coherent whole. And what he provides us is rapturous, deeply involving, and more than a little puzzling.

Basically, *Let's Get Lost* is a manifestation of Weber's crush – a portrait of a pinup. Baker has occupied fantasy space in Weber's head since the photographer was a teenager, and his images of Baker are like his celebrity portraits and his famous Calvin Klein ads – glossy, '40s-style star portraits with an overlay of smoky, '50s cool. Weber is working here out of a highly specialized interest, and what he means to say about his subject comes to us through layers of ambivalence. What Weber is analyzing here is an object of erotic fascination. But of all our passions, those involving sex are simultaneously the most durable and the least resistant to scrutiny. As a result, *Let's Get Lost* is an exercise in hagiography that can't help but deconstruct itself. In his work as a photographer, Weber doesn't so much shoot his subjects as apotheosize them. But Baker resists being mythologized in the generically glamorous manner Weber intends.

At the most fundamental level, the real Chet Baker is a kind of nowhere man. He's too insubstantial for Weber to levitate him into greatness. This fact is the source of the film's dramatic tension, and Weber, to his credit, seems to have realized it. The movie provides the basic outlines of Baker's life, but none of these facts ever attaches itself significantly to a real person. Early on, Baker's style of trumpet playing and singing was marked by a moody insouciance. Later, after years of inactivity – including the three years it took to learn to play his horn with dentures after all his teeth were knocked out – the simplicity and straightforwardness of emotion in his playing seemed forced on him by necessity; he sang as he did because that was all the strength he had left in him.

There's more death than sex in Baker's style, though perhaps this is the tragic dimension that comes from knowing that he died last year by falling out of his hotel room window. In *Let's Get Lost,* his singing is tender and evocative, but detached. He's singing about some dream of love that he is long past believing in. (In this sense, his rendition of Elvis Costello's 'Almost Blue' is perfect – it's about almost feeling something.) He seems equally disembodied speaking into the camera. When near the end Weber asks Baker if he enjoyed making the film, the musician says blandly, 'How could I not? ... It was like a dream.'

Baker lends his image, his music and his past to *Let's Get Lost* but nothing of himself, and if the movie were about Chet Baker – the real Chet Baker – this might have been killing. Instead, the film's true subject is Weber's infatuation; it's about the emotion that, over the years, he has projected onto his idol. These starstruck projections are what we take away from the picture, and the irony is that they're remarkably potent, perhaps partly because we see our own star obsessions mirrored in them. Any illusions that Weber might have had about Chet Baker survive the filmmaker's contact with the flesh-and-blood man. His love is a pure fan's love; everything, even squalor, feeds it. In this sense, Baker has given all of himself that was necessary. For Weber's purposes, the real Chet Baker wasn't irrelevant, but he wasn't that important either.

144 **James Berardinelli** *A Great Day in Harlem* (1995)

Source: James Berardinelli, '*A Great Day in Harlem*,' *ReelViews*, 1995. Internet: http://movie-reviews.colossus.net/

An average picture may be worth a thousand words, but the one around which *A Great Day in Harlem* was formed is worth many, many more. This film tells the story of a legendary jazz photograph – a shot taken in 1958 for *Esquire* magazine by first-time photographer Art Kane. It looks like a class picture, featuring some '58 guys who have never been together in their lives' – performing legends like Thelonious Monk, Dizzy Gillespie, Roy Eldridge, Count Basie, and dozens of others.

Jazz fan Jean Bach turned *A Great Day in Harlem* into a labor of love. This motion picture, with its countless anecdotes about elements of the photograph and the effort that went into taking it, is a joy to watch. We learn why Thelonious Monk wore a light coat and positioned himself next to Marian McPartland and Mary Lou Williams. We're told about Dizzy Gillespie's penchant for sticking his tongue out. We are let in on the truth about why Count Basie was sitting on the curb next to a group of children. Throughout the film's sixty minute running time, many of the surviving participants relate fond memories of the day and each other.

In addition to the interviews, there's plenty of other material to make *A Great Day in Harlem* of interest. First and foremost is the score, a compilation of recorded performances by many of the artists (both living and dead) featured in the picture. Then there are photographs snapped by others during the gathering. Milt Hinton's wife, Mona, came armed with an 8mm movie camera, and her footage adds color and movement. And, to supplement all this material, Bach has included sequences of the performers as they appeared on a 50s TV show, *The Sound of Jazz.*

The picture itself is remarkable – an amazing feat of good fortune that a photographer could gather this many musical luminaries on the corner of Lennox Avenue and 125th Street at 10 o'clock in the morning (an unreasonably early hour for performers used to going to bed at dawn). In many ways, this film is no less worthy of observation and archiving. In addition to being a wonderful mix of culture, memories, and stories, it includes the final filmed interviews with Bud Freeman, Buck Clayton, Max Kaminsky, and Dizzy Gillespie – the man whose last on-camera words (which close out the film) send the audience from the theater smiling and chuckling. If there's such a thing as a magical documentary, *A Great Day in Harlem* is it.

Out-Chorus

There were a raft of books published about jazz history, a lot of them bad, some of them very good as to facts and dates and names; a few were readable, the rest mostly for the fanatics and so packed with names, dates and written either in professors' English or reporters' prose that you had to love the stuff a lot to wade through it. But it all helped, it all made the subject serious because people are impressed by the printed word about anything. (Stephen Longstreet, *The Real Jazz, Old and New*, 1956)

The original job of choosing what merited inclusion and what did not was never an easy one. There was ... the problem of getting permission to reprint from publishers and writers. In some cases, this was impossible ... I was criticized for not including material which I had wanted, but could not get. (Editor Ralph de Toledano, *Frontiers of Jazz*, 1947)

Jazz. As I've said, we do stand by the authenticity of that improvised art. (Jack Gelber, *The Connection*, 1959)

While it has loyal adherents the world over, jazz is at heart an American phenomenon ... and its evolution reflects the struggles and triumphs of American artistry and black Americans. Some ... have even suggested that the jazz band is the embodiment of the American democratic ideal. It invites and thrives on equal participation and input from each contributing member. (Jonny King, *What Jazz Is*, 1997)

In the year 2000 we shall be asking what jazz can do as an encore, now that it has been everywhere and done most things we can think of. In the meantime, looking back is a sumptuous pleasure. (Russell Davies, reviewing Gary Giddins' *Visions of Jazz*, *The Observer*, 1999)

Jazz is still a very big word. (Andrew Clark [ed.], *Riffs & Choruses*, 2001)

Suggested Reading

Useful aids are: Merriam (with Benford), *A Bibliography of Jazz* (1954); Reisner, *The Literature of Jazz: A Selective Bibliography* (1959); Kennington and Read, *The Literature of Jazz: A Critical Guide* (1980 [1970]); Kernfeld (ed.), *The New Grove Dictionary of Jazz* (1988); Feather and Gitler, *The Biographical Encyclopedia of Jazz* (1999). Substantial listings in Tirro, *Jazz: A History* (1993); Walser, *Keeping Time* (ed. 1999).

Details are mostly abbreviated; full information is given in the Bibliography, except running checklist titles of jazz lexicons, fiction, poetry and film (pp. 459–62).

Chorus I: Jazz and definition

Jazz **dictionaries**: see Major's *Juba to Jive: A Dictionary of African-American Slang* (1994); Powell's *The Language of Jazz* (1997), which surveys the term 'jazz' (67–9). **Definitions**: compendia in Pleasants (1955); Ulanov (1952: Ch.1); Ostransky (1977: Ch. 2); detailed discussion in educationalist Gridley's 'Is Jazz popular music?' (1987) and (with Maxham and Hoff) 'Three Approaches to defining jazz' (1989); also Brown's 'The theory of jazz music' (1991). **Meanings** and **origins** are anthologized by editors Kington, *The Jazz Anthology* (1992: Ch. 1), and Meltzer, *Reading Jazz* (ed. 1993: 35–70). Porter, *Jazz: A Century of Change* (1997: Chs 1–5), reprints material on definition, etymology, and responses to early jazz (1919–1934), including Gushee's article (1994) on nineteenth-century origins. Merriam and Garner (**I/6**) cite comprehensively on etymology. For differing perspectives on **jazz evolution**: Morgenstern and Giddins, in *New Perspectives on Jazz* (1990), ed. Baker. Morton's 'Discourse on Jazz' (Library of Congress recordings) is edited in Lomax's *Mister Jelly Roll* (1973 [1950]: 61–6), with comments by Williams, *Jazz Changes* (1992: 137–40). On aesthetics of **jazz appreciation**, Kernfeld's *What to Listen for in Jazz* (1995, with CD) introduces musical concepts, procedures and styles; other listener's guides are Williams' *Where's the Melody?* (1966) and the more pedagogical *Jazz Styles* (Gridley, 1978–99; CDs and teaching manual), *How to Listen to Jazz* (Coker, 1978), and *Jazz: A Listener's Guide* (McCalla, 1982). *What Jazz Is* (King, 1997) is a recommended 'insider's' view from a professional musician. For **sociological approaches** to jazz appreciation and theory, see *Journal of Jazz Studies* articles: Horowitz (1973); Hughes (1974); Horowitz and Nanry (1975). Early full-length studies concentrate on **jazz's status as art**: e.g., Osgood's *So This is Jazz* (1926b), and Mendl, *The Appeal of Jazz* (1927); see also **reception debate** and **analysis** in Engel, 'Jazz: a musical discussion' (1922); Seldes,

'Toujours jazz,' in *The 7 Lively Arts* (1924); Osgood, 'The anatomy of jazz' (1926a); Dodge's later 'Harpsichords and jazz trumpets' (1934) investigates sources of jazz improvisation. A 'new view' of jazz's reception in America is argued by Collier (1988). For McMahon's attacks on jazz's 'unspeakable' degradation: *Ladies' Home Journal* (1921, 1922); *Etude*'s symposium, 'Where is jazz leading America?' (1924), examines 'The Jazz Problem.' On 'Fear and jubilation' of the **Whiteman Aeolian Hall concert** (1924), see DeLong (1983: 3–11); also Meltzer (1993: 116–21). **Early literary treatment** of jazz includes (e.g.): Hughes, *The Weary Blues* (1926); Van Vechten, *Nigger Heaven* (1926); Gade, *Jazz Mad* (1927; **I/17**); March, *The Wild Party* (1928). See also jazz poems: Sandburg, 'Jazz fantasia' (1920); Heyward, 'Jasbo Brown' (1924); Brown, 'Cabaret' (1927); Davis, 'Jazz band' (1935).

Chorus II: Jazz and history

For **jazz history**, see Gioia's *The History of Jazz* (1997); Tirro's comprehensive *Jazz: A History* (1993, with CD [1977]); also Giddins's alternative jazz history and horizons, *Visions of Jazz* (1998), and Walser's readings in jazz history, *Keeping Time* (ed. 1999). Others, of varying value and intention, include Stearns, *The Story of Jazz* (1970 [1956]); Collier, *The Making of Jazz* (1978); Gridley, *Jazz Styles* (1978–); Sales, *Jazz: America's Classical Music* (1984); Megill and Demory, *Introduction to Jazz History* (1984); Porter, Ullman and Hazell, *Jazz: From Its Origins to the Present* (1993); Megill and Tanner, *Jazz Issues: A Critical History* (1995). **Formalist, musicological approaches** are grounded in Schuller's (in-progress) *The History of Jazz* – *Early Jazz* (1968; **I/8**), *The Swing Era* (1989) – and illustrated by Williams' *Smithsonian Collection of Classic Jazz* recordings (1987, with booklet [1973]). The jazz canon and evolutionary development are expounded in Williams' *The Jazz Tradition* (1993 [1970]; **II/22**) and *The Art of Jazz* (ed. 1959), and anticipated in earlier jazz historians: e.g. Panassié, *Hot Jazz* (1936), *The Real Jazz* (1942); Hobson, *American Jazz Music* (1939); Goffin, *Jazz: from the Congo to the Metropolitan* (1944); Blesh, *Shining Trumpets* (1946); Hodeir, *Jazz: Its Evolution and Essence* (1956; **II/24**). For **overviews** of **jazz criticism**: Dodge, 'Consider the critics,' in Ramsey and Smith, *Jazzmen* (1939: Ch. XV); Welburn, 'The American jazz writer-critic of the 1930s' (1989); Gennari, 'Jazz criticism: its development and ideologies,' *Black American Literature Forum* (1991; **II/21**). Giddins examines influences of critics Williams, Balliett and Schuller in 'Fathers and son,' *Faces in the Crowd* (1992: 256–66). For other critiques, see Rasula and Elworth (Gabbard 1995a: 57–75, 134–62). **Oppositional ideologies**, advocating **extra-canonical, contextual approaches**, are focused in Gabbard's influential essay collections: *Jazz Among the Discourses* (1995a) and *Representing Jazz* (1995b): see Gabbard's introduction (jazz canon) and Kenney (jazz history) (1995a: 1–28, 100–16). Carner's essential Literature of Jazz issue, *Black American Literature Forum* (1991), contains Gennari's survey (above); Wallenstein's examination of poetry and jazz (595–620); DeVeaux's influential essay on jazz historiography (525–60; **II/25**) – see also the latter's review article, 'What did we do to be so black and blue?' (1996). From an **African-American perspective**, Baraka (LeRoi Jones) challenges white institutionalizing of jazz in *Blues People* (1963; see also **II/28**); and argues jazz institutions are racist and oppressive with Crouch in 'Jazz criticism and its effect on the art form' (Baker 1990: 55–87). Understanding of black music and its relationship to sociocultural history is urged by Kofsky, 'The jazz tradition: black music and its white critics' (1971). **Women in jazz** are surveyed by Placksin, *Jazzwomen* (1982); Dahl, *Stormy Weather* (1984; **II/29**); Gourse, *Madame Jazz* (1995), which offers a 'status report' on women. See also Lewis Porter, re-evaluating jazz women instrumentalists and composers: *Music Educator's Journal*, Sept.–Oct., 1984. Carby's admired study of sexual politics in women's blues (1986) is reprinted in O'Meally (1998: 469–82) and Walser (1999: 351–65). In addition to the seminal *Hear Me Talkin' to Ya* (1955), see **oral histories** compiled by Spellman (1966), Taylor (1977; **V/63**), Wilmer (1977), Gitler (1985), Stokes (1991); Sidran (1992); also Peretti on oral history archives (Gabbard 1995a: 117–33).

Chorus III: Jazz and style

For an overall **stylistic approach**, see Gridley's compendious *Jazz Styles* (1978–); Kernfeld, *What to Listen for in Jazz* (1995: Ch. 8), offers an introductory 'tour.' See also Hodeir (1956: Ch. 2); Ulanov (1957: Ch. 3); Berendt (1962: Ch. 1); Ostransky (1977: Ch. 5) – on schools, periods, styles. For collected examples of **style analysis** (**recordings, repertoire, performances**), see: William Russell (on Morton) and Ross Russell (on bebop) in Williams' *The Art of Jazz* (1959); Schuller (on Monk, Rollins) in Williams' *Jazz Panorama* (1962); Giddins (on Ellington, Mingus, Coleman) in *Riding on a Blue Note* (1981) and (on Rollins in concert, Gillespie's recordings) in *Faces in the Crowd* (1992). Williams' *Jazz Changes* (1992) includes musicians in rehearsal, studio and club performance (e.g. Jackson recording, Monk at the Five Spot), and technical analysis of style and conventions (Coleman, Morton, Pepper); Balliett's *Goodbyes and Other Messages* (1992) includes jazz repertory (American Jazz Orchestra), 'Mingus at work,' and New York jazz festival performances; Early remembers Mingus, Monk, and Sonny Stitt's saxophone battles, in *Tuxedo Junction* (1989). Wang demonstrates style criticism in 'Jazz circa 1945: a confluence of styles' (1973). Gushee's admired structural analysis of Lester Young ('Shoe Shine Boy') is reprinted in Porter, *Lester Young Reader* (1991a). Hentoff's 1958 *Jazz Review* interview (Miles Davis) comprises performance conventions and jazz repertoire (in Williams [1962]). Giddins traces the 50-year recording history of jazz standard 'Body and Soul' in *Faces in the Crowd* (reprinted in Gottlieb 1997: 1006–12). **Contextualization of jazz styles** in relation to historical and cultural change is exemplified in Russell, *Jazz Style in Kansas City and the Southwest* (1971); also articles by Ellison, 'The golden age, time past' (1959); Hansen, 'Social influences on jazz style' (1960); Erenburg, 'Things to come' (1989); Eric Lott, 'Double V, double-time' (1995). On **jam sessions**, see Russell (1971: Ch. 4); Cameron, 'Sociological notes on the jam session' (1954). **Jazz improvisation**: Berliner's extensive *Thinking in Jazz* (1994) examines the individual and collectivist aspects of jazz performance. Feather's 'Anatomy of improvisation' (1957: Ch. 22) scrutinizes examples of solos, with transcribed charts. Reaction to bebop, reflecting **style wars** in the **1940s**, is treated in Stowe, *Swing Changes* (1994: Ch. 6), and Porter (1997: Ch. 7), who reprints Gottlieb on bebop (1947), the Gillespie vs. Beneke debate (1949), and Armstrong's views. See also Borneman's *Down Beat* contributions (1947, 1948); Gendron's detailed articles on bebop's reception (1994) and 1940s 'moldy figs' and modernists (Gabbard 1995a: 31–75). On **1980s–90s synthesis** and **neoclassicism** in jazz's tradition, Porter (1991) reprints material on avant-garde/fusion opposition (Ch. 10) and traditionalism and revivalism (Ch. 11) – including Pareles' 'Jazz swings back to tradition' (1984), and Jenkins' 'Wynton bites back: addresses his critics' (*c*.1994). See also Marsalis' prescriptive 'What jazz is – and isn't' (1988), reprinted in Walser (1999: 334–9) under 'The neoclassical agenda'; and Sancton's profile of Marsalis, 'Horns of plenty' (1990). Broad surveys of 1980s jazz styles and developments are Davis, *In the Moment: Jazz in the 1980s* (1986), and Nicholson, *Jazz: The 1980s Resurgence* (1990).

Chorus IV: Jazz and culture

For **cultural dimensions** of jazz, important contextual studies are Peretti's *The Creation of Jazz* (1992) and *Jazz in American Culture* (1997; **IV/55**). On the dialectic between jazz and culture, see Levine's influential 'Jazz and American culture' (1989; **IV/54**). O'Meally's innovative collection, *The Jazz Cadence of American Culture* (1998), presents jazz in larger cultural terms, viewing 'jazz as cross-disciplinary beat or *cadence*'; Gabbard's essays (ed. 1995a, 1995b) also expand acceptable subjects for cultural analysis. Tucker's impressive *The Duke Ellington Reader* (1993) combines musicology, analysis, biography and history; DeVeaux documents the large social and musical history of *The Birth of Bebop* (1997); Gioia offers essay reflections on jazz and modern culture in *The Imperfect Art* (1988). Shaw contextualizes jazz period and location in *The Jazz Age* (1987) and *52nd Street: The Street of* Jazz (1971) – as do Charters and Kunstadt, in *Jazz: A History of the New York Scene* (1962); Lax portrays the 1920s era of black musicians (1974). More recent biographies have also brought fuller contextual approaches to their subjects' lives, e.g., Hasse, on Ellington (1993); Woideck, on Parker (1996); Hajdu, on Strayhorn (1996); Gourse, on Monk (1997); Carr, on Davis (1998); Shipton, on Gillespie (1999). On the **jazz audience**, see more recent survey data in DeVeaux's 'Jazz in America: who's listening?' (1995), reprinted in Walser (1999: 389–95). **Sociological approaches** are collected in Nanry's *American Music* (ed. 1972), which contains work by Nanry ('Jazz and all that sociology'); Berger (**IV/51**); Stebbins' celebrated 'A theory of the jazz community'; and Becker – whose 'The professional dance musician and his audience' is reprinted in Walser (1999: 179–91). The social rituals of jazz are found in Leonard's *Jazz: Myth and Religion* (1987). **African-American perspectives** on jazz culture are concentrated in Baraka and Baraka, *The Music: Reflections on Jazz and Blues* (1987); and Kofsky's earlier and later examinations of black nationalism and revolution in music (1970; updated 1998b) and polemical *Black Music, White Business* (1998a), attacking the racial-political economy of jazz. Walling writes on the politics of jazz, through Ellison and Baraka (1974).

Chorus V: Jazz and race

For **African influences** on jazz, see Oliver, *Savannah Syncopators* (1970: 11–27); Weinstein, *A Night in Tunisia* (1992). For **African-American perspectives** on jazz history, see Baraka (LeRoi Jones), *Blues People* (1963); Litweiler, *The Freedom Principle* (1984); Kofsky, *John Coltrane and the Jazz Revolution of the 1960s* (1998b), a revision of his *Black Nationalism and the Revolution in Music* (1970). **Studies of jazz and race** are Sidran, *Black Talk* (1971), on orality and social function; Peretti, *The Creation of Jazz* (1992), on jazz–race relations in urban America, and *Jazz in American Culture* (1997), esp. Ch. 6 ('We insist'); Gerard, *Jazz in Black and White* (1998; **V/57**), examining race, culture and identity in the jazz community; Panish, *The Color of Jazz* (1997); and, for example, collections by Ellison, *Shadow and Act* (1964); Lees, *Cats of Any Color* (1994); and Crouch, *Notes of a Hanging Judge* (1990b) and *The All-American Skin Game* (1995) – see 'On the corner: the sellout of Miles Davis' (166–85). Porter (1997: Ch. 9) has material on race, politics and jazz in the 1950s–1960s, including Taylor's charge, 'Negroes don't know anything about jazz' (1957), and excerpts from a *Down Beat* panel discussion on race (1962), to which Shepp later contributed (16 Dec., 1965). Panel member Hentoff writes on race issues in *Harper's Magazine* (1959) and *The Jazz Life* (1961: Ch. 4). To Feather's 'Blindfold tests,' add 'Jazz and race' (1957: Ch. 5) and his survey 'Race' (1986: 115–26). For reversed racism, see Teachout's 'The color of jazz' (1995), which includes Murray, Feather, Crouch and Marsalis. Relevant **interview collections** are Wilmer's *Jazz People* (1970), with Shepp (Ch. 14); Taylor's extensive *Notes and Tones* (1977; **V/63**); Enstice's and Rubin's *Jazz Spoken Here* (1992). On **racial aesthetics** of **jazz criticism** and **African-American literary theory**, see Gayle, *The Black Aesthetic* (ed. 1971); Baker, *Blues, Ideology, and Afro-American Literature* (1984); Gates, *The Signifying Monkey* (1988). Interesting **literary dimensions of race** are offered by Cayer, on racial imagery in jazz lyrics (1974); Evans, on poet Langston Hughes as 'bop ethnographer' (Oliphant 1994: 119–35); and Mackey, on 'othering' in African-American cultural practice (Gabbard 1995a: 76–99).

Chorus VI: Jazz and myth

Neil Leonard looks extensively at the **jazz myth** in *Jazz: Myth and Religion* (1987), esp. Ch. 6; sociological dimensions are offered by Nanry, *The Jazz Text* (1979: Ch. 8); fabulation of jazz, as modernist art form, by Garber (Gabbard 1995b: 70–103). For mythical treatment of jazz pioneers, see *Jazzmen* (1939), ed. Ramsey and Smith. Dyer's *But Beautiful: A Book About Jazz* (1991; **VI/80**) imaginatively reconstructs jazz myth into fiction. The **Bolden** legend is historically researched by Marquis, *In Search of Buddy Bolden* (1978), and highly mythologized in Ondaatje's impressionistic *Coming Through Slaughter* (1977). Barker (with Shipton) remembers Bolden and the last days of Storyville (1998). On **Beiderbecke**, the standard biography is Sudhalter's and Evans' *Bix: Man and Legend* (1974); see also Sudhalter's recent *Lost Chords: White Musicians and Their Contribution to Jazz* (1999: Ch.17). Ferguson sequeled his famous profile (**VI/75**) with 'Young man with a horn again' (1940), reprinted in *The Otis Ferguson Reader* (1982). Green unravels music from legend in *The Reluctant Art* (1962: Ch. 2). On Johnson's Beiderbecke-based novel and its 1950 film version, see Gabbard's 'Wrong man with a horn' (1989). Brigitte Berman's *Bix* (1981) and Pupi Avati's *Bix: An Interpretation of a Legend* (1990) are later film evocations of Beiderbecke's life and music. The best, most accurate biography of **Young** is Büchmann-Møller's (1990; **VI/79**). Porter's substantial reader (1991a) provides material on Young's biography and music, including interviews. Postif's 1959 *Jazz Hot* interview, reprinted in *Jazz Review* (Williams 1962; **VI/78**), is corrected and restored in Porter (1991a: 173–91). McDonough's account of Young's damaging Army service and racist court-martial (*Down Beat*, Jan., 1981) is reprinted in Campbell's anthology (1995: 245–52); Büchmann-Møller includes 'Private 39729502 Young' (Ch. 6). Young's 'last, sad' days are recorded by Reisner, in Porter (1991a: 89–92), which also has memorial pieces by Gleason and Büchmann-Møller. Tavernier's film, *Round Midnight* (1986), is a fictional composite of Young and Bud Powell (**X/136** and **136**). Earlier **Parker** biographies are Reisner's reminiscences, *Bird: The Legend of Charlie Parker* (1962), and Russell's inventive reconstruction, *Bird Lives!* (1973). Dexter (1964: 145–56) runs censoriously over the Parker story in 'The Bird.' More recent accounts are Giddins' incisive essay, *Celebrating Bird* (1987), which includes players' awe at Parker's mastery; and Woideck's *Charlie Parker* (1996), offering 'A biographical sketch.' Francis Davis pursues an 'extramusical line of enquiry' in the title-piece of *Bebop and Nothingness* (1996). Chan Parker compiles a personal record with photobook *To Bird with Love* (1981) and her *My Life in E-Flat* (1999 [1993]). Fictional versions of the Parker myth include Grennard's 'Sparrow's last jump' (1947), reconstructing Parker's disastrous 'Lover Man' session; Baldwin's 'Sonny's blues' (1957), using Parker's music as reference point; and Cortázar's excellent, Parker-inspired 'The pursuer' (1967). For surveys of Parker's numerous appearances in fiction and poetry, see Albert's bibliography of jazz fiction (1996: x–xiii), and Feinstein's *Jazz Poetry* (1997: Ch. 5). Parker myth material is reworked in Eastwood's film, *Bird* (1988) (**X/137** and **138**).

Chorus VII: Jazz and the jazz life

Anthology material of **jazz musicians' lives** in Travis, *An Autobiography of Black Jazz* (1983), comprising jazz memoir and oral history; numerous first-person narratives and interviews ('Autobiography') in Gottlieb's *Reading Jazz* (ed. 1997). On **professional jazz life**, Hentoff (1961) compiles 'backgrounds' – 'payin' dues,' racial prejudice, drug addiction; Lees meets 'jazz musicians and their world' (1988); Wilmer writes on 'my life in the jazz world' (1989); Crow provides 'scenes from a jazz life' (1992); Giddins recounts the paradigmatic survival 'story' of Red Rodney, 'the Red Arrow,' in *Riding on a Blue Note* (1981); Stan Getz apologizes to *Down Beat*'s editor for his drugstore hold-up (reprinted in Campbell 1995: 309–10); addict Billie Holiday claims she's 'cured for good,' in *Ebony*, 4 (1949): 26–30; Julian Adderley records his 'education' of running a jazz combo, in Williams (1962: 258–63); Maurice Zolotow travels 1,491 band miles, in Condon's *Treasury of Jazz* (1956: 323–34). On **jazz autobiography**, in addition to Harlos' important essay (**VII/88**), see articles by Sudhalter (1991); and Kenney and Ogren, in Buckner and Weiland (1991: 38–59, 112–27). Additionally recommended autobiographies include: Carmichael, *The Stardust Road* (1946); Shaw, *The Trouble with Cinderella* (1952); Armstrong, *Satchmo: My Life in New Orleans* (1954); Bechet, *Treat It Gentle* (1960); Willie the Lion Smith, *Music on My Mind* (1964); Ellington, *Music is My Mistress* (1973); Hodes and Hansen, *Selections from the Gutter* (ed. 1977), and *Hot Man: The Life of Art Hodes* (1992); O'Day, *High Times, Hard Times* (1981); Barker, *A Life in Jazz* (1986); Bigard, *With Louis and the Duke* (1985); McPartland, *All in Good Time* (1987); Hinton and Berger, *Bass Line* (1988); Davis, *Miles: The Autobiography* (1989). Recommended **jazz biographies** are: Priestley, on Mingus (1982); Chilton, on Hawkins (1990); Litweiler, on Coleman (1992); Hasse, on Ellington (1993); Lester, on Tatum (1994); Fraim, on Coltrane (1996); Hajdu, on Strayhorn (1996); Maggin, on Getz (1996); Bergreen, on Armstrong (1997); Gourse, on Monk (1997); Carr, on Davis (1998); Shipton, on Gillespie (1999).

Chorus VIII: Jazz and language

On the **sociolinguistics of jazz**, see Levet's lexographical *Talkin' That Talk* (1992); also Gold's still-authoritative *Jazz Talk* (1975) and 'The vernacular of the jazz world,' *American Speech* (1957); Hart's 'Jazz jargon' (1932) and Webb's 'The slang of jazz' (1937) are timely earlier studies. The most useful **dictionaries** are Powell (1997) and Major (1970, 1994). Other specialist **listings of diction** and **slang** are: Shelly, *Hepcats Jive Talk Dictionary* (1945); Boulware, *Jive and Slang* (1947); Horne, 'The argot of jazz' (Cerulli *et al.*, *The Jazz Word* [1960]) and *Hiptionary* (1963); Reisner, 'The parlance of hip' (*The Jazz Titans* [1960]; **VIII/103**). Sections on **jazz language** are in Ulanov (1957: Ch. 8); Newton (1959: Appendix 2); Nanry (1979: 7–12). Examples of **jive usage** and **transcription** in Frank, 'Now I stash me down to nod' (1944b); Mezzrow, *Really the Blues* (1946), 'The jive section,' with translation (Appendix 2). Mezzrow (119–20) also reproduces Armstrong's 'scat' improvisations on the 1926 'Heebie Jeebies.' For **African-American** folkloric **usage**, see Dundes' compilation, *Mother Wit from the Laughing Barrel* (ed. 1973), which reprints 'The technique of jive' from Burley's *Original Handbook of Harlem Jive* (1944). On Burley and jive talk, see Frank, 'The jive is on!' (1944a); Anon., 'Jive papa,' *Ebony*, 1 (Aug., 1946): 19–24. **Hipster and 'cool'** are examined in Broyard, 'Keep cool, man' (1952); and Mailer's 'The white negro' (1957) – with response from Hentoff (1961: Ch. 8). **Calloway**'s autobiography is *Of Minnie the Moocher & Me* (1976): see Introduction for 'Minnie' lyrics. **Scat singing**, 'From heebie jeebies to bebop,' is reviewed by Gottlieb (1948). For **vocalese**'s 'aesthetic' and comprehensive bibliography-discography, see Grant (Gabbard 1995b: 285–303); Feather explains vocalese (1959). For examination of vocalese's tradition and practitioners, see Friedwald, *Jazz Singing* (1990: 223–50), and Gourse, *Louis' Children* (1984: Chs 12–14, 26). For **jazz-related poems**, see below (**IX**). **Glossaries** of **musical terms** appear in many studies of jazz history and style: comprehensive listings are Gridley (1978–); Megill and Demory (1984); Schuller (1989); Tirro (1993).

Chorus IX: Jazz and literature

For **literary jazz** and **jazz-related literature**, see **anthologies** edited by Meltzer (1993) and Gottlieb (1997), both titled *Reading Jazz*, containing reportage, criticism, autobiography, fiction and poetry. Earlier collections are Condon and Gehman, *Eddie Condon's Treasury of Jazz* (1956); Gleason, *Jam Session* (1958); Cerulli *et al.*, *The Jazz Word* (1960). On **literary and aesthetic analogues**, see Folley-Cooper's illustrative *Seeing Jazz* (ed. 1997); O'Meally's *The Jazz Cadence of American Culture* (ed. 1998); and Jarrett's *Drifting on a Read* (1999); also Jason Berry's explorative 'Jazz literature' (1978). On **jazz fiction** and **criticism**, Albert edits a valuable *Annotated Bibliography* (1996); editors Albert, *From Blues to Bop* (1990) and Breton, *Hot and Cool* (1991), provide excellent collections of jazz short fiction. Parker, *B Flat, Bebop, Scat* (1986) and Lange and Mackey, *Moment's Notice* (1993), collect prose fiction and poetry. Useful survey articles of jazz fiction are Smith (1958) and Bourjaily (1987); also M. Ellison's discussion of blues in fiction, in *Extensions of the Blues* (1989). On **Welty**'s 'Powerhouse,' see numerous articles in Albert's *Bibliography* (1996) entries. Jones (1991: Ch. 8) examines jazz and blues structure in **Petry**'s 'Solo on the drums.' For other recommended **jazz stories**, see Powers, 'He don't plant cotton' (1943); Grennard, 'Sparrow's last jump' (1947); Murray, 'The Luzana Cholly Kick [Train whistle guitar]' (1953); Baldwin, 'Sonny's blues' (1957); Baraka [Jones], 'The screamers' (1963); Cortázar, 'The pursuer' (1967); Škvorecký, 'The bass saxophone' ([novellas] 1979), 'The tenor saxophonist's story' (1997); Biggie, 'St. Louis blues' (1980); Angelou, 'The reunion' (1983). On **'spontaneous composition' aesthetic**, see Kerouac (1958, 1959); Tallman (1959); Weinreich (1987). From often execrable **jazz(-influenced) novels**, these have varied merit: Baker, *Young Man with a Horn* (1938; **VI/76**); Holmes, *Go* (1952), *The Horn* (1958; **VI/87**); Kerouac, *On the Road* (1957; **VIII/105**), *The Subterraneans* (1958); Russell, *The Sound* (1961; **III/37**; **V/70**); Williams, *Night Song* (1961); Simmons, *Man Walking on Eggshells* (1962); Wain, *Strike the Father Dead* (1962); Braly, *Shake Him Till He Rattles* (1963); Green, *Fifty-Eight Minutes to London* (1969); Hunter, *Streets of Gold* (1974); Barnes, *Blue Monday* (1991) (details in Albert [1996]). Jazz and blues influence motival and structural narration in Ellison's *Invisible Man* (1952) and Morrison's *Jazz* (1992). Gelber's *The Connection* (1960) and Ondaatje's *Coming Through Slaughter* (1977) extend the generic treatment of jazz. **Jazz and poetry** 'movement' articles feature in Gleason (1958: 226–30); Cerulli *et al.* (1960: 67–72); Smith (1977). Komunyakaa and Matthews converse (1992); Wallenstein surveys the genre, with excellent discography (1991). See also Rexroth, 'Jazz poetry' (1958a), and 'Some thoughts on jazz,' (1958b); Roskolenko experiences San Francisco jazz poets in 'The sounds of the fury' (1959). See and hear Kerouac's *Mexico City Blues* (1959), *Poetry for the Beat Generation* (Hanover 5006 [1958]), *Blues and Haikus* (Hanover 5000 [1959]). Comprehensive **poetry anthologies** in Feinstein and Komunyakaa (eds.), *The Jazz Poetry Anthology* (1991) and *The Second Set: The Jazz Poetry Anthology, Vol. 2* (1996); Feinstein also examines *Jazz Poetry: From the 1920s to the Present* (1997) and provides *A Bibliographic Guide to Jazz Poetry* (1998). Henderson aligns black speech and music in *Understanding the New*

Black Poetry (ed. 1973); Hartman juxtaposes voice and improvisation in poetry, jazz and song in *Jazz Text* (1991). Examples of **jazz-influenced poetry** (in Feinstein and Komunyakaa) are: Hughes, 'The weary blues' (1926), 'Dream boogie' (1951); Sanchez, 'a/coltrane/poem' (1961); de Legall, 'Psalm for Sonny Rollins' (1963 [in Henderson]); O'Hara, 'The day Lady died' (1964); Kaufman, 'Walking Parker home' (1965); Perkins, 'Jazz poem' (1968); Baraka, 'AM/TRAK' (1969); Cortez, 'Solo finger solo' (*c*.1969); Joans, 'Jazz is my religion' (1969); Harper, 'Dear John, dear Coltrane' (1970); Fabio, 'For Louis Armstrong, a ju-ju' (1973); Jeffers, 'Nina Simone' (1974); Blackburn, 'Listening to Sonny Rollins at the Five-Spot' (1985); Hull, 'Lost fugue for Chet' (1991); Hirsch, 'Art Pepper' (1994); Jauss, 'Black orchid' (1994).

Chorus X: Jazz and film

For **listings** and **surveys**, see Meeker's comprehensive *Jazz in the Movies* (1981 [1977]). Maltin (in Feather, *Encyclopedia* [1976]: 382–6); Smith (in Kernfeld 1988: 375–86); and Priestley (BBC Radio 3: 1997) offer surveys of jazz and film. The standard (only) **critical study** is Gabbard's *Jammin' at the Margins: Jazz and the American Cinema* (1996), which includes a chapter (3) on film's 'art' discourse for jazz; see also his 'Wrong man with a horn' (1989). On the **appropriation of jazz** by **American film industry**, see Giddins, 'Jazz is back on films, too' (1977); Berg, 'Cinema sings the blues' (1978); Williams, 'Jazz at the movies' (in *Jazz in Its Time* [1989]). Hollywood's pejorative **racial roles** and **stereotypes** are examined by Cripps, *Slow Fade to Black* (1977) and *Making Movies Black* (1993), and Bogle (1994; also in Lee [1990]); its **jazz biopics** as 'public history,' by Custen (1992). **Armstrong's film roles** (1931–69) are surveyed in Bogle's essay (in Miller [ed. 1994]: 147–79; **X/134**), and Gabbard (1996: Ch. 6). The **roles** of **race** in **jazz film** are found in individual essays (Garber, Gabbard, Naremore, Knee) in Gabbard (1995b). Knight provides the most detailed analysis of **Jammin' the Blues** (Gabbard 1995b: 11–53); see also review 'Jam session in movieland' (*Ebony*, Nov., 1945: 6–7) and photo-essay, 'Speaking of pictures' (*Life*, 22 Jan., 1945: 6–8). Coursodon's interview with Tavernier (**X/135**) is prefaced by his own remarks on *'Round Midnight*; Crouch (1989) situates *Bird* in the context of Parker, Eastwood and America, and in 'Do the race thing' (*Notes of a Hanging Judge* [1990b]: Ch. 36) reviews Spike Lee's *Do the Right Thing* (1989); Giddins, in 'Spiked jazz' (1992: 52–8), reviews Lee's *Mo' Better Blues* (1990). Francis Davis (1990: 220–2, 223–7) examines *Bird*'s music, and Bruce Weber's obsessive documentary on Chet Baker, *Let's Get Lost*. Additional **biopics** are *The Five Pennies* [Red Nichols] (1959), and *Drum Crazy: The Gene Krupa Story* (1959). **Feature films** more than less focused on jazz are: *The Connection* (1961); *Too Late Blues* (1961); *A Man Called Adam* (1966); *Sweet Love, Bitter* (1966); *Sven Klang's Quintet* (1976); *New York, New York* (1977); *The Gig* (1985); *American Blue Note* (1989); *She's Gotta Have It* (1989); *Mo' Better Blues* (1990); *Kansas City* (1996). Recommended **film (bio)documentaries** on jazz life are: *Mingus* (1968); *New Orleans: Til the Butcher Cuts Him Down* [Punch Miller] (1971); *Jazz is Our Religion* (1972); *Born to Swing* [Count Basie] (1973); *The Last of the Blue Devils* [Kansas City jazz] (1974–9); *Bix: Ain't None of Them Play Like That* (1981); *Jazz* *in Exile* (1982); *Laughin' Louis* [Armstrong] (1983); *The Long Night of Lady Day* [Billie Holiday] (1984); *The Coltrane Legacy* (1985); *Ben Webster: The Brute and the Beautiful* (1986); *Let's Get Lost* [Chet Baker] (1988); *Thelonious Monk: Straight, No Chaser* (1988); *A Great Day in Harlem* (1994). Notable **jazz performance sequences** (some in musicals) feature in *Black and Tan* (1929); *Cabin in the Sky* (1942); *Jam Session* (1944); *New Orleans* (1947); *A Song Is Born* (1948); *Paris Blues* (1961). Distinguished **jazz performance films** are *Jivin' in Be-Bop* (1947); *The Sound of Jazz* (1957); *Jazz on a Summer's* Day (1960); *After Hours* (1961); *L'Aventure du Jazz* (1969–70); *The Great Rocky Mountain Jazz Party* (1977); *Duke Ellington: Reminiscing in Tempo* (1994). Good **jazz music scores** and **soundtracks** in *The Man With the Golden Arm* (1955); *Lift to the Scaffold* (1957); *The Sweet Smell of Success* (1957); *I Want to Live* (1958); *Shadows* (1958–9); *Anatomy of a Murder* (1959); *Jack Johnson* (1970); *The Conversation* (1974). For basic **videography**, see Gridley (1999: 416).

Bibliography

This bibliography lists works referred to in editorial introductions and suggested reading; it also selects from other titles consulted, including those useful for a study and understanding of jazz. Items of anthology content are fully sourced where they appear, and generally not included here. (Where later editions are used, dates of original publication are given in square brackets.)

Albert, Richard N. (ed.) (1990) *From Blues to Bop: A Collection of Jazz Fiction*. Baton Rouge: Louisiana State University Press.
—— (1996) *An Annotated Bibliography of Jazz Fiction and Jazz Fiction Criticism*. Westport, CT: Greenwood Press.
Anonymous (1918) 'Why "Jazz" sends us back to the jungle.' *Current Opinion*, LXV (Sept.): 165.
—— (1924) 'Where is jazz leading America?' [symposium]. *Etude*, 42 (Aug.–Sept.): 517–20, 595–6.
—— (1954) 'Far-out words for cats' [box glossary]. *Time*, 8 Nov.: 42.
—— (1962) 'Racial prejudice in jazz' [panel discussion]. *Down Beat*, 15 March: 20–6; 19 March: 22–5.
Armstrong, Louis (1986 [1954]) *Satchmo: My Life in New Orleans*. New York: Da Capo.
Baker, David N. (ed.) (1990) *New Perspectives on Jazz*. Washington, DC: Smithsonian Institution Press.
Baker, Dorothy (1961 [1938]) *Young Man with a Horn*. Boston: Houghton Mifflin.
Baker, Houston A., Jr. (1984) *Blues, Ideology, and Afro-American Literature: A Vernacular Theory*. Chicago: University of Chicago Press.
Balliett, Whitney (1959) *The Sound of Surprise: 46 Pieces on Jazz*. New York: Dutton.
—— (1962) *Dinosaurs in the Morning*. Philadelphia: Lippincott.
—— (1992) *Goodbyes and Other Messages: A Journal of Jazz, 1981–1990*. New York: Oxford University Press.
—— (2000) *Collected Works: A Journal of Jazz, 1954–2000*. New York: St. Martin's.
Baraka, [as LeRoi Jones] Amiri (1963) *Blues People: Negro Music in White America*. New York: Morrow.
—— (1967) *Black Music*. New York: Morrow.
Baraka, Amiri and Baraka, Amina (1987) *The Music: Reflections on Jazz and Blues*. New York: Morrow.
Barker, Danny (1986) *A Life in Jazz*. Ed. Alyn Shipton. New York: Oxford University Press.
—— with Alyn Shipton (1998) *Buddy Bolden and the Last Days of Storyville*. New York: Oxford University Press.
Bechet, Sidney (1960) *Treat It Gentle: An Autobiography*. New York: Twayne.
Becker, Howard S. (1951–2) 'The professional dance musician and his audience.' *American Journal of Sociology*, 57: 136–44.
—— (1963) *Outsiders*. New York: Free Press.

Berendt, Joachim (1962 [1959]) *The New Jazz Book: A History and Guide*. London: Peter Owen.

Berg, Charles (1978) 'Cinema sings the blues.' *Cinema Journal*, 17, 2: 1–12.

Berger, Morroe (1947) 'Jazz: resistance to the diffusion of a culture-pattern.' *Journal of Negro History*, 32: 461–94. (Reprinted in Nanry, *American Music*, 1972.)

Bergreen, Laurence (1997) *Louis Armstrong: An Extravagant Life*. New York: Broadway.

Berliner, Paul (1994) *Thinking in Jazz: The Infinite Art of Improvisation*. Chicago: University of Chicago Press.

Berry, Jason (1978) 'Jazz literature.' *Southern Exposure*, 6, 3: 40–9.

Bigard, Barney (1985) *With Louis and the Duke: The Autobiography of a Jazz Clarinetist*. Ed. Barry Martyn. New York: Oxford University Press.

Blesh, Rudi (1946) *Shining Trumpets: A History of Jazz*. New York: Knopf.

Bogle, Donald (1994) *Toms, Coons, Mulattoes, Mammies, and Bucks: An Interpretive History of Blacks in American Films*. Oxford: Roundhouse.

Borneman, Ernest (1947) 'Both schools of critics wrong.' *Down Beat*, XIV (30 July): 11; (Aug. 13): 16.

—— (1948) ' "Bop will kill business unless it kills itself first"—Louis Armstrong.' *Down Beat*, XV (7 April): 2–3.

Bourjaily, Vance (1987) 'In and out of Storyville: jazz and fiction.' *New York Times Book Review*, 13, 1 (13 Dec.): 1, 44–5.

Breton, Marcela (ed.) (1991) *Hot and Cool: Jazz Short Stories*. London: Bloomsbury.

Brown, Lee B. (1991) 'The theory of jazz music: "It don't mean a thing".' *Journal of Aesthetics and Art Criticism*, 49: 115–27.

Broyard, Anatole (1952) 'Keep cool, man: the negro rejection of jazz.' *Commentary*, XI (April): 359–62.

Brunn, Harry O. (1960) *The Story of the Original Dixieland Jazz Band*. Baton Rouge: Louisiana State University Press.

Büchmann-Møller, Frank (1990) *You Just Fight for Your Life: The Story of Lester Young*. New York: Praeger.

Buckner, Reginald T. and Weiland, Steven (eds.) (1991) *Jazz in Mind: Essays on the History and Meanings of Jazz*. Detroit: Wayne State University Press.

Burley, Dan (1944) *Dan Burley's Original Handbook of Harlem Jive*. New York: Burley.

Calloway, Cab and Rollins, Bryant (1976) *Of Minnie the Moocher & Me*. New York: Thomas Crowell.

Cameron, William (1954) 'Sociological notes on the jam session.' *Social Forces*, 33 (Dec.): 177–82.

Campbell, James (ed.) (1995) *The Picador Book of Blues and Jazz*. London: Picador.

Carby, Hazel V. (1986) ' "It jus be's dat way sometime": the sexual politics of women's blues.' *Radical America*, 20, 4: 9–22.

Carmichael, Hoagy (1946) *The Stardust Road*. New York: Rinehart.

Carner, Gary (ed.) (1991) 'Introduction.' Literature of Jazz Issue. *Black American Literature Forum*, 25, 3 (Fall): 441–8.

Carr, Ian (1998) *Miles Davis: The Definitive Biography*. London: HarperCollins.

Carr, Roy, Case, Brian and Dellar, Fred (1986) *The Hip: Hipsters, Jazz and the Beat Generation*. London: Faber.

Carruth, Hayden (1986) *Sitting In: Selected Writings on Jazz, Blues, and Related Topics*. Iowa City, IA: University of Iowa Press.

Cayer, David A. (1974) 'Black and blue and black again: three stages of racial imagery in jazz lyrics.' *Journal of Jazz Studies*, I, 2 (June): 38–71.

Cerulli, Dom, Korall, Burt and Nasatir, Mort (eds.) (1960) *The Jazz Word*. New York: Ballantine.

Charters, Samuel B. and Kunstadt, Leonard (1984 [1962]) *Jazz: A History of the New York Scene*. New York: Da Capo.

Chilton, John (1990) *The Song of the Hawk: The Life and Recordings of Coleman Hawkins*. Ann Arbor, MI: University of Michigan Press.

Clayton, Buck, with Nancy Miller Elliott (1986) *Buck Clayton's Jazz World*. London: Macmillan.

Coker, Jerry (1990 [1978]) *How to Listen to Jazz*. New Albany, IN: Jamey Aebersold.

Cole, Bill (1976) *John Coltrane*. New York: Schirmer.

Collier, James Lincoln (1978) *The Making of Jazz: A Comprehensive History*. New York: Dell.

—— (1988) *The Reception of Jazz in America: A New View*. New York: Institute for Studies in American Music.

—— (1989) *Benny Goodman and the Swing Era*. New York: Oxford University Press.

—— (1993) *Jazz: The American Theme Song*. New York: Oxford University Press.

Condon, Eddie and Gehman, Richard (eds.) (1956) *Eddie Condon's Treasury of Jazz*. New York: Dial.

Condon, Eddie with Thomas Sugrue (1992 [1947]) *We Called It Music: A Generation of Jazz*. New York: Da Capo.

Cripps, Thomas (1977) *Slow Fade to Black: The Negro in American Film, 1900–1942*. New York: Oxford University Press.

—— (1993) *Making Movies Black: The Hollywood Message Movie from World War II to the Civil Rights Era*. New York: Oxford University Press.

Crouch, Stanley (1989) 'Bird land.' *New Republic*, 27 (27 Feb.): 25–31.

—— (1990a) 'Jazz criticism and its effect on the art form.' In Baker (1990), 71–87.

—— (1990b) *Notes of a Hanging Judge: Essays and Reviews, 1979–1989*. Oxford: Oxford University Press.

—— (1990c) 'Play the right thing.' *New Republic*, 12 Feb.: 30–6.

—— (1995) *The All-American Skin Game, or, The Decoy of Race: The Long and the Short of It, 1990–1994*. New York: Pantheon.

Crow, Bill (1992) *From Birdland to Broadway: Scenes from a Jazz Life*. New York: Oxford University Press.

Custen, George F. (1992) *Bio/Pics: How Hollywood Constructed Public History*. New Brunswick, NJ: Rutgers University Press.

Dahl, Linda (1984) *Stormy Weather: The Music and Lives of a Century of Jazzwomen*. London: Quartet.

Dance, Stanley with Duke Ellington (1962) 'The art is in the cooking' [interview]. *Down Beat*, 7 June: 13–15.

Dankworth, Avril (1968) *Jazz: An Introduction to Its Musical Basis*. London: Oxford University Press.

Davies, Russell (1999) '100 years of hip' [review]. *The Observer*, 18 April.

Davis, Francis (1986) *In the Moment: Jazz in the 1980s*. Oxford: Oxford University Press.

—— (1990) *Outcats: Jazz Composers, Instrumentalists, and Singers*. New York: Oxford University Press.

—— (1996) *Bebop and Nothingness: Jazz and Pop at the End of the Century*. New York: Schirmer.

Davis, Miles with Quincy Troupe (1989) *Miles: The Autobiography*. New York: Simon & Schuster.

DeLong, Thomas A. (1983) *Pops: Paul Whiteman, King of Jazz*. New York: New Century.

DeVeaux, Scott (1991) 'Constructing the jazz tradition: jazz historiography.' *Black American Literature Forum*, 25, 3 (Fall): 525–60.

—— (1995) 'Jazz in America: who's listening?' *Research Division Report*, 31, National Endowment for the Arts, Carson, CA: Seven Locks.

465

—— (1996) 'What did we do to be so black and blue?' *Musical Quarterly*, 80, 1: 392–430.

—— (1997) *The Birth of Bebop: A Social and Musical History*. Berkeley, CA: University of California Press.

Dexter, Dave (1964) *The Jazz Story: From the '90s to the '60s*. Englewood Cliffs, NJ: Prentice-Hall.

Dodge, Roger Pryor (1934) 'Harpsichords and jazz trumpets.' *Hound & Horn: A Harvard Miscellany*, 7 (July–Sept.): 587–608.

Dundes, Alan (ed.) (1973) *Mother Wit from the Laughing Barrel: Readings in the Interpretation of Afro-American Folklore*. Englewood Cliffs, NJ: Prentice-Hall. (Contains Dan Burley's 'The technique of jive' [1944].)

Dyer, Geoff (1991) *But Beautiful: A Book About Jazz*. London: Cape.

Early, Gerald (1989) *Tuxedo Junction: Essays on American Culture*. New York: Ecco.

Ellington, Duke (1945) 'Why Duke Ellington avoided music schools' [interview]. *PM*, 9 Dec.

—— (1973) *Music is My Mistress*. New York: Doubleday.

Ellison, Mary (1989) *Extensions of the Blues*. London: John Calder.

Ellison, Ralph (1959) 'The golden age, time past.' *Esquire*, Jan. (Reprinted in *Shadow and Act*, 1964.)

—— (1964) *Shadow and Act*. New York: Random.

—— (1970) 'What America would be like without blacks.' *Time*, 95 (6 April): 32–3.

Engel, Carl (1922) 'Jazz: a musical discussion.' *Atlantic Monthly*, CXXX: 182–9.

Enstice, Wayne and Rubin, Paul (1992) *Jazz Spoken Here: Conversations with Twenty-Two Musicians*. Baton Rouge: Louisiana State University Press.

Erenburg, Lewis A. (1989) 'Things to come: swing bands, bebop, and the rise of a postwar jazz scene.' In Lary May (ed.), *Recasting America: Culture and Politics in the Age of the Cold War*, 221–45. Chicago: University of Chicago Press.

Feather, Leonard (1949) 'Pops pops top on sloppy bop.' *Metronome*, LXV (Oct.): 18, 25.

—— (1957) *The Book of Jazz From Then Till Now: A Guide to the Entire Field*. New York: Horizon.

—— (1959) 'An explanation of vocalese.' *Jazz: A Quarterly of American Music*, 3: 261.

—— (1960) *The New Edition of the Encyclopedia of Jazz*. New York: Horizon.

—— (1986) *The Jazz Years: Earwitness to An Era*. London: Quartet.

—— and Gitler, Ira (1976) *The Encyclopedia of Jazz in the Seventies*. New York: Horizon.

—— (1999) *The Biographical Encyclopedia of Jazz*. New York: Oxford University Press.

—— and Tracy, Jack (1963) *Laughter from the Hip*. New York: Horizon.

Feinstein, Sascha (1997) *Jazz Poetry: From the 1920s to the Present*. Westport, CT: Greenwood Press.

—— (1998) *A Bibliographic Guide to Jazz Poetry*. Westport, CT: Greenwood Press.

Feinstein, Sascha and Komunyakaa, Yusef (eds.) (1991) *The Jazz Poetry Anthology*. Bloomington: Indiana University Press.

—— (eds.) (1996) *The Second Set: The Jazz Poetry Anthology, Volume 2*. Bloomington: Indiana University Press.

Ferguson, Otis (1982) *The Otis Ferguson Reader*, ed. Dorothy Chamberlain and Robert Wilson. Highland Park, IL.: December.

Finkelstein, Sidney (1948) *Jazz: A People's Music*. New York: Citadel.

Folley-Cooper, Marquette, Macanic, Deborah and McNeil, Janice (eds.) (1997) *Seeing Jazz: Artists and Writers on Jazz*. San Francisco: Chronicle Books/Smithsonian Institution.

Fraim, John (1996) *Spirit Catcher: The Life and Art of John Coltrane*. West Liberty, OH: Great House.

Frank, Stanley (1944a) 'The jive is on!' *Negro Digest*, July: 11–15.

—— (1944b) 'Now I stash me down to nod.' *Esquire*, 21 (June): 53, 168–70.

Friedwald, Will (1990) *Jazz Singing: America's Great Voices from Bessie Smith to Bebop and Beyond*. New York: Scribner's.

Gabbard, Krin (1989) 'Wrong man with a horn.' *University of Hartford Studies in Literature*, 21: 13–24.

—— (ed.) (1995a) *Jazz Among the Discourses*. Durham, NC: Duke University Press.

—— (ed.) (1995b) *Representing Jazz*. Durham, NC: Duke University Press.

—— (1996) *Jammin' at the Margins: Jazz and the American Cinema*. Chicago: University of Chicago Press.

Gates, Henry Louis, Jr. (1988) *The Signifying Monkey: A Theory of African American Literary Criticism*. New York: Oxford University Press.

Gayle, Addison (ed.) (1971) *The Black Aesthetic*. Garden City, NJ: Doubleday.

Gelber, Jack (1960) *The Connection*. New York: Grove.

Gendron, Bernard (1994) 'A short stay in the sun: the reception of bebop (1944–1950).' *Library Chronicle*, 24, 1–2: 137–59.

—— (1995) ' "Moldy figs" and modernists: jazz at war (1942–1946).' In Gabbard (1995a): 31–75.

Gennari, John (1991) 'Jazz criticism: its development and ideologies.' *Black American Literature Forum*, 25, 3 (Fall): 449–523.

Gerard, Charley (1998) *Jazz in Black and White: Race, Culture and Identity in the Jazz Community*. Westport, CT: Praeger.

Giddins, Gary (1977) 'Jazz is back on films, too.' *Village Voice*, 31 Oct.: 53.

—— (1981) *Riding on a Blue Note: Jazz and American Pop*. New York: Oxford University Press.

—— (1985) *Rhythm-a-ning: Jazz Tradition and Innovation in the '80s*. Oxford: Oxford University Press.

—— (1987) *Celebrating Bird: The Triumph of Charlie Parker*. New York: Morrow.

—— (1992) *Faces in the Crowd: Players and Writers. Essays on Music, Movies and Books*. Oxford: Oxford University Press.

—— (1998) *Visions of Jazz: The First Century*. New York: Oxford University Press.

Gilbert, Edwin (1953) *The Hot and the Cool*. London: Transworld Publications.

Gillespie, Dizzy, with Tex Beneke (1949) 'To bop ... or not to bop.' *Negro Digest*, VIII, 2 (Dec.):11–12. (Reprinted from *The Record Changer*, Sept. 1949.)

—— with Al Fraser (1979) *To Be or Not ... to Bop: Memoirs*. New York: Doubleday.

Gioia, Ted (1988) *The Imperfect Art: Reflections on Jazz and Modern Culture*. New York: Oxford University Press.

—— (1997) *The History of Jazz*. New York: Oxford University Press.

Gitler, Ira (1985) *Swing to Bop: An Oral History of the Transition in Jazz in the 1940s*. New York: Oxford University Press.

Gleason, Ralph (ed.) (1958) *Jam Session: An Anthology of Jazz*. New York: Putnam.

Goffin, Robert (1944) *Jazz: from the Congo to the Metropolitan*. Garden City, NY: Doubleday.

Gold, Robert (1957) 'The vernacular of the jazz world.' *American Speech*, Dec.: 271–82.

—— (1975) *Jazz Talk*. New York: Bobbs-Merrill.

Gottlieb, Bill (1947) 'Jazz grows up into jet-propelled "Bebop".' *New York Herald Tribune*, 26 Sept.: 16.

—— (1948) 'From heebie jeebies to bebop.' *Saturday Review of Literature*, XXXI (30 Oct.): 50–1.

—— (ed.) (1997) *Reading Jazz: A Gathering of Autobiography, Reportage and Criticism from 1919 to Now*. London: Bloomsbury.

Gourse, Leslie (1984) *Louis' Children: American Jazz Singers*. New York: Morrow.

—— (1995) *Madame Jazz: Contemporary Women Instrumentalists.* Oxford: Oxford University Press.

—— (1997) *Straight, No Chaser: The Life and Genius of Thelonious Monk.* London: Books with Attitude.

Grant, Barry Keith (1995) 'Purple passages or fiestas in blue? Notes toward an aesthetic of vocalese.' In Gabbard (1995b), 285–303.

Green, Benny (1962) *The Reluctant Art: Five Studies in the Growth of Jazz.* London: MacGibbon & Kee.

Grennard, Elliott (1947) 'Sparrow's last jump.' *Harper's Bazaar,* 194 (May): 419–26.

Gridley, Mark (1987) 'Is jazz popular music?' *The Instrumentalist,* 41, 8 (March): 17–26, 85.

—— (1999 [1978]) *Jazz Styles: History and Analysis.* Englewood Cliffs, NJ: Prentice-Hall. (With CDs and manual.)

—— Maxham, Robert and Hoff, Robert (1989) 'Three approaches to defining jazz.' *Music Quarterly,* 73, 4: 513–31.

Gushee, Lawrence (1994) 'The nineteenth-century origins of jazz.' *Black Music Research Journal,* 14, 1: 1–24. (Reprinted in Porter, *Jazz,* 1997.)

Hadler, Mona (1983) 'Jazz and the visual arts.' *Arts Magazine,* 57, 10 (June): 91–101.

Hajdu, David (1996) *Lush Life: A Biography of Billy Strayhorn.* New York: Farrar, Straus & Giroux.

Hansen, Chadwick (1960) 'Social influences on jazz style: Chicago, 1920–30.' *American Quarterly,* XII (Winter): 493–507.

Hart, James D. (1932) 'Jazz jargon.' *American Speech,* VII, 4 (April): 241–54.

Hartman, Charles O. (1991) *Jazz Text: Voice and Improvisation in Poetry, Jazz, and Song.* Princeton, NJ: Princeton University Press.

Hasse, John (1975) 'The Smithsonian collection of classic jazz: a review-essay.' *Journal of Jazz Studies,* 3, 1: 66–71.

—— (1993) *Beyond Category: The Life and Genius of Duke Ellington.* New York: Simon & Schuster.

Hawes, Hampton and Asher, Don (1974) *Raise Up Off Me: A Portrait of Hampton Hawes.* New York: Coward, McCann & Geoghegan.

Helland, Dave (1990) 'Wynton: prophet in standard time.' *Down Beat,* 57 (Sept.): 16–19.

Henderson, Stephen (ed.) (1973*) Understanding the New Black Poetry: Black Speech and Black Music.* New York: Morrow.

Hentoff, Nat (1958) 'An afternoon with Miles Davis.' *The Jazz Review,* Dec.: 9–12. (Reprinted in Williams, *Jazz Panorama,* 1962.)

—— (1959) 'Race prejudice in jazz: it works both ways.' *Harper's Magazine,* June: 72–7.

—— (1961) *The Jazz Life.* New York: Dial.

—— (1988) 'Flight of fancy' [interview with Clint Eastwood]. *American Film,* Sept.: 24–31.

Hinton, Milt and Berger, David G. (1988) *Bass Line: The Stories and Photographs of Milt Hinton.* Philadelphia: Temple University Press.

Hobsbawm, E.J. (1989) 'Some like it hot.' *New York Review of Books,* 13 April: 32–4.

Hobson, Wilder (1939) *American Jazz Music.* New York: Vail-Ballou Press.

Hodeir, André (1956) *Jazz: Its Evolution and Essence.* New York: Grove.

Hodes, Art and Hanson, Chadwick (1992) *Hot Man: The Life of Art Hodes.* Oxford: Bayou.

—— (eds.) (1977) *Selections from the Gutter: Jazz Portraits from* The Jazz Record. Berkeley, CA: University of California Press.

Holiday, Billie, with William Dufty (1956) *Lady Sings the Blues.* New York: Doubleday.

Holmes, John Clellon (1952) *Go.* New York: Scribner's.

—— (1958) *The Horn.* New York: Random.

Hopkins, Ernest J. (1913) 'In praise of "jazz," a futurist word which has just joined the language.' *San Francisco Bulletin*, 5 April.

Horowitz, Irving (1973) 'Authenticity and originality in jazz: toward a paradigm in the sociology of music.' *Journal of Jazz Studies*, I, 1: 57–64.

—— and Nanry, Charles (1975) 'Ideologies and theories about American jazz.' *Journal of Jazz Studies*, 2, 2: 24–41.

Hughes, Langston (1926) *The Weary Blues*. New York: Knopf.

Hughes, Phillip S. (1974) 'Jazz appreciation and the sociology of jazz.' *Journal of Jazz Studies*, I, 2: 79–96.

Jarrett, Michael (1999) *Drifting on a Read: Jazz as a Model for Writing*. New York: State University of New York Press.

Jenkins, Willard (1994) 'Wynton bites back: addresses his critics.' *National Jazz Service Organisation Jazz Journal*, 5, 1. (Reprinted in Porter, 1997.)

Johnson, Charles (1925) 'Jazz' [editorial]. *Opportunity: Journal of Negro Life*, May.

Jones, Gayl (1991) *Liberating Voices: Oral Tradition in African American Literature*. Cambridge, MA: Harvard University Press.

Keepnews, Orrin (1987) *The View from Within: Jazz Writings, 1948–1987*. New York: Oxford University Press.

Kenney, William (1993) *Chicago Jazz: A Cultural History, 1904–1930*. New York: Oxford University Press.

Kennington, Donald and Read, Danny L. (1980 [1970]) *The Literature of Jazz: A Critical Guide*. London: Library Association.

Kernfeld, Barry (ed.) (1994 [1988]) *The New Grove Dictionary of Jazz*. London: Macmillan.

—— (1995) *What to Listen for in Jazz*. New Haven, CN: Yale University Press (with CD).

Kerouac, Jack (1957) *On the Road*. New York: Viking.

—— (1958) 'Essentials of spontaneous prose.' *Evergreen Review*, II, 5 (Summer): 73.

—— (1959) 'Belief and technique for modern prose.' *Evergreen Review*, II, 8 (Spring): 57.

King, Jonny (1997) *What Jazz Is: An Insider's Guide to Understanding and Listening to Jazz*. New York: Walker.

Kingsley, Charles (1917) 'Whence comes Jass? Facts from the great authority on the subject.' *New York Sun*, 5 Aug.: 3, 3.

Kington, Miles (ed.) (1992) *The Jazz Anthology*. London: HarperCollins.

Kirchner, Bill (ed.) (1997) *A Miles Davis Reader*. Washington, DC: Smithsonian Institution Press.

Knight, Etheridge (1986) *The Essential Etheridge Knight*, Pittsburgh: University of Pittsburgh Press.

Kofsky, Frank (1970) *Black Nationalism and the Revolution in Music*. New York: Pathfinder.

—— (1971) 'The jazz tradition: black music and its white critics.' *Journal of Black Studies*, I, 4 (June): 403–33.

—— (1998a) *Black Music, White Business: Illuminating the History and Political Economy of Jazz*. New York: Pathfinder.

—— (1998b) *John Coltrane and the Jazz Revolution of the 1960s*. New York: Pathfinder.

Komunyakaa, Yusef and Matthews, William (1992) 'Jazz and poetry: a conversation.' *Georgia Review*, XLVI, 4: 645–61.

Lange, Art and Mackey, Nathaniel (eds.) (1993) *Moment's Notice: Jazz in Poetry and Prose*. Minneapolis: Coffee House.

Larkin, Philip (1970) *All What Jazz: A Record Diary, 1961–68*. London: Faber.

Lax, John (1974) 'Chicago's black musicians in the twenties: portrait of an era.' *Journal of Jazz Studies*, I, 2 (June): 107–27.

Lee, Spike with Lisa Jones (1990) *Mo' Better Blues*. New York: Simon & Schuster.

Lees, Gene (1988) *Meet Me at Jim and Andy's: Jazz Musicians and Their World*. New York: Oxford University Press.

—— (1994) *Cats of Any Color: Jazz Black and White*. Oxford: Oxford University Press.

Leonard, Neil (1962) *Jazz and the White Americans: The Acceptance of a New Art Form*. Chicago: University of Chicago Press.

—— (1975) 'Some further thoughts on jazzmen as romantic outsiders.' *Journal of Jazz Studies*, 2, 2: 45–52.

—— (1987) *Jazz: Myth and Religion*. Oxford: Oxford University Press.

Lester, James (1994) *Too Marvelous for Words: The Life and Genius of Art Tatum*. New York: Oxford University Press.

Levet, Jean-Paul (1992) *Talkin' That Talk: Le Language du Blues et du Jazz*. Paris: Hartie.

Levey, Joseph (1983) *The Jazz Experience: A Guide to Appreciation*. New York: University Press of America.

Levine, Lawrence W. (1977) *Black Culture and Black Consciousness: Afro-American Folk Thought from Slavery to Freedom*. New York: Oxford University Press.

—— (1989) 'Jazz and American culture.' *Journal of American Folklore*, 102, 403 (Jan.–Mar.): 6–22.

Litweiler, John (1984) *The Freedom Principle: Jazz After 1958*. New York: Morrow.

—— (1994 [1992]) *Ornette Coleman: A Harmolodic Life*. New York: Da Capo.

Lomax, Alan (1973 [1950]) *Mister Jelly Roll: The Fortunes of Jelly Roll Morton, New Orleans Creole and 'Inventor of Jazz.'* Berkeley, CA: University of California Press.

Longstreet, Stephen (1956) *The Real Jazz, Old and New*. Baton Rouge: Louisiana State University Press.

Lott, Eric (1995) 'Double V, double-time: bebop's politics of style.' In Gabbard (1995a): 243–55.

McCalla, James (1982) *Jazz: A Listener's Guide*. Englewood Cliffs, NJ: Prentice-Hall.

McMahon, John R. (1921) 'Unspeakable jazz must go!' *Ladies' Home Journal*, XXXVIII (Dec.): 34, 115–16.

—— (1922) 'The jazz path of degradation.' *Ladies' Home Journal*, XXXIX (Jan.): 26, 71.

McPartland, Marian (1987) *All in Good Time*. New York: Oxford University Press.

Maggin, Donald L. (1996) *Stan Getz: A Life in Jazz*. New York: Morrow.

Mailer, Norman (1957) 'The white negro.' *Dissent*, 4 (Summer): 276–93.

Major, Clarence (ed.) (1994) *Juba to Jive: A Dictionary of African-American Slang*. New York: Viking.

Manone, Wingy and Vandervoort II, Paul (1948) *Trumpet on the Wing*. New York: Doubleday.

Marquis, Donald M. (1978) *In Search of Buddy Bolden: First Man of Jazz*. Baton Rouge: Louisiana State University Press.

Marsalis, Wynton (1988) 'What jazz is – and isn't.' *The New York Times*, 31 July: H–21, 24. (Reprinted in Walser, *Keeping Time*, 1999.)

Meeker, David (1981 [1977]) *Jazz in the Movies*. New York: Da Capo.

Megill, David W. and Tanner, Paul O.W. (1995) *Jazz Issues: A Critical History*. Madison, WI: Brown & Benchmark.

Megill, Donald D. and Demory, Richard S. (1984) *Introduction to Jazz History*. Englewood Cliffs, NJ: Prentice-Hall.

Meltzer, David (ed.) (1993) *Reading Jazz*. San Francisco: Mercury House.

Mendl, R.W.S. (1927) *The Appeal of Jazz*. London: Philip Allan.

Merriam, Alan P. with Robert J. Benford (1954) *A Bibliography of Jazz*. Philadelphia: American Folklore Society.

—— and Garner, Fradley H. (1968) 'Jazz – the word.' *Ethnomusicology*, 5: 373–96.

—— and Mack, Raymond W. (1960) 'The jazz community.' *Social Forces*, 38, 3 (March): 211–22.

Mezzrow, Mezz and Wolfe, Bernard (1946) *Really the Blues*. New York: Random.

Miller, Marc H. (ed.) (1994) *Louis Armstrong: A Cultural Legacy*. Seattle: University of Washington Press.

Mingus, Charles (1971*)* *Beneath the Underdog: His World As Composed by Mingus*. Ed. Nel King. New York: Knopf.

Monson, Ingrid (1996) *Saying Something: Jazz Improvisation and Interaction*. Chicago: University of Chicago Press.

Morse, Teddy (1917) 'Sharps and Flats.' *New York Clipper*, 20 June: 4.

Murray, Albert (1976) *Stomping the Blues*. New York: McGraw-Hill.

—— (1990 [1970]) *The Omni-Americans: Black Experience and American Culture*. New York: Da Capo.

Nanry, Charles (ed.) (1972) *American Music: From Storyville to Woodstock*. New Brunswick, NJ: Transaction.

—— with Edward Berger (1979) *The Jazz Text*. New York: Van Nostrand.

Newton, Francis [Eric Hobsbawm] (1975 [1959]) *The Jazz Scene*. London: Weidenfeld & Nicolson.

Nicholson, Stuart (1995 [1990]) *Jazz: The 1980s Resurgence*. New York: Da Capo.

O'Day, Anita, with George Eells (1993 [1981]) *High Times, Hard Times*. New York: Limelight.

O'Meally, Robert G. (ed.) (1998) *The Jazz Cadence of American Culture*. New York: Columbia University Press.

Ogren, Kathy (1989) *The Jazz Revolution: Twenties America and the Meaning of Jazz*. New York: Oxford University Press.

—— (1991) ' "Jazz isn't just me": jazz autobiographies as performance personas.' In Buckner and Weiland (1991), 112–27.

Oliphant, Dave (ed.) (1994) *The Bebop Revolution in Words and Music*. Austin: University of Texas (Harry Ransom Humanities Research Center).

Oliver, Paul (1970) *Savannah Syncopators: African Retentions in the Blues*. New York: Stein & Day.

Ondaatje, Michael (1977) *Coming Through Slaughter*. New York: Norton.

Osgood, Henry O. (1926a) 'The anatomy of jazz.' *American Mercury*, 7, 28 (April): 385–95.

—— (1926b) *So This is Jazz*. Boston: Little, Brown.

Ostransky, Leroy (1977) *Understanding Jazz*. Englewood Cliffs, NJ: Prentice-Hall.

Panassié, Hugues (1936 [1934]) *Hot Jazz: The Guide to Swing Music*. London: Cassell.

—— (1960 [1942]) *The Real Jazz*. New York: A.S. Barnes.

Panish, Jon (1997) *The Color of Jazz: Race and Representation in Postwar American Culture*. Jackson: University Press of Mississippi.

Pareles, John (1984) 'Jazz swings back to tradition.' *New York Times Magazine*, 17 June 1984. (Reprinted in Porter, 1997.)

Parker, Chan (1999 [1993]) *My Life in E-Flat*. Columbia: University of South Carolina Press.

—— and Paudras, Francis (1981) *To Bird with Love*. Poitiers: Wizlov.

Parker, Chris (ed.) (1986) *B Flat, Bebop, Scat: Jazz Short Stories and Poems*. London: Quartet.

Pearson, Nathan W. (1988) *Goin' to Kansas City*. London: Macmillan.

Pepper, Art and Pepper, Laurie (1979) *Straight Life: The Story of Art Pepper*. New York: Schirmer.

Peretti, Burton (1992) *The Creation of Jazz: Music, Race, and Culture in Urban America*. Urbana: University of Illinois Press.

—— (1997) *Jazz in American Culture*. Chicago: Ivan R. Dee.

Pessen, Edward (1989) 'A less than definitive nonhistorical account of the swing era' [review of Schuller's *The Swing Era*]. *Reviews in American History*, 17, 4: 599–607.

Placksin, Sally (1985 ([1982]) *Jazzwomen: 1900 to the Present. Their Words, Lives, and Music*. London: Pluto.

Pleasants, Henry (1955) 'What is this thing called jazz?' *High Fidelity*, Dec.: 50–2, 133–5, 137.

Porter, Lewis (1984) 'She wiped all the men out' [women in jazz]. 2 pts. *Music Educator's Journal*, Sept.–Oct.

—— (1988) 'Some problems in jazz research.' *Black Music Research Journal*, 8: 195–206.

—— (ed.) (1991a) *A Lester Young Reader*. Washington, DC: Smithsonian Institution Press.

—— (1991b) Review of Gunther Schuller: *The Swing Era. Annual Review of Jazz Studies*, 5: 183–200.

—— (1997) *Jazz: A Century of Change: Readings and New Essays*. New York: Schirmer.

—— Ullman, Michael and Hazell, Michael (1993) *Jazz: From Its Origins to the Present*. Englewood Cliffs, NJ: Prentice-Hall.

Porter, Roy (1991) *There and Back: The Roy Porter Story*. Ed. David Keller. Oxford: Bayou.

Postif, François (1959) 'Lester Paris 59.' *The Jazz Review*, II, 8: 7–10. (Reprinted in Williams, 1962.)

Powell, Neil (1997) *The Language of Jazz*. Manchester: Carcanet.

Priestley, Brian (1984 [1982]) *Mingus: A Critical Biography*. New York: Da Capo.

—— (1997) 'Jazz and the movies.' *Jazz Notes*, BBC Radio 3, 24–7 Feb.

Ramsey, Frederic, Jr. and Smith, Charles Edward (1939) *Jazzmen*. New York: Harcourt Brace.

Reisner, Robert George (1959) *The Literature of Jazz: A Selective Bibliography*. New York: New York Public Library.

—— (1960) 'The parlance of hip.' In *The Jazz Titans*, 145–68. New York: Doubleday.

—— (1962) *Bird: The Legend of Charlie Parker*. New York: Citadel.

Rexroth, Kenneth (1958a) 'Jazz poetry.' *The Nation*, 29 March: 231–4.

—— (1958b) 'Some thoughts on jazz as music, as revolt, as mystique.' *New World Writing* 14: 252–68. New York: New American Library.

Rivelli, Pauline and Levin, Robert (eds.) (1979 [1970]) *Giants of Black Music*. New York: Da Capo.

Robbins, Fred (1947) 'Prisoners of WOV.' *Time*, 20 Jan.: 44.

Rollini, Adrian (1987) *Thirty Years with the Big Bands*. Chicago: University of Chicago Press.

Roskolenko, Harry (1959) 'The sounds of the fury.' *The Prairie Schooner*, 39: 148–53.

Russell, Ross (1962 [1961]) *The Sound*. London: Cassell.

—— (1971) *Jazz Style in Kansas City and the Southwest*. Berkeley, CA: University of California Press.

—— (1973) *Bird Lives! The High Life and Hard Times of Charlie (Yardbird) Parker*. New York: Charterhouse.

Sales, Grover (1984) *Jazz: America's Classical Music*. Englewood Cliffs, NJ: Prentice-Hall.

Sancton, Thomas (1990) 'Horns of plenty.' *Time*, 22 Oct.: 64–71.

Sargeant, Winthrop (1975 [1946]) *Jazz: Hot and Hybrid*. New York: Da Capo.

Schuller, Gunther (1968) *Early Jazz: Its Roots and Musical Development*. New York: Oxford University Press.

—— (1989) *The Swing Era: The Development of Jazz, 1930–1945*. New York: Oxford University Press.

Seldes, Gilbert (1924) 'Toujours jazz.' In *The 7 Lively Arts*. New York: Harper.

Shapiro, Nat and Hentoff, Nat (eds.) (1955) *Hear Me Talkin' to Ya: The Story of Jazz as Told by the Men Who Made It*. New York: Rinehart.

Shaw, Arnold (1971) *52nd Street: The Street of Jazz.* New York: Coward, McCann & Geoghegan.

―― (1987) *The Jazz Age: Popular Music in the 1920s.* New York: Oxford University Press.

Shaw, Artie (1952) *The Trouble with Cinderella: An Outline of Identity.* New York: Farrar, Straus & Young.

Shipton, Alyn (1999) *Groovin' High: The Life of Dizzy Gillespie.* Oxford: Oxford University Press.

―― (2001) *A New History of Jazz,* London and New York: Continuum.

Sidran, Ben (1971) *Black Talk.* New York: Holt, Rinehart.

―― (ed.) (1995 [1992]) *Talking Jazz: An Oral History.* New York: Da Capo.

Simmons, Herbert A. (1962) *Man Walking on Eggshells.* Boston: Houghton Mifflin.

Simon, George T. (1981 [1967]) *The Big Bands.* New York: Schirmer.

Smith, Hugh L. (1958) 'Jazz in the American novel.' *English Journal,* XLVII, 8 (Nov.): 467–78.

Smith, Larry R. (1977) 'The poetry-and-jazz movement of the United States.' *Itinerary,* V, 7 (Fall): 89–104.

Smith, Willie, with George Hoefer (1964) *Music on My Mind: The Memoirs of an American Pianist.* Garden City, NY: Doubleday.

Southern, Eileen (1983a [1971]) *The Music of Black Americans: A History.* New York: Norton.

―― (1983b [1971]) *Readings in Black American Music.* New York: Norton.

―― (1989) 'A study in jazz historiography.' *College Music Symposium,* 29: 123–33.

Spellman, A.B. (1966) *Four Lives in the Bebop Business.* New York: Pantheon.

Stearns, Marshall W. (1970 [1956]) *The Story of Jazz.* New York: Oxford University Press.

Stebbins, Robert A. (1968) 'A theory of the jazz community.' *The Sociological Quarterly,* 9, 3 (Summer): 318–31. (Reprinted in Nanry, 1972.)

Stokes, W. Royal (1991) *The Jazz Scene: An Informal History from New Orleans to 1990.* New York: Oxford University Press.

Stowe, David W. (1994) *Swing Changes: Big-Band Jazz in New Deal America.* Cambridge, MA: Harvard University Press.

Sudhalter, Richard M. (1991) 'What's your story, mornin' glory? Reflections on some jazz autobiographies.' *Annual Review of Jazz Studies,* 5: 201–216.

―― (1999) *Lost Chords: White Musicians and Their Contribution to Jazz, 1915–1945.* Oxford: Oxford University Press.

―― and Evans, Philip R. (1974) *Bix: Man and Legend.* New Rochelle, NY: Arlington House.

Tallman, Warren (1959) 'Kerouac's sound.' *The Tamarack Review,* Spring: 58–74.

Taylor, Arthur (1993 [1977]) *Notes and Tones: Musician-to-Musician Interviews.* New York: Da Capo.

Taylor, Billy (1982) *Jazz Piano: History and Development.* Dubuque, IA: Brown.

Teachout, Terry (1995) 'The color of jazz.' *Commentary,* 100, 3: 50–3.

Thomas, J.C. (1975) *Chasin' the Trane: The Music and Mystique of John Coltrane.* New York: Doubleday.

Tirro, Frank (1993 [1977]) *Jazz: A History.* New York: Norton. (With CD).

de Toledano, Ralph (ed.) (1962 [1947]) *Frontiers of Jazz.* New York: Frederick Ungar.

Tomlinson, Gary (1991) 'Cultural dialogics and jazz: a white historian signifies.' *Black Music Research Journal,* 11, 2: 229–64.

Travis, Dempsey J. (1983) *An Autobiography of Black Jazz.* Chicago: Urban Research Institute.

Tucker, Mark (ed.) (1993) *The Duke Ellington Reader.* Oxford: Oxford University Press.

Ulanov, Barry (1952) *A History of Jazz in America.* New York: Viking.

―― (1957) *A Handbook of Jazz.* New York: Viking.

Vincent, Ted (1995) *Keep Cool: The Black Activists Who Built the Jazz Age*. London: Pluto.

Wallenstein, Barry (1991) 'Poetry and jazz: a twentieth-century wedding.' *Black American Literature Forum*, 25, 3 (Fall): 595–620.

Walling, William (1974) 'The politics of jazz: some preliminary notes.' *Journal of Jazz Studies*, II, 1: 46–60.

Walser, Robert (ed.) (1999) *Keeping Time: Readings in Jazz History*. New York: Oxford University Press.

Wang, Richard (1973) 'Jazz circa 1945: a confluence of styles.' *Musical Quarterly*, 59: 531–46.

Webb, H. Brook (1937) 'The slang of jazz.' *American Speech*, XII: 179–84.

Weinreich, Regina (1987) *The Spontaneous Poetics of Jack Kerouac: A Study of the Fiction*. Carbondale: South Illinois University Press.

Weinstein, Norman C. (1992) *A Night in Tunisia: Imaginings of Africa in Jazz*. Metuchen, NJ: Scarecrow.

Welburn, Ron (1989) 'The American jazz writer-critic of the 1930s.' *Jazz-Forschung*, 21: 83–94.

Wells, Dicky, with Stanley Dance (1991 [1971]) *The Night People: The Jazz Life of Dicky Wells*. Washington, DC: Smithsonian Institution Press.

Williams, John (1961) *Night Song*. New York: Farrar, Straus, Giroux.

Williams, Martin (ed.) (1959) *The Art of Jazz: Essays on the Nature and Development of Jazz*. Oxford: Oxford University Press.

—— (ed.) (1962) *Jazz Panorama: From the Pages of* The Jazz Review. New York: Crowell-Collier.

—— (1966) *Where's the Melody? A Listener's Introduction to Jazz*. New York: Random.

—— (1987 [1973]) *The Smithsonian Collection of Classic Jazz*. Washington, DC: Smithsonian Institution Press. (With CD and booklet).

—— (1989) *Jazz in Its Time*. Oxford: Oxford University Press.

—— (1992) *Jazz Changes*. Oxford: Oxford University Press.

—— (1993 [1970]) *The Jazz Tradition*. Oxford: Oxford University Press.

Williams, Mary Lou (1954) 'Mary Lou Williams: a life story' ['My friends the kings of jazz']. *Melody Maker*, 3 April–12 June.

Wilmer, Valerie (1977) *As Serious as Your Life: The Story of the New Jazz*. London: Quartet.

—— (1989) *Mama Said There'd Be Days Like This: My Life in the Jazz World*. London: Women's Press.

—— (1990 [1970]) *Jazz People*. New York: Da Capo.

Woideck, Carl (1996) *Charlie Parker: His Music and Life*. Ann Arbor, MI: University of Michigan Press.

Zwerin, Mike (1983) *Close Enough for Jazz*. London: Quartet.

Index of Names

Boldface page numbers refer to specific items of anthology content, by author.

Abdul-Malik, Ahmed 445
Abrams, Muhal Richard 142
Adorno, Theodor 80, 111, 114
Agee, James 410, **441**
Albert, Richard 9, 32, 363, 365
Alexander, Charles (Chas) 23–4
Alexander, Monty 437
Alger, Horatio 339
Allbrook, Adolphus 232–3
Allen, Henry 'Red' 410, 445, 446
Allen, Steve 319–20, **347–9,** 411
Ammons, Albert 124–5, 386
Anderson, John Murray 412
[Anonymous] 'The Appeal of the Primitive
    Jazz' **32–5**
[Anonymous] 'Delving into the Genealogy
    of Jazz' **35–6**
[Anonymous] 'Vipers, Tea, and Jazz' 319,
    338–9
[Anonymous] 'Why "Jazz" Sends us Back
    to the Jungle' 16
Ansermet, Ernst-Alexandre 16, **42–4**
Appiah, Kwame Anthony 201
Archey, Jimmy 138
Arlington, Josie 242
Armstrong, Lil(lian) Hardin 99
Armstrong, Louis ('Pops,' 'Satch[mo]')
    13, 49–50, 53, 57, 58, 62, 64, 65, 69, 70,
    71, 72, 77, 80, 86, 88, 93, 96, 100, 106,
    108, 112, 114, 142, 146, 161, 172,
    173–5, 187, 196, 199, 204, 209, 210,
    212, 228, 231, 238, 243, 277, 278,
    313-14, 320, 323, 324, 327, 328, 329,
    330, 338, 351, 365, 408, 411, 413, 419,
    420, 421–5, 426, 434, 445
Arnold, Matthew 62
Art Ensemble of Chicago 83, 112, 142,
    181
Asher, Don 277, 305

Astaire, Fred 357
Atlas, Jim 445
Auld, Georgie 225, 227
Austin, Lovie 99
Austin, William Oval 214
Avalon, Frankie 412
Avati, Pupi 420
Ayler, Albert 141, 180, 181

Bach, Jean 411, 448, 449
Bach, Johann Sebastian 44, 47, 48, 71,
    112, 197, 212
Bailey, Donald 306
Bailey, Mildred 98
Baird, Jack 365, **387–90**
Bakay, George 29
Baker, Chet 238, 293, 411, 446–8
Baker, David N. 154
Baker, Dorothy 239, **248–50,** 383, 420
Baker, Houston A. 167, 196
Balanchine, George 384
Baldwin, James 371, 386
Balliett, Whitney 9, 63, 65, 101, 106, 282,
    363–4, 365, 370, **383–6,** 410, **444–6**
Bambara, Toni Cade 385
Baraka, Amiri (LeRoi Jones) 5, 6, 60, 63,
    87, 88, 89, 90, **91–6,** 101, 152, **180–2,**
    193–4, 201, 202, **203–8,** 240, **263–4,**
    319, **336**
  and Baraka, Amina 180, 203, 263
Barbieri, Gato 432
Barker, Danny 138, 277, 282, 445
Barnet, Charlie 413
Barthelme, Donald 364, **380–3,** 385
Bartók, Béla 141
Basie, William 'Count' 69, 107, 121, 128,
    133, 134, 135, 179, 197, 205, 231, 239,
    252–3, 276, 290, 291, 328, 410, 413,
    444, 445, 448

Bauer, Billy   138
Beatles   182
Beaux Arts String Quartet   210
Bechet, Sidney   16, 44, 69, 169, 210, 228, 229, 275, 277, 281, 338, 402, 437
Becker, Howard S.   151
Beeks, Clarence, *see* King Pleasure
Beethoven, Ludwig von   48, 71, 74, 89, 111, 202
Beiderbecke, Bix   6, 69, 92, 172, 173, 174–5, 201, 209, 212, 237, 238, 239, 245-8, 248–50, 270, 329, 338, 383, 410, 416, 419, 420, 421
Bell, Clive   16, **40–2**
Bellson, Louie   321
Benedetti, Dean   240, 261
Beneke, Tex   107
Bennett, Barbara   299–300
Benton, Thomas Hart   160
Berardinelli, James   411, **448–9**
Berendt, Joachim   19, 105, **109–10**
Berger, David   280
Berger, Edward   153
Berger, Morroe   151, **177–8**
Berkeley, Busby   412
Berlin, Irving   17, 46, 49
Berliner, Paul   317
Bernstein, Walter   426
Berry, Chu   136
Berry, Emmett   444
Berry, John   426
Black Benny   304
Blakey, Art   181, 206, 267, 269, 435
Blanton, Jimmy   233
Blesh, Rudi   82, 84, 137–8
Bloom, Harold   112
Blumenthal, Bob   440
Blythe, Arthur   142, 181
Bogle, Donald   408, 409, **421–5**
Bolden, Buddy   6, 28, 31, 237–8, 241, 242–4, 305, 402
Booth, Catherine   164
Bourdieu, Pierre   79
Bourjaily, Vance   408
Bowie, Lester   144
Bradley, Will   290
Braff, Ruby   198–9
Brahms, Johann   74
Brando, Marlon   414
Braxton, Anthony   85, 142

Breton, Marcela   363, 364, 370, 371, 372, 384
Brockway, Howard   35–6
Brossard, Chandler   440
Brown, Clifford   206, 207, 271
Brown, Frank London   364, **376–7**
Brown, James   217
Brown, Jazbo   24
Brown, Ray   138, 213, 437
Brown, Tom   24
Brown, Walter   437
Broyard, Anatole   318, **332–5**
Brubeck, Dave   283
Bruce, Lenny   292
Bryan, William Jennings   166
Bryant, Marie   442, 443
Brynner, Yul   439
Büchmann-Møller, Frank   239, **254–5**
Buckley, Lord   292
van Buren, Paul   325, 332
Burke, Kenneth   325
Burley, Dan   320, **356–8**
Byas, Don   76, 124–5, 232
Byron, Don   121, 123

Caillois, Roger   328
Callender, Red   443
Calloway, Cab   224, 280, 309, 320, 323, **351–6,** 365
  and Rollins, Bryant   351
Cameron, William   176
Capone, Al   166
Carmichael, Hoagy   151, 170–6, 239, 247, 329, 331, 413, 416, 420
Carney, Harry   445–6
Carr, Roy, Case, Brian, and Dellar, Fred   319
Carroll, Joe   320, 349
Carruth, Hayden   106, **124–5,** 368, 370, 372
Carter, Benny   290, 414
Carter, Betty   195, 220, 222–3, 328
Carter, Jimmy   185
Carter, Ron   408, 428, 437
Carvin, Michael   121, 122
Catlett, (Big) Sid   124–5, 442, 443
Cayer, David A.   195
Cerulli, Dom, Korall, Burt, and Nasatir, Mort   268
Cézanne, Paul   41
Challis, Bill   201

Chambers, Leland H.   363, 364, **368–72**
Chambers, Paul   132
Chambers, Tick   28
Charles, Ray   145
Charters, Samuel B. and Kunstadt,
    Leonard   150
Cheatham, Doc   444, 445, 446
Cherry, Don   90
Chicagoans   151, 170–6
Chopin, Frederic   52, 74
Christian, Buddy   29, 313
Christian, Charlie   133
Clarke, Kenny ('Klook')   204
Clarke, Shirley   218
Clayton, Buck   133, 135, 136, 415, 449
Clift, Montgomery   447
Cluzet, François   428, 431
Coker, Jerry   20, 105
Cole, Nat 'King'   419
Coleman, Ornette   65, 69, 90, 93, 94, 96,
    114, 141, 143, 181, 201, 207, 368, 404
Collette, Buddy   232, 233
Collier, James Lincoln   5, 13, 57, 58, 194,
    200–1, **208–12,** 318
Collins, Junior   293
Coltrane, John ('Trane')   65, 80, 93, 94,
    95–6, 107, 111, 130–2, 141, 180, 181,
    196, 201, 206, 207, 212, 230, 253–4,
    263, 264, 305, 367, 399, 404, 410
Columbus, Christopher   396–7
Compendium: Jazz – Formal definitions
    (1913–99)   **18–22**
Condon, Eddie   151, 170–1, 172, 276,
    299–301
Coniff, Frank   138
Coolidge, Calvin   165
Cooper, Gary   435
Corea, Chick   145, 181, 213
Cornish, Willy   244
Cortázar, Julio   7, 386
Cortez, Jayne   365
Coss, Bill   101, 282
Costello, Elvis   447
Coursodon, Jean-Pierre   408–9, **425–30**
Cowell, Stanley   144, 145
Cowley, Malcolm   166
Cox, Ida   98, 214
Cripps, Thomas   408
Criss, Sonny   306, 367, 398–9
Crosby, Bing   416, 417–28
Crosby, Israel   124–5

Crosby, John   444, 445
Crouch, Stanley   409
Curtis, Edward S.   447
Curtiz, Michael   417
Custen, George F.   407, 416, 417

Dahl, Linda   5, 9, 60–1, **96–9,** 328, 331
Dameron, Tadd   195, 224, 404
Dance, Stanley   276, 286
Daniels, Ernest   136
Dankworth, Avril   14, **22–3**
Danton, Georges   396
Dara, Olu   181
Darrow, Clarence   166
Davis, Francis   108, 109, 409, **431–3,**
    437–41
Davis, Miles   60, 63, 65, 66, 69, 77, 78,
    101, 107, 109, 111, 112, 114, 145, 146,
    181, 201, 207, 210, 213, 216, 217, 218,
    222, 223, 232, 233, 255, 277, 279,
    282–3, 284, 298, 305, 307, 364, 367,
    399, 432
Davis, Richard   121
Davison, Wild Bill   138
Daylie, Daddy-0, 310
Dean, James   447
Debs, Eugene   165
Debussy, Claude   228, 263, 396
Delaunay, Charles   254
Desmond, Paul   95, 233
DeVeaux, Scott   4, 9, 59, 60, **79–85,** 106,
    108, 237, 238, 279, 280
De Vries, Peter   384–5
Dewey, John   67
Dickens, Charles   141
Dickenson, Vic   124–5, 444, 445, 446
Dodds, Baby   138, 228
Dodds, Johnny   77, 138, 228, 229
Dodge, Roger Pryor   17, **46–50,** 95
Dolly (family), Jenny and Rosie   34
Dolphy, Eric   180, 181, 367, 397–8, 404
Donahue, Sam   294
Dorn, Larry   137–8
Dorsey, Jimmy   252, 413, 416, 418, 419
Dorsey, Tommy   216, 267, 294, 413, 416,
    418, 419, 435
Downes, Olin   16, **44–5**
DuBois, W.E.B.   206
Dufty, William   225
Dundes, Alan   356
Dunn, Johnny   50

Duval, Reggie   172
Dyer, Geoff   9, 106, 107, **110–16,** 239, **256–9**
van Dyke, Dr. Henry   16, 40
Dylan, Bob   298

Eager, Allen   293
Eaglin, Snooks   93
Early, Gerald   211
Eastwood, Clint   409, 433, 434–5, 436–7, 438, 439, 441
Eckstine, Billy   413
Edison, Harry 'Sweets'   250, 443
Eisenhower, Dwight   207
Eldridge, Roy   70, 112, 146, 194, 195, 215–16, 444, 445, 446, 448
Eliot, T.S.   62, 111, 263
Ellington, Edward Kennedy 'Duke'   13, 29, 49, 58, 65, 69, 78, 80, 85, 96, 106, 111–12, 113, 114, 136, 143, 146, 186, 196, 201, 203, 205, 209, 210, 216, 231, 233, 238, 263, 264, 281, 291, 326, 412, 413, 414–15, 422, 426, 432
Elliott, Bruce   138
Ellis, Herb   213
Ellis, Seger   50
Ellison, Ralph   3, 328, 331
Emge, Charles   410, **442–3**
Engel, Carl   15
Europe, James Reese   15, **25–6**
Evans, Bill   112, 198, 199, 201, 213
Evans, Bill (Lateef, Yusef)   213
Evans, Gil   201, 293
Evans, Herschel   128–9, 136, 253, 431

Faddis, John   437
Farmer, Art   414
Faulkner, Anne Shaw   16, **38–40**
Feather, Leonard   82, 84, 108, 194, **215–16,** 282
and Tracy, Jack   284
Feinstein, Sascha   9, **197,** 366, 367, **398–9**
and Komunyakaa, Yusef   366
Ferguson, Otis   238, 239, **245–8**
Ferlinghetti, Lawrence   320, **350–1,** 366, **394–7**
Fields, W.C.   293, 305
Finkelstein, Sidney   149
Fisher, Rudolph   384
Fitzgerald, Ella   77, 98, 225, 329, 446
Fitzgerald, Scott   6

Flagstad, Kirsten   73
Fletcher, Dusty   424
Ford, Jimmy   293
Forrest, Helen   98, 226
Foster, Frank   427
Foster, Pops   138
Foster, Stephen   418
Frank, Bob   28
Frank, Stanley   320
Freeman, Bud   172, 216, 252, 276, 299, 300–1, 449
Freud, Sigmund   160
Fruscella, Tony   293

Gabbard, Krin   4–5, 6, 7–8, 9, 15, 21, 59, **85–6,** 237, 238, 275, 277, 278, 279, 321, 368, 407, 408, 409, 410, **416–21**
Gable, Clark   309, 432, 435
Gabler, Milt   106, 124–5
Gade, Svend   17, **50–1**
Gaillard, Slim   308, 319, 329, 337, 365
Galloway, Happy   28, 305
Garber, Frederick   237, 409
Gardner, Martin   108, **139–41,** 384, 385
Garner, Erroll   76
Garvey, Marcus   189
Gates, Henry Louis   6, 60, 87, 88, 89, 196
and Lemke, Sieglinde   339
Gayle, Addison   193
Gelber, Jack   384
Gendron, Bernard   5, 107
Gennari, John   5, 9, 58, 59, **62–7,** 107
George, Nelson   161
Gerard, Charley   6, 193, 194, **198–203**
Gershwin, George   17, 46, 48, 49, 73, 127, 207, 416
Getz, Stan   71, 112, 146, 283
Gibson, Harry 'The Hipster'   308, 319
Giddins, Gary   9, 108, **141–3,** 199, 202, 277, 281, 409, **433–7**
Gilbert, Edwin   365
Gillespie, Dizzy   66, 70, 71, 94, 101, 107, 108, 112, 138, 142, 146, 195, 201, 204, 214, 223, 224, 232, 262, 275, 281, 282, **307–10,** 319, 320, 326, 327, 328, 329, 329, 331, 349, 365, 411, 413, 437, 440, 448, 449
and Fraser, Al   277, 278, 307, 329
Gilroy, Frank   383
Ginsberg, Allen   395
Gioia, Dana   238, **245**

Gioia, Ted   57, 58, 106, 109
Gitler, Ira   278
Giuffre, Jimmy   410, 445, 446
Gleason, Ralph   106, 116, 239, 366
Gold, Robert S.   7, 317, 318, 319, **321–4,**
   325, 330, 331
Goldkette, Jean   174, 247, 420
Goodman, Benny   72, 138, 151, 161,
   170–1, 173, 174, 203, 238, 289, 385,
   411, 412, 413, 415, 416–17, 418, 419
Goodman, Harry   174
Goodwin, Charles   133–4
Gordon, Dexter   202, 368, 409, 427–30,
   431, 432, 433, 438
Gottlieb, William   107, 320
Goulden, Wyn   137–8
Gourse, Leslie   5
Grant, Barry   320
Granz, Norman   252, 254, 442
Gray, Glen   290
Gray, Wardell   271
Green, Alfred E.   416
Green, Benny   239
Green, Freddie   121, 445
Greenberg, Clement   67
Gregory, Dick   441
Gridley, Mark   21–2, 57, 88, 105
Grieg, Edvard   74
Griffith, D.W.   32
Grofé, Ferde   200
Guerin, John   437

Hadlock, Richard   91–2
Haig, Al   71, 262
Haley, Bill   182
Hall, Edmond   138
Hall, Jim   198, 199, 213, 445
Hall, Tubby   228
Hamilton, Chico   414
Hamilton, Scott   209
Hampton, Lionel   413, 415
Hancock, Herbie   111, 145, 181, 323, 428,
   432
Handy, W.C.   15, 25, 47, 419
Harding, Warren G.   165
Harlos, Christopher   6, 275, 276, 277,
   279–84
Harper, Michael   9, 196, **230,** 240, **264–5,**
   365, 367, **399–400**
Harrington, Michael   163
Harris, Barry   132, 437

Harris, Estelle   25
Harris, Jerome   120–1, 123
Harris, Sheila   310–12
Harrison, Jimmy   209, 327
Hartman, Charles   365
Hawes, Hampton   6, 13, 240, 277, 281,
   305–7
Hawkins, Coleman ('Hawk')   69, 71, 75,
   107, 111, 128–9, 136, 146, 209, 216,
   239, 252, 253, 256, 257, 370, 435, 444,
   445
Haydn, Franz   44, 48
Hayes, Thamon   133
Haynes, Don C.   95
Hayward, Susan   414
Hearn, Lafcadio   33
Helland, Dave   109
Hemingway, Ernest   166, 263
Henderson, Fletcher   49, 70, 128, 129,
   136, 201, 205, 210, 231, 239, 252–3,
   288, 290, 327, 415, 420
Hendrickson, Robert   15, **23–4**
Hentoff, Nat   62, 63, 107, 194, 199,
   216–20, 370, 409, 444, 445
Herman, Woody   413
Herridge, Robert   410, 444, 445
Heuvelmans, Bernard   78
Heywood, Eddie   268
Hickman, Art   200
Hillyer, Lonnie   132
Hines, Earl   70, 209, 231, 445
Hinson, Hal   411, **446–8**
Hinton, Milt   280, 445, 449
Hobsbawm, E(ric) J., *see* Newton, Francis
Hobson, Wilder   18
Hodeir, André   4, 58, 59, 63, 64–5, **75–9,**
   105, 276, 369–70, 372
Hodes, Art   282, 284, 327, 331
Hodges, Johnny   77, 142, 209, 252, 326
Holiday, Billie   69, 98, 195, 197, 223,
   225–7, 238, 250, 253, 259, 268, 277,
   298, 321, 328, 360, 383, 404, 410,
   412, 415, 417, 419, 421, 431, 434,
   445, 446
Holland, Dave   213
Holmes, John Clellon   241, **270,** 365, 370,
   372, 440
Hope, Bob   413
Hopkins, Ernest J.   18
Hopkins, Lightnin'   93
Horowitz, Harold   149–50, **154–8**

Horowitz, Irving Louis   6, 13, 14, 15
    and Nanry, Charles   13, 14, 200
Horowitz, Vladimir   384
Houseman, John   444
Hubbard, Freddie   145, 195, 220, 221–2,
    323
Hughes, Langston   195, 196, 206, **223–5,**
    263, 365, 367, 370–1, 384, 401
Huizinga, Johan   328
Hurston, Zora Neale   263, 319, **339–47**
Huxley, Aldous   434
Hyams, L'Ana Webster   99
Hyams, Margie   99
Hylton, Jack   49

International Sweethearts of Rhythm   99
Ives, Charles   263

Jablow, Alta, and Withers, Carl   329, 331
Jackson, Angela   321, **359–60**
Jackson, Tony   28, 29
Jacquet, Illinois   77, 442, 443
James, Boisey   24
James, Harry   160, 364, 413
James, Henry   110
Jameson, Fredric   114
Jarman, Joseph   112
Jarrett, Keith   112, 145
Jarrett, Michael   363
Jazz at the Philharmonic (JATP)   129, 269
Jefferson, Eddie   3, 320
Jenkins, Freddy   325
Jenkins, Leroy   142
Johnson, Bunk   32, 94, 108, 139, 238, 243,
    383
Johnson, J.J.   283, 378
Johnson, James P.   201
Johnson, Osie   445
Jolson, Al   416, 418
Jones, Eddie   445
Jones, Jo   121, 255, 442, 443, 445, 446
Jones, Quincy   145
Jones, Thad   145
Jones, Willie   239, 254–5
Joplin, Scott   142
Jung, Carl   62

Kahn, Gus   417
Kaiser, Kay   203
Kaminsky, Max   225, 227, 449
Kane, Art   411, 448

Kazan, Elia   414
Keepnews, Orrin   61
Keil, Charles   327
Kein, Sybil   17, **53**
Kenney, William   150
Kenton, Stan   114, 186, 413
Keppard, Freddie   24, 28, 29, 32, 420
Kernfeld, Barry   13, 105, 107
Kerouac, Jack   7, 319, **337,** 365, **390–1**
Kessel, Barney   442, 443
King, Dr. Martin Luther   114, 189, 230
King, Nel   232, 277
King Pleasure [Clarence Beeks]   320–1,
    358–9, 439
Kingsley, Walter   15, 26, 32
Kirk, Andy   107, 133, 276, 289, 290
Kirk, Rahsaan Roland   195
Klein, Calvin   447
Knight, Arthur   410
Knight, Etheridge   367, **397–8**
de Koenigswarter, Baroness
    Pannonica   240, **266–8,** 435–6, 440
Kofsky, Frank   152
Konitz, Lee   213, 283
Kostelanetz, André   75
Krupa, Gene   160, 276, 300, 301, 411, 413,
    419

Ladnier, Tommy   228
Laine, Jack   187
Laing, R.D.   298
Lala, Pete   313
Lang, Eddie   50
Lang, Fritz   414
LaPorta, John   138
LaRocca, Nick   24, 419–20
Lautrec, Toulouse   415
Lawson, Hugh   132
Leadbelly   433
Lee, Bill   432, 433
Lee, George E.   133, 291
Lee, Peggy   98
Lee, Spike   409, 432
Lees, Gene   6, 9, 101, 194, 198, 200, **212–
    15,** 282
Lemott, Ferdinand   187
Lennon, John   187
Leonard, Herman   257
Leonard, Neil   5, 9, 150, 151, **170–7,** 238,
    317, 318, **324–32**
Levey, Stan   232, 233, 262

Levine, Lawrence W.   5, 152, 162–3, **183–5**
Lewis, John   69, 76, 171, 359, 432
Lewis, Meade Lux   386
Lewis, Ted   16, 37–8, 49, 171, 416
Liebman, Dave   209, 213
Lincoln, Abraham   396
Lindbergh, Charles   394
Lindsay, Vachel   34
Lippincott, Bruce   106, **116–20**
Liston, Melba   99
Liszt, Franz   415
Lomax, Alan   277, 304
Lombardo, Guy   108, 140
Lopez, Jackie   410, **443**
Lott, Eric   5

Mabley, Moms   424
Macdonald, Dwight   143
McBee, Cecil   120, 122
McCalla, James   88–9
McCarthy, Joe   206, 414, 425
McDaniel, Hattie   423
McGhee, Howard   437
McKay, Claude   263
McKee, Lonette   430, 431
McKenzie, Red   276, 299, 300, 301
McKinley, Ray   294
McLaughlin, John   145, 213
McLean, Jackie   111
McMahon, John   16
McPartland, Jimmy   172–3, 276, 299
McPartland, Marian   448
McPherson, Charles   132, 437
McRae, Barry   217
McRae, Carmen   98
McShann, Jay   107, 133, 135, 136
Mahler, Gustav   110
Malcolm X   189, 208, 230
Mangione, Chuck   182
Mann, Anthony   434
Mann, Thomas   434
Manne, Shelly   414
Mao Tse-tung   207, 208
Mares, Paul   420
Markham, Pigmeat   424
Marmarosa, Dodo   232, 233
Marquette, Pee-Wee   431
Marquis, Donald   238
Marsalis, Wynton   57, 80–1, 83, 109, 112, 144, 145, 185, 188, 202, 210
Marsh, Willard   384

Marvin, Lee   414
Marx, Karl   160
Matthews, William   238, 239, **244, 259–60**
Meeker, David   407, 410
Megill, Donald and Demory, Richard S.   57, 88
Meltzer, David   57, 59, **61,** 85–6, 319
Melville, Herman   397
Mencken, Henry Louis   171
Merriam, Alan P.   6
   and Garner, Fradley H.   15, **26–7**
   and Mack, Raymond W.   149, 151–2, **178–80**
Mezzrow, Mezz   6, 151, 170–6, 195–6, **227–9,** 276, 277, 281, 301, **302–3,** 309–10, 319, 324, 329, 331, 338–9
Michelangelo   415
Michelot, Pierre   428
Miley, Bubber   50, 210
Mili, Gjon   410, 441, 442, 443
Miller, Glenn   225, 293, 294, 411, 413, 415, 416, 419, 434
Miller, Marc H.   421
Miller, Punch   410
Milles, James   28
Mills Brothers   254
Mineo, Sal   411, 419
Mingus, Charles   6, 61, 69, **101–2,** 112, 113, 114, 195, 196, **232–4,** 241, 269, 275, 277, 282, 284, 365, 367, 385, 401, 410
Mingus, Sue   9
Mitchell, Red   306
Mitchell, Roscoe   112
Mitchell, Whitey   275–6, **284–6**
Modern Jazz Quartet   143, 145
Moenkhaus, Bill (Monk)   175–6, 329
Mole, Miff   209
Monk, Thelonious   69, 79, 93, 94, 97, 111, 112, 142, 144, 195, 204, 207, 217, 224, 233, 283, 410, 435, 445, 446, 448
Monroe, Clarke   225
Monson, Ingrid   9, 106, **120–4,** 317
Morgenstern, Dan   9
Morris, Marlowe   443
Morris, Thomas   49
Morton, Benny   209, 444, 445
Morton, Ferdinand 'Jelly Roll'   15, **27–30,** 32, 53, 58, 63, 69, 203, 204, 277, 281, **304–5,** 402, 404, 445
Moten, Bennie   107, 133, 134, 291

Mozart, Wolfgang Amadeus   44, 92, 141, 415

Mullen, Harryette   9, 367, **400–1**

Mulligan, Gerry   71, 143, 213, 216, 283, 293, 414, 444, 445, 446

Murphy, Dudley   412

Murray, Albert   6, 196, **231–2**

Murray, David   181

Myers, Helen   198

Namath, Joe   295

Nanry, Charles   6, 9, 13, 14, 149, **153,** 177, 237

Navarro, Fats   271

Neal, Larry   367, **401–4**

Newman, Ernest   46

Newman, Joe   444

New Orleans Rhythm Kings (NORK) 171–2, 420

Newton, Francis (E.J. Hobsbawm)   14, 19, 63, 114

Nichols, Red   49

Nicholson, Stuart   109, 149

Niehaus, Lennie   437, 440

De Niro, Robert   411

Noone, Jimmie   138, 228, 229, 338

O'Bryant, Jimmy   50

O'Connell, Helen   98

O'Day, Anita   98

O'Hara, Frank   365

O'Meally, Robert   7

O'Neill, Eugene   96

Ogren, Kathy J.   6, 150–1, **164–70,** 275, 282, 284

Oliansky, Joel   434, 437, 438, 439

Oliver, King (Joe)   29, 32, 49, 63, 69, 77, 83, 172, 204, 228, 238, 243, 270, 313–14, 325, 338, 383, 418, 420

Ondaatje, Michael   113

Orent, Milton   290

Original Dixieland Jazz Band (ODJB)   24, 28, 31, 92, 171, 416, 419, 420

Ory, Kid   139, 396, 418, 420

Osgood, Henry O.   16, **37–8**

Ostransky, Leroy   19–20

Overstreet, W. Benton   25

Page, Hot Lips   124–5, 133, 328

Page, Walter   121, 136, 291, 328, 445

Palao, Jimmy   29

Panassié, Hugues   18–19, 58, 64, 65, 67, 72, 228

Panish, John   6, 193, 363

Parker (Richardson), Chan   267, 431, 435, 436, 438, 439

Parker, Charlie '(Yard)Bird'   6, 61, 65, 66, 69, 70, 71, 77, 89, 94, 96, 97, 101–2, 107, 111, 130, 133, 138, 142, 146, 187, 195, 196, 201, 204, 210, 218, 221, 223, 224, 232–4, 237, 238, 239–41, 252, 260–70, 293, 295, 298, 306, 307, 320, 325, 358–9, 364–5, 366, 367, 383, 386, 399, 401, 403, 404, 409, 417, 433–7, 437–41

Parks, Gordon   433

Pastor, Tony   225, 226, 227

Patchen, Kenneth   366, **392–3, 393–4**

Patterson, William Morrison   33–4

Paudras, Francis   426, 427, 428, 429, 430, 431, 432

Pearson, Nathan W.   107, **133–7**

Pendergast, Tom   290

Pepper, Art   6, 71, 107, 114, 275, 278, 281, 327, 331

    and Pepper, Laurie   **129–30,** 277, 278, **310–13**

Peretti, Burton W.   5, 6, 105, 109, 149, 152, **185–9,** 278

Perez, Manuel   305, 314

Peterson, Oscar   70, 213, 254

Petit, Buddy   29, 32

Petry, Ann   364, **372–5,** 384

Peyton, Dave   28

Phillips, Flip   435

Picasso, Pablo   41, 263, 384

Pickett, Wilson   217

Pierce, Nat   445

Pleasants, Henry   432

Pollack, Ben   174, 289, 290

Pollack, Jackson   141, 160

Porter, Lewis   16, 50, 239, 251, 279, 280

    Ullman, Michael, and Hazell, Michael   57

Porter, Roy   409

Postif, François   239, **251–4**

Pound, Ezra   263

Powell, Bud   201, 207, 238, 269, 283, 404, 409, 417, 427, 428–9, 431

Powell, Dick   412

Powell, Neil   13, 318

Powell, Richie   404

Powers, J.F.   371

Preminger, Otto   414
Presley, Elvis   182, 187, 412
Price, Sam   135–6, 289
Priestley, Brian   407, 408
Pryor, Richard   441

de Quincey, Thomas   338

Raeburn, Bruce Boyd   211
Ramey, Gene   134, 135, 136
Ramsey, Frederic and Smith, Charles
    Edward   237–8, **242–4**
Rascher, Sigurd   131
Ravel, Maurice   44, 228, 263
Rayfiel, David   426
Razz's Band   23, 25–6
Redd, Vi   99
Redding, Otis   217
Redman, Don   201, 290
Redmond, Eugene   365
Rehak, Frank   445
Reisner, Robert G.   240, 241, 266, 318–19,
    325, 331, **335–6**
Rexroth, Kenneth   366, 368, **392**
Rich, Buddy   70-l
Richards, I.A.   325
Ritt, Martin   426
Rivelli, Pauline and Levin, Robert   216
Rivers, James   437
Roach, Max   13, 20, 111, 113, 138, 181,
    194, 195, 203–8, 255, 269, 283
Robertson, Zue   314
Robeson, Paul   206, 423
Robinson, Jackie   161
Rockwell, Tommy   301
Rodney, Red   435, 437, 439
Rogers, Shorty   414
Rolling Stones   182
Rollins, Sonny   63, 69, 94, 123, 181, 206,
    207, 212–13, 253–4, 255, 410, 427, 432
Roosevelt, Franklin   161
Rosenberg, Harold   67
Rudd, Roswell   202, 219
Rushing, Jimmy   291, 328, 410, 445, 446
Russell, Pee Wee   174–5, 445, 446
Russell, Ross   82, 85, 107, **126–8,** 196, **234,**
    239–40, **260–2,** 438
Ruth, Babe   161

Sabin, Charles   299, 300
Sales, Grover   57, 149

Salinger, Diane   440
Samarin, William J.   329, 332
Sampson, Edgar   290
Sancton, Thomas   81, 85
Sanders, Pharoah   113, 181, 195, 207
Santoro, Gene   81, 85
Sargeant, Winthrop   59, **71–5**
Sargent, Robert   238, **240**
Sartre, Jean-Paul   17, **51–3**
Saunders, William   136, 137
Sawyer, Tom   394
Schoenberg, Arnold   30, 64, 434
Schribman, Sy   225
Schubert, Franz   416
Schuller, Gunther   4, 15, **30–2,** 57, 59, 63,
    106
Scofield, John   209, 213
Scopes, John   166
Scorsese, Martin   426, 431, 438
Scott, Cecil   286
Scott, Hazel   195, 220, 222
Scott, Ronnie   218
Scott, Tony   240, **268–70**
Seaman, Phil   293
Seldes, Gilbert   16
Sennett, Richard   184, 185
Shakespeare, William   212
Shapiro, Nat and Hentoff, Nat   61, 63,
    99–100, 195, 278, 313, 325, 327, 332
Shaw, Artie   195, 225–7, 326, 332, 357, 413
Shearing, George   216
Shepp, Archie   113, 194, 195, 203–8,
    216–20, 223
Sheridan, Chris   276
Shipton, Alyn   8, 9
Shorter, Wayne   145, 146
Sidran, Ben   193, 278, 318
Siegel, Don   414
Silver, Horace   69, 181
Simmons, Herbert A.   365
Simmons, John   443
Simon, George   161, 416
Sinatra, Frank   256, 259, 414
Singleton, Zutty   228
Slonimsky, Nicolas   131
Smight, Jack   410, 444
Smith, Bessie   50, 72, 74, 96, 98, 270, 339
Smith, Buster   133, 136, 439
Smith, Charles Edward   199
Smith, Clara   50
Smith, Hugh L.   365

Smith, Joe   135
Smith, Larry R.   366
Smith, Willie 'The Lion'   282, 402
Snow, Phoebe   182
Snow, Valaida   99
Southern, Eileen   15, **24–5**
Southern, Terry   293, 384
Southern Syncopated Orchestra   16, 43–4
Spanier, Muggsy   326, 416
Spellman, A.B.   87, 95, 278
Spence, Kenneth C.   9, 407–8, **411–16**
Stark, Bobby   288–9
Stearns, Marshall   19, 57–8, 63, 101, 105, 109–10, 282
Stebbins, Robert A.   151
Stein, Gertrude   166
Steiner, George   110–11, 113
Stern, Bert   410
Stewart, Jimmy   411, 414
Stewart, Rex   201, 445, 446
Stitt, Sonny   107, 129–30
Stokes, W. Royal   278
Stokowski, Leopold   167
Stone, Jesse   134–5
Stowe, David W.   6, 108, 150, **158–64**
Stratton, Don   215
Strauss, Richard   48
Stravinsky, Igor   30, 48, 49, 207, 263, 434–5
Strayhorn, Billy   216
Sudhalter, Richard   238, 420
Sugrue, Thomas   276, 299
Sullivan, Joe   301
Sun Ra   181, 404
Susman, Warren   162
Sutton, Ralph   138
Swayze (Swasey), Edwin   50
Sydnor, Doris   435, 439
Szigeti, Josef   72

Tapp, Ferman   287
Tatum, Art   61, 69, 101–2, 419
Tavernier, Bertrand   408–9, 417, 425–30, 431
Taylor, Art(hur)   6, 13, 194–5, **220–3,** 278
Taylor, Billy   65, 106, 199, 201–2, 216
Taylor, Cecil   94, 141, 143, 181, 201, 207, 216, 217
Taylor, Myra   135
Tchaikovsky, Peter Ilyitch   74
Teagarden, Jack   209, 247, 289, 413

Terry, Clark   145, 214–15
Teschemacher, Frank   173, 174, 271, 276, 299, 300, 301
Tesich, Steven   427
Thomas, J.C.   107, **130–2**
Thompson, Chuck   307
Thompson, Lucky   232, 233
Thompson, Sir Charles   250
Thornhill, Claude   276, 292–8, 413
Threadgill, Henry   181
Tirro, Frank   20–1, 57, 58, 80, 85, 88, 105, 196
de Toledano, Ralph   27, 42, 51, 53
Tolliver, Charles   13, 195, 220–1
Tolstoy, Leo   111
Tomlinson, Gary   4, 60, **87–90,** 109, 279, 280
Toomer, Jean   263
Tough, Dave   173
Tourneur, Jacques   439
Traube, Shepherd   410
Tristano, Lennie   138, 283
Troupe, Quincy   277
Trumbauer, Frankie   174, 201, 247, 252
Tucker, Mark   13
Turner, Dale   409, 428, 429, 430, 431, 432
Turner, Frederick Jackson   184
Tyner, McCoy   323

Ulanov, Barry   13, 101, 108, **137–8,** 282

Vaché, Warren   144, 210
Van Vechten, Carl,   357
Vaudreuil, Marquis de   242
Vaughan, Sarah   69, 98
Venora, Diane   439
Venuti, Joe   299
Vian, Boris   78

Wagner, Richard   71
Walder, Herman   128, 136, 291–2
Walder, Woodie   292
Waldron, Mal   410, 445
Walker, Margaret   205
Wallace, Mike   214
Wallenstein, Barry   365, 366
Waller, Fats   101, 209, 270–1, 326, 364, 370, 386, 402, 416
Ward, Frankie   228
Ward, Theodore   205
Warren, Earle   444

Washington, Booker   134, 135
Washington, Dinah   404
Washington, Kenny   121
Waters, Ethel   73
Watrous, Peter   213
Watson, Leo   320
Weather Report   145, 146, 181, 182
Webb, Chick   13, 225, 290
Webb, Jack   417
Weber, Bruce   410–11, 446–8
Webster, Ben   128–9, 133, 135, 136, 206, 218, 410, 444, 445, 446
Weeks, Bryant   420
Wein, George   217
Weiss, Michael   121
Welles, Orson   357
Wells, Dicky   209, 275, 276, **286–9,** 444
Welty, Eudora   7, 363–4, 368–9, 371, 386
Whitaker, Forest   409, 437–8, 439
White, Lulu   242
Whiteman, Paul   16–17, 29, 44–5, 46, 47, 48, 49, 72, 189, 203, 247, 412, 413, 416, 420
Wilder, Joe   444
Williams, Bert   424
Williams, Carlos   263
Williams, Clarence   338
Williams, Cootie   218, 326, 332
Williams, John A.   365, 441
Williams, Martin   4, 14, 57, 58, 61, 62, 63, 65–7, **68–71,** 88, 101, 106, 108–9, **144–6,** 276, 282, 370, 372
Williams, Mary Lou   99, 107, **128–9,** 134,
136, 224, 276, **289–92,** 448
and Orent, Milton   320, **349**
Williams, Mississippi Joe   93
Williams, Ned. E.   325
Williams, Tennessee   96
Williams, Tony   181, 428
Wilson, August   384
Wilson, Dick   136
Wilson, John S.   101, 282
Wilson, Teddy   77, 267, 415
Wilson, Woodrow   165
Winding, Kai   283
Winkler, Irwin   426, 430
Woideck, Carl   240
Wolfe, Bernard   227, 276–7, 302, 324, 338
Wolverines   171
World Saxophone Quartet (WSQ)   181
Wright, Richard   206
Wyler, William   413
Wynn, Neil   9

Yates, Richard   384
Young, Al   9, 239, **250,** 364, 385, **378–80**
Young, Lester ('Prez')   6, 77, 96, 97, 99, 111, 112, 128–9, 133, 135, 136, 146, 201, 206, 218, 237, 238, 239, 250–60, 318, 321, 325, 364, 367, 385, 401–4, 409, 415, 417, 426, 428–9, 431, 435, 442, 443, 445, 446

Zawinul, Joe   145, 146
Zelniker, Michael   437, 439
Zeno, Henry   314
Zwerin, Mike   6, 9, 276, **292–8**

Index of Jazz (and Jazz-related) Films

After Hours   410

Alfie   432

All the Fine Young Cannibals   417

Anatomy of a Murder   414–15, 432

The Benny Goodman Story   408, 411, 416–17, 418, 419, 420

Bird   8, 383, 408, 409, 417, 433–7, 437–41

Birth of the Blues   408, 412–13, 416, 417–18

Bix: An Interpretation of a Legend   420

Black and Tan Fantasy   412

The Fabulous Dorseys   408, 416, 418–19

The Five Pennies   417

The Gene Krupa Story   411, 417, 419

The Gig   383

The Glenn Miller Story   408, 411, 416, 417, 419, 434

A Great Day in Harlem   411, 448–9

Hollywood Hotel   412

I Want to Live   414

Jammin' the Blues   410, 441, 442–3

Jazz on a Summer's Day   410

The Jazz Singer   416

The Jolson Story   416, 418

The King of Jazz   412, 416

Lady Sings the Blues   408, 415, 417, 434

Let's Get Lost   410–11, 417, 446–8

The Man With the Golden Arm   414

Mo' Better Blues   409

New Orleans   408, 419, 421, 434

New York, New York   411–12

Odds Against Tomorrow   432

Orchestra Wives   413

Paris Blues   408, 426

Pete Kelly's Blues   408, 417

A Rhapsody in Black and Blue   408, 422–4

Rhapsody in Blue   416

Round Midnight   8, 383, 408–9, 417, 425–30, 431–3

St. Louis Blues   408, 417, 419

She's Gotta Have It   432

A Song Is Born   413

The Sound of Jazz   410, 444–6

The Sound of Miles Davis   410

Sun Valley Serenade   413

Sweet Love, Bitter   441

The Sweet Smell of Success   414

Symphony in Black   412, 421

Syncopation   408

Talmadge Farlow   417

The Wild One   414

Young Man with a Horn   408, 419, 420–1